The Best of Phlit:

Essays on Literature

Volume 1 of 2

by L. James Hammond

cover design: Elliott Banfield
elliottbanfield.com

Published by: Noontide Press
Seekonk, MA 02771

ISBN: 978-0-9838270-4-7

Contents

Preface

In 1999, I began writing a newsletter (e-zine), and posting it to the web at
ljhammond.com/phlit/newsletter.htm
Since it dealt with philosophy and literature, I called it Phlit. One might describe my newsletter as "philosophy in the present tense," since it not only sets forth ideas, but also describes their origin—the book or discussion or TV show that started me thinking.

In this book, pieces from my newsletter are arranged by subject, not by publication date.

Responses to Phlit: A Newsletter on Philosophy and Literature

"Great great essay from 2005 on the sonnets, Goethe and much more. Really enjoyed your ideas and will come back.... After reading the article on the sonnets, I stayed at your site and read several more articles. Nothing disappointed me. I like your wide breadth of knowledge. I like your balanced and calm presentation of arguments. I like your choice of subjects. I want to read every back issue of the newsletter."
--Chris K.

"I love reading your newsletter... consistently interesting, infectiously readable.... I thought I knew Poe, a favorite of mine, until I read your piece on him. My appreciation of him was at best shallow and at worst misinformed. Thank you for the latest newspaper. Great stuff. I'm an old English major and voracious reader, especially in literature, history and philosophy. It's invigorating to find someone who shares the same loves. Thank you!"
--Vince, San Diego

"I'm always very glad to see another issue of Phlit in my mailbox. Honestly, I have never been a huge fan of *Beowulf*, but I'd still read it again if we could have a reading group here like yours!"
--Sherry

"You impress me with sound reason balanced by spiritual values. I will forward this to a few friends whom I know will appreciate your insights.... Keep up the good work. I do believe it makes a difference."
--Jim F.

"I would like to thank you for sharing your thoughts, insights and data as presented on your masterful website. I enjoy the style of your writing very much. Your writing is lucid and provides one of the most readable humanities websites I have ever encountered.... Thank you for blazing the trail for many of us who will certainly make use of your suggestions."
--Anthony

"I ran across your fascinating site last night and have spent a good deal of time with it.... I love your little, 'popular' essays on writers, philosophers, and so on. Academics naturally have a fit over them because they make things too 'easy'."
--David

"Thank you Hammond. You introduced me to the world of culture, wherein I now live and grow. I should say that were the first great influence in my life. I am 19, from Toronto Canada.... I am very interested in Nietzsche, Emerson, Thoreau...."
--Adam

"Received and perused your Newsletter yesterday.... Zen sounds very intriguing, spiritually grounding and elevating, at once. I love what you say about Buddha holding up a flower.... You've certainly whet the appetite to start reading *The Idiot*."
--Yahia L., Cairo

"Thanks Jim for your inspirational e-mails. I shall be using some of your ideas on Jung with some of my AS Philosophy students on Monday afternoon at a large rural comprehensive school in Devon, UK.... Everyone captivated by Jung—got them all interested—thanks. Please would you place a student of mine on your mailing list."
--Judi

"I am Icelandic (40), and I accidentally found your website.... Thank you, first of all for your work, your page, and your fight for — and defending of 'real' philosophy, and creative thought in general. I love reading your deep, intelligent thoughts in your crystal clear English."
--Ragnar

"Buy this underrated book! Original and interesting. Agree or disagree it's clear that Mr. Hammond put years of work into his book and filled it with his own original ideas and observations. He is obviously very well read and can link different ideas together in interesting ways. The prose is clear and easy to read. You can't beat the price either. Check it out."
--Dustin, February 9, 2017 on Amazon

"Maybe you don't know who Hammond is, and I can't blame you for that. I happened upon his website over 10 years ago and I have been a fan ever since. Give his books a chance! He has a deep and profound understanding of so many subjects. It's easy to read and gives you so much to think about. The fact that he is this unknown is a crime."
--Dustin, January 30, 2022 on Amazon

Jim Hammond grew up in Westport, Connecticut, and graduated from Harvard in 1983. He has published philosophical books and articles in China and Taiwan. He has also published ten books in the U.S. For more information, visit LJHammond.com

1. Poe

A. "The Fall of The House of Usher"

Since the local Great Books group is reading "The Fall of The House of Usher," I decided to read it myself. It's Poe at his best. It's a fun story to read, and it raises the biggest of all philosophical questions: is the universe an organism, in which all the parts are inter-connected, or is it something mechanical that's composed of discrete objects? Can parts of the universe affect each other by mysterious means, occult means, or can parts of the universe only affect each other by direct contact? Is the universe like a billiard table, in which the balls affect each other by direct contact, or is it like two separate billiard tables, the balls on one of which are able—we know not how—to affect the balls on the other? Is the universe rational and comprehensible, or is it mysterious, occult, beyond our grasp? Was primitive man right to believe that everything is inter-connected, or were Newton and Descartes right to believe that "occult influence" is nonsense, superstition?

At the end of "The Fall of The House of Usher," the protagonist, Roderick Usher, and his twin sister, Madeline Usher, die, and then their house collapses. There seems to be some sort of rapport, some occult connection, between the Usher house and the Usher siblings. The story seems like wild fantasy, but could it be true? Stories abound of clocks stopping when their owner dies. Isn't the Usher house similar to a clock, isn't it a clock writ large? Isn't the difference between a clock stopping and a house collapsing just a difference of degree, not a difference of kind? Isn't the essential fact in both cases an occult connection between an inanimate object and a person?

There's an ancient Chinese belief that if an emperor dies, there will be an earthquake in the same year; in other words, the Chinese believed that there was an occult connection, a synchronicity (to use Jung's term) between an emperor's death and an earthquake. Isn't this analogous to the Poe story? Again, we have an inexplicable connection between an inanimate object (in this case, the earth) and a person.

In *Macbeth*, we have a connection between the weather and human affairs: the weather is stormy, and there's a storm in the human realm, too (the king is assassinated). A similar synchronicity between weather and human affairs is found in "House of Usher," where a storm breaks out as the story reaches its climax.

We've looked at several cases of a relationship between a person and an inanimate object. Now let's look at a case of occult connection between two inanimate objects, a case drawn from quantum physics, a case so well authenticated by science that even the most confirmed skeptic couldn't deny it. I refer to The Case of Paired Particles:

> Two paired particles, with opposite spin, are sent in opposite directions. The spin of one of the particles is changed. The other particle's spin also changes, at the same instant, without any apparent cause.[1]

Now let's look at an occult connection between two people. If twins are separated by 1,000 miles, and one of them falls down a flight of stairs and breaks his leg, the other may sense that something is wrong with him, or may have a pain in his own leg. An occult connection between twins exists in "The Fall of The House of Usher": "sympathies of a scarcely intelligible nature had always existed between [Roderick and Madeline]." The phrase "scarcely intelligible" can be paraphrased "mysterious, inexplicable, occult." The mysterious "sympathies" between Roderick and Madeline are further evidence that Poe believes in an inter-connected universe, Poe has a Hermetic worldview.

In the Poe story, Roderick Usher believes in "the sentience of all vegetable things." In a footnote, Poe tells us that Usher's belief was shared by various scientists—"Watson, Dr. Percival, Spallanzani, and especially the Bishop of Landaff." But Usher goes further, goes beyond vegetable things: "in his disordered fancy, the idea had assumed a more daring character, and trespassed, under certain conditions, upon the kingdom of inorganization." That is, Usher believed that even inorganic matter may be sentient. "The belief [was] connected... with the gray stones of the home of his forefathers." So the daring theory fits in with the story, but nonetheless it may be a theory that Poe actually subscribed to, or at least was intrigued by. Is it crazy to believe that "gray stones" are sentient if The Case of Paired Particles shows that particles are sentient? Aren't stones made of particles, and isn't it therefore likely that stones are sentient? Surely Poe would have been fascinated by quantum physics.

The books that Usher reads are major Hermetic texts: "the *Heaven and Hell* of Swedenborg... the *Chiromancy* of Robert Fludd... and the *City of the Sun* of Campanella." These Hermetic thinkers believed that the whole universe was sentient, alive, inter-connected. Usher's daring theory is part of a major school of philosophy, the Hermetic School—the mystical, occult, non-rational school. We have every reason to believe that Poe took these ideas seriously. His story is more than a story of mental collapse, more than a terrifying fantasy. His story is a classic expression of an important philosophical idea. "House of Usher" is part of The Poe Worldview, which is part of the Romantic Worldview, which rejected the mechanical, Newton-Descartes worldview.

Some may object that I'm turning Poe into a philosopher, but it should be remembered that Poe, like Coleridge, wrote philosophy as well as imaginative literature. Poe's *Eureka* is an

---

[1] See the section called "Physics and the Occult" in the Physics chapter of my *Conversations With Great Thinkers*.

> attempt to explain the universe, material and spiritual....[1] [Poe] pursued a unitary theory of metaphysics, nature, art, and the human mind. He conducted his search with astounding vitality and persistence, and surely, by the time he had written *Eureka*, he believed he had arrived at the goal.[2]

It would be surprising if Poe's philosophical ideas didn't find their way into his fiction.

Usher's daring theory (that the whole universe is sentient) may have been influenced by Coleridge, a leading Romantic theorist. In one of his essays, Coleridge

> objects to the division "of all that surrounds us into things with life, and things without life" as an "arbitrary assumption".... He conceives of metals as having a low order of life.[3]

Poe may have acquired his Hermetism from Coleridge, rather than from older Hermetics like Fludd and Campanella.

Like any good Hermetist, Poe not only believed that the universe had a non-rational character (a mysterious, occult character), but also believed that we could grasp the universe best by non-rational means; Poe believed that "intuition is a surer road to truth than either induction or deduction."[4]

One might compare Poe to Balzac, who was born in 1799, just ten years before Poe. Like Poe, Balzac had a keen interest in the occult, in Mesmerism, and in phrenology; Balzac also had a keen interest in Swedenborg. Balzac attempted "to construct a viable theory to unify spirit and matter."[5] Balzac delved into these topics in *Louis Lambert*, *Seraphita*, and *The Magic Skin* (*La Peau de Chagrin*). Since Balzac was renowned for his realistic portraits of French society, the case of Balzac shows that a keen interest in the occult is compatible with a sure grasp of reality.

In his essay on Poe, D. H. Lawrence said that Poe's belief in an interconnected world was justified:

> Surely all material things have a *form* of sentience, even the inorganic: surely they all exist in some subtle and complicated tension of vibration which makes them sensitive to external influence and causes them to have an influence on other external objects, irrespective of contact.

---

[1] See Floyd Stovall's essay, "Poe's Debt to Coleridge," in the Norton Critical Edition of Poe.

[2] See the Joseph Moldenhauer essay, "Murder As A Fine Art," in the Norton Critical Edition.

[3] This is a quote from Coleridge (*Hints towards the formation of a more comprehensive theory of life*) inside a quote from Stovall's essay. Apparently Coleridge used the phrase "mere assumption," and Stovall changed it to "arbitrary assumption."

[4] Quote from Stovall, not Poe.

[5] See the Wikipedia article, "Louis Lambert (novel)"

It's remarkable that Lawrence grasped the Hermetic worldview, the interconnected worldview, and realized that Poe was expressing this worldview, not just writing an entertaining story.

But Lawrence doesn't dwell on Poe's view of the universe, he dwells on Poe's depiction of mental collapse, loss of self. Lawrence says that "House of Usher" is a story of excessive love, and the resulting breakdown of personality. Roderick Usher is so close to his twin sister, so merged in her, that he loses himself.

According to Lawrence, Poe's lovers disintegrate because they

> cannot be separate, cannot be isolate, cannot listen in isolation to the isolate Holy Ghost. For it is the Holy Ghost we must live by.... And the Holy Ghost speaks individually inside each individual: always, for ever a ghost. There is no manifestation to the general world. Each isolate individual listening in isolation to the Holy Ghost within him.
>
> The Ushers, brother and sister, betrayed the Holy Ghost in themselves. They would love, love, without resistance. They would love, they would merge, they would be as one thing. So they dragged each other down into death. For the Holy Ghost says you must not be as one thing with another being. Each must abide by itself, and correspond only within certain limits.
>
> The best tales all have the same burden [that is, Poe's best tales all have the same theme]. Hate is as inordinate as love, and as slowly consuming, as secret, as underground, as subtle. All this underground vault business in Poe only symbolizes that which takes place beneath the consciousness. On top, all is fair-spoken. Beneath, there is awful murderous extremity of burying alive. Fortunato, in "The Cask of Amontillado," is buried alive out of perfect hatred, as the lady Madeline of Usher is buried alive out of love.

This is literary criticism at its best, literary criticism that reaches the level of philosophy. If we substitute the word "unconscious" for "Holy Ghost," Lawrence's view is much like Jung's. (Indeed, Lawrence often uses the term "unconscious," and Jung often uses the term "Holy Ghost.") Both Lawrence and Jung say that it's healthy to listen to our unconscious, unhealthy to lose ourselves in the Other.

In his essay on Friendship, Emerson said "The condition which high friendship demands is ability to do without it.... There must be very two, before there can be very one." Poe's stories show us the danger of becoming "very one" before we've become "very two", the danger of merging with the Other before we've become an individual, an individual capable of standing alone.

Poe's most famous poem, "The Raven," deals with boundless love, love that refuses to give up the beloved even after she dies. Poe epitomizes the Romantic merging of love and death. The linkage between love and death is apparent in some lines that Poe wrote when he was 20:

I could not love except where Death

Was mingling his with Beauty's breath.

The narrator of "The Raven" reminds us of Poe: he's a scholar, pondering "over many a quaint and curious volume of forgotten lore." He's hyper-sensitive to external impressions: "the silken sad uncertain rustling of each purple curtain thrilled me—filled me with fantastic terrors."

B. "Ligeia"

According to Lawrence, Poe's "chief story" is "Ligeia." Like "House of Usher", "Ligeia" is a story of excessive love. According to Lawrence, "Ligeia" is also Poe's own story, the story of his love for his young cousin. Lawrence calls Poe's love "the intensest nervous vibration of unison," and Lawrence says, "the longing for identification with the beloved becomes a lust."

Ligeia's husband wants to know her completely, to probe her inmost soul. "What he wants to do with Ligeia," writes Lawrence, "is to analyze her, till he knows all her component parts, till he has got her all in his consciousness." Lawrence quotes from the story:

> The expression of the eyes of Ligeia! How for long hours have I pondered upon it! How have I, through the whole of a midsummer night, struggled to fathom it! What was it... which lay far within the pupils of my beloved? What *was* it? I was possessed with a passion to discover.

Ligeia is swept away by strong passions: "Of all the women whom I have ever known, she, the outwardly calm, the ever-placid Ligeia, was the most violently a prey to the tumultuous vultures of stern passion." This prompts the following from Lawrence: "Poor Poe, he had caught a bird of the same feather as himself. One of those terrible cravers, who crave the further sensation. Crave to madness or death."

"Ligeia" is a story of immoderate love, and also immoderate hate. Ligeia's love for her husband is "no ordinary passion.... For long hours, detaining my hand, would she pour out before me the overflowing of a heart whose more than passionate devotion amounted to idolatry." After Ligeia dies, her husband marries Lady Rowena, for whom he soon conceives an immoderate hate: "I loathed her with a hatred belonging more to demon than to man."

On the whole, Lawrence seems to be a fan of Poe, but he says that Poe is purely destructive, and fails to be constructive. Poe depicts the personality disintegrating, but doesn't show us a way out, hence he isn't a true artist: "In true art," Lawrence writes, "there is always the double rhythm of creating and destroying." But Lawrence insists that Poe's dark vision has a certain value: "the human soul must suffer its own disintegration, *consciously*, if ever it is to survive."

Lawrence takes a dim view of Poe's poetry. Lawrence says that Poe's personality-collapse makes him hyper-sensitive to external impressions. Lawrence speaks of Poe's extraordinary facility in versification. The absence of real central or impulsive being in himself leaves him inordinately, mechanically sensitive to sounds and effects, associations of sounds, associations of rhyme, for example—mechanical, facile, having no root in any passion.

C. Mesmerism

I read a Poe story called "Mesmeric Revelation." I'm interested in mesmerism because it smacks of the occult. Mesmerism is a path to the unconscious, like hypnotism, dreams, etc. It's also a path to transference—i.e., to a telepathic bond, an unconscious rapport, between mesmerist and patient. After reading "Mesmeric Revelation," I read two essays about it.[1] Neither the story nor the essays were very good, but the essays did whet my appetite to read Poe's other stories about mesmerism: "A Tale of the Ragged Mountains," and "The Facts in the Case of M. Valdemar." That Poe wrote three stories about mesmerism shows how interested he was in the subject. The title "Mesmeric Revelation" suggests that mesmerism (in Poe's view) is the road to deep truths.

"Mesmeric Revelation" isn't a story so much as a philosophical essay. Hence it can be compared to Poe's treatise *Eureka*; one critic called it "a prelude to *Eureka*." As in *Eureka*, Poe confuses things by emphasizing the role of God. Poe also makes the mistake of viewing the universe as created for a purpose, rather than growing up spontaneously. This notion of purpose reminds me of our earlier discussion of The Great Chain of Being; in this discussion, we reviewed the history of Western philosophy, showing how rational thinkers often argued that the world must have been created for a purpose.[2]

According to Poe, life exists for the purpose of pain, and pain is necessary to appreciate pleasure; we can only appreciate heavenly bliss if we've gone through earthly pain. "Pleasure, in all cases, is but the contrast of pain," Poe writes. "Never to suffer would have been never to have been blessed.... The pain of the primitive life of Earth, is the sole basis of the bliss of the ultimate life in Heaven." In my view, Poe's emphasis on pain and pleasure is a sign of superficial thinking. My fundamental principles are that everything is connected and everything is alive. I regard pain and pleasure as secondary things, epiphenomena.

Poe falls into the same error that many rational philosophers fell into—namely, he believes that God must have created many inhabited worlds. We must have earthly pain, Poe reasons, so worlds are created, and each of these worlds is "tenanted by a distinct variety of organic, rudimental, thinking creatures."

---

[1] "Poe and Mesmerism," by Sidney E. Lind, *PMLA*, Vol. 62, No. 4 (Dec., 1947), pp. 1077-1094; "Poe and the Power of Animal Magnetism," by Doris V. Falk, *PMLA*, Vol. 84, No. 3 (May, 1969), pp. 536-546. Lind points out that "'Mesmerism' and 'animal magnetism' were terms used interchangeably in the nineteenth century."

[2] See ljhammond.com/phlit/2009-02.htm#6

But while Poe falls into some errors, he also has some profound ideas. Poe understood that science isn't just a matter of patient experiment. "Science makes its most important advances by seemingly intuitive *leaps*," Poe wrote.[1] Poe believed that everything is connected—a fact that the poet can grasp better than the scientist. Through intuitions and dreams, "the poet can reestablish the network of universal correspondences and the unity of Creation which intelligence and analysis have fragmented."[2]

One of Poe's deepest ideas is that some matter is solid, while other matter is loose, airy, "unparticled." For example, the atmosphere is less solid than a rock, and electricity might be less solid than the atmosphere. "There are gradations of matter of which man knows nothing," Poe writes. "These gradations of matter increase in rarity or fineness, until we arrive at a matter unparticled." I'm reminded of the old alchemical idea of a "subtle body." As I said in an earlier issue,

> Modern physics blurs the boundary between matter and the surrounding space. The whole universe, both "matter" and "emptiness," is buzzing with energy, with a kind of life, with what the Chinese called *ch'i* (also spelled *qi*). Just as there's no "dead matter," so too there's no "dead space." The universe is one, and the universe is alive, and all parts of the universe are connected to, one might say communicating with, all other parts. In classical, Newtonian physics, there were solid particles and empty space. But in modern physics, particles aren't solid, and space isn't empty.[3]

Poe's idea of "unparticled matter" blurs the distinction between matter and void. Likewise, Poe's idea of a "living corpse" blurs the distinction between life and death. All three of Poe's mesmerism stories ("Mesmeric Revelation," "Ragged Mountains," and "M. Valdemar") deal with a living corpse, a person who seems to straddle the fence between life and death. At the end of "Mesmeric Revelation," the narrator wonders if the patient has been speaking to him while dead, "addressing me from out the region of the shadows." Rationalists will dismiss such things as wild fantasy, contrived to sell magazines, but in my view, the line between life and death is unclear, mysterious, and worthy of serious consideration. We simply don't know what is life, what is death. Poe suggests that a "dead" person may have heightened powers of thought, feeling, and action, though his physical senses are gone, just as a mesmerized person seems to have heightened powers, though his physical senses are in abeyance.

In Poe's "Tale of the Ragged Mountains," a man named Bedloe appears to be a living corpse, a second incarnation of a man named Oldeb. So this appears to be a case of reincarnation, metempsychosis. Bedloe has a vision

---

1 *The Genius of Edgar Allan Poe*, by Georges Zayed, Ch. 17, p. 143

2 Ibid, p. 145. These are Zayed's words, not Poe's.

3 See ljhammond.com/phlit/2010-08b.htm

of his former life, as Oldeb, at the very time when his mesmerist, Dr. Templeton, is writing an account of Oldeb's life. So this appears to be a case of unconscious rapport, transference, a telepathic bond.[1]

So which is it, reincarnation or rapport? I would argue that it's both reincarnation and rapport; in earlier issues, I've said that different branches of the occult often overlap. But critics seem to be confused by this overlapping; Lind argues that this is only rapport, not reincarnation, and Falk argues that Lind is wrong, it's reincarnation.

Oldeb is killed, then has an out-of-body experience. "I seemed to rise from the ground.... Beneath me lay my corpse, with the arrow in my temple." Then Oldeb "flitted buoyantly out of the city." Rationalists will dismiss this as wild fantasy, others will regard it as a good description of an out-of-body experience. We discussed out-of-body experiences, or "near death" experiences, in an earlier issue.[2]

In Poe's "M. Valdemar," a mesmerist tries to prolong someone's life by keeping them mesmerized. Here again, rationalists will dismiss this as wild fantasy, but there seem to be such cases. A few months ago, I attended a lecture by Eben Alexander, who wrote a bestseller called *Proof of Heaven*. He said he woke up one morning with a lethal case of meningitis, spent a week in a coma, had an out-of-body experience, then came back to consciousness. The odds of surviving such an illness are slim, and his doctors didn't expect him to live. Was his life prolonged by his out-of-body experience? Did his soul's vitality prevent his body from dying? Can an out-of-body experience be induced, and life be prolonged, by a hypnotist or mesmerist?

Lind points out that Dickens was a defender of mesmerism, while Hawthorne was a critic.[3] Lind speaks of, "Hawthorne's repugnance to spiritualism and mesmerism, and his harsh delineation of Dr. Westervelt, the crafty mesmerist in *The Blithedale Romance*." The founder of mesmerism, Franz Mesmer, coined the term "animal magnetism," meaning a force or energy exerted by living things, and perhaps non-living things, too. Schopenhauer, who was generally receptive to the occult, said

> Considered [from] the philosophical point of view, animal magnetism is the most pregnant of all discoveries that have ever been made, although for the time being it propounds rather than solves riddles. It is

---

[1] "Between Doctor Templeton and Bedloe," Poe writes, "there had grown up, little by little, a very distinct and strongly marked rapport, or magnetic relation.... When I first became acquainted with the two, sleep was brought about almost instantaneously by the mere volition of the operator, even when the invalid was unaware of his presence."

[2] See ljhammond.com/phlit/2002-03.htm#6

[3] For more on this subject, see Fred Kaplan's *Dickens and Mesmerism*. See also Robert Darnton's *Mesmerism and the End of the Enlightenment in France*. For D. H. Lawrence's interest in mesmerism, see ljhammond.com/phlit/2009-01b.htm#9

> really practical metaphysics. [A] time will come when philosophy, animal magnetism, and natural science... will shed so bright a light on one another that truths will be discovered at which we could not otherwise hope to arrive.[1]

Poe shared Schopenhauer's view that mesmerism (animal magnetism) opened up important new fields; in "Ragged Mountains," Poe says, "the soul of the man of today is upon the verge of some stupendous psychal discoveries." Mesmerism opens up the study of the unconscious, and the study of the occult, and thus can lead to "stupendous discoveries."

Lind tells us that a writer who met Poe, Andrew Jackson Davis, said "he is, in spirit, a foreigner." Lind calls this "a keen insight into Poe's personality." Was Poe a "foreigner in spirit" because he spent some of his formative years in Britain? Or was he a foreigner because he was a great intellectual, and many great intellectuals are "foreigners in spirit"? Nietzsche, Joyce, Ibsen—they were all "foreigners in spirit." Did Poe connect with French intellectuals partly because he was a "foreigner," not a "total American"?

D. "The Black Cat"

As I mentioned before, "Mesmeric Revelation" is a rather dull story, and rather unimpressive as a philosophical treatise. "Ragged Mountains" and "M. Valdemar" are better stories. But if you want to see Poe at his best, read "The Black Cat." I admit, it requires a strong stomach, it's a grisly story, but it's one of the best stories by one of the best story-writers.

As for criticism, I recommend *"The Black Cat": Perverseness Reconsidered*, by James Gargano.[2] Gargano notes that the narrator of "The Black Cat" has much to say about

> the spirit of PERVERSENESS. Of this spirit philosophy takes no account. Yet I am not more sure that my soul lives, than I am that perverseness is one of the primitive impulses of the human heart—one of the indivisible primary faculties, or sentiments, which give direction to the character of Man. Who has not, a hundred times, found himself committing a vile or a silly action, for no other reason than because he knows he should not?

Many critics, Gargano says, have argued that "Black Cat" is a story of perverseness. But they're wrong, Gargano says; "Black Cat" is about justice, about how evil actions are punished, how man descends gradually into evil, each step leading to the next step, how evil destroys the soul, how evil destroys the evil-doer from within. In short, it's a story of the workings of moral law, not a story about arbitrary perversity. Gargano speaks of "the narrator's fatuous denial of a moral order at the same time that the reader observes its unfaltering operation."

---

[1] See Wikipedia's article on "Animal Magnetism."

[2] *Texas Studies in Literature and Language*, Vol. 2, No. 2 (Summer 1960), pp. 172-178

Poe's emphasis on perversity is much like Dostoyevsky's. We should take this as Poe's own opinion, not dismiss it as the narrator's opinion. Gargano says that if evil results from a perverse impulse—an impulse that's arbitrary, accidental, uncaused—then there's no moral order. I would argue that evil results from a perverse impulse *and* there's a moral order. Those who give vent to their perverse and evil impulses are punished from within and from without.

In "Black Cat," punishment follows crime with such regularity that one is tempted to invoke the concept of karma. We discussed karma in an earlier issue:

> Science has alerted the West to the importance of causal relationships in the physical world.... India extends this concept of causation to include moral and spiritual life as well.... The present condition of each interior life—how happy it is, how confused or serene, how much it sees—is an exact product of what it has wanted and done in the past. Equally, its present thoughts and decisions are determining its future experiences. Each act that is directed upon the world has its equal and opposite reaction on oneself. Each thought and deed delivers an unseen chisel blow that sculpts one's destiny.[1]

When the narrator of "Black Cat" raps on the very spot where he has immured his wife, it's an example of *frevel*, playful daring that's related to evil.[2] Apparently the "immuration" in "Black Cat" was inspired by an actual murder. And it resembles a later murder: Dr. Hawley Crippen's murder and "immuration" of his wife in 1910.

When did the narrator's chain of crime and punishment begin? When did his descent into evil begin? Gargano shrewdly argues that it began with exaggerated goodness, with a life of sweet innocence:

> Analysis of "The Black Cat" may profitably begin with a consideration of the narrator's professed tenderness of heart. This distinguishing trait expresses itself in such an inordinate fondness for animals as to call forth the ridicule of his playmates....[3] His marriage introduces little change into his life, for his wife shares his docility and tenderness. Indeed, it is almost as if he has acquired another pet rather than a spouse. This congenial triumvirate—narrator, wife, and pets, especially Pluto, the black cat—appears for a time to constitute a family from which all but soft and gentle sensations have been eliminated.

---

1 This is a quote from Huston Smith. See ljhammond.com/phlit/2010-12.htm#2

2 For more on this topic, see *Conversations With Great Thinkers* ==> Psychology ==> "Frevel"

3 Perhaps this "inordinate fondness" conceals something darker. In his essay on Schopenhauer, Hitschmann said that compassion for animals is often accompanied by cruelty toward people.

One is reminded of Poe's own unconsummated marriage to his thirteen-year-old cousin. Does the narrator's fondness for pets also have an analogue in Poe's own life? Certainly the narrator's alcoholism has an analogue in Poe's own life. Gargano shrewdly remarks (following an earlier critic?) that the narrator's "helplessness under the power of 'the Fiend Intemperance' symbolizes his susceptibility to evil through his own divided nature."

The narrator ignores everything but the "soft and gentle," and thereby pushes his shadow to rise up in protest. Nikos Kazantzakis said, "The real meaning of enlightenment is to gaze with undimmed eyes on all darkness." The narrator closes his eyes to the darkness, to his own shadow.

Gargano notes that "Black Cat" has two distinct parts:

> The incidents from the beginning of the story up to and including the fire constitute a distinct artistic unit: a climactic deed has been consummated and a radical moral change has taken place in the protagonist. In a sense, the first section establishes, metaphorically, the conditions that must precede the narrator's murder of his wife. The artistry of the section is remarkable, for in addition to dramatizing what appears a "complete" action, it leaves the protagonist on the brink of total self-destruction.... The hanging of the cat is the clandestine equivalent to the humanly revolting murder of his wife; they are the same deed, in the latter case taking a form which outrages society and must be punished by it.... Thus, the two parts of "The Black Cat" effectively complement each other by revealing in turn the narrator's inner deterioration and his public exposure.

Gargano also notes that the destruction of the house in "Black Cat" is comparable to the destruction of the house in Poe's "Fall of the House of Usher."

> The destruction of the house clearly represents [the narrator's] almost complete moral disintegration, as in "The Fall of the House of Usher" the collapse of the fissure-ridden house corresponds to the death of Roderick Usher. The remaining wall with the "portraiture" of Pluto on it just as clearly signifies that what survives of the narrator will be haunted by his ineradicable sin against his own nature.

Poe's work is full of vitality as well as profundity. Critics have derided the youthful tone of his work. T. S. Eliot, for example, said that Poe has "the intellect of a highly gifted young person before puberty." But perhaps this youthful tone is a virtue; perhaps it's part of Poe's charm.

Henry James said that "enthusiasm for Poe is the mark of a decidedly primitive stage of reflection." Yes, if we take "primitive" in a positive sense. It's precisely this primitive character that James' own work sorely lacks.

E. "The Purloined Letter"

"The Purloined Letter" is one of Poe's best-known stories. It's a detective story, featuring the shrewd C. Auguste Dupin. It's one of Poe's "ratiocination" stories—in other words, it deals with solving a puzzle.

Poe himself was good at solving puzzles, so one wonders if Dupin has some of Poe's own traits. As aids to concentration, Dupin uses smoking, darkness, and silence. Did Poe use the same aids? Poe created the genre of the puzzle-solver because he was himself a puzzle-solver; he was good at it, and enjoyed it.

Sherlock Holmes has some of Dupin's traits; Poe's detective stories influenced Arthur Conan Doyle and others. Like Sherlock Holmes, Dupin is a private detective who has an admiring friend (the narrator), and is more clever than the police.

In "Purloined Letter," the police decide that the letter must be in a certain apartment, and they thoroughly search the apartment. One can't fault their thoroughness or diligence. Dupin thinks more creatively, he considers a wider range of possibilities. If the police are like a scientist who works hard, Dupin is like a scientist who makes a leap to a new paradigm. Dupin puts himself in the mind of the thief, and says that the thief must "reason well" because he's both a poet and a mathematician, he's both imaginative and calculating.

Though there are many critical essays on "The Purloined Letter," I didn't find an essay that I especially liked. I did, however, find a PoeSociety website, eapoe.org, that has many critical essays online. One of these essays is about Coleridge's influence on Poe.[1] Perhaps no thinker influenced Poe more than Coleridge.[2] Coleridge was a deep thinker, a penetrating critic, and a gifted poet. He popularized recent German thinkers and old Hermetic thinkers.

One critic says that Poe's policeman is merely ingenious, not analytic.

> Ingenuity is a mere mechanical skill of combining the facts, obeying the law of cause and effect, [but] analysis is a truly creative power, not determined in its outcome by a strict adherence to such external rules. The close relation of this distinction to Coleridge's differentiation in the *Biographia Literaria* between "fancy" and "imagination" need not even be deduced, it is openly suggested in Poe's text. In a telling aside, the narrator of "The Murders in the Rue Morgue" remarks that "Between ingenuity and the analytic ability there exists a difference far greater, indeed, than that between the fancy and the imagination, but of a character very strictly analogous. It will be found, in fact, that the

---

1 "The Spiritual Descent into the Maelström: A Debt to 'The Rime of the Ancient Mariner,'" by Margaret J. Yonce

2 See

- "Poe's Debt To Coleridge," by Floyd Stovall (*Studies in English*, No. 10 (July 8, 1930), pp. 70-127)
- "Purloined Voices: Edgar Allan Poe Reading Samuel Taylor Coleridge," by Alexander Schlutz (*Studies in Romanticism*, Vol. 47, No. 2 (Summer, 2008), pp. 195-224)
- "Edgar Allan Poe: A Debt Repaid," by Jonathan Bate (this essay can be found in an e-book called *The Coleridge Connection*)

> ingenious are always fanciful, and the truly imaginative never otherwise than analytic." Dupin himself is a true example of the analyst: not confined to a single perspective, his observations are not limited to a specific set of presuppositions.... Because of their imaginative poetic faculties [the thief and Dupin] are both able to outwit the merely ingenious and fanciful Prefect.[1]

F. "The Murders in the Rue Morgue"

This was Poe's first detective story, and it created a sensation—indeed, it created a genre. Wikipedia says,

> "The Murders in the Rue Morgue" established many tropes that would become common elements in mystery fiction: the eccentric but brilliant detective, the bumbling constabulary, the first-person narration by a close personal friend.... Poe also initiates the storytelling device where the detective announces his solution and then explains the reasoning leading up to it.
>
> Modern readers are occasionally put off by Poe's violation of an implicit narrative convention: Readers should be able to guess the solution as they read. The twist ending, however, is a sign of "bad faith" on Poe's part because readers would not reasonably include an orangutan on their list of potential murderers.
>
> Later detective stories would have set up M. Le Bon, the suspect who is arrested, as appearing guilty as a red herring, though Poe chose not to.[2]

"Rue Morgue" begins with a long prologue on analytic thinking. Poe argues that chess doesn't require genuine analytic thinking, because the number of possible moves is finite; chess requires only concentration and calculation. But whist, Poe says, requires analytic thinking; a whist player "notes every variation of face as the play progresses, gathering a fund of thought from the differences in the expression of certainty, of surprise, of triumph, or of chagrin."

Poe mentions the famous French detective Vidocq, whose memoirs may have inspired "Rue Morgue." Vidocq started the world's first detective agency in 1817, when urbanization was causing a rise in crime, and the first police forces were being established. Newspapers were reporting on crime, and the public was becoming interested in crime.

---

1 "Purloined Voices," by A. Schlutz

2 See Wikipedia's article, "The Murders in the Rue Morgue." Wikipedia notes that "there were other stories [before Poe's "Rue Morgue"] that featured similar problem-solving characters. *Das Fräulein von Scuderi* (1819), by E.T.A. Hoffmann... is sometimes cited as the first detective story. Other forerunners include Voltaire's *Zadig* (1748), with a main character who performs similar feats of analysis."

The police are baffled by the murders in the Rue Morgue. But Dupin unravels the mystery by looking for what's odd and unusual:

> It is by these deviations from the plane of the ordinary, that reason feels its way, if at all, in its search for the true. In investigations such as we are now pursuing, it should not be so much asked "what has occurred," as "what has occurred that has never occurred before."

I went back to my old friend Marie Bonaparte, to see if her Freudian study of Poe would impress me as much as it did during my salad days. I read her analysis of "Rue Morgue," which is quite long, and attempts to summarize the story as well as analyze it; you can probably understand her piece without reading the story itself.

Bonaparte's big study of Poe treats his life as well as his work, and she reminded me that Poe went insane for a time, as Dostoyevsky did. Poe said candidly, "I became insane, with long intervals of horrible sanity. During these fits of absolute unconsciousness, I drank—God only knows how often or how much."[1] Bonaparte says that Poe bounced back and forth between healthy women and dying women, and he couldn't find peace in either direction. He could find peace only in drink or drugs or death:

> On the one hand, he was compelled to fly from the dire temptations aroused in him by dead or dying women [like his wife Virginia, who was dying of tuberculosis], on the other, the gruesome fidelity that chained him to the dead woman denied him a right to the living woman. If he turned to them, his way was blocked by the tomb of *Ulalume* while, if he stayed with his dying Virginia, his moral scruples forbade the fearful deeds prompted by his sado-necrophilist sex-urges. Thus both roads were blocked. Then, according as danger threatened most, he would dash for escape in the opposite direction until he found his way blocked and was forced to turn back. Only chastity remained allowed and the means by which to maintain it intact; drinking abroad with his cronies or opium, taken in secret, at home.[2]

Poe's psychological problems were never solved, and may have been insoluble. These problems filled his life with trials and tribulations. His creativity grew out of his suffering.

His works often reflect his life. Bonaparte points out that Dupin the detective resembles Poe in his "doubleness," his "duplicity." Like Poe, Dupin has a "Bi-Part Soul... the creative and the resolvent," the fiction writer and the puzzle solver. Like Poe, Dupin comes from "an illustrious family," but his fortunes have declined.

Bonaparte discusses Poe's influence on Arthur Conan Doyle. Doyle introduced Sherlock Holmes in the novel *A Study in Scarlet*. In that work,

---

[1] *The Life and Works of Edgar Allan Poe*, ch. 36, p. 449

[2] Ch. 17, p. 107

> Holmes reflects on the *outré* character (the very word used by Poe) of the crime he is called upon to solve, considering it a distinguishing feature of the case which should help its elucidation. Even Sherlock Holmes' famous pipe is first smoked by Dupin in "The Purloined Letter."[1]

Bonaparte says that the "ape murder" in "Rue Morgue" is peculiarly violent, and gratifies our aggressive instincts. It also recalls the "primal scene," that is, parental sex as witnessed by the infant. According to Bonaparte, the infant views sex as an aggressive act, and thinks that the man castrates the woman. Beheading is a symbol of castration, hence in "Rue Morgue," the man (the orang-outang) beheads the woman, and hence, in primitive society, beheading is widely practiced.

Bonaparte says that the women, in "Rue Morgue," live in seclusion, in a tightly sealed room, because that's what the son (the author, Poe himself) wished. "No doubt we have here Edgar's wish-fantasy in regard to his mother; the wish of the child to keep all men away."[2]

While Madame L'Espanaye represents the mother, her daughter represents Poe's sister, Rosalie. The ape rams the daughter up the chimney head downwards. The chimney, Bonaparte says, represents the maternal vagina, and the ape implants a child in the vagina. The sex act (castration/beheading of the woman) precedes pregnancy, precedes the implanting of the daughter in the chimney. Bonaparte reminds us that "head downwards [is] the child's position before birth."[3]

If Bonaparte is right, then there's much in "Rue Morgue" that Poe himself wasn't aware of, and his readers weren't aware of, much that doesn't reach the level of consciousness. If Bonaparte is right, then much creativity occurs below the level of consciousness. On the whole, I find Bonaparte's argument persuasive, though some of her points may be stretched.

* * * * *

A critic named John Moore argued that "Rue Morgue" was influenced by Walter Scott's novel *Count Robert of Paris*.[4] This novel features an orang-outang of exceptional size and strength. In many respects, Scott's orang-outang resembles Poe's—his voice, his climbing ability, his size, his agility, his fear of a whip, etc. Scott's orang-outang

> climbs into Agelastes's apartment through a window, unseen. Here he is pacific in his intentions until Agelastes strikes him, when he becomes frenzied, loses all sense of awe for man, and strangles Agelastes. Terrified at what he has done, he escapes by the window through which

---

[1] Ch. 36, p. 430, footnote

[2] Ch. 36, p. 453

[3] Ch. 36, p. 454

[4] "Poe, Scott, and 'The Murders in the Rue Morgue'," by John Robert Moore, *American Literature*, Vol. 8, No. 1 (March, 1936), pp. 52-58.

> he has entered. The strange death of Agelastes remains a mystery to the Emperor's court.

Moore notes another case of Scott's influence on Poe: Scott's *Bride of Lammermoor* influenced Poe's "Fall of the House of Usher"

> with its melancholy young hero, last of his doomed family, dwelling almost alone in a crumbling house the rooms of which are draped in black; the hero's burial of his nearest relative with his own hands in a family vault inside the house; the intensely poetic mood of the narrative; the prophetic foreboding of the interposed lyrics; and the nearby body of water which swallows up the last survivor of his race.

One might say that Moore's argument is the opposite of Bonaparte's. Moore argues that the gruesome quality of "Rue Morgue" doesn't result from Poe's pathology but rather from Poe's source, *Count Robert of Paris*. Moore says that too many critics ignore Poe's sources and focus on his pathology. In my view, these factors work together; Poe has sources, but his pathology molds his choice of sources, and his use of sources. It's a "both/and," not an "either/or."

Poe followed "Rue Morgue" with another detective story, "The Mystery of Marie Roget." "Marie Roget" is based on a real mystery, the death of a young woman named Mary Rogers. Poe uses "Marie Roget" to put forth his solution of the mystery of Mary Rogers. It has been argued that later evidence overturned Poe's solution, and when Poe became aware of this evidence, he modified his story, lest his reputation as a puzzle-solver suffer.[1]

2. Balzac

October 22, 2013
The local GreatBooks group recently read and discussed a Balzac short story, "A Passion in the Desert." It's a great story, and since it can be interpreted various ways, it's a good story for a discussion group. It's a great description of the relationship between man and animal, a great description of the joy of solitude, and it's leavened with wit.

If I were asked to come up with an alternate title for the story, I might call it "Transitions." It deals with the transition from fear of solitude to enjoyment of solitude, the transition from fear of death to acceptance of death, etc. (In an earlier issue, I described a disciple of Jung who went into the mountains in search of solitude, and experienced a transition from fear to serenity.[2])

Balzac was a contemporary of Poe (he was born in 1799, ten years before Poe), and Balzac was interested in the occult, so it isn't surprising that

---

1 See *Poe The Detective: The Curious Circumstances Behind "The Mystery of Marie Roget,"* by John Walsh. New Brunswick, N.J.: Rutgers University Press, 1968, reviewed by W. K. Wimsatt in *American Literature*, Vol. 40, No. 4 (Jan., 1969), pp. 555-557

2 See ljhammond.com/phlit/2004-03.htm#9

he deals with mesmerism (animal magnetism). "The presence of the panther," Balzac writes, "even asleep, could not fail to produce the effect which the magnetic eyes of the serpent are said to have on the nightingale." Later, it's the panther herself who is mesmerized: "He looked at her caressingly, staring into her eyes in order to magnetize her, and let her come quite close to him."

How does the man avoid being eaten by the panther? Balzac says that perhaps "his will powerfully projected had modified the character of his companion." This suggests that mesmerism is a matter of will, the projection of will. We should view mesmerism (animal magnetism) not as a narrow, specialized technique, but as part of the larger issue of the will, how the will can influence the external world. One of Balzac's first writings was a Treatise on the Will, which he mentions in his autobiographical novel *Louis Lambert*. *Louis Lambert* discusses Franz Mesmer, animal magnetism, etc.

I'm curious to know what inspired Balzac to write this story, and how critics have interpreted it, but I haven't found any good essays on it. Surely Balzac knew many old soldiers who were wounded in the Napoleonic wars, but I doubt he knew any who had such strange adventures.

The great Jewish-Austrian writer Stefan Zweig wrote about Balzac in a book called *Three Masters: Balzac, Dickens, Dostoyevsky*.[1] At the time of his death (1942), Zweig was working on a major biography of Balzac, a biography that was never finished. Zweig doesn't seem to grasp the occult, but he realized that Balzac was interested in the occult. Zweig says that, according to Balzac, the shape of one's face reveals one's 'character and inner possibilities.' Zweig continues:

> Mesmer's teaching about the magnetic transference of the will of a medium into another person, was an article of faith with [Balzac]. Nor was he less credulous in his belief that the fingers were endowed with a magnetic power whereby the will could be transmitted from individual to individual. He linked these ideas up with the mystical spiritualizations of Swedenborg. All such ideas he compacted into a more or less systematic theory, and gave utterance to them through the mouth of Louis Lambert, the 'chemist of the will,' cut off in his prime. This Louis Lambert is at one and the same time a portrait of Balzac as he was, and a sketch of the perfected Balzac he would have liked to be; and that is why Lambert embodies more autobiography than any other of Balzac's imaginary figures.

Notice that Zweig describes Balzac as "credulous," which suggests that Zweig himself wasn't receptive to the occult.

3. Hawthorne

---

[1] Zweig wrote about mesmerism in *Mental healers: Franz Anton Mesmer, Mary Baker Eddy, Sigmund Freud.*

A. Survey by Paul Elmer More

I came across an excellent essay on Hawthorne. It was published in *The Atlantic* in 1901. The author, Paul Elmer More, was a prominent writer of the time, a literary critic and a defender of Christianity.

More begins by saying that one theme runs through all of Hawthorne's work: "the penalty of solitude laid upon the human soul." This theme is also apparent in Hawthorne's life; his life is the basis of his work, his work reflects his experience. "Never lived a man," More writes, "to whom ordinary contact with his fellows was more impossible, and the mysterious solitude in which his fictitious characters move is a mere shadow of his own imperial loneliness of soul." I've often argued that imaginative writers tend to express one idea, one theme, in all their work, so I was prepared to believe More's view that one theme runs through all of Hawthorne's works.[1] Hopefully a discussion of Hawthorne's theme will give us an introduction to his work, and inspire us to read his work, without giving away his plots.

The source of Hawthorne's idiosyncrasies can be found in his early childhood. His father was a sea captain who died in 1808, when Hawthorne was just four; his father was probably away from home during much of Hawthorne's first four years. His mother rarely left her room. Of his relationship to his mother, Hawthorne said, "a sort of coldness of intercourse existed between us."[2] One psychologist, C. P. Oberndorf, spoke of Hawthorne's "withdrawal from life, so like his mother's."

Hawthorne experienced "almost continuous depression and feelings of guilt. He was given to punitive self-denials for minor self-indulgences, such as refusing to drink tea because he liked it, a characteristic so typical of neurotic patients." Hawthorne married Sophia Peabody, "an invalid who like his mother had been confined to her room for years." Hawthorne and Sophia seem to have been well matched; she was a fan of his writings, and they had three children.

Hawthorne spent his early years in Salem, Massachusetts and Raymond, Maine. Raymond is on Lake Sebago. "Those were delightful days," Hawthorne later said of Maine, "for that part of the country was wild then, with only scattered clearings, and nine-tenths of it primeval woods." But Hawthorne's memories of Maine weren't entirely positive; he later said that he developed there his "cursed habit of solitude."

When Hawthorne was nine, he was hit on the leg while playing and spent a year in bed, though doctors could find nothing wrong with him; perhaps we should describe this as a childhood neurosis. Perhaps Hawthorne's

---

[1] For a discussion of the central theme of Dickens' work, see ljhammond.com/phlit/2009-06.htm#7. I discussed the central theme of Kafka's work in *Conversations With Great Thinkers*, Ch. 7, "Literature" ==> "Kafka."

[2] "Psychoanalysis in Literature and Its Therapeutic Value," by C. Oberndorf (in *Psychoanalysis and Literature*, edited by H. Ruitenbeek). The next four quotes are also from Oberndorf's essay.

neuroses, idiosyncrasies, and inner conflicts fueled his creativity; genius is often eccentric, often on the border of sanity and insanity.

Hawthorne was especially depressed at age 32, and "thought seriously of suicide." He had another bout of depression at 42. His final bout of depression began in 1860, when he was 56, and lasted until his death in 1864. During this final phase, his wife described him as "so apathetic, so indifferent, so hopeless, so unstrung." As with his childhood "illness," no physical ailment could be identified as the cause of his final "illness." "No organic disease has been established as the cause of his lingering final illness which had all the characteristics of his previous depressions." One infers that Hawthorne died of depression; he had no will to live. Emerson said of Hawthorne's death, "I thought there was a tragic element in the event—in the painful solitude of the man, which, I suppose, could not longer be endured and he died of it." (Emerson was a neighbor of Hawthorne's during the periods when Hawthorne lived in Concord, and Emerson was on friendly terms with Hawthorne.)

During his early-adult years in Salem, Hawthorne "lived as a hermit.... choosing to walk abroad at night, when no one could observe him."[1] When he lived in Concord, he would hide in the woods to avoid meeting a passer-by. Hawthorne once said, "Destiny itself has often been worsted in the attempt to get me out to dinner." "I have not lived," Hawthorne said, "but only dreamed about living."[2]

Hawthorne seemed to regard his solitude as the cruelest of fates. "I have made a captive of myself," Hawthorne wrote to Longfellow, "and put me into a dungeon, and now I cannot find the key to let myself out; and if the door were open, I should be almost afraid to come out. You tell me that you have met with troubles and changes. I know not what these may have been, but I can assure you that trouble is the next best thing to enjoyment, and that there is no fate in this world so horrible as to have no share in its joys or sorrows."

When he was 46, Hawthorne moved with his family to the Berkshires, but he left after 18 months. "I am sick to death of Berkshire," he said, "I have felt languid and dispirited, during almost my whole residence." One of his Berkshire neighbors was Melville, and the two writers became friends.

Hawthorne left the Berkshires in 1851, and moved back to Concord, where he bought a house that he dubbed The Wayside. Perhaps he bought The Wayside with money from *The Scarlet Letter* and *The House of the Seven Gables* (*The Scarlet Letter* sold 2,500 copies in ten days). He wrote a biography of his college friend Franklin Pierce, and when Pierce was elected President in 1852, he appointed Hawthorne to the lucrative post of consul in Liverpool. After four years in England, Hawthorne and his family toured France and Italy, then returned to Concord in 1860.

---

1 "The Solitude of Nathaniel Hawthorne," by Paul Elmer More, *Atlantic Monthly*, November, 1901

2 See Wikipedia's article, "Nathaniel Hawthorne"

[Spoiler Warning: The rest of this section discusses Hawthorne's works, and may "spoil" the fun of reading them.]

Hawthorne's first novel was *Fanshawe*, published when he was just 24. *Fanshawe* is about a man who spends his life in solitary study, cut off from society. The protagonist wins the love of the heroine, Ellen, but then surrenders her to a more worldly man, and "returns to his studies and his death." One is reminded of how Kierkegaard won the love of Regina, then immediately gave her up. The mature Hawthorne took a dim view of *Fanshawe*, and most critics also take a dim view of it, but the psychologist Oberndorf thinks that it reveals much about Hawthorne:

> Many psychoanalysts believe that the first dream that the patient reports after beginning treatment epitomizes his entire life's conflict. So, too, perhaps the earliest writings of an author are more apt to reflect those difficulties by which he is most troubled and with which he is most familiar.

Fanshawe established the theme of Hawthorne's later work:

> Between *Fanshawe*, with its story of the seclusion caused by youthful ambition, and *The Dolliver Romance*, with its picture of isolated old age, there may be found in the author's successive works every form of solitude incident to human existence. I believe no single tale, however short or insignificant, can be named in which, under one guise or another, this recurrent idea does not appear. It is as if the poet's heart were burdened with an emotion that unconsciously dominated every faculty of his mind.[1]

After publishing *Fanshawe* in 1828, Hawthorne concentrated on writing short stories. He didn't publish his second novel, *The Scarlet Letter*, until 1850, when he was 46. "The whole plot of [*The Scarlet Letter*]," writes Paul More, "moves about this one conception of our human isolation as the penalty of transgression.... By his sin Dimmesdale is more than ever cut off from communion with the world, and is driven to an asceticism and aloofness so complete that it becomes impossible for him to look any man in the eye."

Another male character, Chillingworth, is also isolated. More describes Chillingworth as, "The incommunicative student, misshapen from his birth hour, who has buried his life in books and starved his emotions to feed his brain. [Chillingworth's hatred] severs him more absolutely from the common weal, blotting out his life 'as completely as if he indeed lay at the bottom of the ocean.'"

As for the female protagonist, Hester Prynne,

> The Scarlet Letter upon her breast is compared by the author to the brand on the brow of Cain—a mark that symbolizes her utter separation

---

1 "The Solitude of Nathaniel Hawthorne". Apparently *The Dolliver Romance* was published in 1863, a year before Hawthorne died. Yet Wikipedia describes it as "unfinished." Why would a living writer publish an unfinished novel?

> from the mutual joys and sorrows of the world. She walks about the provincial streets like some lonely bearer of a monstrous fate.

More describes *The Scarlet Letter* as a story of

> intertangled love and hatred... love and hatred so woven together that in the end the author asks whether the two passions be not, after all, the same, since each renders one individual dependent upon another for his spiritual food, and each is in a way an attempt to break through the boundary that separates soul from soul.[1]

I made a similar point in an earlier issue:

> Is love the opposite of hate, or are they akin? Proust's narrator half-consciously desires the death of those he loves; thus, his conduct is similar to that of one who hates. And if love often contains a seed of hatred, so too hatred often contains a seed of love. Freud said, "Love is with unexpected regularity accompanied by hate [and] in a number of circumstances hate changes into love and love into hate." Perhaps love and hate aren't opposites, as we're apt to think; perhaps they're two forms of the same thing—namely, attachment, emotional entanglement.[2]

Hawthorne deserves credit for a profound insight—the kinship of hate and love, the way that both hate and love undermine the individual and make him dependent on someone else, attach him to someone else and prevent him from achieving detachment and maturity. Healthy love and friendship require two mature individuals, individuals who aren't emotionally entangled, emotionally dependent.[3]

Hawthorne published his third novel, *The House of the Seven Gables*, in 1851, just one year after *The Scarlet Letter*. He wrote *Seven Gables* during the productive 18 months that he spent in The Berkshires. Again we find the main characters leading solitary lives:

> We know what unwearied care the author bestowed on the description of Miss Hepzibah Pyncheon, alone in the desolate family mansion, and on her grotesque terrors when forced to creep from her seclusion; and how finely he has painted the dim twilight of alienation from himself and from the world into which the wretched Clifford was thrust!

Another fruit of Hawthorne's Berkshire residence was his third novel, *The Blithedale Romance*, which was published in 1852. This novel takes place

---

1 When we discussed Poe, we saw how Poe also describes the sickness of excessive love/hate, excessive attachment to another person.

2 ljhammond.com/phlit/2006-10.htm#4

3 An attachment to another person can also be termed "transference." See ljhammond.com/phlit/2009-01b.htm#10 for a discussion of transference in connection with D. H. Lawrence's "The Fox." For a discussion of transference in connection with Freud and Jung, see *Conversations With Great Thinkers* ==> Psychology ==> "Transference"

in the utopian/socialist community of Blithedale, which is based on Brook Farm, where Hawthorne lived for several months in 1841. Henry James called *Blithedale Romance* "the lightest, the brightest, the liveliest" of Hawthorne's novels, but Paul More dismissed it as "in every way the slightest and most colorless of the novels." Perhaps it's an exception to the rule that all of Hawthorne's works depict solitary characters.

During his years in Europe, Hawthorne didn't publish any novels. In 1860, shortly after he returned to the U.S., Hawthorne published *The Marble Faun*, which is set in Rome. One of the characters, Miriam, moves "with the dusky veil of secrecy about her, among the crumbling ruins and living realities of Rome.... wrapped in the shadows of impenetrable isolation." Paul More suspects that Miriam "suffers for the same cause as Shelley's Beatrice Cenci"—that is, sexual abuse.

More cites several of Hawthorne's short stories as examples of the theme of isolation. More says that the protagonist of "The Gentle Boy" is "severed by religious fanaticism from the fellowship of the world." The protagonist of "Lady Eleanore's Mantle" says,

> The curse of Heaven hath stricken me, because I would not call man my brother, nor woman sister. I wrapped myself in pride as in a mantle, and scorned the sympathies of nature.

The protagonist of "The Minister's Black Veil" says,

> Why do you tremble at me alone? Tremble also at each other! Have men avoided me, and women shown no pity, and children screamed and fled, only for my black veil?.... I look around me, and, lo! on every visage a Black Veil!

The protagonist of "Ethan Brand"

> regarded the men about him as so many problems to be studied. [He] denied the brotherhood of man... in the end he must call on the deadly element of fire as his only friend, and so, with blasphemy on his lips, flings himself into the flaming oven.... The tragic power of the scene lies in the picture of utter loneliness in the guilty breast.[1]

The Blithedale Romance discusses dying in the company of a friend.

> Happy the man that has such a friend beside him when he comes to die! ....How many men, I wonder, does one meet with in a lifetime, whom he would choose for his deathbed companions! At the crisis of my fever I besought Hollingsworth to let nobody else enter the room, but continually to make me sensible of his own presence by a grasp of the hand, a word, a prayer, if he thought good to utter it.

Twelve years after *Blithedale* was published, Hawthorne died in the company of his old friend, Franklin Pierce. Did Hawthorne anticipate that he

---

[1] "The Solitude of Nathaniel Hawthorne," by Paul Elmer More. According to More, "Ethan Brand" is "in many ways the most important of [Hawthorne's] shorter works."

would die in Pierce's company? Or did he will to die in Pierce's company? It's often difficult to distinguish anticipation from will.

Hawthorne also anticipated that he wouldn't live past 60. He died six weeks before his 60th birthday.

If you're looking for a biography of Hawthorne, consider the biography by Edwin Haviland Miller. Hawthorne's son, Julian, wrote two books about his famous father. If you're interested in Hawthorne criticism, Henry James devoted a volume to Hawthorne, and D. H. Lawrence discussed Hawthorne in his book on American literature. Melville and Poe wrote essays on Hawthorne. The Library of America published a book called *True Crime: An American Anthology*; it contains a piece by Hawthorne called "A Collection of Wax Figures."

B. "Rappaccini's Daughter"

Octavio Paz wrote a play called *Rappaccini's Daughter*, based on Hawthorne's story of the same name. Hawthorne's story has various "magical" elements; like Marquez' *One Hundred Years of Solitude*, Hawthorne's story has a beautiful woman who can kill with her breath. Was Hawthorne popular with writers like Paz, Borges, and Marquez? Did the magical elements in Hawthorne appeal to the "magical realists"?

The Hawthorne story is regarded as one of his best, and I thoroughly enjoyed it. It has plot and suspense; it bends reality, but doesn't break it. I also enjoy "magical" writers like Gogol, Poe, and Kafka, and I enjoyed Marquez' "Handsomest Drowned Man in the World." But somehow I wasn't drawn into Borges' "Meeting" or Marquez' *One Hundred Years*.

Hawthorne is even more preoccupied with solitude than Paz and Marquez. In an earlier issue, I argued that solitude is an important theme in all of Hawthorne's work. In "Rappaccini's Daughter," the three main characters are all solitary.

Hawthorne himself was solitary, and he felt that his solitude was a curse. Emerson felt that Hawthorne died from his "painful solitude"; like the Buendias, Hawthorne didn't die from an illness. Perhaps Hawthorne depicted solitude in a more realistic way than Marquez because Hawthorne drew on his own life.

Since "Rappaccini's Daughter" is an important work by an important writer, there's an abundance of criticism about it—an abundance of older criticism, which I prefer to modern criticism. I chose an essay called "Rappaccini's Garden" (1958) by Charles Boewe. Boewe says that the theme of the story is the evil of racial mixing—among people and plants. We don't know who Beatrice Rappaccini's mother is, we only know that her father is Dr. Rappaccini, but we can surmise that Beatrice was the fruit of some sort of adulterous or improper union. Hawthorne says that the garden has been the scene of "such commixture, and, as it were, adultery, of various vegetable species, that the production was no longer of God's making, but the monstrous offspring of man's depraved fancy."

Boewe points out that "the word 'hybrid' originally meant an insult or outrage, especially an outrage connected with sex. The Bible enjoins against hybridization: 'Thou shalt not let thy cattle gender with a diverse kind: thou shalt not sow thy field with mingled seed: neither shall a garment mingled of linen and woolen come upon thee.'" Hybrids are accursed, hence they're often infertile—mules, for example, are infertile.

[Spoiler warning: If you're thinking of reading Hawthorne's story, you might want to skip the rest of this section.]

According to Boewe, Beatrice must die at the end of the story. Hawthorne calls Beatrice "the poor victim of man's ingenuity." Boewe says that Beatrice is "doomed to barren extinction. Like her emblem, the hybrid flowers, she is a living violation of the static order of nature. However much we may pity her as a person, nature imperatively demands that she be purged from the system of created things."

Boewe calls the reader's attention to the Italian critic Mario Praz, who's known for *The Romantic Agony*; Boewe says that Beatrice is one of Praz' "decadent ladies," Beatrice is "literally a *femme fatale*," like Marquez's Remedios the Beauty.

C. "My Kinsman, Major Molineux"

I also read a Hawthorne story called "My Kinsman, Major Molineux." Again, the plot holds your attention, you want to know how it's going to end. It's about a young man from the country, Robin, who comes to Boston in search of his kinsman, Major Molineux. Robin has walked a long way, and reaches Boston as night is falling. Robin is unschooled in the ways of the world, and has too much confidence in himself, his wooden club, and his connection to the Major. Robin suffers a series of bumps and bruises; he's mocked and threatened as he wanders around the city, looking for his kinsman.

One critic, Seymour Gross, says that Robin endures a "dark night of the soul," an introduction to the dark side of human nature. Hawthorne has written a coming-of-age story. By the end of the story, Robin is lonely and afraid, he'd like to return to the comfort of his parents' house. For Robin, solitude isn't a curse, as it often is in Hawthorne; for Robin, solitude is a learning experience, part of the process of growing up and leaving home.

Robin finally encounters his kinsman, Major Molineux, but the major can't help him; the major is an official in the British government, and he's been tarred and feathered by an anti-British mob.[1] Gross argues that Hawthorne often deals with history, but history is merely a setting for Hawthorne; Hawthorne's chief focus is on the moral, the psychological. Robin meets one sympathetic man, who urges him not to flee from Boston too hastily.

Gross argues that "My Kinsman, Major Molineux" is one of Hawthorne's best stories, though it's an early story, written in 1831, when Haw-

---

[1] One might describe Major Molineux as the victim of a charivari. I discussed the charivari in a recent issue, describing it as a "folk custom designed to shame a member of the community" (see ljhammond.com/phlit/2023-03b.htm).

thorne was just 27. "In this tale," Gross writes, "the literal drama is the symbolic drama." In later stories, Hawthorne catered to public taste, and separated "action and idea," so that "the moral [would be] plain and manifest."

D. *The Scarlet Letter*

a. The Kinship of Love and Hate

I recently read Hawthorne's *Scarlet Letter*, and found it most enjoyable and impressive. I prefer it to *Moby-Dick* and *Leaves of Grass*. Hawthorne's prose is "purity itself" (as Poe said), while Melville's prose is quirky and obscure. The plot of *The Scarlet Letter* is exceptionally good—full of drama, almost believable, never dull; the plot has many surprises, yet it feels inevitable. And Hawthorne has a keen sense of humor, evident in "The Custom House" (the long preface to *The Scarlet Letter*). It's not surprising that *The Scarlet Letter* sold briskly when it was published in 1850.

One of the deepest truths in the novel is the kinship of love and hate. When love and hate are carried to the point of obsession (Hawthorne says), we lose ourselves, we lose our center, we become dependent on another person, we become attached to an unhealthy degree, we lose the detachment/independence that are necessary for psychological health.

> It is a curious subject of observation and inquiry [Hawthorne writes], whether hatred and love be not the same thing at bottom. Each, in its utmost development, supposes a high degree of intimacy and heart-knowledge; each renders one individual dependent for the food of his affections and spiritual life upon another; each leaves the passionate lover, or the no less passionate hater, forlorn and desolate by the withdrawal of his subject. Philosophically considered, therefore, the two passions seem essentially the same.

[Spoiler Warning: Skip the rest of this section, if you're planning to read the novel.]

The Scarlet Letter depicts Roger Chillingworth's obsessive hate, and his collapse when the object of his hate dies. At the end of the novel, Chillingworth has lost himself, lost his soul, lost his *raison d'être*. *The Scarlet Letter* is about obsessive hate; it has little to do with love, though it does describe the painful consequences of illicit passion.[1]

How did Hawthorne himself preserve his own soul, his own "calm center"? When he lived at Brook Farm (the utopian-socialist community in West Roxbury), he would periodically retreat to a secluded spot in the woods, a vine-covered "magic circle." Hawthorne wrote about Brook Farm in the

---

[1] One might pity Chillingworth since he's at the mercy of his obsession: "a terrible fascination, a kind of fierce, though still calm, necessity, seized the old man within its gripe, and never set him free again, until he had done all its bidding. He now dug into the poor clergyman's heart, like a miner searching for gold; or, rather, like a sexton delving into a grave, possibly in quest of a jewel that had been buried on the dead man's bosom."

novel *Blithedale Romance*. One critic, Harry West, says that Coverdale, a character in *Blithedale*, is an "author-surrogate." Coverdale

> periodically retreats to his vine-encircled hermitage, "a hollow chamber of rare seclusion" in "the innermost sanctuary" of the woods surrounding Blithedale, for, as he explains, "it symbolized my individuality, and aided me in keeping it inviolate".... All such magic circles for dreaming and meditation are indicative of a retreat inward to the center of consciousness.[1]

I myself walked in the woods near Brook Farm and, after several attempts, managed to find the remains of the utopian community.[2]

b. Black Magic

Since Hawthorne wanted to preserve his individuality, he took a dim view of mesmerism, which he regarded as an invasion of the soul. When his wife, Sophia Peabody Hawthorne, was considering mesmerism as a treatment for headaches, Hawthorne tried to dissuade her. He described mesmerism as "the transfusion of one spirit into another," and he said mesmerism would violate "the sacredness of an individual." He concluded, "If thou wouldst know what heaven is... then retire into the depths of thine own spirit, and thou wilt find it there among holy thoughts and feelings."

Hawthorne's aversion to mesmerism is apparent in his fiction. In an earlier issue, I quoted a critic who spoke of, "Hawthorne's repugnance to spiritualism and mesmerism, and his harsh delineation of Dr. Westervelt, the crafty mesmerist in *The Blithedale Romance*."[3]

Hawthorne's repugnance to spiritualism/magic is also apparent in *The Scarlet Letter*, and Dr. Chillingworth might be compared to Dr. Westervelt. Chillingworth invades the soul, violates the individuality, of Dimmesdale. Hawthorne tells us that before Chillingworth came to Massachusetts, he was seen with another evil doctor, "Doctor Forman, the famous old conjurer, who was implicated in the affair of Overbury." Thomas Overbury was apparently murdered in the Tower of London in 1613, thirty years before the

---

1 "Hawthorne's Magic Circle: The Artist as Magician," Harry C. West, *Criticism*, Vol. 16, No. 4 (Fall 1974), pp. 311-325, jstor.org/stable/23099546

In an earlier issue, I discussed an essay on Hawthorne by Paul Elmer More. More views Hawthorne's retreat from society as a sickness, while Harry West views it in a more positive light. Perhaps the truth is on both sides.

2 The surviving buildings aren't difficult to find if you approach from Baker Street, but I parked on Kendrick Street in Needham.

3 See ljhammond.com/phlit/2013-10b.htm#2

events described in *The Scarlet Letter*. It has been argued that the Overbury murder was a major influence on *The Scarlet Letter*.[1]

Chillingworth also associated with other practitioners of occult arts: "He was heard to speak of Sir Kenelm Digby, and other famous men—whose scientific attainments were esteemed hardly less than supernatural—as having been his correspondents or associates."

As Chillingworth learned from Forman and Digby, so too he appears to have learned from Native Americans:

> During his Indian captivity, [Dr. Chillingworth] had enlarged his medical attainments by joining in the incantations of the savage priests; who were universally acknowledged to be powerful enchanters, often performing seemingly miraculous cures by their skill in the black art.

Chillingworth pursues occult arts like alchemy and astrology, and he's believed to be in league with the devil.

Hawthorne deals with various occult themes, such as the power of intuition, the power of spiritual ills to cause physical ills, the power to foresee the future, and the rapport between nature and man (synchronicity). Hawthorne describes electricity as an occult force, half-physical, half-spiritual:

> Hester silently ascended the steps, and stood on the platform, holding little Pearl by the hand. The minister felt for the child's other hand, and took it. The moment that he did so, there came what seemed a tumultuous rush of new life, other life than his own, pouring like a torrent into his heart, and hurrying through all his veins, as if the mother and the child were communicating their vital warmth to his half-torpid system. The three formed an electric chain.

In the early 19th century, electricity was often viewed as an occult force.

Magic is of two kinds, black magic and white magic. Black magic aims to harm, white magic to help. Hawthorne emphasizes black magic, and depicts Dr. Westervelt, Dr. Chillingworth, and Dr. Forman in a negative light. Is there a single example in Hawthorne's works of a benevolent Magus, like Shakespeare's Prospero?

---

1 See *The Yellow Ruff and the Scarlet Letter*, and *Sir Thomas Overbury's Vision (1616) and other English sources of Nathaniel Hawthorne's The Scarlet Letter*, both by Alfred S. Reid.

Chillingworth doesn't have a medical degree, so perhaps he isn't entitled to be called "Dr. Chillingworth." But he practices medicine in the novel, and Hawthorne says he has a "fair right" to be called a physician.

While *The Scarlet Letter* has English sources, it also has NewEngland sources. Hawthorne was a diligent student of NewEngland history, and his novel has many accurate details. He read Bancroft's *History of the United States*, Hutchinson's *History of Massachusetts*, Caleb Snow's *History of Boston*, Felt's *Annals of Salem*, etc. (See "The New England Sources of *The Scarlet Letter*," by Charles Ryskamp)

c. Hester Hutchinson?

Hawthorne was a student of NewEngland history, and he knew that the Boston colony was fiercely divided, in the 1630s, over the Antinomian Controversy. The Antinomians believed in following the heart, the inner light, the divine voice within, while their opponents emphasized moral law. The Antinomians accused their opponents of preaching a doctrine of works, like the hated Catholics, while they themselves trusted in the grace of God, and the faith of the individual. The Antinomians were akin to the Quakers, and the Boston establishment condemned both Antinomians and Quakers.

The most well-known Antinomian was Anne Hutchinson, who was banished from the Boston colony, and took refuge in Portsmouth, Rhode Island. (Rhode Island was a refuge for Quakers, Jews, Baptists, and others who didn't "toe the line.") While the Antinomian Controversy was raging in Boston, the Boston establishment feared that the Antinomians would resort to armed insurrection, so they sent the constables door-to-door to confiscate the guns of the Antinomians. The Antinomian Controversy brought the Boston colony to the brink of civil war.

A critic named Michael Colacurcio has argued that *The Scarlet Letter* dramatizes the Antinomian Controversy.[1] He compares Hester to Anne Hutchinson, and Dimmesdale to John Cotton, the minister who influenced Hutchinson, but didn't defend her at her trial. Early in the novel, Hester displays "a haughty smile, and a glance that would not be abashed." This description, Colacurcio says, "seems deliberately to recall Mrs. Hutchinson's courtroom defiance."

"From the first," Colacurcio writes, "[Hester] has seemed perilously close to defying her judges with the affirmation that her spirit posits and obeys its own law.... When Hawthorne says of Hester... that 'the world's law

---

[1] "Footsteps Of Ann Hutchinson: The Context Of The Scarlet Letter," *ELH*, Vol. 39, No. 3 (Sep., 1972), pp. 459-494, jstor.org/stable/2872195. Since this essay is written in thorny academic prose, I don't recommend it.

Colacurcio says that Hester "begins in outward conformity, playing the game of 'sanctification'—the single rule of which is that the true Self is the sum of all its outward works." While the Puritan establishment spoke of sanctification, the Antinomians argued that "the significance of a life is not the sum of its legally regulated outward works; or, more radically, what one does has a consecration of its own provided the quality of deep inner feeling is right—i.e., authentic.... The whole antinomian controversy is about the inner and the outer, the private and the public person: what do our outward works, positive and negative, really reveal about our salvation status, or, in naturalized form, about our selves?" John Cotton: "As Justification and the faith of it doth not stand upon his good works, so neither doth it fall or fail upon his evil work."

It can be argued that the Antinomians were the forefathers of the Transcendentalists.

was no law to her mind,' we may well suspect that he intends some conscious pun on the literal meaning of 'antinomianism.'" Hester tries to persuade Dimmesdale that "what they earlier did 'had a consecration of its own'—they having felt it so and said so to each other." Hester eventually concocts "an antinomian plan for adulterous escape."

But Hawthorne, according to Colacurcio, doesn't entirely approve of Hester; Colacurcio calls Hawthorne a "neo-nomian," not an anti-nomian. Hawthorne believes that "the world's law validly exists to restrain our disruptive social excesses."[1] Hawthorne agrees with Roger Williams that the spiritual self is autonomous, but the outward man must obey civil authority.[2]

Colacurcio argues that Antinomianism was a natural reaction to the Puritan emphasis on correct behavior. "Extremes of public legalism seem to breed their antinomian opposite by natural law." The Thesis gives birth to the Antithesis, Puritanism gives birth to Antinomianism.

Colacurcio also argues that, among Antinomians and Quakers, women played a prominent role. Should we compare Anne Hutchinson to modern feminists? Or should we compare her to an ancient priestess, like those at the oracle of Delphi?

d. Proust *Contre* Sainte-Beuve

One might compare the Antinomian Controversy to the literary debate between Proust and Sainte-Beuve. Proust argued, like the Antinomians, that our literary self, our higher self, our true self, isn't expressed in our daily actions, isn't expressed "in our habits, in society, in our vices."[3] The great writer doesn't follow moral law, according to Proust. Proust felt that a great writer could grasp beauty and truth, and express them in his works, though his daily life was stained by vice. He made this argument because his own life was stained by vice; he wanted to justify his life.

Sainte-Beuve, like other 19th-century critics, argued that literature is connected to the author's life/personality. "An author's writing is inseparable from the rest of him," Sainte-Beuve wrote. Proust wrote *Contre Sainte-Beuve*, in which he argued that our daily life doesn't reflect our higher self, our literary self. Proust's argument reminds me of the Antinomian argument that our true self, the state of our soul, isn't reflected in our daily actions. Sainte-Beuve's position is akin to the BostonEstablishment position that, if you want to know the state of the soul, look at the daily life.

e. A New Bible For A New World

Viola Sachs is the Jesse James of Hawthorne criticism—a gun-toting outlaw who strikes fear in the hearts of law-abiding scholars. Sachs was a Jewish emigré from Poland who lived for several years in Brazil, and then had a long academic career in France. Sachs' arguments are so outlandish

---

1 This is a quote from Colacurcio, not from Hawthorne.

2 See footnote 32 in Colacurcio's essay.

3 *Marcel Proust: A Biography*, by George Painter, Vol. 2, Ch. 6

that one scholarly journal prefaced Sachs' essay thus: "*American Quarterly* is pleased to publish this leading example of French work in American Studies. We recognize its provocative and controversial character."

Sachs argues that American writers tried to create a new bible for a New World. One of her books is called *La Contre-Bible de Melville: Moby-Dick Déchiffré* (some of her writings are in French, some in English).

> Emerson repeatedly calls for the scriptures of the New World [Sachs writes]. Whitman viewed his *Leaves of Grass* as a bible chanting the democratic Spirit of the New World.... This obsessive reference to scriptures should not be taken as a mere metaphor: America literally produces its own bible—*The Book of Mormon* (1837).[1]

When I discussed Whitman in 2001, I said, "he dreamed of founding a new religion, for which *Leaves of Grass*—expanded into 365 chapters or psalms, one to be read on each day of the year—would serve as a holy testament."[2] Sachs notes that

> Whitman's *Leaves of Grass*, in the 1867 edition, is built on a hidden numerical framework referring to the yearly calendar; similarly the fifty-two sections of "Song of Myself" identify "Walt Whitman, a Kosmos" with the terrestrial sphere in its annual revolution of fifty-two weeks.

Sachs says that both *The Scarlet Letter* and *Moby-Dick* attempt to be "a revelation of divine Wisdom," a *liber mundi.*

As the Puritans looked for hidden meanings, secret codes, in the Bible, so American writers put hidden meanings in their fiction, their new bibles. Literary codes were an analogue of nature's code: the Puritans believed that nature was the handwriting of God, that we could decipher God's intentions in natural phenomena.[3] The Puritans believed that the Book of Revelation

---

1 Sachs, "The occult language and scripture of the New World," *Social Science Information*, vol. 23, 1: pp. 129-141, first published Jan 1, 1984; available through Sage Journals

2 See ljhammond.com/phlit/2001-01.htm#6. These aren't my words, I was quoting the Introduction to the PenguinClassics edition of *Leaves of Grass*.

3 Sachs: "Just as everyday affairs concealed signs of Divine Providence, and the world of natural phenomena revealed the 'handwriting of God' to the Protestants, so the hidden text of *The Scarlet Letter*, *Moby-Dick*, and others reveals the word/Word of the author/Creator." ("The Gnosis of Hawthorne and Melville: An Interpretation of *The Scarlet Letter* and *Moby-Dick*," *American Quarterly*, Vol. 32, No. 2, Summer 1980, pp. 123-143, jstor.org/stable/2712559)

Let's look at an example of "the handwriting of God" in *The Scarlet Letter*. In Chapter 12, "The Minister's Vigil," Dimmesdale climbs the scaffold in the middle of the night. "The minister, looking upward to the zenith, beheld

contained a prophecy of "the discovery of America and its claimed destiny to be the land of the second coming of Christ."[1]

I've often argued that everything is connected, that the flight of birds (for example) may be connected to human destiny. This is the Hermetic worldview, the view that the universe is an organism, that the parts of the universe are inter-connected. The Puritan view is similar, the Puritans felt that all natural phenomena were controlled by God, and therefore coincidences were more than just coincidences, coincidences were meaningful. Sachs speaks of "Christian Hermeticism." Sachs says that Protestants were interested in "Christian hermeticism, heretical writings, Gnosticism, and neoplatonic thought."[2]

The Hermetic worldview was popular during the Renaissance, popular in the time of Shakespeare and Bruno, popular around 1600, so it's not surprising that Hermetic ideas impact Puritan thinking. And the Hermetic worldview enjoyed a revival in the Romantic period, so writers like Hawthorne and Melville would imbibe Hermetic ideas from both Puritan sources and Romantic sources.

The word "Hermetic" comes from the Greek god Hermes, who corresponded to the Roman god Mercury and the Egyptian god Thoth. Sachs says that "*The Scarlet Letter* and *Moby-Dick* carry numerous references" to Enoch, Thoth, and Hermes.[3]

In the concluding chapter of *The Scarlet Letter*, Hawthorne says that Dimmesdale's life teaches the following moral: "Be true! Be true! Be true! Show freely to the world, if not your worst, yet some trait whereby the worst may be inferred!" Sachs points out that "be true" contains 6 letters, and when it's repeated three times, we have 666, the number of the beast in Revelation.[4]

---

there the appearance of an immense letter—the letter A—marked out in lines of dull red light."

In my view, this is a far-fetched example of synchronicity, an example that isn't realistic, isn't credible. The reader can't believe it, and Hawthorne himself is skeptical. Hawthorne says that a witness of synchronicity "beheld the wonder through the colored, magnifying, and distorting medium of his imagination, and shaped it more distinctly in his after-thought."

If Hawthorne doesn't believe in synchronicity, should we question the sincerity of his writing? Is he just trying to entertain? Or is he expressing genuine experiences, genuine beliefs?

[1] Sachs, "The occult language and scripture of the New World"

[2] Sachs, "The Gnosis of Hawthorne and Melville"

[3] Enoch is a character in Genesis, reputed to be the author of the Book of Enoch, which is discussed in esoteric literature and in the Kabbalah.

[4] Sachs, "The Gnosis of Hawthorne and Melville"

"Let him that hath understanding count the number of the beast: for it is the number of a man; and his number is Six hundred threescore and six." (Revelation, 13:18)

The old rule for coded writing is *Tria Sunt Omnia* [threes are all]. In other words, the hidden meaning is repeated three times. "Be true! Be true! Be true!" seems to exemplify *Tria Sunt Omnia*, the three-fold repetition of the code.[1]

The next sentence ("Show freely to the world, if not your worst, yet some trait whereby the worst may be inferred!") contains 18 words (6 + 6 + 6). The number of words in the entire passage ("Be true! Be true! Be true! Show freely to the world, if not your worst, yet some trait whereby the worst may be inferred!") is 18 + 6, or 24, just as the number of chapters in *The Scarlet Letter* is 24. Sachs says,

> The number of chapters (24), the movement of the narrative from bright sunlight of noon to the darkness of midnight and back again into the bright sun, the period of seven years which elapses in the narrative, all indicate that a cyclical conception of time underlies the mythic structure of the book.

Sachs was influenced by the French scholar Henry Corbin, who specialized in Islamic philosophy/mysticism/Sufism. Corbin was a regular visitor to a Swiss conference called Eranos. Eranos attracts scholars with a mystical bent (Carl Jung, Joseph Campbell, Mircea Eliade, etc.).[2]

Sachs was also influenced by Mircea Eliade, who was born in Romania, lived in France for several years, and spent much of his career at the University of Chicago. In his book *The Sacred and the Profane*, Eliade says

> the profane world is formed of a juxtaposition of phenomena, while an intuitive total apprehension of reality characterizes the sacred. The latter calls for the perception of the world as a meaningful whole, each of its parts partaking in and of the whole.... Wholeness characterizes the sacred world.[3]

Eliade's argument confirms my view that a philosophy of inter-connectedness is a good foundation for a new religion.

As an example of the profane, the un-integrated, Sachs cites the work of American novelist Thomas Pynchon. Though Melville is pessimistic, at least he expresses "chaotic energy... the writing of life. Pynchon's superabundance of information, hieroglyphics, emblems constitutes the 'legacy' of the dead. *The Crying of Lot 49* is the *Book of the Dead* of America."[4]

---

1 For *Tria Sunt Omnia*, I'm indebted to Alexander Waugh and his fascinating Youtube videos about the Shakespeare Controversy.

2 Corbin's mentor was Louis Massignon, who promoted respect for Islam in the West. Massignon was also the mentor of the Iranian intellectual Ali Shariati.

3 This is a quote from Sachs, not Eliade. See Sachs' essay "The Profane and the Sacred: an Initiation to the American Romance," *Revue française d'études américaines*, No. 5 (Avril 78), pp. 73-82, jstor.org/stable/20872698

4 Sachs, "The occult language and scripture of the New World"

Sachs was also influenced by the eminent Melville scholar Harrison Hayford. Hayford taught at Northwestern, and made Northwestern a center of Melville studies. Hayford argued (as Sachs later did) that errors in *Moby-Dick* were intentional, and had a hidden meaning.[1] One of Hayford's students was Hershel Parker, who wrote a two-volume biography of Melville. Parker also edited Melville's complete works, which were published in 15 volumes by Northwestern-Newberry.

Another scholar whom Sachs cites frequently is Sacvan Bercovitch. Born into a Jewish family in Canada, Bercovitch became a prominent figure in American Studies, and taught at Columbia, Harvard, etc. He wrote few books, perhaps because he was busy with teaching, with editing the Cambridge History of American Literature, etc.

One of Bercovitch's best-known books is *The Puritan Origins of the American Self*. He says that the Puritans "conceived of reality... as a system of linked analogies, interlacing every strand of recorded experience, ancient and modem, scientific and humanistic no less than theological." Since Melville was a "direct descendant of the Puritans" (according to Sachs), Melville filled *Moby-Dick* with analogies, correspondences, which must be deciphered by the patient reader.[2] Melville is trying to teach that "the Invisible

---

As for Melville's pessimism, Sachs says, "Melville's *gnosis* denies the existence of anything else than matter in constant movement.... Only matter, chaos, and *Moby-Dick; or, The Whale* exist.... Melville's message reads that no primordial Spirit or Light exists, that all life stems from matter.... Truth is to be found in error and that what the gnostics consider to be the cosmic error of Creation is the only truth.... [In Chapter 49 of *Moby-Dick*, Melville writes,] 'There are certain queer times and occasions in this strange mixed affair we call life when a man takes this whole universe for a vast practical joke, though the wit thereof he but dimly discerns, and more than suspects that the joke is at nobody's expense but his own.'"

Is Hawthorne also pessimistic? *The Scarlet Letter* has little humor, little play, little high-spirits, and much torment and suffering.

1 Sachs, "The Gnosis of Hawthorne and Melville." Sachs refers us to Hayford's essay "Unnecessary Duplicates: A Key to the Writing of *Moby-Dick*" in *New Perspectives on Melville*.

2 And not only *Moby-Dick*: Sachs says that *Mardi* is "entirely structured, as Maxine Moore has brilliantly proved, upon an astrological and astronomical game."

The phrase "linked analogies" calls to mind the Metaphysical Poets, who were probably influenced by the Hermetic worldview. Perhaps some of these poets were Puritans.

The phrase "linked analogies" also calls to mind Joyce's *Ulysses*, which is an elaborate system of analogies. These analogies probably don't indicate that Joyce believed in an inter-connected universe; rather, they seem to be merely a literary device. (See ljhammond.com/phlit/2003-10b.htm)

is but the reversed image of the visible," which reminds us of the Hermetic maxim, "As above, so below."

Melville mentions writers who were preoccupied with numerology, such as Pythagoras and Thomas Browne. Sachs says that 16 is "the number upon which the structure of [*Moby-Dick*] rests."[1] Ishmael is "linked to the hidden architecture of the book, for his story is told in chapter 16 of The Book of Genesis." The doubloon (discussed in chapter 99 of *Moby-Dick*) is worth 16 dollars. Stubb says "At two cents the cigar, that's nine hundred and sixty cigars." But it's actually 1600/2 or 800 cigars. "The mistake of 160 cigars too many," Sachs writes, "or 320 cents too few, serves to call the reader's attention to the importance of the number 16 in this chapter and in the underlying structure of the book."

I don't see much value in Melville's secret codes. Therefore, I don't think we should work very hard to decipher these codes. That said, I find Sachs' essays provocative, and don't regret reading them.

Perhaps the best antidote to all these hidden meanings is Zen, which takes a simple approach, looks at the object, and appreciates it for itself. And perhaps Melville is at his best when he simply describes. In an earlier issue, I noted that D. H. Lawrence

> has high praise for Melville's descriptions, especially his description of the first chase (Chapter 48), which Lawrence calls, "a marvelous piece of true sea-writing.... When [Melville] forgets all audience, and gives us his sheer apprehension of the world, then he is wonderful."[2]

---

[1] Sachs, "The Gnosis of Hawthorne and Melville"

Since the invisible is a mirror-image of the visible, Sachs says that the Puritans were preoccupied with the mirror symbol, which they regarded as "a revealer of the divine image." Melville is also preoccupied with mirrors; "Melville's code is largely based on reflections of numbers in a single or double mirror.... The author even, jokingly, tells us that 'While composing a little treatise on Eternity, I had the curiosity to place a mirror before me.'"

Sachs discusses the "Great Debate" on American literature that took place in the U.S. in the early 1800s. "None of the other young American republics [Mexico, Brazil, etc.] had, so early in its development, shown such a preoccupation bordering on the obsessive with the need to elaborate a national form of art. This widespread debate, with all its anomalies—such as the proposal that a work of art translate the size of America or the demand that American writers discard the English tongue in favor of an Indian one—no doubt sensitized the American writer to the possible correspondence between the very form of writing and the national experience." Perhaps this Great Debate inspired, or helped to produce, writers like Hawthorne and Melville. Can the buzz of literary criticism help to produce great literature?

[2] See ljhammond.com/phlit/2011-12b.htm#8

4. Melville

A. New Bedford

January 18, 2011
I recently went to the Whaling Museum in New Bedford for the annual Moby-Dick Marathon—a public reading of *Moby-Dick* that started at noon on a Saturday, went through the night, and ended at 1 pm on Sunday. About 100 different people read a section of the novel aloud. I didn't see anyone attempt to memorize their section. There are also lectures, quiz games, museum exhibits, banquets, etc., so you might enjoy coming even if you don't want to listen to the reading. The area around the museum is interesting, too; New Bedford is a historic city, and a National Park Visitor Center makes it tourist-friendly. The crime rate is high, however, so you may want to stay in the "historic core."

I was glad I went to the Moby-Dick Marathon; it was the best literature-related event I've ever been to—lots of enthusiastic laymen, and lots of knowledgeable scholars. If you can't make it to New Bedford in January, the Whaling Museum's website has a live video of the reading.

I asked one scholar, Tim Muir, if D. H. Lawrence helped to build Melville's reputation. He said that Melville's reputation had been building in England for 20 or 30 years before Lawrence wrote about Melville in the 1920s. Thus, Melville is one of several writers who were appreciated abroad before they were appreciated at home (Whitman, for example, probably had more fans in England in the 1890s than he had in the U.S., and Nietzsche was first appreciated outside Germany).

Another scholar, Robert K. Wallace, said that Melville made a thorough study of Shakespeare about a year-and-a-half before writing *Moby-Dick.* I told Dr. Wallace that I thought Melville's use of the occult was comparable to Shakespeare's, and I asked Dr. Wallace if Melville was receptive to the occult. He said we don't know.

I suspect, though, that someone as curious and as widely-read as Melville had an opinion on the occult. (Likewise, I would say that Melville probably had an opinion on the Shakespeare controversy, though it may take some research to discover what that opinion was.) Dr. Wallace has written several books that bring together different arts; for example, he wrote a book about Melville and the English painter Turner.

Someone pointed out that, in his latter years, Melville became acquainted with Schopenhauer, and read him with interest.

Someone said that Melville believed he would eventually gain recognition, and Melville compared his work to a plant, the aloe, that blooms every hundred years, and is often dismissed as a weed until it blooms. When I explored this topic on the Internet, though, I found that Melville said that his work might "flower like the aloe, a hundred years hence—or not flower at all, which is more likely by far, for some aloes never flower."[1] This suggests that Melville wasn't sure if he would gain recognition or not.

Melville is popular, and the Melville society seems more active than the Hawthorne society or the Emerson society. Most active of all, however, is the Thoreau society. All four of these societies have conferences and publish periodicals. The Melville society has a conference every year; the next one is in Rome, in June, 2011. The Melville Society publishes a periodical called *Leviathan*.

One of the leading Melville scholars is Hershel Parker, who wrote a giant, two-volume biography of Melville, and edited the Norton Critical Edition of *Moby-Dick*. Edwin Haviland Miller wrote a "psycho-biography" of Melville (Miller also wrote a biography of Hawthorne and a study of Whitman). Edward Edinger wrote a Jungian study called *Melville's Moby Dick: An American Nekyia* (Edinger also wrote *Goethe's Faust: Notes for a Jungian Commentary*).

Warner Berthoff's *The Example of Melville* (1962) looks at Melville's writings as well as his life. Newton Arvin's *Herman Melville* (1950) pays attention to the unconscious and sexuality, as does a recent book, Andrew Delbanco's *Melville: His World and Work*. (Delbanco is the Director of Columbia's American Studies program.)

B. Biographical Notes

When I looked up Melville on Wikipedia, I found this:

> Herman Melville was born in New York City on August 1, 1819, the third child of Allan and Maria Gansevoort Melvill. After her husband Allan died, Maria added an "e" to the family surname. Part of a well-established and colorful Boston family, Melville's father spent a good deal of time abroad as a commission merchant and an importer of French dry goods. The author's paternal grandfather, Major Thomas Melvill, an honored survivor of the Boston Tea Party who refused to change the style of his clothing or manners to fit the times, was depicted in Oliver Wendell Holmes's poem "The Last Leaf."

Notice the phrase "Melville's father spent a good deal of time abroad." Did these absences leave their mark on Melville? In my book of aphorisms, I listed "an absent father" as one of the causes of homosexuality.[2] There may be traces of homoerotic feeling in Melville's works, as when Ishmael and Queequeg share a bed at the Spouter Inn.

> The maternal side of Melville's family was Hudson Valley Dutch. His maternal grandfather was General Peter Gansevoort, a hero of the Battle of Saratoga; in his gold-laced uniform, the general sat for a portrait painted by Gilbert Stuart, which is described in Melville's 1852 novel,

---

[1] *A Herman Melville encyclopedia*, "The American Aloe on Exhibition," by Robert L. Gale

[2] See the section called "Genius and Homosexuality" in the chapter on Genius in my *Conversations With Great Thinkers*.

> *Pierre*, for Melville wrote out of his familial as well as his nautical background. Like the titular character in *Pierre*, Melville found satisfaction in his "double revolutionary descent."

The fortunes of Melville's family declined, prompting Melville to go to sea. But clearly his family had been prominent and upper-class, like that of most American writers, with the exception of Whitman.

After being in the merchant marine, and teaching school, Melville joined a whaling voyage when he was 21. He deserted the ship, ending up in Hawaii.

> While in Honolulu, he became a controversial figure for his vehement opposition to the activities of Christian missionaries seeking to convert the native population.

Melville's respect for the natives is apparent in his portrayal of Queequeg; Ishmael contrasts Queequeg favorably with the Christians he has known.

> Melville married Elizabeth Shaw, daughter of chief justice of the Massachusetts Supreme Judicial Court Lemuel Shaw, on August 4, 1847. In 1866, Melville's wife and her relatives used their influence to obtain a position for him as customs inspector for the City of New York (a humble but adequately paying appointment), and he held the post for 19 years. In a notoriously corrupt institution, Melville soon won the reputation of being the only honest employee of the customs house. (The customs house was coincidentally on Gansevoort St., named after his mother's prosperous family.)

Melville's first book, *Typee* (1846), was a hit, and he became a popular writer. But his popularity waned with *Mardi* (1849), *Moby-Dick* (1851) was coolly received, and *Pierre* (1852) prompted critics to say that Melville had gone mad. He had to abandon writing as a profession. In his later years, he wrote more poetry than prose.

> Melville spent years writing a 16,000-line epic poem, *Clarel*, inspired by his earlier trip to the Holy Land. His uncle, Peter Gansevoort, by a bequest, paid for the publication of the massive epic in 1876. But the publication failed miserably, and the unsold copies were burned when Melville was unable to afford to buy them at cost.

> As his professional fortunes waned, Melville's marriage was unhappy. Elizabeth's relatives repeatedly urged her to leave him, and offered to have him committed as insane, but she refused. In 1867, his oldest son, Malcolm, shot himself, perhaps accidentally.... His wife managed to wean him off alcohol, and he no longer showed signs of agitation or insanity. But recurring depression was added to by the death of his second son, Stanwix, in San Francisco early in 1886.

This passage suggests that neither Melville nor his oldest son were completely sane. In my book of aphorisms, I said that geniuses usually aren't good parents, and I mentioned Melville as an example of a genius whose children turned out badly.[1]

There's a Melville House in Pittsfield, Massachusetts, where Melville lived for 13 years, and there's another Melville House in Troy, New York, where he lived in his early 20s (when he wasn't at sea). Melville is buried next to his wife in Woodlawn Cemetery in The Bronx, New York.

C. Melville and Balzac

In a recent issue, I mentioned that Melville read Schopenhauer with interest. I searched the Internet for more about Melville's reaction to Schopenhauer, and I found an essay by John Haydock that connects Melville's *Billy Budd* to Balzac's *Séraphita* (the essay also connects *Billy Budd* to Schopenhauer).[2] The essay confirmed my hunch that Melville had a deep interest in the occult, and was receptive to the occult.

In my *Realms of Gold*, I mentioned Balzac's interest in the occult: "Balzac had a deep interest in the occult, Swedenborg, mesmerism, phrenology, etc., and he discusses these subjects in his novels *Louis Lambert* and *Séraphita*." According to Haydock,

> Melville had in his library at the time of his death fifteen books of short stories and novels by Honoré de Balzac. One of them was the "philosophical study" *Séraphita*. The novel represents the third and culminating volume of Balzac's trilogy on the power of human will that begins with *The Magic Skin* and *Louis Lambert*, both of which Melville also kept on his bookshelf.

Haydock compares *Séraphita* to Melville's *Mardi*:

> *Séraphita* cannot be forced into the realistic categories of the majority of [Balzac's] fiction. Balzac felt it separate from the rest of his work, in a way similar to Melville's protectiveness of his first philosophic romance, *Mardi*.

Like *Séraphita*, *Mardi* deals with the esoteric (Kabbalah, alchemy, etc.), so Melville was prepared to appreciate *Séraphita*:

> Since the composition of *Mardi*, Melville had displayed his knowledge of esoteric undercurrents in literature, and no doubt felt very familiar with these aspects of Balzac's philosophic system.

Mardi must also deal with Buddhism, for Haydock says "Melville studied Buddhism for many years, as *Mardi* demonstrates."

Melville was interested not only in Buddhism and the occult, but in philosophy in general:

---

[1] See the section called "Genius and Narcissism" in the chapter on Genius in my *Conversations With Great Thinkers*.

[2] "Melville's *Séraphita*: *Billy Budd, Sailor*," by John S. Haydock, originally published in Melville Society *Extracts* (No. 104, March 1996, pp. 2-13).

> Melville had always read philosophy, but in his later years, philosophy became an absorbing interest. As always, he was insistently curious about the relationship between free will and necessity, between individual freedom and impersonal fate.

Moby-Dick contains numerous prophecies. Prophecy is connected to fate: if the future is fated, it can be known in advance; if it's not fated, it can't be known in advance. Fate/Prophecy seems to be the aspect of the occult in which Melville was most interested. He also had some interest in divination—predicting the future based on random events such as rolling dice, drawing cards, etc.

Haydock says,

> *Séraphita* is a story about an androgynous youth (first called Séraphitus, later Séraphita) who possesses great spiritual and physical beauty, and dies... an untimely and unwarranted death voluntarily, quietly and fully self-aware.

Readers of *Billy Budd* will recall Billy's physical beauty and his "untimely and unwarranted" death. Melville says that Billy is "all but feminine in purity of natural complexion." As with Séraphita, Billy's outer beauty is a sign of his inner beauty, his moral beauty: "the moral nature," Melville says, "[is] seldom out of keeping with the physical make." Haydock speaks of, "the externally beautiful, which Balzac believed to reflect moral perfection within."

With their outer and inner beauty, Séraphita and Billy are loved by many.

> In Balzac's novel, the central character is the subject of the love of almost all around him.... When Billy first appears, [we're told] that a ruffian "really loves Billy" and we read later, that "Claggart [who later destroys Billy] could even have loved Billy but for fate and ban."[1]

Séraphita and Billy are androgynous, hermaphroditic, male and female blended. This is related to the esoteric elements of the stories, it represents the "philosophic unity of worldly opposites" and "alchemical perfection."

Séraphita is "loved by both a man and a woman and is opposed by a jealous pastor named Becker." In Melville's novella, the analogue to Becker is Claggart. There are other analogues: Haydock says that Captain Vere, in *Billy Budd*, corresponds to Wilfrid, and

> the wise, old Dansker (i.e., Dane or dweller of the North like Balzac's Norwegians) plays much the same role as the old servant David in *Séraphita*. He is the wise and interpretive substitute grandfather, who shelters his charge but does not interfere in the accomplishment of what is determined for the maturing of "Baby Budd."

According to Balzac, there are three types of people: the Instinctive, the Abstractive, and the Divine. The Instinctive is the lowest, animal level; if

---

[1] Did Claggart initially have positive feelings for Billy? Was his later animosity a reaction to those positive feelings?

the Instinctive has intellect, it is intellect without intuition and wisdom. The Abstractive uses rules and logic, and has the first glimmerings of intuition. The Divine possesses intuition and the wisdom of the heart. Perhaps I shouldn't call them "types," perhaps I should call them "phases," since Balzac seemed to believe in reincarnation, seemed to believe that everyone passes through these three phases.

Different characters in the two stories correspond to different phases in Balzac's scheme.

> Vere is the Abstractive type, who has not yet gained fully the understanding of the issues of the heart but has begun to experience some intuitions of immortality and fate. Because of his Abstractive nature, Vere can only operate from conventional forms, a weakness Melville stresses.... He "leans toward everything intellectual" but this nature in him is not evil but only "pedantic" and "bookish." He is at a stage of transition in metempsychosis that puts him between the Instinctive intellectual and the intuitive Divine.

Claggart represents the Instinctive phase; he was born at that level, and he'll die there, too.

> Claggart is one of those naturally depraved individuals that Balzac would oppose to the higher nature of Billy. He is "the direct reverse of a saint." He is subject to the type of cold depravity "dominated by intellectuality"—not by the objectifying intellect of the Abstractive, but one monitored by a conscience that was "but the lawyer to his will." His depravity is of essence, "born with him and innate".... Significantly, Billy destroys Claggart with a blow to his devious intellectuality—to his forehead, "so shapely and intellectual-looking a feature in the master-at-arms."

The third phase, the Divine phase, is represented by Billy and Séraphita. Billy is called "Apollo," and he's also

> called "bully boy", and is clarified by reference to the worshipped bull of the Assyrians. According to this tradition the bull is born of the sun, and expresses the idea of divinity. This is also, of course, a sacrificial bull, killed for ritual purposes by the priests and people and forming a "communicating link between heaven and earth."

> He is a foundling with no parents (like Séraphitus after the age of 9), whose "lineage is in direct contradiction to his lot": Séraphitus was also of higher birth.... He is twice called a "peacemaker", which of course elicits the promise given in Matthew 5, 9: "Blessed are the peacemakers, for they shall become sons of God." Appropriately, Ratcliffe assigns Billy to a post superior to ordinary humanity on the ship, to the foretop.... Billy is foreshadowed by his foil, the "Handsome Sailor," who is abundantly described in sidereal and divine terms: those primarily of light, stars, and heavenly objects.

Haydock says that Billy's death is an "apotheosis... reminiscent of Balzac's scene of angelic ascension in *Séraphita*, though it is less overtly mystical." Billy dies, says Haydock, with "perfected qualities."

The night before his execution, Billy has an inner "struggle" (Haydock says) comparable to that of Séraphita before her execution, and comparable to the Buddha's "dark night of the soul" before his enlightenment. In all three cases, the result of the struggle seems to be enlightenment, peace, resignation. Séraphita "counsels against active resistance to death, even to an 'unjust' death," and she says, "At the zenith of all virtue is Resignation." Billy also accepts death calmly; his death is a "euthanasia."

After Billy dies, the surgeon and the purser have a debate about his death. The purser sees it as willed death, euthanasia, while the surgeon, who has a rational-scientific-materialistic bent, scoffs at such notions: "Euthanasia, Mr. Purser, is something like your will power: I doubt its authenticity as a scientific term—begging your pardon again. It is at once imaginative and metaphysical." In Melville's time, those who championed the rational-scientific-materialistic worldview were sometimes Utilitarians or Unitarians; according to Wikipedia, "Melville despised Unitarianism and its associated 'ism', Utilitarianism." One thinks of Dostoyevsky, who also despised the rational worldview.[1] Melville admired Emerson, who championed idealism, and criticized materialism.

One of the cornerstones of the occult/mystical worldview is that the will can accomplish much, the will can affect the external world, mold personality, and mold circumstances. We noted above that *Séraphita* is part of a trilogy on "the power of human will." According to Haydock, the theme of both *Séraphita* and *Billy Budd* is that "the power of will can overcome the unjust elements of material life." In our recent discussion of Buddhism, we noted that the Buddha was "a man of enormous will-power," and that he "laid tremendous stress on the will."[2] The importance of will in Schopenhauer's philosophy is evident in the title of his chief work: *The World as Will and Idea*.

D. A Jungian View of *Moby Dick*

I spent months and months reading *Moby Dick*, and I didn't enjoy it. Then I searched for a good critical study of the novel, but couldn't find one. Finally I found a superb book by Edward Edinger, an American Jungian; it's called *Melville's Moby-Dick*. The sub-title is *A Jungian Commentary*, and the sub-sub-title is *An American Nekyia* (a Nekyia is a journey to the underworld, a night sea journey).

Edinger's book is so good that it can serve as an introduction to Jungian psychology, even as an introduction to psychology in general, as well as a guide to *Moby Dick*. It's a short book, but manages to cover the whole span of the novel. It's a readable book, but manages to clarify the obscure depths of the novel. It repays the reader who made the "Long March" through *Moby*

---

1 Dostoyevsky seems to have had less interest in the occult than Melville; one might say that Dostoyevsky was a Freudian, not a Jungian.

2 See ljhammond.com/phlit/2011-01.htm#5

Dick; it makes him feel that his sufferings were not without reward. And it also makes the reader want to read more Edinger.[1]

The epigraph of Edinger's book is a quote from Melville's *Pierre*: "I shall follow the endless, winding way—the flowing river in the cave of man." This quote shows Melville's commitment to exploring the unconscious. Since Melville explores these "winding ways," his works cry out for a psychological study like Edinger's. This quote also shows that Edinger knows not only *Moby Dick*, but other Melville works, too; he even knows Melville's poetry. Thus, Edinger's study of *Moby Dick* throws light on many of Melville's works.

In his introduction, Edinger says that psychology arose as religion declined.

> There can be no scientific approach to the depths of the psyche as long as the contents of these depths are projected into an external system, such as a religious or philosophic creed. The death of religion gives birth to psychology, and the world-phoenix renews itself.

One might say that psychology is the religion of our time.

Turning to "Melville the Man," Edinger says "the psychic atmosphere of Melville's family [was] that of a matriarchy in which the mother is the central figure." Edinger speaks of the "inherent weakness" of Melville's father. According to Edinger, Melville's mother respected her brother more than her husband, and "never committed herself emotionally to her husband." The matriarchal atmosphere in the Melville household may account for the homoerotic elements in Melville's life and work.

Next Edinger discusses Melville's friendship with Hawthorne. When Melville gave Hawthorne a copy of *Moby Dick*, Hawthorne responded with an appreciative, complimentary letter. Melville wrote back, and said that Hawthorne's letter gave him an "infinite fraternity of feeling.... Your heart beat in my ribs and mine in yours." Edinger points out that Hawthorne was fifteen years older than Melville, and Edinger says that this "spiritual love affair" couldn't last:

> Hawthorne of course could not live up to such an intense transference. As with all powerful projections, it came with a possessiveness which

---

[1] Edinger wrote general works—such as *Ego and Archetype* and *Anatomy of the Psyche: Alchemical Symbolism in Psychotherapy*—and also literary studies—such as *Goethe's Faust: Notes for a Jungian Commentary*, *The Psyche on Stage: Individuation Motifs in Shakespeare and Sophocles*, *Eternal Drama: The Inner Meaning of Greek Mythology* and *The Bible and the Psyche: Individuation Symbolism in the Old Testament.*

Another Jungian view of Melville is James Baird's *Ishmael: A Study of the Symbolic Mode In Primitivism* (1956).

If you're interested in Jungian interpretations of literature, consider Maud Bodkin's *Archetypal Patterns in Poetry* (1934). Bodkin also wrote *The Quest for Salvation in an Ancient and a Modern Play*, which compares Aeschylus's *Eumenides* with T. S. Eliot's *The Family Reunion*.

provoked from its object a protective withdrawal. Hawthorne, a shy, introverted man, remained friendly, but did not share Melville's emotional involvement. As the friendship cooled, feeling the inevitable rebuff which excessive expectation brings, Melville was thrown back on himself.

Moby Dick begins with the famous line "Call me Ishmael." In his third chapter, Edinger explores the Ishmael symbol. He starts by saying that Ishmael is "the Biblical figure of the rejected outcast, the alienated man." (In Genesis, Abraham's wife Sarah is unable to bear a child, so she arranges for Abraham to have a child with Sarah's maid, Hagar. An angel tells Hagar to call the boy Ishmael, and tells Hagar that "he shall be a wild ass of a man, his hand against every man and every man's hand against him." When Sarah has a child with Abraham, Hagar and Ishmael are sent away.)

Melville's other writings [Edinger says] show that he was preoccupied throughout his life with the figure of Ishmael, the orphan, the child who was bitterly hurt. In *Mardi* he writes, "sailors are mostly foundlings and castaways and carry all their kith and kin in their arms and their legs," and in *Redburn*, "at last I found myself a sort of Ishmael in the ship, without a single friend or companion. In *Pierre*, the hero feels "entirely lonesome, and orphan-like."

When the young man goes to sea in *Redburn*, he says, "Cold, bitter cold as December, and bleak as its blasts, seemed the world then to me; there is no misanthrope like a boy disappointed; and such was I." Edinger says that Melville's "Ishmael complex," like all major complexes, was rooted in his experience and in identification with an archetype—the Ishmael archetype. Melville's father went insane and died when Melville was 12, "a striking similarity to the Biblical Ishmael, who was replaced by Isaac at the age of thirteen." After the father's death, the family fell on hard times. Furthermore, Melville "was rejected by his mother," Edinger says, "who favored her first son." This first son, Gansevoort, was a lawyer, was involved in politics, supported Polk in the 1844 Presidential election, and after Polk's victory, was repaid with a diplomatic post in London. From his London post, he helped find a publisher for *Typee*.

The relationship between Gansevoort and Herman was, Edinger writes, "molded by the archetype of the hostile brothers.... Gansevoort's life followed a course strangely reciprocal to Herman's."[1] Gansevoort flourished while Herman floundered, but when Herman found success with *Typee*, Gansevoort "died of an obscure illness at the age of thirty." Edinger says of hostile brothers, "as one waxes, the other must wane." The success of *Typee* killed Gansevoort?! A strange idea certainly, and not completely convincing, but interesting, and worthy of further consideration.

Edinger says that hostile brothers like Gansevoort and Herman "embody opposite existential states, acceptance and rejection." A child who experiences only one of these states can't reach full maturity; a child should

---

[1] Edinger mentions other examples of hostile brothers: Cain and Abel, Jacob and Esau, Christ and Satan.

experience both acceptance and rejection—experience them cyclically or alternately. "The one-sided experience of acceptance can be as damaging as rejection." The rejected son, Edinger says, is banished to the wilderness, while the accepted son becomes a "sacrificial victim."

Edinger says that Melville's identification with Ishmael made him take a position "outside the orthodox and conventional," made him take a position counter to the dominant values, counter to Christian values. According to Edinger, Ishmael is not only anti-Isaac, he's anti-Christ. By starting his novel "Call me Ishmael," Melville "prepares for the Luciferian contents to follow."

Perhaps Melville was especially popular in the 1960's, when the counter-culture movement took a position counter to the dominant values—just as Melville had. Edinger sees a kinship between Melville and the twentieth century in general: "His novel speaks so deeply to us today because this state of alienated meaninglessness is so prevalent in twentieth-century man."

Going beyond the opening sentence ("Call me Ishmael"), Edinger looks at the rest of the opening paragraph, and says that it depicts depression—"a damp, drizzly November in my soul." But it's easy to overlook this depression since the tone of the prose is jocular: "With a philosophical flourish Cato throws himself upon his sword; I quietly take to the ship." So Ishmael is depressed, even suicidal, but Melville's tone is light-hearted, as it is throughout much of the novel. Edinger says that depression is the usual starting-point for a Nekyia, a descent into the underworld, into the unconscious. Life is meaningless, our conscious attitude is bankrupt, so we're prepared to turn to the unconscious. Edinger mentions other Nekyias that start with depression: The Odyssey, The Book of Job, The Divine Comedy, Pilgrim's Progress, Faust, etc.

While there are many parallels to Ishmael's "damp, drizzly November in my soul," the closest parallel, according to Edinger, is *Faust*, which begins with the depressed Faust saying "Cooped up among these heaps of books, gnawed by worms, coated with dust..." Both *Moby Dick* and *Faust* involve a pact with the devil. "*Moby Dick* could be called the American *Faust*." Edinger says that *Moby Dick* expresses universal themes from an American perspective; it's the first (the only?) work to explore the "mythological depths" of the American psyche.

Edinger says that while Melville was writing *Moby Dick*, his mind was flooded with unconscious images, and he had to struggle to keep his sanity. "The autonomous archetypal psyche was powerfully and dangerously activated during Melville's writing of *Moby Dick*." Hence the symbolism is richer than in Melville's earlier works; *Moby Dick* is deeper, but also more obscure, than Melville's earlier works.

In the second chapter of *Moby Dick*, Ishmael sets out for New Bedford, or as Edinger puts it, begins the descent into the unconscious. Melville describes New Bedford with the grimmest images: "Such dreary streets! blocks of blackness, not houses, on either hand, and here and there a candle, like a candle moving about in a tomb." According to Edinger,

> This emphasis on blackness and death, characteristic of the early phase of the descent into the unconscious, corresponds to the first phase of the alchemical transformation process, called the *nigredo*, or blackening.

The alchemists experienced the *nigredo* as melancholia.

In the third chapter of *Moby Dick*, Ishmael enters the Spouter Inn and sees a dark and puzzling painting. Is it "the Black Sea in a midnight gale"? Finally Ishmael decides

> The picture represents a Cape-Horner in a great hurricane; the half-foundered ship weltering there with its three dismantled masts alone visible; and an exasperated whale, purposing to spring clean over the craft, is in the enormous act of impaling himself upon the three mastheads.

Edinger says, "This image presages the outcome of the voyage he is about to start."

Ishmael is told that he must share a room with Queequeg, a South Sea native. Edinger says that Queequeg is a personification of the shadow—the first personification encountered in an analysis of the unconscious. Ishmael thinks Queequeg is going to murder him, and calls for the landlord. Edinger says,

> The ego usually assumes the shadow has a hostile intent. This is a projection. The ego feels hostile toward the shadow and expects hostility in return.... As a rule the unconscious shows the ego the same face that the ego shows to it.

One is reminded of the common view that the world will smile at you if you smile at the world; the world shows you the same face that you show to it.

Ishmael soon realizes this, realizes that Queequeg may be afraid of him, and begins to calm down. Edinger says that Queequeg represents not just Ishmael's shadow, but "the original whole man at home with nature and himself." Queequeg's wholeness is symbolized by the "black squares tattooed on his body," and by the Maltese cross with which he makes his mark (he can't write). Queequeg's wholeness is also apparent in his "natural dignity and equanimity," and in his healing effect on Ishmael. Queequeg represents the whole man, the Self. He helps Ishmael achieve "a reconnection with the Self," and this in turn brings about "a capacity for love and human feeling." Queequeg redeems Ishmael, so that when the ship is destroyed, Ishmael survives.

In addition to tattoos in the shape of black squares, Queequeg also has tattoos in a labyrinth design. Edinger says the labyrinth is a symbol of the unconscious.

Edinger points out that Queequeg was very eager to leave his South Sea island, and join a whaleship. "His urgent need to make contact with civilization is important. It represents the striving of the shadow for consciousness." This reminds me of *Dracula*, in which the Englishman's need for the

Romanian vampire is matched by the vampire's need for the Englishman. As I said in an earlier issue,

> Stoker [i.e., Bram Stoker, author of *Dracula*] depicts both Victorian England and Dracula's Transylvania as wastelands. Both areas need the other in order to be rejuvenated. Victorian England needs the passion, energy, and spontaneity of Transylvania, and Dracula needs the "man-brain", the self-consciousness, of England.

Melville depicts Ishmael and Queequeg as "a cozy, loving pair, almost a married couple. In other of Melville's writings also we find intense, emotional relationships between men." Edinger thinks that Melville hadn't realized his masculine side because his relationship with his father was "inadequate." This lack of masculinity affected Melville's writings, Edinger argues. Melville lacks "the discriminating, structuring, clarifying function of the masculine principle," and his work has "a certain wild unpredictability." One might say that Melville possesses the Dionysian, but not the Apollonian. "Queequeg's harpoon symbolizes this missing rationality" (Apollo was the god of archery). Queequeg is everything that Melville/Ishmael isn't, "Queequeg is full of strength, dignity, and purposefulness, a harpooner who has his harpoon with him constantly."

Queequeg also represents everything that 19th-century American society isn't—that is, he has a cultural significance as well as a personal significance. He is "the shadow and adversary of the nineteenth-century collective canon of religious orthodoxy." Here again, Melville appeals to modern man, since modern man has started to respect his "Queequeg side"—the whole man, the natural man, the pagan man. As Edinger puts it, Queequeg represents "an aspect of the collective psyche which is only now, one hundred years later, beginning to emerge into consciousness."

In Chapter 10 of *Moby Dick*, Ishmael joins Queequeg in idol-worship. This suggests, says Edinger, that Ishmael/Melville isn't an orthodox Christian. Edinger reminds us that Melville made "some caustic remarks" about Christian missionaries in his earlier books.

Edinger notes that the word "vocation" comes from *vocare*, to call. As Jung said, "Anyone with a vocation hears the voice of the inner man: he is called." Edinger says that Melville himself felt called to be an "artist-prophet," and "To preach the Truth to the face of Falsehood." But the more he heeded this inner voice, the less money his writing brought in, so he was torn between his calling and his necessities. As he wrote to Hawthorne,

> Try to get a living by the Truth—and go to the soup societies.... What I feel most moved to write, that is banned—it will not pay. Yet, altogether, write the other way I cannot. So the product is a final hash, and all my books are botches.

Edinger says that many of us are in Melville's predicament, many of us are torn between our calling and our practical situation. Edinger thinks that we can't give ourselves entirely to our calling, or entirely to our practical situation; we have to unite the opposites.

Before the *Pequod*'s voyage begins, Ishmael receives two warnings: Ahab is nowhere in sight, so Ishmael can't see his captain before entrusting himself to him, and then a "ragged old sailor" named Elijah makes some dire comments about Ahab.

Edinger says that Ahab and his three officers represent the four functions of Jungian theory. "Ahab, as captain, stands for the superior function, which is thinking." Thinking isn't the superior function for everyone, only for "thinking types," such as Melville.

The first mate, Starbuck, represents the auxiliary function. When a person's superior function is thinking, his auxiliary function is intuition, and Starbuck represents intuition. Melville says that Starbuck's intuition was an intelligent superstition; "outward portents and inward presentiments were his."

The second mate is Stubb, and he represents sensation, the opposite of intuition. As Ahab says of Starbuck and Stubb, "Ye two are the opposite poles of one thing; Starbuck is Stubb reversed, and Stubb is Starbuck." Stubb is described as a "good-humored, easy and careless." Edinger says, "Thoughts of death, if he has any, are easily dispelled by a good dinner."

When thinking is the superior function, feeling is the inferior function. The last officer, the third mate, is Flask, who represents feeling. Since the inferior function is unconscious and undeveloped, Flask isn't described in detail. We're told that he's "very pugnacious concerning whales," and tries to "destroy them whenever encountered."

These four officers tell us about Melville himself:

> We might outline Melville's personality through the officers he created for the *Pequod*: thinking, his superior function; intuition, its well-developed auxiliary; sensation, a rather poorly developed third; and feeling, his fourth function, undifferentiated and inferior. *Moby Dick* shows a striking lack of differentiated feeling. It is notable that the novel contains no significant female (anima) figure! And Melville's personal relationships and feeling adaptations were correspondingly precarious. Likewise, his relatively inferior sensation function was evident in his life—in his shaky relation to reality, requiring support by relatives.

The *Pequod*'s most balanced personality, Edinger says, is Starbuck. Starbuck says it's proper to fear whales. In Starbuck's view, "an utterly fearless man is a far more dangerous comrade than a coward." Edinger remarks, "In the coming voyage, Ahab is to demonstrate the truth of this remark."

In his seventh chapter, Edinger turns to Ahab, and notes that Ahab is "the prototype of the heretic" since, in the Old Testament, Ahab violates the covenant with Yahweh, and permits the worship of Baal. "That Melville too was a heretic there can be no doubt."

One who descends into the unconscious is bound to be a heretic—if he weren't, if he were at home with the orthodox, he wouldn't make the descent. "Ahab and Ishmael are the two sides of the heretical outsider. Ishmael the passive victim, Ahab the active rebel."

Edinger says that the matriarchal religion of Baal is receptive to the unconscious ("the maternal unconscious"), and respects images, while the patriarchal religion of Yahweh abhors "graven images," and has a profound antipathy to the imagination. Islam, too, is opposed to images, as is Protestant Christianity.

Edinger says there's a good reason for the taboo against images: one must repress the unconscious in order to develop consciousness.

> During a certain phase of ego development, it is absolutely necessary to depreciate the unconscious, the maternal womb of the ego, which is also the source of imagination. The conscious personality must separate itself from its origins if it is to achieve some measure of autonomy. This is the goal of all patriarchal initiation. The artist seems to have never completed this patriarchal initiation. In him, the door to the maternal unconscious with its rich store of images that feed the imagination remains open. He never gives complete allegiance to the masculine principle, but rather maintains an ambiguous relation to the feminine.

In my book of aphorisms, I discussed how youth represses the unconscious.[1] And I argued that the artist (the male artist) is often feminine.[2] Melville's bond with his father was weak (as we saw above), so he was open to unconscious images.

Edinger says that, while it's necessary for the youth to depreciate the unconscious, this process "carries serious dangers of inflation and alienation from the source of one's being." In my book of aphorisms, I noted that "pride is as characteristic of youth as stoicism." And when we discussed the Grail legend, we saw that "It is natural that a young person who sets himself a lofty ideal... should, without noticing it, succumb to a certain arrogance."[3]

Edinger says that pride is a necessary element in the growth of consciousness: "The Prometheus myth symbolizes the necessary act of inflation or hubris which must be risked in each new step in the growth of consciousness." Prometheus stole fire from the gods—a symbol of proud daring—and then he was tormented by a vulture—a symbol of the suffering that comes with greater consciousness, a suffering that Melville experienced and depicted in Ahab.[4]

As Ahab can be compared to Prometheus, so too he can be compared to Christ. When he first appears on deck, Ahab has "a crucifixion in his face... some mighty woe." Edinger says there are also links between Pierre and Christ. Edinger says that Pierre and Ahab have much in common: "A careful

---

[1] See "Stages of Youth" in the Psychology chapter of my *Conversations With Great Thinkers*.

[2] See "Woman, Child, Genius" in the Genius chapter of my *Conversations With Great Thinkers*.

[3] ljhammond.com/phlit/2003-01.htm

[4] See my later chapter on Mary Shelley's *Frankenstein*, where I discuss the Promethean quest for knowledge, and the feeling of guilt that accompanies it.

reading of *Pierre* can leave no doubt that its central figure represents the same one-sided, heaven-storming attitude as does Ahab."

When Ahab first appears on deck, we see his scar:

> Threading its way out from among his grey hairs, and continuing right down one side of his tawny scorched face and neck, till it disappeared in his clothing, you saw a slender rod-like mark, lividly whitish.

Edinger says that Ahab is a "marked man," that he has been "marked by God." Such a mark is ambiguous: it could be the mark of Cain, or it could mean "belonging to the elect or the chosen people."

Edinger mentions another "marked man" in Melville's works, a renegade in *Omoo*. This renegade rejects civilization because he was a foundling, and had a hard childhood. Does Ahab also reject civilization because he had a hard childhood? His mother died when he was a year old, his father even earlier.[1] "If one's early experiences have been too harsh," Edinger writes, "one has had no basis laid for an allegiance to society and the collective human enterprise; no safeguards exist against the regressive nihilism of primitive affect." The psychology of the criminal.

What does Ahab's missing leg signify? "The presence of such an image in Melville's imagination," Edinger writes, "indicates that he had suffered a profoundly crippling psychic trauma." This trauma, Edinger argues, was in his relationship to his parents—his mother's preference for his older brother, and his father's "masculine inadequacy, mental breakdown, and subsequent death." A parent's mental breakdown, Edinger says, is probably more traumatic than a parent's death. Melville mentions this early trauma in *Redburn*:

> Talk not of the bitterness of middle-age and after life; a boy can feel all that, and much more.... Never again can such blights be made good; they strike in too deep, and leave such a scar that the air of Paradise might not erase it.

Both in *Redburn* and *Pierre* there are hints of the father's moral failing, which is followed by the son's disillusionment. What was the nature of this moral failing? Perhaps a sexual indiscretion, Edinger says, but more likely "his father's general weakness." Both Redburn and Pierre idealize their father, and then become disillusioned; as the narrator of *Pierre* says, "Thy sacred father is no more a saint... Truth rolls a black billow through thy soul!"

A parent trauma leaves a hole in the child's soul, Edinger says, and this hole exposes the child to "violent eruptions of primitive, unmediated archetypal images." These violent eruptions caused problems in Melville's personal life, but fueled his creativity. Melville seemed to recognize this, and he makes Ahab say, "My topmost greatness lies in my topmost grief."

Let's return to the subject of Ahab's missing leg. Edinger points out that many mythical heroes were dismembered—Osiris, Dionysus, etc. And he points out that a stage in the alchemical process is represented by "a lion

---

1 "Captain Ahab did not name himself," Melville tells us. "'Twas a foolish, ignorant whim of his crazy, widowed mother, who died when he was only a twelvemonth old." (Ch. 16)

with his paws cut off." Dismemberment symbolizes separation between ego and unconscious: "the original state of unconscious wholeness must be torn apart if a higher level of conscious development is to be achieved." Both Ishmael and Ahab have lost their original wholeness. Ishmael's reaction is "passive escape and thoughts of suicide." Ahab's reaction is a defiant vow to "dismember his dismemberer."

Edinger discusses several dreams in Melville's works, and says that they might represent Melville's own dreams. Edinger makes the bold suggestion that Melville may have dreamed of losing his leg. Edinger mentions Stubb's dream, in which he tries to kick Ahab and kicks his own leg off. Edinger also mentions a dream that Pierre has, in which a Titan named Enceladus rams himself against a cliff in an expression of "immitigable hate" and ends up losing his arms.

Edinger mentions a shipwreck image in *Pierre*: "His soul's ship foresaw the inevitable rocks, but resolved to sail on, and make a courageous wreck." The narrator speaks of Pierre's "profound willfulness"; such willfulness reminds us of Ahab. *Pierre* itself was an act of willfulness, a courageous wreck, a book that didn't try to win over the public, but instead thumbed its nose at the public.

Edinger discusses a poem by Melville in which a ship steers directly into an iceberg, and is destroyed.

> This is surely an actual dream of Melville's. Using different images, it presents the same basic content as Ahab's assault on the white whale, Stubb's dream of kicking the pyramid, and Enceladus' attack on the mountain of Zeus. Such dreams carry a warning. The ship, representing the dreamer's conscious life-orientation, is willfully pursuing a suicidal course, deliberately ramming a solid iceberg.... This image indicates a grave mal-adaptation to reality.... We know Melville's sanity was in grave danger for several years after *Moby Dick*.... Apparently, the message of this and other dreams did get through to him, since he did not suffer a total shipwreck.

Turning from Ahab to the white whale, Edinger says that the whale has a "multitude of meanings." At the front of the novel, Melville collects comments on whales from many sources. Edinger says that Melville discovered "the amplification method" on his own, "and used it to gain entrance to the collective unconscious.... The entire book can be seen as an elaborate amplification of the psychological meaning of the whale and whale hunting."

One of the many things that Moby Dick represents, Edinger says, is the deity. In chapter 71 of *Moby Dick*, the *Pequod* meets a ship called the Jeroboam, which has a strange prophet, Gabriel, who "pronounced the white whale to be the Shaker God incarnated, and he prophesied 'speedy doom to the sacrilegious assailants of his divinity.'"

Melville emphasizes the darkness. Edinger insists that this darkness is true, that the world really has a dark side, though it may have a bright side, too. "Melville had a vision of radical evil. Although one-sided and conditioned by childhood trauma, it is none the less true." Melville brought this "radical evil" to God's doorstep, and asked, "Why did you make such a world? You're responsible for this radical evil." As Edinger says, "The acute, tortured awareness of radical evil as an aspect of God is a theme that runs through all of *Moby Dick*."

In Chapter 40 of *Moby Dick*, the ringed horizon is compared to a boxing ring. "In that ring Cain struck Abel. Sweet work, right work! No? Why then God, mad'st thou the ring?" Is the Christian God of Love a deceit? Jung often complained about the one-sided view of God found in modern Christianity. Jung's awareness of evil is on a par with Melville's, and Jung felt that God Himself must have a dark side.

When people see the dark side, when they're preoccupied with radical evil, they seize upon a scapegoat: "The resentment accumulates which must have some object." For Ahab, the scapegoat was Moby Dick. All the "intangible malignity" in the world, Ahab transferred to the "abhorred White Whale, he pitted himself, all mutilated, against it."

Melville understood that evil is embedded in the world, and embedded in our unconscious, whether or not we actually experience it. He understood that the unconscious isn't just personal, it's collective, and therefore it contains more than just our personal experience, it contains the experience of mankind.

Melville also understood that this collective unconscious is like instinctive behavior in animals. In Chapter 42 of *Moby Dick*, Melville says that a "young colt" in Vermont is terrified of a buffalo robe because he knows instinctively that buffaloes can gore him and trample him, though he's never seen a buffalo. "Here thou beholdest even in a dumb brute," Melville says, "the instinct of the knowledge of the demonism in the world." This is Melville's metier, "the demonism in the world."

Edinger is deeply impressed by Melville's grasp of the workings of the unconscious, and its analogy in the animal world. But Edinger also thinks that Melville's grasp of the unconscious is somewhat one-sided. Because of his personal experience, because of his troubled relationships with both of his parents, the unconscious

> carried a darker and more negative aspect than it might for someone else. Melville might say with Ahab, "So far gone am I in the dark side of earth, that its other side, the theoretic bright one, seems but uncertain twilight to me."

Now Edinger turns to the shadowy figure of Fedallah, who lurks around Ahab, and has some sort of influence over him. Edinger says that "Fedallah is clearly related to the devil; if he is not the devil himself, at least he is one of his subordinates." Fedallah's companions are said to have "a certain diabolism of subtlety."

As Ishmael is linked to Queequeg, so Fedallah is linked to Ahab. As Queequeg is the shadow/unconscious of Ishmael, so Fedallah is the shadow/unconscious of Ahab. As Queequeg represents wholeness and the Self, so Fedallah represents wholeness and the Self. Fedallah's wholeness is suggested by his clothes, "which combine the opposite colors, black and white," and also by his connection to the "primal generations," the "first man," the Anthropos.

Six years ago, when I discussed Conrad's *Heart of Darkness*, I pointed out that Conrad uses the very word "shadow" to refer to Kurtz. Likewise, Melville compares Fedallah to a shadow: "Ahab chanced so to stand, that the Parsee occupied his shadow; while, if the Parsee's shadow was there at all it seemed only to blend with, and lengthen Ahab's."(Ch. 73). In Chapter 130, Melville says that Ahab and the Parsee often stared at each other, "as if in the Parsee Ahab saw his forethrown shadow, in Ahab the Parsee his abandoned substance." Jung didn't choose the word "shadow" at random; man seems naturally disposed to apply the word "shadow" to the unconscious, the dark side of human nature.

But while there are similarities between Fedallah and Queequeg, there are also differences. Queequeg is the noble savage, Fedallah the diabolical savage. Queequeg's fortitude complements Ishmael's weakness, while Fedallah's "moral inferiority" complements Ahab's "conscious sense of nobility." So *Moby Dick* has two pairs—Ishmael-Queequeg and Ahab-Fedallah—and these two pairs add up to a quaternity. (Edinger mentions in passing that Pip also forms a "character pair" with Ahab; Pip's weakness complements Ahab's strength.)

Now Edinger turns to "The Town-Ho's Story," Chapter 54 of *Moby Dick*, which is a digression, a story-within-a-story. Like *Moby Dick* itself, "The Town-Ho's Story" is about vengeance; one might say it's not a digression, it's an aspect of the main story. "The Town-Ho's Story" is about an officer, Radney, who could not endure a sailor, Steelkilt, because Steelkilt is handsome and noble and has a "natural superiority." (One is reminded of Melville's novella *Billy Budd*, in which an officer named Claggart can't endure the handsome, noble Billy. "A biblical precedent is Saul's jealousy of the young David."[1])

Radney mistreats and insults Steelkilt.

> When an individual's essential human dignity is attacked, as happened to Steelkilt, the deity within, the Self, is affronted; and contrary to all reasonable and personal considerations, it insists on executing nemesis.

Steelkilt makes plans to kill Radney, but before he can do so, Radney chases Moby Dick, and is killed by Moby Dick.

In the story of the conflict between Radney and Steelkilt, we have a capsule version, presented in the context of an interpersonal relationship, of the larger conflict between Ahab and Moby Dick. Radney is even described in terms reminiscent of Ahab. Concerning Radney's compulsion to humiliate Steelkilt, it is said that 'Radney was doomed and made mad.' In his compulsion, Radney is called 'the predestined mate' and 'the infatuated man who sought to run more than halfway to meet his doom.' All of these remarks apply to Ahab.

In his chapter "Linked Analogies," Edinger says that Melville presents the natural world, and man's everyday pursuits, as symbols of deeper truths. Edinger quotes Ahab's remark, "O Nature, and O soul of man! how far beyond all utterance are your linked analogies! not the smallest atom stirs or

---

1 Norton Critical Edition, ch. 54, footnote 2

lives on matter, but has its cunning duplicate in mind." Edinger says that Melville's long descriptions of whaling have a significance that's more than practical. He notes that Emerson also subscribed to the idea of "linked analogies": "Every natural fact," Emerson wrote, "is a symbol of some spiritual fact." Edinger calls this "the theory of correspondences."

Such a correspondence is the basis of *Moby Dick*'s best sentence:

> The rushing *Pequod*, freighted with savages, and laden with fire, and burning a corpse, and plunging into that blackness of darkness, seemed the material counterpart of her monomaniac commander's soul.

This may be the best sentence Melville ever wrote, but it would be better without the analogy, better without "seemed the material counterpart of her monomaniac commander's soul." Zen literature gives us the fact, the image, without constantly looking for analogies.

Such correspondences and analogies should not be confused with synchronicities because they don't occur at the same moment; a cloudless sky and a calm mind may be analogous, but they aren't events that occur at the same moment. But if we say that analogous things occur together, or are seen together, then the theory of analogies begins to merge with the theory of synchronicity. For example, if we say that the eagle is analogous to the king, and the eagle is seen when the king dies, or when a new king takes over, then we have an analogy that's also a synchronicity.

Moby Dick is based on an 1820 incident: the whaleship *Essex* was rammed by an angry sperm whale and sunk. In late 1851, just when *Moby Dick* was coming off the press, another whaleship, the *Ann Alexander*, was rammed by an angry sperm whale and sunk. Melville was struck by the coincidence: "Ye Gods! What a commentator is this *Ann Alexander* whale. What he has to say is short and pithy and very much to the point. I wonder if my evil art has raised this monster." Was it just a coincidence, or was it a synchronicity?

Is the *Ann Alexander* the best example of synchronicity from Melville's biography? Are there examples of synchronicity in Melville's works? I find three synchronicities in *Moby Dick*:

1. During the storm in Chapter 119, Ahab approaches Starbuck "and almost at the same instant a volley of thunder peals rolled overhead." Ahab notices the coincidence/synchronicity and calls himself "Old Thunder."
2. In Chapter 130, a hawk carries off Ahab's hat, later dropping it in the ocean. This prompts the following remark from Melville: "An eagle flew thrice round Tarquin's head, removing his cap to replace it, and thereupon Tanaquil, his wife, declared that Tarquin would be king of Rome. But only by the replacing of the cap was that omen accounted good. Ahab's hat was never restored." The Roman legend involves an eagle, symbol of royalty. Melville implies that the theft of Ahab's hat is a bad omen; perhaps dropping it in the ocean suggests that Ahab himself will have a watery grave.
3. In Chapter 135, another synchronicity occurs, also involving animals: "Scarce had [Ahab] pushed from the ship, when numbers of sharks,

seemingly rising from out the dark waters beneath the hull, maliciously snapped at the blades of the oars, every time they dipped in the water; and in this way accompanied the boat with their bites. It is a thing not uncommonly happening to the whale-boats in those swarming seas; the sharks at times apparently following them in the same prescient way that vultures hover over the banners of marching regiments in the east." What makes the sharks significant is that they appear on the decisive third day of the chase, when Ahab and most of the crew are about to perish; the sharks didn't appear earlier. So their appearance is like the hat theft: a synchronicity that hints of coming events.

Let's return to the night when the *Pequod* was plunging along, "freighted with savages, and laden with fire, and burning a corpse." Ishmael is at the tiller, and he falls asleep briefly. When he wakes up, he finds that he has turned around, and the ship is in danger of capsizing. Edinger says that Ishmael's unconscious is rebelling against the *Pequod*'s suicidal course, it wants to turn around, but it can't get the attention of his conscious mind, so it seizes control of his body.

> When one fails to permit an inner reaction to become conscious, it may then seize our bodily functions and force an expression through them, concretizing the image it wishes to convey. So it is with psychosomatic illnesses, and so it is with the majority of so-called accidents.

Edinger says we should interpret accidents as we interpret dreams; like dreams, accidents carry an "unconscious message." One might compare an accident to a "slip of the tongue."

At the start of the voyage, Ahab nailed a gold doubloon to the mast, promising it to the first person who sighted Moby Dick. Edinger says the doubloon is a mandala, an image of the Self. In Chapter 94, several members of the *Pequod*'s crew approach the doubloon, and interpret its images according to their own personalities. "Each projects his own psychic contents on it and thereby reveals his own attitude and relation toward the Self." The doubloon represents three mountains, a part of the zodiac, and in the middle, the sun.

The first to approach the doubloon is Ahab. "If we did not already know it, Ahab's inflation would now stand revealed. He identifies himself with the three proud mountain peaks, the ego is identified with the Self." Next, Starbuck approaches. "Where Ahab sees the mountain peaks, Starbuck sees the dark valley. [Starbuck] is caught in the valley of Ahab's mountains." Stubb, who represents the sensation function, sees only the zodiac signs, and consults an almanac to discover their meaning. Flask, who represents the repressed feeling function, calculates how many cigars the coin will buy. "Fedallah pays obeisance to the doubloon by bowing down to it. This indicates that despite his diabolical aspects, he is related to wholeness. In his role as 'avenging angel,' he is in the service of the Self." Like Goethe's devil, Fedallah seeks evil, but effects good (by compensating for Ahab's nobility, and checking Ahab's hubris).[1]

Finally Pip, the mad black boy, approaches the doubloon and "provides the wisest answer": "Here's the ship's navel, this doubloon here, and they are all on fire to unscrew it. But, unscrew your navel, and what's the consequence?" The *Pequod* has lost its center, it's controlled by a madman, it's doomed. Just as, in fairy tales, the simpleton often represents wisdom, so the mad Pip represents wisdom.

> Pip is an example of a well-known archetypal figure, the fool. One thinks, for instance, of *Parsifal* and the fool in *King Lear*.[2] The figure of the fool represents that orientation which although apparently stupid and inept in relation to the conscious world of material expediency, is in tune with the eternal verities of the objective psyche.

As the novel approaches its conclusion, Ahab becomes more human, more self-aware. When Starbuck tells him that some of the barrels of whale-oil are leaking, Ahab at first dismisses him, preoccupied with the pursuit of the white whale. Starbuck says, "Let Ahab beware of Ahab." Instead of responding angrily, Ahab admits, "There's something there," and he reverses his position on the oil-leak, and orders a search for the leaking barrels. Ahab isn't as headstrong as he was earlier in the novel. Soon after, we find Ahab gazing at a vial of Nantucket sand, "a small indication that his frozen feelings were beginning to thaw."

When Ahab thinks the fight with Moby Dick is imminent, he has the blacksmith make him a special harpoon, which he tempers in the blood of the three harpooners. He calls this a baptism, a baptism not in the name of the Father, but in the name of the devil: "*Ego non baptizo te in nomine patris, sed in nomine diaboli*!" "This ritual," Edinger writes, "confirms what has been suspected all along, that Ahab's pact with Fedallah is a pact with the devil." Edinger says that Melville made a pact with the devil in writing *Moby Dick*; in a letter to Hawthorne, Melville said that the secret motto of the novel is the above-quoted line ending *in nomine diaboli*, and Melville said that his "whale book" was boiled in "hell-fire."

In *Mardi*, Melville had said, "he who hates is a fool." But in a later poem, Melville gives us a deeper view of hatred; Melville says that hatred grows out of love, out of "Amor incensed." To restore the capacity to love, one must live through hatred. Edinger quotes an Indian aphorism: "He who loves God takes seven reincarnations to reach perfection; and he who hates God

---

1 In Goethe's *Faust*, Mephistopheles says that he's
"Part of that power which would
Do evil constantly and constantly does good."
Ein Teil von jener Kraft,
Die stets das Böse will und stets das Gute schafft.

2 Parsifal means "pure fool" in Arabic, or at least that's what Wagner thought.

takes only three, for he who hates God will think of him more than he who loves him." As love can turn into hatred, so hatred can turn into love. If hatred is repressed, Edinger says, then love may be frozen, too.

Edinger says that, in *Moby Dick*, Melville gave full vent to his hatred, hence *Moby Dick* has a "power and depth of imagination" far beyond his other works. *Moby Dick* overthrows Puritan ideals, and releases all that Puritanism represses. To accept one's dark side, to confront one's shadow, to make a pact with the devil, is a stage in the process of maturing. Many leading 19th-century writers, Edinger says, explored the dark side, and tried to overcome the split between dark and light, tried to "reclaim and redeem for conscious use the repressed human energies which had been consigned to hell by the Christian dissociation." Among these redeemers of the dark side are Melville, Goethe, and Nietzsche.

By redeeming the dark side, Melville released his imagination. "The writing of *Moby Dick* was an experiment in active imagination." Edinger says that Melville's method of writing was much like what Jungians call active imagination. Edinger quotes *Mardi*, in which Melville describes a writer named Lombardo:

> When Lombardo set about his work, he knew not what it would become. He did not build himself in with plans; he wrote right on; and so doing, got deeper and deeper into himself; and like a resolute traveler, plunging through baffling woods, at last was rewarded for his toils.

Melville understood (Edinger says) that "all ideas and images that come to us are 'infused,' that is, come from a source other than the ego." In order for these images to reach consciousness, one must relax conscious control. Jung said that active imagination is "based on a deliberate weakening of the conscious mind and its inhibiting effect, which either limits or suppresses the unconscious." Melville showed "extraordinary courage," Edinger says, in his exploration of the unconscious, an exploration that had "absolutely no collective sanction," an exploration that could have resulted in madness.

As the end approaches, Ahab has a recurrent dream of hearses. He fears that this dream portends his own death. This leads Edinger into a discussion of premonitory dreams, and the ability of the unconscious to transcend space and time.

Fedallah makes prophecies similar to those that the witches make in *Macbeth*. He assures Ahab, "I shall still go before thee thy pilot.... Hemp only can kill thee." One is reminded of

Macbeth shall never vanquished be until
Great Birnam wood to high Dunsinane hill
Shall come against him.

Like Macbeth, Ahab trusts these prophecies, and believes that he's invulnerable.

Ahab gets angry at a quadrant, calling it a "foolish toy" that presumes to insult the sun. Edinger reminds us that Ahab himself threatened to "strike the sun." Ahab is projecting his own arrogance onto the quadrant. "Whenever we observe an excessive affect reaction to a person or an object, we can suspect a psychological projection to be operating." Ahab's anger at the quadrant is actually anger at his own hubris; he's beginning to turn against his own psychic inflation. As we noted above, his frozen feelings are starting to thaw, his unconscious is starting to compensate for his one-sided conscious attitude. "The fiery reaction that bursts out of Ahab against the quadrant is the first manifestation of the rectifying energies which appear subsequently as the typhoon, the fire of the corpusants, and finally the white whale itself."

Edinger notes that wind is a symbol of the spirit, the unconscious. Starbuck points out that the typhoon comes from the east, where Ahab is heading, and that the typhoon has damaged Ahab's whale-boat, in the very place where Ahab stands. "His stand-point is stove, man!" Edinger comments, "The same power that destroyed the quadrant for its hubris is destroying Ahab's standpoint."

Now the divine fire appears—the corpusants, also called St. Elmo's Fire. Ahab has united the crew, molded them to his own purpose, but the divine fire breaks up this unanimity. "Starbuck urges that the ship turn for home and a few chapters later contemplates killing Ahab."

As Ahab addresses the divine fire, he suggests that God is incomplete, that God needs man, that the unconscious needs human consciousness. "I know that of me," Ahab says, "which thou knowest not of thyself, oh, thou omnipotent." This is the same insight, Edinger says, that Job has (here Edinger is following Jung's argument in *Answer to Job*). Job discovered "that Yahweh is not human but, in certain respects, less than human, that he is just what Yahweh says of leviathan." Yahweh is an unconscious being, a phenomenon.

As *Moby Dick* draws to a close, "a radical change is occurring within [Ahab]." Ahab becomes "a feeling human being," and shows kindness and love in his dealings with Pip. "Ahab, although he dies, is healed."

> Pip is Ahab's shadow, his opposite half. Together they make a whole. As the old Manxman put it, "One daft with strength, the other daft with weakness." The fact that Ahab is able to relate feelingly to Pip means that he is at last approaching an acceptance of his own weak side and even finding value in it.... The relationship between Ahab and Pip thus represents a reconciliation of opposites, which is one of the features of the integrated personality.

Shortly after Ahab has this change of attitude, the *Pequod* meets the *Rachel*, a whaleship that's looking for a lost whale-boat. Edinger notes the significance of Rachel in the Old Testament, and says that *Rachel* represents "the positive archetypal mother.... A positive feminine, feeling element has entered the situation. It is this ship and what it symbolizes that is later the agent of salvation for Ishmael."

In Chapter 132, Edinger says, "the demonisms are stripped away entirely and Ahab is revealed to himself and to us in his full humanity." Ahab tells Starbuck that he's "away, whole oceans away, from that young girl-wife I wedded past fifty, and sailed for Cape Horn the next day, leaving but one dent in my marriage pillow—wife? wife?—rather a widow with her husband alive! Aye, I widowed that poor girl when I married her, Starbuck."

> In this stunning passage [Edinger comments], we finally meet Ahab as a full human being. Now we see his life in a larger perspective. A new level of consciousness has dawned on Ahab. He now realizes the compulsive, demonic nature of his previous state, and, for the present at least, is released from it. The missing anima appears, Ahab's wife, and feeling for her transforms the situation. This point marks the climax of *Moby Dick*. Ahab's hate has spent itself, and in its place comes sorrow for his folly. Now Ahab can contemplate with Shakespeare, how "strange it is that nature must compel us to lament our most persisted deeds."

In his last chapter, Edinger notes that the pursuit of Moby Dick lasts three days. He notes the significance of three: "In fairy tales, we frequently encounter the theme of the crucial act which must be repeated three times." He notes that there are three Fates in Greek mythology, and three Norns in Teutonic mythology. He notes that Starbuck understands the "three theme":

> This the critical third day? For when three days flow together in one continuous intense pursuit; be sure the first is the morning, the second the noon, and the third the evening and the end of that thing—be that end what it may.

Edinger also notes that three is in stories of death and rebirth. Jonah was in the belly of the whale for three days, and Jesus was in the tomb for three days (before being resurrected).

Edinger says that the image of spiral motion occurs twice in the final pages: first when Moby Dick swims in a circle around a wrecked whale-boat, and next when the *Pequod* is sucked into a "wheeling circle" of water. Edinger notes the religious significance of spiral motion, and says it's a "symbol for the process of individuation, which is a kind of circumambulation in ever smaller circles of the Self."

At the end of the novel, Ishmael takes refuge in Queequeg's coffin. The coffin signifies death and rebirth; it's a "container of death," but also a "cradle and womb." And it's significant, Edinger says, that the coffin is Queequeg's:

> The same whirlpool wheel of the Self which sucked the ill-fated *Pequod* down to death, threw up out of its center the protective vessel of rebirth for Ishmael. In this final scene, Queequeg's redemptive function for Ishmael, which was noted earlier, is verified. Ishmael's words shortly after meeting Queequeg came back to us with added meaning: "I felt a melting in me. No more my splintered heart and maddened hand were turned against the wolfish world. This soothing savage had redeemed it."

In closing, Edinger notes how deeply moved Melville was when, as a young sailor in the middle of the Pacific Ocean, he read about the whaleship

Essex. Edinger says that the story of the *Essex* must have stirred up an unconscious complex or archetype in Melville, "the Job archetype, man's encounter with an apparently malevolent deity." Like Job and Ahab, we're battered and bruised and defeated, and become wiser in the process. As Jung said, "the experience of the self is always a defeat for the ego."

Eventually, Edinger says, Melville was healed and found wholeness: "he experienced the *coniunctio* that was prefigured at the end of *Moby Dick*." In a late poem, Melville wrote

Speak not evil of the evil:
Evil and good they braided play
Into one cord.

In another late poem, Melville wrote

Healed of my hurt, I laud the inhuman sea—
Yea, bless the Angels Four that there convene;
For healed I am even by their pitiless breath
Distilled in wholesome dew named rosemarine.

E. More Views of *Moby Dick*

a. Lawrence

I read D. H. Lawrence's essay on *Moby Dick*, which is in his *Studies in Classic American Literature*. It's a good essay, I recommend it, I'm surprised it's not anthologized more often. Though Lawrence is much impressed with *Moby Dick*, he isn't blind to the book's faults.

> At first you are put off by the style.... Nobody can be more clownish, more clumsy and sententiously in bad taste, than Herman Melville, even in a great book like *Moby Dick*. He preaches and holds forth because he's not sure of himself. And he holds forth, often, so amateurishly.... One wearies of the *grand serieux*.

Melville is far too ready to philosophize, to look for deep, dark truths in the universe. And he's far too ready to imitate other writers, especially Shakespeare—to imitate Shakespeare's philosophical asides, and Shakespeare's emphasis on fate. Melville imitates because, as Lawrence notes, "he's not sure of himself." Melville was determined to be a Great Writer, so he imitated other Great Writers, especially the Greatest of them, Shakespeare.

Lawrence has high praise for Melville's descriptions, especially his description of the first chase (Chapter 48), which Lawrence calls,

> a marvelous piece of true sea-writing.... When [Melville] forgets all audience, and gives us his sheer apprehension of the world, then he is wonderful, his book commands a stillness in the soul, an awe.... Melville is a master of violent, chaotic physical motion; he can keep up a whole wild chase without a flaw.

And Lawrence also has high praise for Melville's descriptions of a calm sea. He even praises the chapters that describe the process of whaling ("magnificent records of actual happening"). Lawrence calls *Moby Dick* "a surpassingly beautiful book.... the greatest book of the sea ever written. It moves awe in the soul."

When I read *Moby Dick*, I too was struck by Melville's descriptions, such as the chase scene in Chapter 61. For me, however, Melville's obscure prose makes *Moby Dick* unenjoyable to read; perhaps obscurity bothers me more than it bothered Lawrence. I'm ready to admit that *Moby Dick* is a classic, and deserves to be considered a classic, but it's a classic that I don't enjoy, and don't recommend.

Lawrence notes that Melville "hardly reacts to human contacts any more," perhaps because he's intent on philosophizing. Ishmael becomes friends with Queequeg, but soon "Queequeg is forgotten like yesterday's newspaper.... Queequeg must be just 'KNOWN', then dropped into oblivion."

At the end of Lawrence's essay, he says that everyone dies at the end of *Moby Dick*, including Ishmael. Perhaps Lawrence is unaware that Ishmael survives because the first English edition of *Moby Dick* didn't mention Ishmael's survival, and thus left the impression that everyone perished.

b. Leonard Woolf

Leonard Woolf (husband of Virginia Woolf) is tougher on Melville than Lawrence—more critical of his style, less impressed with his virtues. But even Woolf admits that *Moby Dick* attains greatness, and *Mardi* is "on the verge of" greatness. Woolf thinks that Melville's early prose (the prose of *Typee*, for example) is better than the prose of *Moby Dick*.

> It seems to me that after 1846 Dickens had a deep, and in some respects a disastrous, influence on Melville. From Dickens he derived the exaggerated, and in his case unspontaneous, humor which disfigures so many pages of *Moby Dick* [and] the loose torrent of his unending sentences.[1]

I think this is true, though I haven't found any confirmation of Dickens' influence on Melville. It stands to reason that a writer as popular as Dickens was in 1846 would influence the young Melville. We noted above that Melville was prone to imitate.

With respect to style, Woolf is Melville's toughest critic:

> The first thing which must be said of Melville is that he writes the most execrable English. Take a sentence like the following [describing Ahab's authority]: "That certain sultanism of his brain, which had otherwise in a good degree remained unmanifested; through those forms that same sultanism became incarnate in an irresistible dictatorship."[Ch. 33] This is a thoroughly bad sentence, and its badness is

[1] Woolf's remarks can be found in an early Norton Critical Edition (made in 1967, probably the first Norton edition).

> quite pointless, and there are thousands like it in *Mardi* and *Moby Dick*. (The use of the semi-colon in this sentence is worth noting; it is characteristic of Melville, who bespatters his sentences with semi-colons without regard to meaning or convention.) His second great vice is rant or rhetoric. When he wants to say that a sailor looked angrily at the mate, he describes him as "stabbing him in the eye with the unflinching poniard of his glance."[Ch. 54] I cannot see the slightest point in this kind of bombast, and, when it raves on for page after page, I almost pitch the book into the waste-paper basket and swear that I will not read another line.

I agree with this criticism, and I think that Melville's style ruins *Moby Dick*—for me, and for many other readers. I remember chatting with a guide at the New Bedford whaling museum, who said he had tried to read *Moby Dick* several times, but couldn't do it. *Moby Dick* isn't a book that a teacher should assign, unless he wants to persuade students that classic literature is obscure, difficult, and unenjoyable.

But I agree with Woolf that Melville sometimes writes well, and there are some fine sentences in *Moby Dick*, such as the sentence I quoted in the last issue: "The rushing *Pequod*, freighted with savages, and laden with fire, and burning a corpse, and plunging into that blackness of darkness..." If Melville had written nothing but this sentence, he would be immortal.

c. Charles Olson

Charles Olson wrote a study of *Moby Dick* entitled *Call Me Ishmael* (1947). Olson grew up in Massachusetts (Worcester and Gloucester) and became a prominent poet. For a person with a modern sensibility, like Olson, Victorian fiction would have little appeal, and Melville's darkness and nihilism would be refreshing and impressive. But now that Western culture has spent a century wallowing in darkness, Melville's darkness is neither refreshing nor impressive.

Olson compares Ahab to Faust, who made a pact with the devil. Olson says that Ahab's diabolism reaches its peak in the Candles chapter (Chapter 119), when a storm lights the masts with "corpusants," or St. Elmo's fire, and Ahab brandishes his harpoon at the crew. The following morning, Ahab puts a new needle on the damaged binnacle, and he appears "in all his fatal pride."

Shortly after, a change sets in, Ahab is softened by contact with the mad cabin-boy, Pip, as Ishmael was once softened by contact with Queequeg. "The lovely association of Ahab and Pip," Olson writes, "is like the relations of Lear to both the Fool and Edgar." Olson says that Pip has seen God, and so he's able to mock the Pequod's "black tragedy." Though Pip is below decks in the last chapters, the change he has wrought in Ahab is lasting; Ahab's "insistent diabolism" melts away, and he becomes a sympathetic figure.

d. William Ellery Sedgwick

William Ellery Sedgwick is the author of *Herman Melville: The Tragedy of Mind* (1944). Sedgwick discusses Shakespeare's influence on Melville:

> There are numerous and diverse parallels in language, in emotional effect, in situation and tragic action between *Moby Dick* on the one hand, and, on the other, *King Lear*, *Hamlet*, *Macbeth*, *Othello*, and *Timon*.

Sedgwick quotes Melville's remark on Shakespeare:

> Those deep faraway things in him; those occasional flashings forth of the intuitive Truth in him; those short, quick probings at the very axis of reality—those are the things that make Shakespeare, Shakespeare.

Sedgwick quotes a "probing" from *Moby Dick*: "Oh God! [Ahab cries,] that man should be a thing for immortal souls to sieve through!" As a second example of a probing, Sedgwick quotes Ahab's "angry retort to the ship's carpenter, 'Thou art as unprincipled as the gods, and as much of a jack-of-all-trades.'" I doubt that such probings are what make Shakespeare great, and I doubt that Melville's probings add to *Moby Dick*.

Sedgwick says that "in *Moby Dick*, as in Shakespeare's tragedies, there is a solid, crowded foreground of material things and of human characters and actions." But unlike Shakespeare, Melville is continually looking behind this foreground, in order to obtain "a more immediate view into the ultimate." According to Sedgwick, Melville was bound by "his inherited and his temperamental Calvinism... to confront the truth as directly and comprehensively as possible."

A modern critic, Joyce Carol Oates, makes the same point; she speaks of "Melville's conception of the art of fiction as primarily moralizing allegory. [Melville] is basically an essayist for whom drama is not an end in itself but the mere pretext for speculation."[1] Oates also speaks of "Melville's notorious stylistic difficulty, his lengthy and frequently graceless sentences." These were all factors, Oates says, in Melville's unpopularity with his contemporaries, along with "the unremitting bleakness of his vision" and his "cosmic pessimism." The mystery is not that Melville was unpopular, but that he has become popular.

Sedgwick tries to explain the horror of whiteness that Melville discusses in Chapter 42, "The Whiteness of the Whale." Sedgwick says that it stems from "the preoccupation with truth, with ideality.... In the white light of the soul's preoccupation with truth all its earthly satisfactions seem illusory—all stale, flat and unprofitable."

---

[1] *Billy Budd and Other Tales*, Afterword; Signet Classics. It has been argued that Ahab is unrealistic, one-dimensional. Oates says that only in *Pierre* did Melville attempt a realistic novel, with three-dimensional characters. But she thought *Pierre* was "fatally marred" by its style.

e. Melville's Doubloon and Homer's Shield

I read an essay that compares the doubloon that Ahab nails to the mast with the shield that Hephaestus makes for Achilles.[1] The essay argues that the doubloon-shield parallel is just one aspect of something larger: Homer's influence on *Moby Dick.*

The author, Daniel Garrison, begins with some remarks on a literary device called ecphrasis—describing a work of art in another work of art.

> Keats's "Ode On A Grecian Urn" is ecphrastic virtually in its entirety; usually the device is set in a larger whole. Often the work of art described is imaginary, as is the case with Keats's Urn; occasionally the object of an ecphrastic description is real, as happens to be the case with Melville's Ecuadorian Doubloon.

Melville is fond of ecphrasis, Garrison says, and uses it "not as a showpiece but as a vehicle of meaning." Garrison says that *Mardi* has a description of

> a carved oaken box of sea biscuit.... The glass ship in *Redburn* and the small oil painting of the protagonist's father in *Pierre* are prominent visual objects which symbolize a state of mind essential to the novel's meaning.

Early in *Moby Dick*, Ishmael sees a painting in an inn, and tries to figure out its meaning. According to Garrison, Melville is "preoccupied with visual images and he repeatedly appeals to our remembrance of paintings, sculpture, and architecture."

After these preliminary remarks, Garrison compares the doubloon and the shield. He says that both are round and gold, both depict the sun, and both appear to be symbols of the world. Furthermore, Melville's doubloon description is found in the same place in his work as Homer's shield description—the beginning of the fourth quarter.

Now Garrison turns to other parallels between Melville and Homer. He says that *Moby Dick* is about the wrath of Ahab, as the *Iliad* is about the wrath of Achilles. He says that Ahab sequesters himself in his cabin (especially at the start of the novel) as Achilles sequesters himself in his tent. One critic, F. O. Matthiessen, said that *Moby Dick* "is more consistently alive on the Homeric than on the Shakespearean level."

I'm not convinced that Homer had much influence on Melville, and I certainly don't think he had as much influence as Shakespeare. But Garrison is convincing when he writes about the importance of visual art in Melville's work, and when he argues that Homer's shield influenced the doubloon.

---

1 "Melville's Doubloon and the Shield of Achilles," by Daniel H. Garrison, *Nineteenth-Century Fiction*, Vol. 26, No. 2 (Sep., 1971), pp. 171-184

f. Final Thoughts

Now I'd like to comment on a few passages that caught my eye as I read *Moby Dick*, passages that I haven't yet commented on. First, in Father Mapple's sermon (Chapter 9), Jonah is said to have an evil eye, an evil air; Jonah is a "shadow figure," and the people around him sense that immediately.

> [Jonah] finds the Tarshish ship receiving the last items of her cargo; and as he steps on board to see its Captain in the cabin, all the sailors for the moment desist from hoisting in the goods, to mark the stranger's evil eye. Jonah sees this; but in vain he tries to look all ease and confidence; in vain essays his wretched smile. Strong intuitions of the man assure the mariners he can be no innocent.

The captain also detects Jonah's evil air:

> "I seek a passage in this ship to Tarshish; how soon sail ye, sir?" Thus far the busy captain had not looked up to Jonah, though the man now stands before him; but no sooner does he hear that hollow voice, than he darts a scrutinizing glance.[1]

Melville takes a bleak view of New Bedford whaling:

> One most perilous and long voyage ended, only begins a second; and a second ended, only begins a third, and so on, for ever and for aye. Such is the endlessness, yea, the intolerableness of all earthly effort.

Melville seems preoccupied with time; in his view, time stretches out endlessly. He doesn't grasp the present, the moment, the "eternal now." Melville's preoccupation with time is the antithesis of Zen. Melville's view is false, insofar as he sees endless repetition of the same, and he overlooks change. New Bedford whaling only seemed "for ever and for aye"; in fact, it ended not long after Melville sailed. So the whaling industry exemplifies change, not endless repetition.

Melville takes a dim view of the world in general:

> The sun hides not Virginia's Dismal Swamp, nor Rome's accursed Campagna, nor wide Sahara, nor all the millions of miles of deserts and of griefs beneath the moon. The sun hides not the ocean, which is the dark side of this earth, and which is two thirds of this earth. So, therefore, that mortal man who hath more of joy than sorrow in him, that mortal man cannot be true—not true, or undeveloped. With books the same. The truest of all men was the Man of Sorrows, and the truest of

---

[1] I see nothing like this in the Book of Jonah. Is Melville writing from his own experience? Is he writing about himself rather than Jonah? Was Melville himself a "shadow figure" with a "wretched smile"? Elsewhere I discussed Hardy's character Boldwood, who doesn't fit in with the group; when Boldwood appears in the barn, the workers fall silent (ljhammond.com/phlit/2010-07.htm#2).

> all books is Solomon's, and Ecclesiastes is the fine hammered steel of woe. 'All is vanity.' ALL.

One suspects that Melville regarded the pessimistic Schopenhauer as a kindred spirit. Nietzsche's objection to Schopenhauer applies also to Melville: a negative judgment about the world tells us more about the judger than about the world. Melville's pessimism is a product of his experiences, of his own temperament.

Melville seems to make a deliberate effort to write a Great Book, and to create characters that resemble Shakespeare's characters. He says that a tragic hero should have

> a half willful overruling morbidness at the bottom of his nature. For all men tragically great are made so through a certain morbidness. Be sure of this, O young ambition, all mortal greatness is but disease.

Ahab is certainly morbid, and he has an "overruling" passion, a monomania. In an earlier issue, we discussed A. C. Bradley's view of the tragic hero: "Bradley says that Shakespeare's tragic characters fail to achieve balance, wholeness, and restraint:

> In almost all we observe a marked one-sidedness, a predisposition in some particular direction; a total incapacity, in certain circumstances, of resisting the force which draws in this direction; a fatal tendency to identify the whole being with one interest, object, passion, or habit of mind. This, it would seem, is, for Shakespeare, the fundamental tragic trait.... It is a fatal gift, but it carries with it a touch of greatness.[1]

Bradley's remarks fit Ahab perfectly. Bradley's view of the tragic hero agrees with Melville's view: one-sidedness, lack of balance and restraint, a touch of greatness, a touch of evil.

Melville realizes that the future is foretold by both externals (omens) and internals (hunches). And he realizes that our inner being shapes circumstances:

> Ye admonitions and warnings! ....not so much predictions from without, as verifications of the foregoing things within. For with little external to constrain us, the innermost necessities in our being, these still drive us on.

Ahab is driven on by his inner being, his obsession, and nothing external can deflect him from his destiny. Queequeg shows that death comes from the will, not from externals, and if we don't will to die, we won't die:

> Now that he had apparently made every preparation for death; now that his coffin was proved a good fit, Queequeg suddenly rallied; soon there seemed no need of the carpenter's box: and thereupon, when some expressed their delighted surprise, he, in substance, said, that the cause of his sudden convalescence was this: at a critical moment, he had just

---

[1] ljhammond.com/phlit/2006-03.htm#3

> recalled a little duty ashore, which he was leaving undone; and therefore had changed his mind about dying: he could not die yet, he averred. They asked him, then, whether to live or die was a matter of his own sovereign will and pleasure. He answered, certainly. In a word, it was Queequeg's conceit, that if a man made up his mind to live, mere sickness could not kill him: nothing but a whale, or a gale, or some violent, ungovernable, unintelligent destroyer of that sort.

One might go even further, and say that even whales and gales can be molded by our inner being, our will.

But the opposite is also true: circumstances can mold our will, and Melville is aware of this, too. He shows how the depressed *Pequod* is enlivened by an encounter with the cheerful *Bachelor*:

> Not seldom in this life, when, on the right side, fortune's favorites sail close by us, we, though all adroop before, catch somewhat of the rushing breeze, and joyfully feel our bagging sails fill out. So seemed it with the *Pequod*. For next day after encountering the gay *Bachelor*, whales were seen and four were slain; and one of them by Ahab.

Malcolm Gladwell has argued that our circumstances, our environment, molds our mind. When I discussed Gladwell's Tipping Point, I wrote thus:

> In earlier issues of this e-zine, I've often discussed thinkers like James Allen, who believe that our mind, our attitude, molds our circumstances. Gladwell argues the opposite—that our environment molds our mind, "our inner states are the result of our outer circumstances." Gladwell calls this the Power of Context.

Melville has the genius to grasp both the Power of Will and the Power of Context.

In the middle of his novel, Melville places a story-within-a-story, a digression called "The Town-Ho's Story." A later novelist, a novelist in the realistic tradition, like Hardy or Tolstoy, wouldn't digress in this manner. Is Melville part of the pre-realistic tradition? Should we compare him to Cervantes and Fielding, rather than Hardy and Tolstoy?

At the climax of the Town-Ho's story, the Captain prepares to lash Steelkilt, but suddenly desists:

> Steelkilt here hissed out something, inaudible to all but the Captain; who, to the amazement of all hands, started back, paced the deck rapidly two or three times, and then suddenly throwing down his rope, said, "I won't do it—let him go—cut him down: d'ye hear?"

Why does the Captain release Steelkilt? Some scholars argue that Steelkilt is a woman dressed as a man, and when the Captain realizes that, he releases Steelkilt. But Steelkilt is said to have a "flowing golden beard," and there doesn't seem to be anything feminine about him. What other theory could account for the Captain's surprising decision to release Steelkilt? I remember hearing about an American prisoner who was about to be executed by a Japanese officer. The prisoner told the officer that, if he was killed, he would haunt the officer for the rest of his life. The officer released him.

But could Steelkilt make such a threat? Steelkilt is going to be flogged, not executed. The Captain's decision to release Steelkilt is a difficult puzzle to unravel.

Melville makes a striking observation about the whale's eyes:

> While in most other animals that I can now think of, the eyes are so planted as imperceptibly to blend their visual power, so as to produce one picture and not two to the brain; the peculiar position of the whale's eyes, effectually divided as they are by many cubic feet of solid head, which towers between them like a great mountain separating two lakes in valleys; this, of course, must wholly separate the impressions which each independent organ imparts. The whale, therefore, must see one distinct picture on this side, and another distinct picture on that side; while all between must be profound darkness and nothingness to him. Man may, in effect, be said to look out on the world from a sentry-box with two joined sashes for his window. But with the whale, these two sashes are separately inserted, making two distinct windows, but sadly impairing the view.

Analysis of the eye leads to some remarks on the whale's brain:

> Both his eyes, in themselves, must simultaneously act; but is his brain so much more comprehensive, combining, and subtle than man's, that he can at the same moment of time attentively examine two distinct prospects, one on one side of him, and the other in an exactly opposite direction? If he can, then is it as marvelous a thing in him, as if a man were able simultaneously to go through the demonstrations of two distinct problems in Euclid.

Melville also discusses how the whale breathes—or rather, how he swims underwater without breathing:

> The whale, who systematically lives, by intervals, his full hour and more (when at the bottom) without drawing a single breath, or so much as in any way inhaling a particle of air; for, remember, he has no gills. How is this? Between his ribs and on each side of his spine he is supplied with a remarkable involved Cretan labyrinth of vermicelli-like vessels, which vessels, when he quits the surface, are completely distended with oxygenated blood. So that for an hour or more, a thousand fathoms in the sea, he carries a surplus stock of vitality in him, just as the camel crossing the waterless desert carries a surplus supply of drink for future use in its four supplementary stomachs.

Melville also comments on the whale's size—bigger than a whole town!

> According to my careful calculation... a Sperm Whale of the largest magnitude, between eighty-five and ninety feet in length, and something less than forty feet in its fullest circumference... will weigh at least ninety tons; so that reckoning thirteen men to a ton, he would considerably outweigh the combined population of a whole village of one thousand one hundred inhabitants.

One of the most memorable chapters in *Moby Dick* is Chapter 119, "The Candles," which deals with the typhoon, and the "corpusants" (also known as "St. Elmo's Fire"). The corpusants are fires at the ends of the masts; they make the masts resemble candles.

> While this pallidness was burning aloft, few words were heard from the enchanted crew; who in one thick cluster stood on the forecastle, all their eyes gleaming in that pale phosphorescence, like a far away constellation of stars. Relieved against the ghostly light, the gigantic jet negro, Daggoo, loomed up to thrice his real stature, and seemed the black cloud from which the thunder had come. The parted mouth of Tashtego revealed his shark-white teeth, which strangely gleamed as if they too had been tipped by corpusants; while lit up by the preternatural light, Queequeg's tattooing burned like Satanic blue flames on his body.

Passages like these remind one of Hawthorne's remark: "What a book Melville has written! It gives me an idea of much greater power than his preceding ones."

After the storm, Starbuck goes below to speak to Ahab in his cabin.

> The loaded muskets in the rack were shiningly revealed, as they stood upright against the forward bulkhead. Starbuck was an honest, upright man; but out of Starbuck's heart, at that instant when he saw the muskets, there strangely evolved an evil thought; but so blent with its neutral or good accompaniments that for the instant he hardly knew it for itself.

Starbuck asks himself,

> Shall this crazed old man be tamely suffered to drag a whole ship's company down to doom with him? Yes, it would make him the willful murderer of thirty men and more, if this ship come to any deadly harm; and come to deadly harm, my soul swears this ship will, if Ahab have his way. If, then, he were this instant—put aside, that crime would not be his.

In a similar way, some of the people around Hitler knew that he was carrying Germany to destruction, and they thought about trying to kill him before he did so. (In the last issue, we discussed other parallels between Ahab and Hitler.[1])

The final battle:

> Moby Dick had turned, and was now coming for the three crews. Ahab's boat was central; and cheering his men, he told them he would take the whale head-and-head—that is, pull straight up to his forehead—a not uncommon thing; for when within a certain limit, such a course excludes the coming onset from the whale's sidelong vision. But ere that close limit was gained, and while yet all three boats were plain as the ship's three masts to his eye; the White Whale churning

---

1 ljhammond.com/phlit/2011-12.htm#5

himself into furious speed, almost in an instant as it were, rushing among the boats with open jaws, and a lashing tail, offered appalling battle on every side; and heedless of the irons darted at him from every boat, seemed only intent on annihilating each separate plank of which those boats were made.

5. Mark Twain

A. Shakespeare's Influence on Twain

Twain tried to compete with Shakespeare, and he studied Shakespeare assiduously, hoping to learn everything that Shakespeare had to teach. As a result of his close study of Shakespeare, Twain's mind was saturated with Shakespeare's works, and his own works contain countless allusions to Shakespeare.

Shakespeare's influence on Twain is the subject of an essay called "Samuel Clemens and the Ghost of Shakespeare," by James Hirsh.[1] Hirsh says that even when Twain retired from writing, it was a retirement à la Shakespeare:

> When Clemens wrote in a 1905 letter to his daughter Clara that he had broken his bow and burned his arrows, "His expression recalls Prospero's—and supposedly Shakespeare's—valedictory speech in *The Tempest*." For Clemens, Shakespeare was not merely a figure to idolize or to parody but someone to emulate.

Perhaps this shouldn't surprise us, perhaps every gifted young writer at that time emulated Shakespeare. Shakespeare was more important then, since German literature was just beginning to be appreciated, and Russian literature was scarcely known outside Russia. Goethe emulated Shakespeare, as did G. B. Shaw, Whitman, Melville, and Hawthorne. "Whitman 'considered himself Shakespeare's rival in the New World and was even jealous of his fame'.... *Moby Dick* is openly and pervasively influenced by Shakespeare." Twain wasn't content to achieve anything less than Shakespeare achieved; if his work didn't match up, then he was uneasy, then he tried to explain why it didn't match up.

Even minor episodes in *Huck Finn* are Shakespeare-influenced.

> In the opening chapter of the novel, Huck hears 'twelve licks' of the clock, determines 'something was a stirring,' and then hears Tom's identifying signal. In the opening scene of *Hamlet*, after Barnardo says the clock has 'struck twelve,' Francisco reports 'Not a mouse stirring,' but at that point Horatio and Marcellus arrive and give the identifying passwords.

More important scenes of *Huck Finn* are also Shakespeare-influenced.

---

[1] *Studies in the Novel*, 24, no. 3 (fall 1992): 251-72

Colonel Sherburn's contemptuous dismissal of the mob in Chapter 22 ("droop your tails and go home") re-enacts Coriolanus's defiance of the Roman populace ("You common cry of curs... I banish you!").

Another memorable scene in *Huck Finn* was influenced by *Hamlet.* "The passage generally regarded as Clemens' greatest accomplishment, Huck's meditation in Chapter 31, consists in large part of paraphrases of Claudius' soliloquy." This seems to be Hirsh's discovery. Many of Hirsh's Shakespeare-Twain connections seem tenuous, forced, but this one seems solid. How did it escape so many readers? What a thrill for Hirsh to discover it! Hirsh was the perfect candidate to make this discovery since he's an expert on Shakespeare soliloquies, and wrote a book on the subject. Let's match Huck's soliloquy against Claudius':

Claudius	**Huck**
Pray can I not, though inclination be as sharp as will.	I about made up my mind to pray... But words wouldn't come.
And, like a man to double business bound, I stand in pause where I shall first begin.	I knowed very well why they wouldn't come ...it was because I was playing double.
I am still possess'd of those effects for which I did the murder.	I was letting *on* to give up sin, but ...I was holding on to the biggest one of all.
Bow, stubborn knees.	So I kneeled down.
My words fly up, my thoughts remain below. Words without thoughts never to heaven go.	I was trying to make my mouth *say* I would do the right thing ...but deep down in me I knowed it was a lie.... You can't pray a lie.... All right, then, I'll *go* to hell.

"The final words of Huck's meditation," Hirsh points out, "are even spoken aloud, like a soliloquy by a Shakespearean character."

Considering how Twain used Shakespeare, one might say, "Shakespeare was an original, Twain wasn't." But Shakespeare wasn't entirely original, he too was in debt to earlier writers, such as Ovid. Perhaps every writer is "in debt," just as every writer has a father.

B. Gentleman and Mudcat: Social Class in *Huck Finn*

My daughter and I are reading *Huck Finn* together. It's a good book to read aloud—full of action and humor. It's good for children, even better for adults.

Twain reminds me of Nietzsche insofar as he scorns the common man, and admires the aristocrat. This attitude is apparent early in the novel when he describes Huck's father, who is from the lower class. Huck's father is a vagrant and a drunk. Judge Thatcher takes him in, and tries to reform him:

> Then they tucked the old man into a beautiful room, which was the spare room, and in the night some time he got powerful thirsty and clumb out on to the porch-roof and slid down a stanchion and traded his new coat for a jug of forty-rod, and clumb back again and had a

> good old time; and towards daylight he crawled out again, drunk as a fiddler, and rolled off the porch and broke his left arm in two places, and was most froze to death when somebody found him after sun-up. And when they come to look at that spare room they had to take soundings before they could navigate it.
>
> The judge he felt kind of sore. He said he reckoned a body could reform the old man with a shotgun, maybe, but he didn't know no other way.

Twain's description of the Arkansas rabble fairly drips with contempt:

> All the stores was along one street. They had white domestic awnings in front.... There was empty drygoods boxes under the awnings, and loafers roosting on them all day long, whittling them with their Barlow knives; and chawing tobacco, and gaping and yawning and stretching—a mighty ornery lot. They generly had on yellow straw hats most as wide as an umbrella, but didn't wear no coats nor waistcoats, they called one another Bill, and Buck, and Hank, and Joe, and Andy, and talked lazy and drawly, and used considerable many cuss words. There was as many as one loafer leaning up against every awning-post, and he most always had his hands in his britches-pockets, except when he fetched them out to lend a chaw of tobacco or scratch.

Now listen to Huck's description of Col. Grangerford:

> Col. Grangerford was a gentleman, you see. He was a gentleman all over; and so was his family. He was well born, as the saying is, and that's worth as much in a man as it is in a horse, so the Widow Douglas said, and nobody ever denied that she was of the first aristocracy in our town; and pap he always said it, too, though he warn't no more quality than a mudcat himself. Col. Grangerford was very tall and very slim, and had a darkish-paly complexion, not a sign of red in it anywheres; he was clean shaved every morning all over his thin face, and he had the thinnest kind of lips, and the thinnest kind of nostrils, and a high nose, and heavy eyebrows, and the blackest kind of eyes, sunk so deep back that they seemed like they was looking out of caverns at you, as you may say.

Twain's hero-aristocrats always stand alone, against the mob; they never appear in twos or threes. They have a particular physical appearance, and occupy a particular place in society—often a judge, in this case an officer (colonel). Later in the novel, we meet another colonel, Colonel Sherburn, who is being taunted by the local drunk, Boggs:

> And so he went on, calling Sherburn everything he could lay his tongue to, and the whole street packed with people listening and laughing and going on. By and by a proud-looking man about fifty-five—and he was a heap the best dressed man in that town, too—steps out of the store, and the crowd drops back on each side to let him come. He says to Boggs, mighty ca'm and slow—he says: "I'm tired of this, but I'll endure it till one o'clock. Till one o'clock, mind—no longer. If you open your mouth against me only once after that time you can't travel so far but I will find you." Then he turns and goes in. The crowd looked mighty sober; nobody stirred, and there warn't no more laughing.

Sherburn shoots Boggs, killing him. A lynch mob goes after Sherburn:

> They swarmed up towards Sherburn's house, a-whooping and raging like Injuns.... Just then Sherburn steps out on to the roof of his little front porch, with a double-barrel gun in his hand, and takes his stand, perfectly ca'm and deliberate, not saying a word. The racket stopped, and the wave sucked back.
>
> Sherburn never said a word—just stood there, looking down. The stillness was awful creepy and uncomfortable. Sherburn run his eye slow along the crowd; and wherever it struck the people tried a little to outgaze him, but they couldn't; they dropped their eyes and looked sneaky.[1]

In addition to Colonel Grangerford and Colonel Sherburn, another character who is favorably portrayed is Dr. Robinson. Again we see the high position in society (doctor), again we see the aristocratic appearance ("a big iron-jawed man"). When the two rapscallions (whom Huck refers to as the king and the duke) pretend to be the heirs of Peter Wilks, Dr. Robinson realizes that they're frauds, and laughs in their face. The crowd, however, sides with the king and the duke. When the king and the duke talk privately, the duke says he's worried about Dr. Robinson, but the king says, "Cuss the doctor! What do we k'yer for HIM? Hain't we got all the fools in town on our side? And ain't that a big enough majority in any town?" Twain's contempt for the majority reminds one of Ibsen's Dr. Stockman (as well as Nietzsche). Likewise, Twain's belief that breeding is "worth as much in a man as it is in a horse" reminds one of Stockman.

When the king and the duke put on a nonsense-show called The Royal Nonesuch, the crowd is angry until "a big, fine looking man" addresses them, and suggests a response to the swindle. Later we learn that the "big, fine looking man" is a judge.

Notice how Twain emphasizes that his hero-aristocrats are "big," "very tall," etc. I'm reminded of a chapter in Gladwell's *Blink*, a chapter in which he discusses how people are impressed by stature, and often choose tall men to fill high positions. "In the U.S. population," Gladwell writes, "about 14.5 percent of all men are six feet or taller. Among CEOs of Fortune 500 companies, that number is 58 percent.... Most of us... automatically associate leadership ability with imposing physical stature."[2] Are we choosing the tall to be leaders, or are natural leaders tall? What is cause and what is effect?

Most of the characters in *Huck Finn* are based on people Twain knew: Pap, Huck, Tom, Jim, the duke and the dauphin, Boggs and Col. Sherburn.

---

[1] Can anyone doubt that Twain's sympathies are with Sherburn? "Several points which Sherburn makes were made by Twain as his own in a chapter discarded from *Life on the Mississippi*."(See Walter Blair's essay, "The French Revolution and Huckleberry Finn," in *Twentieth Century Interpretations of* Adventures of Huckleberry Finn)

[2] See Ch. 3, #2

Twain's fiction has a ring of truth because it's based on fact; as Twain put it,

> If you attempt to create a wholly imagined incident, adventure or situation, you will go astray and the artificiality will be detectable, but if you found on *fact* in your personal experience, it is an acorn, a root, and every created adornment that grows out of it, and spreads its foliage and blossoms to the sun will seem reality, not invention.

Twain preferred fact to fiction. He said, "I like history, biography, travels, curious facts and strange happenings, and science. And I detest novels, poetry and theology." Twain's favorite book was Carlyle's history of The French Revolution; Twain read that book over and over again, he was reading it on his deathbed. Twain also read and re-read Dickens' novel about The French Revolution, *A Tale of Two Cities*. One might say that Twain didn't learn by reading, he learned by re-reading; he read Carlyle and Dickens until his mind was saturated with them, until he could re-create their scenes in his own fiction.

Carlyle describes The Mob and The Leader—two topics that play prominent roles in *Huck Finn*. Like Twain, Carlyle scorns The Mob and admires The Leader.

Carlyle often expresses pity for the unfortunate—even for people like Robespierre, of whom many would say, "he deserved it." Likewise, Twain expresses pity for the King and Duke: "I was sorry for them poor pitiful rascals."

C. Conscience in *Huck Finn*

As you read *Huck Finn*, you repeatedly encounter the theme of conscience, guilt. For example, when the two rapscallions (the "king" and the "duke") finally receive their comeuppance, and get tarred and feathered, Huck's conscience blames him for not doing something to save them. Huck says,

> So we poked along back home, and I warn't feeling so brash as I was before, but kind of ornery, and humble, and to blame, somehow—though I hadn't done nothing. But that's always the way; it don't make no difference whether you do right or wrong, a person's conscience ain't got no sense, and just goes for him anyway. If I had a yaller dog that didn't know no more than a person's conscience does I would pison him. It takes up more room than all the rest of a person's insides, and yet ain't no good, nohow. Tom Sawyer he says the same.

Huck has ample reason to hate the rapscallions, and to welcome their defeat, so it's difficult to see why his conscience would upbraid him for not coming to their aid. Likewise, it's difficult to see why his conscience would upbraid him for helping Jim to reach his freedom. Huck's conscience seems to be blind, unreasonable.

One wonders why Huck, an uncivilized child of nature, would so often fall prey to the feeling of guilt. Perhaps this feeling of guilt fits better with

Huck's creator (Twain) than with Huck himself; it seems somewhat out of place with Huck.

Twain himself described *Huck Finn* as "a book of mine where a sound heart and a deformed conscience come into collision and conscience suffers a defeat."[1] One critic said that "Huck's spontaneously good heart has dictated his actions, but his conscience has remained depraved, for it represents the community." In Twain's world, virtue is a matter of the heart, not the head. "In a crucial moral emergency," Twain wrote, "a sound heart is a safer guide than an ill-trained conscience."[2] Twain's view of morality resembles that of the Philosophy of Today, which also prefers spontaneity to reasoning.

Huck's conscience tells him that he shouldn't steal a slave, he shouldn't liberate a slave. Twain regards this as an example of a perverse moral principle that is instilled by society: "That strange thing, the conscience—that unerring monitor—can be trained to approve any wild thing you *want* it to approve if you begin its education early and stick to it." The view that conscience isn't innate, that it comes from society, was championed in antiquity by the epicurean school.

In the characters of Miss Watson and Widow Douglas, Twain depicted two different kinds of morality. Miss Watson represents the epicurean/utilitarian/selfish school, and tries to induce Huck to behave with promises of heaven and threats of hell. On the other hand, Widow Douglas tells Huck that the reward for prayer is "spiritual gifts"; she tells Huck to "help other people" and doesn't mention reward or punishment. Her approach to morality is that of the stoic school, which believed that man has a natural sense of right and wrong, that conscience is innate rather than acquired.

Twain was troubled by a severe conscience, and he wrote a story ("The Facts Concerning the Recent Carnival of Crime in Connecticut") in which the protagonist does away with his conscience entirely. In this story, the protagonist is visited by his conscience in the form of a deformed dwarf. The conscience-dwarf tells him, "'It is my *business*—and my joy—to make you repent of *every*thing you do.' The narrator kills the troublesome dwarf and begins a life of crime."[3]

One can divide *Huck Finn* into three parts:

1. the preliminary part, in which the action takes place in Huck's "hometown";
2. the middle part, in which Huck and Jim float down the Mississippi on their raft, and meet various memorable characters;
3. the final part, in which Tom Sawyer plays an elaborate game of prisoner, using romantic novels as his guide, and Jim as his prisoner.

---

[1] See "Society and Conscience in Huckleberry Finn", Leo B. Levy, *Nineteenth-Century Fiction*, Vol. 18, No. 4 (Mar., 1964), pp. 383-391

[2] See Kaufman, Will, "Mark Twain's Deformed Conscience," *American Imago*, Volume 63, Number 4, Winter 2006, pp. 463-478.

[3] See "So Noble... and So Beautiful a Book," in *Twentieth Century Interpretations of* Adventures of Huckleberry Finn

For most readers, the middle part is doubtless the heart of the book, and the last part is a letdown. But it can't be denied that Twain's humor sparkles as brightly in this last part as in anything he ever wrote. When Tom Sawyer plays his game of prisoner, I'm reminded of Osama bin Laden, who gives his henchmen titles like "Caliph of Baghdad". Like Tom Sawyer, al Qaeda has a romantic conception of the past.

In the middle part, Twain satirizes Southern society, especially its religion and culture.

> The satire of the towns along the banks insists again and again that the dominant culture is decadent and perverted. Traditional values have gone to seed. The inhabitants can hardly be said to live a conscious life of their own; their actions, their thoughts, even their emotions are controlled by an outworn and debased Calvinism, and by a residue of the eighteenth-century cult of sensibility. With few exceptions they are mere bundles of tropisms, at the mercy of scoundrels like the Duke and the King who know how to exploit their prejudices and delusions.[1]

Twain took a dim view of Christianity, referring to it as "an odious religion." Twain didn't work his way to Eastern religion, or to the Hermetic religion, so one might say that Twain had no religion. Does this explain his pessimism, his dark view of the human condition? Should he be grouped with other 19th-century pessimists like Schopenhauer and Leopardi, pessimists who had broken with the old religion, and not yet found a new one?

6. Henry James

A. Ezra Pound and Henry James

In a recent issue, I noted that James Joyce was a HenryJames fan.[2] Ezra Pound was also a HenryJames fan. Like Henry James, Ezra Pound left the U.S., and tried to make his way as a man-of-letters in Europe (Joyce was also an expat; he left Ireland and spent most of his life in Italy and France).

Pound met Henry James several times in London around 1912, when Pound was 27, and James was about 70. At first, they glared at each other; perhaps James was put off by Pound's bohemian appearance (Pound was known to wear an earring, green pants, a purple hat, a hand-painted tie, etc.). Later Pound reported that "he had met James again and liked him 'still more on further acquaintance.' He reported yet another meeting, when he lunched with a group that included James, whom he found 'quite delightful.' Six years later he said of James: 'The man had this curious power of founding affection in those who had scarcely seen him.'"[3]

---

1 See "A Sound Heart and a Deformed Conscience," by Henry Nash Smith in *Twentieth Century Interpretations of* Adventures of Huckleberry Finn

2 See ljhammond.com/phlit/2021-10.htm

3 jstor.org/stable/2923022

"He talked exactly as he wrote," Pound said of James. "It is with his own so beautiful talk, his ability to hear his own voice in the rounded paragraph, that he is aptest to charm one." In his poetry, Pound alluded to James and his works. "In the *Cantos* Pound is referring to James when he says 'the old voice lifts itself / Weaving an endless sentence.'"

Pound complained that James was under-appreciated in the U.S. "[Pound] writes to his mother in 1915, 'If your unfortunate continent had only familiarized itself more fully with his excellent works it would be a far pleasanter, a far more possible habitat.'" In 1918, Pound wrote a 40-page piece on James for the *Little Review*. "As preparation for his essay, he went through, from first to last, all the volumes of the Macmillan edition of James, a prodigious task." In his essay, Pound makes some criticisms of James, but on the whole, "James emerges from the essay a literary giant. What author could ask for more unstinted praise than being designated 'the greatest writer of our time and of our own particular language'?"

Pound felt that James was at least as good a writer as Proust; Pound said that Proust is "the nearest the French can get to Henry James." James' interest in structure/form appealed to Pound. "Pound's concern with craftsmanship, his insistence that the literary artist bring an abundance of conscious techniques to the act of composition, is reflected in the relatively large amount of space he gives in his essay to James' notes for *The Ivory Tower*. The interest in form that these notes reveal makes James, according to Pound, unique among novelists who have written in English."

Pound admired James' criticism as well as his fiction. Pound "included James on his list of recommended writers in *ABC of Reading*, saying that James' prefaces are 'the one extant great treatise on novel writing in English.'"

B. "Poor Richard"

I read "Poor Richard," a story by Henry James, a story that William James was a fan of. "Poor Richard" was published in 1867, when Henry was only 24. It's one of his "American stories"; it takes place in the rural North, and several of the characters are CivilWar soldiers. It's often called the best of Henry's early stories. I enjoyed it, and I can understand why it's well-regarded.

"Poor Richard" was published in *Atlantic* magazine, where William Dean Howells was assistant editor. Howells was impressed with "Poor Richard," and wanted to publish everything that James wrote; Howells promoted James, as he promoted Mark Twain. One critic said that "Poor Richard" "led to the beginning of a friendship between James and Howells which may be considered as one of the great literary friendships in the annals of literature."[1]

---

[1] *A Landscape Painter*, New York, Scott and Seltzer, 1919, Preface by Albert Mordell

But Howells didn't trust readers to appreciate James. Howells wrote, "I cannot doubt that James has every element of success in fiction. But I suspect that he must in a very great degree create his audience. In the meantime, I rather despise existing readers."

I'm reminded of Proust, who felt that an original writer or artist had to form his audience, educate his audience. "People of taste and refinement," Proust wrote, "tell us nowadays that Renoir is one of the great painters of the last century. But in so saying they forget the element of Time, and that it took a great deal of time, well into the present century, before Renoir was hailed as a great artist."[1] In several respects, Proust reminds me of Henry James: the refinement (of both feelings and language), the wit, the interest in painting (and culture in general), the dedication to literature, the bachelor life, the penchant for socializing.[2]

While Howells gave James a chance to "create his audience," sales of the *Atlantic* were falling behind sales of illustrated magazines like *Harper's* and *Century*. By 1890, *Atlantic* editors were no longer eager to publish James; the *Atlantic* was aiming at a broader audience, and James' work was becoming subtler and less popular.

I mentioned James' refinement. Here's an example:
Richard visits Gertrude when she's hoping for a visit from another man. Gertrude calls out, "What do you want? Can I do anything for you?" James writes, "A certain infinitesimal dryness of tone on Gertrude's part was the inevitable result of her finding that that whispered summons came only from Richard."[3] This sentence shows James' penchant for refinement of both feeling and language. Most writers would be satisfied with "A certain dryness of tone." "Infinitesimal" and "inevitable" are unnecessary, and obscure the author's meaning.

One critic said that "Poor Richard" shows James' "growing fondness for analysis. He allowed it to run away with him.... The psychologist unfortunately predominated over the novelist."[4]

"Poor Richard" contains characters and themes that appear in James' later writings. For example, "Poor Richard" has a female character, Gertrude,

---

1 *The Guermantes Way*, Part II, Ch. 1

Jacques Barzun said that, to enjoy James' fiction, one needs an "ear trained to catch the nuances of a subdued rhetoric."

2 Ezra Pound "said that Proust is 'the nearest the French can get to Henry James.'"(jstor.org/stable/2923022)

3 When James revised "Poor Richard" for publication in book form, he changed this sentence to, "A certain indefinable dryness of tone on Gertrude's part was the inevitable result of her finding that this whispered invocation came from poor Richard." This revised version, like the original version, has the refinement of feeling and language that I think is typical of James.

4 *The Early Development of Henry James*, by Cornelia Kelley, Ch. 5, p. 72

who captivates men, not with her beauty, but with her character. One critic spoke of James' "gravely sweet girls."[1]

And "Poor Richard" has a male character, Richard, who finally wins the heart of the woman he pursues, but then steps back. One critic wrote,

> In [James'] later works such renunciation nearly always involves a turning away from sexual union, from the natural consummation of passion. As Edmund Wilson remarks, "the men are always deciding not to marry the women in Henry James."[2]

Another critic says that Richard's renunciation of Gertrude is "an early version of the Jamesian 'renunciation,' made famous by characters like Christopher Newman, Isabel Archer, Fleda Vetch, and Lambert Strether."[3] This

---

[1] "Howells Reviews James: The Transcendence of Realism," Sarah B. Daugherty, *American Literary Realism, 1870-1910*, Spring-Autumn, 1985, jstor.org/stable/27746179

Is Daisy Miller also one of James' "gravely sweet girls"? Daisy's beauty is striking, and she seems exuberant rather than grave, but she's innocent, she has little interest in sex or money. James describes Daisy's glance as "perfectly direct and unshrinking. It was not, however, what would have been called an immodest glance, for the young girl's eyes were singularly honest and fresh.... She was very quiet; she sat in a charming, tranquil attitude.... [Daisy] was not a coquette."

[2] "Henry James: Money and Morality," Alice Morgan, *Texas Studies in Literature and Language*, Spring 1970, Vol. 12, No. 1, jstor.org/stable/40754083k

Peter Collister says that Richard is one of "the series of romanticized young and fragile males cherished by James." (*Writing the Self: Henry James and America*, by Peter Collister, p. 91) Sarah Daugherty calls Richard "an early exemplar of the 'poor gentleman'... a sensitive youth."

Richard's fragility and sensitivity suggest that he represents James himself, just as I suspect that Winterbourne (in "Daisy Miller") represents James himself. Leon Edel says that, as Richard is pushed to the periphery of the social circle by two soldiers, so James was pushed to the periphery by Oliver Wendell Holmes Jr. and John Gray, both veterans. As three men pay attention to Gertrude, so Holmes, Gray, and James paid attention to Minnie Temple. "Richard's feelings," Edel writes, "have all the vividness of personal experience."

Edel says that when Richard recovers his health, Gertrude falls ill. Edel calls this James' "vampire theme"; Edel says that this theme can be found in other works by James.(See Volume 1 of Edel's 5-volume biography of James, pp. 236-238)

[3] "Flirtations in Early James," David Southward, *Nineteenth-Century Literature*, March 1998, jstor.org/stable/2934063

theme of stepping back from marriage has an obvious parallel with James' own life.

C. "Daisy Miller"

"Daisy Miller" was published in 1878, when James was 35. It launched his career, becoming popular in both England and America. It's about 50 pages long, so it should probably be called a novella. Like many James stories, it deals with an American in Europe. James contrasts Daisy's spontaneity with the propriety of her elders. One might call "Daisy Miller" a novel of manners, since much of it deals with the question, What is proper behavior? How should a well-mannered person act? I enjoyed it, it's a readable story, a sketch of scenic spots in Europe, an introduction to James' *modus operandi*. But I missed James' subtler touches, I needed to read critical essays to appreciate James' artistry.
[Spoiler Warning: If you're thinking of reading "Daisy Miller," you may want to skip the rest of this section.]

One critic said that James often introduces his theme in his opening paragraph. The opening paragraph of "Daisy Miller" introduces the theme of the spontaneous, exuberant American and the proper, staid European:

> At the little town of Vevey, in Switzerland, there is a particularly comfortable hotel. There are, indeed, many hotels, for the entertainment of tourists is the business of the place, which, as many travelers will remember, is seated upon the edge of a remarkably blue lake—a lake that it behooves every tourist to visit.... In this region, in the month of June, American travelers are extremely numerous; it may be said, indeed, that Vevey assumes at this period some of the characteristics of an American watering place. There are sights and sounds which evoke a vision, an echo, of Newport and Saratoga. There is a flitting hither and thither of "stylish" young girls, a rustling of muslin flounces, a rattle of dance music in the morning hours, a sound of high-pitched voices at all times. [But] there are other features that are much at variance with these suggestions: neat German waiters, who look like secretaries of legation; Russian princesses sitting in the garden; little Polish boys walking about held by the hand, with their governors; a view of the sunny crest of the Dent du Midi and the picturesque towers of the Castle of Chillon.

A critic named Motley Deakin compared "Daisy Miller" to *Corinne*, a novel by Mme de Stael. *Corinne* is half novel, half travel book; it describes many scenic spots in Italy. Like "Daisy Miller," *Corinne* is about a strong-willed woman who comes into conflict with society and dies.[1]

The Colosseum in Rome had a special significance for James as for Mme de Stael. Mme de Stael calls the Colosseum "the most beautiful ruin

---

1 "Daisy Miller, Tradition, and the European Heroine," Motley F. Deakin, *Comparative Literature Studies*, Vol. 6, No. 1 (1969), pp. 45-59, jstor.org/stable/40467801

of Rome." Deakin says that the Colosseum is a "magnet to the Romantic spirit." Corinne and Daisy both view the Colosseum at night, "the time favored by romantic devotees of this scene."

Deakin argues that Daisy is more than an-American-in-Europe, she's also part of a European tradition, the tradition of the Romantic Rebel. But the Romantic tradition evolved in the decades between Mme de Stael and James; Romanticism became mixed with Realism. Deakin says, "The romantic sentiment felt for the Colosseum is still strong enough to draw Daisy to it, but the attenuation of its attraction becomes evident in Daisy's incapacity to see this somber scene as anything more than 'pretty.'" Perhaps we should call James "half Romantic, half Realist," rather than "full Romantic."

As Daisy's feeling for the Colosseum is attenuated, so too the erotic passion in "Daisy Miller" is attenuated; James is not a "full Romantic." Corinne was a far more ardent lover than Daisy:

> [Corinne's] love for Oswald [is] overpowering and total.... Corinne exudes an erotic sentiment characteristic of the Romantic Movement and reminiscent of a host of earlier heroines—a sentiment that, though later diminished and viewed negatively as scandalous impropriety, still informs "Daisy Miller."

The element of political rebellion in Mme de Stael is also attenuated in "Daisy Miller." The protagonist of Mme de Stael's *Delphine* is enthusiastic about the American Revolution and the French Revolution. For Delphine, freedom is both a personal ideal and a political ideal. "By the time it reaches Daisy, this ideal is flattened and attenuated; it is diminished to deportment and manners. As a result, Daisy comprehends only dimly the ideal of freedom which she symbolizes."

Like James, Mme de Stael contrasts different cultures. Corinne is part-British, part-Italian. She finds the Italian spirit liberating—as Shakespeare did, as Goethe did, as E. M. Forster did.[1]

Was James directly influenced by Mme de Stael? Or was he influenced through intervening writers? Probably both. In "Daisy Miller," James mentions one of these intervening writers—Victor Cherbuliez, author of *Paule Méré*. Thus, James gives us a hint about who influenced "Daisy Miller," and what tradition "Daisy Miller" belongs to. Deakin says,

> the stories of James and Cherbuliez have much in common. They both explore the theme of social disorientation, examining the effects of rigid conventions on a young girl not sympathetic to them.... The male protagonists in both novels cannot resist the pressures of convention, thus exposing the unprotected heroines to the crushing power of these pressures. Both novels present a protest against these inhuman social

---

[1] Victor Cherbuliez's protagonist, Paule Méré, whom I discuss below, has a Swiss father and an Italian mother. She also feels the Italian spirit to be liberating. Deakin writes, "Though [Paule Méré] combines qualities of both countries, she responds most evidently to Italy and its attributes of beauty, spontaneity, pleasure, and freedom."

> forces, but both also contain the bitter recognition that they are invincible, destroying as they do the young innocents.

Another critic writes,

> Like James' novel, *Paule Méré* takes its title from the name of its heroine and concerns a spirited, independent-minded young woman whose unchaperoned excursions with a man excite the censure of European society and make her an object of scandal. Even the settings of the two novels are similar: both open at a Swiss hotel and end in Italy.[1]

Since *Paule Méré* ends with the death of the protagonist, the reference to *Paule Méré* in "Daisy Miller" might be viewed as a foreshadowing of Daisy's death. There are other, more obvious foreshadowings: When Daisy says she's going for a walk, her mother says, "You'll get the fever as sure as you live." And Daisy tells Winterbourne, "We are going to stay [in Rome] all winter, if we don't die of the fever; and I guess we'll stay then."

A critic named Carol Ohmann says that James links Daisy to the natural world, and to the natural cycle of birth and death, thereby preparing the reader for Daisy's death.[2] Daisy walks with Giovanelli in the Pincian Garden, overlooking the Villa Borghese, and later she walks with Giovanelli at "the Palace of the Caesars" on Palatine Hill. Both these locations afford the visitor a broad prospect, and James describes both with a kind of poetic rapture. James had a special fondness for Rome, and doubtless he enjoyed these two places many times. Ohmann is probably right when she says that James is subtly connecting Daisy to natural processes. "Once Daisy is identified with the world of nature.... her death is inevitable."

I mentioned above that James was influenced by the French Romantic tradition, including Mme de Stael and Victor Cherbuliez. Another writer in this tradition is George Sand. James admired Sand. Like Daisy, the heroines of Sand's novels are spontaneous, willful women who clash with society and die. "Forced back upon themselves by their unwillingness to accede to the demands of society, they have developed habits of introspection and self-examination. They are superior women in their dedication, their moral virtue, or their genius."[3]

Like Mme de Stael, Sand "intended her works as defenses of herself, as vindications of her own unorthodox opinions and actions." Like Mme de Stael, Sand was drawn to revolution/reform; Sand even started her own newspaper. Wikipedia says that Sand "was a member of the provisional government of 1848, issuing a series of fiery manifestos." The Romantic spirit is passionate in love, unconventional in manners/lifestyle, revolutionary in politics, immoderate in all things.

Daisy's death is somewhat puzzling. Does she die because society frowns on her free-spirited ways? Does she die because Winterbourne

---

1 sparknotes.com/lit/daisy/section3/page/2/

2 "Daisy Miller: A Study of Changing Intentions," Carol Ohmann, *American Literature*, Vol. 36, No. 1 (Mar., 1964), pp. 1-11, jstor.org/stable/2923496

3 See the essay by Motley Deakin

doesn't commit himself to her decisively? If we view Daisy as part of a Romantic tradition, it helps us to make sense of her death. This tradition includes Mme de Stael (born 1766), George Sand (born 1804), and Victor Cherbuliez (born 1829). Henry James (born 1843) drew on these earlier writers.[1]

Perhaps one cause of Daisy's death is her own *frevel*; she's "asking for trouble," she tempts fate, she teases the numinous powers. "'I don't care,' said Daisy in a little strange tone, 'whether I have Roman fever or not!'" Some readers might say, "This remark is out of character, it doesn't ring true. It has no connection to what precedes it." But perhaps this remark rings true insofar as *frevel* is a constant in human nature, especially in one as young and willful as Daisy.[2]

The name "Daisy" suggests a person who's open and spontaneous, as Daisy is. The name "Winterbourne," on the other hand, suggests a person who's more controlled. Did James put part of himself into Winterbourne? Daisy says to Winterbourne, "I noticed you were as stiff as an umbrella the first time I saw you." When Winterbourne says to Daisy, "I don't dance," Daisy responds, "Of course you don't dance; you're too stiff." When Winterbourne advises Daisy to get into Mrs. Walker's carriage, Daisy says, "I never heard anything so stiff!" When Winterbourne tells Daisy, "I wish you would flirt with me, and me only," Daisy responds, "You are the last man I should think of flirting with. As I have had the pleasure of informing you, you are too stiff."[3]

Winterbourne is rather solitary, as the bachelor James may have been. When Winterbourne encounters Daisy on the Palatine Hill, Daisy says, "I should think you would be lonesome.... You are always going round by yourself. Can't you get anyone to walk with you?"

Did James put part of himself into the character of Winterbourne, as Shakespeare put part of himself into Hamlet? And does Winterbourne spread a lethal chill around him, as Hamlet seems to? In an earlier issue, I said that Wilson Knight regards Hamlet as "a shadow figure, a 'negative thinker,' one who kills people with negative thoughts, an example of the power of negative thinking." Is Winterbourne also a shadow figure, a "thought killer"?[4]

When Daisy and Giovanelli see Winterbourne in the Colosseum, Daisy feels that Winterbourne is casting an Evil Eye on them. James writes,

---

[1] Cornelia Kelley argues that "Daisy Miller" was influenced by *A Foregone Conclusion*, a novel by James' friend William Dean Howells. This Howells novel has a lively heroine named Florida Vervain. But Motley Deakin points out that Howells' heroines have "a happier future with marriage and children," while Daisy dies the untimely death of the French Romantic heroine.

[2] For more on *frevel*, see my *Conversations With Great Thinkers* ==> "Psychology" ==> "*Frevel*"

[3] Did James describe himself as "stiff" in his correspondence, or in his autobiographical writings?

[4] Winterbourne is described as "a man of imagination and, as our ancestors used to say, sensibility." Couldn't this be said of James himself?

> Presently the sound of the woman's voice came to [Winterbourne] distinctly in the warm night air. "Well, he looks at us as one of the old lions or tigers may have looked at the Christian martyrs!" These were the words he heard, in the familiar accent of Miss Daisy Miller. "Let us hope he is not very hungry," responded the ingenious Giovanelli. "He will have to take me first; you will serve for dessert."

Perhaps the lonely, stiff Winterbourne is emotionally hungry.

Daisy's death has multiple causes, as real events have multiple causes. The notion that Daisy is killed by a dark, mysterious, evil force, such as the Evil Eye, is consistent with an argument made by Jacques Barzun. Barzun calls James a "melodramatist." Barzun divides literature into melodrama and comedy; he views tragedy as a subset of melodrama. He says that melodrama deals with "terrifying evil.... man's horror in the face of evil.... freezing fear, the mysteriousness of the force [of evil] at work."[1]

Barzun speaks of "Aesthetic Melodrama," and he distinguishes Aesthetic Melodrama from tragedy and from low-grade melodrama. He says that many novelists, including James and Balzac, write Aesthetic Melodrama. Some novelists, like George Meredith, write comedy; according to Barzun, Meredith "believes in faults, errors, follies, but not in terrifying evil." Barzun says, "I have long puzzled over the undoubted fact that relatively few persons are admirers of both Henry James and Meredith." So Barzun sees a fundamental difference between James and Meredith, between Melodrama and Comedy.

Barzun says that James is somewhat critical of the older melodrama of Dickens, Balzac, etc. And James is also somewhat critical of realists like Flaubert; Flaubert's work is "tame and, in the end, life-denying." James tries to "purge and renovate" the old Romantics; he uses subtler methods than they used, he uses "the nuances of a subdued rhetoric." But there's "fire and force beneath the surface."

Barzun says that James depicts "the friction of two men." We find this friction in "Daisy Miller"; Winterbourne and Giovanelli look askance at each other. In "Poor Richard," we find friction between three men, all of whom are interested in Gertrude.

In "Daisy Miller," it's difficult to tell who's the hero and who's the villain. Barzun says that the hero and the villain want the same things: the girl and the money.[2] The reader of "Daisy Miller" may sympathize with Winterbourne rather than Giovanelli, but at the end of the novella, Giovanelli rises in our estimation. As Barzun says, James often gives the reader a "moral shock," James says, "Look! It is not as you think!"

---

[1] I found Barzun's essay, and other essays, in *Tales of Henry James*, which is part of Norton Critical Editions. Barzun may be the only HenryJames scholar who's also a WilliamJames scholar.

[2] Barzun says that "most of [James'] novels and tales deal with middling people pursuing the two simplest objects of human concern—love and money."

At the end of both "Poor Richard" and "Daisy Miller," nobody gets the girl. This is typical of James. One critic wrote, "Like so many Jamesian heroes, Winterbourne has lost the capacity for love, and he has lost the opportunity to come to life."

In describing the death of Daisy, James does a superb job of combining two dark forces, *frevel* and the Evil Eye. In his discussion of "Daisy Miller," Leon Edel seems oblivious of both *frevel* and the Evil Eye. But Edel grasps the theme of the disobedient child. He speaks of "the unerring vision which James had of the total abdication, by the mass of American parents, of all authority over their children."[1]

The film version of "Daisy Miller," made in 1974, is faithful to the novella, and takes you to all the scenic spots in the novella.

D. "The Madonna of the Future"

In his conversation with Einstein, Bernard Cohen said, "The historian often encountered this problem: Can a scientist's contemporaries tell whether he is a crank or a genius when the only evident fact is his unorthodoxy?" Einstein agreed that this was a difficult problem; "There is no objective test," Einstein said.

The same question arises in Henry James' short story "The Madonna of the Future." The narrator, an American visiting Florence, meets an American painter named Theobald, who has been living in Florence for years. Theobald guides the narrator through Florence's galleries and streets, while the narrator wonders whether Theobald is a genius or a crank. When someone calls Theobald a "magnificent genius," the narrator says,

> "I am sure I don't know," I answered with a shrug. "If you are in a position to affirm it, you have the advantage of me. I have seen nothing from his hand but the bambino yonder, which certainly is fine."

The narrator says that Theobald has "a certain pallid leanness of visage, which I hardly knew whether to refer to the consuming fire of genius or to a meager diet.... He seemed always hungry.... His velvet coat was threadbare."

Is Theobald actually creating any works? Is he above the art market, or below it? Theobald says,

> "As a proof of my conscientiousness"—and he stopped short, and eyed me with extraordinary candor, as if the proof were to be overwhelming—"I have never sold a picture!"

The narrator isn't sure what to make of this. "The fact that he had never sold a picture was more obvious than glorious." But the narrator is impressed with Theobald's commitment, enthusiasm, inspiration:

> I was more and more impressed with my companion's remarkable singleness of purpose. Everything was a pretext for some wildly idealistic rhapsody or reverie. Nothing could be seen or said that did not lead him sooner or later to a glowing discourse on the true, the beautiful,

---

[1] See Edel's biography of James, Volume 2, Book 6, "Daisy," Section 3

> and the good. If my friend was not a genius, he was certainly a monomaniac.

Surely this is an allusion to Goethe's creed, "Live resolutely in the good, the whole, and the beautiful" (*Im guten, ganzen, shonen resolut zu leben*). Goethe was an important figure in James' time; in a recent issue, I discussed how William James admired Goethe. Goethe died in 1832, just ten years before William was born.

Note that Henry James has modified Goethe's creed, he's omitted "the whole," and replaced it with "the true." Is this because he himself didn't try to achieve wholeness, and focused instead on art and literature? Goethe was involved in three things that James wasn't involved with: science, politics, and family. William James faulted his brother's writing for "over-refinement" and "want of blood." Was Goethe a greater writer because he included wholeness among his goals, because he wasn't focused entirely on art?

Though William found fault with Henry's writings, he called "Madonna of the Future" a "masterpiece." I agree with William that it's a first-rate story, a lively and readable story; I'm more impressed with the style than I am with the style of Henry's later works. "Madonna of the Future" contains some profound remarks on art, as when the narrator says, "Besides being strong in his genius, Raphael was happy in a certain good faith of which we have lost the trick." The Renaissance artist is distinguished not only by his genius and his skill but by his faith in life.[1]

* * * * *

Theobald complains about his American roots:

> An American, to excel, has just ten times as much to learn as a European.... We have neither taste, nor tact, nor power. How should we have them? Our crude and garish climate, our silent past, our deafening present, the constant pressure about us of unlovely circumstance, [are] void of all that nourishes and prompts and inspires the artist.

To which the narrator responds:

> Nothing is so idle as to talk about our want of a nutritive soil, of opportunity, of inspiration, and all the rest of it. The worthy part is to do something fine! There is no law in our glorious Constitution against

---

1 In an earlier issue, I discussed Panofsky's view that "a portrait of an individual is more than a portrait of an individual—it is sometimes a portrait of the spirit of an age." The Renaissance spirit was confident and balanced, as was the Renaissance portrait. Henry James says that Raphael had "a certain good faith," and Panofsky speaks of being "free and open to the world." The Renaissance had confidence in the world, and this is apparent in their portraits. James says that his contemporaries have "lost the trick" of this "good faith." What would he say about more modern works, such as Munch's *Scream*? Surely he'd use a stronger phrase than "lost the trick." Perhaps he'd say, as Kafka did, that the spine of the soul had broken.

> that. Invent, create, achieve! No matter if you have to study fifty times as much as one of these! What else are you an artist for?

James probably subscribed to both these views—he thought it was a handicap not to be European, but he thought that this handicap could be overcome. In his book on Hawthorne, James listed all the things that America lacked:

> No sovereign, no court, no personal loyalty, no aristocracy, no church, no clergy, no army, no diplomatic service, no country gentlemen, no palaces, no castles, nor manors, nor old country-houses, nor parsonages, nor thatched cottages nor ivied ruins; no cathedrals, nor abbeys, nor little Norman churches; no great Universities nor public schools—no Oxford, nor Eton, nor Harrow; no literature, no novels, no museums, no pictures, no political society, no sporting class—no Epsom nor Ascot! Some such list as that might be drawn up of the absent things in American life—especially in the American life of forty years ago.

This long list helps us to understand why James left the U.S., and spent most of his adult life in Europe. James speaks of, "the coldness, the thinness, the blankness" of the American scene. What is there for an American novelist to write about?

> Our foremost feeling is that of compassion for a romancer looking for subjects in such a field. It takes so many things, as Hawthorne must have felt later in life, when he made the acquaintance of the denser, richer, warmer European spectacle—it takes such an accumulation of history and custom, such a complexity of manners and types, to form a fund of suggestion for a novelist.

But at least the American can laugh. "It would be cruel, in this terrible denudation, to deny [the American] the consolation of his national gift, that 'American humor' of which of late years we have heard so much." I enjoy James' humor, and I enjoy Mark Twain's humor even more.

One source of inspiration for American writers is nature; Melville is our great marine writer, Thoreau our great terrene writer. If we lacked "old country-houses" and "Norman churches," we didn't lack nature.

* * * * *

Henry James spent much of his life around museums and artists. As a teenager, he studied painting with William Morris Hunt. One of his fellow-students, John La Farge, introduced him to the poetry of Robert Browning. Browning's poem "Andrea del Sarto" influenced "Madonna of the Future." Browning's protagonist is a painter who is productive but uninspired, James' protagonist is a painter who is inspired but unproductive. Browning says "A man's reach should exceed his grasp." Andrea doesn't reach high enough, Theobald reaches for the stars but grasps nothing.[1]

Another influence on "Madonna of the Future" is a Balzac story called "The Unknown Masterpiece" (*Le Chef-d'Oeuvre Inconnu*). Balzac describes a painter who believes he has found the secret of depicting living, breathing people, but after working on his masterpiece for ten years, he suddenly loses faith in his work after a casual remark by a young man. Likewise, James' painter keeps his faith for many years until a casual remark by a young man deflates his inspiration, breaks the spell.

Like Browning, Balzac was a major influence on Henry James; like Browning, Balzac was introduced to James by the artist John La Farge, who was eight years older than James. As Henry's brother William was fond of Browning, so too William was fond of Balzac; in an earlier issue, I quoted William's resolve to "read all Balzac." Browning and Balzac were both important writers in Henry James' youth; they both seemed to explore human nature more deeply than it had been explored before.

But taste changes, and our view of human nature changes. Browning and Balzac were hot new writers in Henry's youth, but they didn't keep that position for long. By the time Henry was in the evening of his life, young people were losing interest in Balzac. In 1902, when Yeats mentioned Balzac to a 20-year-old James Joyce, "Joyce burst out laughing so that everyone in the café turned round to look at him. 'Who reads Balzac today?' he exclaimed."

We find the same thing in philosophy; the hot philosopher of today doesn't stay hot for long. For many years, the philosopher struggles to gain recognition, and soon after he's recognized, another thinker comes along and

---

1 See "Henry James' 'Half-Man': The Legacy of Browning in 'The Madonna of the Future,'" by Michael L. Ross, *Browning Institute Studies*, 1974, Vol. 2 (1974), pp. 25-42, jstor.org/stable/25057596. Ross says he's indebted to Cornelia Kelley's book *The Early Development of Henry James*.

I noted elsewhere that William James, like his brother, was a fan of Browning, especially his "Grammarian's Funeral."

We should aim high, Browning says, even if we produce something imperfect. This is called Browning's "doctrine of the imperfect." Ruskin would have agreed with Browning (were they fans of each other?). Ruskin wrote, "It is, perhaps, the principal admirableness of the Gothic schools of architecture, that they... receive the results of the labor of inferior minds; and out of fragments full of imperfection, and betraying that imperfection in every touch, indulgently raise up a stately and unaccusable whole. It seems a fantastic paradox, but it is nevertheless a most important truth, that no architecture can be truly noble which is not imperfect.... The principle may be stated more broadly still. I have confined the illustration of it to architecture, but I must not leave it as if true of architecture only.... No good work whatever can be perfect, and *the demand for perfection is always a sign of a misunderstanding of the ends of art*."(*The Stones of Venice*)

renders him obsolete. As Schopenhauer put it, "To truth only a brief celebration of victory is allowed between the two long periods during which it is condemned as paradoxical, or disparaged as trivial."[1] Schopenhauer himself enjoyed "a celebration of victory" from about 1860 to 1890, then everyone started talking about Nietzsche.

But we shouldn't push this argument too far, it's only half-true.[2] It would be equally true to say that Homer and Shakespeare are still interesting to modern readers, Balzac and Schopenhauer are still interesting. The cutting-edge moves, but the classics endure.

E. "The Aspern Papers"

"The Aspern Papers" (1888) is one of Henry James' most highly-regarded novellas. Set in Venice, it describes an American scholar's effort to obtain letters written by an American poet, Jeffrey Aspern. The letters are in the possession of Juliana Bordereau, an elderly woman who, many years ago, had a liaison with Aspern.

[Spoiler Warning: If you're thinking of reading "The Aspern Papers," you may want to skip the rest of this section.]

"The Aspern Papers" reminds me of James' "Madonna of the Future," which I discussed in a recent issue. Both novellas are set in Italy, both have suspense, both deal with cultural matters ("Madonna" with art, "Aspern" with literature). "Madonna of the Future" was influenced by multiple literary works—a Browning poem, a Balzac story, a Musset play. Likewise, "The Aspern Papers" echoes Pushkin's "Queen of Spades," Pushkin's "Bronze Horseman," and perhaps Poe's "Tell-Tale Heart."

Since I'm a big fan of "Queen of Spades," I enjoyed tracing the links between it and "Aspern." In both stories, an elderly woman has something that a young man longs for. In both stories, the young man spends much time trying to penetrate the old woman's quarters. In both stories, the young man looks up at the old woman's windows from outside, while she watches him through the same windows; when he finally enters her inner sanctum, the old woman dies. In both stories, the old woman lives with a young female companion, a submissive woman, a woman whom the young man ingratiates himself with, a woman whom the old woman would like to marry to the young man. In both stories, the young man is focused on obtaining the "treasure" from the old woman; the young man is obsessed, ruthless, heartless, he doesn't care if the old woman dies, and he doesn't have any interest

---

[1] *The World as Will and Representation*, vol. 1, Preface to first edition

[2] As Berenson put it, "Nothing we can say, except perhaps in the quantitative sciences, can be more than a half-truth."(*Aesthetics and History in the Visual Arts*, Introduction)

in the young woman. In both stories, if the young man had married the young woman, he probably would have obtained the treasure.[1]

We don't know for certain that James read "Queen of Spades," but I think he probably did (in a French translation). We do know that James was a friend of the Russian novelist Turgenev, and we know that Turgenev was a kind of apostle of Russian literature, so Turgenev could have described Pushkin's "Queen of Spades" to James.[2]

While there are numerous parallels between "Aspern" and "Queen of Spades," there's only one parallel between "Aspern" and Pushkin's "Bronze Horseman," but it's a significant one. In "Aspern," the narrator encounters the statue of Bartolomeo Colleoni, which is outside the Church of John & Paul (the Basilica di Santi Giovanni e Paolo, known in Venetian as San Zanipolo).

---

1 I believe that the Queen of Spades appears at the end of Pushkin's story because the old woman is annoyed that the young man (Hermann) has ignored the young woman. When the old woman appears to Hermann as a ghost, she says, "I forgive you my death, on condition that you marry my ward, Lizaveta Ivanovna." Since Hermann ignores this condition, the old woman doesn't forgive him, the old woman becomes the Vengeful Dead. She gets her revenge by preventing Hermann from winning the final card game.

I discussed "Queen of Spades" in 2010. At that time, I didn't notice the Freemason symbolism in the story, especially the importance of the numbers 3 and 7. Pushkin himself was a Mason.

2 Briggs speaks of "Turgenev whose self-imposed task it was to spread the good name of his literary compatriots abroad."

Anthony Briggs, "Alexander Pushkin: A Possible Influence on Henry James," *Forum for Modern Language Studies*, Volume VIII (1), Jan 1, 1972

Statue of Bartolomeo Colleoni by Verrocchio
photo by Didier Descouens

The reader familiar with Pushkin [writes a Pushkin critic] will be astounded at this moment by the similarity between this scene... and that between Yevgeny and the statue of Peter in The Bronze Horseman. It is all there: the mental confusion, physical wandering, a sudden stop, self-awareness and recognition of a large building... a huge bronze equestrian statue towering aloft, indifferent to the petty egoist and his tiny troubles below.[1]

Statue of Peter the Great, Saint Petersburg
photo by Andrew Shiva

[1] ibid

Leon Edel, perhaps the preeminent HenryJames scholar, says that “The Aspern Papers” is “the most brilliant of Henry’s tales,” and Edel says that “the most exquisite” passage in “Aspern” is the encounter with the statue. Should we give credit to Pushkin for inspiring this passage? Or should we give credit to James for appreciating the Pushkin passage, and for being able to utilize it? As Emerson said, “Next to the originator of a good sentence is the first quoter of it.” Next to the originator of a good passage is the first utilizer of it. James was a good utilizer of world literature; Briggs calls James “a supreme eclectic, an assimilator of the best available.” James’ father called him “a devourer of libraries.”

Was there an affinity between Pushkin and James? The American critic Edmund Wilson said that Pushkin and James both had a combination of “hard realism with formal harmony,” and both had a “classical equanimity.”[1]

* * * * *

As a youngster, James read a good deal of Poe. In his autobiography, James said that he shared his fondness for Poe with his brother William. As one critic put it,

> An “enthusiasm for Poe” had been passed from brother to brother... with the siblings taking turns mounting on “little platforms” to declaim such Poe classics as “The Raven” and “Annabel Lee.”[2]

Scholars have argued that Poe influenced Henry James. “Aspern” has several things in common with Poe’s “Tell-Tale Heart.” In both stories, “the narrator never reveals his name... nor his age or place of birth or residence.” In both stories, the old person has some sort of cover or veil or film over his eye.

---

1 Quoted in Briggs

I recently discovered that Joyce was a fan of Henry James. Joyce’s biographer, Richard Ellman, says that, when Joyce was about 22, James “continued to interest him.” Joyce called James, “that nice old Henry James,” he said that James’ “Madonna of the Future” was “very pleasant writing,” he said that James’ review of Baudelaire was “damn funny,” and he liked the depiction of Isabel Archer in James’ *Portrait of a Lady*.(Ellman, Ch. 11, p. 193)

2 Leonardo Buonomo, “Echoes of the Heart: Henry James’s Evocation of Edgar Allan Poe in ‘The Aspern Papers,’” mdpi.com/2076-0787/10/1/55

Buonomo puts “enthusiasm for Poe” in quotation marks because James had written, “enthusiasm for Poe is the mark of a decidedly primitive stage of reflection.” Later James showed more respect for Poe. “Calling him ‘a man of genius,’ whose ‘intelligence was frequently great,’ James had singled out for praise Poe’s early perceptive assessment of Hawthorne’s worth.” It’s not uncommon for a writer to be both positive and negative about another writer. Tolstoy, for example, said both positive and negative things about Dickens.

> In Poe, especially in "The Tell-Tale Heart," James found the prototype of an obsessive narrator, oscillating between exhibitionism and shame, maniacal reporting and self-deception.[1]

But James' narrator has a more calm, mature tone.

> In reinventing the Poe narrator, James considerably toned down the frantic, oral quality, the theatricality of the original (which had made it ideal for reading aloud), endowing it with a more controlled, subdued tone.

When I discussed James' "Daisy Miller," I said that the protagonist (Winterbourne) may have caused Daisy's death through some sort of negative energy, through his Evil Eye. The same could be said of the protagonist of "Aspern"; he seems to cause the death, will the death, of the old woman (Juliana).[2]

I said that Daisy's own *frevel*, her own recklessness, may have contributed to her death. Likewise, the "Aspern" protagonist may be a *freveler*, and that may contribute to his failure. In the beginning of "Aspern," the protagonist says he will "make love" to Juliana's niece (Tita), but at the end he says that remark was "a joke without consequences." Was he recklessly playing with Tita's feelings—was he *freveling*?

One could argue that the entire effort to obtain Aspern's letters was *frevel*. The protagonist ends by cursing "the extravagant curiosity" that had motivated him. "We had more than enough material without [the letters], and my predicament was the just punishment of that most fatal of human follies, our not having known when to stop." Was this Daisy's mistake, too? Can we define *frevel* as "not knowing when to stop"?[3] Should we credit James with a deep understanding of *frevel*?

---

1 Buonomo, quoting William Veeder

It has been argued that Poe and James subscribed to the same theory of fiction. "Allen Tate noted that Poe's 'insistence upon unity of effect, from first word to last, in the famous review of Hawthorne's *Twice-Told Tales*' anticipated 'the high claims of James in his essay *The Art of Fiction*.'"

It has also been argued that the "Aspern" narrator has the "exaggerated male fear of women" that we find in some Poe stories.

2 Buonomo: "Even though he never contemplates doing Juliana any bodily harm—should she refuse to part with the papers—the military metaphors that come so easily to his mind betray a barely-suppressed hostility towards her, as do the many instances in which he foreshadows—and perhaps secretly wishes for—her death."

3 In an earlier issue, I discussed Philippe Petit, who became famous for walking on a tight-rope stretched between Manhattan's Twin Towers. "[Petit] said it was easy being on the wire, and he felt happy there. Finally he decided to get off; he said he didn't want to tempt fate, didn't want to annoy the gods that are in the buildings, in the wire, in everything.... Petit was successful because he wasn't a *freveler*, he knew when to stop."

When I discussed "Daisy Miller," I said that the solitary, stiff Winterbourne resembled James himself. The protagonist of "Aspern" also reminds one of James. When Tita asks him, "Shall you study—shall you read and write—when you go up to your rooms?" he responds, "I don't do that at night, at this season. The lamplight brings in the [insects]."
Tita asks, "And in winter do you work at night?"
"I read a good deal, but I don't often write."[1]

"Aspern" seems to give us a glimpse of James' own life. Many James stories seem to have this autobiographical element, seem to have a male protagonist who reminds one of James himself. If the "Aspern" protagonist causes Juliana's death by his ruthlessness, is James expressing his own ruthlessness, his own dark side, his own capacity for injuring others?

Like other James stories, "Aspern" depicts a man who chooses not to marry, who runs from women. Does this reflect James' own attitude toward women?

Like other James stories, "Aspern" was revised for the "New York Edition" of James' works. These revisions underline the heartlessness of the "Aspern" narrator, underline the narrator's loss of "human decency," and perhaps his loss of an emotional link to Tita.[2] In the original version, the narrator thinks that Juliana "would die next week, she would die tomorrow—then I could seize her papers." In the NewYork version, Juliana "would die next week, she would die tomorrow—then I could pounce on her possessions and ransack her drawers."

In the original version, "Aspern" ends with the narrator saying that a portrait of Aspern "hangs above my writing table. When I look at it my chagrin at the loss of the letters becomes almost intolerable." In the NewYork

---

[1] Like Trollope, Schopenhauer, and many other writers, James probably did most of his writing in the morning. Here's a description of Schopenhauer's day: "He rose every morning at seven and had a bath but no breakfast. He drank a cup of strong coffee before sitting down at his desk and writing until noon. At noon he ceased work for the day."

[2] Wayne Booth, *The Rhetoric of Fiction*, pp. 354-364, excerpted in the Norton Critical Edition of *Tales of Henry James*.

Borrowing a phrase from Wallace Stevens, Booth says that the "Aspern" narrator is "the lunatic of one idea," he has an *idée fixe*. Thus, he resembles one of Shakespeare's tragic heroes, his obsession is a tragic flaw. In an earlier issue, I quoted A. C. Bradley, who said that Shakespeare's tragic heroes have "a marked one-sidedness, a predisposition in some particular direction... a fatal tendency to identify the whole being with one interest, object, passion, or habit of mind. This, it would seem, is, for Shakespeare, the fundamental tragic trait.... It is a fatal gift, but it carries with it a touch of greatness."

This one-sidedness might seem permanent, unalterable, but Hartsock suggests that it can be altered, overcome. "The evil in the ["Aspern"] narrator," Hartsock writes, "is the evil that Lambert Strether [a character in James' *Ambassadors*] is finally able to excise: the failure to be fully conscious."

version, the last sentence subtly suggests that the narrator has lost more than the letters: "When I look at it I can scarcely bear my loss—I mean of the precious papers." This revision, Booth says, "beautifully reminds us of what the narrator has really lost."

As the narrator reminds us of other James males, so Tita reminds us of other James females. As I noted elsewhere, James' females are "gravely sweet," they have moral beauty. After Tita's hints about marriage are rebuffed, she's disappointed but not angry.

> She stood in the middle of the room with a face of mildness bent upon me, and her look of forgiveness, of absolution, made her angelic. It beautified her.... She smiled strangely, with an infinite gentleness.... She had the force of soul [to] smile at me in her humiliation.

One critic, Mildred Hartsock, said that Tita is the real hero of "Aspern," and her quest for emotional satisfaction is the real subject of the story: "The heart of the matter is not the papers but the tragedy of a woman. [Tita] is a pathetic spinster whose pathos becomes true tragedy as she sees what her choice must be—and makes it with dignity."[1]

* * * * *

Twain said that a fiction-writer often starts with facts:

> If you attempt to create a wholly imagined incident, adventure or situation, you will go astray and the artificiality will be detectable, but if you found on *fact* in your personal experience, it is an acorn, a root, and every created adornment that grows out of it, and spreads its foliage and blossoms to the sun will seem reality, not invention.

All of the James stories that I've discussed, including "Aspern," start from fact, start from something that James saw or heard about. As there are several literary sources for "Aspern," so there are several facts behind "Aspern." One of these facts is that Henry met a Countess Gamba, who had a family connection to a mistress of Byron's (Teresa Guiccioli). The Gambas had numerous letters that Byron had written to Teresa, and they had burned one that they deemed particularly obscene. The Gambas refused to show anyone their "literary hoard."[2]

Another fact behind "Aspern" is that an elderly lady named Mary Jane ("Claire") Clairmont lived for many years in Florence, and possessed "certain Shelley and Byron papers." She had been a mistress of Byron. A Shelley fanatic named Silsbee tried to obtain Claire's papers, and even rented a room in Claire's house. Like Juliana in "Aspern," Claire lived with her niece.

---

[1] Mildred Hartsock, "Unweeded Garden: A View of *The Aspern Papers*," *Studies in Short Fiction*, V, 1967, pp. 60-68, included in the Norton Critical Edition of *Tales of Henry James*.

[2] Surely James understood the feelings of the scholar who wanted the precious papers. But he also understood the feelings of the writer who burned his papers to keep them from the prying eyes of the scholar. James himself guarded his privacy and burned his letters.

When Claire died, Silsbee spoke to the niece about the precious papers. The niece said he could have the papers if he married her. He didn't accept the bargain, he abandoned his quest for the papers.

James was fascinated by this story, partly because Claire had been living in his own time, and he had often walked past her house. Claire represented for James the "visitable past"—around her hovered the glory of the great poets of the past, yet she was a living person whom you could visit. She was both the past and the present, she was the "visitable past." In "Aspern," the protagonist feels that he's in the presence of the past—he's in proximity to Juliana, who was in proximity to the great Jeffrey Aspern.

In addition to the "Gamba fact" and the "Clairmont fact," there's a third fact behind "Aspern": James' own relationship with Constance Fenimore Woolson. Woolson was a writer, and the great-niece of James Fenimore Cooper. Woolson had a strong attachment to James, and probably hoped they would get married. While James was writing "Aspern," he was sharing a house with Woolson near Florence. He was friendly to Woolson—as the "Aspern" narrator is to Tita—but he wouldn't go further, and this was probably disappointing to Woolson. Perhaps James asked himself, like the "Aspern" narrator, Did I mislead her? Should I have married her? Woolson died at age 53, six years after "Aspern" was published; she fell from her Venetian apartment; her death was almost certainly a suicide.[1]

One could ask, "Since the plot of 'Aspern' is drawn from these three 'facts'—Gamba, Clairmont, and Woolson—was Pushkin really an important influence on 'Aspern'?" Briggs argues that the two most dramatic episodes in "Aspern" are

1. the nocturnal encounter with the old woman that ends in her death
2. the encounter with the statue

Briggs says that these two episodes "owe nothing whatever to the source material, real life, anecdotal or biographical. They seem, both of them, very close to Pushkin."

James works within a realistic tradition. He wrote, "the only reason for the existence of a novel is that it does attempt to represent life." The novelist aims at truth, just as the philosopher, the historian, and the scientist aim at truth. The narrator of "Aspern" tells Juliana, "The great philosophers and poets of the past.... often lay bare the truth." Juliana says, "The truth is God's, it isn't man's; we had better leave it alone." The narrator responds,

---

[1] See Edel's 5-volume biography of James, Vol. 3, Book 4, "The Aspern Papers"

Doubtless Woolson read "The Aspern Papers." Did she feel that Tita was based on herself? (The name "Tita" comes from a character in Woolson's novel *Anne.*) Did she feel that the relationship between herself and James was echoed in the relationship between the "Aspern" narrator and Tita? As for James, when he heard about Woolson's death, did he feel that he should have done more to satisfy her emotional needs?

> We are terribly in the dark, I know... but if we give up trying what becomes of all the fine things? What becomes of the work I just mentioned, that of the great philosophers and poets? It is all vain words if there is nothing to measure it by.

This kind of philosophical reflection is rare in James; I think it would be difficult to find a deeper philosophical reflection than this one in all of his work.

Some critics say that James doesn't depict life as a whole. Gide said, "the skillfully made network spun out by [James'] intelligence captivates only the intelligence.... All the weight of the flesh is absent, and all the shaggy, tangled undergrowth, all the wild darkness." But we've seen a "subterranean evil" in the protagonists of "Daisy Miller" and "Aspern." James indicates evil, but doesn't wallow in it, as modern writers often do. And he balances evil with moral beauty. As for *frevel*, what could be darker, shaggier, more irrational than that? And what writer in the English language has depicted *frevel* more skillfully than James?

Some readers say that James is too subtle, too obscure, they wish he would speak more plainly. Booth says that readers dismiss James for his "obscurities," or idolize him for his "subtle ambiguities." Booth says, "both positions are wholly safe, backed by troops in rank on rank, with traditions of honorable battle going back many decades." If James is sometimes obscure, isn't this also true of life itself?

F. "The Lesson of the Master"

I read a novella by Henry James called "The Lesson of the Master." I chose this story because, while reading a biography of William James, I came across William's comment on this story, in a letter to Henry: "I think it exquisite all through—the most finished and mature execution of anything yet." William is my guide to Henry's works.

"The Lesson of the Master" is about a young writer, Paul Overt, who has a growing reputation, as Henry James himself did when he wrote the story. Paul meets an older writer, Henry St. George, a "master" who's more established than Paul. But Henry has sold out to the marketplace, and no longer produces first-rate work. Henry tells Paul to stay true to his highest goals, not to sell out as he has done; Henry advises Paul not to marry and have a family, as he has done, but to dedicate himself entirely to producing great literature. So "the lesson of the master" seems to be, Don't do as I've done.

Paul reminds me of James himself, as other James protagonists remind me of James himself; Paul is a typical James male. Paul falls in love with a young woman, Marian Fancourt, who has recently returned from India, where she lived with her soldier father. Marian is a typical James female protagonist—noble, high-minded, candid. "She gave such an impression of the clear and the noble combined with the easy and the natural.... She suggested no sort of sisterhood with the 'fast' girl.... no cheap coquetry."[1]

Since Paul is a typical James male, and Marian a typical James female, one might suppose that the story is a bit dull, especially for one who has met these characters in other James stories. But it's not dull, it's impressive, even moving, since James describes the young writer's literary aspirations, and Marian's purity, with such eloquence. One does wonder, however, if the story has broad appeal, and one isn't surprised that the *Atlantic* lost interest in publishing James; James writes for a literary audience, not a broad audience.

[Spoiler warning: if you're thinking of reading the novella, you may want to stop here.]

Like most James males, Paul flees from his beloved, perhaps influenced by Henry's warnings about marriage. But Paul doesn't forget Marian. After completing a book while staying on the north shore of Lake Geneva, Paul returns to London and goes straight to Marian's. There he's shocked and angered to learn that Henry's wife has died, and Henry is marrying Marian! This is the sort of plot twist that we often find at the end of a James story; James' dexterity in handling plot gave his work a broader appeal than it would otherwise have had.

Paul wonders if Henry has played a trick on him, if Henry viewed him as a rival for Marian's affections, if Henry was trying to get rid of him by warning him about the dangers of marriage. At the end of the story, the reader is faced with a choice: "Was Henry St. George, the Master of the tale, genuinely concerned with 'saving' and converting Paul Overt, the budding genius, for the glory of England and literature, or was he simply manipulating him for his own ends and steering him away from Marian Fancourt... so that he could marry her himself when the time came?"[2]

I'm a fan of literary criticism, so I always read critical essays after finishing a story. There seem to be few essays on this story, but I found one good one, and one is all I need. It's by a scholar named Adeline Tintner, who has written about other James stories. Tintner points out that the master's

---

1 In 1895, the Emmet sisters (Rosina and Ellen) stayed with William James and his family. William wrote to Henry, "They are the most wholesome, innocent, free-hearted and generous girls." William's description reminds me of Henry's female protagonists, such as Marian. Is this personality-type the ideal of the James family? Or is it the ideal of American Protestants in general?

2 "Iconic Analogy in 'The Lesson of the Master': Henry James' Legend of Saint George and the Dragon," by Adeline R. Tintner, *The Journal of Narrative Technique*, May 1975, Vol. 5, No. 2, pp. 116-127, jstor.org/stable/30225556

name, Henry St. George, fairly screams to be interpreted symbolically, St. George being the patron saint of England.[1]

In "The Lesson of the Master," James takes his stock characters, and relates them to the legend of St. George. Such legends were popular in James' day, and James' friend Edward Burne-Jones made a series of paintings about the St. George legend.

The legend of St. George is found in a collection of "saint stories" called *Golden Legend*, which was originally written in Latin around 1250 AD, then printed in English by William Caxton in 1483, then reprinted by William Morris in 1892, with help from Burne-Jones.

Golden Legend is one of the fundamental works of medieval civilization. James seems to have read the Caxton version of the St. George story; "The Lesson of the Master" uses phrases from the Caxton version.

Tintner points out that, in writing his stories, James often used other literary works as a template; "Master Eustace," for example, draws on *Hamlet*, and *The Princess Casamassima* draws on Keats' poetry. And James often underlines the connection by mentioning, in his own story, the story to which it's connected; in "The Lesson of the Master," the legend of St. George and the dragon is explicitly mentioned.

If the master, in James' story, represents St. George, who represents the dragon? The dragon is Mrs. St. George, a worldly woman who dominates her husband, then conveniently dies so Henry can marry Marian. Dragons breathe fire, as all the world knows; accordingly, Mrs. St. George burns one of her husband's books.

As the color blue pops up repeatedly in *Blue is the Warmest Color*, so the color red pops up repeatedly in James' novella, which might be called "Red is the Dragon's Color." Tintner speaks of "Mrs. St. George, who burns his book, whose spirit presides over the smoking room, who represents the devil and the idols of the market, whose color is red, whose soul is worldly, who loves celebrities and the show of society." Mrs. St. George wears a "crimson dress," and walks with Paul around the park, a "red wall" on their left. Mrs. St. George has built a windowless cage for her husband to write in, and has outfitted the cage with a "band of crimson cloth" that stretches from the entrance to the writing desk.[2]

---

[1] What does the name "Paul Overt" signify? Overt is from the French *ouvert*, open. Tintner speaks of, "Paul Overt, who is 'overt,' 'open' to being saved or not, as only he may decide, for the literary glory of England." I think we should view the name "Overt" more broadly, view it as a general openness of character.

[2] Doubtless it's easier to notice symbols like the saint and the dragon if you read the story twice. According to Tintner, "James frequently stated, either through fictive characters or through his own letters and critical writings, that he expected his reader to give his prose a second reading." James said that he wanted "analytic appreciation." As I said in an earlier issue, James creates structure by careful selection, unlike a "saturation novelist," who

If the story ended here, if the story ended with Henry marrying the angelic Marian, and Paul sad, lonely, and angry, it might seem that the bachelor life wasn't the good life, and that Paul regretted his decision to flee Marian. But the story doesn't end here, there's a final scene, a scene that justifies Paul's (and James') renunciation of marriage. In this final scene, "[Marian] was in white, there were gold figures on her dress and her hair was a casque of gold. [Paul] saw in a single moment that she was happy, happy with an aggressive splendor."

Marian appears worldly, focused on material things; her color is gold. Her literary interests make her even more dangerous for a writer than Mrs. St. George. As Henry says, "They think they understand, they think they sympathize. Then it is that they are most dangerous." Henry, committed to Marian, abandons writing altogether.

The story ends by saying that Paul was right to dedicate himself to literature, and Henry was right to advise Paul not to marry. James justifies his bachelor life. "St. George was essentially right... Nature dedicated [Paul] to intellectual, not to personal passion."

James has written a story that works on two levels, realistic and symbolic. "The Lesson of the Master" can be enjoyed with or without its symbolism.

G. "A London Life"

I read a novella by Henry James called "A London Life." It's not one of his most popular works, perhaps because the plot is rather dark. It's the classic HenryJames plot: Americans in Europe. A young American woman, Selina Berrington, is married to an Englishman, has two children, and divides her time between a country house and a city house. Her younger sister, Laura Wing, is visiting for an extended period, and tries to rescue her sister from marital shipwreck and messy divorce.

[Spoiler Warning: If you're thinking of reading the story, you may want to stop here.]

As the story proceeds, Laura begins spending time with a young man named Mr. Wendover. But when she's ready to get married, he's not ready, and when he's ready to get married, she's not ready, so in classic HenryJames fashion, they don't marry.

James thought highly enough of the story to include it in the New York Edition of his works (it's in Volume 10 of 26). He grouped "A London Life" with "The Spoils of Poynton" and "The Chaperon," and in the Preface to the volume, he said that all three stories feature young women who exemplify "the free spirit." These young women have a "moral and aesthetic con-

---

pours out his soul, his thoughts, his experiences. Perhaps a saturation novelist doesn't need to be read twice.

science [that] obeys commands unheard by others, whose vision of an uncorrupted social order is both isolating and exhilarating."[1] These young women have a "high lucidity... acuteness and intensity, reflection and passion."[2]

And what exactly are the commands heard by Laura Wing's "moral and aesthetic conscience"? The short answer is, She disapproves of Selina's headlong pursuit of pleasure. Leon Edel and other critics have argued that Laura is an "unbending Puritan" who feels "righteous indignation at the sexual weaknesses of others"; Laura is "bristling with righteousness."[3] These critics insist that James is not on Laura's side, he's on Selina's side; James is "indulgent" toward Selina's adulteries; James is saying that "social indiscretions are sometimes committed without consequences."[4]

A critic named Heath Moon says that this reading is "totally misguided." Moon points to James' preface to Volume 10, in which he calls Selina "the wicked woman of my story," and speaks of her "perversity." According to Moon, James had a "strongly conservative social ideology." James was troubled by the decline of the British aristocracy, a decline that resulted (in part) from adultery, divorce, and public scandal. The scandals of the aristocracy were being printed by the new gossip magazines, and eagerly read by millions of readers. After leaving England for Italy in December 1886, James wrote to Charles Eliot Norton,

> The subject of the moment, as I came away, was the hideous Campbell divorce case, which will besmirch exceedingly the already very damaged prestige of the English upper class. The condition of that body seems to me to be in many ways very much the same rotten and *collapsible* one as that of the French aristocracy before the revolution—minus cleverness and conversation; or perhaps it's more like the heavy, congested and depraved Roman world upon which the barbarians came down.[5]

---

1 "James's 'A London Life' and the Campbell Divorce Scandal," by Heath Moon, *American Literary Realism*, 1870-1910, Autumn, 1980, Vol. 13, No. 2, pp. 246-258, jstor.org/stable/27745952

2 James' preface to Vol. 10, p. xv

3 I'm quoting Heath Moon. The last phrase ("bristling with righteousness") is from James himself, but Moon insists that this is Selina's view, not James'.

4 I'm quoting Heath Moon, who's quoting Edel.

5 Quoted in Moon. Heath Moon was a teacher at two private schools in the LosAngeles area, Pilgrim School and Harvard-Westlake. This is an unusual background for someone who publishes scholarly articles; perhaps Moon's unusual background is related to his heterodox theories. Moon died in early 2021, at about age 79. He published at least four articles on Henry James, including

James is fighting for civilization. He's troubled by adultery because it leads to divorce and scandal, it threatens civilization. In the second paragraph of the story, we find tradition being undermined by hedonism.

> Our attention is drawn at the start [Moon writes] to Laura's concern for the fate of the estate, a property under a dark sentence even while outwardly emanating serenity and security.... "In the park [James writes], half-way, suddenly, Laura stopped, with a pain—a moral pang—that almost took away her breath; she looked at the misty glades and the dear old beeches (so familiar they were now and loved as much as if she owned them); they seemed in their unlighted December bareness conscious of all the trouble."[1]

James speaks of the park, with its "air of happy submission to immemorial law." If only the Berringtons, who own the park, were happily submitting to immemorial law! Laura's walk through the park brings her to a "dower house," that is, a house for widows. Like the park, the house (known as "Plash") is redolent of culture and tradition, and thus clashes with the hedonism and scandal of the Berringtons.

> The room had its bright, durable, sociable air, the air that Laura Wing liked in so many English things—that of being meant for daily life, for long periods, for uses of high decency. But more than ever today was it incongruous that such an habitation, with its chintzes and its British

---

- "Saving James from Modernism: How to Read The Sacred Fount," *Modern Language Quarterly*, 49.2 (1988), 120-41
- "Is the Sacred Fount a Symbolist Novel?"
- "More Royalist Than the King"

Two useful resources for readers of James are

- *The Cambridge Companion to Henry James* edited by Jonathan Freedman (1998)
- The Cambridge Edition of the Complete Fiction of Henry James (in 34 volumes)

[1] Moon says that Laura has become the protector of the estate, an estate that's neglected, even undermined, by its owners. Thus, Laura is the "thematic cousin" (Moon argues) of three other James characters who become protectors of an estate that doesn't belong to them: Clement Searle (*The Passionate Pilgrim*), Hyacinth Robinson (*The Princess Casamassima*), and the Bly governess (*The Turn of the Screw*).

One could add another name to this list: Henry James. One could argue that James himself is protecting an estate, a tradition, a culture that doesn't belong to him, namely, English civilization. Like the four characters he created, James is an "appreciative outsider who must salvage and preserve the 'property' of spoiled or abdicated insiders."

> poets, its well-worn carpets and domestic art—the whole aspect so unmeretricious and sincere—should have to do with lives that were not right.

When Laura goes to the Berringtons' city house, she's again struck by the contrast between the "peace and decorum" of the house and the "contentious and impure" spirit of its owners. When Lionel Berrington (Selina's husband) indicates to Laura that he's planning to terminate his marriage, Laura explodes:

> "I don't think you care any more for your home than Selina does. And it's so sacred and so beautiful, God forgive you! You are all blind and senseless and heartless and I don't know what poison is in your veins. There is a curse on you and there will be a judgment!" the girl went on, glowing like a young prophetess.

The British aristocracy was indeed on the brink. "A London Life" was published in 1888, and by the 1920s, the British aristocracy was in retreat, and old estates were being subdivided and sold off. One might say that James foresaw the fall of the aristocracy, while Proust, 28 years younger than James, lived long enough to see this fall and describe it. The aristocracy fell throughout the Western world at about the same time.

In this story, as in other stories, James shows his grasp of frevel. When Selina slips off to Paris for a few days of dissipation, James says that this excursion

> had the mark of Selina's complete, irremediable frivolity—the worst accusation (Laura tried to cling to that opinion) that she laid herself open to. Of course frivolity that was never ashamed of itself was like a neglected cold—you could die of it morally as well as of anything else. Laura knew this and it was why she was inexpressibly vexed with her sister.

Like the common cold, frivolity/frevel seems trivial, yet it can grow into something serious. One can die of it, as Daisy Miller does.

If the meaning of the story is plain, Moon asks, and if it's reinforced by the author's notebooks, letters, and preface, how could Edel and other critics misconstrue the story? How could they think that James was on Selina's side, that James was condemning Laura? Moon says that these critics didn't share James' respect for tradition. They weren't on intimate terms with the aristocracy, as James was, and they didn't see the positive aspects of the aristocracy. They couldn't relate to James' love of tradition—old houses, old parks, etc.

> Without any internal or external evidence [Moon writes], critics have assumed that Laura reacts because of righteous indignation at the sexual weaknesses of others. On the contrary, she is not a Puritan and her reaction is not "moral" in the sense of a disapproval based on prescriptive metaphysical beliefs. Instead, what commands her loyalty is a historically circumscribed institution rich in aesthetic associations.... For [Laura] divorce is wicked not because it violates general principles of

> sexual purity, but because it violates the heritage of a social class.... Hers is not a moralist's but a Tory's fanaticism.

The quarrel between Edel and Moon might be compared to the quarrel between Socrates and the Sophists, or the quarrel between Strauss and Nietzsche. Edel's view implies that morality is absolute, universal, timeless, while Moon's view implies that morality is relative. Edel, Socrates, and Strauss would say that adultery is either eternally and absolutely right, or eternally and absolutely wrong, while Moon, the Sophists, and Nietzsche would say that adultery is wrong in some situations but not all, morality depends on time and place, James' condemnation of adultery applies only to a particular society. Moon argues that James is defending a specific cultural tradition, not (as Edel thinks) mocking a moral absolute.

Many of the other James stories that I've discussed are based on a literary template, that is, their theme is taken from another literary work. "A London Life," on the other hand, is based on current events, on highly-publicized divorce trials, such as the Dilke trial and the Campbell trial. "There are curious similarities," Moon writes, "between Lord and Lady Campbell and the Berringtons. In both cases an injured husband initiates divorce proceedings, followed by the wife's counter suit, in spite of the chivalric custom according to which the husband allows the wife to file so that her reputation will endure minimal smudging." Since Selina has several lovers, Lionel's suit is called "Berrington vs. Berrington and Others," as the real-life suit was called "Campbell vs. Campbell and Others."

Laura is a "free spirit," as James says, not a person with "an inflexible conception of what is good and right," as Edel says. Laura has her own views about the good and the beautiful, she's not an unthinking adherent of Puritan morality. Heath Moon has rescued "A London Life" from a mis-reading. This story should occupy a more prominent position in James' *oeuvre*.

H. "The Pupil"

"The Pupil" is about an American family, the Moreens, who wander about European capitals, leaving behind a trail of unpaid bills. The Moreens engage a young man named Pemberton to tutor their youngest child, a boy named Morgan; Morgan is "the pupil."

Morgan is a sickly, intelligent boy, and Pemberton has a good relationship with him. Morgan and Pemberton take a dim view of Morgan's parents, who care only for social graces and social connections. Morgan warns Pemberton that his parents are bad payers—they didn't pay Morgan's nurse, and they aren't paying Pemberton.

[Spoiler warning: if you're thinking of reading "The Pupil," you might want to stop here.]

Mr. and Mrs. Moreen are eager to marry their daughters to somebody, preferably to a man of the "right sort." But as with many James characters, the girls remain unwed. As Morgan says of his sisters' suitors, "Just when we think we've got them fast, we're chucked!" In the New York Edition,

James changed this to, "Just when we think we've landed them, they're back in the deep sea!"[1]

As the suitors pull back from a commitment to Morgan's sisters, so Pemberton pulls back from a commitment to Morgan. At the climax of the story, Morgan's parents urge Pemberton to take Morgan under his wing, manage Morgan, but Pemberton hesitates, in classic HenryJames fashion, and the moment passes. Morgan realizes that Pemberton is afraid to make a commitment to him, and this realization seems to trigger the heart attack that kills Morgan.

We find something similar in James' "Daisy Miller." In "Daisy Miller," Winterbourne hesitates to commit himself to Daisy, as Pemberton hesitates to commit himself to Morgan. "Like so many Jamesian heroes, Winterbourne has lost the capacity for love, and he has lost the opportunity to come to life." James' heroes avoid commitment, remain on the sidelines, and miss opportunities.

At the end of "The Pupil," as at the end of "Daisy Miller," we find tragedy, the death of the young innocent. As James' secretary, Theodora Bosanquet, said, Morgan is one of James' "children of light" (Bosanquet wrote a critical biography of James, *Henry James At Work*). Morgan's death, like Daisy's death, is "over-determined," it has multiple causes. This is how life works, in my view, so James is being true-to-life. Morgan's parents and Morgan's tutor both contribute to his death, and it's difficult to say who contributes more.[2]

---

1 I read the Norton Critical Edition of "The Pupil" (in a volume called *Tales of Henry James*). Norton chose the original version of "The Pupil," not the later version from the New York Edition. I agree with the widespread view that James didn't improve his works when he edited them for the New York Edition, and therefore it's best to read the earlier versions. On the other hand, I find the New York Edition to be useful for filtering out James' second-rate works.

2 As Seymour Lainoff writes, "The Moreens, it is true, are chiefly instrumental in bringing on Morgan's death. But Pemberton, the boy's tutor and the narrator of the story, should not be allowed to get off scot-free, as he customarily is; he must be held culpable, too. If not as guilty as the governess in *The Turn of the Screw*, he is at least accessory to the crime. Acting always upon motives acceptable enough by the world's lights and yet revealing a limited morality when judged by more heroic standards, he is incapable of making the bold gesture needed to liberate Morgan from his blighting surroundings. The devoted Morgan dubs his tutor a 'hero' on several occasions; the undeserved title acquires irony before the story ends."

At the critical moment, Pemberton keeps a distance from Morgan. "The theme of the story," according to Lainoff, is "the isolation, the eternal loneliness, of the human spirit. The soul has no true home; family bonds are limited; even friendship has its limits."

I don't blame James for the ambiguity of his action, I blame him for the ambiguity of his sentences. His strength is that he creates characters that come alive, that the reader can connect with. His weakness is that he doesn't write clear prose, he's too fond of subtleties, refinements, obscurities.

As I read "The Pupil," it was clear that Morgan's parents were portrayed in a negative way, Pemberton in a more positive way. I expected a twist ending, a reversal, a justification of Morgan's parents. As Jacques Barzun said, James often gives the reader a "moral shock," James says, "Look! It is not as you think!" And there is at least a partial reversal at the end of "The Pupil": Pemberton seems to kill Morgan by shrinking back from commitment, while Morgan's parents seem to love him deeply. At the critical moment, when Morgan is dying, Mrs. Moreen "bounded forward.... 'Ah, his darling little heart!' ...she caught him ardently in her arms." Mr. Moreen is "trembling all over [and] in his way, as deeply affected as his wife."

In "The Pupil," James shows the "marked moral intensity" that many of his works have, and that many great novels have.[1]

* * * * *

In the first chapter of "The Pupil," James writes, "[Morgan] passed out of one of the long windows; Pemberton saw him go and lean on the parapet of the terrace." You can't walk through today's windows (even if they're open), but it was once common to have windows that reached all the way to the floor. On a hot day, such windows could be opened to allow people to pass through (and perhaps to allow breezes to pass through).

Below is a picture of The Grange, Alexander Hamilton's house in upper Manhattan, now owned by the National Park Service. Note how the windows reach all the way to the ground. Outside is a balcony, so if you opened a window, you could walk out to the balcony, as Morgan does in James' story.

Another critic, Thomas Canavan, says that "The Pupil" deals with money from its opening sentence. "All of these references to money," Canavan writes, "further the central theme of the tale and identify the focus of James' attention: the effects of rapaciousness on the human spirit.... Deserted by mother, father, and tutor... Morgan falls victim to selfishness and rapacity, vices which may find their origin in a diseased heart, and illustrates, through the death of his own 'good' heart, the heartlessness that is bred of worldliness."

1 See my remarks on F. R. Leavis (ljhammond.com/phlit/2008-11.htm#2).

These tall windows are triple-hung, as opposed to today's double-hung windows. If you have a triple-hung window, you can raise the bottom two sections to the level of the top section. These tall windows are a good indication of an old house. Over time, the bottom section is often boarded up, leaving a shorter, double-hung window, but also leaving signs that the window was once taller.

I. *The Turn of the Screw*

Our book group recently discussed *The Turn of the Screw*, by Henry James. Several people had missed the previous discussion (on Jung's autobiography), perhaps because of summer travels. We spent some time discussing Jung, and everyone agreed that Jung's autobiography was a marvelous book—a mind-blowing, jaw-dropping book. Jung seems to be the prophet of our time, the writer who moves people most and impresses people most, as Nietzsche was the prophet of a century ago.

Most people in the group felt as I did about *The Turn of the Screw*: the ornate, wordy style makes the book painful to read, or at least less pleasurable than it would otherwise be. It's a ghost story, and since I'm interested in ghosts, and think that ghosts probably exist, the story engaged me. Critical opinion is sharply divided about *The Turn of the Screw*: according to one view, the ghosts are real, and Henry James believed in ghosts; this view might be called the occult view, or the Jungian view. According to another view, the ghosts are hallucinations of the governess-narrator; this view might be called the rationalist view, or the Freudian view.

Here's an example of James' style: "My question had a sarcastic force that I had not fully intended, and it made her after a moment inconsequently break down." My objection to this sentence (and to James' style in general) is that it is obscure. The word "inconsequently" is unnecessary, it muddies the water. Mark Twain said that if you see an adverb, kill it, and "inconsequently" is richly deserving of death. "But you just used an adverb yourself! 'Richly' is an adverb, isn't it?" Perhaps it is, I know nothing about grammar, but I do know that "richly deserving" is a common expression, easily understood, while "inconsequently" is an unusual word, almost never heard in spoken English, and "inconsequently break down" is a strange, obscure phrase.

Here's another example of James' style: "It was impossible to have given less encouragement than he had administered to such a doctrine." This sentence would be clearer, easier for the reader to grasp, if James had written "it was impossible to have given less encouragement than he had given..." Repetition is easier for the reader to grasp than variety, and repeating the word "given" makes the sentence clearer than replacing "given" with "administered". Furthermore, who ever heard of 'administering encouragement to a doctrine'?

One final example: "I dare say I fancied myself in short a remarkable young woman and took comfort in the faith that this would more publicly appear." This sentence is wordy, in my view, and could be improved by deleting the phrase "in short". "But the phrase 'in short' is needed for the sake of summing up and concluding." Then move 'in short' to the start of the sentence, and delete "I dare say", so the sentence would run: "In short, I fancied myself a remarkable young woman..." James forfeits the right to use the phrase "in short" because he's never "short", he always chooses to take the long way around. James' prose has no music, no rhythm, no force. James' prose is obscure, and for a writer, obscurity is the sin against the Holy Ghost, the sin for which there is no forgiveness.

James' style may have become even more obscure after he wrote *The Turn of the Screw*. His brother, William, struggled to understand one of Henry's late works, *The Wings of the Dove*. William said that he read "many pages and innumerable sentences twice over to see what the dickens they could possibly mean."[1]

William also struggled with *The Golden Bowl*, the last novel that Henry completed. While admitting Henry's "extreme success in this book," William wished that Henry would "sit down and write a new book, with... no psychological commentaries, and absolute straightness in the style. Publish it in my name, I will acknowledge it, and give you half the proceeds."

An Englishman once asked Tocqueville, "What do you consider your Golden Age?" Tocqueville responded, "The latter part of the seventeenth century.... Style then was the mere vehicle of thought. First of all to be perspicuous, and then being perspicuous, to be concise, was all they aimed at.... In the eighteenth century... ornament was added."[2]

---

1 See Robert D. Richardson's biography of William James, Ch. 70

2 *Correspondence and Conversations of Alexis de Tocqueville With N. W. Senior*, 8/26/50

A writer should aim to be clear and concise, he should aim to communicate something to the reader. Henry James, however, seems to regard style as an end itself, not as a vehicle of thought. Unlike all other English writers, James inserts a space within contractions; for example, James writes *did n't* instead of *didn't*. He's so wordy that he can't resist the opportunity to make two words out of one!

But whatever flaws he may have, James deserves our respect because he had high regard for literature, and because he made a lasting contribution to literature. The James family (Henry, William, and Alice) is one of the most talented families in literary history. Every writer we read, like every person we meet, has some traits that annoy us, but these annoying traits shouldn't blind us to their virtues. The style of James' earlier works (the works written before *The Turn of the Screw*) is clearer. One of these earlier works, *The Portrait of a Lady*, is said to be his masterpiece, and until I read that book, I can't give my opinion of James as a novelist.

Now our book group is reading Joseph Conrad's *The Nigger of the "Narcissus"*. After reading James, Conrad is like a breath of fresh air because his prose is straightforward. Conrad is in touch with life, in touch with earthy reality (or perhaps I should say, "watery reality"). James, on the other hand, seems detached from life, and this may explain his preoccupation with language-for-its-own-sake.

7. Robert Louis Stevenson

A. "The Lantern-Bearers"

William James was a big fan of an essay by Robert Louis Stevenson called "The Lantern-Bearers." He quotes Stevenson's essay at length in "On A Certain Blindness in Human Beings." James inspired me to read Stevenson's essay. In his essay, Stevenson reminisces about his boyhood on the east coast of Scotland:

> These boys congregated every autumn about a certain easterly fisher-village, where they tasted in a high degree the glory of existence. The place was created seemingly on purpose for the diversion of young gentlemen.... There was nothing to mar your days, if you were a boy summering in that part, but the embarrassment of pleasure.

The village looked out on Bass Rock, and was within walking distance of a castle named Tantallon, and a hill called The Law.

> You might climb The Law, [Stevenson writes] where the whale's jaw-bone stood landmark in the buzzing wind, and behold the face of many counties, and the smoke and spires of many towns, and the sails of distant ships.... Or perhaps pushing to Tantallon, you might lunch on sandwiches and visions in the grassy court, while the wind hummed in the crumbling turrets.... The Bass, in the eye of fancy, still flew the colors of King James; and in the ear of fancy the arches of Tantallon still rang with horse-shoe iron, and echoed to the commands of Bell-the-Cat.... You might bathe, now in the flaws of fine weather, that we pathetically

> call our summer, now in a gale of wind, with the sand scourging your bare hide, your clothes thrashing abroad from underneath their guardian stone.

Stevenson's prose has a clarity, simplicity, and poetry that Henry James can't match. Henry James was a close friend of Stevenson's; William James never met Stevenson. Stevenson died in Samoa at the age of 44. In an earlier issue, I quoted the epitaph that Stevenson wrote for himself:

Under the wide and starry sky,
Dig the grave and let me lie.
Glad did I live and gladly die,
And I laid me down with a will.
This be the verse you grave for me:
Here he lies where he longed to be;
Home is the sailor, home from sea,
And the hunter home from the hill.

This is how a great writer copes with death: he makes literature out of it. Even imminent death couldn't quench what Henry James called the "gaiety" of Stevenson's writing. This gaiety is characteristic of Zen. The Zen poet Basho wrote a haiku that expresses the same attitude toward death—the same positive spirit in the face of imminent death:

Nothing in the voice of the cicada
Intimates
How soon it will die

Stevenson calls his essay "The Lantern-Bearers" because it describes how the boys walked abroad at night with a small lantern (a "bull's-eye lantern") under their coats.

> We wore them buckled to the waist upon a cricket belt, and over them, such was the rigor of the game, a buttoned top-coat. They smelled noisomely of blistered tin; they never burned aright, though they would always burn our fingers; their use was naught; the pleasure of them merely fanciful; and yet a boy with a bull's-eye under his top-coat asked for nothing more.

Once the boys had gathered,

> The coats would be unbuttoned and the bull's-eyes discovered; and in the chequering glimmer, under the huge windy hall of the night, and cheered by a rich steam of toasting tinware, these fortunate young gentlemen would crouch together in the cold sand of the links or on the scaly bilges of the fishing-boat, and delight themselves with inappropriate talk.

For Stevenson, the hidden lantern is a metaphor for the joy and poetry that's hidden in the individual. For Stevenson, as for William James, the inner life of other people is a closed book.

One of the purposes of Stevenson's essay is to criticize the realistic novelists who describe a person's external life, but miss the hidden joy. Stevenson was a neo-Romantic who took a dim view of realism. In Stevenson's time, the leading realist was Zola. Stevenson says that, if Zola described the lantern-bearers, he would miss their hidden joy. "To the eye of the observer," Stevenson writes, "they are wet and cold and drearily surrounded; but ask themselves, and they are in the heaven of a recondite pleasure, the ground of which is an ill-smelling lantern."

Realists like Zola say that they don't depict artists, they depict The People. Realists say (according to Stevenson) "our works must deal exclusively with... the average man, who was a prodigious dull fellow, and quite dead to all but the paltriest considerations." But the average man has a hidden poetry, Stevenson says. While Stevenson criticizes Zola, he praises Whitman, he says that Whitman grasped the average man: "Whitman knew very well, and showed very nobly, that the average man was full of joys and full of poetry of his own."

Stevenson's essay appealed to William James because it reinforced his view that each individual has a unique perspective, and it's hard for us to understand another person. Realism gives us only the outer man, only the surface. "No man lives in external truth," Stevenson writes, "among salts and acids, but in the warm, phantasmagoric chamber of his brain, with the painted windows and the storied walls."

When we dig into the most prosaic life, when we dig into the mind of a miser, "which seems at first a dust-heap, we unearth some priceless jewels," such as a "disdain of many pleasures," a "disdain of the inevitable end," and a "scorn of men's opinions." The miser may have an inner life that belies his outer life:

> Looking in the bosom of the miser, consideration detects the poet in the full tide of life, with more, indeed, of the poetic fire than usually goes to epics; and tracing that mean man about his cold hearth, and to and fro in his discomfortable house, spies within him a blazing bonfire of delight. And so with others, who do not live by bread alone, but by some cherished and perhaps fantastic pleasure; who are meat salesmen to the external eye, and possibly to themselves are Shakespeares, Napoleons, or Beethovens; who have not one virtue to rub against another in the field of active life, and yet perhaps, in the life of contemplation, sit with the saints.[1]

Great literature doesn't give us drab "reality," it gives us "the quick of life," it gives us dreams and passions. Sometimes it depicts ecstasy, sometimes suffering. "These are notes that please the great heart of man.... We love to think of them, we long to try them, we are humbly hopeful that we may prove heroes also."

---

[1] I myself exemplify Stevenson's theory since my external life may seem dreary to an observer, but I have all sorts of dreams and ambitions within—I have a bull's-eye lantern attached to my belt.

Stevenson uses a parable to contrast the passionate life with the mechanical life:

> There is one fable that touches very near the quick of life: the fable of the monk who passed into the woods, heard a bird break into song, hearkened for a trill or two, and found himself on his return a stranger at his convent gates; for he had been absent fifty years, and of all his comrades there survived but one to recognize him.

This monk was transported by song, by natural beauty, and time disappeared.

> All life that is not merely mechanical is spun out of two strands: seeking for that bird and hearing him. And it is just this that makes life so hard to value, and the delight of each so incommunicable; and just a knowledge of this, and a remembrance of those fortunate hours in which the bird has sung to us, that fills us with such wonder when we turn the pages of the realist. There, to be sure, we find a picture of life in so far as it consists of mud and of old iron, cheap desires and cheap fears, that which we are ashamed to remember and that which we are careless whether we forget; but of the note of that time-devouring nightingale we hear no news.

Stevenson is a Zennish writer; he focuses on the moment, the moment of joy; he makes time disappear.

Stevenson's essay ends with a somewhat puzzling paragraph: "We have heard, perhaps, too much of lesser matters. Here is the door, here is the open air. *Itur in antiquam silvam* [Going to the ancient wood]." Perhaps this means, "Let's go outside, and experience the beauty of nature—enough of words and books."

I'm a big fan of Stevenson's essay, and I can understand why William James was a big fan of it. Stevenson is an extraordinary prose writer. All good prose is poetic, and no one writes more poetic prose than Stevenson. He probably over-states his case, the average man probably doesn't conceal a hidden Shakespeare. But his argument is at least partly true, and on the whole, this is an extraordinary essay.

* * * * *

Stevenson and Henry James first met in 1879, when Stevenson was 29, and James 36. They weren't impressed with each other. Stevenson said that James was "a mere club fizzle... and no out-of-doors, stand-up man whatever."[1] James described Stevenson as "a shirt-collarless Bohemian and a great deal (in an inoffensive way) of a poseur."

A few years later, James praised *Treasure Island* in his essay "The Art of Fiction." James said he had been a child, but had never sought buried treasure. Stevenson responded with an essay of his own, remarking that if James "had never been on a quest for buried treasure, it can be demonstrated

---

[1] This resembles Hemingway's criticism of T. S. Eliot: "He never hit the ball out of the infield in his life." Is there an affinity between Hemingway and Stevenson, as there is between Eliot and Henry James?

that he has never been a child."[1] Youthful romanticism is the source of Stevenson's work.

James had argued that the novel "competes with life... the novel is history."[2] Stevenson responded, the novel "could not compete with life. It had to be 'make-believe.'"[3] The novel takes one aspect of life, Stevenson said, and simplifies it; life is monstrous and infinite, while a literary work is a neat package. James is defending the realistic novel, Stevenson the neo-Romantic novel.

After reading Stevenson's essay, James sent him a letter, saying he enjoyed everything Stevenson wrote; "the current of your admirable style floats pearls and diamonds." Stevenson wrote back, inviting James to visit him at Bournemouth; Stevenson said he liked visitors because he was bedridden (Stevenson's health had always been precarious). Stevenson had dubbed his Bournemouth house "Skerryvore" after a lighthouse built by his uncle (Stevenson came from a family of lighthouse-builders).[4]

---

[1] Stevenson used the same reasoning in a fable called "The Tadpole and the Frog":

"Be ashamed of yourself," said the frog. "When I was a tadpole, I had no tail."

"Just what I thought!" said the tadpole. "You never were a tadpole."

[2] This quote is partly from Edel, partly from James. See p. 122 of Edel's *Henry James: The Middle Years*.

[3] I'm quoting Edel, p. 124

Stevenson was friends with the novelist George Meredith, and he was a big fan of Meredith's novels, such as *The Egoist*. Stevenson wrote, "I have just re-read for the third and fourth time *The Egoist*. When I shall have read it the sixth or seventh, I begin to see I shall know about it. You will be astonished when you come to re-read it; I had no idea of the matter—human, red matter, he has contrived to plug and pack into that strange and admirable book."

Meredith used Stevenson as the model for Gower Woodseer, a character in Meredith's novel *The Amazing Marriage*.

[4] James' friend John Singer Sargent got to know Stevenson before James did. Sargent wrote to James, "I was very much impressed by [Stevenson]; he seemed to me the most intense creature I had ever met."(Edel, *Henry James: The Middle Years*, p. 149)

Stevenson's cousin and biographer, Graham Balfour, described how Stevenson played billiards: "He played with all the fire and dramatic intensity that he was apt to put into things. The balls flew wildly about, on or off the table as the case might be, but seldom indeed ever threatened a pocket."(quoted in Blyth, *Zen in English Literature*, Ch. 4, p. 62)

Balfour joined Stevenson on Samoa, and remained there until Stevenson died.

At one point, James himself was living in Bournemouth, so he visited Stevenson and his wife daily. James moved to Bournemouth to be near his ailing sister, Alice. James would spend part of the day working on his latest novel, *The Princess Casamassima*, and part of the day visiting the two invalids, Alice and Stevenson.

Stevenson greatly enjoyed James' visits. Stevenson wrote two poems about James' visits. One pretends that James is visiting with a group of women — fictional women from his stories.

Lo, how these fair immaculate women walk
Behind their jocund maker.

The other poem is written from the perspective of a Venetian mirror, an actual mirror that James had given Stevenson.

Where the bells peal far at sea
Cunning fingers fashioned me.
There on palace walls I hung
While that Consuelo sung...
  there
In my grey face, faces fair
Shone from under shining hair...
So awhile I glowed, and then
Fell on dusty days and men;
Long I slumbered packed in straw,
Long I none but dealers saw;
Till before my silent eye
One that sees came passing by.
Now with an outlandish grace,
To the sparkling fire I face
In the blue room at Skerryvore;
Where I wait until the door
Open, and the Prince of Men,
Henry James, shall come again.

Stevenson admired many of James' works, but criticized *Washington Square*. James himself took a dim view of *Washington Square*, and didn't include it in the "New York Edition" of his works. Stevenson objected to the harsh, lemon-juice realism of Zola, but he didn't object to James' realism, which might be called classical realism or upbeat realism.

James stays close to life; in the last issue, I discussed James' "London Life," which is based on an actual divorce, a much-publicized divorce. Stevenson, on the other hand, didn't get his plots from the contemporary world; like Walter Scott, Stevenson often set his stories in past ages.[1] At the end of

---

[1] Stevenson's grandfather was apparently a friend and traveling-companion of Walter Scott.

Stevenson's wife, Fanny, was an American, divorced with three children, made a living writing for magazines, and was ten years older than Stevenson.

his life, however, Stevenson turned toward realism, partly because he was angry at the conduct of the Western powers in the South Pacific, and he wanted to publicize the plight of the natives.

James' *Princess Casamassima* deals with the political turmoils of the 1880s. James was horrified that politics was coming to dominate England's national consciousness, but he was also fascinated by the political situation. In 1885, James wrote,

> The ministry is still in office but hanging only by a hair, Gladstone is ill and bewildered, the mess in the Sudan unspeakable, London full of wailing widows and weeping mothers, the hostility to Bismarck extreme, the danger of complications with Russia imminent, the Irish in the House of Commons more disagreeable than ever, the dynamiters more active, the income tax threatening to rise to its maximum, the general muddle, in short, of the densest and darkest.[1]

B. *Fables*

I've been reading the *Fables* of Robert Louis Stevenson. They're a forgotten corner of Stevenson's *oeuvre*. They constitute a tiny volume—less than 100 pages. One might say they were neglected by Stevenson himself; at the time of his death, they were an unfinished fragment.

I learned of Stevenson's *Fables* more than twenty years ago, while reading a Zen writer, R. H. Blyth. Blyth is a little-known writer, but he has a high reputation among students of Zen. Blyth finds Zen in Stevenson, Dickens, Shakespeare, Wordsworth—he finds Zen in many writers who never heard the word "Zen."

Blyth quotes many writers in foreign languages—French, German, Italian, even Chinese and Japanese. He may be the greatest quoter in world literature, but sometimes he's too fond of quotations. Blyth was widely read, and had a knack for learning languages. I recommend Blyth's *Zen in English Literature and Oriental Classics*.

Blyth rarely quotes Stevenson's novels, such as *Kidnapped*; Blyth focuses on Stevenson's poems and fables. For example, he quotes a poem from Stevenson's *Child's Garden of Verses*:

The friendly cow all red and white,
I love with all my heart:
She gives me cream with all her might,
To eat with apple-tart.

The child and the cow are both whole-hearted, and this whole-hearted quality is Zen. "The Zen of the cow ('with all her might') appeals to the child's Zen ('with all my heart')."[2] Stevenson puts himself into the mind of

---

1 Quoted in Edel, *Henry James: The Middle Years*, p. 85

2 *Zen in English Literature and Oriental Classics*, Ch. 23, pp. 359, 360

the child. "The Zen of *A Child's Garden of Verses* can be tested by the fact that in most of them it is impossible to think that they were not written by the child himself." Stevenson grasps the child's Zen, and expresses it in poetry. "What is most remarkable about Stevenson's *A Child's Garden of Verses* is that he sees the child's Zen and reflects it back to the child in the form of poetry."

There are 20 fables in Stevenson's little volume, and Blyth comments on 7 of them. I found one critical essay on Stevenson's *Fables*: "Stevenson's Conception of the Fable," by Alice D. Snyder, *The Journal of English and Germanic Philology*, January, 1922, Vol. 21, No. 1, pp. 160-168, jstor.org/stable/27702630

I haven't found any Stevenson critic who's aware of Blyth, aware of the "Zen view" of Stevenson.

I found a book called *The Proper Pirate: Robert Louis Stevenson's Quest for Identity*, by Jefferson Singer. This book comments on some of Stevenson's fables, such as "The House of Eld." Singer calls his book *The Proper Pirate* because he thinks that Stevenson was torn between propriety/civilization and piracy/bohemianism. According to Singer, "The House of Eld" represents revolt against home/parents, but also an admission that revolt doesn't necessarily bring happiness. (One could also read "The House of Eld" as revolt against traditional religion/morality, which didn't bring happiness, but instead led to Communism, Fascism, etc.)

On the "proper" side, we have statements like this: "I defend civilization for the thing it is, for the thing it has *come* to be, the standpoint of a real old Tory." On the bohemian side, we have statements like this: "If I had to begin again... I believe I should try to honor Sex more religiously. The worst of our education is that Christianity does not recognize and hallow Sex. It looks askance at it.... Well, it is so; I cannot be wiser than my generation."(letter to cousin Bob, September 1894; see also *The Proper Pirate*, p. 170)

D. H. Lawrence, 35 years younger than Stevenson, did just what Stevenson said he'd do if he was starting his career again: Lawrence respected the body and sex, focused on the body and sex.

According to Jefferson Singer, "The Argentinian writer Borges counted [Stevenson's *Fables*] as a great influence on his own allegorical and enigmatic tales."(p. 39)

Stevenson's *Fables* may have been inspired by Bulwer-Lytton's *Fables in Song*. Stevenson wrote a review of Bulwer-Lytton's work.

If you want a biography of Stevenson, the first and most intimate is the one by Stevenson's cousin, Graham Balfour. Another Stevenson biography is *Voyage to Windward: The Life of Robert Louis Stevenson*, by J. C. Furnas. Consider also *Robert Louis Stevenson: Interviews and Recollections*, edited by R. C. Terry.

Stevenson's *Fables* are remarkable for their style and wit as well as their Zen. Here's a fable called "The Sick Man and the Fireman":

> There was once a sick man in a burning house, to whom there entered a fireman.
>
> "Do not save me," said the sick man. "Save those who are strong."
>
> "Will you kindly tell me why?" inquired the fireman, for he was a civil fellow.
>
> "Nothing could possibly be fairer," said the sick man. "The strong should be preferred in all cases, because they are of more service in the world."
>
> The fireman pondered a while, for he was a man of some philosophy. "Granted," said he at last, as a part of the roof fell in; "but for the sake of conversation, what would you lay down as the proper service of the strong?"
>
> "Nothing can possibly be easier," returned the sick man; "the proper service of the strong is to help the weak."
>
> Again the fireman reflected, for there was nothing hasty about this excellent creature. "I could forgive you being sick," he said at last, as a portion of the wall fell out, "but I cannot bear your being such a fool." And with that he heaved up his fireman's axe, for he was eminently just, and clove the sick man to the bed.

Kierkegaard said, "The comical always lies in a contradiction." Stevenson's fable is comical because of the contradiction between the relaxed tone of the conversation, and the fact that it takes place in a burning building. The fireman has none of the urgency that one would expect in such a situation; he says he's talking "for the sake of conversation."

We saw above that Zen is whole-hearted. This whole-hearted quality prompts decisive action. Zen doesn't split hairs, it doesn't get bogged down in knotty questions. The fireman in the fable acts decisively, he cleaves the sick man with his axe. Blyth says,

> Most of our talk about duty, religion, patriotism, Zen, is of this useless, circular character. In Buddhism, the body is called "a burning house." We talk and talk while our life burns away.... Fine words butter no parsnips. The question is, what are we to do in this continual, continuous dilemma which we call human life? ...The Gordian knot must be cut.

The fireman ends the discussion, he cuts the Gordian knot. Stevenson isn't recommending violence, he's using violence as a metaphor; he's recommending decision, action.[1]

---

[1] Sidney Colvin, a friend of Stevenson's, published an edition of Stevenson's letters after Stevenson's death. Colvin introduced these letters with an interesting sketch of Stevenson. Colvin speaks of the "maxims of life which he was accustomed to forge for himself and to act by." Colvin quotes two maxims that recommend decision/action:

This decisive quality can be a virtue in literature as well as in life. We see this decisive quality in the epitaph that Stevenson wrote for himself, in which he summarizes life and death in eight lines:

Under the wide and starry sky,
Dig the grave and let me lie.
Glad did I live and gladly die,
And I laid me down with a will.
This be the verse you grave for me:
Here he lies where he longed to be;
Home is the sailor, home from sea,
And the hunter home from the hill.

Stevenson slices through the problems of life and death, he cuts the Gordian knot, he simplifies. Great literature often simplifies. In his essay on Wagner, Nietzsche praised Wagner for being "a simplifier of the universe."[1]

---

1. "Acts may be forgiven; not even God can forgive the hanger-back."
2. "Choose the best, if you can; or choose the worst; that which hangs in the wind dangles from a gibbet."

Colvin says that Stevenson had a gift for conversation. "It was only in talk... that all the many lights and colors of this richly compounded spirit could be seen in full play.... The talk would stream on in endless, never importunate, flood and variety. A hundred fictitious characters would be invented, differentiated, and launched on their imaginary careers; a hundred ingenious problems of conduct and cases of honor would be set and solved, in a manner often quite opposed to conventional precept; romantic voyages would be planned and followed out in vision, with a thousand incidents, to all the corners of our own planet and of others."

Colvin quotes W. E. Henley, a friend of Stevenson's: "He will discourse with you of morals, music, marbles, men, manners, metaphysics, medicine... with equal insight into essentials and equal pregnancy and felicity of utterance... He will stop with you to make mud pies in the first gutter, range in your company whatever heights of thought and feeling you have found accessible, and end by guiding you to altitudes far nearer the stars than you have ever dreamed of footing it... He makes you wonder which to admire the more—his easy familiarity with the Eternal Veracities or the brilliant flashes of imbecility with which his excursions into the Infinite are sometimes diversified. He radiates talk, as the sun does light and heat."

[1] *Untimely Essays*, "Wagner in Bayreuth," #4

Years later, when Nietzsche wrote his autobiography, he said that his essay on Wagner was really about himself: "The essay 'Wagner in Bayreuth' is a vision of my future." Nietzsche would have been proud to be called "a simplifier of the universe."

The professional scholar goes in the opposite direction; he's fond of complexity. For example, a scholar who was trying to boost the reputation of Stevenson's *Black Arrow* said that it offered "insight into the complexity of the human condition." For scholars, "complexity" is a compliment, "simplicity" a pejorative. In this respect, as in many other respects, the professional scholar is the opposite of the real writer.

Stevenson has simplicity in his style as well as his content. His epitaph is notable for its simple language as well as its simple thoughts—no complexity here. Stevenson has boyish high spirits, and a boyish love of adventure. He's not a favorite with contemporary scholars. In the Norton Critical Editions, only one volume is devoted to Stevenson. For many years, he was entirely excluded from the Norton Anthology of English Literature.

So a whole-hearted attitude is Zennish, and it expresses itself in decision/action. The opposite of a whole-hearted attitude is an attitude of boredom, indifference, half-heartedness. As Blyth says, "Stagnation of life is the real tragedy of this world, for it is the waste of life."[1] Stevenson asks God to awaken him violently, lest he stagnate:

Lord, thy most pointed pleasure take
And stab my spirit broad awake;
Or, Lord, if too obdurate I,
Choose thou, before that spirit die,
A piercing pain, a killing sin,
And to my dead heart run them in!

Zen is about being awake, about appreciating the present moment. Thoreau is a Zennish writer; at the end of *Walden*, Thoreau says, "Only that day dawns to which we are awake."

But there's a difference between Thoreau and Stevenson. Thoreau lived deliberately, Stevenson impetuously. Thoreau generally stayed close to home, Stevenson traveled widely. Thoreau was a bachelor who's famous for living alone in a tiny house, Stevenson was married and had a large group of relatives around him on Samoa. Stevenson was Thoreau's toughest critic; he said Thoreau was a "skulker," a "prig," who lacked manliness and "dash."[2]

Blyth is evidently impressed with Stevenson's *Fables*; he quotes them at length, as examples of the Zen spirit. One early reviewer of the *Fables*

In his essay on Wagner, Nietzsche uses the GordianKnot metaphor, but he reverses its meaning. He says that the simplifier is the person who doesn't cut the knot, but rather the person who binds together the loose ends after the knot has been cut. Nietzsche praises Wagner because "he rivets and locks together all that is isolated." This is a good description of my work, I try to bring together the various disciplines, I try to combine and simplify.

[1] *Zen in English Literature*, Ch. 19, p. 297

[2] Sidney Colvin says, "effeminacy, or aught approaching sexlessness, was perhaps the only quality in man with which he had no patience." Does this explain his harsh criticism of Thoreau?

said they're "almost more remarkable than any of [Stevenson's] more elaborate compositions."

Alice Snyder argues that an old-fashioned fable, like "The Hare and the Tortoise," presents an appearance and a moral—the appearance being that the hare is faster, the moral being that the persistence of the tortoise wins the race. Stevenson's fables are different: "The interesting thing about Stevenson's fables is that they prove morals, not appearances, to be deceptive, and ask us to invert them, as it were."

Is Stevenson upending traditional morality, as Nietzsche did? One critic said that Stevenson's fables "are essentially modern in their structure, and go to the very root of the paradox that all the deep modern thinkers find in human life, though they do not pretend to find any solution of that paradox, but leave it where they found it." This critic doesn't explain what that paradox is, but perhaps Stevenson's fable "The Sinking Ship" will help us to grasp it.

"Sir," said the first lieutenant, bursting into the Captain's cabin, "the ship is going down."

"Very well, Mr. Spoker," said the Captain; "but that is no reason for going about half-shaved. Exercise your mind a moment, Mr. Spoker, and you will see that to the philosophic eye there is nothing new in our position: the ship (if she is to go down at all) may be said to have been going down since she was launched."

"She is settling fast," said the first lieutenant, as he returned from shaving.

"Fast, Mr. Spoker?" asked the Captain. "The expression is a strange one, for time (if you will think of it) is only relative."

"Sir," said the lieutenant, "I think it is scarcely worthwhile to embark in such a discussion when we shall all be in Davy Jones' Locker in ten minutes."

"By parity of reasoning," returned the Captain gently, "it would never be worthwhile to begin any inquiry of importance; the odds are always overwhelming that we must die before we shall have brought it to an end. You have not considered, Mr. Spoker, the situation of man," said the Captain, smiling, and shaking his head.

"I am much more engaged in considering the position of the ship," said Mr. Spoker.

"Spoken like a good officer," replied the Captain, laying his hand on the lieutenant's shoulder.

On deck they found the men had broken into the spirit-room, and were fast getting drunk.

"My men," said the Captain, "there is no sense in this. The ship is going down, you will tell me, in ten minutes: well, and what then? To the philosophic eye, there is nothing new in our position. All our lives long, we may have been about to break a blood-vessel or to be struck by lightning, not merely in ten minutes, but in ten seconds; and that has not prevented us from eating dinner, no, nor from putting money in the Savings Bank. I assure you, with my hand on my heart, I fail to comprehend your attitude."

The men were already too far gone to pay much heed.

"This is a very painful sight, Mr. Spoker," said the Captain.

"And yet to the philosophic eye, or whatever it is," replied the first lieutenant, "they may be said to have been getting drunk since they came aboard."

"I do not know if you always follow my thought, Mr. Spoker," returned the Captain gently. "But let us proceed."

In the powder magazine they found an old salt smoking his pipe.

"Good God," cried the Captain, "what are you about?"

"Well, sir," said the old salt, apologetically, "they told me as she were going down."

"And suppose she were?" said the Captain. "To the philosophic eye, there would be nothing new in our position. Life, my old shipmate, life, at any moment and in any view, is as dangerous as a sinking ship; and yet it is man's handsome fashion to carry umbrellas, to wear india-rubber over-shoes, to begin vast works, and to conduct himself in every way as if he might hope to be eternal. And for my own poor part I should despise the man who, even on board a sinking ship, should omit to take a pill or to wind up his watch. That, my friend, would not be the human attitude."

"I beg pardon, sir," said Mr. Spoker. "But what is precisely the difference between shaving in a sinking ship and smoking in a powder magazine?"

"Or doing anything at all in any conceivable circumstances?" cried the Captain. "Perfectly conclusive; give me a cigar!"

Two minutes afterwards the ship blew up with a glorious detonation.

Blyth says that this fable "shows Zen on its destructive side." He says, "The most important word in the fable is 'glorious.' Glorious means Good, as distinguished from good. The word 'good' is a relative word as opposed to 'bad.' The word 'Good' is absolute and has no contrary."[1] Perhaps Stevenson is suggesting that the world is good in an absolute sense, good simply because existence is better than non-existence, good despite the death and

---

[1] Blyth, Ch. 1, p. 12. Note the similarity between Stevenson's sinking ship (as a metaphor for human life) and Buddhism's burning house. In fact, Stevenson himself uses the burning-house metaphor in one of his fables, as we saw above.

If Stevenson has something in common with Nietzsche (as I suggested above), perhaps that's because he and Nietzsche were contemporaries; perhaps that generation looked askance at conventional morality. Another member of that generation was Oscar Wilde, who also criticized conventional morality; for example, Wilde said, "Moderation in all things—including moderation." Nietzsche was born in 1844, Stevenson in 1850, Wilde in 1854. Stevenson seemed to realize that he was a product of his time; earlier I quoted his remark, "I cannot be wiser than my generation."

Another factor to consider is that Stevenson may have written some of his fables in Samoa. He may have felt that Christian missionaries were interfering with healthy native traditions. This may have strengthened his animus against conventional Western morality.

suffering that are embedded in life.[1] In a piece called "The End," I argued that human existence might be good in this absolute sense, even if the sun burned out and life came to an end.

If the U.S. is in terminal decline, and the earth is in terminal decline, and the sun is in terminal decline, should we give way to loud wailing and lamentation? Or should we accept the fact that existence is temporary, and make the most of the present moment? Blyth says, "'The skill to please without eternity,' is the property of all existing things. Eternity, infinity, are not necessary to the true life, which is complete, with which we can be satisfied and pleased, at any moment, in any place."

We can't listen to our favorite song an infinite number of times, it would cease to be pleasurable. We can't grab happiness and hold onto it. Blyth quotes Blake:

He who bends to himself a Joy,
Doth the wingèd life destroy;
But he who kisses the Joy as it flies,
Lives in eternity's sunrise.

Let's return to Stevenson's fable "The Sinking Ship." Blyth calls our attention to the phrase "Doing anything at all in any conceivable circumstances." This phrase, according to Blyth, is "the freedom of Zen. A man must be able (that is, willing) to do anything on any occasion whatever. Hundreds of verses in the writings of Zen express this perfect freedom, which alone allows us to act perfectly." Blyth quotes several of these verses, such as

Stones rise up into the sky;
Fire burns down in the water.

The freedom of Zen makes it a popular guide for artists, athletes, etc. Freedom means creativity, it's the opposite of stagnation.

The freedom of Zen is sometimes at odds with ethics. Stevenson's Zen sometimes violates conventional morality. Any mysticism/religion some-

---

[1] In "The Sinking Ship," Stevenson uses a violent image, just as he uses a violent image in "The Sick Man and the Fireman." Some readers in our time might be troubled by this, it hits too close to home, it reminds them of contemporary terrorists who actually view such violence as glorious. But when we read Stevenson, I think we should try to see things from his perspective; we shouldn't let contemporary terrorists shape how we read literature.

The image of a "glorious detonation" could be viewed aesthetically, could be viewed as an example of the sublime. In an earlier issue, I quoted Grant's description of a battle: "The enemy were evidently expecting our fleet, for they were ready to light up the river by means of bonfires... and by firing houses.... The sight was magnificent, but terrible." Magnificent but terrible is a good definition of the sublime; Stevenson's "glorious detonation" could be called magnificent but terrible, i.e., sublime.

times conflicts with morality. Kierkegaard said that religion sometimes involves a "suspension of the ethical." Kierkegaard said that when Abraham raised his arm to slay Isaac, Abraham was following a religious command, and violating an ethical command.

C. "Thrawn Janet"

I read a short story by Robert Louis Stevenson called "Thrawn Janet." Henry James said that "Thrawn Janet" is the best of Stevenson's short works, as *Kidnapped* is the best of his longer works. The word "thrawn" is a Scottish word meaning "twisted." In Stevenson's story, Janet has a twisted neck.

The story is written largely in the Scottish dialect, which makes it somewhat difficult to read. Other Scottish writers, like Walter Scott and Robert Burns, also use the Scottish dialect from time to time. So if you become somewhat familiar with Scottish, it will help you not only with "Thrawn Janet," but with other works.

Some Scottish words are close to English; for example, the Scottish "twa" means "two," "muckle" means "much," "muir" means "moor," "abune" means "above," "craig" means "crag" ("craig" can also mean "neck"). One can usually gather the meaning from the context; for example, "the auld aik cabinet" is "the old oak cabinet." One can also use a Scottish dictionary (an online dictionary). Some Scottish words seem unrelated to English; for example, "bairn" means "child," and "burn" means "stream."

"Thrawn Janet" is a horror story, a story about the devil taking over the body of a dead witch. It was believed that the devil had a particular hatred for ministers; "Thrawn Janet" is about a minister who is harassed by the devil. "Thrawn Janet" appealed strongly to Stevenson himself; one might say that the story cast a spell on its own creator. His wife said that when Stevenson read the story to her, he "fairly frightened himself, and we crept down the stairs clinging hand in hand like two scared children."[1]

---

[1] Quoted in "Stevenson's Use of Witchcraft in 'Thrawn Janet,'" by Coleman O. Parsons, *Studies in Philology*, July, 1946, Vol. 43, No. 3, pp. 551-571, jstor.org/stable/4172769

Stevenson uses the Scottish word "collieshangie" (quarrel). Collieshangie comes from collie, so it could be translated "collie-fight" or "dog-fight." A collieshangie is an arranged fight, a staged fight, between collies. One of man's oldest pleasures is watching animals tear each other to pieces. Man thirsts for blood. Perhaps this thirst can be controlled by modern civilization, and eventually outgrown.

Let's look at the passage in which "collieshangie" appears. Stevenson is describing how the village women attack Janet (this kind of attacking is sometimes called "rabbling" because it's done by a mob or rabble). Stevenson writes, "The carline skirled till ye could hear her at the Hangin' Shaw, and she focht like ten; there was mony a guidwife bure the mark of her neist day

The Scottish dialect had a strong attraction for Stevenson. As a child, Stevenson heard bits of dialect, and he heard stories about the devil from his nurse, that "overflowing treasury of ghost, goblin, witch, warlock, spunky, and fairy stories, which she told him with the curdling realism that comes of wholehearted belief."

But Stevenson had mixed feelings about horror stories, and about "Thrawn Janet" in particular. He decided that "Thrawn Janet" wasn't universal; "It is true only historically, true for a hill parish in Scotland in old days, not true for mankind and the world." He questioned the value of dark literature: "I do not think it is a wholesome part of me that broods on the evil in the world and man; but I do not think that I get harm from it; possibly my readers may, which is more serious; but at any account, I do not purpose to write more in this vein."[1]

At the start of "Thrawn Janet," the minister is skeptical of stories about devils and witches. He's learned, enlightened. But the events recounted in the story convert him to the old beliefs; he becomes gloomy and solitary. "His eye was wild, scared, and uncertain." At the start of the story, the minister takes pity on Janet and tries to help her, but this approach backfires.

So what's the moral of the story? Perhaps it's the Biblical teaching, "Thou shalt not suffer a witch to live." Or perhaps it's the Biblical teaching, "Be sober, be vigilant; because your adversary the devil, as a roaring lion, walketh about, seeking whom he may devour." One critic wrote,

> Stevenson in this story turned about the normal moral balance. Soulis' kindness toward Janet brings him horror; the persecution of witches is justified. The morality of the story troubled Stevenson: "Poor Mr. Soulis' faults," he later wrote, "we may eagerly recognize as virtues, and we feel that by his conversion he was merely worsened; and this, although the story carries me away every time I read it, leaves a painful impression on my mind."[2]

---

an' mony a lang day after; and just in the hettest o' the collieshangie, wha suld come up... but the new minister"
(the old woman screamed till you could hear her at the Hanging Wood [i.e. the manse where Soulis lived], and she fought like ten; there was many a goodwife bore the mark of her next day and many a long day after; and just in the hottest of the quarrel, who should come up... but the new minister).

1 But if Stevenson abandoned horror fiction, he didn't abandon the theme of the encounter with evil. Warner says that Stevenson's "principal concern in all his best fiction [is] man's struggle against a palpable malevolence." See "Stevenson's First Scottish Story," by Fred B. Warner, Jr., *Nineteenth-Century Fiction*, December, 1969, Vol. 24, No. 3, pp. 335-344, jstor.org/stable/2932862

2 Warner

In the last issue, we saw how Stevenson upended traditional morality in his *Fables*. Is he doing the same thing in "Thrawn Janet"? Perhaps Stevenson's generation had grown tired of traditional morality, perhaps a spirit of rebellion was in the air.

The moral witch tale would start with a minister persecuting a witch, then becoming enlightened and feeling remorse. Stevenson takes the opposite course; his minister moves "from skepticism to superstitiousness."[1] As Stevenson upends morality, so he upends history; his minister is skeptical about witchcraft around 1700, when Scottish ministers weren't skeptical, and his minister believes in witchcraft around 1750, when ministers didn't believe.[2]

Walter Scott, whom Stevenson admired, devoted a volume to witchcraft. Scott also wrote a story on the subject—"Wandering Willie's Tale," which can be found in his novel *Redgauntlet*. Scott didn't upend morality as Stevenson did; one critic spoke of "Sir Walter's morally sound order."[3]

"Thrawn Janet" is remarkable for its direct presentation of evil. Henry James, in his "Turn of the Screw," leaves the reader guessing whether the ghost is real or imagined. But there's no guessing in "Thrawn Janet," no uncertainty, everything is described with stark directness.

Henry James had said that a horror writer should merely hint at horror, and let the reader fill in: "'Make him think the evil, make him think it for himself, and you are released from weak specifications.' In James' story, the most important things are left unsaid. In 'Thrawn Janet,' all is specified, and not weakly."

Stevenson's wife said that he was always looking for "euphonious and expressive names." She said he was especially fond of the names in "Thrawn

---

1 Parsons

2 What is true of Scotland is probably true of other places, such as New England. The Salem witch trials took place in the late 1600s. By 1750, witchcraft was probably regarded as superstition in New England.

Soulis was shattered by his encounter with evil. Other Stevenson heroes encounter evil and become wiser. "It is in his best novel, *Kidnapped*, that he creates the character able to respond most satisfactorily to a revelation of the world's iniquities. David Balfour, like many a hero of Scott, goes to the Highlands a boy and returns a man.... David can do what Soulis cannot: he can accept the world as it is." (Warner)

Warner says that "Thrawn Janet" may have influenced James' "Turn of the Screw":

"Mrs. Grose implies that Miss Jessel left Bly because she was pregnant with an illegitimate child; Janet also has had a child out of wedlock. In both stories the house is near water; black figures appear and disappear; Janet, Quint, and Jessel all return from the dead. In each story birds, stairways, and blown-out candles figure in the mystery."

3 Parsons

Janet." "Murdoch Soulis of Balweary in the Vale of Dule he believed he could never better."

Stevenson felt a connection to Scottish history through his mother's family and his father's family. He felt that, in general, Scots had a stronger tie to the past than English:

> That is the mark of the Scot of all classes [Stevenson wrote]: that he stands in an attitude towards the past unthinkable to Englishmen, and remembers and cherishes the memory of his forebears, good or bad; and there burns alive in him a sense of identity with the dead even to the twentieth generation.

Though much of Stevenson's life was spent abroad, and many of his books are set outside Scotland, he had a strong feeling for his homeland:

> There is no special loveliness in that grey country, with its rainy, sea-beat archipelago; its fields of dark mountains; its unsightly places, black with coal; its treeless, sour, unfriendly-looking corn-lands; its quaint, grey castled city [i.e., Edinburgh], where the bells clash of a Sunday, and the wind squalls, and the salt showers fly and beat. I do not even know if I desire to live there; but let me hear in some far land, a kindred voice sing out, "Oh, why left I my hame?" and it seems at once as if no beauty under the kind heavens, and no society of the wise and good, can repay me for my absence from my country. And though I think I would rather die elsewhere, yet in my heart of hearts I long to be buried among good Scotch clods. I will say it fairly, it grows on me with every year: there are no stars so lively as Edinburgh street-lamps. When I forget thee, auld Reekie, may my right hand forget its cunning!
>
> The happiest lot on earth is to be born a Scotsman. You must pay for it in many ways, as for all other advantages on earth. You have to learn the Paraphrases and the Shorter Catechism; you generally take to drink; your youth, as far as I can find out, is a time of louder war against society, of more outcry and tears and turmoil, than if you had been born, for instance, in England. But somehow life is warmer and closer.[1]

At the end of "Thrawn Janet," Janet's devil-inhabited body is destroyed, apparently by a lightning bolt. Her body "lowed up like a brunstane spunk and fell in ashes to the grund" (rose up like a brimstone spark and fell in ashes to the ground). Then "the thunder followed, peal on dirling peal, the

---

[1] Doubtless Stevenson is thinking of his own experience when he speaks of taking to drink and warring against society. Stevenson, an only child, fought hard to break free of his parents' orbit. In his religious attitude and his career choice, he was a big disappointment to his parents. The young Stevenson had what might be called an "identity crisis." In the last issue, I mentioned a book called *The Proper Pirate: Robert Louis Stevenson's Quest for Identity.*

Edinburgh is called "Old Reekie" (Old Smoky) because of all the smoke from burning coal and burning peat.

rairing rain upon the back o' that; and Mr. Soulis lowped through the garden hedge, and ran, wi' skelloch upon skelloch, for the clachan" ("lowped" is related to "leapt," "skelloch" means "scream," "clachan" means "village"). "But it was a sair dispensation for the minister; lang, lang he lay ravin' in his bed; and frae that hour to this, he was the man ye ken the day" (But it was a sore dispensation for the minister; long, long he lay raving in his bed; and from that hour to this, he was the man you see today).[1]

Did Stevenson himself ever feel the immediate presence of evil? Did he ever feel panic fear? Did he ever have an urge to run for the clachan, skelloch upon skelloch? We know that his contemporary William James did have this experience. James said that he

> went one evening into a dressing room in the twilight to procure some article that was there, when suddenly there fell upon me without any warning, just as if it came out of the darkness, a horrible fear of my own existence.... Not the conception or intellectual perception of evil, but the grisly blood-freezing heart-palsying sensation of it close upon one, and no other conception or sensation able to live for a moment in its presence.... I became a mass of quivering fear. After this the universe was changed for me altogether. I awoke morning after morning with a horrible dread at the pit of my stomach.... For months I was unable to go out into the dark alone.[2]

One is reminded of the experience of the Reverend Murdoch Soulis, and one wonders what James would have thought of Stevenson's story. James' father (Henry James Sr.) had a similar experience.

> One day... towards the close of May [1844], having eaten a comfortable dinner, I remained sitting at the table after the family had dispersed, idly gazing at the embers in the grate, thinking of nothing, and feeling

---

[1] Notice how the weather is in sync with the events. First the weather is oppressively hot, "uncanny weather." After Janet's body is destroyed, there's thunder and rain.

Stevenson says this about the night before the climax: "That was a nicht that has never been forgotten in Ba'weary, the nicht o' the seeventeenth of August, seventeen hun'er' an twal'. It had been het afore, as I hae said, but that nicht it was hetter than ever. The sun gaed doun amang unco-lookin' clouds; it fell as mirk as the pit; no a star, no a breath o' wund; ye couldnae see your han' afore your face."

The behavior of animals is also in sync with the events. Before he encounters the devil, Soulis sees first two, then four, then seven crows flying around the old churchyard. It was clear to Soulis that something had changed their ordinary behavior ("first twa, an syne fower, an' syne seeven corbie craws fleein' round an' round abune the auld kirkyaird.... It was clear to Mr. Soulis that something had put them frae their ordinar").

[2] See Richardson's biography of William James, Ch. 65. This passage can also be found in James' *Varieties of Religious Experience*.

> only the exhilaration incident to a good digestion, when suddenly—in a lightning flash as it were—"fear came upon me, and trembling, which made all my bones to shake." To all appearance it was a perfectly insane and abject terror, without ostensible cause, and only to be accounted for, to my perplexed imagination, by some damned shape squatting invisible to me within the precincts of the room, and raying out from his fetid personality influences fatal to life. The thing had not lasted ten seconds before I felt myself a wreck.

"The depression he felt in the wake of this experience took him two years to pull out of."[1] Henry Sr. referred to this experience as his "vastation." I don't see any evidence that Stevenson experienced such fear, but I think some horror writers, like Poe and Lovecraft, experienced the sort of fear that they wrote about.

D. "Dr. Jekyll and Mr. Hyde"

The novella "Jekyll and Hyde" is one of Stevenson's best-known works. It made a big impression when it was published in 1886, and it has become a symbol of man's duality.

This duality is a central theme in Stevenson's work. As a teenager, Stevenson wrote a play about Deacon Brodie, a respectable Edinburgh cabinet-maker who led a secret life as a house-breaker.[2] Stevenson was also fascinated by the case of Eugene Chantrelle, a French teacher in Edinburgh and an acquaintance of Stevenson; Chantrelle was convicted for murdering his wife, and suspected of murdering other people, too.

Was Stevenson interested in man's duality because he himself led a double life? One critic describes Stevenson as "the only child of very pious parents. [He] suffered from their Puritan restrictiveness." Apparently he resorted to drink and prostitutes, "leaving home for a bohemian love-life in the Edinburgh slums."

Another reason why Stevenson was interested in man's duality is that he felt his works were created by a muse, an inner voice, something outside his conscious self. As one critic wrote, Stevenson believed that "his creative projects are produced not by him, but by a shadowy character he calls 'the other fellow,' for whom Stevenson himself acts only as an amanuensis."[3]

---

1 See Richardson's biography, Ch. 2

2 "Stevenson had been long familiar with the story of Deacon Brodie, an Edinburgh cabinet maker by day and burglar by night, and as early as 1865 [at age 15] he was at work on a drama based on the man's life. (He later completed the work with W. E. Henley, titling it, *Deacon Brodie, or The Double Life*.)"(Miyoshi, p. 474)

3 "Robert Louis Stevenson and his 'Other Fellow': The Dreaming Self and the Death of the Author," by Audrey Murfin, Victorians Institute Journal Digital Annex 41 (2013), nines.org/exhibits/Robert_Louis_Stevenson_and_his

Stevenson described this "other fellow" in a letter to Frederic Myers. Myers did research on the occult, and was a leading member of The Society for Psychical Research, of which Stevenson was a member. Stevenson was interested in the occult, and in dreams; he wrote an essay called "A Chapter on Dreams." His works often allude to occult phenomena. For example, in "Jekyll and Hyde," Utterson has a hunch that he's finally going to meet Mr. Hyde:

> In the course of his nightly patrols, he had long grown accustomed to the quaint effect with which the footfalls of a single person, while he is still a great way off, suddenly spring out distinct from the vast hum and clatter of the city. Yet his attention had never before been so sharply and decisively arrested; and it was with a strong, superstitious prevision of success that he withdrew into the entry of the court.

In his "Chapter on Dreams," Stevenson notes that a dream sometimes tells an involved story, and the dreamer is surprised by the plot twists, though his own unconscious, his "other fellow," created the whole story.[1] So Stevenson understood that dreams are created by this "other fellow," just as fictional works are, just as Hyde's crimes are. Man's duality is evident, Stevenson believed, in dreams, fictional works, and crimes.

Stevenson noted that people sometimes take action while in a dream, while sleeping. People who are sleeping sometimes act in a way that their waking self wouldn't, as Hyde acts in a way that Jekyll wouldn't. In his letter to Myers, Stevenson describes a night of illness and pain, a night in which he was struggling with various dreams and hallucinations. His conscious self knew that he shouldn't tell his wife about the dream, but finally his other self "called my wife to my bedside, seized her savagely by the wrist, and, looking on her with a face of fury, cried, 'Why do you not put the two ends together and put me out of pain?'"

This other self, this unconscious self, might be compared to Mr. Hyde. This incident took place in 1884, two years before Stevenson wrote "Jekyll and Hyde." This experience of duality, of split personality, may have strengthened Stevenson's interest in duality, and may have inspired him to create "Jekyll and Hyde." The theme of duality looms large in both Stevenson's work and his life; I mentioned it fifteen years ago when discussing *Treasure Island* (see ljhammond.com/phlit/2008-02.htm#5).

"Jekyll and Hyde" was born in dreams and intuitions. Before Stevenson began writing it, he was casting about for a subject, and had a dream about a man transforming himself into a monster, into a Hyde character. While still asleep, Stevenson screamed in terror. This roused his wife, who roused Stevenson himself. Stevenson was annoyed with his wife, annoyed that she had pulled him out of what he called "a fine bogey tale."

Though the "bogey tale" was interrupted, it provided the seed for a novella, and Stevenson set to work. Stevenson's stepson, Lloyd Osbourne, later said,

---

[1] Stevenson describes a dream in which he kills his father, then becomes very close with his widowed mother—not unlike Oedipus.

> I remember the first reading as though it were yesterday. Louis [i.e., Robert Louis Stevenson] came downstairs in a fever; read nearly half the book aloud; and then, while we were still gasping, he was away again, and busy writing. I doubt if the first draft took so long as three days.[1]

"Jekyll and Hyde" made a strong impression on the public, as well as on Stevenson and his family. It sold rapidly, and was turned into a play starring Richard Mansfield. But soon the public was engrossed by the serial killings of "Jack the Ripper," and Mansfield was mentioned as a suspect! So Mansfield closed down the successful production.

Is it possible that Jack the Ripper himself read the story, and was inspired by it? Did Stevenson consider this possibility? Did life imitate art? In a recent issue, I noted that Stevenson was concerned about the effect of his work on the reader.

Surely one reason why the story made such an impression was its graphic violence—violence that had no cause, violence motivated by pure evil, satanic evil. In the following passage, a maid is looking out the window and sees

> an aged beautiful gentleman with white hair, drawing near along the lane; and advancing to meet him, another and very small gentleman, to whom at first she paid less attention. When they had come within speech (which was just under the maid's eyes) the older man bowed and accosted the other with a very pretty manner of politeness. It did not seem as if the subject of his address were of great importance; indeed, from his pointing, it sometimes appeared as if he were only inquiring his way; but the moon shone on his face as he spoke, and the girl was pleased to watch it, it seemed to breathe such an innocent and old-world kindness of disposition, yet with something high too, as of a well-founded self-content.
>
> Presently her eye wandered to the other, and she was surprised to recognize in him a certain Mr. Hyde, who had once visited her master and for whom she had conceived a dislike. He had in his hand a heavy cane, with which he was trifling; but he answered never a word, and seemed to listen with an ill-contained impatience. And then all of a sudden he broke out in a great flame of anger, stamping with his foot, brandishing the cane, and carrying on (as the maid described it) like a madman. The old gentleman took a step back, with the air of one very much surprised and a trifle hurt; and at that Mr. Hyde broke out of all bounds and clubbed him to the earth. And next moment, with ape-like fury, he was

---

[1] Stevenson's wife read the manuscript and wrote comments in the margin. "She observed that in effect the story was really an allegory, but Robert was writing it as a story. After a while, Robert called her back into the bedroom and pointed to a pile of ashes: he had burnt the manuscript in fear that he would try to salvage it, and thus forced himself to start again from nothing, writing an allegorical story as she had suggested."(Wikipedia)

> trampling his victim under foot and hailing down a storm of blows, under which the bones were audibly shattered and the body jumped upon the roadway. At the horror of these sights and sounds, the maid fainted.

Notice the phrase "ape-like fury." Hyde is also described as a "monkey," "troglodytic," "hardly human." It seems that Stevenson was influenced by Darwin's theory. As a consequence of Darwin's work, man was viewed, not as a relative of God, but as a relative of animals. Was a savage beast lurking beneath the veneer of civilization? (In recent weeks, we've seen this savage beast in Ukraine.)

One critic wrote, "In 'Jekyll and Hyde,' as in 'Thrawn Janet' and 'The Merry Men,' Stevenson probes the Calvinist tradition of personified evil largely for Gothic effect."[1] Stevenson was concerned about the effect of "personified evil" on the reader, yet he kept coming back to the subject, perhaps because of his Calvinist upbringing, perhaps because of his experience of duality, perhaps because he knew that "personified evil" struck a chord with the public.

When people see Hyde's face, they feel "disgust, loathing and fear." But they can never explain why. Hyde "gave an impression of deformity without any nameable malformation." Stevenson doesn't describe Hyde in detail, Hyde is obscure; the reader learns nothing about his hair or his eyes or his nose. One might compare Stevenson's depiction of Hyde to Milton's description of Death. Milton wrote,

> The other shape,
> If shape it might be called that shape had none
> Distinguishable in member, joint, or limb,
> Or substance might be called that shadow seemed,
> For each seemed either; black it stood as Night,
> Fierce as ten Furies, terrible as Hell,
> And shook a dreadful Dart; what seemed his head
> The likeness of a Kingly Crown had on.

In his essay on the sublime, Edmund Burke praised the "judicious obscurity" of Milton's description of Death, and Burke considered this obscurity characteristic of the sublime. Burke said that the sublime is that which arouses terror, horror, and astonishment—just what is aroused in Enfield by his first sight of Hyde. Enfield says,

> I saw two figures: one a little man who was stumping along eastward at a good walk, and the other a girl of maybe eight or ten who was running as hard as she was able down a cross street. Well, sir, the two ran into one another naturally enough at the corner; and then came the horrible part of the thing; for the man trampled calmly over the child's body and left her screaming on the ground. It sounds nothing to hear,

---

[1] *Robert Louis Stevenson and the Fiction of Adventure*, by Robert Kiely, p. 209

> but it was hellish to see. It wasn't like a man; it was like some damned Juggernaut.

Hyde has a mysterious power, a satanic power, a power that makes him seem inhuman. As beauty causes pleasure, according to Burke, so sublimity causes pain; the sight of Hyde causes pain to other characters.

But the sublime is often associated with reverence, while Hyde awakens loathing rather than reverence. Should we describe Hyde's effect as horror rather than sublimity? Or should we extend the concept of sublimity to include the loathsome Hyde?

* * * * *

The main characters in "Jekyll and Hyde" represent joyless life, lifeless life, death-in-life. "The important men of the book," one critic wrote, "[are] all unmarried, barren of ideas, emotionally stifled, joyless."[1] The lawyer Utterson, for example, "enjoyed the theatre, [but] had not crossed the doors of

---

1 "Dr. Jekyll and the Emergence of Mr. Hyde," by Masao Miyoshi, *College English*, Mar., 1966, Vol. 27, No. 6 (Mar., 1966), pp. 470-474 and 479-480, jstor.org/stable/374021

Saposnik writes, "The four prominent men in the story are gentlemen and, as such, are variations of standard gentlemanly behavior. Three are professional men—two doctors, one lawyer—and the only non-professional, Richard Enfield, is so locked into his role that his description as 'the well-known man about town' might as well be a professional designation." When a Jungian like myself hears of four characters, he wonders if this might be a Jungian quaternity. (See "The Anatomy of 'Dr. Jekyll and Mr. Hyde,'" by Irving S. Saposnik, *Studies in English Literature, 1500-1900*, Autumn 1971, Vol. 11, No. 4, Nineteenth Century (Autumn, 1971), pp. 715-731, jstor.org/stable/449833)

Miyoshi points out that Hyde isn't violent at first. Compared to Jekyll, Hyde is "younger, lighter, happier in body." He has a "heady recklessness" and a "current of disordered sensual images running like a mill-race in my fancy." One might say that, at first, Hyde is just "Jekyll on vacation," just "Jekyll having a good time," but then Hyde gets out of control.

Stevenson said that Jekyll's chief vice is neither repressed violence nor repressed sexuality, but rather hypocrisy; Jekyll makes too brave a show of virtue and respectability.(Saposnik, p. 727) Saposnik says that Hyde represents "vitality," "life force"—just what is lacking in Jekyll and the other leading characters.

Miyoshi says that "Jekyll and Hyde" is a "romance," not an "orthodox realistic novel." Miyoshi says that Stevenson compared romance and realism in several essays, such as "A Gossip on Romance." Miyoshi says that romance and realism were "clearly distinguishable throughout the greater part of the

one for twenty years." Jekyll metamorphoses into Hyde in order to experience joy, spontaneity, vitality.

These men aren't bums or bohemians, they're lawyers and doctors, they're successful, comfortable, respectable. "In this society of respectables Dr. Jekyll stands out as 'the very pink of the proprieties.'"

Jekyll craves respectability, he speaks of, "my imperious desire to carry my head high, and wear a more than commonly grave countenance before the public." But he also has "a certain impatient gaiety of disposition." Torn between respectability and gaiety, unable to reconcile these tendencies, Jekyll became "committed to a profound duplicity of life."

He begins making scientific experiments, hoping to create an alter ego who can express his repressed gaiety. He dabbles in his laboratory, like Faust and Frankenstein, pursuing "the mystic and the transcendental." Finally he concocts a potion that will turn him into Mr. Hyde, then back to Dr. Jekyll.

Stevenson's London is a wasteland, both in its people and its landscape. Here is how Stevenson describes Utterson's visit to Hyde's house in Soho:

> It was by this time about nine in the morning, and the first fog of the season. A great chocolate-colored pall lowered over heaven, but the wind was continually charging and routing these embattled vapors; so that as the cab crawled from street to street, Mr. Utterson beheld a marvelous number of degrees and hues of twilight; for here it would be dark like the back-end of evening; and there would be a glow of a rich, lurid brown, like the light of some strange conflagration; and here, for a moment, the fog would be quite broken up, and a haggard shaft of daylight would glance in between the swirling wreaths. The dismal quarter of Soho seen under these changing glimpses, with its muddy ways, and slatternly passengers, and its lamps, which had never been extinguished or had been kindled afresh to combat this mournful re-

---

nineteenth century, [but] the two merge in the last decade to form the new symbolic novel."

Miyoshi says that, at the end of the eighteenth century, Gothic romances like *The Castle of Otranto* and *Caleb Williams* explored "the theme of double personality." This theme also looms large in Romantic poets, who dealt with "the schism between the ineffable imagination and the demands of reason." In the Victorian era, the schism between imagination and reason became "a problem of personal faith vs. social responsibility.... The Victorian writer wanted above all to 'stay in touch'.... The world was waiting to be improved upon." One thinks of Mill's preoccupation with social reform.

When we say that Stevenson wrote romances, this doesn't mean that his work was concerned with romantic relationships, erotic passions. To avoid this misinterpretation, one might use the word "fantasy" rather than the word "romance." In fact, Stevenson's work is rarely erotic. "Critics have often complained that the London of ['Jekyll and Hyde'] is singularly devoid of women. [One critic] likens the atmosphere to 'a community of monks.'"(Saposnik)

> invasion of darkness, seemed, in the lawyer's eyes, like a district of some city in a nightmare.

Perhaps the theme of "Jekyll and Hyde" is the same as that of many literary works: the quest for wholeness, balance, happiness, the good life. But "Jekyll and Hyde" doesn't present this theme through characters who have achieved wholeness, but rather through characters who have failed to achieve it. Theologians can portray God positively by describing what He is, or negatively by describing what He isn't; the negative approach was called the *via negativa*. Likewise, imaginative writers can depict wholeness through positive examples or through negative examples. In "Jekyll and Hyde," Stevenson pursues the *via negativa*, he portrays characters who are lifeless, or who achieve vitality only through a dramatic split of their personality.[1]

In his essay "Lay Morals," Stevenson discusses wholeness/vitality:

---

[1] Miyoshi says that "Jekyll and Hyde" depicts "the late Victorian wasteland," which is "unfit to sustain a human being simultaneously in an honorable public life and a joyful private one."

The critic F. R. Leavis said that D. H. Lawrence was concerned with the difference between vitality and death-in-life. Leavis wrote, "[Lawrence] has an unfailingly sure sense of the difference between that which makes for life and that which makes against it; of the difference between health and that which tends away from health."

According to Leavis, Lawrence depicts love as a quest for wholeness (you'll recall that the leading characters of "Jekyll and Hyde" are bachelors, men without a love life):

> Though Leavis sees erotic elements in "The Fox," he realizes that eros is part of something larger, part of the quest for a fulfilling life and a whole personality. Leavis calls "The Fox" "a study of human mating; of the attraction between a man and a woman that expresses the profound needs of each and has its meaning in a permanent union." Though Henry wants "to have this place [i.e., Bailey Farm] for his own," Leavis says that it's essentially a spiritual quest, "there is nothing mercenary about his attitude." "The Fox" is a love story, and it deals with love in the deepest sense of the word, love as a quest for wholeness.(See ljhammond.com/phlit/2009-01b.htm#14)

When we speak of balance/wholeness, perhaps we're speaking of an ideal that can never be completely attained. Saposnik says that Jekyll's experiments lead to "the inescapable conclusion that man must dwell in uncomfortable but necessary harmony with his multiple selves." Saposnik compares wholeness to the elusive El Dorado.

Saposnik points out that Jekyll's house symbolizes his split personality; Saposnik speaks of, "Jekyll's house, with its sinister rear entrance through which Hyde passes and its handsome front 'which wore a great air of wealth and comfort.'"

> [The soul] demands that we shall not live alternately with our opposing tendencies in continual see-saw of passion and disgust, but seek some path on which the tendencies shall no longer oppose, but serve each other to a common end. It demands that we shall not pursue broken ends, but great and comprehensive purposes, in which soul and body may unite like notes in a harmonious chord. That were indeed a way of peace and pleasure, that were indeed a heaven upon earth. It does not demand, however... that I should starve my appetites for no purpose under heaven but as a purpose in itself; or, in a weak despair, pluck out the eye that I have not yet learned to guide and enjoy with wisdom. The soul demands unity of purpose, not the dismemberment of man; it seeks to roll up all his strength and sweetness, all his passion and wisdom, into one.[1]

E. M. Forster described the quest for wholeness in similar language:

> Only connect! ....Only connect the prose and the passion, and both will be exalted, and human love will be seen at its height. Live in fragments no longer. Only connect, and the beast and the monk, robbed of the isolation that is life to either, will die.

Jekyll fails to connect, he isolates his beast from his conscious self, from his public persona.

* * * * *

The main characters of "Jekyll and Hyde" are professional men, men from the upper middle class. Stevenson himself was born into this class, his family was well-to-do. But Stevenson had no interest in building a career that would ensure he remained in this class. On the contrary, he liked to drop into a lower class; when he traveled to California as a young man, he traveled "on the cheap," and consorted with the working class. He notes that Christianity doesn't preach respectability:

---

1 This ideal of wholeness may become clearer if we apply it to one facet of life, namely, sexuality. Stevenson writes, "Man is tormented by a very imperious physical desire; it spoils his rest, it is not to be denied.... In the satisfaction of this desire, as it first appears, the soul sparingly takes part; nay, it oft unsparingly regrets and disapproves the satisfaction. But let the man learn to love a woman as far as he is capable of love; and for this random affection of the body there is substituted a steady determination, a consent of all his powers and faculties, which supersedes, adopts, and commands the other. The desire survives, strengthened, perhaps, but taught obedience and changed in scope and character. Life is no longer a tale of betrayals and regrets; for the man now lives as a whole; his consciousness now moves on uninterrupted like a river; through all the extremes and ups and downs of passion, he remains approvingly conscious of himself." I'm indebted to Saposnik for drawing my attention to Stevenson's "Lay Morals."

> There is a kind of idea abroad that a man must live up to his station, that his house, his table, and his toilette, shall be in a ratio of equivalence, and equally imposing to the world. If this is in the Bible, the passage has eluded my inquiries. If it is not in the Bible, it is nowhere but in the heart of the fool....
>
> A man who has not experienced some ups and downs, and been forced to live more cheaply than in his father's house, has still his education to begin. Let the experiment be made, and he will find to his surprise that he has been eating beyond his appetite up to that hour; that the cheap lodging, the cheap tobacco, the rough country clothes, the plain table, have not only no power to damp his spirits, but perhaps give him as keen pleasure in the using as the dainties that he took, betwixt sleep and waking, in his former callous and somnambulous submission to wealth.

Stevenson notes that one who looks like a Bohemian, may be merely pursuing a different kind of respectability, while one who looks like a burgher may be a genuine Bohemian, may be following his own drummer:

> The Bohemian of the novel, who drinks more than is good for him and prefers anything to work, and wears strange clothes, is for the most part a respectable Bohemian, respectable in disrespectability, living for the outside.... But the man I mean lives wholly to himself, does what he wishes, and not what is thought proper, buys what he wants for himself, and not what is thought proper, works at what he believes he can do well and not what will bring him in money or favor. You may be the most respectable of men, and yet a true Bohemian.

Stevenson's "true Bohemian" knows what he wants, he knows himself. The chief ingredient of personal growth, Stevenson seems to say, is self-consciousness:

> There is plainly one thing more unrighteous than all others.... And this is to lose consciousness of oneself. In the best of times, it is but by flashes, when our whole nature is clear, strong and conscious, and events conspire to leave us free, that we enjoy communion with our soul....
>
> It is to keep a man awake, to keep him alive to his own soul and its fixed design of righteousness, that the better part of moral and religious education is directed; not only that of words and doctors, but the sharp ferule of calamity under which we are all God's scholars till we die.

* * * * *

In "Jekyll and Hyde," Stevenson uses a Latin phrase that I hadn't heard before, *pede claudo*. When I googled this phrase, I found that it was short for *pede poena claudo*, meaning "punishment moves with halting gait" (*poena* = punishment, *pede* = foot, *claudo* = closed/crippled/limping). The criminal escapes initially, but punishment slowly catches up with him, as the tortoise overtakes the hare. The phrase *pede poena claudo* comes from an ode by Horace:

saepe Diespiter
neglectus incesto addidit integrum,
raro antecedentem scelestum
deseruit pede Poena claudo.

(If Jupiter is disrespected, he often punishes the innocent with the guilty. Rarely does punishment, moving with halting step, fail to catch up with earlier crime.)

Diespiter is another name for Jupiter. *Diespiter* is from *dies* meaning day or sky. *Diespiter* means DiesPater, SkyFather. *Deus* means god, sky, shining. Likewise, the Chinese *tian* means sky or god. (The Chinese emperor was called *tian-zi*, son of heaven. A successful emperor had the *tian-ming*, the mandate of heaven.) "Jupiter" is from *djous-pater*. "Zeus" is from *dzeus* or *zdeus*. So both "Jupiter" and "Zeus" are related to *deus* (god), and both *deus* and *dies* are related to sky/shining.

E. "The Pavilion on the Links"

"The Pavilion on the Links" is a novella by Robert Louis Stevenson. It was written in 1880, about one year before *Treasure Island*, and it might be called a short version of *Treasure Island*. Like *Treasure Island*, "The Pavilion on the Links" is an adventure story that could be enjoyed by a 12-year-old. One reason I read "Pavilion" is that Arthur Conan Doyle had high praise for it (Doyle also had high praise for Stevenson's "Jekyll and Hyde").

Fiction is often based on a kernel of fact. *Treasure Island* seems to be an exception, it seems to be purely imaginary. "Pavilion," on the other hand, is based on a real event, a "defaulting banker picked up by a yacht upon the coast of Wales."[1]

The "bad guys" in "Pavilion" are Italian *carbonari*. The *carbonari* were revolutionaries who wanted a more liberal, more democratic Italy. They were often irredentists who wanted cities like Venice to be redeemed for Italy, reclaimed from the Austrians. (The word "irredentist" was originally an Italian word meaning "unredeemed." The phrase *Italia irredenta* occurs in "Pavilion." Irredentism is at the root of today's disputes over Ukraine and Taiwan.) In "Pavilion," the *carbonari* deposited money with a banker named Huddlestone, who lost the money in the stock market. Now Huddlestone is on the run, the Italians are in pursuit and are determined to kill him.

Huddlestone and his supporters barricade themselves in a house (a "pavilion") on the links. The word "links" has its original meaning—a sandy, grassy, rolling terrain. Stevenson writes, "*links* being a Scottish name for sand which has ceased drifting and become more or less solidly covered with

---

[1] "Robert Louis Stevenson's Art of Revision: 'The Pavilion on the Links' as Rehearsal for 'Treasure Island,'" by William H. Hardesty and David D. Mann, *The Papers of the Bibliographical Society of America*, September 1988, Vol. 82, No. 3, pp. 271-286, jstor.org/stable/24303898

turf." We use the word "links" to mean "golf course" since golf was originally played in Scotland on this sort of terrain.

Some similarities between "Pavilion" and *Treasure Island*:

- both stories are "a formulaic adventure told by a rather naive first-person narrator"
- the situation of the narrator, originally safe, "unexpectedly becomes dangerous as a result of threatening intruders"
- "the action centers on concealed treasure and involves betrayal by an apparently loyal and trustworthy person (Huddlestone, Long John Silver)"
- "a band of ruthless and alien villains (Italian conspirators, pirates) confronts an outnumbered loyal party in isolated circumstances"
- the loyal party "makes a stand under siege"

What a contrast between "Pavilion" and a HenryJames story! James often deals with visual art and literature—not much here to entertain a 12-year-old. Stevenson writes "blood and thunder" tales that seem best suited for youngsters. In my view, Stevenson writes better prose than James, but Stevenson's stories don't stay as close to his own experience, they seem more artificial than James' stories.

I found one critical essay on "Pavilion" (jstor.org/stable/24303898). It says that the hot-tempered Northmour is "probably the most interesting character that Stevenson created before Long John Silver." Northmour is

> an enigma—so much so that we never even learn his first name, only the initial R.... His "dark satanic" being glowers over the events, like the Byronic hero whom he resembles. The reader is fascinated by his violent temper, his almost obsessive concern for honor, and his wry, devilish remarks.... It is Northmour's duality—almost schizophrenia—that makes [the narrator] constantly unsure of how to treat him, or how far to trust him.

Northmour resembles Long John Silver. As I wrote elsewhere, "One of the themes of Stevenson's work is moral ambiguity, 'the co-presence of good and evil qualities in the same person.' Long John Silver [is] initially good, then evil, then good again."

I don't regret reading "Pavilion"—the prose is excellent, and the story holds your interest. On the other hand, I wouldn't recommend it enthusiastically—it's obviously a tall tale written to entertain, and it's difficult for the reader to "suspend his disbelief," to view these characters as real people. Are we making a mistake by thinking of Stevenson as a fiction writer? Perhaps his best works are his essays and travel books.

8. Holmes and Howells

I often confuse Oliver Wendell Holmes and William Dean Howells.

The first thing to be said about Oliver Wendell Holmes is that there are two of them: father and son, Senior and Junior. Senior was an eminent physician and a professor at Harvard Medical School; he invented the term "anesthesia." Junior was an eminent lawyer and Supreme Court Justice. Senior was a man-of-letters who knew many New England writers, wrote a biography of Emerson, and a prose miscellany called *The Autocrat of the Breakfast-Table*. Senior was also a well-respected poet; Poe said that his poem "The Last Leaf" (about Thomas Melville, Herman Melville's grandfather) was one of the best in the English language. Junior, on the other hand, wasn't a man-of-letters, and confined himself to legal writing. Senior was over 50 when the Civil War broke out, and didn't participate in the war, Junior was in numerous battles, and was wounded several times.

William Dean Howells was the son of a newspaper editor, and he was a published author at an early age. In 1860, when he was just 23, Howells wrote a campaign biography for Lincoln, and when Lincoln won the election, Howells was rewarded with diplomatic posts in Venice and other European cities. Howells is chiefly remembered for his realist fiction. His best-known work, *The Rise of Silas Lapham*, describes "the rise and fall of an American entrepreneur in the paint business."[1] Howells championed realism in the pages of *Atlantic Monthly*, which he edited in the 1870s. He was a close friend of Mark Twain, and wrote a book called *My Mark Twain: Reminiscences*.

9. Jack London

I'm reading Jack London's *White Fang*. London reminds me of Thomas Wolfe. Like Wolfe's novels, *White Fang* doesn't have one, all-embracing plot; rather, it has a series of episodes. London is rougher than Wolfe—closer to the frontier, closer to nature. Wolfe has more education, more degrees, more literary ambition, and is more introspective than London.

I enjoy *White Fang*—good style, exciting story—but I never lose the feeling that this is a novel, this is an author trying to entertain the reader. *White Fang* doesn't draw you in, it doesn't make you suspend your disbelief, it doesn't convince you that it's a real world, it doesn't make you empathize with the characters as if they were real.

London draws on his experiences in Alaska, at the time of the Yukon Gold Rush. The novel opens with two men transporting a coffin through the Alaska wilderness, during the winter. The coffin sits on a sled, which is pulled by a dog team. The men are pursued by ravenous wolves. One of the men, Bill, says "They're goin' to get us. They're sure goin' to get us, Henry." Henry responds, "They've half got you a'ready, a-talkin' like that.... A man's half licked when he says he is." Sure enough, the wolves get Bill.

Did Bill's negative thinking bring about his death? Or was his thinking an anticipation of his death? In other words, is this a case of the power of thought/attitude, or is it a case of precognition? The vast field of the occult

---

[1] See the Wikipedia article, "William Dean Howells"

can be divided into different categories, but these categories often overlap, and it's often difficult to tell which category a particular phenomenon belongs to.

Bill's situation resembles that of a soldier who anticipates death, and then dies—for example, the Civil War soldier, Sullivan Ballou, whose letter to his wife figures prominently in Ken Burns' documentary on the Civil War. In this letter, Ballou anticipates death:

> O Sarah! If the dead can come back to this earth and flit unseen around those they loved, I shall always be near you; in the garish day and in the darkest night—amidst your happiest scenes and gloomiest hours—always, always; and if there be a soft breeze upon your cheek, it shall be my breath; or the cool air fans your throbbing temple, it shall be my spirit passing by. Sarah, do not mourn me dead; think I am gone and wait for thee, for we shall meet again.

Ballou died a few days after this letter was written. How did Ballou know that he would die soon? Is this a case of precognition, or is it a case of negative thinking bringing about a negative result?

Much of *White Fang* is about animals (especially wolves and dogs), much of it tries to get inside the head of an animal. Chapter 7, for example, tries to see the world as a wolf cub sees it. Through some sort of telepathy or intuition, the cub senses trouble:

> As he lay there, suddenly there came to him a feeling as of something terrible impending. The unknown with all its terrors rushed upon him, and he shrank back instinctively into the shelter of the bush. As he did so, a draught of air fanned him, and a large, winged body swept ominously and silently past. A hawk, driving down out of the blue, had barely missed him.

London's animals often use their intuition, their sixth sense; London's interest in the occult intersects with his interest in animals. In the following passage, London describes White Fang's attitude toward a man named Beauty Smith:

> He did not like the man. The feel of him was bad. He sensed the evil in him, and feared the extended hand and the attempts at soft-spoken speech.... From the man's distorted body and twisted mind, in occult ways, like mists rising from malarial marshes, came emanations of the unhealth within. Not by reasoning, not by the five senses alone, but by other and remoter and uncharted senses, came the feeling to White Fang that the man was ominous with evil, pregnant with hurtfulness, and therefore a thing bad, and wisely to be hated.

In the following passage, White Fang senses that his new owner, the kindly Weedon Scott, is preparing to leave the Klondike region, and return to California:

> It was in the air. White Fang sensed the coming calamity, even before there was tangible evidence of it. In vague ways it was borne in upon him that a change was impending. He knew not how nor why, yet he

got his feel of the oncoming event from the gods themselves. In ways subtler than they knew, they betrayed their intentions to the wolf-dog that haunted the cabin-stoop, and that, though he never came inside the cabin, knew what went on inside their brains.

10. Faulkner

A. *The Sound and the Fury*

Our book group recently read William Faulkner's *The Sound and the Fury*. At first, I regretted the choice because it seemed so difficult, so obscure, but eventually I grew to like it, other people in the group liked it, and I was glad I chose it. It was the first Faulkner novel I've ever read. In the past, I tried several times to read *The Sound and the Fury*, but I never made it through the first page. Now I realize that if one makes an effort, and reads some commentary, it's a fine novel. After I finished it, I went back to page 1, and read the beginning again—something I haven't done with any of the other 60 books we've read in our group. Now I understand why this novel had a special place in Faulkner's heart, why Faulkner was in ecstasy while writing the first section—an ecstasy that he never experienced again in his literary career.

The characters are more alive than living people, the scenes more vivid than reality. One rarely finds a novel that has so much energy, so much life. The first two chapters require patience, especially on a first reading, but the last two chapters are delightful. I strongly recommend reading this novel in the Norton Critical Edition, which contains many interesting essays. But even these essays don't give a first-time reader as much help as he needs, hence I also recommend Volpe's *Reader's Guide to William Faulkner*, which holds your hand, and takes you through each page, each scene. I suggest that you alternate between text and commentary; keep going back and forth until you get the rhythm of the book, until you know the characters and the story.[1]

One of Faulkner's strengths is his ability to re-create the speech, the accent, of his characters; he catches the flavor of southern black language, the cynical tone of the cold-hearted Jason Compson, etc. Though Faulkner is sometimes described as a great humorist, equal to Mark Twain, this novel contains only a few flashes of humor. It's tragic rather than comic.

Faulkner's reputation grew slowly. The only one of Faulkner's novels that was a bestseller and a money-maker was *Sanctuary*, which he intended to be popular. Malcolm Cowley put together a book called *The Portable Faulkner*, which arranges sections of Faulkner's novels in chronological sequence; *The Portable Faulkner* made Faulkner's work more accessible, and played a key role in boosting Faulkner's reputation.

---

[1] The Internet might help; I recommend this site: mwp.olemiss.edu//dir/faulkner_william

In 1949, Faulkner received the Nobel Prize, and the speech that he delivered on that occasion was considered one of the best speeches ever delivered at a Nobel ceremony:

> Our tragedy today [Faulkner said] is a general and universal physical fear so long sustained by now that we can even bear it. There are no longer problems of the spirit. There is only the question: When will I be blown up? Because of this, the young man or woman writing today has forgotten the problems of the human heart in conflict with itself which alone can make good writing.... Until he relearns these things, he will write as though he stood among and watched the end of man. I decline to accept the end of man....

The Sound and the Fury is often read in high school English classes. Is it a good choice? Yes and no. Yes, insofar as it's one of the classics of American literature, and deservedly so. No, insofar as students can't learn to write good prose by reading slang. Yes, insofar as students would find it a difficult book to read on their own. No, insofar as it may give students the impression that classic literature is a struggle, not a pleasure.

In his *Art of the Novel*, Kundera says that Flaubert discovered everyday life. If this is true, then Faulkner may be said to be working in the tradition of Flaubert, because Faulkner depicts the everyday, depicts the minute details that make up everyday life, depicts very ordinary people doing very ordinary things. If you want discussions of the existence of God, the future of civilization, or the symphonies of Beethoven, you won't find them here. The pettiness, the absurdity that one finds in *The Sound and the Fury* reminds one of Beckett's *Waiting for Godot.*

Faulkner's characters are often at odds with each other, and sometimes at each other's throats; like all great writers, Faulkner shows us the dark side of human nature, the evil that dwells in the human heart. But Faulkner balances this with scenes of tenderness, fidelity, and virtue. In short, Faulkner explores the heights and depths of human nature. He also shows us how character has its roots in upbringing, how the children are molded by the parents.

One of Faulkner's characters, Mrs. Compson, turns against life, preaches morality, and stays in bed. Quentin, one of Mrs. Compson's sons, also loses touch with present realities, and also turns against life. Quentin is preoccupied with honor, with pride, with "fine, dead sounds," with "an ethical order based on words." Quentin's ethical order separates him from reality; as one critic wrote, "the constant references to the shadows and the mirror emphasize the barrier between Quentin and reality."[1] Quentin eventually commits suicide. Clearly, Faulkner isn't holding up Quentin as a model. Like Nietzsche, Faulkner takes a dim view of moral phrases, moral concepts.

---

1 See the essay by Olga Vickery in the Norton Critical Edition; the essay is excerpted from her book, *The Novels of William Faulkner: A Critical Interpretation.* For more on Mrs. Compson, see the section "Talking, Acting" in the Ethics chapter of my *Conversations With Great Thinkers.*

Borrowing a phrase from Kierkegaard, one can describe Quentin as a "knight of infinity"; his lofty thoughts take him away from everyday reality. Quentin has outgrown what Kierkegaard called "immediacy," but he hasn't become a "knight of faith," he hasn't achieved "immediacy after reflection."

Faulkner grew up in Mississippi, and he writes about Mississippi. He's considered part of the "Southern Renaissance." He was born in 1897, three years before the North Carolina writer, Thomas Wolfe, who is also considered part of the Southern Renaissance. Faulkner praised Wolfe for his daring and originality. On the other hand, Faulkner criticized Hemingway for his lack of daring, for his restraint and clarity. Faulkner said Hemingway "has no courage, has never climbed out on a limb... has never used a word where the reader might check his usage by a dictionary"; Hemingway didn't have the courage to risk "bad taste, over-writing, dullness, etc."[1]

My own taste is the opposite of Faulkner's: I loathe obscurity, I love E. M. Forster because he's clear, because he's devoid of "bad taste, over-writing, dullness." I love clarity, simplicity, the grand style. But if a writer has great talent, as Faulkner does, then I enjoy his work, even though he sometimes irritates me, even if his taste isn't mine.

Perhaps one reason for Faulkner's obscurity is that the most famous writer in the English-speaking world during Faulkner's formative years (James Joyce) was known for his obscurity. Faulkner admired Joyce, and when Faulkner was living in Paris, he frequented the café that Joyce frequented, but didn't muster the nerve to speak to Joyce. The young writers who grew up in Joyce's shadow (such as Faulkner) came to believe that, if a writer wanted to be taken seriously, he couldn't be lucid, he couldn't use a conventional technique. Faulkner used the stream-of-consciousness technique that Joyce had pioneered, and some passages of *The Sound and the Fury* resemble *Ulysses*. For example, this passage: "the swing the cedars the secret surges the breathing locked drinking the wild breath the yes Yes Yes yes."

While Forster's work contains a hopeful philosophy, Faulkner's *Sound and Fury* is often viewed as despairing, nihilistic. Sartre noted that Faulkner always looked back, he couldn't face the future:

> For [Faulkner], as for all of us, the future is closed. Everything we see and experience impels us to say, "This can't last." And yet change is not even conceivable, except in the form of a cataclysm. We are living in a time of impossible revolutions, and Faulkner uses his extraordinary art to describe our suffocation and a world dying of old age.[2]

Faulkner's world has a past, but no future; Faulkner felt that the American South was "dead, killed by the Civil War." One of his characters says, "*Fui. Non sum.* [I was. I am not.]" Faulkner views the world in the past tense.

---

1 Faulkner made these remarks in question-and-answer sessions with English classes at the University of Mississippi, April, 1947. Hemingway was offended, and Faulkner apologized.

2 See the Sartre essay in the Norton Critical Edition.

Faulkner's generation lived during a time of world war and genocide; religious and moral systems were tottering, and no replacements were at hand. Thus, it isn't surprising that this generation couldn't face the future, that their worldview was one of despair. A discussion of despair in modern fiction would be incomplete without mentioning Kafka, the most pessimistic and despairing of all modern writers. Is despair the dominant note of modern literature? Will the writers of our time be able to overcome despair, and face the future with a positive attitude?

B. "All the Dead Pilots"

The local Great Books group recently read a Faulkner story called "All the Dead Pilots." I didn't like it much at first reading—it was puzzling, obscure. But I read some commentary that I found on the Internet, then went back to the story, and liked it more. Faulkner is often difficult at first reading. Perhaps the example of Joyce's *Ulysses* made him think that great literature was obscure, that a serious writer shouldn't be clear.

In 1929, the well-known English writer Arnold Bennett heard some buzz about the young Faulkner, read *The Sound and The Fury*, and said that Faulkner had "great and original talent," but that, influenced by Joyce, Faulkner was "exasperatingly, unimaginably difficult to read. He seems to take malicious pleasure in mystifying the reader."[1] Bennett later read Faulkner's first novel, *Soldiers' Pay*, and said,

> Faulkner is the coming man. He has an inexhaustible invention, powerful imagination, a wondrous gift of characterization, a finished skill in dialogue; and he writes, generally, like an angel. None of the arrived American stars can surpass him in style when he is at his best.... He has in him the elements of real greatness.

But Bennett complained that, while not as obscure as *The Sound and The Fury*, *Soldiers' Pay* was still

> difficult to read.... To read it demands an effort.... There is no excuse for this. The great masters are not difficult to read.... A novel ought to be easy to read; it ought to please immediately. But too many young novelists seem to be actuated by a determination not to please.

Bennett said that Faulkner was little appreciated in his own country. Bennett said that Dreiser was also little appreciated in the U.S. until Bennett's review of *Sister Carrie* appeared in the U.S. In 1945, all of Faulkner's

---

1 See *William Faulkner: The Critical Heritage*, edited by John Bassett, published by Routledge. See also *A Reader's Guide to William Faulkner: The Short Stories*, by Edmond Loris Volpe, and *Reading Faulkner: Glossary and Commentary: Collected stories*, by Theresa M. Towner and James B. Carother. There's an excellent short biography of Faulkner in *Critical Companion to William Faulkner: A Literary Reference to His Life and Work*, by A. Nicholas Fargnoli, Robert W. Hamblin, and Michael Golay (previously published as *William Faulkner A to Z*).

17 books were out of print in the U.S. except *Sanctuary*. In France, however, Faulkner was highly regarded. Writers are sometimes appreciated more in foreign countries than in their own countries. Schopenhauer, for example, was first appreciated in England, and Nietzsche was first appreciated in Denmark and other foreign countries.

"All the Dead Pilots" is about World War I pilots. Faulkner himself served in the Canadian Air Force during World War I, and he often wrote about this experience, especially in his early years ("All the Dead Pilots" was written in 1931, when Faulkner was 34). "All the Dead Pilots" has the pessimistic worldview that is characteristic of Faulkner. As one critic wrote,

> Faulkner's conspicuous melancholy seems to have been contributed to by two wars—not only the first World War, but the American Civil War [perhaps we should speak of "Faulkner's double melancholy"]. His disillusionment was indicated in his first novel, *Soldiers' Pay*, with its ghastly portrait of the disfigured flier's return and his frivolous sweetheart's revulsion and infidelity. Intensification of melancholy by World War experiences may be traced also in a short story, "Ad Astra." Herein the concept attributed by Hemingway to Gertrude Stein—"You are all a lost generation"—recurs in a still more somber form; Faulkner's character remarks, "All this generation which fought in the war are dead tonight. But we do not yet know it."
>
> In Faulkner's novels the post-bellum South seems to stand like Lot's wife, petrified in a morbid backward glance at the holocaust consuming a damned people.[1]

In Faulkner's view, there's no glory in war, or only a fleeting glory. In the story's concluding paragraph, Faulkner writes,

> The courage, the recklessness, call it what you will, is the flash, the instant of sublimation; then flick! the old darkness again.... It can be preserved and prolonged only on paper: a picture, a few written words that any match... can obliterate in an instant. A one-inch sliver of sulphur-tipped wood is longer than memory or grief.

So much for the immortality of literature.

According to the traditional view, war is glorious because it affords an opportunity to display courage. But Faulkner doesn't believe in courage: "No man deserves praise for courage or opprobrium for cowardice, since there are situations in which any man will show either of them."

"Faulkner" is a Scottish name meaning falconer; Faulkner's family may have been Scots-Irish.

11. Hemingway

---

1 "Faulkner and the South," by Warren Beck, *The Antioch Review*, Vol. 1, No. 1 (Spring, 1941), pp. 82-94

A. "Fathers and Sons"

I read a Hemingway story called "Fathers and Sons." Good stuff. The central character, Nick Adams (a recurring character in Hemingway's fiction), remembers his late father, while his son sits next to him, and has filial feelings for him such as he had for his father. Nick remembers his Michigan summers, his Indian girlfriend, and hunting with his father:

> His father came back to him in the fall of the year, or in the early spring when there had been jacksnipe on the prairie, or when he saw shocks of corn, or when he saw a lake, or if he ever saw a horse and buggy, or when he saw, or heard, wild geese, or in a duck blind.... His father was with him, suddenly, in deserted orchards and in new-plowed fields, in thickets, on small hills, or when going through dead grass, whenever splitting wood or hauling water, by grist mills, cider mills and dams and always with open fires.

Could even the harshest Hemingway critic say anything against this passage? Notice that phrase "the fall of the year." It may seem that "of the year" is superfluous, and "the fall" is sufficient. But "of the year" adds poetry, rhythm, and it also adds clarity. This is literature of a high order.

Hemingway is writing about what Proust called the "intermittences of the heart." You start to recover from your grief, and then suddenly something recalls the deceased, and your grief returns; your grief is intermittent. These intermittences are so important in Proust's work that he thought of calling his novel *The Intermittences of the Heart*.

Hemingway was an excellent athlete. Near the end of his life, his Idaho neighbors were much impressed with his shooting ability. Perhaps his talent for shooting fed his passion for shooting. Aren't we fond of the things we're good at? Hemingway's athletic ability reminds me of Shakespeare, as does his thirst for travel and adventure, his preoccupation with war and violence, his multiple marriages/affairs, etc.

B. "A Clean, Well-Lighted Place"

I also read one of Hemingway's most famous stories, "A Clean, Well-Lighted Place." Set in Spain, it's about a lonely, perhaps suicidal old man drinking brandy at a café. "It was late and every one had left the café except an old man who sat in the shadow the leaves of the tree made against the electric light." Two waiters talk about the old man, and about whether to close the café and go home.

Perhaps the real protagonist of the story is the feeling of nothingness that comes at 2 in the morning. "What did he fear? It was not fear or dread. It was a nothing that he knew too well. It was all a nothing and a man was nothing too. It was only that and light was all it needed and a certain cleanness and order." Unlike the younger waiter, the older waiter sympathizes with the old man because he too feels the chill of nothingness, he too dreads the dark and the solitude, he too wants a "clean, well-lighted place" as a bulwark against nothing.

Why this preoccupation with nothing? Is it because Hemingway's was a lost generation—nothing to believe in? Is nihilism at the core of this story? Is this story an epitome of the nihilism of the lost generation?

> "Last week he tried to commit suicide," one waiter said.
> "Why?"
> "He was in despair."
> "What about?"
> "Nothing."

Like the old man, Hemingway himself later tried to commit suicide, and was prevented. Soon after being prevented, Hemingway did commit suicide, like his father before him. Does this story anticipate Hemingway's own end? If someone asks us, "what prompted Hemingway to commit suicide?" should we answer, "nothing"?

Students of Kundera may feel that Hemingway's nothingness (*nada*) resembles Kundera's "unbearable lightness of being." Maybe I'm stupid, like the younger waiter in the story, or maybe I don't stay up late enough, but I don't feel this nothingness, I don't feel the "unbearable lightness of being." Zen thrives on nothing, it flourishes in the void, it loves emptiness. In this *nada*, Zen finds its *todo*.

Joyce was a big fan of this story. I'm starting to like it, though I didn't like it much at first. It was apparently the inspiration for a Hopper painting, *Nighthawks*.

C. "The Snows of Kilimanjaro"

This is one of Hemingway's most famous short stories. The setting is an African safari, like the one Hemingway himself took in 1933. It's a pleasant read, with lively scenes of Africa, and of places where Hemingway lived previously. The protagonist ("Harry") is an aging writer who is dissatisfied with himself, his life, his writing, and his wife. His decision to go on safari was prompted by a feeling that he had grown lazy and comfortable. Harry takes a no-frills safari in order to regain his youthful vigor and "work the fat off his soul." But while on safari, he cut himself on a thorn, his leg has gangrene, and his life is in danger—just as Hemingway himself became seriously ill on his safari.

When I read "Kilimanjaro," I thought it was written in the Fifties; Harry seems like Hemingway at 55. I thought that, in "Kilimanjaro," Hemingway was looking back on his three failed marriages. I was surprised to learn that "Kilimanjaro" was written in 1936, when Hemingway was only 37. Was Hemingway foreseeing his future? Hemingway matured quickly, and aged quickly. Harry's feelings are doubtless Hemingway's own:

> He had had his life and it was over and then he went on living it again with different people and more money, with the best of the same places, and some new ones.... I'm getting as bored with dying as with everything else, he thought. "It's a bore," he said out loud. "What is, my dear?" "Anything you do too bloody long."

I'm reminded of Beckett's grim comment about the world: "It has gone on long enough." I'm also reminded of Sartre's argument that Faulkner was a "lost man" because he couldn't look to the future, he could only look back: "*Fui. Non sum* [I was, I am not]." Perhaps we should classify Hemingway, Faulkner, and Beckett as members of "The Lost Generation." According to Wikipedia, Harry (the protagonist of "Kilimanjaro"), lives "only for the moment, with no regard to the future."

When it first appeared, "Kilimanjaro" mentioned Fitzgerald in a derogatory way. It described Fitzgerald as a "wrecked" man, and Harry is "contemptuous of those who wrecked." Naturally Fitzgerald was offended. Fitzgerald published a piece about his own problems ("The Crack-Up"), but he didn't want other writers writing about his problems. Fitzgerald objected to Maxwell Perkins (Perkins was Hemingway's editor and also Fitzgerald's editor) and to Hemingway himself:

> Dear Ernest:
>
> Please lay off me in print. If I choose to write *de profundis* sometimes it doesn't mean I want friends praying aloud over my corpse. No doubt you meant it kindly but it cost me a night's sleep. And when you incorporate it in a book would you mind cutting my name? It's a fine story—one of your best—even though the "Poor Scott Fitzgerald etc." rather spoiled it for me.
>
> Ever Your Friend
> Scott

In later printings, Fitzgerald's name was replaced by the name Julian (Julian English was the protagonist of John O'Hara's *Appointment in Samarra*; Julian drinks too much, ruins his life, and finally commits suicide).

Hemingway also finds time to throw a stone at Malcolm Cowley, describing him as an "American poet with... a stupid look on his potato face." Hemingway's quarrels with fellow writers are legendary.

"Kilimanjaro" contains many cutting remarks about Harry's wife (Hemingway's wife?): she's a "rich bitch," Harry doesn't really love her, Harry doesn't mind dying "except that he would rather be in better company." Should we praise Hemingway for being brutally honest, or criticize him for being brutally tasteless? How did Hemingway's wife feel about this story? During the safari and the writing of "Kilimanjaro," Hemingway was married to his second wife, Pauline Pfeiffer, but this marriage disintegrated soon afterwards.

Wikipedia says this about Hemingway's early novel, *The Torrents of Spring*:

> The hero of this novel suffers from impotence, while the hero of *The Sun Also Rises* suffered from an undescribed war wound that prevented intercourse. Many of Hemingway's short stories from this period (such as "God Rest Ye Merry Gentlemen") also treat themes of sexual dysfunction.

In "Kilimanjaro," Hemingway seems to say that this problem diminished with the passing of time:

> It was strange that when he did not love her at all and was lying, that he should be able to give her more for her money than when he had really loved.... He had sold vitality, in one form or another, all his life and when your affections are not too involved you give much better value for the money.... He had chosen to make his living with something else instead of a pen or a pencil.

As the ailing Harry lies in his cot, vultures and hyenas closing in, he thinks he's going to die, and he recalls incidents from his past life that he hasn't yet written about. He recalls his early days in Paris at the Place Contrescarpe:

> In that poverty, and in that quarter across the street from a Boucherie Chevaline and a wine cooperative he had written the start of all he was to do. There never was another part of Paris that he loved like that, the sprawling trees, the old white plastered houses painted brown below, the long green of the autobus in that round square, the purple flower dye upon the paving, the sudden drop down the hill of the rue Cardinal Lemoine to the River, and the other way the narrow crowded world of the rue Mouffetard.... There were only two rooms in the apartments where they lived and he had a room on the top floor of that hotel that cost him sixty francs a month where he did his writing, and from it he could see the roofs and chimney pots and all the hills of Paris.

Harry/Hemingway also recalls winters in the Austrian Alps, and ski runs:

> As you ran down the last stretch to the steep drop, taking it straight, then running the orchard in three turns and out across the ditch and onto the icy road behind the inn. Knocking your bindings loose, kicking the skis free and leaning them up against the wooden wall of the inn, the lamplight coming from the window, where inside, in the smoky, new-wine smelling warmth, they were playing the accordion.

Perhaps the high point of the story is Harry's dream of flying to a Nairobi hospital. He's in a tiny plane, piloted by "old Compton":

> Compie turned his head and grinned and pointed and there, ahead, all he could see, as wide as all the world, great, high, and unbelievably white in the sun, was the square top of Kilimanjaro.

Hemingway's description is so good that one is convinced that Hemingway saw that himself. As you read it, you feel that you're seeing it. And when you're done, you want to go there, and see Kilimanjaro for yourself.

Hemingway wrote another safari story, "The Short Happy Life of Francis Macomber." It's a fine story, at least as good as "Kilimanjaro". If you like stories in which the protagonist changes, "Macomber" is for you. On the other hand, if you dislike violent hunting scenes, you may want to avoid "Macomber."

"Macomber" deals with overcoming fear, the sudden death of fear. Hemingway suggests that he witnessed the death of fear when he was a soldier. In an earlier issue, I described a woman's experiences "Alone in the Mountains"—how she was terrified initially, but later her terror disappeared, suddenly and completely.[1]

D. Brooks and Warren on Hemingway

The best Hemingway criticism that I've found is an essay by Cleanth Brooks and Robert Penn Warren in their textbook *Understanding Fiction*. The essay focuses on "The Killers," one of Hemingway's best-known stories, but it also comments on Hemingway in general.

One of the themes of "The Killers" is inaction. As Wyndham Lewis said, the Hemingway hero isn't a person who acts, but rather a person "things are done to." As we saw earlier, Sartre argued that Faulkner and Proust created a world with no future; "Proust's heroes never undertake anything." For the Lost Generation of Hemingway, Faulkner, and Proust, the world wasn't pregnant with possibilities, but rather "dying of old age."

Brooks and Warren argue that "The Killers" is "about the discovery of evil. The theme [is] the Hamlet theme." According to Brooks and Warren, young Nick Adams is the focus of "The Killers," and Nick is changed by the events of the story. The gangsters follow the gangster code. They're bored with the laymen who aren't initiated into the gangster code. Nick is shocked to find that the gangster movie has suddenly become reality. He's even more shocked to find that the gangsters' intended victim, Ole Andreson, accepts the gangster code, and doesn't even try to overturn the gangsters' plans.

According to Brooks and Warren, the boarding-house manager, Mrs. Bell, is introduced as a contrast to the gangsters' world: "She is the world of normality, which is shocking now from the very fact that it continues to flow on in its usual course."

Turning to Hemingway's other works, Brooks and Warren write:

> The situations and characters which interest Hemingway [are] usually violent ones: the hard-drinking and sexually promiscuous world of *The Sun Also Rises*; the chaotic and brutal world of war as in *A Farewell to Arms*, *For Whom the Bell Tolls*, or "A Way You'll Never Be"; the dangerous and exciting world of the bull ring or the prize ring as in *The Sun Also Rises*, *Death in the Afternoon*, "The Undefeated," "Fifty Grand"; the world of crime, as in "The Killers," *To Have and Have Not*, or "The Gambler, the Nun, and the Radio." Hemingway's typical characters are usually tough men, experienced in the hard worlds they inhabit, and apparently insensitive.... They are, also, usually defeated

---

[1] See ljhammond.com/phlit/2004-03.htm#9

> men. Out of their practical defeat, however, they have managed to salvage something.... They have maintained... an ideal of themselves, formulated or unformulated, by which they have lived.[1]

Hemingway's world is "violent and meaningless" but his characters

> make one gallant effort to redeem the incoherence and meaninglessness of this world: they attempt to impose some form upon the disorder of their lives, the technique of the bullfighter or sportsman, the discipline of the soldier, the code of the gangster.

Brooks and Warren are doubtless correct: Hemingway has a certain admiration for the disciplined soldier, the skilled bullfighter, etc. Doesn't Hemingway also have a certain admiration for animals? For example, the wounded lion in "Kilimanjaro" who charges the hunters with his dying breath, and keeps charging as he's being shot, or the fighting cocks mentioned in *The Old Man and the Sea*, who fight after one eye is destroyed, and keep fighting even after both eyes are destroyed. Surely these animals deserve mention when Brooks and Warren discuss "the gallantry of defeat."

Let's accept the Brooks-Warren argument that Hemingway admires those who "impose some form upon the disorder of their lives." Now let's ask, where did this worldview come from? Did Hemingway get this worldview from experience, from life itself? Or did Hemingway acquire this worldview from books, from a favorite author?

One of his favorite authors was Conrad. Perhaps the adventurous quality in Hemingway's life was inspired by Conrad; perhaps Conrad was an inspiration for Hemingway's life as well as his writing. At any rate, Conrad's heroes seem to follow a code, just as Hemingway's do. Conrad's heroes follow the code of the seaman in the face of danger. In *Heart of Darkness*, Conrad mentions a seaman named Towser who writes a sailing manual with "a singleness of intention, an honest concern for the right way of going to work." For Conrad and Hemingway, a code of behavior provides focus, concentration, "singleness of intention," a way of imposing form on the chaos of experience. It seems likely that Hemingway acquired his worldview from Conrad, and then found this worldview verified by experience.[2]

Some of Conrad's heroes exemplify "the gallantry of defeat"—such as Captain Beard in "Youth." So this is another Hemingway theme that may be derived from Conrad.

Brooks and Warren note that the Hemingway hero, in addition to being "tough and apparently insensitive," is also "simple." Here again, the parallel with Conrad is striking. Conrad describes Captain Beard as "immense in the singleness of his idea."

Let's assume I'm right, let's assume Hemingway was profoundly influenced by Conrad. Should this make us think less of Hemingway? Not at all,

---

[1] One thinks of Santiago (in *The Old Man and the Sea*) who is defeated, but salvages something, upholds his ideal, the fisherman's ideal.

[2] In another issue (ljhammond.com/phlit/2012-04.htm#19), I discussed Kipling's influence on Hemingway.

just as evidence of Shakespeare's influence on Twain doesn't make us think less of Twain, and evidence of Homer's influence on Vergil doesn't make us think less of Vergil. If it's valuable for an individual to have a code of behavior that can give structure to his life, so too it's valuable for a young writer to have a model, a pole star, to guide his literary career.

Two points should be noted concerning The Hemingway Code. First, it runs counter to what we might expect, since we might expect authors to frown on those who follow rules, conventions, rather than natural feelings. Doesn't Tolstoy frown on Alexey Karenina because he lives by social convention? Second, if we depict people living by a code, it leaves little room for unconscious motivation, shadow impulses, which many writers are preoccupied with. Ahab, for example, is driven by a shadow impulse, not by a sea-captain code. If Hemingway depicts people who live by a code, a Hemingway critic can argue that his psychology is somewhat flat. According to Brooks and Warren, Hemingway "rarely indulges in any psychological analysis, and is rarely concerned with the detailed development of a character."

According to Brooks and Warren, one of Hemingway's characteristics is "a little streak of poetry or pathos" in a world that seems violent and insensitive. Though Hemingway's heroes follow a strict code, their spontaneous feelings aren't completely dead, and they occasionally express these feelings with "ironic understatement." For example, the guide in "Macomber," Robert Wilson, is a tough character who follows the hunting code, but at the end of the story, he says he was beginning to like Macomber, and he's "a little angry" at his murder. "Just as there is a margin of victory in the defeat of the Hemingway characters," write Brooks and Warren, "so there is a little margin of sensibility in their brutal and violent world."

"The typical character," write Brooks and Warren, "is sensitive, but his sensitivity is never insisted upon; he may be worthy of pity, but he never demands it. [When I read this, I thought of Santiago in *Old Man and the Sea.*] The underlying attitude in Hemingway's work may be stated like this: pity is only valid when it is wrung from a man who has been seasoned by experience, and is only earned by a man who never demands it, a man who takes his chances."

Let's look at a Hemingway story called "In Another Country." It's a simple, touching portrait of human suffering, set in Milan in the last year of World War I. At the end of the story, we find that 'streak of poetry or pathos' that (according to Brooks and Warren) is characteristic of Hemingway. The major is suffering, but doesn't demand pity. He keeps his dignity, like other Hemingway heroes, and carries himself "straight and soldierly."

While many of Hemingway's heroes follow a code, some of his characters, like young Nick Adams, haven't yet been initiated into a code. According to Brooks and Warren, there are two types of Hemingway character: the hard-bitten initiated, and the young un-initiated. In "The Killers," Nick is the un-initiated, while the other characters, with the possible exception of Mrs. Bell, have all adopted some sort of code.

Turning to Hemingway's style, our authors say

> there is an obvious relation between this style and the characters and situations with which the author is concerned: unsophisticated characters and simple, fundamental situations are rendered in an uncomplicated style.

Our authors proceed to connect Hemingway's style with his metaphysics, his view of the universe:

> The short simple rhythms, the succession of co-ordinate clauses, and the general lack of subordination—all suggest a dislocated and ununified world. Hemingway is apparently trying to suggest in his style the direct experience—things as seen and felt, one after another, and not as the mind arranges and analyzes them.... It is as though he should say: despite the application of the human intellect to the problems of the world, the world is still a disorderly and brutal mess, in which it is hard to find any sure scale of values; therefore, it is well for one to remember the demands of fundamental situations—those involving sex, love, danger, and death, in which the instinctive life is foremost—which are frequently glossed over or falsified by social conventions or sterile intellectuality, and to remember the simple virtues of courage, honesty, fidelity, discipline.

Brooks and Warren conclude their essay thus:

> The various (and often quite different) stories done by a good writer always have some fundamental unifying attitudes—for a man can be only himself.... A good writer does not offer us, for instance, a glittering variety of themes. He probably treats, over and over, those few themes that seem to him most important in his actual living and observation of life.

E. *The Old Man and the Sea*

Carlos Baker, the prominent Hemingway critic, finds many parallels between *Old Man* and Conrad's story "Youth." Hemingway must have drawn on Conrad's work, must have used it as a model. We know that Hemingway was an admirer of Conrad, and read him assiduously.

Santiago, the protagonist of *Old Man and the Sea*, is a blend of Conrad's characters, Marlow and Beard. As Santiago remembers his youthful vision of lions on an African beach, so Marlow remembers his youthful vision of natives on a Java dock. As Santiago is distinguished by his eyes ("Everything about him was old except his eyes and they were the same color as the sea and were cheerful and undefeated"), so Beard is distinguished by his eyes ("He had blue eyes in that old face of his, which were amazingly like a boy's, with that candid expression some quite common men preserve to the end of their days by a rare internal gift of simplicity of heart and rectitude of soul"). Santiago's heroic determination is captured in the motto of Conrad's ship: Do or Die. But despite his determination and skill, Santiago is overcome (like Beard) by the forces of nature: the gallantry of defeat.

In an earlier issue, we discussed Faulkner's character, Dilsey, whose attitude is "whatever happens must be met with courage and dignity in which there is no room for passivity or pessimism."[1] One might compare Hemingway's Santiago with Faulkner's Dilsey; they both keep going. Virtue is persistent, it's always beginning (*semper incipere*, to use Luther's phrase).

> "I told the boy I was a strange old man [Santiago says]. Now is when I must prove it." The thousand times that he had proved it meant nothing. Now he was proving it again. Each time was a new time and he never thought about the past when he was doing it.

A passage in *Old Man* reminded me of an idea that we've discussed in many previous issues, von Franz's idea of *frevel*.[2] Here's the passage:

> When he and the boy fished together they usually spoke only when it was necessary.... It was considered a virtue not to talk unnecessarily at sea and the old man had always considered it so and respected it.

Santiago is respectful—respectful of the sea, of nature. He's not a *freveler*.

Von Franz relates a Swiss folk tale about a herdsman who doesn't respect the numen of the mountains, a herdsman who exemplifies *frevel*.[3] When the herdsman hears a voice in the mountains saying "Shall I let it go?" he answers back, rather impudently, "Oh, you can hold it still longer!" This is repeated the next day, and then the voice says, "I can't hold it any longer!" and the mountain collapses, killing the herdsman. While Santiago has a pious respect for the numen, the divine power, of the sea, the herdsman is somewhat impious and disrespectful, he's a *freveler*. Carlos Baker noticed that piety is one of Santiago's salient traits: "Santiago is evidently a pious old man. The piety appears unobtrusively in his constant, accepted, and unquestioning awareness of supernal power."[4]

Let's assume I'm right, let's assume that Santiago is pious and serious and devoid of *frevel*. Can we extend this view to all of Hemingway's heroes? Do all of Hemingway's heroes follow a code that keeps them within certain boundaries, keeps them away from *frevel*? Does von Franz's idea throw light on Hemingway's work? If *frevel* is a common path to evil, as von Franz argues, then is Hemingway right to recommend a code that keeps us on "the straight and narrow," keeps us away from *frevel*?

Von Franz says that the word "*frevel*" is now usually used in connection with hunting; one who violates the hunting code is guilty of *jagdfrevel*. Examples of *jagdfrevel* are "shooting pregnant deer or hunting in the closed season... or shooting badly and wounding without killing, and then not bothering about the wounded animal afterwards." This is the very situation that

---

1 See the section called "Talking, Acting" in the Ethics chapter of my *Conversations With Great Thinkers*.

2 For more on *frevel*, see the section on *Frevel* in the Psychology chapter of my *Conversations With Great Thinkers*.

3 *Shadow and Evil in Fairytales*, part 2, ch. 2, p. 143

4 *Hemingway: The Writer as Artist*, ch. 12

arises in "Macomber": the guide insists on going after the wounded animal, dangerous as this may be. The guide follows the hunting code, and doesn't commit *jagdfrevel*. The Hemingway hero is not a *freveler*.

F. "Fifty Grand"

"Fifty Grand" features a boxer who is a typical Hemingway hero: aging, experienced, understated, able to master intense pain and keep going. His opponent is a younger boxer who appeals to the crowd, who seeks "popularity," whose motto is "Be yourself," who can't master pain but instead "rolled [on the ground] and twisted around," who lacks grace under pressure.

The hero seems cynical, seems to care about nothing but money. But he has his pride, his code of honor: "He wanted to finish it off right to please himself. He didn't want to be knocked out." The hero says, "I think I can last. I don't want this bohunk to stop me." His motto seems to be "Control yourself," rather than "Be yourself."

His code of honor isn't a traditional moral code, so he doesn't scruple to bet against himself, to "fix" the fight. He's a loser; he loses the fight on a foul, and even without the foul he would have lost. But he wins a subtle kind of victory by maintaining his self-respect, keeping the code, mastering his pain, not being knocked out.

"Fifty Grand" was published in *The Atlantic* in 1927, then in a short-story collection called *Men Without Women*. Joseph Wood Krutch described the collection as "sordid little catastrophes" involving "very vulgar people." There is something sordid in "Fifty Grand," but it also has something heroic. And Hemingway is certainly a master of the language of vulgar people; every word has truth and weight.

When Hemingway was in high school, he was tall and somewhat uncoordinated, he wasn't very good at baseball, football, etc. But he liked boxing, and became somewhat proficient at it. When he lived in Cuba, he offered $250 to anyone who could stay in the ring with him for three minutes. He also refereed youth boxing.[1]

G. "A Way You'll Never Be"

Hemingway is often called an innovator, and this may be partly true. But he can also be viewed as a follower, a follower of Joyce and other moderns.

"A Way You'll Never Be" is a story that Hemingway published in 1933. It's an autobiographical story, a story drawn from Hemingway's WorldWarOne experience; Hemingway was on the Italian side when Italy was fighting Austria.

Hemingway dwells on the harsh realities of war. He speaks of "rape in which the woman's skirts are pulled over her head to smother her, one comrade sometimes sitting upon the head." Hemingway says of helmets,

---

[1] See the Burns/Novick documentary on Hemingway. And see Wikipedia, "Fifty Grand."

"They're absolutely no damned good.... I remember when they were a comfort when we first had them, but I've seen them full of brains too many times."

Before he turned 19, Hemingway was wounded in the head, legs, etc. The protagonist of "A Way You'll Never Be," Nick Adams, has an assortment of wounds. Nick says, "If you are interested in scars I can show you some very interesting ones." Hemingway describes how Nick struggles with the effects of his wounds and his traumas. Nick has bad dreams, he can't sleep without a light on, etc.

On the day described in the story, Nick lies down, and his mind wanders; he thinks of a dancing girl in Paris. Hemingway uses the stream-of-consciousness technique that Joyce popularized:

> And there was Gaby Delys, oddly enough, with feathers on; you called me baby doll a year ago tadada you said that I was rather nice to know tadada with feathers on, with feathers off, the great Gaby, and my name's Harry Pilcer, too, we used to step out of the far side of the taxis when it got steep going up the hill and he could see that hill every night when he dreamed with Sacré Coeur, blown white, like a soap bubble.[1]

In the past, writers usually aimed at clarity, but Hemingway seems to aim at obscurity. After Joyce, it seemed that obscurity was a virtue, a characteristic of serious writers.

"A Way You'll Never Be" has little action, little plot; this is baffling to young readers, but it impresses sophisticated critics. One might say that Hemingway doesn't try to give pleasure to the reader; this is characteristic of modern artists—painters as well as writers.

In an earlier issue, I discussed Arnold Bennett's response to Faulkner. Bennett said that Faulkner is "difficult to read.... There is no excuse for this.... Too many young novelists seem to be actuated by a determination not to please." Despite these objections, Bennett was a fan of Faulkner, and I think it's possible to be a fan of Hemingway despite his occasional obscurity, despite his "determination not to please."

H. "The Gambler, the Nun, and the Radio"

This story deals with a question that has been present in literature since ancient times, but acquired a new urgency in Hemingway's time: What does it all mean? Does life have any meaning or value? Or is it just a long sequence of the sun rising, and the sun setting?

The story was published in 1933. The setting is a Montana hospital. "The story 'evidently grew out of Hemingway's hospitalization in Billings, Montana, following an automobile accident in November 1930.'"[2] The protagonist, Frazer, is a writer who seems to represent Hemingway.

---

[1] Nick steps out of "the far side," the side away from the driver, because he wants to get away without paying. He hopes they won't see that driver again, and he has a "fear that they might take the same driver twice."

[2] Edward Stone p. 378, quoting Carlos Baker

Frazer may feel the hopelessness of The Depression, but he isn't hopeful about revolution, he isn't captivated by Communism or Fascism. Revolution is ecstasy, Frazer thinks, but it can't last, it can't fill up the 24 hours of the day, it "can only be prolonged by tyranny."

Frazer is weary of life. "Mr. Frazer had been through all this before." But Frazer finds some relief in a radio, turned very low, which he listens to all night. "Living... requires the aid of opiates."[1] The story depicts several kinds of opiate: Liquor, gambling, music, religion, radio, etc.

In *A Farewell to Arms*, Hemingway wrote, "Always another day starting and then another night."[2] This attitude was widespread in Hemingway's time. Fitzgerald wrote in *The Crack-Up*, "No choice, no road, no hope—only the endless repetition of the sordid and the semi-tragic."[3] Beckett said of the world, "It has gone on long enough."

Edward Stone argues that even one of Hemingway's upbeat stories like "Big Two-Hearted River" can be viewed in terms of the "*nada*-concept."[4] *Nada*, nothing, meaninglessness. There's a certain nihilism in Hemingway's world even when the sun is shining and the fish are biting. Hemingway's generation struggled to find meaning/value. It's easier for our generation to find meaning/value because we start with lower expectations, we start from zero, we start from Hemingway's *nada*. Every sunrise is a bonus.

In "The Gambler, the Nun, and the Radio," Cayetano Ruiz, the gambler, has some traits of the Hemingway hero. He endures intense pain in silence, he controls himself. He becomes paralyzed in one leg but still has laughing eyes.

12. John O'Hara

I became acquainted with an American fiction writer, John O'Hara. He was born in 1905, six years after Hemingway. Like Hemingway, O'Hara was known initially for his short stories, and like Hemingway, he was a well-known writer by age 30. His first novel, *Appointment in Samarra*, is his most highly-regarded. Hemingway wrote, "If you want to read a book by a man who knows exactly what he is writing about and has written it marvelously well, read *Appointment in Samarra*."[5]

O'Hara grew up in Pottsville, Pennsylvania. His family was probably upper-middle-class. He attended boarding school, but when his father died,

---

"Hemingway's Mr. Frazer: From Revolution to Radio," by Edward Stone, *Journal of Modern Literature*, March, 1971, Vol. 1, No. 3, pp. 375-388

1 Stone, p. 386

2 Quoted in Stone, p. 382

3 Quoted in Stone, p. 381

4 Stone p. 380, quoting Carlos Baker. The *nada*-concept is discussed in Hemingway's "Clean, Well-Lighted Place" (see above).

5 O'Hara became interested in the Samarra legend through Somerset Maugham's play *Sheppey*.

O'Hara couldn't afford to attend college (his goal had been to attend Yale). This seems to have left him with a deep sense of social inferiority. Hemingway said, "Someone should take up a collection to send John O'Hara to Yale." Issues of class loom large in O'Hara's writings. O'Hara was often described as a bitter, difficult person. In some towns, his fiction was banned because of its sexual content. In Pottsville, the public library banned his works because of their acerbic remarks on locals.

O'Hara (right) with Hemingway about 1934

O'Hara hungered for prizes and glory: "I want the Nobel prize... so bad I can taste it." When Steinbeck won the Nobel Prize in 1962, O'Hara wrote him, "I can think of only one other author I'd rather see get it." Wikipedia speaks of O'Hara's "vigorous self-promotion." O'Hara wrote the epitaph for his own tombstone: "Better than anyone else, he told the truth about his time."

He published more than 200 short stories in *The New Yorker*. Many of his stories, and some of his novels, are set in Gibbsville, a fictionalized version of Pottsville. John Updike was one of O'Hara's fans; Updike compared him to Chekhov. Several of O'Hara's works were made into films, including *BUtterfield 8* and *From the Terrace*.[1]

In addition to fiction, O'Hara wrote for newspapers. His political views were somewhat conservative; in this respect, he reminds me of Dos Passos.

13. Dos Passos

The American novelist John Dos Passos is rarely read today, but perhaps he deserves more attention. He was born in 1896, shortly before Fitzgerald, Hemingway, Faulkner, and Thomas Wolfe, and he lived until 1970, outliving those four writers. In 1936, Sartre called Dos Passos "the greatest

---

[1] I enjoyed watching *From the Terrace*, though it's somewhat sugary and silly. It deals with the Morgan bank, which I have some interest in.

writer of our time." Dos Passos was a prolific writer, producing 42 novels, as well as historical books, travel books, and a memoir. His fiction has been described as experimental, non-linear, a collage. One of his most popular novels is an early work, *Manhattan Transfer*, which deals with life in New York City. Perhaps his *magnum opus* is *U.S.A.*, a trilogy that he wrote in his thirties.

Dos Passos's father was a wealthy lawyer of Portuguese descent. Dos Passos attended a boarding school, The Choate School, toured Europe with a private tutor, then attended Harvard. During World War I, he and his friend E. E. Cummings volunteered for the Ambulance Corps, and were sent to Europe.

In the 1920s, Dos Passos strayed from his father's pro-business creed, became sympathetic to socialism, and studied socialism in Russia. In the 1930s, however, he went to Spain during the Spanish Civil War, and became an anti-communist, partly because he blamed the Soviets for murdering his friend and translator, José Robles. While he was in Spain, Dos Passos broke with Hemingway, perhaps because Hemingway didn't share his anti-communist views. In the early 1950s, Dos Passos admired the anti-communist crusader Joe McCarthy, and in the late 1950s, he wrote for the conservative *National Review*. This drift to the Right probably contributed to the decline of Dos Passos's popularity, but it wasn't the sole cause of this decline; according to Wikipedia, "there is a consensus among critics that the quality of his novels drastically declined following *U.S.A.*"

Dos Passos was a painter as well as a writer. "While Dos Passos never gained recognition as a great artist, he continued to paint throughout his lifetime and his body of work was well respected."

Though I haven't read Dos Passos, his photo on Wikipedia convinces me of his genius.

John Dos Passos

14. Sinclair Lewis

Sinclair Lewis was born in Minnesota in 1885, so he was about ten years older than Dos Passos. Lewis was the son of a doctor, and he attended Yale. In his late teens, he had spells of religious enthusiasm (religious and moral enthusiasm is often found among adolescents).

Like Dos Passos, Lewis is rarely read today, but in his time, no American writer, not even Hemingway, was more prominent or more widely read. Lewis was the first American writer to win a Nobel Prize, and his novel *Main Street* sold millions of copies; *Main Street* has been called "the most sensational event in twentieth-century American publishing history." Published in 1920, *Main Street* is "a realistic novel about small-town life." Among Lewis's other novels are *Babbitt*, *Dodsworth*, and *Arrowsmith*. Several of his novels were made into movies; *Dodsworth* is especially esteemed by film critics.

Lewis drank heavily, and died at 65.

Sinclair Lewis should not be confused with Upton Sinclair, who was born in 1878, seven years before Sinclair Lewis. When Upton Sinclair was 28, he published *The Jungle*, a novel that exposed the Chicago meat-packing industry. A champion of left-wing causes, Upton Sinclair ran for Congress on the Socialist ticket. He was interested in the occult, and he wrote a book about telepathy called *Mental Radio*. He lived to the age of 90, and wrote close to 100 books.

15. Nathanael West

I discovered an American novelist, Nathanael West. His real name was Nathan von Wallenstein Weinstein. He was born in 1903, and died in a car accident at age 37. His death may have been a "willed death," a quasi-suicide, prompted by the recent death of his friend F. Scott Fitzgerald. Like Fitzgerald, West spent part of his career in Hollywood, writing screenplays. He attended Brown University, where he was friends with the comic writer S. J. Perelman. West's writing has been described as "a sweeping rejection of political causes, religious faith, artistic redemption and romantic love." Perhaps his best-known works are the novels *Miss Lonelyhearts* (set in Manhattan) and *The Day of the Locust* (set in Hollywood); both these novels have been made into movies.

16. Jack Kerouac

I recently read Wikipedia's article on Jack Kerouac, and learned that

- He was born in 1922 in Lowell, Massachusetts, to French Canadian parents. His first language was French, and he often wrote in French.
- He was an outstanding athlete, and went to Columbia on a football scholarship (while there, he "argued constantly" with his coach).
- As a Columbia student, his literary talent caught the eye of professor Mark Van Doren.
- He read Thomas Wolfe, and was influenced by him.
- During World War II, he was discharged from the navy "on psychiatric grounds (he was of 'indifferent character' with a diagnosis of 'schizoid personality')."
- He called his writing style "Spontaneous Prose, a literary technique akin to stream of consciousness." To avoid interrupting the "stream," he made long scrolls of paper that allowed him to type for hours without a pause.
- The publication of *On the Road* in 1957 brought him instant fame. "He soon found he had little taste for celebrity status."
- From *On the Road*: "The only people for me are the mad ones, the ones who are mad to live, mad to talk, mad to be saved, desirous of everything at the same time, the ones who never yawn or say a commonplace thing, but burn, burn, burn, like fabulous yellow Roman candles exploding like spiders across the stars, and in the middle, you see the blue center-light pop, and everybody goes ahh..."
- From *On the Road*, describing a visit to Denver: "The air was soft, the stars so fine, the promise of every cobbled alley so great, that I thought I was in a dream." What poetic prose! This sentence alone guarantees Kerouac's immortality.
- He was interested in Buddhism, and was friends with Alan Watts. He wrote a biography of the Buddha (*Wake Up*).
- A heavy drinker, he died of cirrhosis of the liver in 1969, at 47, and is buried in Lowell with his third wife, Stella.

- Several documentaries have been made about Kerouac, including "Kerouac, the Movie," "Jack Kerouac: King of the Beats," and "What Happened to Kerouac?"

17. *Stoner*

I read a novel called *Stoner*, by John Williams. Highly recommended. Simple, plain, flat, like a piece of high-quality bread that has no butter or jam on it. Contains little humor or action. Readable and rather short, never dull. It feels like a memoir or biography, it feels true, and you connect with the characters as if they were real people. It deals with the basic facts of existence—love, death, marriage, enmity. One can't imagine *Stoner* being written by anyone but an American; it seems to capture the essence of a region of the U.S.—The Plains. Perhaps its chief weakness is that it doesn't achieve any spiritual victory, any mystic vision.

A kind of cult has arisen around *Stoner*. It has ardent fans, but somehow it isn't widely known. It's sometimes called "the best novel you never heard of." Here are some critical remarks on *Stoner*:

- "Something rarer than a great novel—it is a perfect novel, so well told and beautifully written, so deeply moving, it takes your breath away." (Morris Dickstein)
- "I had never encountered a work so ruthless in its devotion to human truths and so tender in its execution." (Steve Almond)
- "There is entertainment of a very high order to be found in *Stoner*, what Williams himself describes as 'an escape into reality' as well as pain and joy. The clarity of the prose is in itself an unadulterated joy." (John McGahern)

Williams' prose is a model of simplicity and clarity, so his work should be read by students.

Williams grew up in a working-class family in Texas, and became an English professor at the University of Denver. He's best known for

- *Stoner*, which he published in 1965
- *Augustus*, a novel about the Roman emperor, which he published in 1972. *Augustus* was the co-winner of the National Book Award in 1973, perhaps because the judges knew that *Stoner* should have won the award, and were making up for their earlier mistake. One critic compared *Augustus* to Robert Graves' *I, Claudius*, Hermann Broch's *Death of Virgil*, and Marguerite Yourcenar's *Memoirs of Hadrian*. Perhaps we can also compare *Augustus* to a series of novels called Masters of Rome, by the Australian writer Colleen McCullough.
- *Butcher's Crossing* (1960), which deals with Kansas in frontier times

"Critic Morris Dickstein noted that, while *Butcher's Crossing*, *Stoner*, and *Augustus* are 'strikingly different in subject,' they 'show a similar narrative arc: a young man's initiation, vicious male rivalries, subtler tensions between men and women, fathers and daughters, and finally a bleak sense of disappointment, even futility.'"[1] Williams died in 1994. He apparently wrote little in his last twenty years, though he left a novel unfinished at the time of his death.

In addition to his novels, Williams wrote two volumes of poetry, and edited an anthology called *English Renaissance Poetry.*

[Spoiler warning: If you're thinking of reading *Stoner*, you should skip the rest of this section.] The following passage has the bleak beauty that's characteristic of *Stoner*:

> They buried his father in a small plot on the outskirts of Booneville, and William returned to the farm with his mother. That night he could not sleep. He dressed and walked into the field that his father had worked year after year, to the end that he now had found. He tried to remember his father, but the face that he had known in his youth would not come to him. He knelt in the field and took a dry clod of earth in his hand. He broke it and watched the grains, dark in the moonlight, crumble and flow through his fingers. He brushed his hand on his trouser leg and got up and went back to the house. He did not sleep; he lay on the bed and looked out the single window until the dawn came, until there were no shadows upon the land, until it stretched gray and barren and infinite before him.

When Stoner becomes a grad student, he makes friends with two other grad students, Gordon Finch and Dave Masters.

> The three of them—Stoner, Masters, and Finch—got in the habit of meeting on Friday afternoons at a small saloon in downtown Columbia, drinking large schooners of beer and talking late into the night.

This passage reminded me of Joyce's remark about Stephen Dedalus: "Stephen... had told Cranly of all the tumults and unrest and longings in his soul, day after day and night by night." The early chapters of Stoner might be called *A Portrait of the English Professor As A Young Man.*

One of the high points of the novel, and of Stoner's life, is Stoner's affair with a grad student, Katherine Driscoll. Finally Stoner and Katherine separate in order to save their careers; they believe that without a career, a person is nothing. Stoner says that if he elopes with Katherine,

> I almost certainly wouldn't be able to teach, and you—you would become something else. We both would become something else, something other than ourselves. We would be—nothing.

Williams describes the end of the affair with his usual directness:

> He didn't see Katherine Driscoll again. After he left her, during the night, she got up, packed all her belongings, cartoned her books, and left word with the manager of the apartment house where to send them. She mailed the English office her grades, her instructions to dismiss her classes for the week and a half that remained of the semester, and

---

[1] See Wikipedia's article, "John Edward Williams"

> her resignation. And she was on the train, on her way out of Columbia, by two o'clock that afternoon. She must have been planning her departure for some time, Stoner realized; and he was grateful that he had not known and that she left him no final note to say what could not be said.

One might say that the theme of *Stoner* is love—love of literature as well as people. When Stoner is an undergrad, his professor (Archer Sloane) recommends that he continue his study of literature at the graduate level; Sloane realizes that Stoner has a passion for literature: "It's love, Mr. Stoner," Sloane said cheerfully. "You are in love. It's as simple as that."

As a teacher, Stoner finds it difficult to communicate his love of literature:

> From the time he had fumbled through his first classes of freshman English, he had been aware of the gulf that lay between what he felt for his subject and what he delivered in the classroom. He had hoped that time and experience would repair the gulf; but they had not done so. Those things that he held most deeply were most profoundly betrayed when he spoke of them to his classes; what was most alive withered in his words; and what moved him most became cold in its utterance.

Eventually, though, Stoner learns to express his feeling for literature in the classroom:

> The love of literature, of language, of the mystery of the mind and heart showing themselves in the minute, strange, and unexpected combinations of letters and words, in the blackest and coldest print—the love which he had hidden as if it were illicit and dangerous, he began to display, tentatively at first, and then boldly, and then proudly.

On his deathbed, Stoner reflects on his passion:

> In his youth he had given it freely, without thought; he had given it to the knowledge that had been revealed to him—how many years ago?—by Archer Sloane; he had given it to Edith, in those first blind foolish days of his courtship and marriage; and he had given it to Katherine, as if it had never been given before.... It was a passion neither of the mind nor of the flesh; rather, it was a force that comprehended them both.

18. *Fifth Business*

I read *Fifth Business*, a novel by the Canadian writer Robertson Davies. When it was published in 1970, *Fifth Business* was very popular; bookstores couldn't keep it on the shelf. It's often called Davies' best novel. It's the first novel in Davies' *Deptford Trilogy*; in the 1950s, Davies published *The Salterton Trilogy*, and in the 1980s, he published *The Cornish Trilogy*. In addition to novels, Davies wrote plays and essays.

Davies is a great storyteller and a deep thinker. There's never a dull moment in *Fifth Business*, the prose is highly readable, and the plot keeps your attention until the last page. On the debit side of the ledger, Davies has the faults of many modern writers: he often descends to the vulgar and sordid, his prose is clear but rarely arresting or moving, he's content to entertain and doesn't aspire toward the great or the noble. When the narrator of *Fifth Business*, Dunstan Ramsay, writes a book, he describes it in words that could be applied to *Fifth Business* itself:

> It was full of romance and marvels, with a quiet but sufficient undertone of eroticism and sadism, and it sold like hot-cakes.... It was a lively piece of work, and all I regretted was that I had not made a harder bargain for my share of the profit.

In an earlier issue, I noted that older writers like Agatha Christie (born 1890) have a certain dignity and courtesy.[1] Younger writers, including Davies (born 1913), take the low road to popularity. There are many examples of this in *Fifth Business*, such as the passage in which Boy Staunton is explaining to Dunstan why Dunstan can be a teacher but not a Headmaster:

> Don't you think the way you rootle in your ear with your little finger delights the boys? And the way you waggle your eyebrows—great wild things like moustaches, I don't know why you don't trim them—and those terrible Harris tweed suits you wear and never have pressed. And that disgusting trick of blowing your nose and looking into your handkerchief as if you expected to prophesy something from the mess.[2]

But while Davies is too fond of the low road, one can't deny that *Fifth Business* is filled with shrewd psychological insights. On the very first page, the young Dunstan is sledding with another youngster, Percy Boyd Staunton. He describes Percy as his "lifelong friend and enemy." I immediately thought of my own boyhood friends, who were friends one day, enemies the next. Even among adults, relationships change over time, and today's friend can be tomorrow's enemy.

Davies says that childhood traits recur later in life:

> I have never thought that traits that are strong in childhood disappear; they may go underground or they may be transmuted into something else, but they do not vanish; very often they make a vigorous appearance after the meridian of life has been passed. It is this, and not senility, that is the real second childhood.

Davies remarks on the complex, multi-faceted nature of man. When Dunstan is in the army, he reads the Bible and also entertains his comrades with dirty jokes. His comrades

---

1 ljhammond.com/phlit/2011-10.htm#9

2 One might ask, What caused the decline of courtesy and the rise of vulgarity? What happened between the AgathaChristie generation and the RobertsonDavies generation that might have caused the rise of vulgarity? This is when the aristocracy fell. I'm reminded of Pessoa's remark, "The ruin of aristocratic influence created an atmosphere of brutality."

> could hardly conceive that anybody who read the Testament could be other than a Holy Joe—could have another, seemingly completely opposite side to his character. I cannot remember a time when I did not take it as understood that everybody has at least two, if not twenty-two, sides to him.

In earlier issues, I quoted Nietzsche's remark, "The ultimate art is the art of self-love."[1] Dunstan has a friend named Liesl, who criticizes him for being too altruistic: "You are a decent chap to everybody, except one special somebody, and that is Dunstan Ramsay. How can you be really good to anybody if you are not good to yourself?"

Davies admired Jung, and he incorporates Jungian ideas into his fiction. He says, for example, that "Religion and Arabian Nights were true in the same way.... They were both psychologically rather than literally true... Psychological truth was really as important in its own way as historical verification." Davies uses Jungian terms like *mysterium coniunctionis* [synthesis of opposites]: "In a movement that reached its climax in 1924," Davies writes, "the Presbyterians and Methodists had consummated a *mysterium coniunctionis* that resulted in the United Church of Canada." Davies says, "I was myself much concerned with that old fantastical duke of dark corners, C. G. Jung."

Like Jung, Davies is conscious of the dark side, the shadow. Davies speaks of, "the Bollandist tradition of looking firmly at the shadow as well as the light." According to one critic, Davies believed that good and evil are interwoven in the striving for wholeness.[2] God is not absolutely good, nor is the devil absolutely evil. Dunstan can't achieve wholeness until he compromises with the devil. Liesl says to Dunstan, "Why don't you, just for once, do something inexplicable, irrational, at the devil's bidding, and just for the hell of it? You would be a different man."

Like Jung, Davies is receptive to the occult. "As to the reality of ghosts," Davies said, "I am not of the sceptical party."

[Spoiler Warning: If you're thinking of reading Fifth Business, you may want to skip the rest of this section.]

Dunstan's childhood friend, Percy Boyd Staunton, becomes a wealthy businessman. He gives himself a new name: Boy Staunton. Davies discusses a subject that we've often discussed in this e-zine, the death of love. Davies discusses the quarrels ("rows") between Boy and his wife, Leola:

> Rows between them seemed to be single affairs, and it was only when I looked backward that I could see that they were sharp outbreaks in a continuous campaign.... Boy needed me as someone in whose presence he could think aloud... a lot of his thinking was about the inadequacy of the wife he had chosen to share his high destiny.

---

1 See, for example, ljhammond.com/phlit/2011-08.htm#4

2 "Three Times Three: The Novels of Robertson Davies," by Edward L. Galligan, *The Sewanee Review*, Vol. 98, No. 1 (Winter, 1990), pp. 87-95

Davies discusses another subject we've often discussed in this e-zine, willed death—a person who dies because he doesn't have the will to live. Leola, Boy's wife, loses the will to live, and brings about her own death: "I have always thought it suspicious that Leola opened her windows one afternoon, when the nurse had closed them, and took a chill, and was dead in less than a week."

As the will can cause death, so it can cause life. Mrs. Dempster, Davies' saint figure, brings the narrator's brother to life when he has apparently died. Mrs. Dempster doesn't use physical means, she uses the power of will.

The novel ends with the question, Who killed Boy Staunton? One critic said that all three novels in *The Deptford Trilogy* deal with this question.[1] Davies' answer to this question:

> He was killed by the usual cabal: by himself, first of all; by the woman he knew; by the woman he did not know; by the man who granted his inmost wish; and by the inevitable fifth, who was keeper of his conscience and keeper of the stone.

This is a profound answer because it suggests that events don't have one cause, they have multiple, inter-locking causes. In earlier issues, I spoke of Mutual Arising—multiple causes arise together. Causality is a net, not a chain.

19. F. Scott Fitzgerald

A. "Some Sort of Epic Grandeur"

F. Scott Fitzgerald (Francis Scott Key Fitzgerald) was born into an upper-middle-class family in 1896. He was named after Francis Scott Key, a distant relative. His mother's family was from Ireland and had money; his father's family was from Maryland and had class. Maryland had long been associated with Catholicism; both Fitzgerald's parents were Catholic.

In the first five years of his life, Fitzgerald was the only child in the house. One Fitzgerald biographer says that his mother

> had spoiled him so badly that with other boys he showed off and bragged and belittled and was desperately unpopular.... At St. Paul Academy he was known as the freshest boy in school. "If anybody can poison Scotty or stop his mouth in some way, the school at large and myself will be obliged," a letter in the school paper observed.... [Fitzgerald wrote about] his prep school unpopularity in "The Freshest Boy" (1928), the most moving of the Basil Duke Lee stories.[2]

---

[1] "All three books hinge to some extent on the mystery of who killed Boy Staunton." ("Robertson Davies as a Modern Instance," by Douglas Paschall, *The Sewanee Review*, Vol. 87, No. 1 (Winter, 1979), pp. 180-186

[2] *Fool for Love: F. Scott Fitzgerald*, by Scott Donaldson, Ch. 1. In an earlier issue, I discussed how the genius often has an unusually close relationship

Fitzgerald spent part of his childhood in St. Paul, Minnesota, part in Buffalo, New York. He went to several Catholic schools, including "the Newman School... in Hackensack, New Jersey. At Newman, Father Sigourney Fay recognized his literary potential and encouraged him to become a writer."[1] Fitzgerald dedicated his first novel to Sigourney Fay.

---

with his mother. This close relationship has been called "Jocasta mothering"; I called my essay "The Sons of Jocasta." "As a result of Jocasta mothering," I wrote, "the boy feels swallowed by the mother's love, and has difficulty becoming independent. The boy's feeling for his mother is ambivalent—a mix of love and hate"(ljhammond.com/phlit/2020-10b.htm). This seems consistent with Fitzgerald's biography.

Donaldson shrewdly links Fitzgerald's Jocasta mothering with his unpopularity. Fitzgerald's unpopularity at school is characteristic of genius, and can be compared to Thomas Wolfe's experience at school. Wolfe writes, "Eugene's first year at the university was filled for him with loneliness, pain, and failure. Within three weeks of his matriculation, he had been made the dupe of a half-dozen classic jokes.... As he walked across the campus, he heard his name called mockingly from a dozen of the impartial windows, he heard the hidden laughter.... It seemed to him... that the best he could do would be to seek out obscurity for the next four years.... There was no one to whom he could turn: he had no friends."(*Look Homeward Angel*, Ch. 28)

This situation proved to be temporary for Wolfe, as for Fitzgerald. Wolfe eventually became involved in many activities at the University of North Carolina, and enjoyed his time there, as Fitzgerald enjoyed his time at Princeton.

Perhaps the best example of Jocasta mothering and unpopularity is Proust. As I wrote in an earlier issue, "As a student, Proust didn't fit in socially; one of his classmates later wrote, 'There was something about him which we found unpleasant. His kindnesses and tender attentions seemed mere mannerisms and poses, and we took occasion to tell him so to his face. Poor, unhappy boy, we were beastly to him.'" As he became an adult, though, Proust became increasingly social, like Fitzgerald and Wolfe.

Fitzgerald himself links his Jocasta mothering not with his unpopularity but with his poor academic record: "An indulgent mother had given him no habits of work."("The Freshest Boy")

Another characteristic of genius is timidity, which is a cause of unpopularity, and an effect of Jocasta mothering. I discussed timidity with reference to Joyce, Kipling, Ibsen, and Graham Greene.

[1] Wikipedia ==> F. Scott Fitzgerald. About a year before he died, Fitzgerald wrote his daughter, "I am not a great man, but sometimes, I think the impersonal and objective quality of my talent, and the sacrifices of it, in pieces, to preserve its essential value has some sort of epic grandeur." Matthew Bruccoli's biography of Fitzgerald is called *Some Sort of Epic Grandeur*.

Fitzgerald entered Princeton in 1913. He was "one of the few Catholics in the student body." He failed math and science classes. His favorite class was English, but he felt that his English professors didn't understand poetry. "I got in a series of scraps with them," he later told his daughter, "so that I finally dropped English altogether." Fitzgerald joined a social club, and a theater club, and he wrote lyrics for musicals.

Fitzgerald was particularly fond of football. In a story called "The Bowl," Fitzgerald wrote, "I reveled in football, as audience, amateur statistician and foiled participant—for I had played in prep school." As a freshman, he tried out for the football team, hoping to recapture his prep-school glory, but he was skinny, and didn't make the first cut.

Fitzgerald "formed close friendships with classmates Edmund Wilson and John Peale Bishop, both of whom would later aid his literary career. Determined to be a successful writer, Fitzgerald wrote stories and poems for the Princeton Triangle Club, the Princeton Tiger, and the Nassau Lit." Fitzgerald read novelists from the previous generation, such as H. G. Wells and Compton Mackenzie; both Wells and Mackenzie influenced his early work.

Fitzgerald also read Keats. He was drawn to Keats "for his richness of language.... Fitzgerald read and reread Keats, memorized passages. He wrote Keatsian poems and turned them into evocative prose for *This Side of Paradise*. As early as his college years he imagined that he too had tuberculosis and would die young."

At Princeton, Fitzgerald was socially and economically inferior to the WASP elite. He described his mother's family as "straight 1850 potato famine Irish." But he thought that this inferiority might be an asset; the elite came from old families, families that might be somewhat complacent, somewhat decadent. Fitzgerald described the elite as,

> the men who when he first went to college had entered from the great prep schools with graceful clothes and the deep tan of healthy summers. He had seen that, in one sense, he was better than these men. He was newer and stronger. Yet in acknowledging to himself that he wished his children to be like them he was admitting that he was but the rough, strong stuff from which they eternally sprang.[1]

One of the salient facts of American history is the decline of the WASP elite. Perhaps we can explain this decline by saying that immigrant families were rough and strong, elite families complacent and decadent.

In his later life, Fitzgerald remained fascinated by Princeton. In 1927, he wrote, "Looking back over a decade one sees the ideal of a university become a myth, a vision, a meadow lark among the smoke stacks.... [One seeks in vain] for any corner of the republic that preserves so much of what is fair, gracious, charming and honorable in American life." When he died of a heart attack in 1940, he was reading the *Princeton Alumni Weekly*.

---

[1] See Fitzgerald's short story "Winter Dreams."

Fitzgerald dropped out of Princeton to join the Army; he never graduated. The U.S. was entering World War I; young men were dreaming of military glory. Also, he had been spurned by the girl he loved, Ginevra King. Wikipedia says "he hoped to die in combat."

Wikipedia says that Ginevra was the inspiration for several Fitzgerald characters, including Daisy Buchanan. "As a parting gift before their relationship ended, Ginevra... wrote a story that she sent to Fitzgerald. In her story, she is trapped in a loveless marriage with a wealthy man yet still pines for Fitzgerald, a former lover from her past. The lovers are reunited only after Fitzgerald has attained enough money to take her away from her adulterous husband." So Ginevra's story contained the kernel of *The Great Gatsby*, and was surely the source of *Gatsby*.[1]

As a soldier in 1917, Fitzgerald was stationed near Montgomery, Alabama. "At a country club, Fitzgerald met Zelda Sayre, a 17-year-old Southern belle and the affluent granddaughter of a Confederate senator whose extended family owned the White House of the Confederacy." Fitzgerald and Zelda became engaged, though one suspects that Fitzgerald's real love was Ginevra.

In June 1919, Zelda broke off their engagement, probably because Fitzgerald had little money. Fitzgerald was then living in New York City. "Fitzgerald felt defeated and rudderless: two women had rejected him in succession; he detested his advertising job; his stories failed to sell; he couldn't afford new clothes, and his future seemed bleak.... Fitzgerald publicly threatened to jump to his death from a window ledge of the Yale Club, and he carried a revolver daily while contemplating suicide."

While he was in the army, Fitzgerald had written a novel called *The Romantic Egotist*. Though it was rejected by Scribner's, the reader at Scribner's, Maxwell Perkins, was somewhat encouraging. Perkins "praised Fitzgerald's writing and encouraged him to re-submit it after further revisions."

In July 1919, "Fitzgerald quit his advertising job and returned to St. Paul. Having returned to his hometown as a failure, Fitzgerald became a social recluse and lived on the top floor of his parents' home.... He decided to make one last attempt to become a novelist and to stake everything on the success or failure of a book. Abstaining from alcohol and parties, he worked day and night to revise *The Romantic Egotist* as *This Side of Paradise*—an autobiographical account of his Princeton years and his romances....

"While revising his novel, Fitzgerald took a job repairing car roofs at the Northern Pacific Shops in St. Paul. One evening in the fall of 1919, after an exhausted Fitzgerald had returned home from work, the postman rang and delivered a telegram from Scribner's announcing that his revised manuscript had been accepted for publication. Upon reading the telegram, an ecstatic Fitzgerald ran down the streets of St. Paul and flagged down random automobiles to share the news.

---

[1] Wikipedia says that, as Ginevra was the model for Daisy Buchanan, so Max Gerlach was the model for Jay Gatsby, and Edith Cummings was the model for Jordan Baker.

"Fitzgerald's debut novel appeared in bookstores on March 26, 1920 and became an instant success. *This Side of Paradise* sold approximately 40,000 copies in the first year. Within months of its publication, his debut novel became a cultural sensation in the United States, and F. Scott Fitzgerald became a household name. Critics such as H. L. Mencken hailed the work as the best American novel of the year, and newspaper columnists described the work as the first realistic American college novel.... Magazines now accepted his previously rejected stories, and *The Saturday Evening Post* published his story 'Bernice Bobs Her Hair' with his name on its May 1920 cover."[1]

After the success of *This Side of Paradise*, Zelda decided she wanted to marry Fitzgerald after all. When they were married in 1920,

> Fitzgerald claimed neither he nor Zelda still loved each other.... "I wouldn't care if she died [Fitzgerald told a friend], but I couldn't stand to have anybody else marry her" ....Alcohol increasingly fueled the Fitzgeralds' social life, and the couple consumed gin-and-fruit concoctions at every outing. Publicly, their alcohol intake meant little more than napping at parties, but privately it led to bitter quarrels. As their quarrels worsened, the couple accused each other of marital infidelities. They remarked to friends that their marriage would not last much longer.

They had one child, a girl called Scottie, who became a journalist. It wasn't a good marriage. They spent too much money, drank too much, partied too much. It was as if Fitzgerald wasn't aiming for a good life, but rather for a life that would make a lively story. One might say that Scott and Zelda were living an unreal life.

Reality, however, eventually caught up with them, in the form of health problems, psychological problems, financial problems, etc. In 1934, H. L. Mencken wrote in his diary, "The case of F. Scott Fitzgerald has become distressing. He is boozing in a wild manner and has become a nuisance." Fitzgerald had hit bottom.

How did Fitzgerald cope with this? He wrote about it. He published an essay called "The Crack-Up," which was followed by two similar essays. These three essays were collected (with various other material) in a volume called *The Crack-Up*, which was published after his death.

After he died, Zelda saw his virtues more clearly: "He was as spiritually generous a soul as ever was," she wrote a friend. "It seems as if he was always planning happiness for Scottie and for me. Books to read—places to go. Life seemed so promising always when he was around.... Scott was the best friend a person could have."

* * * * *

---

1 Wikipedia ==> F. Scott Fitzgerald

Fitzgerald's novels didn't sell well, with the exception of his first novel; in the last year of his life, he earned $13.13 in royalties.[1] His short stories, however, brought him a substantial income. Now the situation is reversed: his novels sell briskly, his stories are often overlooked.

A leading Fitzgerald scholar, Matthew Bruccoli, writes, "During his lifetime Fitzgerald was far better known and more widely read as a short-story writer than as a novelist."[2] Fitzgerald published 65 stories in the *Saturday Evening Post*, which paid him as much as $4,000 per story, about $60,000 in today's dollars.

But his ability to write and sell short-stories gradually dried up. In the last year of his life, Fitzgerald wrote to Zelda, who was then in an asylum with psychological problems: "My old talent for the short story vanished.... I got my public with stories of young love," but he could no longer relate to young love. Stories of young love, which resonated in the 1920s, seemed out of place in the 1930s, a time of depression and war.

The Fitzgerald revival started soon after his death. *The Great Gatsby* was given to American soldiers serving overseas, and the Red Cross gave it to American POWs. "By 1945, over 123,000 copies of The Great Gatsby had been distributed among U.S. troops."

B. Fitzgerald in Westport

In May, 1920, F. Scott Fitzgerald and his wife Zelda rented a house in Westport, Connecticut (my hometown). Scott was 23, Zelda 19. Scott's first novel, *This Side of Paradise*, had been published two months earlier, and the first printing had sold out in three days (there were many more printings to come, as the publisher tried to keep up with demand). Scott was becoming famous, and he could sell short stories for large sums. Scott and Zelda married right after *This Side of Paradise* became successful. They lived in a NewYorkCity hotel, but their wild parties disturbed other residents, so they were asked to leave.

They bought a car, and headed for the country. They stopped in Rye, New York, but didn't like it, so they kept driving, following the coast. (Zelda had grown up in Montgomery, Alabama; among her relatives were senators and judges. Having seen little of the coast, Zelda was intrigued by beaches.) In Westport, Zelda drove into a fire hydrant, destroying their new car. They took a trolley to the Westport beach, where they found a house for rent. They remained in the house from May to October.[3]

---

1 See the end of the excellent Fitzgerald documentary, *Winter Dreams*.

2 *The Short Stories of F. Scott Fitzgerald*, Preface

3 The address was 244 South Compo Road, just north of the Longshore property, and just south of Hedgerow Lane. There's a plaque in front of the house. The house was often referred to as "The Wakeman Cottage"; in 1920, it was owned by the Wakeman family. It was built about 1760.

Scott and Zelda, with their Westport abode in the background

Fitzgerald describes the house in his second novel, *The Beautiful and the Damned*. This novel has been called "a sort of trial run for *The Great Gatsby*" (*Gatsby* was his third novel).[1]

The young couple continued to lead a fast life. The literary critic Edmund Wilson, a classmate of Scott's at Princeton, visited them and said they were "reveling nude in the orgies of Westport." Zelda's motto, printed in her high-school yearbook, was

Why should all life be work, when we all can borrow.
Let's think only of today, and not worry about tomorrow.

When Zelda was still living with her parents, she came home late one night, and her father said, "You little hussy, do you know what time it is?" She replied, "It's the time when all hussies come home."

In 1920, Westport was a small town with onion farms and a few big mansions. The onion crop had been ruined by a blight, and the onion storehouses on the coast were being used to store illicit liquor (Prohibition had begun in January, 1920). It was said that Westport's leading rum-runner was Jack Rose, who had been involved in the famous 1912 murder of Manhattan gangster Herman Rosenthal. This murder is mentioned in *Gatsby*.

Jack Rose is apparently one model for the mobster in *Gatsby*, Meyer Wolfshiem. Another model for Wolfshiem is Arnold Rothstein, who fixed the 1919 World Series.

In addition to rum-running, Jack Rose was involved in the movie business. In *The Beautiful and the Damned*, there's a film producer named Joseph Bloeckman, and in *Gatsby*, there's a producer named Newton Orchid.

Fitzgerald's Westport house was near two big estates, the estate of Frederick E. Lewis, which later became Longshore Country Club, and the estate of Edward T. Bedford. It's believed that the Lewis estate is the model for Jay Gatsby's estate, the Bedford estate is the model for Tom and Daisy Buchanan's estate, and Fitzgerald's own house is the model for the humble abode of the *Gatsby* narrator, Nick Carraway.

---

[1] See the *NewYorker* article by Barbara Probst Solomon, online at newyorker.com/magazine/1996/09/09/westport-wildlife. This article has the cool, fashionable tone that many *NewYorker* articles have.

> The setting of Fitzgerald's Westport place—the cottage next to the millionaire's estate, the view of grand houses on the shore across the bay [toward Norwalk and Saugatuck Shores]—corresponded with striking accuracy to Nick's setup next door to Gatsby.

Edward T. Bedford had made his fortune in the oil business, and had built a private race track in Westport; he may be the model for a *Gatsby* character, "Demaine, the oil man."

Frederick E. Lewis had a tower or "imitation lighthouse" on his beach. In *Gatsby*, Nick says,

> At high tide in the afternoon, I watched his guests diving from the tower of his raft, or taking the sun on the hot sand of his beach while his two motor-boats slit the waters of the Sound, drawing aquaplanes over cataracts of foam.

An article by Barbara Probst Solomon says,

> The description in *Gatsby* of the train station, the drawbridge, the road running by the railroad tracks... and the Italian child playing nearby sounded like the station in Saugatuck [a section of Westport], which was then largely Italian.... The sadness of the summer houses closed down in late fall.

Gatsby appears to be set on the north shore of Long Island, where Fitzgerald spent 18 months; Fitzgerald lived in Great Neck after leaving Westport, and before going to the French Riviera. It's often said that Little Neck and Great Neck are the models for *Gatsby*'s West Egg and East Egg. But Solomon says that, while in Great Neck, the Fitzgeralds lived in "a landlocked suburban house," a house that doesn't match *Gatsby* as well as the Westport house. Doubtless *Gatsby* was influenced by both Westport and Great Neck.

Solomon says that around 1925, a new society was developing in New York City, a society that fused Jew and Gentile. Fitzgerald discusses this in an essay called "My Lost City"; for Fitzgerald, the marriage of Irving Berlin and Ellin Mackay symbolizes the new, multi-ethnic New York. Solomon says that Westport was on the cutting edge of Jew-Gentile fusion. Neighboring towns like Darien were known for a "Gentleman's Agreement" whereby realtors agreed not to sell to Jews. Westport was different.[1]

When I was growing up in Westport, one of the town's most famous residents was Paul Newman, who was half-Jewish, and was married to a Gentile (actress Joanne Woodward).

The best documentary on Fitzgerald is surely *Winter Dreams*, by DeWitt Sage. A BBC documentary, *Sincerely, F. Scott Fitzgerald*, is also good. The best film version of *The Great Gatsby* is probably the one made in 2013. More recently, Amazon made a 10-part series about Zelda and Scott,

---

[1] In nearby New Canaan, Fitzgerald's editor, Maxwell Perkins, lived in a historic house at 63 Park Street. Thomas Wolfe often visited Perkins in New Canaan.

Z: The Beginning of Everything. Amazon is also making a series called *The Last Tycoon*, based on Fitzgerald's last, unfinished novel.

The Last Tycoon is set in Hollywood, where Fitzgerald spent his last years (1937-1940). Zelda was then in an institution (she had become mentally unstable around 1930). Fitzgerald had a three-year relationship with Sheilah Graham, a Hollywood gossip columnist. Graham's memoir about Fitzgerald, *Beloved Infidel*, became a bestseller, and was made into a movie. "During those three years, Scott outlined an educational 'curriculum' for [Graham] and guided her through it, which she later wrote about in detail in *A College of One*."[1] (In an earlier issue, I described how the Russian writer Isaak Babel designed a curriculum for his girlfriend.[2])

According to Wikipedia, "Cambridge University Press has published the complete works of F. Scott Fitzgerald in authoritative annotated editions." Many of the volumes are edited by Matthew J. Bruccoli, a leading authority on Fitzgerald. According to Wikipedia, "[Bruccoli's] 1981 biography of Fitzgerald, *Some Sort of Epic Grandeur: The Life of F. Scott Fitzgerald*, is considered the standard Fitzgerald biography." Broccoli edited *F. Scott Fitzgerald: A Life in Letters*, and he edited an 800-page collection of Fitzgerald's short stories.

C. Fitzgerald and the Occult

Fitzgerald, like other great writers, was fascinated by the intuitive, the unconscious, the non-rational. Here's a passage from Fitzgerald's short story about football (a story called "The Bowl"):

> Princeton moved steadily down the field. On the Yale twenty-yard line things suddenly happened. A Princeton pass was intercepted; the Yale man, excited by his own opportunity, dropped the ball and it bobbed leisurely in the general direction of the Yale goal. Jack Devlin and Dolly Harlan of Princeton and somebody—I forget who—from Yale were all about the same distance from it. What Dolly did in that split second was all instinct; it presented no problem to him. He was a natural athlete and in a crisis his nervous system thought for him. He might have raced the two others for the ball; instead, he took out the Yale man with savage precision while Devlin scooped up the ball and ran ten yards for a touchdown.

Emerson spoke of, "that source, at once the essence of genius, of virtue, and of life, which we call Spontaneity or Instinct." Emerson and Fitzgerald are both fascinated by "Spontaneity or Instinct."

In a story called "A Short Trip Home," Fitzgerald describes a young man (Eddie) on a train with a young woman (Ellen); Eddie and Ellen are in a private room; Eddie is trying to prevent a "tough guy" from being alone with Ellen. "Just at that moment I became aware, with the unquestionable knowledge reserved for facts, that he was just outside the door. She knew it,

---

[1] See Wikipedia, "Sheilah Graham"

[2] ljhammond.com/phlit/2010-10.htm

too; the blood left her face." I'm reminded of a passage from Emerson: "Every man discriminates between the voluntary acts of his mind and his involuntary perceptions, and knows that to his involuntary perceptions a perfect faith is due." Eddie has an "involuntary perception" of the presence of the "tough guy."

Emerson and Fitzgerald are dealing with different things: Fitzgerald is dealing with the unseen presence of a person, Emerson with philosophical ideas. But intuition works in both cases. Eddie has an intuition that the tough guy is standing outside the door, Einstein has an intuition that $e = mc^2$, Mendeleev sees in a dream the Periodic Table. As Emerson said, "When we discern truth, we do nothing of ourselves, but allow a passage to its beams." Intuition works in everyday life, and in discovering new theories. Hence Emerson calls it, "the essence of genius, of virtue, and of life."

Consider the following passage from a Fitzgerald story called "The Diamond as Big as the Ritz":

> About half-way to the steep summit the trees fell away.... Just before he reached this point he slowed down his pace, warned by an animal sense that there was life just ahead of him. Coming to a high boulder, he lifted his head gradually above its edge.... This is what he saw: Braddock Washington was standing there motionless, silhouetted against the gray sky without sound or sign of life.

Fitzgerald's interest in this sort of intuition or hunch could be the product of his own experience, or it could be the product of his reading; perhaps his experience and his reading reinforced each other. He may have found such passages in writers he admired, such as Compton Mackenzie and Joseph Conrad.

D. *The Great Gatsby*

a. The Breaking Point

In *The Great Gatsby*, Jay Gatsby is the protagonist, Tom Buchanan the antagonist. Jay decides to confront Tom, and tell him that his wife (Daisy) has never really loved him, she loves Jay. Meanwhile, Tom decides to confront Jay, and tell him to stay away from Daisy.

Jay and Tom collide on a hot summer day at the Plaza Hotel in Manhattan. Daisy is complaining about the heat.

> "The thing to do is to forget about the heat," said Tom impatiently. "You make it ten times worse by crabbing about it." He unrolled the bottle of whiskey from the towel and put it on the table. "Why not let her alone, old sport?" remarked Gatsby. "You're the one that wanted to come to town." There was a moment of silence. The telephone book

> slipped from its nail and splashed to the floor.... Gatsby examined the parted string.[1]

Just when Jay and Tom are colliding, just when the tension is reaching a "breaking point," the string holding the telephone book breaks. Could this happen in real life? Can tension between people affect inanimate objects? Is it just a coincidence that the string breaks at that moment, or is there some sort of relationship between mankind and inanimate objects? Were we right to say, "Everything is connected"? If a clock stops when its owner dies, is that just a coincidence? Is the universe an organic whole in which everything is connected, and everything—even a clock, even a string—has some sort of energy, consciousness, life?

In 1909, Jung visited Freud in Vienna, and asked him about the occult.

> Because of [Freud's] materialistic prejudice, [Jung later said,] he rejected this entire complex of questions as nonsensical... I had difficulty in checking the sharp retort on the tip of my tongue.... At that moment there was [a] loud report in the bookcase.... I said to Freud: "There, that is an example of a so-called catalytic exteriorization phenomenon.... I now predict that in a moment there will be another such loud report!" Sure enough, no sooner had I said the words than the same detonation went off in the bookcase.[2]

The quarrel between Freud and Jung, like the quarrel between Jay and Tom, seems to be manifested in a disturbance in the world around them, in the inanimate objects around them. How did Fitzgerald grasp this profound truth? It's possible that he experienced something like this, but I think it's more likely that he found something like this in the work of another novelist, such as Conrad. It's impossible to over-state Conrad's influence on Fitzgerald.[3]

---

[1] Am I the first critic to notice this incident? Both movie versions of *Gatsby*—the 1974 movie and the 2013 movie—skip over the falling phone book.

Fitzgerald writes, "Gatsby examined the parted string, muttered 'Hum!' in an interested way, and tossed the book on a chair." Why does Gatsby examine the string "in an interested way"? Perhaps he suspects the breaking string isn't a random occurrence, but rather a synchronicity, a "meaningful coincidence." Perhaps he suspects that the string has some sort of rapport with the people in the room; the tension among the people has impacted the string.

[2] Jung, *Memories, Dreams, Reflections*, Ch. 5, p. 155. Similar cases could be found in Jung's writings; for example, he says that the mental energy of a medium once caused a steel knife in his family's house to break into pieces (he preserved the pieces for the rest of his life).

[3] Fitzgerald was especially impressed by Conrad's *Nostromo*. Jeffrey Meyers: "Fitzgerald's letters reveal that Conrad's art was a constant touchstone for his own. He cited *Nostromo* as 'the great novel of the past fifty years.... I'd rather have written Conrad's *Nostromo* than any other novel... because

Doubtless we could find countless examples, in literary works, of a connection between people and inanimate objects. And doubtless we could find countless examples in the real world of such a connection. A connection between people and inanimate objects can also be demonstrated through controlled experiments, as we saw in an earlier issue.[1]

b. Fortune's Wheel

The Great Gatsby is often called Fitzgerald's best novel. It was written when he was about 27, and in the prime of his career. When he wrote *Gatsby*, Fitzgerald was already a famous writer, already married to Zelda. Did he anticipate that his best days were behind him, that ahead lay trouble and early death? In my book of aphorisms, I said, "People can often foresee the time of their death."[2] The narrator of *Gatsby*, Nick, says

> "I just remembered that today's my birthday." I was thirty. Before me stretched the portentous, menacing road of a new decade.... We drove on toward death through the cooling twilight.

People who are 27 or 30 don't usually feel that they're moving toward death, they don't usually view the next decade as "portentous, menacing." In Fitzgerald's essay "My Lost City," one finds the same sense of impending decline:

> I remember riding in a taxi one afternoon between very tall buildings under a mauve and rosy sky; I began to bawl because I had everything I wanted and knew I would never be so happy again.

In his early days, Fitzgerald seemed to have everything—fame, money, a beautiful wife. But beneath the surface, trouble lurked—Zelda's mental problems, Scott's alcohol problems, etc. When Fitzgerald wrote *Gatsby*, Fortune was about to turn her wheel, and Fitzgerald sensed it.

The magic of his early days with Zelda was gone. When Gatsby returns from the war, he visits Louisville, where his relationship with Daisy had blossomed, but "he knew that he had lost that part of it, the freshest and the best, forever." Zelda was no longer a princess, she was a responsibility. Gatsby tells Nick how he hesitated to kiss Daisy:

> Out of the corner of his eye Gatsby saw that the blocks of the sidewalks really formed a ladder and mounted to a secret place above the trees—

Nostromo, the man, intrigues me so much. [Conrad] took this man of the people and imagined him with such a completeness that there is no use of anyone else pondering over him for some time. He is one of the most important types in our civilization... one that always made a haunting and irresistible appeal to me.'" ("Conrad's Influence on Modern Writers," by Jeffrey Meyers, *Twentieth Century Literature*, Vol. 36, No. 2, Summer, 1990, pp. 186-206, jstor.org/stable/441821)

[1] See ljhammond.com/phlit/2006-06.htm#3

[2] See the section called "Anticipating Death" in Chapter 13, "Life- and Death-Instincts"

> he could climb to it, if he climbed alone, and once there he could suck on the pap of life, gulp down the incomparable milk of wonder.... He knew that when he kissed this girl, and forever wed his unutterable visions to her perishable breath, his mind would never romp again like the mind of God. So he waited, listening for a moment longer to the tuning-fork that had been struck upon a star. Then he kissed her.

c. Lost Illusions

Gatsby is a dreamer, and Daisy is the woman of his dreams. When he finally comes face-to-face with Daisy, it's difficult for her to live up to Gatsby's dreams:

> There must have been moments even that afternoon when Daisy tumbled short of his dreams—not through her own fault, but because of the colossal vitality of his illusion. It had gone beyond her, beyond everything. He had thrown himself into it with a creative passion, adding to it all the time, decking it out with every bright feather that drifted his way. No amount of fire or freshness can challenge what a man will store up in his ghostly heart.[1]

Don Quixote is also a dreamer. Does Western literature have a tendency in this direction, a tendency that began in the Renaissance period, a tendency that sets it apart from Greco-Roman literature? Is there an introspective tendency in the Western psyche, a tendency created by, or at least strengthened by Christianity? Does introspection create an inner life, a fantasy life, and a corresponding dissatisfaction with reality? Even in a modern writer like Proust, dreams/illusions play an important role.

A critic named Robert Emmet Long has argued that *The Great Gatsby* is influenced by Conrad's works, especially *Almayer's Folly*, *Lord Jim*, and *Heart of Darkness*.[2] Long argues that Conrad's early work, such as *Almayer's Folly*, is about romantic illusions that are shattered by reality.

---

[1] Is the character of Gatsby credible? Can someone make a fortune in organized crime, but also be a dreamy romantic?

[2] See "The Great Gatsby and the Tradition of Joseph Conrad," Texas Studies in Literature and Language, Vol. 8, No. 2 (Summer 1966), pp. 257-276, jstor.org/stable/40753900. Long's article is continued in Vol. 8, No. 3 (Autumn 1966), pp. 407-422, jstor.org/stable/40753911.
Long summarizes the parallels between Gatsby and Conrad thus: "*Almayer's Folly* sets up a framework for the illusionist hero, whose 'future' is in conflict with the realities of the present, and whose dream is destroyed symbolically by a 'betraying heroine.' With this as scaffolding, *Lord Jim* adds the dimension of the attempt to recover the past, and thus to reinstate a Platonic identity. Finally, *Heart of Darkness* adds a cultural reference and theme, contrasting the 'exuberant imagination' of a defeated hero with a visionless society."

Thus, Conrad's early work resembles Flaubert's *Madame Bovary*, which depicts the protagonist's illusions with ironic detachment (Flaubert's work had considerable influence, even outside France).[1]

Beginning with *Lord Jim*, however, Conrad starts to sympathize with his dreamer, to see his dreamer as a better man than those around him.[2] If the dreamer isn't an unqualified hero, he at least has some heroic qualities. This is the template that Fitzgerald follows in *Gatsby*. Gatsby is corrupt but also noble, and his nobility shines more brightly when set against the pettiness of those around him. As the narrator, Nick, puts it,

> "They're a rotten crowd," I shouted across the lawn. "You're worth the whole damned bunch put together."[3]

Gatsby's large soul is manifest in his smile: "It was one of those rare smiles with a quality of eternal reassurance in it, that you may come across

---

1 See the section called "Chekhov" in the Literature chapter of my *Conversations With Great Thinkers*.

Long thinks that Conrad was influenced by Baudelaire as well as Flaubert: "The use of a great modern city as a culture symbol relates *Heart of Darkness* and *The Great Gatsby* to a tradition of social criticism developing from the nineteenth century. The city of Paris in Baudelaire's *Les Fleurs du mal* has already been one of the great culture symbols of the nineteenth century, and its influence upon *Heart of Darkness* is very probable. Baudelaire was among Conrad's favorite poets, and he had used a passage from one of Baudelaire's poems, 'Le Voyage' (which contains the phrase 'the horror!') as an epigraph to one of his own works. Baudelaire had written that evil, though destructive, is more human than passive nonentity; and this vision of evil forms a criticism of the spiritual inertia of modern culture. The same criticism applies in *Heart of Darkness*, where the infinite potentialities of the human soul are evoked by Kurtz, contrasted with the complacency of the 'monstrous town.'"

2 According to Long, Conrad goes beyond Flaubert, beyond Flaubert's ironic detachment. Conrad draws on an older tradition, the Romantic tradition. "The moral problem raised by Jim," Long writes, "is really the same issue which had been created by nineteenth-century romanticism: the moral conflict between personal or social duty, and the perhaps higher duty of self-realization." Kurtz violates moral precepts in the name of self-realization.

3 Long notes that the people who surround Gatsby are described in the same way as the people who surround Conrad's Jim: "Jim's idealism is challenged by a world peopled by... depraved characters, who heap upon him the full measure of their imprecation. Cornelius passes judgment upon Jim in the name of all of his kind. 'He throws dust into everybody's eyes; he throws dust into your eyes, honorable sir, but he can't throw dust into my eyes.' Tom Buchanan, speaking for the subordinate characters of *The Great Gatsby* who are alike in the meanness and confusion of their lives, makes a similar indictment of Gatsby: 'He threw dust into your eyes just like he did in Daisy's, but he was a tough one.'"

four or five times in life." Here again, Fitzgerald seems to be following a Conrad template; the protagonist of Lord Jim also has a memorable smile.

> While Jim is talking about his plans, Marlow notices that a "strange look of beatitude overspread his features.... He positively smiled! ....It was an ecstatic smile that your face—or mine either—will never wear, my dear boys."[1]

Perhaps the most famous image in Gatsby is the green light at the end of the Buchanan dock, a light that symbolizes Gatsby's great love (Daisy), but also belongs to Gatsby's adversary (Tom). Likewise, in *Almayer's Folly*, the houses of the protagonist and antagonist are separated by water, and Almayer can see his foe's lights at night. As Gatsby's dreams for the future center on Daisy, so Almayer's dreams for the future center on his daughter, Nina.[2]

d. Car Accidents

Though Fitzgerald often follows a Conrad template, his plot revolves around a contemporary situation that Conrad doesn't deal with: the car accident. Car accidents raise various moral issues: How should we respond when we hit a person or an animal? Should we stop if we see a stranger having a problem? In an earlier issue, I discussed "driving dilemmas" in the work of the American writer Andre Dubus, and I wrote, "Driving seems to be a fertile field for moral choice because when we're driving, we have to make split-second decisions, and we're often dealing with strangers."[3]

After Daisy hits Myrtle, Gatsby pretends that he was driving. I was reminded of the Chappaquiddick accident, when Mary Jo Kopechne drove off a bridge, but Ted Kennedy pretended that he was driving.[4]

---

[1] In an earlier issue, I compared *The Great Gatsby* and *Heart of Darkness* (see ljhammond.com/phlit/2005-09b.htm#3). I discussed how the protagonists, Gatsby and Kurtz, are flawed but noble—more noble than those around them. Elsewhere I discussed Conrad's influence on Hemingway, and how the eyes of a Conrad character resemble those of a Hemingway character (see ljhammond.com/phlit/2008-05c.htm#5). Finally, I discussed Conrad's influence on Raymond Chandler (see ljhammond.com/phlit/2012-11.htm#5).

[2] Long notes other parallels between *Gatsby* and *Almayer's Folly*: "In the backgrounds of Almayer and Gatsby—in the progression of events bringing them to Sambir and West Egg, with their beliefs in a 'splendid future'—there is a remarkable parallel. Almayer is 'adopted' by Lingard, 'the old adventurer' who takes him as a young man aboard his yacht, the *Flash*, on a cruise in which every island of the archipelago is visited.... In *The Great Gatsby*, the role of Lingard is played by Dan Cody, who brings young James Gatz aboard his yacht, the *Tuolomee*, for a voyage which takes them three times around the continent."

[3] See ljhammond.com/phlit/2014-11b.htm#3

[4] See ljhammond.com/phlit/2004-12c.htm#2

After Daisy hits Myrtle, Gatsby tries to hide the evidence: "He gave instructions that the open car wasn't to be taken out under any circumstances—and this was strange, because the front right fender needed repair." If people hit someone and keep going, they often try to hide the evidence. I even heard of a case where someone killed a pedestrian and kept going, then later drove their car into a stone wall, so the damage from the second accident would hide the damage from the first accident.

e. Weak Ego

In an earlier issue, I said, "One of the chief characteristics of the intellectual is a weak ego."[1] I discussed photos of Proust, Forster, and Joyce, concluding that their weak ego "manifests itself in a posture that isn't erect, but rather tilted." I noted that, in group photos, they're usually on the edge of the group, not in the middle.

Because of his weak ego, the intellectual is poor at wielding authority, and is frequently the butt of ridicule. This lack of authority, lack of force, makes it difficult for the intellectual to be a teacher. Joyce, Thoreau, Aldous Huxley—all tried their hand at teaching, but couldn't control the students. Joyce said his students were "aware of my lack of rule and of the fees their papas pay."

Fitzgerald doubtless had a weak ego, and he was impressed by people of the opposite type, impressed by people with a strong ego. Instead of the phrase "strong ego," Fitzgerald uses the phrase "self-sufficiency." He describes a self-sufficient woman who doesn't even look at him when he enters the room: "If she saw me out of the corner of her eyes she gave no hint of it." He says, "Almost any exhibition of complete self-sufficiency draws a stunned tribute from me."[2] Fitzgerald is "stunned" by self-sufficiency because it's foreign to him, because he doesn't possess it himself.

f. The Fitzgerald Theme

Gatsby is a dreamer, a romantic. A critic named Stephen Tanner has spoken of "The Gatsby Complex". Tanner argues that the fundamental idea behind Fitzgerald's work is dream followed by disappointment, illusion followed by disillusion:

> Combining two of [Fitzgerald's] favorite words, I have labeled the first part Romantic Promise. By this term I wish to signify the complex of hope, dream, yearning, aspiration, expectation, anticipation, idealism, mystery, confidence, and future possibility characteristic of so many of his characters.... Since Romantic Promise always tends to outstrip reality, it leads inevitably to the second part of the story, a concomitant disillusionment that I denote, using a phrase from Frost's "Oven Bird,"

---

1 ljhammond.com/phlit/2006-09.htm#4

2 Though much in *Gatsby* is Conrad-influenced, I suspect that this passage is "pure Fitzgerald." I also suspect that I'm the first critic to trace this passage to Fitzgerald's own lack of "self-sufficiency."

> a Diminished Thing. I intend Diminished Thing to mean the unavoidable aftermath of Romantic Promise: hopes and dreams thwarted, the mystery and excitement become commonplace, the future devoid of expectation and possibility. The Diminished Thing takes many forms in Fitzgerald's fiction—indeed he was fascinated with exploring its many varieties and manifestations—but its typical versions are loss of youth, losing the girl or discovering she does not equal the dream, emotional bankruptcy, declining health, or in general losing the gift of looking to the future with anticipation.[1]

Fitzgerald himself was aware that his stories kept repeating the same theme.

> Generalizing from his own experience, Fitzgerald once asserted that authors usually repeat themselves. They have two or three really significant experiences in their lives and retell in various disguises their two or three stories "maybe ten times, maybe a hundred, as long as people will listen." He confessed that he worked best when he faced the fact that all his stories were going to have "a certain family resemblance."

In earlier issues, I've often argued that one theme runs through all a writer's work. I quoted a Proust critic: "Proust saw in Hardy's *Jude the Obscure*, *The Well-Beloved*, and *A Pair of Blue Eyes* the same nucleus. He recognized the same basic content in all the work of any one artist." I discussed The Shakespeare Theme, The Dickens Theme, The Kafka Theme, etc.[2]

Fitzgerald's theme is dream followed by disappointment. This theme grows out of his own life, his own experience. Fitzgerald's own mind was torn between dream and disappointment, Romantic Promise and the Diminished Thing. Fitzgerald said, "the test of a first-rate intelligence is the ability to hold two opposed ideas in the mind at the same time and still retain the ability to function." And what are the "opposed ideas" that Fitzgerald held in his own mind? "The sense of the futility of effort and the sense of the necessity to struggle." Dream and disappointment.

One of the themes of this e-zine is that we must often live with tension, contradiction, opposition. Life isn't either/or, it's both/and. As Whitman put it, "Do I contradict myself? Very well then... I contradict myself."[3]

---

[1] "Fitzgerald's Lost City," Stephen L. Tanner, *Rocky Mountain Review of Language and Literature*, Vol. 35, No. 1 (1981), pp. 55-62, jstor.org/stable/1347727

[2] The quote about Hardy is from ljhammond.com/phlit/2007-09.htm#10; I discussed Shakespeare at ljhammond.com/phlit/2003-07.htm#4, Dickens at ljhammond.com/phlit/2009-06.htm#7, and Kafka at ljhammond.com/cwgt/07.htm#24

[3] For more on contradiction, see ljhammond.com/phlit/2002-05a.htm

g. The James-Wells Debate

Henry James distinguished between 'selection novels' and 'saturation novels.' His own novels were selection novels, the material being selected to create structure; a selection novel has "a controlling idea and a clear center of interest." Academics are impressed with this sort of novel, impressed with structure. James felt that younger novelists (like Compton Mackenzie, Arnold Bennett, and H. G. Wells) were creating saturation novels "which he associated with discursiveness and 'the affirmation of energy, however directed or undirected.'"[1] Perhaps the best example of a saturation novelist is Thomas Wolfe, who is ignored in The Academy.

The young Fitzgerald was much impressed with Compton Mackenzie. Fitzgerald's first novel, *This Side of Paradise*, was "written under the spell of Compton Mackenzie, one critic even pointing out nearly a hundred points of similarity between *This Side of Paradise* and Mackenzie's *Sinister Street*." Fitzgerald once wrote, "I sent [*This Side of Paradise*] to Mencken with the confession that it derives from Mackenzie and Wells" (Mackenzie's *Sinister Street* and Wells' *Tono-Bungay*).

But *Gatsby* was written under the spell of Conrad, whom James cited as a selection novelist. When you read *Gatsby*, you feel that it has structure, it isn't just a record of experience. Fitzgerald's earlier work isn't as carefully structured. In *This Side of Paradise*, Fitzgerald identifies with the protagonist, but in *Gatsby*, Fitzgerald detaches himself from the protagonist. In *Gatsby*, Fitzgerald uses a Conrad-style narrator who can observe the protagonist with a blend of admiration and blame. *This Side of Paradise* deals with lost illusions, as Gatsby does, but it uses the 'saturation approach' rather than the 'selection approach.'

Henry James had a debate with H. G. Wells about the novel as a genre. James championed structure, form, craft, and his arguments resonated with The Academy and with Highbrow Culture. James' arguments were "one of the first and most significant formulations in Anglo-American letters of what will serve as one of the central tenets of high literary modernism."[2] Like T. S. Eliot, James champions the formal and the impersonal. The Academy admired Eliot and James, while ignoring Wells and Wolfe.

Wells celebrates the novel's "moral persuasive" force. He believes that the novel can make us want to change ourselves or change the world, the novel can be social or political. For Wells, the world isn't stable, it's in flux; his interest in social change made him a pioneer of science fiction. While James is interested in method, Wells is interested in matter.

---

1 Robert Emmet Long, "The Great Gatsby and the Tradition of Joseph Conrad," Part 1, Summer

2 "The Possibilities of the Novel: A Look Back on the James-Wells Debate," by Phillip E. Wegner, *The Henry James Review*, Volume 36, Number 3, Fall 2015, pp. 267-279. For more on the James-Wells debate, see *Henry James and H. G. Wells: A Record of their Friendship, their Debate on the Art of Fiction, and their Quarrel*, Ed. Leon Edel and Gordon N. Ray

> We are going to write about it all [said Wells]. We are going to write about business and finance and politics and precedence and pretentiousness and decorum and indecorum, until a thousand pretenses and ten thousand impostures shrivel in the cold, clear air of our elucidations.[1]

James viewed the novel as a self-contained whole, an artistic whole. The novelist assumes that a stable world is "established in advance."[2]

The debate between James and Wells, between structure and content, reminds one of Schiller's theory that art is divided between *Formtrieb* (Form Drive) and *Stofftrieb* (Content Drive). Schiller and other Romantics sided with *Stofftrieb*.

E. Karl Polanyi

I read a Fitzgerald story called "The Diamond as Big as the Ritz." It's about a young student, John Unger, who visits a classmate, Percy Washington, at his home in Montana during the summer (Fitzgerald himself made a similar visit when he was halfway through Princeton). Young love figures prominently in the story; John falls for Percy's sister:

> He saw a girl coming toward him over the grass. She was the most beautiful person he had ever seen. She was dressed in a white little gown that came just below her knees.... Her pink bare feet scattered the dew before them as she came. She was younger than John—not more than sixteen.

---

1 Wells wrote a popular book called *The Outline of History: The Whole Story of Man*, as if to fulfill his promise, "We are going to write about it all." Can you imagine Henry James writing such a book?

2 Ibid. Virginia Woolf seemed to side with James in this debate. "Virginia Woolf, in another of the most influential documents of British literary modernism, the 1924 essay 'Mr. Bennett and Mrs. Brown,' makes claims for the 'proper' work of the modern novel that are strikingly similar to those advanced earlier by James. Woolf offers the axiom that 'all novels, that is to say, deal with character, and that it is to express character—not to preach doctrines, sing songs, or celebrate the glories of the British Empire, that the form of the novel, so clumsy, verbose, and undramatic, so rich, elastic, and alive, has been evolved.' But this focus is exactly what we do not see in her predecessors, the Edwardian writers Wells, Bennett, and Galsworthy. Their works, Woolf maintains, 'leave one with so strange a feeling of incompleteness and dissatisfaction. In order to complete them it seems necessary to do something—to join a society, or, more desperately, to write a cheque.'"(Wegner, "The Possibilities of the Novel")

Kundera had much to say about the novel. He was a champion of the loosely-structured novel, so he would probably side with Wells rather than James.

The Washington family is fabulously wealthy because Percy's grandfather, Fitz-Norman Washington, found an enormous diamond, "a diamond as big as the Ritz." Fitz-Norman

> had estimated that the diamond in the mountain was approximately equal in quantity to all the rest of the diamonds known to exist in the world. There was no valuing it by any regular computation, however, for it was *one solid diamond*—and if it were offered for sale not only would the bottom fall out of the market, but also... there would not be enough gold in the world to buy a tenth part of it. And what could anyone do with a diamond that size? It was an amazing predicament. He was, in one sense, the richest man that ever lived—and yet was he worth anything at all? If his secret should transpire there was no telling to what measures the Government might resort in order to prevent a panic, in gold as well as in jewels. They might take over the claim immediately and institute a monopoly. There was no alternative—he must market his mountain in secret.

As you can see from this passage, it's a wild story; one can't believe in the plot or the characters. Fitzgerald fails to achieve "suspension of disbelief."

I read an essay by Richard Godden called "A Diamond Bigger Than the Ritz: F. Scott Fitzgerald and the Gold Standard." Godden's specialty is the intersection of literature and economics. Godden's prose is thorny and obscure; he's fond of jargon from economics. Godden's essay was published in 2010. One should never read literary criticism written after 1980—it's not intended for the general reader, and the prose is obscure.

I must admit, though, that I learned something from Godden's essay, I learned about economists such as Karl Polanyi. Polanyi was born into a distinguished Jewish family; he was born in Vienna, grew up in Budapest, then returned to Vienna after World War I. When Hitler came to power in 1933, Polanyi left Austria, spent several years in London, then lived in the U.S. and Canada, while teaching at Bennington and Columbia.

Polanyi was critical of the Austrian School of economics, skeptical of laissez-faire economics, and sympathetic toward Christian socialism and Fabian socialism. The Austrian School emphasized the abstract individual, Polanyi sees the individual within a social and cultural milieu, hence Polanyi is sometimes called an "economic anthropologist"; Polanyi draws on the research of anthropologists like Malinowski. In Polanyi's view, "man's economy [is] submerged in his social relationships."[1] Godden writes,

> Karl Polanyi... describes "belief in the Gold Standard" during the twenties as "the faith of the age," adding that since, in the modern economy, "currency had become the pivot of national politics... nobody could fail to experience the daily shrinking or expanding of the financial yardstick; populations became currency conscious; the effect of inflation on real income was discounted in advance by the masses; men and women everywhere appeared to regard stable money as the supreme

[1] Wikipedia ==> The Great Transformation (book), quote from Polanyi

need of human society." Such "faith" rested on the assumption, Polanyi argues, "that bank notes have value because they represent gold": "Whether gold itself has value for the reason that it embodies labor, as the socialists held, or for the reason that it is useful and scarce, as the orthodox doctrine ran, made no difference."

After World War I, all political leaders needed to stabilize the currency: "Faced with immediate postwar inflation, the need to restore a country's currency via gold, so that that country might trade, repay loans or pay reparations, was shared by Herbert Hoover, Vladimir Lenin, Winston Churchill and Benito Mussolini."[1]

Polanyi is best known for *The Great Transformation: The Political and Economic Origins of Our Time* (1944), which he wrote in English. Polanyi argues that the modern market society represents a "great transformation" from traditional society. In a traditional society, economic activity is based on

1. Householding (individual households work to meet their own needs)
2. Reciprocity (I help you build a barn, you help me build a barn; "On a macro level, this would include the production of goods to gift to other groups")
3. Redistribution ("trade and production is focused to a central entity such as a tribal leader or feudal lord and then redistributed to members of their society")

In traditional society, everyone loaned and everyone borrowed, but in the new market society, debt (overdue debt) is a crime, and debtors are imprisoned. In traditional society, there are common lands, grazing lands, but in the market society, these common lands are replaced by "enclosures," i.e., private lands enclosed by fences. So land and labor are "sold on the market at market-determined prices instead of allocated according to tradition, redistribution, or reciprocity." This is a "great transformation" because "it was both a change of human institutions and human nature."

Is socialism the natural state, the original state? The market society is a new development, "laissez-faire was planned... social protectionism was a spontaneous reaction to the social dislocation imposed by an unrestrained free market." The new market society of modern times has brought great wealth, but at what cost? Polanyi says we're seeing a double movement: the spread of a market society, and a movement to protect people from the market. Our best hope, Polanyi argues, is some sort of socialism, some sort of buffer against the excesses of a free market.

* * * * *

So Polanyi believes that wealth is only valuable if it makes people's lives better. He would have agreed with Ruskin's remark, "There is no wealth but life." David Brooks made a similar argument in a recent NewYorkTimes column:

---

[1] This is a quote from Godden, not Polanyi.

"Each year Gallup surveys roughly 150,000 people in over 140 countries about their emotional lives. Experiences of negative emotions—related to stress, sadness, anger, worry and physical pain—hit a record high last year.

"Places like China and India have gotten much richer. But development does not necessarily lead to gains in well-being, in part because development is often accompanied by widening inequality.... We conventionally use G.D.P. and other material measures to evaluate how nations are doing. But these are often deeply flawed measures of how actual people are experiencing their lives.

"James Carville famously said, 'It's the economy, stupid.' But that's too narrow. Often it's human flourishing, stupid, including community cohesion, a sense of being respected, social connection."

* * * * *

Godden discusses the importance of the Gold Standard in the new market society:

> Exponents of the liberal market needed a device whereby people of different nations might freely trade with one another, confident that monies so earned (whatever their currency) would be "as good as gold." The International Gold Standard, widely adopted by the 1870s, and rendering currencies commensurate via a golden mean, was that device—for Polanyi, "an extraordinary intellectual achievement." Confidence, on the back of gold, ensured that labor and land (or all things manufactured and grown), might increasingly be viewed not (in the case of labor) as an activity inseparable from life, or (in the case of land) as a gift of geography and history, but as prices-in-waiting, or profits to be made in the global marketplace. Gold [was,] however, subject to what Polanyi describes as "double movement": "While the organization of world commodity markets, world capital markets and world currency markets under the aegis of the Gold Standard gave an unparalleled momentum to the mechanisms of markets, a deep-seated movement sprang into being to resist the pernicious effects of a market controlled economy."

Since the Gold Standard was the keystone of the market society, the Gold Standard was the target of many critics, such as William Jennings Bryan. Polanyi would probably have agreed with Bryan, and Polanyi supported Britain's decision in 1931 to abandon the Gold Standard. When Britain abandoned gold, the British pound immediately lost 25% of its exchange value. Polanyi "argues that Britain went off the gold standard due to pressures from labor, which had grown stronger over time. Labor opposed the gold standard because maintaining it meant that the British government had to implement austerity."[1]

Polanyi was a critic of the free market, as Hayek was a champion of the free market. Polanyi compares the free market to primitive and traditional societies; he says the free market produces wealth, but also solitude and stress. Hayek compares the free market to a centrally-planned economy, such as Stalin's Soviet Union or Mao's China; Hayek says the planned economy produces poverty, a loss of freedom, a form of "serfdom." Is it possible to have the cooperation and community of traditional society, while leaving room for freedom and individuality?

We saw above that the Washington family had a huge diamond, but couldn't do much with it. Godden says that the U.S. was in a similar position after World War I: it possessed much of the world's gold, but gold sitting in a vault is of little use. Godden writes,

> The United States emerged from the First World War with a great capital surplus and owning much of the world's gold. To sell abroad it had to transfer wealth to potential buyers. From 1921, the government encouraged private overseas loans as a way of recycling cash for the purchase of U.S. exports. As a result, between 1924 and 1929, 80% of the capital borrowed by German credit institutions came from American banks.

Fitzgerald describes how the first Washington, Fitz-Norman, used his wealth to buy "rare minerals," which he deposited in various banks around the world. Fitz-Norman's son, Braddock, carried this a step further: "The minerals were converted into the rarest of all elements—radium—so that the equivalent of a billion dollars in gold could be placed in a receptacle no bigger than a cigar box." In 1922, when Fitzgerald wrote the story, it was suspected that radium might be unsafe. "In 1904," Godden writes, "Clarence Dally, glassblower and laboratory employee in Edison's Menlo Park laboratory, died as a result of long-term exposure to radiation poisoning." In the same year, "Edison discontinued experiments on the commercial potential of radium as a source of light."

At the end of Fitzgerald's story, Braddock Washington detonates the diamond mountain, killing everyone at the estate except John Unger and Percy's two sisters. Godden calls the explosion a "prefiguration of the Crash of '29." Perhaps it's also a prefiguration of the use of radioactive material as an explosive. So "The Diamond as Big as the Ritz" is a rather dark and pessimistic story.

---

[1] Wikipedia ==> The Great Transformation (book). Nowadays there are a few people, such as Judy Shelton, who advocate a return to the Gold Standard. As Bryan and others wanted to leave the Gold Standard, so some Europeans want to leave the Euro; the Euro seems to entail the kind of austerity that was once associated with the Gold Standard. The argument over the Gold Standard, around 1900, might be compared to the argument in recent years over globalization.

Jeffrey Hart divides Fitzgerald's work into three periods:

1. his early period, when he aims to "bring out a meaning in life.... Write biographical novels with a burst of ideas toward the close"[1]; example: *This Side of Paradise*
2. his second period, the "ironical pessimistic," emphasizing "the meaninglessness of life"; example: *The Beautiful and Damned* (1922); Hart says that *The Beautiful and Damned* is spoiled by its "heaviness and pessimism"
3. his third period, which is his best period, when he's inspired by Conrad; example: *The Great Gatsby* (1925); in *Gatsby*, Fitzgerald manages to achieve a certain objectivity, a certain detachment

"The Diamond as Big as the Ritz" exemplifies Fitzgerald's second period, his pessimistic period. According to Matthew Bruccoli, "The meaning of 'Diamond' is sufficiently clear: Absolute wealth corrupts absolutely and possesses its possessors."[2] The story may contain images that an economist would find interesting, but I think it's a second-rate story nonetheless.

23. J. D. Salinger

February 11, 2010
Salinger died recently. I discovered him rather late, since he wasn't on my list of Great Writers. But once I started reading him, I fell madly in love, since he spoke my language, and discussed my world, in a way that Homer, Proust, and Tolstoy didn't.

I wasn't alone, Salinger was extremely popular. Astute readers, like Edmund Wilson and Hemingway, were impressed with Salinger. He seemed to enjoy writing, and to make reading enjoyable:

> If only you'd remember [Salinger wrote] before ever you sit down to write that you've been a *reader* long before you were ever a writer. You simply fix that fact in your mind, then sit very still and ask yourself, as a reader, what piece of writing in all the world Buddy Glass would most want to read if he had his heart's choice.

And what piece of writing did Salinger The Reader most want to read? "What I like best," he wrote, "is a book that's at least funny once in a while." So Salinger The Writer gave us books that were at least funny once in a while.

His specialty was the little details of home and family:

> It was dark as hell in the foyer.... I certainly knew I was home, though. Our foyer has a funny smell that doesn't smell like anyplace else. I

---

[1] Hart is quoting Edmund Wilson. Hart and Wilson say that the pessimistic Fitzgerald was inspired by certain writers, but they don't identify those writers.

[2] *Some Sort of Epic Grandeur*, Ch. 20

> don't know what the hell it is. It isn't cauliflower and it isn't perfume—I don't know what the hell it is—but you always know you're home.

Salinger was receptive to Eastern wisdom, and to the occult. When his protagonist (Holden Caulfield) wants to talk to his sister on the phone, he wonders what he should do if she doesn't answer: "I thought of maybe hanging up if my parents answered, but that wouldn't've worked, either. They'd know it was me. My mother always knows it's me. She's psychic."

Here's another example of telepathy from *The Catcher in the Rye*:

> I started playing golf when I was only ten years old. I remember once, the summer I was around twelve, teeing off and all, and having a hunch that if I turned around all of a sudden, I'd see Allie. So I did, and sure enough, he was sitting on his bike outside the fence.

If you want to try Salinger, I suggest one of his *Nine Stories*, or his novel, *The Catcher in the Rye*. As for Salinger criticism, I recommend an essay called "J. D. Salinger: Some Crazy Cliff."[1]

24. Salinger in Westport

In a recent issue, I discussed Fitzgerald's stay in Westport, Connecticut (my hometown), and I mentioned in a footnote that "J. D. Salinger wrote *Catcher in the Rye* in 1950, while living on South Compo Road in Westport." When *Catcher* became a bestseller, Salinger fled the limelight, moved to Cornish, New Hampshire, and lived as a recluse.

A correspondence school, as you may know, is a school where teacher and student correspond; before there were online schools, there were correspondence schools. Westport was home to an art correspondence school, the Famous Artists School, which purported to turn people into artists. Prominent artists like Norman Rockwell lent their names to the scam. One is reminded of that august educational institution, Trump University.

You would send in a sample of your work, and then they would write back, saying you had great potential, and you should enroll in their school. Salesmen combed the country, recruiting gullible art students. Ads filled the newspapers. Money rolled in.

It was so profitable that a Famous Writers School was also established in Westport, and it used the same business template as the Famous Artists School. Prominent writers like Clifton Fadiman, Bruce Catton, and Mignon Eberhart lent their names; Bennett Cerf of Random House was one of the founders. By 1969, the annual revenue of the Famous Writers School reached $48 million, and the business's stock price had gone from $5 to $40. A successful scam indeed.

In 1970, Jessica Mitford published an exposé in the *Atlantic Monthly*; her article was called "Let Us Now Appraise Famous Writers." After Mitford's exposé, investigations were launched, the stock price fell, and in 1972, the Famous Writers School went bankrupt.

---

[1] A. Heiserman and J. Miller, *Western Humanities Review*, 1956 (10)

In 1950, when Salinger came to Westport, the Famous Artists School had been going for two years. It's likely that he heard about the school. In 1952, Salinger published a short story about an art correspondence school; the story was called "De Daumier-Smith's Blue Period."

Daumier-Smith is a "teacher" at the school. He quickly forms an emotional bond with a student/correspondent, a nun named Sister Irma. He writes Irma "a long, almost an endless, letter.... I asked her to please tell me how old she was.... I asked if she were allowed to have visitors at her convent." He tells Irma,

> I think you are greatly talented and would not even be slightly startled if you developed into a genius before many years have gone by.... The days will be insufferable for me till your next envelope arrives, it goes without saying.

Before falling asleep, the young art teacher thinks of Irma:

> I tried to visualize the day I would visit her at her convent. I saw her coming to meet me—near a high, wire fence—a shy, beautiful girl of eighteen who had not yet taken her final vows and was still free to go out into the world with the Peter Abelard-type man of her choice. I saw us walking slowly, silently, toward a far, verdant part of the convent grounds, where suddenly, and without sin, I would put my art around her waist.

When I was growing up in Westport around 1970, the phrase "Famous Artists" was constantly ringing in my ears. The School rented space from Eddie Nash on Riverside Avenue. Since money was rolling in, they decided to build a new headquarters, and they decided that my neighborhood was just the place for it. According to Rumor (spread by my mother in countless phone conversations), the parking lot would have space for 1,000 cars.

My mother banded together with other neighbors, and formed a group called Families For A Residential Westport. (They could have called their group NIMBY, Not In My Back Yard.) This was the beginning of my mother's long involvement in local politics.

My mother's group referred to their opponents as The Boyd Group (or, "The Boyds"). John Boyd was a prominent lawyer in Westport, and he favored business and development. He was probably hired by businesses who wanted permission to build. One of Boyd's allies, Lou Villalon, ran the local newspaper, *The Town Crier*.

My parents were Republicans, and so were The Boyds; the battle over Famous Artists wasn't a Republican-Democrat battle, or a Conservative-Liberal battle, it was a Development Battle. Doubtless the Development Battle was fought in thousands of American towns.

My mother's group won the battle, Famous Artists never moved to my neighborhood. The next Development Battle in Westport was over Cockenoe Island, where an electric utility proposed building a power plant. Anti-development forces created their own newspaper, the *Westport News*, which became the town's chief newspaper. The Battle of Cockenoe Island was also won by anti-development forces. A third battle was fought over a dairy farm, Nyala Farms, where a chemical company proposed building their headquarters. This battle was won by the development forces.

25. Salinger's Mysticism

J. D. Salinger is one of the most remarkable talents in the history of American literature. It's hard to believe that he can be so funny and entertaining, and at the same time so profound and philosophical. Only a supremely great writer can manage this "double play."

I once discussed E. M. Forster with a Brown professor, who insisted that Forster was funny, not philosophical. I argued that Forster was funny *and* philosophical, just as Salinger is. I think Forster would have been a Salinger fan, he would have seen the Zennish element in Salinger, and laughed out loud at Salinger's humor. Like Forster, Salinger was a student of Eastern wisdom.

After reading Salinger's story "De Daumier-Smith's Blue Period," I found an essay called "Salinger, from Daumier to Smith" by John Russell.[1] Russell appears to be a leader in the field of Salinger criticism.[2] Though his essay isn't easy to read, it throws much light on "De Daumier-Smith's Blue Period" and on Salinger's entire *oeuvre*.

Russell divides Salinger's work into three groups:

1. The early stories—the first seven stories in Salinger's collection *Nine Stories*
2. *The Catcher in the Rye*, Salinger's only novel, his longest and most popular work
3. Salinger's late works, beginning with the stories "De Daumier-Smith's Blue Period" and "Teddy," and continuing with "Franny," "Zooey," "Raise High the Roof Beam, Carpenters," and "Seymour: An Introduction."

The early stories are well-crafted, the late stories disdain craft and pursue ultimate truth. The late stories "seem to loosen," Russell writes, "as if in obedience to a new, anti-aesthetic principle." One is reminded of Tolstoy who, at the height of his powers and fame, began to disdain literature, and pursue ultimate truth.

Russell argues that "De Daumier-Smith" is a pivotal story in Salinger's *oeuvre* because it has the craft of the early stories, and also the philosophical depth of the late work. Russell calls his essay "From Daumier to Smith" because he believes that, at the beginning of the story, the protagonist is an aesthete, Daumier, but by the end of the story, he's become Smith, one who

---

1 *Wisconsin Studies in Contemporary Literature*, Vol. 4, No. 1, Special Number: Salinger (Winter, 1963), pp. 70-87. Online at jstor.org/stable/1207186.

2 In 1966, the journal *Modern Fiction Studies* devoted an issue to Salinger. The issue began with an essay by John Russell called "Salinger's Feat."

respects the sanctity of everyone and everything, one who says "Everybody is a nun."[1]

The aesthete Daumier wants to "escape the world," Russell says. Daumier is disgusted by reality: "Through his aesthetic reaction he has made a moral condemnation of the normal world." (One thinks of the young aesthete in Kierkegaard's *Either/Or*, whom Kierkegaard juxtaposes with a sober, mature, ethical character, Judge William.) Daumier is disgusted by a shop window, horrified that he'll always be "a visitor in a garden of enamel urinals and bedpans." Later, however, he has a mystical experience at the same shop window, and he learns non-discrimination, he learns the sanctity of everyone and everything.

Russell divides Salinger's protagonists into two groups: mystics and striving artists. Teddy and Seymour are the mystics. (Such mystics may create art but they aren't "striving artists," they're "pure artists.") Seymour preaches non-discrimination:

> I'll champion indiscrimination till doomsday, on the ground that it leads to health and a kind of very real, enviable happiness. Followed purely it's the way of the Tao, and undoubtedly the highest way.

According to Russell, such direct preaching is characteristic of Salinger's later works.

Daumier-Smith is a young teacher at an art correspondence school. His student, Sister Irma, is a nun. According to Russell, the plot resembles a poem by Emerson:

> Using first the young man's discovery and then his loss of Sister Irma, Salinger is paralleling exactly the theme of Emerson's "Each and All." In both poem and story the narrators begin by trying to possess and end by relinquishing—at which point wisdom and joy reach them.[2]

"Wisdom and joy" have supplanted the "blue period." Daumier-Smith has come to understand, Russell says, that "things and people are to be loved in their places, without any impulse to appropriate and change them." Salinger's un-enlightened characters often try to "appropriate and change"; Russell speaks of, "Holden Caulfield's rage to be protective."

Salinger's story ends with an idea that we often find in his later work: "Everybody is a nun." Every activity is sacred, as long as we're just doing

---

1 Russell says that the sanctity of everyone and everything is also the theme of Browning's "Pippa Passes" and Anatole France's "Our Lady's Juggler." Russell doesn't suggest, however, that Salinger was influenced by Browning or France.

2 Russell: "What does it mean to give Sister Irma her release? For de Daumier-Smith, it involves a rejection of living for art's sake and an acceptance of life unrecorded, untrumpeted, unappeased or made tragic or forced to chime in any other way with the customary drives of the artist. In making the rejection, our hyphenated hero has ceased being Daumier and has become Smith."

it, as long as we're "not governed by mind, logic, conscious furthering of self." Salinger often focuses on people's movements: "Salinger's work is filled with a kind of reverent record of the motions of people's hands and especially their feet." At the conclusion of "Seymour: An Introduction," Seymour's enlightenment is suggested by his graceful movements: "A thinking Seymour didn't cross a twilit street quickly, or surely didn't seem to. In that light, he came toward us much like a sailboat."

26. Louis Auchincloss

February 11, 2010

Louis Auchincloss, a prominent American writer, died recently. He was 92, and was still publishing novels in his 80s. He was born into New York City's WASP establishment ("Auchincloss" is a Scotch name), and often wrote about that establishment. An obituary in the *New York Times* said,

> Although he practiced law full time until 1987, Mr. Auchincloss published more than 60 books of fiction, biography and literary criticism in a writing career of more than a half-century. He was best known for his dozens and dozens of novels about what he called the "comfortable" world.

Was there something unfashionable about Auchincloss's fiction, something politically-incorrect? When the counter-culture movement of the 60s began, his reputation seemed to decline. I never heard of him until I saw his obituary. If I heard the name "Auchincloss" a few times, it was because of a connection between Jackie Kennedy's family and the Auchincloss family.

Auchincloss was more than a novelist, he was a man-of-letters. Among his non-fiction works are biographies of Woodrow Wilson and Teddy Roosevelt, and an autobiography called *A Writer's Capital*. He also wrote critical studies of Dreiser, Henry James, and others. According to the *Times*,

> Mr. Auchincloss's greatest influence was probably Edith Wharton, whose biography he wrote and with whom he felt a direct connection. His grandmother had summered with Wharton in Newport, R.I.; his parents were friends of Wharton's lawyers. He almost felt he knew Wharton personally, Mr. Auchincloss once said.

According to the *New Criterion*, "Since the deaths of Edmund Wilson and Lionel Trilling... Auchincloss now stands out as our most distinguished and versatile man of letters." If you want to try Auchincloss's fiction, consider one of his many short stories, or his novel *The Rector of Justin*, which was "a best seller and a finalist for the National Book Award, [and] is regarded by many critics as Mr. Auchincloss's best and most important novel."[1] Its protagonist is the headmaster (or "rector") of a New England private school. Among his other novels, *The Embezzler* was also a bestseller; *East Side*

---

[1] "Louis Auchincloss, Chronicler of New York's Upper Crust, Dies at 92," *New York Times*, January 27, 2010

Story traces an upper-class New York City family from the Civil War to the Vietnam War.

While Salinger was reclusive, Auchincloss was involved in civic affairs. "Mr. Auchincloss was a man of the city he knew so intimately, serving as president and chairman of the Museum of the City of New York."

I read his story, "The Cathedral Builder," which is in a volume called *Second Chance: Tales of Two Generations*. I found it intelligent, cultured, well-written, clear, readable. If it has no brilliant virtues, it has no conspicuous vices, either. It's just what one would expect from the author's reputation and biography. Auchincloss doesn't dig very deep, or soar very high, but he's enjoyable to read.

27. Miscellaneous

A.

While reading Harding's biography of Thoreau, I'm struck by how easily writers contact each other: Whitman contacts Emerson, Emerson contacts Carlyle, etc. Today things are very different, today it's difficult for an aspiring writer to contact an established writer, today established writers build walls around themselves (Solzhenitsyn, Salinger) or hide from the world like an outlaw (Pynchon), today established writers complain that they're besieged by hordes of aspiring writers. Today the literary world suffers from overpopulation, and from the bright light of the mass media, which makes fame burdensome.

B.

Many intellectuals have relationships with older women: Thomas Wolfe (his girlfriend Aline was 20 years older than he was), Hemingway (his first wife, Hadley, was 8 years older), D. H. Lawrence (his wife Frieda was 6 years older, and was married with three children when they met), Robert Louis Stevenson (his wife Fanny was 10 years older), Robert Musil (his wife Martha was 7 years older), Pablo Neruda (his second wife, Delia, was 20 years older), Erwin Panofsky (his first wife, Dora, was 8 years older), etc.

C.

Someone once said to Ibsen, "Your work is talked-about now, but I don't think it will appeal to future generations." Ibsen was horrified: "If you take away posterity, you take away everything." Walter Scott wanted to reach distant generations, as Shakespeare did. "What good is a reputation that only lasts for a couple of generations?" Scott asked.

Literature has always been a conversation between generations. Writers were inspired by authors who were dead, and tried to reach readers who were not yet born. In our time, however, writers seem to write for their contemporaries, perhaps because they don't revere the dead, as writers once did, perhaps because they don't care about the opinion of posterity.

28. Thomas Mann

I read a story by Thomas Mann called "A Man and His Dog" (sometimes called "Bashan and I"; the original German title is *Herr und Hund*).[1] Koestler calls this story "a masterpiece." It is indeed a first-rate story. Written during World War I, it depicts simple, domestic pleasures, and the beauty of the local park. Mann has an exceptional gift of style, tone, narrative voice.

It's an upbeat story, it takes a positive attitude toward the world, but Mann doesn't ignore the sordid aspects of dog-ownership. Mann's family purchased a young dog, and walked home with it.

> The homeward way [was] scarcely a triumphal procession.... [Bashan] proved to be suffering from an apparently chronic diarrhea, which obliged us to make frequent pauses under the villagers' eyes. At such times we formed a circle round him to shield his weakness from unfriendly eyes.

Mann is working within the great tradition of the European novel, he depicts life in all its aspects, while creating a work that's generally upbeat. He depicts the dark and sordid, but doesn't wallow in it, or underline it.

Mann was born in 1875, so he matured before Western civilization was traumatized by World War I. His tastes seem classical rather than avant-garde. He sees nature through the eyes of Claude Lorrain: "Nothing more agreeable to the eye," Mann writes, "than looking from the wild garden beneath one's feet to the humid massing of fine-leafed foliage that shuts in the view—foliage such as Claude Lorrain used to paint, three centuries ago."

Mann and Bashan encounter a hunter. Mann describes the hunter as "only a man in velveteens... not a gentleman.... rather rough-looking." Another translation describes the hunter as "only a plain man in corduroys and no particular class, but in your eyes [i.e., Bashan's eyes] he is the finest gentleman in the world." I couldn't find the German original, but I think it's clear that Mann is distinguishing between a man and a gentleman. In Mann's day, Western society still had class distinctions; not every man was a gentleman, and not every woman was a lady. But by the time Mann died in 1955, class distinctions had crumbled; any member of the male gender could be called "man" or "gentleman."

Mann realizes that much of the beauty of nature is water.

> I am very fond of brooks [he writes] as indeed of all water, from the ocean to the smallest reedy pool. If in the mountains in the summertime

---

[1] The standard translation of this work, and of Mann's other works, is by H. T. Lowe-Porter. Project Gutenberg has "Bashan and I" in a translation by Herman George Scheffauer. I think the Lowe-Porter translation is better than the Scheffauer translation. Old, classic translations like those by Lowe-Porter are always being re-done, perhaps to fix mistakes, perhaps to provide income for translators. John E. Woods criticized Lowe-Porter's translations, and made several Mann translations of his own. I think it's a bad idea for each generation to make its own translations.

> my ear but catch the sound of plashing and prattling from afar, I always go to seek out the source of the liquid sounds, a long way if I must.... I can lean on the rail of a little bridge over a brook and contemplate its currents, its whirlpools, and its steady flow for as long as you like.

I said above that "contact with nature may contain some elements of the mystic vision."[1] Mann's response to nature has these mystical elements. Koestler said that, in the mystical experience, "The 'I' ceases to exist because it has... established communication with, and been dissolved in, the universal pool." In the following passage, note the parallel between Mann's experience and the mystical experience: "The sight of water in whatever form or shape," Mann writes, "is my most lively and immediate kind of natural enjoyment; yes, I would even say that only in contemplation of it do I achieve true self-forgetfulness and feel my own limited individuality merge into the universal."

In an earlier issue, I discussed Lamarck's theory of evolution. This theory is often summarized as "the inheritance of acquired characteristics." I posed the question, Do animals inherit acquired knowledge? For example, is a dog born with a fear of bees, because its ancestors learned that a bee-sting is painful? Mann ponders these same questions; he speaks of "inborn experiences, unconscious memories."[2]

Mann gives us objective description as well as subjective response. He lists the various tree-species in the park; he approaches nature scientifically as well as aesthetically. As one critic put it, "the distinction of this narrative does not lie in its scientific accuracy but rather in the unique and fascinating fusion of *Wahrheit und Dichtung* [truth and poetry]."[3]

Mann's house still stands, just north of Bad Tölz, just east of the Isar River, and 30 miles south of Munich; the house probably isn't open to the public. Mann's LosAngeles house, and his family's Lübeck house, are open to the public.

29. Kafka

I'm now reading Kafka's novel, *The Trial.* It's described on the back cover as a "terrifying tale," but it strikes me as playful and humorous. Example: K. is walking to his "first interrogation." As he climbs a flight of stairs, he has to push his way through children who are playing on the stairs; "he had actually to wait for a moment until a marble came to rest, two children...holding him meanwhile by his trousers." A "terrifying tale"?

---

[1] See ljhammond.com/phlit/2023-02b.htm

[2] I wrote, "How is it possible that a dog is afraid of a bee, though it's never been stung? Perhaps it has an 'inherited memory,' a 'race memory,' a 'species memory,' a 'Lamarckian memory,' perhaps the acquired knowledge of its ancestors has been passed down." (See ljhammond.com/phlit/2023-01.htm#down30)

[3] See jstor.org/stable/30160379

Kafka's work is sprinkled not only with humor, but also with poetry. In the first chapter of *The Trial*, K. comes home from his job and speaks to his landlady, Frau Grubach. Frau Grubach assures him that Fraulein Bürstner's room is in good order, despite having been used by court officials earlier that day. She invites K. to look at the room himself. "'Thanks, I believe you,' said K., but went in through the open door all the same. The moon shone softly into the dark chamber." This soft moonlight is, in my view, poetry of the highest order: natural, realistic, and described in the simplest possible language. Surely such passages meant much to Kafka, and surely they contribute much to his place in world literature. As Kundera said, Kafka not only described the situation of modern man, he also found beauty in it.

Kundera writes like a professional writer: every step is planned, and every plan is executed. Kafka, on the other hand, wrote like an amateur: nothing is planned, nothing is finished. In Kafka's work, the parts mean more than the whole; Kafka was in love with the trees, and lost sight of the forest. Kafka didn't seem to think about his novel as a whole, he wrote without knowing where he was going, he was preoccupied with the act of writing, he sought the perfect sentence, he tried to make every sentence perfect.

While reading the final chapters of *The Trial*, I was impressed by the cathedral scene, which is certainly one of the novel's most memorable scenes. And I was struck once again by Kafka's obsession with moonlight; at the end of the novel, when Joseph K. is brought to a quarry to be executed, we're told that "the moon shone down on everything with that simplicity and serenity which no other light possesses."

The worst chapter in the novel is, in my opinion, Chapter 8, the chapter about Block. It's the only chapter that ends with the phrase, "[This chapter was never completed.]" Perhaps Chapter 8 should have been published in an appendix, along with the other unfinished chapters. If Kafka disliked that chapter as much as I do, that might explain why he left it in an unfinished state. I suspect that Kafka would be pained to hear that Chapter 8 is now read all over the world.

Why do I dislike that chapter so much? It's perverse, morbid; it shows the utter degradation of a human being. Like K., Block is a client of a lawyer named Huld. Block's attitude toward Huld is one of trembling submission:

> the client ceased to be a client and became the lawyer's dog. If the lawyer were to order this man to crawl under the bed as if into a kennel and bark there, he would gladly obey the order.

I'm fascinated by Nietzsche's remarks on the ideal poet:

> he will scent out those cases in which, in the *midst* of our modern world... the great and beautiful soul is still possible, still able to embody itself in the harmonious and well-proportioned and thus acquire visibility, duration and the status of a model, and in so doing through the excitation of envy and emulation help to create the future.[1]

---

1 *Assorted Opinions and Maxims*, #99

I'm fascinated by the idea that an imaginative writer can "help to create the future," can mold and inspire people. Nietzsche's ideal poet is the opposite of the modern poet; the modern poet doesn't depict a "great and beautiful soul," but rather concentrates on the morbid, the perverse, the sadistic, characters like Block.

When I read Nietzsche's remark at our discussion group, one person said that Nietzsche's "great and beautiful soul" would be awfully boring, and nobody in our group thought that Nietzsche's ideal poet was possible or desirable. But Nietzsche's idea isn't as far-fetched as it might seem; after all, Greek and Latin poets generally depicted people who were larger-than-life, better than actual people. As Aristotle said, "Sophocles might be called an imitator of the same kind as Homer, for they both represent good men."[1] Greek sculptors also depicted people who were idealized, but close enough to us that we respond to them. Greek art had an idealizing tendency. Renaissance culture, which followed ancient models, also had an idealizing tendency. Is an idealizing tendency possible today? Will Nietzsche's ideal poet arise in our time?

30. *The Leopard*

A. The Life of Lampedusa

The Leopard is an Italian novel, published in 1958, and quickly recognized as a classic. The author, Lampedusa, was from Sicily, and the novel is set in Sicily in the late 1800s, when Italy is being unified by Garibaldi and others. The Leopard isn't avant-garde, it's clear, realistic, classical. It's often humorous; indeed, much of its charm comes from its humor. In the original Italian, the title of the novel is *Il Gattopardo.*

In the novel, the name "Lampedusa" is changed to "Salina." The Leopard is the heraldic symbol or logo of the Prince of Salina. The protagonist of the novel is the Prince, i.e., The Leopard; the Prince is based on Lampedusa's great-grandfather.

There's an island south of Sicily called Lampedusa; it was owned by the Lampedusa family for almost 200 years, then sold in the 1840s to the Kingdom of Naples. And there's an island north of Sicily called Salina. The Lampedusa family is related to another "literary leopard," the Italian poet/essayist Giacomo Leopardi, whom Wikipedia calls, "the greatest Italian poet of the nineteenth century and one of the most important figures in the literature of the world."[2]

---

1 *Poetics*

2 On the link between Leopardi and Lampedusa, see <a href=https://www.theatlantic.com/magazine/archive/1963/02/lampedusa-in-sicily-the-lair-of-the-leopard/658778/ target=_blank>an article</a> in *Atlantic* magazine (February 1963) by Archibald Colquhoun, Lampedusa's English translator. The article can be read on the *Atlantic* website, or downloaded as a pdf. The pdf version is somewhat different, or at least differently arranged, than the website version.

Lampedusa is class-conscious; one might say he's more conscious of class than of anything else. The Leopard deals with the decline of the aristocracy. Lampedusa himself was a member of the aristocracy, he was the Prince of Lampedusa.

Lampedusa's Leopard takes a pessimistic view of the future, similar to the view I took in a recent issue.[1] The aristocracy is losing power, Lampedusa says, and the new regime will be worse. After the Prince sees peasants living in squalor,

> The Prince was depressed: "All this shouldn't last; but it will, always; the human 'always,' of course, a century, two centuries... and after that it will be different, but worse. We were the Leopards, the Lions; those who'll take our place will be little jackals, hyenas."[2]

A representative of the new regime asks the Prince to join the Senate. He responds, "For the moment, for a long time yet, there's nothing to be done. I am sorry; but I cannot lift a finger in politics. It would only get bitten."

We saw a similar attitude when we discussed *The Book of Ebenezer Le Page*. The author, G. B. Edwards, is writing about a young man named Neville:

> Edwards believes that we must endure the political situation: "As bad as Guernsey is, I hope [Neville] will not butt in and try and change it. It will change quick enough without his help; and for the worse and worse. He must endure it."

As the Portuguese philosopher Pessoa wrote,

> A terrible, progressive illness has fallen on our civilization.... The horror of action, which has to be vile in a vile society, sullied our spirit. The soul's higher activity sickened; only its lower activity, because it was more vital, did not decay.... The only recourse for souls born to command was abstention.

Pessoa was born in 1888, Lampedusa in 1896, Edwards in 1899. Is today's political situation confirmation of their dark predictions? Has our political situation become "worse and worse"?

Lampedusa is often compared to Edwards: both are known for one novel, both wrote their *magnum opus* late in life, both died before their novel was published. Lampedusa's novel is very good, but Edwards' is better—more humorous, more hopeful, more ecstatic. Edwards' language has a charm that a translation can't match (I read Lampedusa in translation).[3]

---

1 See ljhammond.com/phlit/2024-01.htm

2 *The Leopard*, Ch. 4

3 Lampedusa's translator, Archibald Colquhoun, describes Lampedusa's prose thus: "elaborate, allusive, has no equivalent in modern Italian and for us recalls Proust's.... It totally ignores the new stripped style of Italian writing since the war."(*Atlantic* article)

One might argue that the U.S. was started by people from the middle-class, or upper-middle-class; one might argue that the U.S. never had an aristocracy. But Lampedusa would probably say that the U.S. had an aristocracy, a different kind of aristocracy, an aristocracy not based on blood, but on "the length of time lived in a place."[1]

Length of time is important in the U.S., hence Americans often claimed Mayflower ancestry. Assuming "length of time" is important in the U.S., is it also important in Canada, Australia, Brazil, etc.?

Is "length of time" the only factor shaping class in America? In an earlier issue, I mentioned another factor: the social position that your ancestors occupied in the "mother country."[2] I mentioned the art historian Bernard Berenson, who felt that he was the social equal of anyone since his ancestors were in the upper class of their Jewish village in the "old country."

Lampedusa mentions another possible basis for an aristocracy: "greater knowledge of some text considered sacred." This might apply to China, where political power was given to those who excelled at literary exams. Or it might apply to Muslim society, where people are respected if they've memorized the Koran. Or it might apply to traditional Jewish society, where knowledge of the sacred texts was admired.

Lampedusa's aristocrats are losing power and losing estates. New men like Sedara are gaining power and gaining estates. Sedara rose from the peasant class, and ends up in the Senate (the same Senate that the Prince declines to join). Sedara is a swindler, a type I've often written about; Sedara is an expert at "the finding or weaving of hidden plots."[3] Aristocrats can be taken in by these plots; they have an "incapacity for self-defense."

The movie version of *The Leopard* is impressive, and enjoyable to watch. It's faithful to the novel, and it has a certain vitality. It's three hours long, but it holds your attention; it's in Italian, with subtitles; it was made in 1963. There are wonderful scenes of the Sicilian countryside. Wikipedia says, "The film is now widely regarded as a classic and one of the greatest

---

Edward Chaney discovered and promoted Edwards, and was close friends with Edwards. Edwards died in 1976, almost twenty years after the publication of *The Leopard*. I asked Chaney in an e-mail if Edwards were familiar with *The Leopard*. Chaney responded, "I don't think I have any documentary evidence that he read *The Leopard* (and don't remember him talking about it) but feel sure he would have done (since he was so very well-read and it received such a lot of acclaim when it was published and it would have been his kind of book)." I think it's likely that Edwards read *The Leopard* around 1960, and by the time he met Chaney around 1972, it was no longer on the front of his mind, so he didn't discuss it with Chaney.

1 *The Leopard*, Ch. 5

2 See ljhammond.com/phlit/2020-05b.htm#3

3 *The Leopard*, Ch. 4. In Chapter 6, Lampedusa speaks of "the rise of this man [i.e., Sedara] and a hundred others like him... their obscure intrigues and their tenacious greed." For more on swindlers, see ljhammond.com/phlit/2021-02c.htm#2

movies ever made." It brings the past to life, but it has neither idea nor humor nor suspense; it doesn't move the viewer. I would recommend it, but I wouldn't rave about it.

Lampedusa led a bookish, retired life; Wikipedia calls him, "A taciturn, solitary, shy, and somewhat misanthropic aristocrat, he opened up only with a few close friends." Much of his time with friends was spent reading aloud, teaching literary history, etc.

According to Wikipedia,

> In 1953, Lampedusa began to spend time with a group of young intellectuals, one of whom was future literary critic Francesco Orlando.... Their conversations soon turned into an intensive series of classes taught by Lampedusa. He taught Orlando English... and then began a series of classes on European literature. Lampedusa's notes for these classes were the most extensive piece of writing he ever did; they included a 1,000-page critical history of English literature from Bede to Graham Greene, including an effort to place the various writers in their historical-political contexts. This was followed by a less formal course on French literature and some less formal studies (Goethe, Spanish literature, Sicilian history) with individual members of the group.[1]

Doubtless no money changed hands in this "classroom." Would anyone in our time have such a passion to teach, such a passion to learn, so much respect for literature? In a democratic society like ours, where everyone needs to make a living, is it possible to have so much dedication to literature?

Lampedusa and his wife read aloud to each other in the evening.[2] (Characters in *The Leopard* sometimes read aloud to each other.) Lampedusa admired the famous military writer Clausewitz. His wife told Archibald Colquhoun, "I *begged* him not to read Clausewitz aloud to me."

It's characteristic of a great writer like Lampedusa to be more focused on reading than on writing. As I wrote in an earlier issue,

> Berenson's passion for reading distracted him from writing. Berenson says that, if he didn't achieve much, it's due to "an intemperate lust for reading, which has not diminished but grown with the years.... It is a commonplace that the more one loves to read the less one is likely to write." Perhaps Berenson was familiar with Wilde's remark, "I am too fond of reading books to care to write them."[3]

---

[1] Orlando's grandfather was the Prime Minister of Italy during World War I.

Lampedusa isn't the only great writer who did this sort of teaching. In an earlier issue, I mentioned the teaching efforts of F. Scott Fitzgerald and Isaak Babel (see ljhammond.com/phlit/2017-02b.htm#5).

[2] *Atlantic* article by Archibald Colquhoun

[3] See ljhammond.com/phlit/2003-12.htm

Lampedusa was finally inspired to write when his cousin Lucio Piccolo had some literary success, prompting Lampedusa to think, "If he can do it, I can too."

Lucio was one of the leading Italian poets of his generation; his work was esteemed by Yeats and Pound. He had a deep interest in the occult, which was then called "spiritualism." He corresponded with Yeats about fairies. Lampedusa scoffed at Lucio's spiritualism, and said to him, "You are immersed in the lowest superstitions." Lampedusa's failure to appreciate the occult is doubtless related to his failure to develop a mystical/Zennish/affirmative attitude.

As Lampedusa was writing *The Leopard*, he often read sections to his friends. His friends noticed "how close it came to the factual history of Palermo in days gone by."[1] Many great novels are rooted in fact.

One of the first people to appreciate *The Leopard*'s merit was Lampedusa's wife, Alessandra (Licy) Wolff Stomersee. Like Lampedusa, Licy was a cultured aristocrat; at her first meeting with Lampedusa, they talked about Shakespeare. Licy was a practicing psycho-therapist, and the president of the Italian Psychoanalytic Society; she died in 1982.

Lampedusa wanted to live in the family palace where his mother lived, and Licy couldn't get along with his mother, so Licy and Lampedusa didn't live together steadily until the last decade of Lampedusa's life. They had no children. Licy had been married previously; she married Lampedusa when she was 38 and Lampedusa was 36.

Though Lampedusa was a bookish man who seems to have had few *affaires de coeur*, his novel is filled with references to sex. For example, at the end of the novel, when his main characters have grown old, he writes, "They had had a very short affair thirty years before, and kept the intimacy—for which there is no substitute—conferred by a few hours spent between the same pair of sheets." Lampedusa's view of love is unromantic, disillusioned: "Flames for a year, ashes for thirty."

Lampedusa's protagonist (the Prince, The Leopard) takes a similar view of life in general:

> "I'm seventy-three years old, and all in all I may have lived, really lived, a total of two... three at the most."And the pains, the boredom, how long had they been? Useless to try to make himself count those; all of the rest: seventy years.

---

[1] *The Leopard*, preface by Lanza Tomasi. Great novels often start from reality. As I wrote in an earlier issue, "Most of the characters in Huck Finn are based on people Twain knew: Pap, Huck, Tom, Jim, the duke and the dauphin, Boggs and Col. Sherburn. Twain's fiction has a ring of truth because it's based on fact; as Twain put it, 'If you attempt to create a wholly imagined incident, adventure or situation, you will go astray and the artificiality will be detectable, but if you found on fact in your personal experience, it is an acorn, a root, and every created adornment that grows out of it, and spreads its foliage and blossoms to the sun will seem reality, not invention.'"(See ljhammond.com/phlit/2007-12.htm#9)

The preface to *The Leopard* is written by Gioacchino Lanza Tomasi, whom Wikipedia describes as Lampedusa's "distant cousin [and] adoptive son." Lanza Tomasi writes, "Lampedusa's readings of Stendhal had made him a disciple." Surely Stendhal influenced Lampedusa's approach to novel-writing.

Lampedusa was also fond of Dickens, Graham Greene, the Spanish playwright Lope de Vega, and many others. Lampedusa could read in many different languages, even Russian. Below is a photo of Lampedusa (right) with Lucio Piccolo (center) and Lanza Tomasi.

The Prince of Salina, the protagonist of The Leopard, has some loyalty to the old Kingdom of the Two Sicilies. The Prince's nephew, Tancredi, is fighting on the side of the new king, Victor Emmanuel II of Piedmont-Savoy, who hopes to unite Italy, with help from Garibaldi and others. (Tancredi is said to be based on Lanza Tomasi.)

The Prince tries to dissuade Tancredi from fighting for Victor Emmanuel. Tancredi says, "Unless we ourselves take a hand now, they'll foist a republic on us. *If we want things to stay as they are, things will have to change*."[1] This is the most famous line in the novel. The historian Gordon Wood called it, "A wonderful line that captures the dynamics of history—history is always changing."[2] It has been called The Lampedusa Strategy.

For more on Lampedusa, see *The Last Leopard: A Life of Giuseppe Tomasi di Lampedusa*, by David Gilmour. Lampedusa properties can be seen today in Palermo, Palma di Montechiaro, and Santa Margherita di Belice.

---

1 *The Leopard*, Ch. 1, italics added. The original is, "*Se vogliamo che tutto rimanga come è, bisogna che tutto cambi.*"

2 See c-span.org/video/?295328-1/depth-gordon-wood

The property at Santa Margherita di Belice belonged to Lampedusa's mother's family, and Lampedusa spent summers there as a youngster. It inspired "Donnafugata" in *The Leopard.* Lampedusa also wrote about this property in a fragment called "Places of My Infancy."

In *The Leopard,* the Prince of Salina daydreams about "Donnafugata and his palace, with its many-jetted fountains, its memories of saintly forebears, the sense it gave him of everlasting childhood." The property was lost to the family when an uncle abruptly sold his share. Lampedusa's widow encouraged him to write about the property to assuage his grief.

When the Prince of Salina is dying, he makes "a general balance sheet of his whole life, trying to sort out of the immense ash heap of liabilities the golden flecks of happy moments." Among the happy moments are "the first few hours of returns to Donnafugata, the sense of tradition and the perennial... time congealed." Also among the happy moments are

> many hours in the observatory.... Then, the dogs: Fufi, the fat pug of his childhood, the impetuous poodle Tom, confidant and friend, Speedy's gentle eyes, Bendicò's delicious nonsense, the caressing paws of Pop, the pointer at that moment searching for him under bushes and garden chairs and never to see him again.

Shakespeare grew up in a castle that had its own theater. Likewise, the palace at Santa Margherita had its own theater, so the young Lampedusa could watch plays without leaving home. He saw *Hamlet* for the first time at the family theater.

In Shakespeare's day, the aristocracy was richer and more powerful, so his family had actors on their own payroll. Lampedusa's family, on the other hand, rented their theater to the actors, who charged admission for their plays.

B. Jeffrey Meyers on *The Leopard*

Jeffrey Meyers, the most prolific of all literary critics, wrote about *The Leopard* in a short essay published in 1974.[1] The essay analyzes a painting by the French painter Greuze, a painting that gets the Prince's attention while he's resting by himself during a ball. The painting depicts the death of an elderly man, and foreshadows the Prince's own death. Meyers mentions other such foreshadowings: the soldier found dead in the garden at the start of the novel, the rabbit killed by the Prince and his hunting partner, the priest going to administer the last rites as the Prince is driving to the ball, etc.

The theme of *The Leopard,* Meyers argues, is in its first sentence, "*Nunc et in hora mortis nostrae* [now and in the hour of our death]."[2] The theme

---

1 "Greuze and Lampedusa's *Il Gattopardo*," by Jeffrey Meyers, *The Modern Language Review*, April, 1974, Vol. 69, No. 2, pp. 308-315, jstor.org/stable/3724577

2 For more on death in *The Leopard,* see
Kuhns, Richard F. "Modernity and Death: *The Leopard* by Giuseppe di Lampedusa." *Contemporary Psychoanalysis* 5.2 (1969): 95-119.

of *The Leopard* is "aristocratic pride in a moment of decline, and the erosion and extinction of a noble fortune, fame and family."

Lampedusa deals with death and decline, but his novel also has vitality, even *joie de vivre*. Lampedusa wrote, "Art has two constant unending preoccupations: it is always meditating upon death and it is always creating life."[1]

Meyers compares the ball scene near the end of *The Leopard* to a similar scene at the end of Proust's novel:

> Ponteleone's grand ball at the end of *Il Gattopardo* is closely modelled on the last scene of Proust's novel, "The Princess de Guermantes Receives," which illuminates the themes of change and decay, and the triumph of bourgeois over aristocratic values.

Meyers argues that another scene in The Leopard is comparable to a scene in *War and Peace*. Meyers writes,

> The moving scene of Tancredi's return from the wars with his friend Cavriaghi is influenced... by the similar return of Nicholai Rostov and his friend Denisov from the campaigns against Napoleon in War and Peace (iv.i).... In both *War and Peace* and *Il Gattopardo* the young warriors are greeted with excitement by the faithful retainer at the entrance to the great house... rush to the surprised and highly emotional reception of the large family circle, forget to introduce their weary companions, and search distractedly for their most beloved—Nicholai's mother and Tancredi's fiancée—who arrive after the climactic entrance.

C. Stendhal and Lampedusa

Meyers wrote another essay that discusses the influence of Stendhal's *Charterhouse of Parma* on *The Leopard*.[2] Like his Greuze essay, this essay is difficult to read for a monoglot like myself, since it has un-translated quotations from French and Italian. But it throws considerable light on Lampedusa and on Stendhal.

The Charterhouse of Parma was written in 1839, nine years after Stendhal's most famous novel, *The Red and the Black*. The protagonist of *Char-*

For another essay by Meyers, see
Meyers, Jeffrey. "Symbol and Structure in *The Leopard*." *Italian Quarterly* 9.34-35 (1965): 50-70.

1 This quote can be found in the *Atlantic* article, but I'm not sure which of Lampedusa's works it comes from. Colquhoun discusses some of Lampedusa's minor works, such as his short story "The Professor and the Mermaid," a re-writing of H. G. Wells' *The Sea Lady*.

2 "The Influence of *La Chartreuse de Parme* on *Il Gattopardo*," by Jeffrey Meyers, *Italica*, Sep., 1967, Vol. 44, No. 3, pp. 314-325, jstor.org/stable/477766

terhouse is Fabrice del Dongo, a young Italian nobleman who has some liberal ideas and joins Napoleon's army. Stendhal himself was born and raised in Grenoble, a French city that's near Italy and Switzerland. Stendhal was from the upper-middle-class (his father was a lawyer and landowner). Like Fabrice del Dongo, Stendhal had some liberal ideas and fought in Napoleon's army.

Both Stendhal and Lampedusa had good military records. Stendhal was known for staying cool during the disastrous retreat from Russia—he even stuck to his routine of shaving every morning. Lampedusa was taken prisoner by the Austro-Hungarian army; his family received no news, and thought he had died.

> Then his father learned that in a prisoner-of-war camp at Szombathely in Hungary there was an officer called Tomasi who read all day long [Tomasi was one of Lampedusa's many names]. This description made his father re-open the search and get him traced through the Vatican.... Lampedusa made two attempts to escape, the second time successfully. He crossed Europe alone, in disguise and on foot. He did not leave regular service until 1921, and when he did, it was with a very good military record.[1]

Lampedusa often told stories about his war experiences, and some of his closest friends were men he met in the prisoner-of-war camp.

One scholar says that Lampedusa's mother was "an adored figure in his life, while he was partially estranged from his father."[2] The same could be said of Stendhal. Should we view the two novelists as Sons of Jocasta?[3]

Fabrice, the protagonist of *Charterhouse*, turns away from society in disgust, and lives in a world of imagination. Discussing Fabrice's career possibilities, Stendhal writes, "Unfortunately, a gentleman can't become either a doctor or a lawyer, and this age belongs to the lawyers." The aristocracy has disintegrated, we live in the age of The Schemer. And the best schemers are lawyers, because they get the power of the law and the state behind their schemes. Stendhal writes, "Everyone here steals... There is nothing real, nothing that survives disgrace, save money."

Both Fabrice and The Leopard find peace in astronomy.

> For both heroes [Meyers writes] astronomy and contemplation-reverie are closely connected. [The Leopard's] evasion of reality, his solitude, and his isolation from society are all synthesized in his passion for astronomy.

Fabrice is assisted in his star-study by Priore Blanès, as The Leopard is assisted by Father Pirrone.

Meyers says that The Leopard's observatory is analogous to Fabrice's prison tower. "We are told again and again," Meyers writes, "that Fabrice

---

1 *Atlantic* article

2 *Atlantic* article

3 For more on Sons of Jocasta, see ljhammond.com/phlit/2020-11.htm#2

[enjoys] '*les douceurs de la prison*' [the pleasant hours spent in prison] and that '*jamais il n'avait été aussi heureux*' [he had never been so happy]. When finally released, '*il était au désespoir d'être hors de prison* [he was depressed to be out of prison].'"[1] Eventually Fabrice becomes a monk and enters the Charterhouse, voluntarily imprisoning himself. Meyers says that "Fabrice, like The Leopard, despises the class struggle, the fight for money and position, and the intrigues at court." Fabrice's prison tower, like The Leopard's observatory, is a refuge from the hurly-burly of life, from the struggle to get ahead.

Fabrice and The Leopard both choose inaction, both choose to abstain. The Leopard despises the scheming Sedara, but doesn't bother to resist him. Likewise, he doesn't bother to join the Senate. One critic, Martin Turnell, says that characters like The Leopard aren't escaping from life, they have their own set of values, and their values are opposed to society's values.[2] One could argue that characters like The Leopard aren't rejecting society, society is rejecting them. The Marxist literary critic Gyorgy Lukacs said of Stendhal,

> He depicts with admirable realism the inevitable catastrophe of these [lonely] types, their inevitable defeat in the struggle against the dominating forces of the age, their necessary withdrawal from life or more accurately, their necessary rejection by the world of their time.[3]

The Leopard's "defeat" is an indictment of his society, modern society, the society that arose in the 19th century. As Lukacs wrote of *Charterhouse*, "The fate of these characters is intended to reflect the vileness, the squalid loathesomeness of the whole epoch, an epoch in which there is no longer any room for the noble-minded." Meyers writes, "The heroes of Stendhal and Lampedusa are isolated from society by their own extraordinary gifts of intelligence and refinement. Because they are unique, their exceptional values and abilities die with them while the values they detest live on." Both Fabrice and The Leopard are disillusioned with all political parties: "A change of government would mean little more than a change of personalities."[4]

In his essay on Stendhal, Lampedusa said that Stendhal wanted to make us indignant at schemers, indignant at "such men and such methods [*Stendhal voleva indignare il lettore contro tali uomini e tali metodi*]." Meyers writes, "Surely Lampedusa arouses our indignation against the unscrupulous

---

1 In an earlier issue, I discussed a character created by Evelyn Waugh, and said that he enjoyed prison (see ljhammond.com/phlit/2022-07.htm#2).

2 In his Stendhal essay, Meyers quotes Turnell's book, *The Novel in France*. Turnell isn't discussing *The Leopard*, but his remarks seem to fit *The Leopard*.

3 In his Stendhal essay, Meyers quotes from Lukacs' *Studies in European Realism*.

4 Turnell, quoted in Meyers' essay on Stendhal. In a letter, Lampedusa said that his protagonist "completely expresses my own ideas."(*Atlantic* article)

Sedara." By arousing indignation, can novelists like Stendhal and Lampedusa mold behavior? Can they inspire people not to become schemers, but rather to pursue higher ideals—inside or outside society? If people like Stendhal and Lampedusa become extinct, will civilization be submerged beneath a sea of Sedaras?

The Leopard opts to "swallow the toad" and "cut a deal" with Sedara, he opts to adjust to a society that he despises, rather than engage in quixotic attempts at reform. The Leopard opts to "cling to the status quo and avoid leaps in the dark."

Meyers says that Lampedusa calls his protagonist "Fabrizio" after Stendhal's protagonist. But Lampedusa's great-grandfather (the model for Lampedusa's protagonist) actually had the name Fabrizio (his full name was Don Giulio Maria Fabrizio, Prince of Lampedusa). Likewise, Lampedusa makes his protagonist a star-gazer, not only because Stendhal's protagonist is a star-gazer, but also because Lampedusa's great-grandfather really was a star-gazer (he discovered two asteroids, and named them Palma and Lampedusa).

Perhaps Lampedusa was interested in *Charterhouse* partly because the protagonist had the same name (Fabrice/Fabrizio) as his great-grandfather, and the same hobby (astronomy). More importantly, Stendhal's protagonist had the same attitude toward life that Lampedusa had—disillusioned, detached, solitary. Lampedusa's views on Stendhal can be found in his essay "*Lezioni su Stendhal*."[1]

In *The Leopard*, the Prince's wife is "Maria Stella." The real Leopard (Lampedusa's great-grandfather) was also married to "Maria Stella." And the symbol of the Lampedusa family really was a leopard (or a similar animal). When Archibald Colquhoun visited Palma di Montechiaro around 1960, he found "an occasional leopard rampant clambering legless above a doorway."

Colquhoun says,

> The various members of the Lampedusa family of a hundred years ago [are] mentioned in the novel by their real Christian names, including the old Leopard himself, his mother, wife, sons, and daughters.... Even the most minor characters, the most glancingly mentioned places, seem transferred from the existing originals.

Even the dog Bendico is based on a real original; indeed, even the stuffed Bendico has a parallel in history.

Does this help to explain why *The Leopard* has what Colquhoun calls an "extraordinary sense of actuality, of the reader's being right there"? Of course, this "sense of actuality" is more than just a matter of names and

---

[1] Published in 1959 in *Paragone*, CXII, 40, Florence. Meyers refers to this essay.

Meyers argues that a particular scene in *The Leopard* is based on a scene in *Charterhouse*: "Fabrizio's audience with the Bourbon King Ferdinand, [is] closely modelled on a similar scene in *La Chartreuse*, Fabrice's audience with the Prince of Parma."

places, it's about Lampedusa's deep connection to those names and places; the novel's vitality reflects the author's vitality.

E. M. Forster was a fan of *The Leopard*, and called it, "One of the great *lonely* books."[1] This is a perceptive comment. On the surface, the Prince of Salina is quite social: he has a large family, a mistress, a hunting buddy, he attends a ball, etc. Only when you look beneath the surface does the Prince seem lonely.

Forster also said that Lampedusa's novel "has certainly enlarged my life—an unusual experience for a life which is well on into its eighties." Does all great literature enlarge our life?

31. Kundera

November 2, 1999
Last night, I picked up Kundera's book, *The Art of the Novel*, wondering if it would be suitable for our discussion group. I was deeply impressed. It's literature about literature—one of my favorite genres. It's a semi-philosophical work, a witty, profound, cultured book. I was fascinated by a chapter called "Sixty-three Words." This chapter consists of sixty-three definitions—or rather, sixty-three aphorisms (Kundera points out that the Greek word for definition is *aphorismos*). A few of these definitions are humorous:

LETTERS They are getting smaller and smaller in books these days. I imagine the death of literature: Bit by bit, without anyone noticing, the type shrinks until it becomes utterly invisible.

Others are serious:
COLLABORATOR ....In the course of the war against Nazism, the word "collaboration" took on a new meaning: putting oneself voluntarily at the service of a vile power.... Now that the word has been found, we realize more and more that man's activity is by nature a collaboration. All those who extol the mass media din, advertising's imbecilic smile, the neglect of the natural world, indiscretion raised to the status of a virtue—they deserve to be called "collaborators with modernity."

Such passages as this reveal Kundera as a fighter against philistinism, a fighter for culture, a fighter for culture by example as well as by precept. And isn't that the best that can be said of a writer?

In the last edition of Phlit, I suggested that one of you, my dear subscribers, might write a biographical sketch of Kundera, but no one took up the suggestion. My curiosity about Kundera drove me to scour the web for information, but all I found (as often happens with web searches) was links, links to more links, fancy fonts, fancy wallpapers, etc.

Finally, in despair, I wrote e-mail to a Kundera fan in Iceland:

Re: the elusive Kundera

---

1 Quoted in the *Atlantic* article, and in Meyers' Stendhal essay. Did Forster write an essay on Lampedusa? Where is this quote from?

> I'm curious to know: Is Kundera still alive? In good health? Living in Paris? Reclusive, or receptive to visitors? Involved in contemporary Czech affairs? Has children? Did he have the military camp experience that Ludvik has in *The Joke*? Does Ludvik = Kundera? Was his father killed by the Nazis, as Ludvik's father was? Etc., etc.

I received the following response:

> Dear sir, I recommend you to re-read his novels, it's all that counts. As you probably know, in *The Art of the Novel* he says that he wants, just like Flaubert, to disappear behind his work.

Thus I found myself in a debate about whether literature is subjective or objective. I began by asking, "did Flaubert really disappear behind his work?" Flaubert endowed his most famous character, Madame Bovary, with his own distaste for everyday reality; he once said, "*Madame Bovary, c'est moi.*" Flaubert said that he didn't want to have children: "I desire my flesh to perish, and have no wish to transmit to anyone the humiliating impotencies and the ignominies of existence."

True, Flaubert aimed to be objective, just as Kundera aims to be objective and to 'disappear behind his work,' but I don't think either Flaubert or Kundera succeeded in attaining objectivity. Their work is all the more vivid and absorbing because it reflects their own feelings and experiences. Flaubert's most interesting work, in my view, is his letters.

Kundera disagrees. Kundera thinks that we should ignore the creator, and concentrate on the creation:

> The moment Kafka attracts more attention than Joseph K., Kafka's posthumous death begins.... I refuse to put the *Letters to Felice* on the same level as *The Castle*.

But Kafka himself (according to his friend, Max Brod) liked biographies and autobiographies more than any other kind of literature. Indeed, Kafka took pains with his famous *Letter to Father*, and treated it as a literary work to be preserved with his other works; one might say that it was a *Letter to Posterity*, not a *Letter to Father*.

The best literature blends subjective and objective elements. Kundera and Flaubert aspired after objectivity, but didn't attain it. I admire their fiction, but I disagree with their fiction-theory.

February 5, 2000
Kundera's book, *The Art of the Novel*, contains a chapter on Kafka. I was pleased to see that Kundera shares my view that Kafka is fundamentally a humorous writer: "When Kafka read the first chapter of *The Trial* to his friends, everyone laughed, including the author.... The comic is inseparable from the very essence of the *Kafkan*."[1] Kundera argues that Dostoyevsky's *Crime and Punishment* is about an offender who seeks punishment, while *The Trial* is about an arrested person who seeks his offense, who seeks an

---

[1] Milan Kundera, *The Art of the Novel*, Harper & Row (paperback), V, 2, p. 104

answer to the question, "What have I done wrong?" I think this is a misreading of Kafka. K. isn't preoccupied with the cause of his arrest.

Paul Goodman, author of a book called *Kafka's Prayer*, says that the reader may wonder why K. is arrested, but K. himself "takes the unknown charge quite for granted."[1] Goodman's book is a penetrating Freudian view of Kafka and Kafka's work. Kundera's disdain for Freudian interpretations has, in my view, caused him to fall into some mis-readings of Kafka. But Kundera's *Art of the Novel* is a masterpiece of literary style, while Goodman's book is unimpressive as literature. It's difficult to make Freudian theories into good literature; Freudian theories can be applied everywhere, and they must be used with restraint and taste.

The Spanish philosopher Ortega wrote, "The genre of the novel, if it is not yet irretrievably exhausted, has certainly entered its last phase."[2] Pessimism about the future of the novel is widespread. But Kundera doesn't share that pessimism; Kundera is bullish on the future of the novel. He thinks that future novelists can explore four avenues: play, dream, thought, time:

Play	Kundera praises Sterne's *Tristram Shandy* and Diderot's *Jacques le Fataliste*: "They reach heights of playfulness, of lightness, never scaled before or since. Afterward, the novel got itself tied to the imperative of verisimilitude, to realistic settings, to chronological order."[3] Kundera is fond of the older novelists, of the pre-Balzac novelists. He's fond of their wide-ranging, free-spirited approach; they admit frankly that they are writers, novelists, they don't try to create a realistic world.
Dream	Kafka achieved "the fusion of dream and reality.... His enormous contribution is less the final step in a historical development than an unexpected opening that shows that the novel is a place where the imagination can explode as in a dream."
Thought	Musil and Broch made the novel "the supreme intellectual synthesis. Is their achievement the completion of the novel's history, or is it instead the invitation to a long journey?"[4] Broch seems to be Kundera's favorite novelist, the novelist who had the greatest influence on him.
Time	The novelist of the future can break the boundaries of one lifetime, and discuss an entire civilization, an entire millennium. "Aragon and Fuentes have already tried this."[5]

While lavishing praise on Kafka, Broch and Musil, Kundera is less fond of Joyce and Proust. He doesn't think that Joyce and Proust are in touch with modern realities:

---

[1] IV, 7

[2] *Notes on the Novel*

[3] I, 8, p. 15

[4] I, 8, p. 16

[5] ibid

> The time was past when man had only the monster of his own soul to grapple with, the peaceful time of Joyce and Proust. In the novels of Kafka, Hasek, Musil, Broch, the monster comes from outside and is called History ... it is impersonal, uncontrollable, incalculable, incomprehensible—and it is inescapable.[1]

I reject the notion that we're controlled by outside forces, that the modern world is a trap. I believe that we can find peace and freedom within ourselves, perhaps with the help of Zen. Kundera's description of the world may be true of Stalin's Russia, or of Stalin's Prague, but it isn't true of the world that I live in. The modern economy isn't an economy of obedient functionaries, like the economy of Kafka's time. The modern economy prizes initiative and creativity. The industrial age has given way to the information age, but Kundera doesn't take account of this change.

Don't misunderstand me, I'm not a fan of the modern world, I'm not more fond of the modern world than Kundera is. I disagree with some aspects of Kundera's description of the modern world, but I share his view that the modern world is an inhospitable place for culture. Kundera wrote, "The novel cannot live in peace with the spirit of our time;" it must develop "against the progress of the world."[2] I agree. I agree that the modern world, pervaded by business, media, etc., is not a friendly environment for the novel, for literature in general, for any type of higher culture. Where I differ with Kundera is that I believe it's possible for us to retire from the world, to create a space within ourselves that is beyond the reach of historical forces.

Descartes called man the "master and proprietor of nature." Kundera says that man is no longer the master of anything, he "is master neither of nature (it is vanishing, little by little, from the planet), nor of History (it has escaped him), nor of himself (he is led by the irrational forces of his soul)."[3] There is a deep truth here, but Kundera has carried it too far; man has more mastery than Kundera thinks. Kundera goes on to say that if God is no longer master, and man is no longer master, then the earth is hurtling through the void with no one at the steering wheel. "There it is, the unbearable lightness of being."[4] No, I don't agree! It's true that being is light, but this lightness isn't at all unbearable. Zen teaches us to become as light as being itself, Zen teaches us not only to find the lightness of being "bearable," but to rejoice in this lightness.

September 22, 2000
The Unbearable Lightness of Being
I didn't enjoy this novel as much as I enjoyed Kundera's first novel, *The Joke*. Methinks his first was his best—his most natural, his most spontaneous. *The Unbearable Lightness of Being* strikes me as somewhat contrived,

---

[1] I, 6, p. 11
[2] I, 10, p. 19
[3] II, p. 41
[4] ibid

as if Kundera were following certain theoretical principles, following a recipe. The plot is swallowed up by philosophical asides; in *The Joke*, on the other hand, the plot had considerable vitality.

But *Unbearable Lightness* is not without virtues: like all of Kundera's works, it's clear, readable and highly intelligent; it sheds much light on Communist society; it contains some interesting ideas and some memorable scenes. Nietzsche said (apropos of Schopenhauer) that the value of a philosopher's work lay not in his Big Ideas but in his Little Ideas, his casual observations. This is also true of Kundera's work. In *Unbearable Lightness*, the Big Ideas are rather dull, but there are many interesting little observations, such as the following insight into the nature of vertigo:

> What is vertigo? Fear of falling? Then why do we feel it even when the observation tower comes equipped with a sturdy handrail? No, vertigo is something other than the fear of falling. It is the voice of the emptiness below us which tempts and lures us, it is the desire to fall, against which, terrified, we defend ourselves.[1]

One of the novel's main characters, Tomas, is a doctor. Kundera says,

> he had come to medicine not by coincidence or calculation but by a deep inner desire. Insofar as it is possible to divide people into categories, the surest criterion is the deep-seated desires that orient them to one or another lifelong activity.[2]

Here again Kundera shows his gift for shrewd psychological insight. Incidentally, Kundera does such a good job of putting himself into the mind of a doctor that one almost suspects that he was a doctor himself.

Around 1970, a congressman visited my parents' house for a political-social evening. He sat on the floor—as my father long remembered, and remembered with disapproval. This incident came back to me when I read the following passage in Kundera's novel:

> Sitting on the floor when you had guests was at the time [late 1960s] a gesture signifying simplicity, informality, liberal politics, hospitality, and a Parisian way of life. The passion with which Marie-Claude sat on all floors was such that Franz began to worry she would take to sitting on the floor of the shop where she bought her cigarettes.[3]

Here again Kundera shows his gift for minute observation; in this case, the truth of the observation was confirmed by my own experience.

Kundera's *Unbearable Lightness* is a cold work, and no one will shed a tear over the human relationships that it describes. But like *The Joke*, it becomes warmer and sweeter at the end. *Unbearable Lightness* ends with a chapter on country life, a chapter so vivid that the reader is convinced that

---

[1] II, 17

[2] V, 7

[3] III, 6

Kundera must have lived in the country himself. This final chapter is a dog story, a touching story that must have caused many tears to flow.

In conclusion, permit me to quote Goethe: "a man's virtues are his own, his faults are those of his time." Kundera is imperfect, but so is every writer. Kundera's virtues are virtues that no other contemporary writer possesses.

June 26, 2003
The Book of Laughter and Forgetting
My reaction to this book was similar to my reaction to Kundera's *Unbearable Lightness of Being*: the story didn't engross me, but the book is highly readable, the ideas are interesting, and the union of plot and idea is often impressive. One interesting idea in *The Book of Laughter and Forgetting* is the idea of borders—more specifically, the idea that there is a border separating the meaningful from the meaningless, and we're always close to that border, we're always close to the feeling that life is meaningless:

> The woman he had loved most (he was thirty at the time) would tell him (he was nearly in despair when he heard it) that she held on to life by a thread. Yes, she did want to live, life gave her great joy, but she also knew that her 'I want to live' was spun from the threads of a spiderweb. It takes so little, so infinitely little, for someone to find himself on the other side of the border, where everything—love, convictions, faith, history—no longer has meaning. The whole mystery of human life resides in the fact that it is spent in the immediate proximity of, and even in direct contact with, that border, that it is separated from it not by kilometers but by barely a millimeter.[1]

As Hamlet put it, "How weary, stale, flat and unprofitable,/Seem to me all the uses of this world!" We have all felt this way at one time or another. What is the meaning and value of human life? This is a question that philosophy has never completely answered, and it's also a question that people ask themselves many times in the course of their lives.

Is this idea of "borders" an original idea? Or did Kundera get it from another writer? We find the same idea in Sainte-Beuve: "Extreme happiness just barely separated, by a trembling leaf, from extreme despair—isn't this life? (L'extrême félicité à peine séparée par une feuille tremblante de l'extrême désespoir, n'est-ce pas la vie?)" We also find this idea in Kierkegaard: "I live continually on the border of the happy and the desert Arabia."

32. Cioran, etc.

I recently received e-mail from Richard Costa, a Phlit subscriber in Brazil. Richard asked me what I thought of Cioran. I told him I had never heard of Cioran, and I asked Richard to tell me about him.

Cioran was a Romanian writer who lived most of his life in France, and wrote in French. Cioran was born in 1911, and died in 1995. Cioran said, "I

---

[1] Part VII, ch. 6, p. 281

have no nationality—the best possible status for an intellectual." While attending college in Bucharest, he became friends with Eugène Ionesco, the playwright, and Mircea Eliade, who became known for his work on the history of religion.

Cioran was influenced by Nietzsche, and like Nietzsche, he wrote aphorisms and short essays. Richard calls him "the king of pessimists," and his books have titles like *On the Heights of Despair* and *The Trouble With Being Born*. Cioran also wrote *Anathemas and Admirations*, which contains a vivid portrait of his friend Samuel Beckett. Beckett wrote an article on Cioran that introduced Cioran to the English-speaking world; in his article, Beckett said "[Cioran] is not a writer of despair, there is always a little blue light." Cioran's financial situation was precarious; "I don't make a living," he said, "I eke one out."

33. Gabriel Garcia Marquez

A. "The Handsomest Drowned Man in the World"

The local GreatBooks group, which has often inspired me to try new authors, recently inspired me to try the Colombian author Gabriel Garcia Marquez. Marquez was born in 1927, won the Nobel Prize in 1982, and died in 2014. Marquez was a friend of Castro, and Marquez's harsh criticism of the U.S. led to his being banned from the U.S. (the ban was finally lifted during Clinton's tenure; Clinton said that Marquez's *One Hundred Years of Solitude* was his favorite novel).

Marquez and Castro knew each other as students in Bogota in the late 1940s. Marquez said of Castro, "Ours is an intellectual friendship. It may not be widely known that Fidel is a very cultured man. When we're together, we talk a great deal about literature."

Marquez is known for a literary genre called "magical realism." This approach may have been inspired by his grandmother, who often spoke of occult things in a matter-of-fact way. Or it may have been inspired by Kafka, who mixed wild fantasy with precise realism.

Perhaps my own writings should be called "magical realism" since I have a keen interest in the magical/occult, and an equal interest in concrete realism. At any rate, I was immediately attracted to Marquez. The GreatBooks group discussed a Marquez story called "The Handsomest Drowned Man in the World." I would describe the story as short, readable, and poetic; I recommend it without qualification.

In Kafka's "Metamorphosis," the protagonist turns into an insect. This kind of wild fantasy can't be found in Marquez's story. Marquez describes things that you can almost believe—if you're receptive to the occult. But Marquez goes slightly beyond the occult into the fantastic.

For example, the drowned man seems to influence the weather, there seems to be some correspondence between nature and the human sphere. This is a classic example of the occult; we've discussed this in connection with *Macbeth*, etc. If you're receptive to the occult, then you probably believe that nature and the human sphere may indeed be connected.

However, Marquez takes this ancient theme a little further than is believable; he goes beyond the "believable occult" into "fantasy occult." In the last sentence of the story, Marquez says that the drowned man has had a permanent effect on the weather in the village. This is hard for anyone to believe—even someone who's receptive to the occult.

The story deals with another ancient occult theme: the significance of names. The villagers think that the drowned man must be named Esteban: "Most of them had only to take another look at him to see that he could not have any other name." In 1952, Marquez wrote an article called "One Must Be Like the Name." Marquez says that he once heard the remark, "He had the face of someone named Roberto, but his name was José."[1]

A critic named Paul Hedeen has given us a good summary of the story. He says that the drowned man represents the "introduction of a new god":

> Here redemption for a town comes in the form of death, the drowned man, and his appearance completely reorders the town, giving it purpose and saving it from its narrow existence and its solitude. The people even bury the body in the sea without an anchor "so that he could come back if he wished and whenever he wished." The drowned man becomes a fertility symbol when in his memory the people of the town completely decorate with flowers a promontory that can be seen from far out to sea.[2]

B. *One Hundred Years of Solitude*

I read the famous novel by Gabriel Garcia Marquez, *One Hundred Years of Solitude*. Wikipedia has this to say about the novel:

> Since he was 18, Garcia Marquez had wanted to write a novel based on his grandparents' house where he grew up. However, he struggled with finding an appropriate tone and put off the idea until one day the answer hit him while driving his family to Acapulco. He turned the car around and the family returned home so he could begin writing. He sold his car so his family would have money to live on while he wrote. Writing the novel took far longer than he expected; he wrote every day

---

1 Goethe was receptive to the occult, and inclined to believe in the occult significance of names. He said, "I shall always be Goethe.... When I say my name, I say everything that I am." Wikipedia says, "Nominative determinism is the theory that a person's name can have a significant role in determining job, profession or even character. It was a commonly held notion in the ancient world." (Wikipedia, "Nominative Determinism") According to the ancients, *nomen est omen*. One might compare one's name with the time of one's birth, which is significant in astrology. For more on names, consider *The Language of Names*, by Justin Kaplan and Anne Bernays.

2 Paul M. Hedeen, "Gabriel Garcia Marquez's Dialectic of Solitude" (originally published in *Southwest Review*, Autumn, 1983, #68), included in *Bloom's Modern Critical Interpretations: Gabriel Garcia Marquez's One Hundred Years of Solitude*, edited and with an introduction by Harold Bloom

> for 18 months. His wife had to ask for food on credit from their butcher and baker as well as nine months of rent on credit from their landlord.
>
> During the 18 months of writing, Garcia Marquez met with two couples... every night and discussed the progress of the novel, trying out different versions. When the book was published in 1967, it became his most commercially successful novel... selling over 50 million copies.... The story chronicles several generations of the Buendia family from the time they founded the fictional South American village of Macondo, through their trials and tribulations, and instances of incest, births, and deaths. The history of Macondo is often generalized by critics to represent rural towns throughout Latin America or at least near Garcia Marquez's native Aracataca.

Perhaps a Marquez scholar could tell us more about this "Acapulco moment," this Eureka moment. What was the idea that brought the book together, that inspired Marquez to turn his car around, abandon his vacation plan, and start writing? In an earlier issue, I wrote, "After Dostoyevsky lost all his money in a German casino, the plot of *Crime and Punishment* came to him in a flash, a vision." I wouldn't say that Marquez' Acapulco moment was a vision; I would call it an idea, a strategy. And I wouldn't describe Marquez' strategy as a plot because *One Hundred Years* doesn't really have a plot; perhaps the term "plot device" would be more appropriate.

[Spoiler warning: If you're thinking of reading Marquez' novel, you might want to skip the rest of this section.]

So what was the plot device that prompted Marquez to turn his car around? Perhaps it was the device that appears at the end of the novel—the prophecies of the gypsy alchemist, Melquiades, prophecies which describe the whole history of the Buendia family, prophecies which are finally deciphered at the end of the novel by the last of the Buendias, who reads of his own demise as his life is ending. It's a clever ending, but does it touch the reader? Does the reader care about these characters?

Marquez has a deep grasp of the occult, but he stretches the occult beyond truth, beyond credibility. Nobody can really believe that Melquiades prophesied the whole history of the Buendia family, or that the last Buendia was simultaneously reading the prophecy and living it. Marquez frequently refers to Nostradamus; Melquiades is a small-town Nostradamus. The prophecies of Nostradamus are a serious matter; Jung wrote a serious study of them.[1] But with Marquez, prophecy becomes an amusement, a device. If you're interested in the occult, as I am, you'll find Marquez continually interesting, but continually disappointing.

In the last chapter of *One Hundred Years*, Marquez says that, in the prophecies of Melquiades, "Melquiades had not put events in the order of man's conventional time, but had concentrated a century of daily episodes in such a way that they coexisted in one instant." This is an interesting idea, especially if the reader is interested in the occult, but is it believable? Does

---

[1] See Ch. 7 of Jung's *Aion*. *Aion* is Volume 9 in Jung's Collected Works—more specifically, Volume 9, Part 2.

it touch the reader? Marquez is overthrowing our everyday conception of time, he's overthrowing linear time; he's saying that the future exists already, and can be grasped by prophets like Nostradamus and Melquiades. All of this is interesting in an intellectual way, and it's an amusing fantasy, but it doesn't come out of the author's own experience, and it doesn't touch the reader's heart.

In my *Realms of Gold*, I said that Thomas Wolfe anticipated his early death: "Something has spoken to me in the night," Wolfe wrote, "burning the tapers of the waning year; something has spoken in the night, and told me I must die.... A wind is rising, and the rivers flow." Here we have a prophecy that's both touching and realistic, it comes out of the author's heart, and it touches the reader's heart. But the prophecies of Marquez seem like mere devices, wild fantasies.

Furthermore, the prophecies of Melquiades are written in a complicated code: "He had written it in Sanskrit, which was his mother tongue, and he had encoded the even lines in the private cipher of the Emperor Augustus and the odd ones in a Lacedemonian military code." So instead of genuine prophecy, we have wild fantasy.

One day, four boys attempt to destroy the prophecies. "But as soon as they laid hands on the yellowed sheets an angelic force lifted them off the ground and held them suspended in the air until Aureliano returned and took the parchments away from them." Again we have a wild fantasy, a story that lacks the ring of truth.

Marquez depicts twins who die at the same time. This is interesting to a student of the occult; twins are often "entangled," they often have a telepathic bond. But dying at the same time? Why would a telepathic rapport lead twins to die at the same time? Again, Marquez is taking an occult notion and giving it a strange twist, he's changing it from a deep truth to a wild fantasy. A more likely situation would be for one twin to die, and the other to sense this death; or for one twin to die, and the other to hear himself called, at the moment of death, by the dying twin.

When twins die at the same time, I'm reminded of Adams and Jefferson dying on July 4; Adams and Jefferson wanted to live until July 4; their will-to-live enabled them to reach the 4th. But Marquez' twins have no such reason to die together.

Arthur Koestler died with his wife in a "suicide pact," as did the Austrian writer Stefan Zweig, and the German writer Kleist. But with Marquez' twins, there's no such pact, no desire to die together. So the simultaneous death of Marquez' twins doesn't have the ring of truth.

Marquez plays with the idea of entangled twins, as he plays with many occult ideas. He carries the idea to an extreme, so it becomes absurd or humorous:

> Until the beginning of adolescence they were two synchronized machines. They would wake up at the same time, have the urge to go to the bathroom at the same time, suffer the same upsets in health, and they even dreamed about the same things.... Santa Sofia de la Piedad

gave one of them a glass of lemonade and as soon as he tasted it the other one said that it needed sugar.

As in his story "The Handsomest Drowned Man in the World," Marquez plays with the idea that your name is your destiny (*nomen est omen*). Many of the male characters in *One Hundred Years* are named Aureliano or Jose Arcadio. Marquez says, "While the Aurelianos were withdrawn, but with lucid minds, the Jose Arcadios were impulsive and enterprising, but they were marked with a tragic sign." Your name determines your personality, your destiny.

One of the basic truths of the occult is mind over matter. Matter is, in some sense, conscious and alive, and can therefore be influenced by mind, will. People can will themselves to live longer, or to die sooner, as we see in the case of Adams and Jefferson. Nietzsche had limited interest in the occult, but he did realize that the will plays a role in death; he said that the deaths of Socrates and Jesus were willed deaths, and he said, "One perishes by no one but oneself."[1]

Marquez often deals with willed death. He says, "Buendias died without any illness." When Amaranta Ursula is bleeding profusely, she tells her husband "not to worry because people like her were not made to die against their will." It's their own will that kills people, Marquez and Nietzsche say, not physical causes.

Ursula says that she's "waiting for the rain to stop in order to die." When it finally stops raining, "Ursula had to make a great effort to fulfill her promise to die when it cleared." Here again, Marquez takes a classic occult situation—mind over matter, willed death—and gives it a twist. Usually a person wills to stay alive, as Adams and Jefferson willed to stay alive until July 4. Or they have a will to die, but this will is unconscious, or semi-conscious. But with Marquez, we have something new and different and strange: Ursula makes a "great effort" to die, but doesn't commit suicide.

Why does Marquez give occult situations a strange twist? Perhaps because LatinAmerican literature is saturated with the occult, so the occult became boring, and needed a dash of spice, a new twist. When I discussed a Brazilian novel, *The Alchemist*, I noted the many occult themes. When I discussed Marquez' "The Handsomest Drowned Man in the World," I noted the many occult themes. And when I discussed a story by Borges called "The Meeting," I said that it had "a whiff of the occult." So perhaps Marquez thought that the occult was old and stale, and needed a twist.

Another possibility is that Marquez was influenced by Borges, who stretches the occult into wild fantasy. In an earlier issue, I wrote,

> Borges seems to regard the occult not as real, but as something that can add spice to a fictional work. The occult element in this story [i.e., in "The Meeting"] (knives with a vendetta against each other) is unreal,

---

[1] *Twilight of the Idols*, "Expeditions of an Untimely Man," #36. On Socrates and Jesus, see Nietzsche's *Assorted Opinions and Maxims*, #94 (this book is part of the second volume of Nietzsche's *Human, All-Too-Human*). See also Nietzsche's *Twilight of the Idols*, "The Problem of Socrates," #12.

> unconvincing, false. Many great literary works deal with the occult and stay within the boundaries of truth—for example, Lawrence's "The Fox"—but Borges goes beyond these boundaries. Perhaps this makes Borges popular with critics and academics—people who are interested in art, in craft, not in truth, not in reality. Great literature speaks to your own experience, and grabs you by the throat. But "The Meeting" doesn't speak to anyone's experience, it's just a story; it shouldn't be called magical realism, it should be called unreal magic.

So perhaps Marquez wasn't bored with the occult, but rather he felt that the occult should be blended with wild fantasy, because his mentor (Borges) had written this way.

The *paterfamilias* of the Buendia clan is Jose Arcadio Buendia, a giant man who goes mad and is tied to a tree. When his wife, Ursula, decides to move him to his bedroom, "Not only was he as heavy as ever, but during his prolonged stay under the chestnut tree he had developed the faculty of being able to increase his weight at will, to such a degree that seven men were unable to lift him and they had to drag him to the bed." Here we have another example of mind over matter; the will can make one heavier. This idea isn't as wild as it might seem; I've seen karate experts appear to make themselves heavier to avoid being lifted.

In a recent issue, I discussed the character of the "holy fool," the "dummling" with deep wisdom.[1] Marquez' novel has a holy fool named Remedios the Beauty.

> She reached twenty without knowing how to read or write, unable to use the silver at the table, wandering naked through the house because her nature rejected all manner of convention.... It seemed as if some penetrating lucidity permitted her to see the reality of things beyond any formalism.

When Fernanda sees Remedios the Beauty "eating with her hands, incapable of giving an answer that was not a miracle of simplemindedness," she thinks Remedios the Beauty is an idiot. But the Colonel takes a different view; he thought "Remedios the Beauty was in no way mentally retarded, as was generally believed, but quite the opposite." The Colonel says, "It's as if she's come back from twenty years of war." War enables one to penetrate "beyond any formalism" to the "reality of things." The Colonel and Remedios the Beauty have both gone beyond conventions and formalities. The Colonel is disillusioned, Remedios the Beauty is naive, a holy fool.

So Marquez is capable of creating interesting characters, but he doesn't seem to create a fictional world that you can believe in, a fictional world that makes you "suspend your disbelief." You don't feel that his characters are real people, that his novel is a real world.

When the Colonel is captured and sentenced to death, he's surprised to find that he has no premonition of death. The Colonel is a prophet, and he trusts his premonitions. "Since the beginning of adolescence, when he had

---

1 See ljhammond.com/phlit/2023-03.htm

begun to be aware of his premonitions, he thought that death would be announced with a definite, unequivocal, irrevocable signal, but there were only a few hours left before he would die and the signal had not come."

Why doesn't the signal come? Because he isn't going to die; his executioners don't dare to kill him, they're afraid that the townspeople will rise up against them. Marquez has a deep grasp of the occult; Marquez realizes that premonitions can foretell the future, and the lack of a premonition can also foretell the future.[1]

As a stylist, Marquez is impressive, even when read in translation. His work holds your attention; it has clarity, force, life. But do his characters come alive? Can the reader empathize with these characters? Proust's narrator comes alive because he's Proust himself—his loves, his losses, his dreams. Each of the Karamazov brothers represents a facet of Dostoyevsky himself, and each of them comes to life. Hamlet has often been said to reflect Shakespeare himself. But Marquez' characters don't represent Marquez; it's difficult to believe in these characters. They remain at "arm's length" for the author, and for the reader.

When one of the Buendia boys asks his brother what sex feels like, the answer is, "It's like an earthquake." This is great writing: it's a poetic image, it's a description, it's a witticism, and it's very concise. Marquez is a first-rate stylist. But the earthquake metaphor isn't enough to draw the reader into this fictional world. Sex plays an important role in Marquez' novel, but it's never beautiful or touching. *One Hundred Years* doesn't have plot or suspense; it has great writing, and an abundance of ideas, an abundance of occult situations.

Marquez has a firm grasp of politics and war, at least in the context of Latin America. He probably knew many people who had experienced war, and he may have experienced war himself. One of the Buendias, Colonel Aureliano Buendia, fights a long war against the Conservative forces. After many years of fighting, the Colonel says to a comrade,

> "Tell me something, old friend: why are you fighting?" "What other reason could there be?" [the comrade] answered. "For the great Liberal party." "You're lucky because you know why," [the Colonel] answered. "As far as I'm concerned, I've come to realize only just now that I'm fighting because of pride." "That's bad."

Perhaps wars are often fought from pride, to avoid humiliation. The original cause of war is forgotten, but the war goes on, it has a momentum of its own, neither side wants to admit defeat, both sides want power for the sake of power.

---

[1] D. H. Lawrence also realized that the lack of a premonition is significant. He writes, "On the Sunday afternoon he went to Keston to meet Clara at the station. As he stood on the platform he was trying to examine in himself if he had a premonition. 'Do I *feel* as if she'd come?' he said to himself, and he tried to find out. His heart felt queer and contracted. That seemed like foreboding. Then he *had* a foreboding she would not come!"

Both sides commit atrocities. War takes a toll on the conscience, the soul. When the Colonel has a widow's house reduced to ashes, his comrade says, "Watch out for your heart, Aureliano.... You're rotting alive."

Finally the Colonel decides to stop fighting, and says to his comrade,

> "Put on your shoes and help me get this shitty war over with." When he said it he did not know that it was easier to start a war than to end one. It took him almost a year of fierce and bloody effort to force the government to propose conditions of peace favorable to the rebels and another year to convince his own partisans of the convenience of accepting them.

At the end of the war, the Colonel is utterly disillusioned, with no hopes or dreams, no notion of glory. He keeps busy by making metal fish, he tries to numb his mind, so "there was not the smallest empty moment left for him to fill with his disillusionment of the war."

Marquez seems to be angry at the foreigners (Americans?) who come to Macondo to profit from the banana business. But the people suffer as much from civil wars as from the foreigners.

A critic named Linda B. Hall wrote an essay on Marquez' novel; she called her essay "Labyrinthine Solitude," a reference to the title of Marquez' novel and to the title of a book by Octavio Paz, *The Labyrinth of Solitude.* Paz was about 15 years older than Marquez, and his *Labyrinth of Solitude* was published about 15 years before *One Hundred Years of Solitude.* In her essay, Hall says that modernity has made Latin Americans solitary. Traditional society was "peaceful, static, rural," while modernity means "the throwing of the individual, alone and unaided, onto the urban labor market." Hall quotes Paz, who says that modern solitude doesn't strengthen the soul, it's "utter damnation... the random solitude of hotels, offices, shops and movie theaters."

But Marquez' characters are in a small town, not in the "urban labor market." I'm not convinced that Marquez has depicted modern solitude, though I accept the argument that he was influenced by Paz. The solitude in Marquez' novel is often strange and unreal, as when a dead man (Prudencio Aguilar) seeks the company of the living. Another dead man, Melquiades, "had been through death, but he had returned because he could not bear the solitude."

According to Paz, "death and birth are the two extreme solitary experiences."[1] People want to die with someone else, as in the suicide pacts that I mentioned above. As for the state of death, I don't think we know whether there's life after death, what sort of life it is, and whether it involves the feeling of loneliness.

Hall says that, for Paz and Marquez, "the deepest form of communion and the closest antidote to solitude is sexual love.... The act of love is a combination of the forces of creation and destruction that furnishes to man, for a fraction of a second, a 'more perfect state of being.'" This strikes me as a valid point, but does Marquez embody this in his novel? For example, the

---

[1] This is a quote from Hall, not Paz.

young man who describes sex as an earthquake—is he seeking communion, or is he seeking pleasure and experience? And the older woman, Pilar Ternera, has sex with various men, but I don't think she's seeking an "antidote to solitude."

Isaak Babel said of Nabokov, "He can write, but he's got nothing to say." This is how I feel about Marquez. What is Marquez trying to say? He's a brilliant stylist, and he has an astonishing grasp of occult situations, but he doesn't take the occult seriously, he twists it into wild fantasy. He doesn't try to reach truth, or provide a reason for hope.

34. Borges

"The Meeting," by Jorge Luis Borges, has a touch of magic, a whiff of the occult; it's a good example of what critics call "magical realism". Though I enjoyed it, I have some objections; I'm still not willing to include Borges among the great writers. A great writer is fascinated by reality, and he depicts reality, but Borges seems to be immersed in books, and unable to depict reality. "It was obvious," the narrator says, "that everybody was drunk; I do not know whether there were two or three emptied bottles on the floor or whether an excess of movies suggests this false memory to me." Borges seems to suffer from an excess of books and movies. He doesn't see reality face to face, he sees it through the lens of culture.

Borges seems to regard the occult not as real, but as something that can add spice to a fictional work. The occult element in this story (knives with a vendetta against each other) is unreal, unconvincing, false. Many great literary works deal with the occult and stay within the boundaries of truth—for example, Lawrence's "The Fox"—but Borges goes beyond these boundaries. Perhaps this makes Borges popular with critics and academics—people who are interested in art, in craft, not in truth, not in reality. Great literature speaks to your own experience, and grabs you by the throat. But "The Meeting" doesn't speak to anyone's experience, it's just a story; it shouldn't be called magical realism, it should be called unreal magic.

The dying man in Borges' story says, "How strange. All this is like a dream." It's not like reality.

35. *The Alchemist*, by Paulo Coelho

I read a popular novel called *The Alchemist*. It was written in 1988 by Paulo Coelho, a Brazilian, and it has become an international bestseller. One might call it self-help literature in fictional form. It says that you can live your dream. It says that when we're young, we have hopes and dreams, but later we lose hope and we stop dreaming. "The world's greatest lie," Coelho writes, is that "at a certain point in our lives, we lose control of what's happening to us, and our lives become controlled by fate."

But if we live our dream, the universe will assist us through some sort of synchronicity, through the power of will, the power of intuition. We can make our dream a reality by the power of will. As Goethe said, "What one longs for in youth, one has in old age in abundance."[1] As an epigraph for *The Alchemist*, Coelho could have used this Nietzsche quote: "Do not reject the hero in your soul! Keep holy your highest hope!"[2] And Coelho would approve of the quote that Melville kept on his desk: "Stay true to the dreams of thy youth." Writers like Goethe, Nietzsche, and Melville are dreamers; they're driven by their dreams, not by the hope of a paycheck or a position. So *The Alchemist* would strike a chord with them.

There are deep truths in *The Alchemist*, and in self-help literature: mind over matter, the power of will, the wisdom of dreams/intuitions. *The Alchemist* is short and easy to read. The plot holds your attention, and there are many interesting thoughts. I wouldn't recommend it enthusiastically, and I wouldn't call it a great book, but I don't regret reading it.

[Spoiler Warning: If you're thinking of reading *The Alchemist*, you may want to stop here.]

At the start of the novel, the protagonist, a Spanish shepherd boy named Santiago, has a recurring dream that a treasure awaits him at the Pyramids. He decides to sell his flock of sheep and pursue his dream. Much of the novel consists of Santiago's journey through the desert to the Pyramids. Coelho talks much about the desert, and the people who live there.

Soon after Santiago sells his sheep, his money is stolen. Later he loses his money a second time. His guru, an alchemist, tells him that he will lose his money a third time because everything happens in threes: "You have already lost your savings twice.... I'm an old, superstitious Arab, and I believe in our proverbs. There's one that says, 'Everything that happens once can never happen again. But everything that happens twice will surely happen a third time.'"

Coelho seems to understand desert culture, and this proverb about things happening three times is probably a genuine piece of Arab wisdom. It may well correspond with reality, and if it does, we would expect to find it in other cultures. In his Youtube videos, Alexander Waugh often quotes

---

1 This is the epigraph of Goethe's autobiography. The German is, *Was man in der Jugend wünscht, hat man im Alter die fülle*. (Another epigraph of Goethe's autobiography is Menander's remark, "He who has not been thrashed has not been educated." Perhaps the Menander epigraph appears in the second volume of Goethe's autobiography?)

The Alchemist is saturated with the occult. Brazilians are probably more interested in the occult than Western Europeans, Americans, etc. Russians, too, have a strong interest in the occult. "To believe in esoteric, mind-reading or alchemy is typical for Russian elites."(quote from Twitter, Sergej Sumlenny) In an earlier issue, I said that the Russian intellectual Alexander Dugin was "drawn to Hermetism."

2 From Nietzsche's *Thus Spoke Zarathustra*, "Of the Tree on the Mountainside"

the Elizabethan maxim *Tria Sunt Omnia* (threes are all).[1] When I discussed the Hermetic aspect of Hawthorne's fiction, I mentioned the "three theme."[2]

Coelho says that the vast desert makes people feel small, and reduces them to a respectful silence:

> In the desert, there was only the sound of the eternal wind, and of the hoofbeats of the animals. Even the guides spoke very little to one another. "I've crossed these sands many times," said one of the camel drivers one night. "But the desert is so huge, and the horizons so distant, that they make a person feel small, and as if he should remain silent." The boy understood intuitively what he meant, even without ever having set foot in the desert before. Whenever he saw the sea, or a fire, he fell silent, impressed by their elemental force.

I discussed this respectful attitude earlier in connection with Hemingway, in connection with the filmmaker Werner Herzog, and in connection with the psychologist Marie-Louise von Franz. Hemingway wrote, "When he and the boy fished together, they usually spoke only when it was necessary.... It was considered a virtue not to talk unnecessarily at sea and the old man had always considered it so and respected it." The fisherman's respectful silence in the midst of the sea is similar to the respectful silence in the midst of the desert that Coelho writes of.

Instead of using the word "dream," Coelho sometimes speaks of a "Personal Legend." He says that your Personal Legend is

> what you have always wanted to accomplish. Everyone, when they are young, knows what their Personal Legend is. At that point in their lives, everything is clear and everything is possible. They are not afraid to dream.... To realize one's Personal Legend is a person's only real obligation.

But if your dream is to be a pro athlete, is this likely to come true? To make you happy? To make the world better? Perhaps not all dreams/ambitions are equally valuable, equally worthy of being pursued. Perhaps the little boy who dreams of being Tom Brady would be better off trying to learn a humble skill, like carpentry.

One's dreams may distract one from worldly matters and family responsibilities. Perhaps Melville's wife wished that he did less dreaming, and paid more attention to practical matters (his wife's family urged her to leave him). As Coelho says, "We know what we want to do, but are afraid of hurting those around us by abandoning everything in order to pursue our dream." Santiago is ambivalent about pursuing his dream because he doesn't want to leave his sheep:

---

[1] I say "Elizabethan" but actually the idea may originate before Elizabethan times, it may originate in medieval times, or in the Gnostics, or in prehistoric folk wisdom.

[2] See ljhammond.com/phlit/2018-12.htm#11

> He knew everything about each member of his flock: he knew which ones were lame, which one was to give birth two months from now, and which were the laziest. He knew how to shear them, and how to slaughter them. If he ever decided to leave them, they would suffer.

When we're close to attaining our dream, we sometimes shrink back. Coelho says we have a "fear of realizing the dream for which we fought all our lives.... This is the most dangerous of the obstacles because it has a kind of saintly aura about it: renouncing joy and conquest." Coelho has thought much about dreams, and looked at the subject from various angles.

In an earlier issue, I discussed James Allen, one of the creators of self-help literature. Allen said, "He who cherishes a beautiful vision, a lofty ideal in his heart, will one day realize it.... The greatest achievement was at first and for a time a dream. The oak sleeps in the acorn.... Dreams are the seedlings of realities." What Allen expresses as non-fiction, Coelho expresses as fiction.

Scholars have placed folk stories into categories. According to Wikipedia, *The Alchemist* belongs in Category 1645, "The Treasure At Home." In this type of story, the hero leaves home in search of treasure, then finds that the treasure is actually at his home.

36. Pushkin's "Queen of Spades"

I read a Pushkin short story, "The Queen of Spades," which is being discussed by the local GreatBooks group. An excellent short story, I highly recommend it. The story is saturated with magic and the occult, but manages to keep two feet on the solid ground of reality. The story has a high reputation; it's considered one of Pushkin's best, and one of the best in all of Russian literature.

Pushkin is said to have had a strong interest in the occult, and he's said to have been an avid card-player and gambler. Perhaps his interest in the occult is typical of the Romantic period. Pushkin always felt that he would die young and die violently, and he did so (he died at age 37, from wounds received in a duel). His art and his life reflect each other.

The story's epigraph is, "The queen of spades signifies secret ill-will." Thus, playing cards are given an occult significance, like tarot cards. A card game isn't just a game of chance, it has a magical significance, an occult significance, it's connected to human destiny; perhaps it foretells the future, or offers guidance for the future. In short, a card game is a kind of divination. Perhaps this is why Pushkin had a keen interest in cards, and includes card games in many of his works.

The story touches on other aspects of the occult, besides divination. There's life-after-death, and a Swedenborg quote about life-after-death. (One is reminded of another Romantic writer, Poe, who also mentions Swedenborg in connection with the occult.) There's also telepathy: the servant girl, Lizaveta, can always feel when Hermann is watching her. And when Hermann is wandering the streets, an "unknown power" draws him to the home of the Countess. And finally, there's a reference to a famous occultist,

St. Germain. St. Germain traveled to Russia (among other places), and was a member of the same Freemason lodge that Pushkin himself was in.

One member of the GreatBooks group did some research on faro, the card game played in the story. He said that Hermann had the winning card, and could have played it, but played the Queen of Spades by mistake. This suggests that Hermann had a self-destructive impulse, it suggests that (on some level) he didn't want to win. Hermann's inner divisions cause him to err, just as, when he's looking at the Countess's casket, his inner divisions cause him to stumble and fall. Ultimately, his inner divisions land him in a mental hospital.

Hermann lacks a heart. He embodies calculating self-interest—greed. The Countess has a heart; after she dies, she still cares about Lizaveta, and tries to arrange for her marriage. And Lizaveta also has a heart; after she's married and wealthy, she takes care of a poor relative. One might say that, in Pushkin's story, the characters get what they deserve.

According to some critics, Hermann is the model for a later creation, Dostoyevsky's Raskolnikov, protagonist of *Crime and Punishment*. It is also argued that Svidrigailov (a character in *The Brothers Karamazov*) is Raskolnikov's "double," and thus has some of Hermann's traits. Svidrigailov sees a ghost, as Hermann does; Svidrigailov's girlfriend, Dunia, is a Lizaveta-figure, as his late wife (Marfa) is a Countess-figure. The triangle Svidrigailov-Marfa-Dunia reproduces the triangle Hermann-Countess-Lizaveta. Likewise, the triangle in *Crime and Punishment* of Raskolnikov-Pawnbroker-Sonia reproduces Pushkin's triangle.[1]

Dostoyevsky's attitude toward ghosts reflects his reading of "The Queen of Spades." Since Hermann eventually goes mad, one might say that the ghost of the Countess is Hermann's hallucination. But in *The Brothers Karamazov*, Dostoyevsky says the fact that "ghosts appear only to the sick... only proves that ghosts *can* appear to no one but sick people—and not that there are no ghosts *per se*." In sum, Pushkin's story had a profound effect on Dostoyevsky.

37. Chekhov

February 7, 2005
I recently read an excellent 10-page story by Chekhov: "In Exile." I read the story because the local Great Books club was discussing it at their monthly meeting, and I wanted to attend the meeting. It's a superb short story—philosophically profound, yet realistic and credible.

"In Exile" deals with one of the oldest debates in ethics: the debate between the Active Life and the Contemplative Life. One finds this debate in ancient philosophy and in Renaissance philosophy. In China, this debate was

---

[1] See *Canadian Slavonic Papers*, May-June 1996, "Everyone Knew Her... Or Did They?" by Svetlana Grenier, footnote 30. Unfortunately, this essay is written in the scholarly jargon that I call LitSpeak, so it makes painful reading.

called "Kong-Meng, Lao-Zhuang"; that is, the worldly philosophers Confucius and Mencius versus the hermit-philosophers Lao Zi and Zhuang Zi.

Even today, this debate lives on; on one side are Western philosophers who say that we should try to make ourselves better, and make the world better, and on the other side are Eastern philosophers who say that we should accept ourselves as we are, and accept the world as it is. One might describe this debate as Nietzsche versus Zen. Perhaps this debate can never be resolved, because truth is on both sides, just as the debate in physics between the wave theory of light and the particle theory of light can never be resolved, because truth is on both sides. Some contradictions are irreconcilable.

Chekhov's story is the best version of this debate that I've ever seen. Both sides are given a hearing, and it's impossible to tell which side the author is on. My only complaint is that Chekhov depicts both sides as flawed, and so the reader is left with nothing but nihilism, despair. Instead of depicting both sides as true, instead of depicting a clash between two truths, Chekhov depicts both sides as false, bankrupt, and he leaves the reader empty-handed.

Pretend your neighbor knocks on your door today, and says, "I can see no reason to go on living, so I'm going to commit suicide tomorrow. I've come to bid you an eternal farewell." You couldn't raise his spirits by handing him "In Exile" because it's a bleak, pessimistic story.

In the introduction to the story, we find a quote from Gorky; Gorky praises Chekhov as a "great, wise, and observant man" who said to his countrymen, "You live badly, my friends. It is shameful to live like that." Okay, we live badly (his countrymen should have responded), so tell us how we should live. Don't just shake your head, don't just criticize. Make some constructive suggestions, show us how we might live better.

Why was Chekhov content to criticize? Perhaps he couldn't point the way because he hadn't found the way himself. He lived in a nihilistic society; in the late 1800s, there was an epidemic of suicide in Russia. We're all products of our time, and Chekhov's time was nihilistic, so the best he could offer was nihilism, despair. As the son of a serf, perhaps Chekhov didn't feel responsible for solving the big problems. On the other hand, the nobleman Tolstoy strove to find The Way, and to tell the world about it.

When I said this at the meeting, when I said that Chekhov failed to show us The Way, people responded, "a fiction writer shouldn't be expected to solve philosophical problems. A fiction writer explores problems, he doesn't solve them." Thoreau said that "the mass of men lead lives of quiet desperation." And then Thoreau proceeded to show the reader how he might live a good life; Thoreau didn't just criticize, he offered a positive vision. "But Thoreau was a philosopher, we're talking about fiction." But what about Whitman? Whitman offered a positive vision, a mystic vision, much as Thoreau did. "But Whitman wasn't a fiction writer, he was a poet. Fiction is different." But what about E. M. Forster? Forster was a fiction writer, and he offers a positive vision. Forster was influenced by Whitman, and Forster offers a mystic vision, a Zennish vision; Forster also points the way toward personal growth. A fiction writer is, after all, a human being, and it's natural for a human being to seek The Way, to seek The Good Life, and to tell other people what he has found.

Let's look at some passages from "In Exile", and let's see how Chekhov depicts the debate between Action and Contemplation. Chekhov makes strong arguments for both sides in this debate, but his characters don't embody these arguments in a positive way. Chekhov wisely puts the argument for Contemplation in the mouth of an older man, the argument for action in the mouth of a younger man, just as, in China, the young man goes out into the world, and listens to Confucius and Mencius, while the old man retires from the world, goes into the mountains, and listens to Lao Zi and Zhuang Zi.

Chekhov's old man is Semyon, who operates a ferry on a Siberian river (the story is called "In Exile" because it's about people who have been exiled from Russia, and are living in Siberia). "I stay here," Semyon says, "going back and forth, from one bank to the other. For twenty-two years now that's what I've been doing. Day and night. The pike and the salmon under the water and me on it. That's all I want. God give everyone such a life."

People who want a wife, or money, or freedom (i.e., freedom to leave Siberia) are, according to Semyon, being tempted by the Devil; they should close their ears to the Devil, and be content with what they have. "I can sleep naked on the ground and eat grass," says Semyon; "I don't want anything, I'm not afraid of anyone, and the way I see it, there's no man richer or freer than I am."

When someone on the other bank calls for the ferry, Semyon says, "'All right, plenty of time!' ...in the tone of a man who is convinced that there is no need to hurry in this world—that it makes no difference, really, and nothing will come of it." Semyon reminds one of Stoicism, and of Zen. Zen doesn't say, however, that one shouldn't hurry because everything is meaningless, Zen says one shouldn't hurry because one should be aware of the present moment, savor the present moment.

Semyon isn't depicted in a positive light: he enjoys vodka, and drinks it on the sly lest his fellow boatmen ask for some. At the end of the story, he goes to sleep with the door to his hut still open, because he's too lazy to get up and close it.

Semyon converses with a young Tartar, who rejects his Stoic worldview. In broken English (or rather, broken Russian), the Tartar says, "God created man to live, be joyful, be sad and sorrow, but you want nothing... You not live, you stone, clay! Stone want nothing and you want nothing... God not love you." The Tartar longs for the company of his wife, and he says that

> if his wife came to him even for one day, even for one hour, he would be willing to accept any torture whatsoever, and thank God for it. Better one day of happiness than nothing.

Though there's wisdom in the Tartar's remarks, he isn't presented in a positive light; at the end of the story, the Tartar is lonely and miserable, and he cries "like the howling of a dog."

Though Chekhov fails to present a positive vision, or a model character, "In Exile" is a masterpiece nonetheless, and a perfect choice for a discussion group.

38. Isaak Babel

October 9, 2010
In a recent issue of *Commentary*, the editor (John Podhoretz) affirmed the magazine's commitment to literature, and said that *Commentary* often published unsolicited short fiction. Podhoretz said that *Commentary* had long been committed to literature, and that in one of its first issues, it had published a story by the Jewish-Russian writer, Isaak Babel. The story was called "First Love," and Podhoretz said it was "universally considered among the greatest short works of the 20th century." I decided to have a look at the story, and try to learn more about Babel.

"First Love" is about a young Jewish boy's love for an older woman, and about a 1905 pogrom in which his family suffers. Not bad, some touching scenes, but I wouldn't recommend it. Like many modern works, it's often obscure, and often morbid. As Gorky put it, Babel has "a Baudelairean predilection for rotting meat."[1]

One of Babel's major works is a short-story collection, *Red Cavalry*, which deals with the Russo-Polish War of 1920. Babel also wrote *Odessa Tales*, about Jewish gangsters. As for Babel criticism, two of the most famous American critics have written about Babel: Lionel Trilling wrote an introduction to Babel's *Collected Stories* (New York, 1955), and Harold Bloom wrote *Isaac Babel* (1987).

Babel had numerous affairs, and had children with at least three different women. One of these women later wrote,

> Before I met Babel, I used to read a great deal, though without any particular direction. I read whatever I could get my hands on. Babel noticed this and told me, "Reading that way will get you nowhere. You won't have time to read the books that are truly worthwhile. There are about a hundred books that every educated person needs to read. Sometime I'll try to make you a list of them." And a few days later he brought me a list. There were ancient writers on it, Greek and Roman—Homer, Herodotus, Lucretius, Seutonius—and also all the classics of later European literature, starting with Erasmus, Rabelais, Cervantes, Swift, and Coster, and going on to 19th century writers such as Stendhal, Mérimée, and Flaubert.

Once an enthusiastic communist, Babel gradually became disillusioned with communism. Since his writings sometimes strayed from the Party line, they were criticized by the authorities, so he stopped writing. At age 44,

---

1 For a more positive view of Babel, see ljhammond.com/phlit/2014-11b.htm#2

Babel was arrested by Stalin's police and executed, leaving some of his writings unfinished. His last recorded words, uttered the day before his execution, were "I am asking for only one thing—let me finish my work."

Did Babel have a self-destructive streak? He had been living in Paris, and might have survived if he had stayed there, but he chose to return to the Soviet Union, though he knew he might be in danger there. Perhaps he returned to the Soviet Union because there he was a professional writer, a respected writer, even a celebrity, while in Paris, he didn't enjoy that status, and he would have had to scramble to make a living.

Babel made the most devastating criticism ever made of Nabokov: "He can write, but he's got nothing to say." We find a similar view in Wikipedia:

> Nabokov's detractors fault him for being an aesthete and for his over-attention to language and detail rather than character development.... Danilo Kis wrote that Nabokov's is "a magnificent, complex, and sterile art." Russian poet Yevgeny Yevtushenko said... that he could hear the clatter of surgical tools in Nabokov's prose.[1]

When I read *Lolita*, I was initially overwhelmed by the verbal fireworks and the sparkling wit, but I eventually tired of it, and didn't finish it; it didn't seem to be going anywhere. I didn't include Nabokov in my *Realms of Gold*. Perhaps Nabokov's popularity is due to the fact that some critics share his preoccupation with language; perhaps some critics are uneasy when a novelist "has something to say."

39. Modern Russian Writers

I discovered a modern Russian novelist, Andrei Bely. He's best known for *Petersburg* (1913), which is described as a Symbolist novel; Bely is often compared to Joyce. Bely wrote poetry and criticism as well as fiction. In addition to *Petersburg*, several other Bely novels have been translated into English, as well as a volume of short stories and a volume of essays. Bely wrote three volumes of memoirs.

Bely grew up in a prominent Moscow family; his father was a well-known intellectual, specializing in math. Bely had a strong interest in philosophy, he's considered part of the Russian neo-Kantian school. Wikipedia says that Bely's works "feature a striking mysticism"; in his later years, Bely was influenced by Rudolf Steiner, and became a friend of Steiner's. "Andrei Bely" was actually his pen name; his real name was Boris Nikolaevich Bugaev. Bely died in 1934 at age 53, apparently of natural causes.

I also discovered a Russian critic from more recent times, Mikhail Bakhtin. Like Bely, Bakhtin came from a prominent Russian family. Several of his books deal with Dostoevsky and Rabelais. Bakhtin is popular with modern literary theorists and critics. He wrote about aspects of philosophy that don't interest me, such as the philosophy of language.

---

[1] Article on "Vladimir Nabokov"

Finally, I discovered the Soviet writing team known as Ilf and Petrov (Ilya Ilf and Yevgeny Petrov). Both "Ilya Ilf" and "Yevgeny Petrov" were pen names. Both men hailed from Odessa, Ukraine. Ilf and Petrov were active in the 1930s. They're known for two satirical novels, *The Twelve Chairs* and *The Little Golden Calf*; both novels feature a con man named Ostap Bender. According to Wikipedia, these two novels are "among the most widely read and quoted books in Russian culture," and have often been turned into movies. Ilf and Petrov travelled across the U.S. in the 1930s. The trip resulted in a book, *Little Golden America*, and a photo essay. Both men died young—Ilf from illness, Petrov from a plane crash.

40. Dostoyevsky

July, 2001
A couple months ago, our book group read Dostoyevsky's novel, *The Idiot*. The edition that we chose is part of a series called Oxford World's Classics; it's a good edition in every respect—translation, introduction, bibliography, notes, maps, etc. One book mentioned in the bibliography caught my fancy: *Unconscious Structure in The Idiot: A Study in Literature and Psychoanalysis*, by Elizabeth Dalton. I've always been fond of Freudian (and Jungian) interpretations of literature, and *The Idiot* seemed ripe for such interpretation.

Apparently most people don't share my fondness for Freudian interpretations; I found that *Unconscious Structure* was a rare book, difficult to obtain, and impossible to buy. (I like to own the books that I read, so that I can mark passages in the book, and then lay the book aside; when I read a library book, I feel compelled to make notes in my computer, which is a tedious task. Typing page after page leaves me with tired fingers and wrists; I've tried voice-recognition software, but it makes so many mistakes that I gave up on it.)

When I began reading *Unconscious Structure*, I soon found that it lived up to my highest hopes. It allowed me to review and re-experience the novel. It also allowed me to review Freud's theories. Truth, said Schopenhauer, agrees with itself and confirms itself. In this case, Dostoyevsky and Freud agreed with each other and confirmed each other, and one was left with greater respect for both writers. *Unconscious Structure* deserves to be considered a classic in its field, along with Marie Bonaparte's *Life and Works of Edgar Allan Poe*, Phyllis Greenacre's *Swift and Carroll: A Psychoanalytic Study*, and Maud Bodkin's *Archetypal Patterns in Poetry*. (Is it just a coincidence that all four of these books are by women? Or do women have a greater sensitivity for grasping the unconscious?)

The chief character in *The Idiot* is Prince Myshkin. "The main idea of the novel," said Dostoyevsky, "is to depict the positively good man," and Myshkin is that man. Myshkin is a Christ figure—honest, ingenuous, indifferent to wealth and to physical pleasure. Myshkin is a very attractive character indeed. Whether or not Dostoyevsky succeeded in 'depicting the positively good man,' he deserves credit for making the attempt. Things that are truly great can never be completed perfectly; credit should go to those who make the attempt.

The author of *Unconscious Structure*, Elizabeth Dalton, argues that Myshkin's personality has its share of violent and lustful drives, but these drives are repressed; "Myshkin's goodness is obviously problematic; it has a dark underside of which Myshkin himself is aware in the form of what he calls 'double thoughts.'"[1] In an earlier issue, we discussed how Freud and Nietzsche believed that morality is related to the death-instinct, that morality springs from the super-ego raging against oneself.[2] Dalton argues that Myshkin's morality is related to a death-instinct, a masochistic impulse; Myshkin derives a sort of sexual pleasure from suffering. Dalton summarizes thus:

> In the person of Myshkin, the novel poses a radical question. We are presented with an apparently 'good' man whose character embodies Christian ideals of self-sacrifice and compassion ...yet this figure is treated in such a way as to raise the most disturbing questions about the origins of his goodness and the concealed gratifications afforded by his self-abnegation. By its presentation of the good man, the novel calls into question the very nature of goodness, and its relation to what we call evil.[3]

The character of Myshkin confirms Freud's view of morality; it confirms Freud's view that morality is ambiguous, not as simple, pure and lily-white as some people suppose. Likewise, the character of Myshkin confirms Nietzsche's view that the "good" man, the saint, has a variety of motives; his motives are "human, all-too-human."

Both Dostoyevsky and Freud see aggression as a widespread, deep-seated instinct in human nature. Dalton writes thus:

> Aggression has a particularly disturbing quality in *The Idiot*. One does not of course actually see the instinct or the drive itself; but its effects are felt everywhere in the novel. Violence is a constant brooding threat in the dark coloration and atmosphere of the novel; it appears explicitly

---

[1] Part II, ch. 2. Dalton notes that the people Myshkin interacts with later meet disaster. "Myshkin's conscience seems to have lost contact with the realities of the external situation, to be functioning instead in the service of some more obscure inner purpose; thus instead of preventing harm and doing good, it wreaks havoc." Thus, Myshkin reminds us of another "sweet prince," Hamlet, who also "wreaks havoc" among the people around him.

[2] See ljhammond.com/phlit/2001-05.htm#3. My theory of history says that when the life-instinct is dominant, as in a renaissance period, you find amoral philosophers. Conversely, when the death-instinct is active, you find moral philosophers.

[3] Ch. 12

> in imagery and action, and in the ideas and fantasies of the characters. The final action toward which everything in the novel tends is murder.[1]

Like many of Dostoyevsky's works, *The Idiot* was inspired by a newspaper story, a story about a 15-year-old girl who was tortured by her parents, and who tried to burn their house down. The aggressive impulses depicted in Dostoyevsky's works were not hatched in the author's own imagination, they were manifested in the world around him—the world described in the daily newspaper, and also the world of the Siberian prison system, of which Dostoyevsky had firsthand knowledge.

There is one final point on which Dostoyevsky and Freud are in agreement: the importance of guilt in the human psyche. Freud says that the sense of guilt is

> the most important problem in the development of civilization... The price we pay for our advance in civilization is a loss of happiness through the heightening of the sense of guilt.[2]

The sense of guilt is often unconscious, and it's often accompanied by an unconscious need for punishment.

Dalton argues that, in *The Idiot*, Nastasya and Myshkin both have "an irrational guilt and a need to suffer."[3] Nastasya's guilt, and her need for punishment, lead her to give herself to Rogozhin, even though she expects that Rogozhin will murder her.

A person like Myshkin, who represses much, is prone to guilt; guilt springs from intentions, as well as from actions. "A sense of guilt," says Freud, "could be produced not only by an act of violence that is actually carried out (as all the world knows), but also by one that is merely intended (as psycho-analysis has discovered)."[4] The more Myshkin represses his aggressive impulses, the more guilty he feels; as Freud said, "a person's conscience becomes more severe and more sensitive the more he refrains from aggression against others."

Guilt goes hand-in-hand with aggression because the repression of aggressive impulses creates the sense of guilt. If *The Idiot* is pervaded by aggression, as Dalton argues, it is also pervaded by guilt. Dalton says that Myshkin has a

> pervasive sense of guilt.... On the day Rogozhin tries to murder him, Myshkin feels overcome with guilt. Speaking of the murder attempt afterwards with Rogozhin, Myshkin says, "Our sin was the same." It is evidently as much a sin to be murdered as to murder![5]

---

[1] Ch. 8

[2] *Civilization and Its Discontents*, ch. 8

[3] Ch. 4

[4] Ch. 8

[5] Ch. 2

Doubtless some people will argue that a Freudian analysis of *The Idiot* violates the work of art. But if such an analysis can throw light on human nature, on the dark side of human nature, is it not worthwhile? To be aware of man's darker impulses is the first step in dealing with them. As Nikos Kazantzakis put it, "The real meaning of enlightenment is to gaze with undimmed eyes on all darkness."

41. Pride and Prejudice

A. An English Epictetus

Jane Austen's fiction is philosophical as well as entertaining. Her philosophy might be described as Johnsonian Stoicism. She tells us not to live in the past and the future, not to live on hopes and regrets. When Darcy is regretting a letter he wrote, Elizabeth tells him, "You must learn some of my philosophy. Think only of the past as its remembrance gives you pleasure." A wise maxim, but not easy to follow!

When Elizabeth tells her father not to let Lydia go to Brighton, her father doesn't follow her advice. Elizabeth is stoical:

> It was not in her nature... to increase her vexations by dwelling on them. She was confident of having performed her duty, and to fret over unavoidable evils, or augment them by anxiety, was no part of her disposition.

[Spoiler Warning: If you're thinking of reading *Pride and Prejudice*, I suggest you skip the rest of this section.] Sometimes the stoicism of Austen's characters is tested by everyday annoyances, as when Mrs. Bennett complains constantly about Bingley abandoning Jane: "It needed all Jane's steady mildness to bear these attacks with tolerable tranquillity."

Instead of getting annoyed by the comments of the people around us, Austen says, we can find amusement in them. Mr. Bennett finds amusement in his wife:

> To his wife he was very little otherwise indebted, than as her ignorance and folly had contributed to his amusement. This is not the sort of happiness which a man would in general wish to owe to his wife; but where other powers of entertainment are wanting, the true philosopher will derive benefit from such as are given.

Austen describes the folly of living in the future, living in hope; this is a favorite Stoic theme. Elizabeth is eager for Wickham to leave town, but

> she found, what has been sometimes found before, that an event to which she had been looking with impatient desire did not, in taking place, bring all the satisfaction she had promised herself. It was consequently necessary to name some other period for the commencement of actual felicity—to have some other point on which her wishes and hopes might be fixed, and by again enjoying the pleasure of anticipa-

> tion, console herself for the present, and prepare for another disappointment. Her tour to the Lakes was now the object of her happiest thoughts.

Austen explores the feeling of guilt, and her characters often blame themselves. Darcy, for example, blames himself for the haughty style of his first proposal to Elizabeth. He says to Elizabeth,

> Your reproof, so well applied, I shall never forget: "had you behaved in a more gentlemanlike manner." Those were your words. You know not, you can scarcely conceive, how they have tortured me—though it was some time, I confess, before I was reasonable enough to allow their justice.

Darcy's feeling of guilt may be a healthy emotion since it makes him humbler, makes him a better person. Wisdom comes through suffering, so if the keenest suffering is self-reproach, then self-reproach may be our best teacher. As Darcy says, "Painful recollections will intrude which cannot, which ought not, to be repelled." Is the feeling of guilt a teacher whom we should listen to and learn from—experience to the full? Mr. Bennett says, "Lizzy, let me once in my life feel how much I have been to blame. I am not afraid of being overpowered by the impression. It will pass away soon enough."

Darcy says that his hauteur has its roots in his early childhood: he was an only son, and an eldest child; he was spoiled and he looked down on other people. But he has been educated by Elizabeth, by her criticisms, and by his own self-reproaches:

> Such I was, from eight to eight and twenty; and such I might still have been but for you, dearest, loveliest Elizabeth! What do I not owe you! You taught me a lesson, hard indeed at first, but most advantageous. By you, I was properly humbled. I came to you without a doubt of my reception. You showed me how insufficient were all my pretensions to please a woman worthy of being pleased.

The feeling of guilt, though painful for Darcy, may have made him a better person. Darcy is eager to show Elizabeth that he has learned, grown, improved: "I hoped to obtain your forgiveness, to lessen your ill opinion, by letting you see that your reproofs had been attended to."

The union of Darcy and Elizabeth is a union of opposites, reminding us of the saying, "opposites attract." We can learn from our opposite, and become more whole.

> [Elizabeth] began now to comprehend that he was exactly the man who, in disposition and talents, would most suit her. His understanding and temper, though unlike her own, would have answered all her wishes. It was an union that must have been to the advantage of both; by her ease and liveliness, his mind might have been softened, his manners improved; and from his judgment, information, and knowledge of the world, she must have received benefit of greater importance.

As I wrote in an earlier issue, "According to Jungians, marriage means seeking wholeness by joining with someone who complements you, someone who supplies your deficiencies."[1] Perhaps Austen's message is, "Marriage should be about achieving wholeness, not simply about obtaining wealth or pleasure."

One of the themes of *Pride and Prejudice* is that first impressions can be deceiving; this may be why an early draft of the novel was entitled *First Impressions*. Elizabeth's first impression of Darcy is negative, and her first impression of Wickham is positive. Darcy is cold on the outside, but good on the inside, while Wickham is warm on the outside, but cold on the inside. "There certainly was some great mismanagement in the education of those two young men. One has got all the goodness, and the other all the appearance of it." Both Darcy's goodness and Wickham's wickedness have their origins in their early childhood, their "education."

I hope these remarks have shown that Austen is a good philosophical writer, and her aphorisms are often impressive. Virginia Woolf said of Austen, "of all great writers she is the most difficult to catch in the act of greatness." I hope I've shown that it's possible to catch Austen in "the act of greatness."

B. Critical Essays

I read several essays about *Pride and Prejudice*, but I haven't found one that I can recommend enthusiastically.

Austen works on a small scale, a domestic scale. She told her niece, an aspiring writer, "You are now collecting your people delightfully, getting them exactly into such a spot as is the delight of my life—3 or 4 Families in a Country Village is the very thing to work on." Austen described her work as a "small square two inches of ivory." Her work is clear and readable; she doesn't explore deep passions. "The prevailing tone... is brisk and dry."[2]

One might say that the first half of *Pride and Prejudice* is about the hostility that drives Elizabeth and Darcy apart, while the second half is about their coming together. As one critic wrote,

> This pattern is formed by diverging and converging lines, by the movement of two people who are impelled apart until they reach a climax of mutual hostility, and thereafter bend their courses towards mutual understanding and amity. It is a pattern very common in fiction, but by no means easy to describe plausibly.[3]

The relationship between Elizabeth and Darcy may have been modeled after a relationship in Fanny Burney's popular novel, *Cecilia*. Q. D. Leavis (wife

---

[1] See ljhammond.com/phlit/2004-08.htm#3

[2] See "Pride Unprejudiced," by Mark Schorer, *The Kenyon Review*, Vol. 18, No. 1 (Winter, 1956), pp. 72-91

[3] Mary Lascelles, "The Narrative Art of Pride and Prejudice," in the Norton Critical Edition of *Pride and Prejudice*.

of critic F. R. Leavis) argued that *Pride and Prejudice* is an attempt to "re-write the story of *Cecilia* in realistic terms." In *Cecilia* we find the remark, "The whole of this unfortunate business has been the result of Pride and Prejudice," so we know where Austen got her title.[1]

One critic, Mark Schorer, argues that Darcy represents Pride, while Elizabeth represents Prejudice. Schorer regards Mr. Collins as a "hilarious caricature" of Pride, and Lady Catherine as a caricature of Prejudice. Like many novels, *Pride and Prejudice* deals with personal growth.

> Elizabeth and Darcy are rewarded because they are capable of altering.... The interest of a novel... lies in the processes of human alteration.... In their alteration, [Darcy and Elizabeth] are free to merge.

Schorer argues that, in Austen's time, the landed aristocracy was declining, and the merchant class was rising. Austen uses marriage as a symbol of this change; the marriage between Elizabeth and Darcy, for example, is a marriage between the merchant class and the landed aristocracy. (Proust also depicted the merging of the aristocracy with the middle class, as in the marriage of Mme Verdurin with the Prince de Guermantes, and the marriage of Gilberte with Saint-Loup.) Austen also depicts "marriage as a brutal economic fact in an essentially materialistic society." Schorer concludes that "all this is the groundwork out of which *Pride and Prejudice*, together with Jane Austen's other novels, arises."

Though Austen is highly respected today, she has had many critics. Charlotte Bronte, for example, said

> She does her business of delineating the surface of the lives of genteel English people curiously well; there is a Chinese fidelity, a miniature delicacy in the painting: she ruffles her reader by nothing vehement, disturbs him by nothing profound: the Passions are perfectly unknown to her.... No open country, no fresh air, no blue hill.

Emerson was also critical of Austen: "Never was life so pinched and narrow.... All that interests in any character [is], has he (or she) the money to marry with?" I hope I've shown that Austen deals with some large subjects, and handles them well; the fact that she places these large subjects on a small stage, on the stage of everyday life, shouldn't make us conclude that she deals only with trivial matters.

42. F. R. Leavis on Early English Novelists

As part of my Jane Austen study, I looked at *The Great Tradition*, by the famous English critic F. R. Leavis. It starts with this sentence: "The great English novelists are Jane Austen, George Eliot, Henry James and Joseph Conrad—to stop for the moment at that comparatively safe point in history." I discovered, though, that while *The Great Tradition* discusses Eliot, James,

---

[1] See "Pride Unprejudiced," by Mark Schorer

and Conrad, it doesn't discuss Austen, whom Leavis says "needs to be studied at considerable length."

Leavis does, however, make some general remarks about Austen in his introduction. He starts the introduction by commenting on older novelists like Defoe and Sterne, who enjoyed a certain vogue with the Bloomsbury Group (Virginia Woolf, E. M. Forster, etc.). He dismisses these older novelists; he speaks of Sterne's "irresponsible (and nasty) trifling." He says that Fielding is important in literary history, but he's monotonous, simplistic. Once you start to appreciate Jane Austen, Leavis says, then you realize that "life isn't long enough to permit of one's giving much time to Fielding.... What [Fielding] *can* do appears to best advantage in *Joseph Andrews*."

Leavis agrees with Samuel Johnson that Richardson has "a more inward interest" than Fielding. Leavis praises Richardson's "analysis of emotional and moral states... *Clarissa* is a really impressive work." Leavis says that Richardson's fame spread throughout Europe, and that he helped to make Austen possible. Nonetheless, "it's no use pretending that Richardson can ever be made a current classic again." His work is "limited in range and variety," and he demands too much time from the reader.

While Richardson focused on the middle class, Fanny Burney wrote about "educated life," and thus influenced Austen more directly.

> Here we have one of the important lines of English literary history: Richardson ==> Fanny Burney ==> Jane Austen. It is important because Jane Austen is one of the truly great writers, and herself a major fact in the background of other great writers.

Leavis says that a study of Austen allows us to see what's important in Fielding, Richardson, and other earlier writers: "Her work, like the work of all great creative writers, gives a meaning to the past." This is an astute remark, and it's as true in philosophy as it is in fiction; an important philosopher prompts us to reinterpret the tradition.

Leavis says that Austen has

> an intense moral interest of her own in life... a preoccupation with certain problems that life compels on her as personal ones.... Without her intense moral preoccupation she wouldn't have been a great novelist.

All great novelists, according to Leavis, have this "intense moral preoccupation." All great novelists have "an unusually developed interest in life. They are all distinguished by a vital capacity for experience, a kind of reverent openness before life, and a marked moral intensity." One might compare Leavis' argument with that of American novelist John Gardner, who wrote a controversial book called *On Moral Fiction*. "In this work, Gardner attacks what he sees as contemporary literature's lack of morality, which he calls the highest purpose of art."[1]

Leavis has little respect for Walter Scott: "Of his books, *The Heart of Midlothian* comes the nearest to being a great novel, but hardly *is* that." As for the fiction of H. G. Wells, Leavis says that Wells *discusses* problems and

---

1 See Wikipedia's article "On Moral Fiction"

ideas, but a great novelist *embodies* problems and ideas in his fiction. Leavis has some praise for Arnold Bennett, but says "Bennett seems to me never to have been disturbed enough by life to come anywhere near greatness."

I like the phrase "disturbed by life"; a writer who is disturbed by life has an "intense moral preoccupation." A moral preoccupation should not be confused with moralizing, with preaching. Proust, for example, is preoccupied with life—with obsessive love, with grief, etc.—but he doesn't moralize.

Leavis says that Austen's famous irony has a "serious background," and is related to Austen's "essential moral interest." I'm reminded of Kierkegaard's view that Socrates' famous irony was related to his moral interest, his moral passion. As I wrote in an earlier issue,

> In his book *The Concept of Irony*, Kierkegaard argued that the famous irony of Socrates wasn't based on indifference or cynicism, but rather on depth of spirit, ethical passion.[1]

43. Dickens

A. Dickens and John Forster

The most well-known biography of Dickens is John Forster's. Forster was a close friend of Dickens during most of Dickens' adult life. Forster's biography is known for being lively and intimate. Such a book can never be rendered obsolete by later scholarship. If only it were written in a simpler, clearer style!

Like David Copperfield, Dickens learned shorthand as a teenager. (Doubtless he taught himself, as Thoreau taught himself surveying.) Starting at age 17, Dickens worked as a court reporter for two years, then as a Parliamentary reporter for four years. His job was to take down in shorthand Parliamentary debates, and political speeches delivered around England, then transcribe the shorthand, then get his pages to the newspaper's office in time for the deadline.

---

1 See ljhammond.com/phlit/2009-06.htm#5

Dickens at 27
engraving by Robert Graves
from a painting by Daniel Maclise

Dickens often worked all night, sometimes by candlelight in a coach that was galloping along at 15 miles an hour. Dickens says that he once charged his newspaper for damage to his coat "from the drippings of a blazing wax candle, in writing through the smallest hours of the night in a swift-flying carriage-and-pair." Not infrequently, the coach broke down, turned over, or got stuck in a ditch.

This was around 1832, just before the advent of railroads. Forster says, "[Dickens] saw the last of the old coaching-days, and of the old inns that were a part of them." Dickens preserved this world in his novels. (The name "Pickwick" comes from the Pickwick family of Bath—Eleazer Pickwick ran a coaching business, and his nephew, Moses Pickwick, ran the adjacent inn.)

Dickens later said, "To the wholesome training of severe newspaper work, when I was a very young man, I constantly refer my first successes." For the young Dickens, reporting meant stimulation, travel, experience.

When Forster meets Dickens, Forster is working for a newspaper, Dickens is a 19-year-old reporter for that newspaper. Forster and his colleagues have a big problem: the reporters have gone on strike. The strikers have chosen Dickens as their leader. Forster says,

> I well remember noticing at this dread time, on the staircase of the magnificent mansion we were lodged in, a young man of my own age, whose keen animation of look would have arrested attention anywhere, and whose name, upon inquiry, I then for the first time heard. It was coupled with the fact, which gave it interest even then, that "young Dickens" had been spokesman for the recalcitrant reporters, and conducted their case triumphantly.

Forster continues:

> There was that in the face as I first recollect it which no time could change, and which remained implanted on it unalterably to the last. This was the quickness, keenness, and practical power, the eager, restless, energetic outlook on each several feature, that seemed to tell so little of a student or writer of books, and so much of a man of action and business in the world. Light and motion flashed from every part of it.... "What a face is his to meet in a drawing-room!" wrote Leigh Hunt to me, the morning after I made them known to each other. "It has the life and soul in it of fifty human beings." In such sayings are expressed not alone the restless and resistless vivacity and force of which I have spoken, but that also which lay beneath them of steadiness and hard endurance. [Jane Carlyle said of Dickens' face] "It was as if made of steel."

As Chesterton put it, "in the matter of concentrated toil and clear purpose and unconquerable worldly courage—[Dickens] was like a straight sword."

Forster describes the start of Dickens' literary career. At age 21, Dickens wrote a piece called "Mr. Minns and his Cousin," which was later published in *Sketches by Boz*. He dropped this piece "stealthily one evening at twilight, with fear and trembling, into a dark letter-box in a dark office up a dark court in Fleet Street." The piece appeared in the *Old Monthly Magazine*, and Dickens was on his way.

Forster's first visit to Dickens took place shortly after the death of Dickens' beloved sister-in-law Mary, who lived with Dickens and his wife. "His heart opened itself to mine," Forster wrote. "I left him as much his friend, and as entirely in his confidence, as if I had known him for years."

A few weeks later, Dickens wrote to Forster, "I look back with unmingled pleasure to every link which each ensuing week has added to the chain of our attachment. It shall go hard, I hope, ere anything but Death impairs the toughness of a bond now so firmly riveted." Forster says, "It remained unweakened till death came," and death didn't come for almost 35 years.

Writers value feedback, and feedback is especially valuable prior to publication. Forster read all of Dickens' writings prior to publication, or listened as Dickens read them aloud. Forster provided valuable feedback to Dickens.

Every year, Forster dined with Dickens and his wife on their wedding anniversary, which was also Forster's birthday. They dined at the Star and Garter in Richmond. "It was a part of his love of regularity and order, as well as of his kindliness of nature, to place such friendly meetings as these under rules of habit and continuance." They kept up this tradition for twenty years, except when Dickens and his wife were abroad. Perhaps this tradition lapsed as a result of the growing estrangement between Dickens and his wife.

Forster says that, in a circle of friends, there was nothing pretentious about Dickens:

> Displays of conversational or other personal predominance, were no part of the influence he exerted over friends. To them he was only the pleasantest of companions, with whom they forgot that he had ever

written anything.... His talk was unaffected and natural, never bookish in the smallest degree. He was quite up to the average of well-read men, but as there was no ostentation of it in his writing, so neither was there in his conversation. This was so attractive because so keenly observant, and lighted up with so many touches of humorous fancy.

Like many intellectuals, Dickens found relief from mental work in physical exercise—long rides or walks into the country, stopping for lunch at an inn. He usually invited Forster:

> "What a brilliant morning for a country walk!" [Dickens] would write, with not another word in his dispatch. Or, "Is it possible that you can't, oughtn't, shouldn't, mustn't, won't be tempted, this gorgeous day?" Or, "I start precisely—precisely, mind—at half-past one. Come, come, come, and walk in the green lanes. You will work the better for it all the week. Come! I shall expect you." Or, "You don't feel disposed, do you, to muffle yourself up and start off with me for a good brisk walk over Hampstead Heath? I knows a good 'ous there where we can have a red-hot chop for dinner, and a glass of good wine," which led to our first experience of Jack Straw's Castle, memorable for many happy meetings in coming years.

Dickens was fond of sports. One summer, he rented a house outside London, and invited friends and relatives to visit. They played various games, and

> Dickens for the most part held his own.... Bar-leaping, bowling, and quoits were among the games carried on with the greatest ardor; and in sustained energy, what is called keeping it up, Dickens certainly distanced every competitor. Even the lighter recreations of battledoor and bagatelle were pursued with relentless activity. [Quoits was similar to horseshoes, battledoor was similar to badminton, bagatelle might be described as miniature golf played on a board.]

Sometimes Dickens visited a seaside town, and took long beach walks, or watched as a storm raged.

The vivacity that we find in Dickens' biography is similar to the vivacity we find in his fiction. What I wrote about Proust and Kafka is also true of Dickens:

> Proust wasn't bookish or pedantic. Like Kafka, Proust was more fascinated by life itself than by literature. Kafka and Proust viewed life from a literary standpoint, and found life to be the most profound and the most humorous of authors. Proust would have agreed with Kafka's remark: "From life one can extract comparatively so many books, but from books so little, so very little, life." The greatness of Kafka and Proust lies less in their learning than in their living. Proust learned a great deal from life, and his work is based on his own experience.

On one Saturday night in April 1838, Dickens and Forster dined in London, then set out for a late-night ride to Richmond. Dickens had just published *Nicholas Nickleby* (this was his fourth book, following *Sketches by Boz*, *The Pickwick Papers*, and *Oliver Twist*). Forster writes,

> The smallest hour was sounding from St. Paul's into the night before we started, and the night was none of the pleasantest; but we carried news that lightened every part of the road, for the sale of *Nickleby* had reached that day the astonishing number of nearly fifty thousand!

B. Films

The Man Who Invented Christmas (2017) is a movie about Dickens, based on a non-fiction book of the same name by Les Standiford. The movie focuses on the writing of *A Christmas Carol*. It depicts Dickens' friendship with John Forster, his crowded household, his "prodigal father," his negotiations with publishers, etc. Not a great movie, but it's moderately effective both as Dickens biography and as Christmas tale, so I recommend it.

The Invisible Woman (2013) is a movie about Dickens' relationship with Ellen Ternan; Dickens "kept company" with Ellen for the last 10-15 years of his life, and provided for her in his will. The movie does an excellent job of depicting Dickens—his passion for sports and games, his interest in amateur theatricals, his friendship with Wilkie Collins, his harsh treatment of his wife, his penchant for punctuality and order, his interest in mesmerism and the occult, etc. But when the movie depicts Dickens' relationship with Ellen, it enters the realm of speculation—little is known with certainty about their relationship. I can't recommend the movie with enthusiasm, it doesn't grab the viewer, it doesn't achieve "suspension of disbelief," you're never drawn in, you never forget that these are actors.

C. Chesterton and Dickens

In a recent issue, I discussed Joseph Conrad. I focused on an essay that Conrad wrote in 1905, an essay called "Autocracy and War." I wrote, "Conrad could sense that the atmosphere in Europe was darkening."[1]

When World War I broke out in 1914, it seemed at first that this would dispel the oppressive atmosphere; people were thrilled at the prospect of a big war, young men were walking on air in anticipation of military glory. But once the war settled into a muddy and bloody mess, the excitement faded, the dark atmosphere returned and intensified, the prospects for European civilization seemed bleaker than ever.

Conrad doesn't try to explain why the atmosphere, in 1905, was darkening, though he speaks of, "the general effect of the fears and hopes of the time." Perhaps the atmosphere was darkening as a result of developments in the realm of thought—the breakdown of religious belief, the so-called "death of God," the tendency of modern science to reduce everything to physical

---

[1] See below, "Conrad ==> On Russia," or see ljhammond.com/phlit/2021-01.htm#6

causes, the struggle for survival depicted by Darwin, etc. In the last issue, I mentioned how, in 1901, Jacques Maritain and his wife

> became disenchanted with scientism, which could not, in their view, address the larger existential issues of life.... In light of this disillusionment, they made a pact to commit suicide together if they could not discover some deeper meaning to life within a year.[1]

Now I'm reading one of G. K. Chesterton's most highly-regarded works, his study of Dickens. Chesterton's book was published in 1906, one year after Conrad's essay. Chesterton noticed the same darkening atmosphere that Conrad noticed, and Chesterton ascribes this darkening to modern science.

Chesterton says that Dickens and his generation were more optimistic, more hopeful; the early 1800s were more hopeful than the late 1800s. The early 1800s were influenced by the French Revolution, which aimed to build a new world, which gave the average person confidence that he could advance, he could do anything. As Wordsworth put it,

Bliss was it in that dawn to be alive,
But to be young was very heaven!

Dickens' own life seemed to justify these high hopes. Hadn't he risen from modest origins to dizzy heights of fame and fortune by his own hard work and talent?

In Chesterton's time, however, people didn't feel what Dickens felt, they didn't have the high hopes that Dickens had, hence they couldn't relate to Dickens' novels, and Dickens' popularity was on the wane. The high hopes of the Revolution and liberalism, the high hopes of democracy and universal education, were withering, the atmosphere was darkening. Chesterton says that "a pessimistic science" is one of the chief factors in the crumbling of Dickensian optimism.

I believe that a new philosophy, and a new approach to evolution, can put pessimism to rout, and perhaps restore our taste for Dickens. Zen can help us to achieve what Chesterton calls "an ecstasy of the ordinary," and Zen doesn't require belief in God.

A receptive attitude toward the occult will restore what Chesterton calls "a faith in the infinity of human souls." Every human being has mind-boggling capacities, including a capacity to transcend space and time. As Jung put it, "Nobody can say where man ends. That is the beauty of it, you know; it's very interesting. The unconscious of man can reach God knows where. There we are going to make discoveries."[2]

---

[1] See ljhammond.com/phlit/2021-01b.htm#2

[2] Chesterton says, "The note of the last few decades in art and ethics has been that a man is stamped with an irrevocable psychology, and is cramped for perpetuity in the prison of his skull." But Zen says that man is free; each of us is free to awaken to the present moment, to appreciate the sights and

Chesterton is a deep thinker and a superb stylist. It's easy to understand why he has a high reputation, and why his study of Dickens has a particularly high reputation. Chesterton grasps that a great artist like Dickens doesn't use reason, doesn't use conscious thinking, he uses "passionate unconsciousness.... No man by taking thought can add one cubit to his stature; but a man may add many cubits to his stature by not taking thought." This passage shows how Chesterton is fond of taking a proverbial saying and giving it a twist, reversing it.

Chesterton advocates a retreat to Christianity, he's one of the great champions of Christianity. I believe we can overcome pessimism, not by retreating to Christianity or Judaism or Islam, but by going forward, by extending the boundaries of knowledge, and by founding spiritual life on a solid intellectual basis.

* * * * *

When I discussed Conrad, I mentioned that he had various illnesses as a child, illnesses that were regarded as psycho-somatic. Chesterton says that Dickens, too, was sickly as a child; he speaks of, "the touch of ill-health.... The streak of sickness was sufficient to take him out of the common unconscious life of the community of boys.... He was thrown back perpetually upon the pleasures of the intelligence." The young Dickens enjoyed comic novelists like Smollett and Fielding. When he became an adult and started writing fiction, he wrote in the comic tradition.

Shakespeare, especially the comedies of Shakespeare, also influenced Dickens. Chesterton says that Falstaff "might well have been the spiritual father of all Dickens's adorable knaves, Falstaff the great mountain of English laughter and English sentimentalism."

After enjoying a happy childhood until age 12, Dickens was suddenly thrown into the hell of a shoe-polish factory. His father had been imprisoned for debt, his mother and younger siblings lived with his father in the debtors prison, and Charles was on his own, working long hours at a factory, and living at a boarding house. The experience was so painful, so traumatic, that Dickens could scarcely speak of it in later years. It was a soul-crushing experience; Chesterton compares it to torture.

One might suppose that talented people become successful, and un-talented people are unsuccessful, but Chesterton (sometimes called The Prince of Paradox) argues that talented and interesting people are often found among the poor, among the unsuccessful. Chesterton argues that Dickens takes his liveliest characters from the lower classes.

> These great, grotesque characters are almost entirely to be found where Dickens found them—among the poorer classes.... Our public life consists almost exclusively of small men. Our public men are small because they have to prove that they are in the commonplace interpretation clever, because they have to pass examinations, to learn codes of

---

sounds of Now. And if we're receptive to Jung's teachings, then we aren't imprisoned in our own skull, we can "reach God knows where."

> manners, to imitate a fixed type. It is in private life that we find the great characters. They are too great to get into the public world.[1]

The unsuccessful have lots of corners, which make them more interesting, but prevent them from rising in the world.

* * * * *

Chesterton admires the novelist and critic George Gissing. Chesterton calls Gissing “a man of genius” and “the soundest of the Dickens critics.” Gissing said that Dickens’ poor characters are never intellectual. Chesterton goes further and argues that none of Dickens’ characters are intellectual. Dickens’ characters have personality, a large personality, perhaps an exaggerated personality, and they express themselves fully, express themselves without reserve.

> The present that each man brings in hand [Chesterton writes] is his own incredible personality. In the most sacred sense, and in the most literal sense of the phrase, he “gives himself away.” Now, the man who gives himself away does the last act of generosity; he is like a martyr, a lover, or a monk.

So Dickens’ novels are full of life because they feature lively characters, marked individualities, who express themselves fully, hold nothing back, give themselves away.

Chesterton applies the idea of “giving oneself away” to martyrs, lovers, and monks. Does it also apply to writers? Is literature a “giving oneself away”? On Nietzsche’s highest flight of inspiration, he speaks of giving oneself away:

> I love him whose soul is lavish, who neither wants nor returns thanks, for he always gives and will not preserve himself.... I love him whose soul is overfull, so that he forgets himself and all things are in him: thus all things become his downfall.[2]

Those who spent time with Nietzsche noticed that he wasn’t polished or controlled or reserved. One acquaintance said,

---

[1] Perhaps my earlier remarks on Thomas Wolfe throw light on Dickens (see ljhammond.com/phlit/2006-05.htm#6). I said that Wolfe believed that the common man loves life. I quoted a Wolfe critic: “It seems to [Wolfe’s protagonist] that most men have known the wisdom of loving life and their fellow men and have hated the death-in-life.... Although man can be base, obscene, cruel, and treacherous, he remains noble through his love of life. This power binds men together.... Man’s spirit wills to live in spite of everything. Seldom do men deliberately ally themselves with death.” One thinks of Micawber, who experiences various setbacks, but seems to preserve a love of life. Doubtless we should also ascribe this love of life to Dickens himself.

[2] *Thus Spoke Zarathustra*, Prologue, #4. See also *Beyond Good and Evil*, #206, where Nietzsche contrasts the reserved scholar with the genius.

> The emotivity in his temperament struck me as strange. Especially his monologues on Wagner, which began calmly with rationally founded judgments, but soon accelerated into an avalanche of words that stirred up psychic depths and ended in tears.[1]

Nietzsche gives himself away, holds nothing back, and like many Dickens characters, ends in tears. Nietzsche lacked the reserve that makes for worldly success.

The contemporary poet Galway Kinnell said that poetry is about giving oneself away, revealing oneself: "Poetry is somebody standing up, so to speak, and saying, with as little concealment as possible, what it is for him or her to be on earth at this moment." Kinnell and Dickens and Nietzsche wrote with "as little concealment as possible."

Proust contrasted the courteous aristocrat (Saint-Loup) with the artist who gives himself (Elstir):

> [Elstir] lavished on me a friendliness which was as far above that of Saint-Loup as that was above the affability of a mere tradesman. Compared with that of a great artist, the friendliness of a great gentleman, charming as it may be, has the effect of an actor's playing a part, of being feigned. Saint-Loup sought to please; Elstir loved to give, to give himself. Everything that he possessed, ideas, work, and the rest which he counted far less, he would have given gladly to anyone who could understand him.

In *David Copperfield*, Dickens writes about his own life. *David Copperfield* is often called his most autobiographical novel, and his best novel. Tolstoy said, "Sift the literature of the world and you get Dickens. Sift the works of Dickens and you get *David Copperfield*."[2]

If people have a high opinion of themselves, one might expect them to conceal it. But Dickens doesn't conceal, he reveals, he "gives himself away,"

---

[1] This is a quote from Resa von Schirnhofer. It can be found in *Conversations With Nietzsche*, #62, edited by Sander L. Gilman.

According to Chesterton, Dickens was "a man who might at any moment cry like a child." Dickens was "dangerously close to tears."

[2] Chesterton also felt that David Copperfield was Dickens' best novel. See *Appreciations and Criticisms of the Works of Charles Dickens* (1911).

George Gissing said, "Dickens held [*David Copperfield*] to be his best book, and the world has agreed with him. In no other does the narrative move on with such full sail from first to last. He wrote from his heart; picturing completely all he had suffered as a child, and even touching upon the domestic trouble of his later life."

Tolstoy and Dostoyevsky were both big fans of Dickens. They were roughly contemporary with Dickens. On the other hand, Chesterton was from a later generation, a gloomier generation, a generation that couldn't relate to Dickens. Dickens was born in 1812, Dostoyevsky in 1821, Tolstoy in 1828, Chesterton in 1874.

he tells us that he had a higher opinion of his work than anyone else had. In *David Copperfield*, Dickens writes about the beginning of his literary career, his fame, the many letters he receives, etc. He writes, "I was not stunned by the praise which sounded in my ears, notwithstanding that I was keenly alive to it, and thought better of my own performance, I have little doubt, than anybody else did."

Chesterton noticed that Dickens thought highly of his own work: "A definite school regarded Dickens as a great man from the first days of his fame: Dickens certainly belonged to this school." Here, too, there's a parallel with Nietzsche, who expresses a high opinion of his own work in *Ecce Homo* and elsewhere.

One of the impressive things about Dickens' novels is how many he wrote. As Chesterton put it, "One of the godlike things about Dickens is his quantity, his quantity as such, the enormous output, the incredible fecundity of his invention." In my chapter on genius, I noted that genius has "exceptional passion and energy." In *David Copperfield*, Dickens speaks of his "patient and continuous energy." He describes how he developed the habit of hard work, and how "my success had steadily increased with my steady application." Perhaps he worked too hard, perhaps he wore himself out; his public readings were especially tiring. He died at 58.

As for Chesterton, he seems to be a genius of a lower grade than Dickens, exemplifying my theory that "there are various grades of genius."

* * * * *

Chesterton says that many Dickens characters are exaggerated, even unrealistic, but he doesn't see this as a fault in Dickens. "Exaggeration is the definition of art," Chesterton says.

Exaggeration also plays a role in non-fiction writing. The American philosopher Eric Hoffer said, "To think out a problem is not unlike drawing a caricature. You have to exaggerate the salient point and leave out that which is not typical."[1] Hoffer quotes Bagehot: "To illustrate a principle, you must exaggerate much and you must omit much."

Dickens' popularity is waning, Chesterton says, not because he exaggerates, but because he exaggerates the wrong things, he exaggerates feelings that are foreign to modern readers. "The truth he exaggerates," Chesterton says, "is exactly this old Revolution sense of infinite opportunity and boisterous brotherhood." The modern writer also exaggerates, but he exaggerates the perverse and morbid. I've often complained that contemporary movies exaggerate the perverse and morbid.[2]

---

1 *The True Believer*, #43

"To those who would class Dickens' creations as caricatures, Poe asserted that 'a certain amount of exaggeration is essential in the proper depicting of truth itself.'"(jstor.org/stable/3044218)

2 In my *Conversations With Great Thinkers*, I wrote, "Evil has become as fashionable in art as good was formerly. Twentieth-century art, including

D. Dickens and Poe

Chesterton says that Dickens has a "natural turn for terrors" as well as a "natural turn for joy and laughter." Chesterton says that Dickens' first novel, *Pickwick Papers*, is comic and light-hearted, while his second, *Oliver Twist*, is full of horror and darkness.[1] (I'm reminded of Nietzsche, who expressed the positive in *Zarathustra*, and the negative in his next book, *Beyond Good and Evil.*) "In *Oliver Twist*," Chesterton writes, "the smoke of the thieves' kitchen hangs over the whole tale, and the shadow of Fagin falls everywhere."

When Dickens writes in a dark vein, his work can have a striking similarity to that of Poe. One of Dickens' early stories, "A Confession Found in a Prison in the Time of Charles II," has the tone of a Poe story, and doubtless influenced two of Poe's best-known stories, "The Tell-Tale Heart" and "The Black Cat." Before Poe wrote these stories, he read the Dickens story, and described it as "a paper of remarkable power, truly original in conception, and worked out with great ability."[2]

---

film, has become obsessed with the morbid and the immoral. Many modern artists seem to think that profundity consists in concentrating on the evil, irrational, morbid side of human nature. The morbidity of modern art is as one-sided, as exaggerated, as fraudulent, as was the sentimentality of early-nineteenth-century art. The moral anarchy of modern art, especially that of popular music and film, contributes to the moral anarchy of modern society." See also my remarks on the movie *Sophie's Choice* (ljhammond.com/phlit/2011-10.htm#4).

1 *Charles Dickens*, 1906

When I wrote this, I hadn't read *Pickwick*. I now realize that *Pickwick* has several horror stories, several stories that might have been written by Poe. The main story in *Pickwick* deals with the adventures of a learned society, The Pickwick Club. But there are several "digression stories," and these sub-stories are often horror stories. Chapter 3, for example, contains "The Stroller's Tale," which is about a man who's dying and losing his mind, and fears his wife is going to kill him. Chapter 6 contains a tale called "The Convict's Return," about a man who beats his wife and child; the child eventually grows up, fights his father, his father dies. Chapter 11 contains "The Madman's Manuscript," about a man who goes mad and kills his wife, and tries to kill her brother. So I don't understand why Chesterton said, "[Dickens'] natural turn for terrors was kept down in *Pickwick*."

2 "The Personal and Literary Relationships of Dickens and Poe: Part Three: Poe's Literary Debt to Dickens," by Gerald G. Grubb, *Nineteenth-Century Fiction*, December, 1950, Vol. 5, No. 3, pp. 209-221; jstor.org/stable/3044119

Clearly Dickens influenced Poe, but who influenced Dickens? Where did Dickens get the "horror style"?

Poe was born in 1809, just three years before Dickens. Poe was quick to appreciate Dickens' genius, and sing his praises. In 1836, when Dickens was just 24, and hadn't published his first novel, Poe praised Dickens' *Sketches by Boz*: "'*Sketches by Boz* are all exceedingly well managed, and never fail to *tell* as the author intended.' After listing the contents of the volume, [Poe] says, 'There are here some as well conceived and well written papers as can be found in any collection of any kind.'"

Later in the same year, Poe hailed the appearance of *Pickwick Papers*. "The author possesses nearly every desirable quality in a writer of fiction.... His general powers as a prose writer are equaled by few." When Dickens was 28, he began publishing *The Old Curiosity Shop* (in serial form in a periodical, as most of his works were published). *The Old Curiosity Shop* deals with the love between a girl and her grandfather. Poe said,

> This conception is indeed most beautiful. It is simple and severely grand. The more fully we survey it, the more thoroughly are we convinced of the lofty character of that genius which gave it birth.... If the conception of this story deserves praise, its execution is beyond all.... In all higher elements which go to make up literary greatness, it is supremely excellent.

Poe noted that Dickens has a double popularity: he's popular with the masses, and with "the informed and intelligent." When Dickens burst on the scene, the most popular novelist in England was Edward Bulwer-Lytton. Poe realized that Bulwer-Lytton was a skillful craftsman, while Dickens was a genuine genius. As Gerald Grubb wrote, "It took unusual insight to enable a critic to recognize the rising Dickens as a greater genius than the accomplished Bulwer-Lytton."

When Dickens was 30, he made his first trip to the U.S. When Dickens reached Philadelphia in March, 1842, Poe wrote to him, asked for a meeting, and sent him two volumes of his short stories. Poe and Dickens met twice, and Poe asked Dickens to help him publish his works in England.

In November, 1842, Dickens wrote Poe from London, and said that he'd failed to find a publisher for Poe's works. Though Dickens and Poe were always amicable, they never became close friends (Dickens did become close friends with Washington Irving and several other Americans). It seems

---

In an earlier issue, I noted that Poe's "Murders in the Rue Morgue" was influenced by Walter Scott's *Count Robert of Paris*, and "The Fall of the House of Usher" was influenced by Scott's *Bride of Lammermoor*. Grubb points out that Poe's famous poem "The Raven" was influenced by the raven in Dickens' *Barnaby Rudge*.

Grubb has high regard for *The Mind of Poe*, by Killis Campbell. Campbell mentions many examples of Poe borrowing from earlier writers, including Dickens. Campbell says that Poe's story "The Man of the Crowd" is Dickens-influenced; perhaps Campbell is referring to the way the narrator observes the passing crowd, and tries to infer all sorts of things from a person's appearance.

that Dickens later described Poe as "our friend in Philadelphia, who is a miserable creature; a disappointed man in great poverty, to whom I have ever been most kind and considerate."[1]

In late 1842, Dickens published *American Notes*, which dealt with his recent trip to the U.S. Dickens discussed the U.S. at greater length in his novel *Martin Chuzzlewit*, which was published a few months after *American Notes*. Chesterton has high praise for *Chuzzlewit*, calling it a "great satire," and saying that it "may survive America as *The Knights* has survived Athens." Chesterton says that *Chuzzlewit* satirizes sins that are

> not merely American, but English also. The eternal, complacent iteration of patriotic half-truths; the perpetual buttering of one's self all over with the same stale butter; above all, the big defiances of small enemies, or the very urgent challenges to very distant enemies; the cowardice so habitual and unconscious that it wears the plumes of courage.... The thing which is rather foolishly called the Anglo-Saxon civilization is at present soaked through with a weak pride.... It uses its organs of public opinion not to warn the public, but to soothe it. It really succeeds not only in ignoring the rest of the world, but actually in forgetting it.

When Dickens was in the U.S. in 1842, slavery was a hot topic. Dickens was vehemently opposed to slavery. A defender of slavery once asked him, Why would a slave-owner mistreat his own slave, his own property? Isn't it in his own interest to treat his slave decently? Dickens responded,

> It was not a man's interest to get drunk, or to steal, or to game, or to indulge in any other vice; but he did indulge in it for all that.... Cruelty and the abuse of irresponsible power were two of the bad passions of human nature, with the gratification of which considerations of interest or of ruin had nothing whatever to do.

Dickens visited southern states as well as northern states, and he paints a grim picture of slavery.

Dickens visited prisons, mental hospitals, etc. At the Perkins School for the Blind, near Boston, Dickens met Laura Bridgman, who was both deaf and blind, but had managed to get an education. "His account of this meeting in *American Notes* would inspire Helen Keller's parents to seek an education for their daughter."[2] Both Keller and her teacher, Anne Sullivan, attended the Perkins School. Dickens donated £1700 to the Perkins School so they could obtain special copies of *The Old Curiosity Shop*, copies that could be read by blind students.

Dickens had a love of life and a love of mankind. He had compassion for those who suffered, especially children who suffered; he remembered his

---

[1] See Part 3 of Grubb's essay. The adjective "miserable" should perhaps be interpreted as an expression of pity rather than contempt. Grubb says there's "an undertone of respect and even of sympathy" in Dickens' references to Poe.

[2] See Wikipedia ==> "American Notes"

own sufferings as a child. He was a social reformer as well as an artist, hence he was interested in jails, mental hospitals, schools for the blind, etc.

Before he started writing *Nicholas Nickleby*, Dickens traveled to Yorkshire, to visit schools that were "notorious for cruelties." He traveled with his illustrator, Hablot Browne, who was known as "Phiz." *Nicholas Nickleby* called attention to abuses in schools, as *Pickwick* had called attention to abuses in debtors' prisons, and *Oliver Twist* had called attention to abuses in workhouses (also known as "poorhouses"). By exposing abuses, Dickens could effect change and reduce suffering.[1]

Perhaps Dickens could also effect change of a less tangible kind by changing the reader's values, the reader's morals. George Gissing said that Dickens presented moral ideals:

> the ideal of goodness and purity, of honor, justice, mercy, whereby the dim multitudes falteringly seek to direct their steps.... It was the part of Dickens to show the beauty of moral virtues.... When sending forth [David Copperfield] into the world Betsy Trotwood gave him this brief counsel, "Never be mean; never be false; never be cruel." Better advice she could not have bestowed; and it was the ideal of conduct held up by Dickens to all his readers.[2]

In 1867, when Dickens was 55, he made a second (and last) visit to the U.S. By this time, both Poe and his wife had died. Dickens looked up Poe's mother-in-law in Baltimore, and "generously entreated her acceptance of one hundred and fifty dollars with the assurance of his sympathy."[3]

E. Dickens on America

Chesterton dismisses Dickens' *American Notes* as a "squib," and says "they are no true picture of America." But I'm impressed with *American Notes*. Dickens notices something that I've often discussed—namely, that

---

[1] In *David Copperfield*, Agnes says to David, "'Your growing reputation and success enlarge your power of doing good; and if I could spare my brother,' with her eyes upon me, 'perhaps the time could not.'" Dickens felt that he had a responsibility, a mission. In addition to furthering reforms in his fiction, he set up a house for "fallen women," and managed it for ten years, "setting the house rules, reviewing the accounts and interviewing prospective residents."(Wikipedia, "Charles Dickens")

[2] Gissing's view of the power of fiction to mold people and influence society reminds me of Shaw's view of the power of drama. Shaw felt that the theater was replacing the church, and he called the theater, "a factory of thought, a prompter of conscience, an elucidator of social conduct, an armory against despair and dullness, and a temple of the Ascent of Man."

[3] This is a quote from American author and publisher James T. Fields. It can be found in Part 3 of Grubb's essay.

Poe's wife, Virginia Clemm, was his first cousin. Poe's mother-in-law, Maria Poe Clemm, was his aunt; Maria's father was Edgar's grandfather.

the U.S. is full of swindlers. A successful swindler is respected, perhaps even elevated to the Presidency. His conduct is excused, he may even be praised as a smart deal-maker, a sharp operator.

Americans blame, not the swindler, but the victim of the swindle, they say that the victim should have been more alert, they quote the maxim "buyer beware" (*caveat emptor*). Americans don't ask, Is this how someone should treat other people? Is this how the swindler would want people to treat him? Dickens' moral sense was outraged by swindlers, and by Americans' toleration of swindlers.

A "prominent feature" in American society, Dickens wrote, is

> the love of "smart" dealing: which gilds over many a swindle and gross breach of trust; many a defalcation, public and private; and enables many a knave to hold his head up with the best, who well deserves a halter.... The following dialogue I have held a hundred times:
>
> "Is it not a very disgraceful circumstance that such a man as So-and-so should be acquiring a large property by the most infamous and odious means, and notwithstanding all the crimes of which he has been guilty, should be tolerated and abetted by your Citizens? He is a public nuisance, is he not?"
>
> "Yes, sir."
> "A convicted liar?"
> "Yes, sir...."
> "And he is utterly dishonorable, debased, and profligate?"
> "Yes, sir."
> "In the name of wonder, then, what is his merit?"
> "Well, sir, he is a smart man."
>
> The merits of a broken speculation, [Dickens writes,] or a bankruptcy, or of a successful scoundrel, are not gauged by its or his observance of the golden rule, "Do as you would be done by," but are considered with reference to their smartness.

I made a similar argument in earlier issues:
"In a civilized society, where open combat is rare, the sneaky person is more dangerous than the violent person. The sneaky person operates within the law, or turns the law to his advantage.... In business situations, Americans treat each other savagely.... Our society has become a free-for-all, a no-holds-barred scramble for wealth, a war of all against all (*bellum omnium contra omnes*).... Greed and moral decay are tearing our society apart.... Trust is the life-blood of society. He who betrays trust strikes at the heart of society."

I quoted Freud: "The law is not able to lay hold of the more cautious and refined manifestations of human aggressiveness." Freud understood the swindler, and he understood the pain of the swindler's victim—one of the most acute kinds of pain. Though Freud briefly visited the U.S., his remarks are doubtless based on his experiences in Europe. Swindlers exist in every corner of the world, and they've existed since time immemorial. But they're especially prevalent in the U.S., and Americans are especially tolerant of them. And the problem may be worse today than in Dickens' time.

You can't guard against the swindler because he strikes when you don't expect it, he utilizes the element of surprise, which plays such an important role in war. The PearlHarbor attack, the 9/11 attacks—many attacks depend on the element of surprise. The swindler will find a novel way to trick you, a way you aren't expecting, and he'll find a way to win your trust before he stabs you in the back.

You can't prevent the surprise attack because you aren't aware that you're at war, your enemy strikes during peace-time. Once the war starts, both sides are on high alert, and it's more difficult to take the other side by surprise. But a surprise attack in peace-time is difficult to prevent, and this is true among neighbors as well as among nations.

It's almost impossible to prevent a clever swindle. Your only hope is to bring the swindler to justice after-the-fact, and that's almost impossible, too. The swindler turns a profit, and goes on to his next swindle. Gradually society becomes full of swindlers. Americans need to be permanently on high alert against swindlers.

It's our virtues that make us vulnerable to the swindler; as I wrote elsewhere, "The Greek word *agathos* means noble, good, naive, gullible, trusting. One's virtues make one easy to deceive and rob, one's virtues make one a tempting target for a con man." Since we wouldn't think of perpetrating a swindle, it doesn't occur to us that our neighbor might be plotting a swindle against us.

William James would have agreed with Dickens, though he probably didn't read *American Notes*. James believed, "we must not explain away indifference to justice as 'pragmatism.'" James said, "Exactly that callousness to abstract justice is the sinister feature... of our U.S. Civilization." Around 1900, James asked, "What are the bosom vices of the level of culture which our land and day have reached? ....Swindling and adroitness and the indulgence of swindling and adroitness."

James lamented the "exclusive worship of the bitch-Goddess SUCCESS," and he said that "the squalid cash interpretation put on the word success—is our national disease." Elsewhere James said, "the prevalent fear of poverty among the educated classes is the worst moral disease from which our civilization suffers."[1]

* * * * *

According to Dickens, American journalists say the worst about politicians, and the American public believes the worst about politicians, so decent people don't want to enter the political arena.

> One great blemish in the popular mind of America [Dickens writes] and the prolific parent of an innumerable brood of evils, is Universal Distrust.... "You carry," says the stranger, "this jealousy and distrust into every transaction of public life. By repelling worthy men from

---

[1] See Richardson's biography of James, Ch. 73, Ch. 82, and Ch. 67

> your legislative assemblies, it has bred up a class of candidates for the suffrage, who... disgrace your Institutions and your people's choice."

Americans don't believe good reports about people, but they do believe bad reports: "You will strain at a gnat in the way of trustfulness and confidence, however fairly won and well deserved; but you will swallow a whole caravan of camels, if they be laden with unworthy doubts and mean suspicions." A caravan of camels—like the story that Hillary Clinton was chopping up children.

Such wild stories may seem to flourish on the Internet, but Dickens says that they have a long history; Dickens has boundless contempt for American journalism. The U.S. has some newspapers, Dickens says,

> of character and credit.... But the name of these is Few, and of the others Legion; and the influence of the good, is powerless to counteract the moral poison of the bad....
>
> To those who are accustomed to the leading English journals, or to the respectable journals of the Continent of Europe; to those who are accustomed to anything else in print and paper; it would be impossible, without an amount of extract for which I have neither space nor inclination, to convey an adequate idea of this frightful engine in America....
>
> Schools may be erected, East, West, North, and South; pupils be taught, and masters reared, by scores upon scores of thousands; colleges may thrive, churches may be crammed, temperance may be diffused, and advancing knowledge in all other forms walk through the land with giant strides: but while the newspaper press of America is in, or near, its present abject state, high moral improvement in that country is hopeless. Year by year, it must and will go back; year by year, the tone of public feeling must sink lower down.

The American press not only publishes the false and degrading, it also stifles truth; it censors unfashionable views, politically-incorrect views:

> When any man in that free country has freedom of opinion, and presumes to think for himself, and speak for himself, without humble reference to a censorship which, for its rampant ignorance and base dishonesty, he utterly loathes and despises in his heart; when those who most acutely feel its infamy and the reproach it casts upon the nation, and who most denounce it to each other, dare to set their heels upon, and crush it openly, in the sight of all men: then, I will believe that its influence is lessening, and men are returning to their manly senses.

Dickens notes that many Americans read only newspapers: "With ribald slander for its only stock in trade, it is the standard literature of an enormous class, who must find their reading in a newspaper, or they will not read at all." At the present time, Dickens says, the only "national amusement" in the U.S. is "newspaper politics." (It should be noted that, in 1868, during his second visit to the U.S., Dickens believed there was "much improvement in the press.")

Dickens says that Americans aren't a happy people, perhaps because we're striving to get rich. Americans

> certainly are not a humorous people [Dickens writes] and their temperament always impressed me as being of a dull and gloomy character.... In travelling about, out of the large cities... I was quite oppressed by the prevailing seriousness and melancholy air of business.... Healthful amusements, cheerful means of recreation, and wholesome fancies, must fade before the stern utilitarian joys of trade.

Dickens paints a harsh portrait of America. He says that America isn't a model for the nations, it's a warning to the nations. "I do fear," Dickens said, "that the heaviest blow ever dealt at liberty will be dealt by this country, in the failure of its example on the earth." *American Notes* generated considerable controversy in the U.S.; American journalists leapt to the defense of their country, and castigated Dickens.

For a long time, it must have seemed that Dickens was too pessimistic, it must have seemed that the U.S. *was* a model for the nations, that the U.S. was unusually successful both politically and economically. Now, however, it seems that the U.S. is beginning to come unraveled, and Dickens' dire forebodings seem to deserve a closer look. Dickens knew that his predictions wouldn't immediately be realized. "I can bide my time," he said.

American Notes contains a charming account of Dickens' attempt to buy new boots. He says that this incident shows the spirit of equality in the U.S., shows how the working-class doesn't bow to a higher class, shows how "the Republican Institutions of America undoubtedly lead the people to assert their self-respect and their equality."

> I wanted a pair of boots at a certain town.... I therefore sent a message to an artist in boots, importing, with my compliments, that I should be happy to see him, if he would do me the polite favor to call. He very kindly returned for answer, that he would 'look round' at six o'clock that evening.
>
> I was lying on the sofa, with a book and a wine-glass, at about that time, when the door opened, and a gentleman in a stiff cravat, within a year or two on either side of thirty, entered, in his hat and gloves; walked up to the looking-glass; arranged his hair; took off his gloves; slowly produced a measure from the uttermost depths of his coat-pocket....
>
> [I] looked with some curiosity at his hat, which was still upon his head. It might have been that, or it might have been the heat—but he took it off. Then, he sat himself down on a chair opposite to me; rested an arm on each knee; and, leaning forward very much, took from the ground, by a great effort, the specimen of metropolitan workmanship which I had just pulled off: whistling, pleasantly, as he did so. He turned it over and over; surveyed it with a contempt no language can express; and inquired if I wished him to fix me a boot like that?
>
> I courteously replied, that provided the boots were large enough, I would leave the rest to him; that if convenient and practicable, I should

> not object to their bearing some resemblance to the model then before him; but that I would be entirely guided by, and would beg to leave the whole subject to, his judgment and discretion. 'You an't partickler, about this scoop in the heel, I suppose then?' says he: 'we don't foller that, here.' I repeated my last observation.
>
> He looked at himself in the glass again; went closer to it to dash a grain or two of dust out of the corner of his eye; and settled his cravat. All this time, my leg and foot were in the air. 'Nearly ready, sir?' I inquired. 'Well, pretty nigh,' he said; 'keep steady.' I kept as steady as I could, both in foot and face; and having by this time got the dust out, and found his pencil-case, he measured me, and made the necessary notes.
>
> When he had finished, he fell into his old attitude, and taking up the boot again, mused for some time. 'And this,' he said, at last, 'is an English boot, is it? This is a London boot, eh?' 'That, sir,' I replied, 'is a London boot.' He mused over it again, after the manner of Hamlet with Yorick's skull; nodded his head, as who should say, 'I pity the Institutions that led to the production of this boot!'; rose; put up his pencil, notes, and paper—glancing at himself in the glass, all the time—put on his hat—drew on his gloves very slowly; and finally walked out.
>
> When he had been gone about a minute, the door reopened, and his hat and his head reappeared. He looked round the room, and at the boot again, which was still lying on the floor; appeared thoughtful for a minute; and then said 'Well, good arternoon.' 'Good afternoon, sir,' said I: and that was the end of the interview.

Dickens says that this incident wasn't typical, it was an exaggerated case; usually his interactions with American tradesmen were amicable, and it didn't offend him that American tradesmen were less deferential than their British counterparts.

This anecdote about boots illustrates Forster's remark that Dickens' "leading quality was humor." Did Dickens get his sense of humor from his father? Or from novelists like Fielding and Smollett? An aristocrat's pride may inhibit his humor. Tolstoy, an aristocrat, is rarely (if ever) humorous, but Dostoyevsky, who was from the middle-class, wrote some humorous works, such as "Crocodile."

Perhaps humor is connected to national character; perhaps certain peoples, like the English and the Jews, are more inclined toward humor. Among the English, even someone from the pinnacle of the aristocracy, like Shakespeare, has a comic bent. As for humorous Jewish writers, Kafka and Woody Allen come to mind. Joyce said that a sense of humor is

> a thing which Stendhal lacked—and which some Frenchmen lack... they cannot but take life seriously, and no Frenchman will admit his

> inferiority before life. His vanity prevents it. But an Englishman is better balanced, and he will admit his powerlessness before fate by means of his humor.[1]

Dickens' *American Notes* is often humorous. Is there a single example of humor in Tocqueville's *Democracy in America*?

Chesterton said that Dickens' humor emphasizes that everyone is interesting, everyone is different. Chesterton writes, "Dickens' sense of democracy.... rested on the sense that all men were wildly interesting and wildly varied." But Chesterton says that Dickens lacks a sense that all men have dignity, even sublimity. Perhaps it took an aristocrat to emphasize the dignity of all men, an aristocrat like Walter Scott. Chesterton says that Scott's "rich and dramatic effects are gained in almost every case by some grotesque or beggarly figure rising into a human pride and rhetoric.... All his characters are kings in disguise."

Dickens also lacks a sense of stillness, of Zen. Perhaps the first English novelists to express the Zen spirit in their fiction were Walter Pater and E. M. Forster.

One of Dickens' strengths is that his fictional world seems like a real world. The reader "suspends his disbelief," the reader connects with Dickens' characters as if they were real people. Dickens himself connected with his characters, and when he finished a novel, he hated to part from his characters.

F. *David Copperfield*

i. The Mind of the Heart

I recently read *David Copperfield.* It was more enjoyable than I had expected, easier to read than I had expected. It's a long novel, but it doesn't seem long because the narrative moves along at a brisk pace, and holds your interest. Only the last chapters drag a bit; Chesterton said that the early chapters were written from the heart, and reflect the author's own experience, but the last chapters are invented, artificial.[2]

[Spoiler Warning: If you're thinking of reading *David Copperfield*, you may want to skip the rest of this section, i.e., you may want to skip all the sub-sections related to *Copperfield.*]

One of the themes of David Copperfield is "the mind of the heart," the wisdom of the unconscious, non-rational wisdom, intuitive wisdom. We find this wisdom in a *Copperfield* character named Mr. Dick, who is a "holy fool," an innocent lunatic. Mr. Dick enjoys flying kites and playing with children. Mr. Dick can be compared to other Dickens characters who represent "the mind of the heart," such as Sleary (in *Hard Times*), Guppy (in *Bleak House*), Glubb (in *Dombey and Son*), and Fezziwig (in *Christmas Carol*). These

---

1 *Conversations With James Joyce*, by Arthur Power, Ch. 11

2 See *Appreciations and Criticisms of the Works of Charles Dickens*. Elsewhere Chesterton said, "the early pages of the book are in particular astonishingly vivid."(*Charles Dickens*, 1906)

characters contrast with rational, calculating, heart-less characters like Gradgrind (in *Hard Times*) and Scrooge (in *Christmas Carol*).

Mr. Dick visits David's school:

> He soon became known to every boy in the school; and though he never took an active part in any game but kite-flying, was as deeply interested in all our sports as anyone among us. How often have I seen him, intent upon a match at marbles or pegtop, looking on with a face of unutterable interest, and hardly breathing at the critical times!

In *Copperfield*, Dickens not only shows us "the mind of the heart," he states this theme explicitly. When Doctor Strong and his wife Annie are at an impasse in their marriage, and no one seems able to break the impasse, Mr. Dick saves the day. He has "a subtlety of perception... which leaves the highest intellect behind," a "mind of the heart." Mr. Dick has no ego, he just wants to help his friends:

> "A poor fellow with a craze, sir," said Mr. Dick, "a simpleton, a weak-minded person—present company, you know!" striking himself again, "may do what wonderful people may not do. I'll bring them together, boy. I'll try. They'll not blame me. They'll not object to me. They'll not mind what I do, if it's wrong. I'm only Mr. Dick. And who minds Dick? Dick's nobody!"[1]

At another important moment in the story, when Betsey is wondering whether to bring David into her household, Dick again plays a key role.

> "Mr. Dick," said my aunt, "what shall I do with this child?" Mr. Dick considered, hesitated, brightened, and rejoined, "Have him measured for a suit of clothes directly."

Once we realize that the holy fool is a recurring character in Dickens' works, the question arises, Where did Dickens get this character? From his own experience and observation? From his reading of novelists like Fielding? I suspect that he got it from fairy tales; the Dickens biographer Edgar Johnson spoke of, "those echoes from the fairy tales which constantly recur in Dickens."[2] Sixteen years ago, I discussed the Jungian Marie-Louise von Franz:

---

[1] The crisis in Doctor Strong's marriage to Annie is caused by Uriah Heep, who drops hints that Annie is unfaithful. One might compare Doctor Strong to Othello, Uriah to Iago, and Annie to Desdemona.

[2] *Charles Dickens: His Tragedy and Triumph*, Vol. 2, Ch. 6, p. 698

Chesterton may have perceived the importance of the dummling in Dickens' works. "The key of the great characters of Dickens," Chesterton wrote, "is that they are all great fools. There is the same difference between a great fool and a small fool as there is between a great poet and a small poet. The great fool is a being who is above wisdom rather than below it."

> Von Franz's specialty is fairy tales, and she believes that one of the stock characters of fairy tales represents integrity. She speaks of, "the famous fairy tale motif of the Dummling, the simpleton, who appears in an infinite number of fairy tales. For instance, a king has three sons and the youngest is a fool whom everybody laughs at; but it is always this fool who becomes the hero in the story.... This kind of simple-minded, candid integrity is a great mystery and is already the secret of an individuated personality. The gift of guileless integrity is a divine spark in the human being. In analysis, I would say that it is the decisive factor as to whether an analysis goes right or wrong."

Mr. Dick is a good example of a dummling, and the dummling is a recurring character in Dickens' works. The dummling has naivete, integrity, and enthusiasm; he has non-rational wisdom, the mind of the heart.

* * * * *

Mr. Dick's keen interest in a game of marbles contrasts with calculating characters like Gradgrind, who see no purpose in play. It also contrasts with another Dickens character-type: the cool, ironic, sophisticated character who's bored with everything, indifferent to everything. In *Copperfield*, the cool character is Jack Maldon.

> "Have you breakfasted this morning, Mr. Jack?" said the Doctor. "I hardly ever take breakfast, sir," he replied, with his head thrown back in an easy-chair. "I find it bores me."

Maldon is as bored with current events as he is with breakfast:

> "Is there any news today?" inquired the Doctor. "Nothing at all, sir," replied Mr. Maldon. "There's an account about the people being hungry and discontented down in the North, but they are always being hungry and discontented somewhere.... There's a long statement in the papers, sir, about a murder," observed Mr. Maldon. "But somebody is always being murdered, and I didn't read it." A display of indifference to all the actions and passions of mankind was not supposed to be such a distinguished quality at that time, I think, as I have observed it to be considered since. I have known it very fashionable indeed.

When I discussed Dickens' *Hard Times*, I noticed this same attitude of cool sophistication in a character named James Harthouse.[1]

ii. The Undisciplined Heart

Mr. Dick represents the wisdom of the unconscious, the wisdom of the Self (to use a Jungian term). But there's also a shallower impulse of the body,

---

The novelist and critic George Gissing says that Mr. Dick "served a very practical purpose, that of recommending rational treatment of the insane." I don't deny this, but I think Mr. Dick also shows "the mind of the heart."

[1] See below, "*Hard Times* ==> Irony and Sophistication"

of the ego; it can be argued that a major theme of *Copperfield* is "the undisciplined heart." The undisciplined heart can lead one into a bad marriage—*Copperfield* has several bad marriages—and a bad marriage can ruin one's life, and even lead to one's death.

One bad marriage is Clara Copperfield's marriage to Edward Murdstone. Clara was widowed by the early death of her husband, David's father. What leads her into the fatal blunder of choosing Murdstone? Betsey Trotwood, David's aunt, can't understand it: "Whatever possessed that poor unfortunate Baby, that she must go and be married again... I can't conceive." Mr. Dick puts forward what is probably the correct explanation: "Perhaps she did it for pleasure."

Clara's undisciplined heart has led her into a fatal mistake. Once Murdstone has her firmly tied in the bonds of matrimony, he brings his sister Jane into the household, and together they tyrannize over Clara and David. Clara bends to the Murdstones, Clara can't "live under coldness or unkindness." One critic says that, with her undisciplined heart, Clara "cannot bear either responsibility or discomfort."[1] Clara becomes ill and dies. Betsey later excoriates Murdstone for killing Clara: "You must begin to train her, must you? begin to break her, like a poor caged bird, and wear her deluded life away, in teaching her to sing YOUR notes?"

Many English novelists explore the dark side of marriage. When I discussed D. H. Lawrence, I wrote,

> For Lawrence, love is often "a very terrible thing," because Lawrence understands the death of love, death by love, and death for love. Lawrence understands the dark side of love, the dark side of marriage. Perhaps this understanding came not from his own experience but from his mother's experience.[2]

---

1 See "The Undisciplined Heart of David Copperfield," by Gwendolyn Needham (*Nineteenth-Century Fiction*, September, 1954, Vol. 9, No. 2, pp. 81-107, jstor.org/stable/3044322). If I were to recommend one essay on *Copperfield*, it would be Needham's.

2 Hardy also depicts the dark side of marriage. In an earlier issue, I said that Hardy's *Jude the Obscure* depicts two men "who appear to die from flawed relationships with women." Wikipedia says of *Jude the Obscure*, "From the original pairing of Arabella and Jude to their eventual reunion, Hardy depicts marriage as an oppressive social necessity, propelling the characters into a downward spiral of unhappiness."

Kipling also depicts the dark side of marriage. The protagonist of *The Light That Failed*, Dick, tells Maisie, "We've both nice little wills of our own, and one or other of us has to be broken." "It is not Maisie who is destroyed," one critic writes. "Very early, by her unremitting preoccupation with her work, by the invincible coldness of her character, she succeeds in reducing Dick to a condition in which the erstwhile confident young braggart turns on her silently the 'look of a beaten hound waiting for the word to crawl to his

Clara's death is death by love—"a relationship that drives one party to death." David's own relationship with Dora might be called the death *of* love, "a gradual loss of respect/love." David falls head-over-heels for Dora, but both of them are too young to understand what they're getting into, too young to understand that marriage is more than physical pleasure.[1]

David's heart is undisciplined, like Clara's, he's attracted by beauty, he doesn't realize that Dora isn't the right life-partner for him. David doesn't understand what Lawrence's mother learned by painful experience: "Nothing is as bad as a marriage that's a hopeless failure. Mine was bad enough,

---

mistress's feet.' The degradation is total: deprived of all initiative in the relationship, Dick is allotted the feminine and subservient role." Kipling's understanding of the dark side of marriage couldn't save him from getting into a marriage in which he himself was "deprived of all initiative."

Tolstoy admired Dickens, especially *Copperfield.* He opens *War and Peace* with an unhappy marriage, a marriage that resembles the marriage of David and Dora. Tolstoy's Prince Andrew treats his wife, Lisa, with "a cold and insulting politeness." His father senses his unhappiness, and says, "One can't un-marry." Prince Andrew escapes his marital problems by going off to war. When he returns, Lisa dies in childbirth. Her expression seems to say, "What have you done to me?" Prince Andrew feels "guilty of a sin he could neither remedy nor forget."(See *Dickens the Novelist*, by F.R. and Q.D. Leavis, Ch. 2, pp. 39-41)

In "The Short Happy Life of Francis Macomber," Hemingway depicts a troubled marriage that ends with the wife killing the husband.

The death of David's mother makes David an orphan. There are numerous orphans in *Copperfield,* and in other Dickens novels; Edgar Johnson speaks of, "that long sequence of rejected children, fatherless or motherless... who move through almost all Dickens' stories."(Vol. 2, Ch. 6, p. 684) Does this reflect Dickens' own feelings of abandonment when he was sent to the shoe-polish factory?

[1] Perhaps one reason for the popularity of *Copperfield* is that Dickens portrays young love through David and Dora. George Gissing writes, "Little Em'ly has, after all, but a subordinate part in *David Copperfield.* The leading lady is Dora. Dora is wooed, Dora is wed—the wooing and wedding of a butterfly. Yet it is Dickens' prettiest bit of love."

David realizes that all husbands discover that marriage is different from their romantic dream. But he also thinks there's something special in his case, a special incompatibility between himself and Dora. He speaks of, "these two irreconcilable conclusions: the one, that what I felt was general and unavoidable; the other, that it was particular to me, and might have been different.... It would have been better for me if my wife could have helped me more, and shared the many thoughts in which I had no partner; and that this might have been, I knew."

God knows, and ought to teach you something; but it might have been worse by a long chalk."[1]

Betsey suspects that David is making a mistake, and tries to warn him, but he's too far gone in amorous passion. As Needham puts it, Betsey asks "leading questions about Dora—'Not silly?' 'Not light-headed?'" Betsey utters an ominous verdict on David's infatuation: "Blind, blind, blind." What David should look for in a spouse, Betsey says, is "Deep, downright, faithful earnestness."[2]

David's marriage to Dora doesn't bring him the happiness he dreamed of; the marriage goes downhill, and nothing can get it back on track. David's marriage to Dora probably reflects Dickens' own marriage to Kate Hogarth. Kate was the mother of Dickens' ten children. Dickens and Kate separated when Dickens was 45. This separation prompted a public statement from Dickens, in which he spoke of, "Some domestic trouble of mine, of long standing...." The phrase "long standing" implies that these domestic troubles existed when Dickens was writing *Copperfield*.[3]

Did these domestic troubles prompt Dickens to wish his wife dead, and is this wish behind the death of Dora? Discussing Dora's death, Edgar Johnson says it may have been a "wish fulfillment." The breakdown of David's marriage "hints all the unspoken feelings that lurked below the surface of [Dickens'] relationship to Kate."[4] One wonders what Kate felt as she read *David Copperfield.*

---

1 Needham says that the undisciplined heart is selfish, not really loving. When Dora's father dies, David doesn't sympathize with Dora and the deceased; rather, he's annoyed that Death has displaced him in Dora's thoughts. Needham writes, "David's confession of a 'lurking jealousy of Death' which pushes him out of Dora's thoughts shows the instinctive selfishness of undisciplined love."

2 This deep earnestness is what David himself has: "Whatever I have tried to do in life," David says, "I have tried with all my heart to do well... whatever I have devoted myself to, I have devoted myself to completely... in great aims and in small, I have always been thoroughly in earnest." David is earnest, committed, diligent; he could take as his motto the sea chanty that Dickens quotes: "A long pull, and a strong pull, and a pull altogether, my hearties, hurrah!"

3 Dickens' public statement shows what a tumultuous time this was for him. "I most solemnly declare..." Dickens writes, "that all the lately whispered rumors touching the trouble... are abominably false. And whosoever repeats one of them after this denial, will lie as willfully and as foully as it is possible for any false witness to lie, before heaven and earth."

When David reflects on his marriage to Dora, he realizes that their incompatibility showed itself in many small ways: "I think of every little trifle between me and Dora, and feel the truth, that trifles make the sum of life."

4 *Charles Dickens: His Tragedy and Triumph*, Vol. 2, Ch. 6, p. 689

We can use the phrase "death of love" for the gradual withering of love under the pressure of day-to-day life, the gradual exposure of differences, or the creation of differences by the growth/change of one person. We can use the phrase "death by love" for a relationship that turns sour, and drives one person to an early death (as Lawrence put it, love sometimes degenerates into "a fearful, bloody battle that ended only with the death of one"). We can use the phrase "death for love" when someone dies so that others can be together. In *David Copperfield*, Ham is sacrificed so Steerforth and Emily can be together. When Steerforth and Emily elope, Ham becomes depressed, hopeless, careless of his own safety. Ham dies *for* love, he's a casualty of the Steerforth-Emily relationship.[1]

Steerforth and Emily both have undisciplined hearts. Steerforth is attracted to Emily because she's young and pretty, Emily hopes to become a lady, and raise her social rank.[2]

A letter from Dickens to John Forster may reveal Dickens' attitude toward Kate. "Kate wants to know," Dickens writes, "whether you have any books to send her, so please to shoot here any literary rubbish on hand." Doesn't this resemble David's attitude toward Dora?

Dickens was probably a difficult man to live with, especially in his headstrong youth. Edgar Johnson says, "Dickens did not realize what a strain his furious energies, his wild alternations of exhilaration and gloom, and his tyrannical insistence on precision all put upon his wife and family."(Vol. 2, Ch. 6, p. 689)

[1] These three categories—death of love, death by love, and death for love—are somewhat artificial. Dora's death could be placed in any of these categories, or in all three.

[2] George Gissing and other critics have mocked Dickens for his use of coincidence. Gissing writes, "When Steerforth returns to England from his travels with Emily, his ship is of course wrecked on the sands of Yarmouth, and his dead body washed up at the feet of David Copperfield, who happened to have made a little journey to see his Yarmouth friends on that very day." When I read about Steerforth's death, however, I was impressed by how Dickens had brought the various strands of his plot together. Dickens is often called a mediocre craftsman, but the average reader probably doesn't notice flaws of craftsmanship.

Gissing also criticizes Dickens for the awkwardness of his conclusion, where Dickens brings back all his characters, even characters whom we haven't seen in hundreds of pages, like Mr. Mell, the usher at David's school. All the characters seem to be thriving.

Gissing says that Dickens was "humbly born," and he became the spokesman of the growing middle class. Gissing thinks that Dickens wanted to improve his social status: "[Dickens] wore himself to a premature end in striving to found his title of gentleman on something more substantial than glory." Was Dickens too eager for a large fortune and a large property?

David is finally enlightened by Annie Strong, who says, "There can be no disparity in marriage, like unsuitability of mind and purpose." Annie avoided a liaison with Jack Maldon. Annie is happy in her marriage to Doctor Strong, who's considerably older than she is. Annie says, "If I were thankful to my husband for no more, instead of for so much, I should be thankful to him for having saved me from the first mistaken impulse of my undisciplined heart." David realizes that he gave way to "the first mistaken impulse of my undisciplined heart."

Needham says that the model for *David Copperfield* is Fielding's *Tom Jones*. She writes,

> At the time when Dickens' mind was "running like a high sea" on plans for *Copperfield*, his sixth son was born (January 16, 1849), and Dickens wrote John Forster that he had changed the child's name from the intended "Oliver Goldsmith" to "Henry Fielding," as "a kind of homage to the style of work he was now bent on beginning."

Fielding advises his young readers to learn prudence because virtue alone isn't sufficient, "no man can be good enough to enable him to neglect the rules of prudence." But Needham says that Dickens goes further than Fielding, Dickens has a deeper conception of personal growth. Perhaps the soul itself grew in the century between *Tom Jones* and *David Copperfield*; self-knowledge evolves, psychology evolves, just as technology evolves. Needham writes,

> Dickens' theme of the undisciplined heart encompasses [Fielding's theme] and goes further; natural goodness plus prudence may win affectionate respect, but one must learn a higher wisdom of the heart if he would achieve inner strength and peace.... It must be self-reliant and possess constancy and fortitude in order to be strengthened, not conquered or merely softened, by adversity and sorrow.... This is the discipline which David and every good man must achieve.

Needham says that, in his early years, David has "passive fortitude" but not "active courage. Delicate as a child, he was soon hurt bodily or mentally." Needham says that David is "naturally timid" and "exhibits courage only when driven by desperation." This is doubtless a portrait of Dickens himself.

Needham says that David's "modesty often sinks into lack of self-confidence, his judgment into self-distrust." David speaks of, "A distrust of myself, which has often beset me in life on small occasions, when it would have been better away." Needham bids us to "Recall how often [David's] lack of self-assertion makes him an easy victim to the tyranny of waiters, coachmen, and landladies."[1]

---

[1] David says, "I get so miserable and worried, and am so unsteady and irresolute in my power of assuring myself."

Some readers might ask, "How can David be a portrait of Dickens? David lacks self-confidence, but Dickens had a high opinion of his work, as you

David resembles not only Dickens, but the intellectual in general. In an earlier issue, I discussed the "weak ego" of the intellectual—the timidity, the self-doubt, the lack of authority. Perhaps Dickens overcame some of these flaws as he grew older.[1]

Betsey sees David's flaws and tries to fix them:

> Aunt Betsey fears his lack of firmness [Needham writes]. She urges him to be "A fine firm fellow, with a will of your own.... with strength of character that is not to be influenced, except on good reason, by anybody, or by anything."

Betsey herself didn't always have this firmness. Needham points out that Betsey is the novel's first example of an "undisciplined heart." Betsey was led by her "undisciplined heart" into a bad marriage. She became embittered, "closed to the world." But she grows during the novel. Needham writes,

> Care and responsibility for the orphaned child [i.e., for David] opens her heart first to love for David, then for mankind; thus she achieves the disciplined heart and proves it by extending the charitable love to Dora that she had denied to Mrs. Copperfield.[2]

---

pointed out in a recent issue." I would respond with three arguments, any one of which might meet the challenge.

1. Dickens could compare himself to Fielding, perhaps even think that he was a better writer than Fielding, but that doesn't mean he could confront a waiter or a landlady. A person can be assertive in some situations, but not in others.
2. Dickens could have lacked self-confidence in his early years, but developed it later. When he was 60, perhaps he could compare himself to Fielding and confront a waiter.
3. Human nature is complicated and contradictory, people can be self-confident on Monday, and self-doubting on Tuesday.

1 See ljhammond.com/phlit/2017-04.htm#7 and ljhammond.com/phlit/2012-04.htm#7

2 This movement from love of an individual to love of mankind reminds me of Thomas Wolfe. In an earlier issue, I wrote, "Friendships are important to Wolfe's hero, but they don't last forever. One by one, the protagonist's relationships collapse, and his focus gradually shifts from individuals to mankind as a whole."

Needham says that we find personal growth even in minor characters like Mrs. Gummidge. "The calamity befalling the Yarmouth household," Needham writes, "also disciplines Mrs. Gummidge, hitherto selfishly engrossed in her own misfortunes. Aroused by others' sorrow, that 'lone lorn creetur' ceases moaning about 'everythink going contrairy,' feels herself needed, and becomes a cheerful prop to Mr. Peggotty in his affliction."

Mr. Wickfield, instead of loving mankind, focuses on one person, his daughter. His weaknesses make him vulnerable to Uriah Heep's wiles.

> Enslaved by alcohol [Needham writes], entrapped by Heep, Mr. Wickfield is shocked into the realization that he, rather than Uriah, is ultimately responsible for the ruin.... "Weak indulgence has ruined me [Wickfield says]. Indulgence in remembrance, and indulgence in forgetfulness. My natural grief for my child's mother turned to disease; my natural love for my child turned to disease.... I thought it possible that I could truly love one creature in the world, and not love the rest... that I could truly mourn for one creature gone out of the world, and not have some part in the grief of all who mourned."

* * * * *

Needham says that David's immaturity is apparent in his reactions to other characters. David is much impressed with Steerforth, who proves to be deeply flawed. Meanwhile, David laughs at Traddles, who proves to have a solid character.

"The boy cannot perceive Steerforth's faults nor Traddles' merits," Needham writes. "David's erroneous valuation of his two friends, so long held, is the first example of his heart's 'mistaken impulses.'" David introduces Steerforth to the Yarmouth household—Daniel Peggotty, Ham, Emily, etc.—and thereby David brings "grave trouble to others—sorrow for which David feels partly responsible." When Traddles helps to overthrow Uriah, David finally appreciates his merit: "This was the first occasion on which I really did justice to the clear head, and plain, patient, practical good sense of my old schoolfellow."

David's romantic passion for Dora contrasts with Traddles' patient love for Sophy. Traddles and Sophy have a long engagement, their motto is "Wait and hope." David

> cannot comprehend their unselfish consideration for Sophy's preposterous family; [David's] impatient ardor rejects their motto, "Wait and hope." Only when the finally disciplined David returns from Europe does he appreciate how rich in happiness such a marriage as theirs will prove.

* * * * *

Dickens not only shows us moral failings, he traces them to their roots in childhood. Steerforth understands his own moral failings, and ascribes them to the lack of father-influence. He says, "I wish to God I had had a judicious father these last twenty years! I wish with all my soul I had been better guided! I wish with all my soul I could guide myself better!"

Another minor character, Mrs. Steerforth, exemplifies lack of personal growth. She's selfish and proud, and fostered those vices in her son, hence Rosa castigates her for her son's misdeeds. Needham says that Mrs. Steerforth is "embittered" by grief, and feels "no compassion for others."

As for the diabolical Uriah Heep, he isn't the product of a loving household. Uriah says, "Father and me was both brought up at a foundation school for boys; and mother, she was likewise brought up at a public, sort of charitable, establishment." Dickens understood that evil isn't the product of spontaneous generation, evil has a cause, a history.

Uriah Heep is eventually defeated by Micawber and Traddles, as the Murdstones were defeated by Betsey. Good overcomes evil. Is this shallow optimism? Gwendolyn Needham speaks of, "Dickens' basic belief that 'real love and truth are stronger in the end than any evil and misfortune in the world.'" What Needham calls a "basic belief" does seem excessively optimistic—a lot of innocent people suffer, and die young, in this world.

But what Needham calls a "basic belief" is actually only a hope. Agnes says, "I hope that real love and truth are stronger in the end than any evil or misfortune in the world." Needham has removed two important words from the start of the quotation: "I hope." What Needham calls a "basic belief" is actually only a hope.

Dickens isn't naively optimistic; he sees darkness and light, suffering and joy. He tries to emphasize the positive, he tries to call the glass half-full rather than half-empty. Whatever life is, he seems to say, let's make the best of it, and if we write a novel, let's try to raise the reader's spirits. Needham says that the "prevailing tone" of *Copperfield* is "a melodic blend of bright humor, tender sorrow, and firm hope."

Dickens depicts moral failings, he depicts the causes of these failings, and he depicts the overcoming of these failings. David learns from experience, learns from his mistakes, and learns to discipline his heart. He becomes older and wiser during a long, lonely trip to Europe. During this trip, he falls into despair: "Listlessness to everything but brooding sorrow was the night that fell on my undisciplined heart." Slowly he climbs back to health and joy, helped by natural beauty, a letter from Agnes, his literary work, etc.

When he returns from Europe, David thinks that Agnes is out of reach. David

> determines to convert what might have been between him and Agnes into a means "of making me more self-denying, more resolved, more conscious of myself, and my defects and errors." After three years' absence, David is ready to return home, confident that he "could think of the past now, gravely, but not bitterly, and could contemplate the future in a brave spirit." He has learned that real love has no "alloy of self," that sorrow should strengthen, and—his final step toward emotional maturity—that one must himself develop the firmness, fortitude, and courage to guide his life in the right path.[1]

When David finally bonds with Agnes, Dickens expresses David's maturity with images that a reader of Jung will recognize: the center, the circle,

---

[1] David's maturity resembles detachment, as I described it in an earlier issue (see ljhammond.com/phlit/2006-10.htm#3).

the stone: "Clasped in my embrace, I held the source of every worthy aspiration I had ever had; the center of myself, the circle of my life, my own, my wife; my love of whom was founded on a rock!"

David Copperfield is about personal growth, about attaining maturity and wisdom through suffering. It stays close to reality, close to the author's life, close to its theme, hence *Copperfield* doesn't contain Dickens' wildest flights of fancy; John Forster said, "The masterpieces of Dickens' humor are not in [*Copperfield*]." But *Copperfield* is Dickens' most popular work—most popular with the public, with critics, and with Dickens himself. It contains a ripe wisdom, an affirmation of life in the face of suffering.

* * * * *

I said above that the moral lapses of Steerforth and Uriah Heep were caused by their upbringing. Did Dickens' sufferings in the shoe-polish factory leave their mark on his own character? Was there a dark side to Dickens' sunny personality?

Forster says that Dickens was "often uneasy, shrinking, and over-sensitive" in society. Dickens learned to force himself; Forster speaks of, "bearing down and overmastering the feeling." Dickens was sometimes too willful, and pushed himself too hard; Forster speaks of "self-imposed burdens greater than might be borne by any one with safety." Even his exercise was excessive, as when he took walks of more than 15 miles at night. Perhaps Dickens' intensity contributed to his early death (he died at 58). Schopenhauer said, "The greatest mental abilities are found only with a vehement and passionate will."[1] Dickens had such a will. Strong will, weak ego.

His intensity was apparent in his domestic habits. Every morning, he toured his house, and "if a chair was out of its place," his daughter later wrote, "or a blind not quite straight, or a crumb left on the floor, woe betide the offender.... Even in his hours of relaxation, he was still... always busy."[2]

---

1 *The World as Will and Representation*, Vol. 2, Ch. 19

2 The following anecdote shows Dickens' tension, his attempts to "overmaster" his feelings, and how he was sometimes overcome by his feelings. The anecdote comes from his son Henry Fielding Dickens. Henry says that it's "typical of a strange reticence on [my father's] part, an intense dislike of 'letting himself go' in private life or of using language which might be deemed strained or over-effusive....

In the year 1869... I was fortunate enough to gain one of the principal scholarships at Trinity Hall, Cambridge.... I knew that this success, slight as it was, would give him intense pleasure, so I went to meet him... to tell him of it. As he got out of the train I told him the news. He said, 'Capital! capital!'—nothing more. Disappointed to find that he received the news apparently so lightly, I took my seat beside him in the pony carriage he was driving. Nothing more happened until we had got half-way to Gad's Hill, when he broke down completely. Turning towards me with tears in his eyes and giving me a warm grip of the hand, he said, 'God bless you, my boy; God bless you!'

Forster says there was something "hard and aggressive" in Dickens at times, a "tone of fierceness," "a stern and even cold isolation of self-reliance side-by-side with a susceptivity almost feminine and the most eager craving for sympathy."[1] But Dickens' dark side was only apparent on rare occasions, perhaps only when he was around 50.

When Dickens was 50, he asked Forster to remember what he'd been through, remember that the "never-to-be-forgotten misery of that old time bred a certain shrinking sensitiveness in a certain ill-clad ill-fed child." He tells Forster that this "shrinking sensitiveness" has returned "in the never-to-be-forgotten misery of this later time." Perhaps the "misery" that Dickens is referring to is the breakdown of his marriage, which brought with it scandals, quarrels, etc.

* * * * *

Dickens is often a subtle psychologist. Dickens describes Micawber's state of mind when he's ensnared by Uriah. Micawber tries to make punch, his specialty, but he's distracted. When something is troubling us, we can't focus on everyday tasks, we make mistakes. David speaks of,

> The strange proceedings in which I saw [Micawber] engaged; whereof his putting the lemon-peel into the kettle, the sugar into the snuffer-tray, the spirit into the empty jug, and confidently attempting to pour boiling water out of a candlestick, were among the most remarkable. I saw that a crisis was at hand.

Dickens says that when Emily was living in Italy, she spoke Italian, but she reverted to English when she was sick: "Em'ly was took bad with fever, and, what is very strange to me is—maybe 'tis not so strange to scholars—the language of that country went out of her head, and she could only speak her own." This is what happened to Joseph Conrad:

> Conrad's wife Jessie wrote that, during Conrad's malaria attack on their honeymoon in France in 1896, he "raved... speaking only in his native tongue and betraying no knowledge of who I might be. For hours I remained by his side watching the feverish glitter of his eyes... and listening to the meaningless phrases and lengthy speeches, not a word of which I could understand.

Conrad describes a similar situation in his short story "Amy Foster."

That pressure of the hand I can feel now as distinctly as I felt it then, and it will remain as strong and real until the day of my death."

This anecdote comes from Henry's book, *Memories of My Father*. Perhaps Dickens was overcome with emotion because he was so thrilled that his son was succeeding at Cambridge, and thereby rising into the upper class.

[1] There was probably a feminine streak in Dickens. In my essay on genius, I argued that genius, especially artistic genius, usually has a feminine streak. (See *Conversations With Great Thinkers*, "Genius.")

iii. Dickens and the Occult

There are many branches of the occult—telepathy, astrology, life-after-death, etc.—and different branches are popular at different times. It's often difficult to tell whether an occult phenomenon should be placed in this branch or that branch; some Jungians placed many occult phenomena in the branch they called Synchronicity. In Dickens' day, mesmerism was a popular branch of the occult, and many occult phenomena were placed within the category of mesmerism. (In an earlier issue, I said that Poe, who was a contemporary of Dickens, had a strong interest in mesmerism, and discussed it in several stories.[1])

Dickens' daughter, Mary, says that he liked to tell the following story:

> Meeting someone in the busy London streets, he was on the point of turning back to accost the supposed friend, when finding out his mistake in time he walked on again until he actually met the real friend, whose shadow, as it were, but a moment ago had come across his path.[2]

I would call this telepathy or anticipation-of-the-future, but Dickens and his daughter viewed it as an illustration of "mesmerism, and the curious influence exercised by one personality over another." Mary says that her father "believed firmly in the power of mesmerism, as a remedy in some forms of illness, and was himself a mesmerist of no mean order; I know of many cases, my own among the number, in which he used his power in this way with perfect success."

The most well-known mesmerist of Dickens' time was John Elliotson. After watching one of Elliotson's demonstrations, Dickens said, "I am a believer [and] I became so against all my preconceived opinions."

Here's an occult experience that Dickens had:

> I dreamed that I saw a lady in a red shawl with her back towards me.... On her turning round I found that I didn't know her, and she said "I am Miss Napier." All the time I was dressing next morning, I thought, What a preposterous thing to have so very distinct a dream about nothing! and why Miss Napier? for I never heard of any Miss Napier. That same Friday night, I [gave a public reading]. After the reading, came into my retiring-room, Mary Boyle and her brother, and the Lady in the red shawl whom they present as "Miss Napier!"

Wikipedia says that, in the latter part of his life, Dickens "furthered his interest in the paranormal, becoming one of the early members of The Ghost Club." Doubtless Dickens should be classed among the many great writers who had a strong interest in the occult.

---

1 See above, Poe ==> Mesmerism, or see ljhammond.com/phlit/2013-10b.htm#2

For more on mesmerism, see Fred Kaplan's *Dickens and Mesmerism.*

2 See *My Father As I Recall Him*, by Mary (Mamie) Dickens

iv. The Occult in *David Copperfield*

One doesn't need to go far to find an example of the occult in *Copperfield.* In the first paragraph, we read, "I was born (as I have been informed and believe) on a Friday, at twelve o'clock at night. It was remarked that the clock began to strike, and I began to cry, simultaneously." David's nurse, and "sage women in the neighborhood," make various deductions about his future based on "the day and hour of my birth."

Astrology deals with the day of one's birth, and also the time of one's birth. Astrology is one branch of the occult. It's difficult to know whether Dickens believed in astrology or not; my guess is that he kept an open mind about it, he neither believed nor disbelieved.

David and his mother (Clara) receive a visit from David's aunt (actually great-aunt), Betsey Trotwood. Betsey has a stern appearance but a good heart. Since David's father has died, Clara is a widow, and Betsey is sympathetic to her plight. Dickens tells us that Clara "had a fancy that she felt Miss Betsey touch her hair, and that with no ungentle hand." But Betsey isn't touching Clara's hair, she's "frowning at the fire." Clara's feeling indicates that Betsey looked at Clara's hair, Betsey intended to touch Clara's hair. This passage is a perfect illustration of one of the basic truths of the occult: the power of looking, the power of intention, the power of will.

In the above example, looking has a friendly significance. Looking, like willing, can be friendly or unfriendly; there's an Evil Eye as well as a "benevolent eye." Dickens describes how Uriah Heep's mother watches David and Agnes with an Evil Eye (Uriah wants to marry Agnes, so Uriah and Mrs. Heep oppose any warm feelings between David and Agnes):

> [Mrs. Heep] sat on one side of the fire; I sat at the desk in front of it; a little beyond me, on the other side, sat Agnes. Whensoever, slowly pondering over my letter, I lifted up my eyes, and meeting the thoughtful face of Agnes, saw it clear, and beam encouragement upon me... I was conscious presently of the evil eye passing me, and going on to her, and coming back to me again, and dropping furtively upon the knitting.

Notice that David doesn't say he *saw* Mrs. Heep looking at him, he says he was "conscious" of her looking at him, just as Clara, in the earlier passage, was conscious of Betsey looking at her. Both passages show the power of looking; when someone is looked at, they often feel it. The occult is about the power of looking and willing, the power of the mind, whether for good or evil; the occult is about mind over matter. Those who reject the occult believe that mind can't influence matter.

In *Copperfield*, mind is a force that can make a person healthy or unhealthy, a force that can make a person live or die. When Dora dies, her dog loses his will to live, her dog promptly dies. Mr. Wickfield's wife dies because her father disapproves of her marriage, and renounces her; Mr.

Wickfield's wife dies of a broken heart, dies because she loses her will to live. In earlier issues, I discussed "willed death."[1]

One of the most important branches of the occult is fate—the idea that the future already exists, and that a prophetic dream or hunch can reveal the future. Many occult phenomena involve leaping over space or time. This suggests that space and time (as Kant tried to tell us) are illusions, they exist in the mind but not in reality.[2]

When David leaves home, his mother has a premonition that she won't see him again: "I never shall see my pretty darling again. Something tells me so, that tells the truth, I know." When she parts from David for the last time, she puts a special significance into the parting. First she embraces David. "Then I was in the carrier's cart when I heard her calling to me. I looked out, and she stood at the garden-gate alone, holding her baby up in her arms for me to see."[3]

Dickens himself had a premonition of impending death, and put a special significance into his last farewell to his daughter Katie. At the time, he was busy writing his last novel, *The Mystery of Edwin Drood.* Another daughter (Mary) wrote,

> As a rule when he was so occupied, my father would hold up his cheek to be kissed, but this day he took my sister in his arms saying: "God bless you, Katie," and there, "among the branches of the trees, among the birds and butterflies and the scent of flowers," she left him, never to look into his eyes again.

One branch of the occult is *déjà vu*—the feeling that you've experienced this before, and you know what will happen next. The feeling of *déjà vu* may be based on a prior anticipation of the future. In other words, you feel you've been here before because you have been here before—in a prophetic dream or hunch. When David is talking to Uriah, "the strange feeling (to which, perhaps, no one is quite a stranger) that all this had occurred before, at some indefinite time, and that I knew what he was going to say next, took possession of me."[4] E. C. Bentley said that *déjà vu* "is no mystery for those philosophers who hold that all which we shall see, with all which we have seen and are seeing, exists already in an eternal now." Time is an illusion, reality is an eternal now, the future already exists.

---

[1] See, for example, ljhammond.com/phlit/2010-11.htm#11

[2] For more on Kant, see ljhammond.com/phlit/1999-11.htm

[3] Elsewhere I described how Thomas Wolfe anticipated his early death: "Something has spoken to me in the night... and told me I must die."

[4] Later, when David is talking to Micawber, he has another feeling of *déjà vu*. David says, "We have all some experience of a feeling that comes over us occasionally, of what we are saying and doing having been said and done before, in a remote time—of our having been surrounded, dim ages ago, by the same faces, objects, and circumstances—of our knowing perfectly what will be said next, as if we suddenly remembered it!" I discussed *déjà vu* in an earlier issue (see ljhammond.com/phlit/2018-10b.htm).

Just as the time of one's birth may have some occult significance, so too one's name may have some significance. When we think of Dickens' fiction, we think of his names—Copperfield, Steerforth, Murdstone, etc. When Barkis is interested in Peggotty, David says, "'Her Christian name is Clara.' 'Is it though?' said Mr. Barkis. He seemed to find an immense fund of reflection in this circumstance, and sat pondering and inwardly whistling for some time." In the film *The Man Who Invented Christmas*, we see Dickens making notes of interesting names. Eight years ago, I wrote,

> Goethe was receptive to the occult, and inclined to believe in the occult significance of names. He said, "I shall always be Goethe.... When I say my name, I say everything that I am." Wikipedia says, "Nominative determinism is the theory that a person's name can have a significant role in determining job, profession or even character. It was a commonly held notion in the ancient world." According to the ancients, *nomen est omen.*

The name "Murdstone" drips with malignity. Murdstone could repeat Goethe's remark, "When I say my name, I say everything that I am."[1]

When I discussed Arthur Conan Doyle, I said that he had a keen interest in the occult, and he alludes to the occult in the SherlockHolmes stories. For example, he depicts a character who can feel whether her husband is alive or not.[2] We find the same thing in *Copperfield*: Daniel Peggotty can feel that Emily is alive, and that his search for her won't be in vain:

> "Mas'r Davy, I have felt so sure as she was living—I have know'd, awake and sleeping, as it was so trew that I should find her—I have been so led on by it, and held up by it—that I doen't believe I can have been deceived. No! Em'ly's alive!" He put his hand down firmly on the table, and set his sunburnt face into a resolute expression. "My niece, Em'ly, is alive, sir!" he said, steadfastly. "I doen't know wheer it comes from, or how 'tis, but I am told as she's alive."

Daniel has a telepathic bond with Emily, and can feel whether she's alive or dead. Likewise, there's a telepathic bond between David and his aunt (Betsey). David knows that Betsey is thinking about Agnes, and Betsey knows that David is thinking about Agnes, but they tacitly agree not to talk about Agnes:

> Between my aunt and me there had been something, in this connection, since the night of my return, which I cannot call a restraint, or an avoidance of the subject [i.e., Agnes], so much as an implied understanding

---

1 For more on this topic, see Alastair Fowler's *Literary Names*.

Steerforth says, "Ride on! Rough-shod if need be, smooth-shod if that will do, but ride on! Ride on over all obstacles, and win the race!" Ride on, steer forth! His philosophy of life is embedded in his name. "When I say my name, I say everything that I am."

2 See below "Arthur Conan Doyle," or see ljhammond.com/phlit/2007-09.htm#5

> that we thought of it together, but did not shape our thoughts into words. When, according to our old custom, we sat before the fire at night, we often fell into this train; as naturally, and as consciously to each other, as if we had unreservedly said so. But we preserved an unbroken silence. I believed that she had read, or partly read, my thoughts that night; and that she fully comprehended why I gave mine no more distinct expression.

Later David can feel Betsey's presence: "I was roused by the silent presence of my aunt at my bedside. I felt it in my sleep, as I suppose we all do feel such things." When David is feasting with the Micawbers, he can feel Littimer's presence: "I was aware of a strange presence in the room, and my eyes encountered those of the staid Littimer, standing hat in hand before me." When David visits Traddles, he feels he's being watched: "I walked in [and] walked upstairs; conscious, as I passed the back parlor-door, that I was surveyed by a mysterious eye."

When Betsey is far away from home, she can feel what's happening at home: "'If ever there was a donkey trespassing on my green,' said my aunt, with emphasis, 'there was one this afternoon at four o'clock. A cold feeling came over me from head to foot, and I know it was a donkey!'"

Another branch of the occult is synchronicity—the occurrence of analogous events at the same time, or nearly the same time. I can find only one example of synchronicity in *Copperfield*, and it's not a good example, it's rather awkward and artificial. Betsey is skeptical about David's relationship with Dora, Betsey thinks Dora is too childish and irresponsible. David is determined to go forward, determined to marry Dora. Betsey says, "Blind, blind, blind!" When the chapter concludes, David says, "There was a beggar in the street, when I went down... he made me start by muttering, as if he were an echo of the morning: 'Blind! Blind! Blind!'"

The critic Gwendolyn Needham says of this scene, "Dickens contrives a typical theatrical coincidence." Synchronicity can be dismissed as coincidence, and if it's not well handled, it can seem to be done for effect, it can seem theatrical, rather than a depiction of how the world works.

When David goes to school, he's enchanted by an older student, Steerforth. Steerforth has a "delightful voice," a "handsome face," and "some inborn power of attraction besides (which I think a few people possess), to have carried a spell with him to which it was a natural weakness to yield." Steerforth's "spell" doesn't seem plausible to me, but perhaps it deserves to be mentioned in a discussion of Dickens' views on the occult.

We can see Dickens' deep interest in the occult in his works and also in his life. If one collected examples of the occult from all of Dickens' works, it would doubtless be a long list, and it could serve as an introduction to the occult. The occult is full of mysteries, full of unknowns, and it fascinates many great writers, including Dickens. The occult is at the cutting edge of human thought, it's the philosophical subject *par excellence*.

G. *Hard Times*

i. Introduction

I recently read *Hard Times*, by Dickens. I enjoyed it; it's amusing, and the plot draws you in. It has a light, witty tone, but also a serious, impassioned tone; it's the perfect balance of light and heavy.

Hard Times is about a hyper-rational man, Mr. Gradgrind, and his effort to stuff facts into the heads of his children. Gradgrind seems much impressed by the science of economics, and he names two of his children "Adam Smith" and "Malthus." One might describe *Hard Times* as a satire of economics, and of rational thinking in general. Ruskin was also a critic of economics, and as I read *Hard Times*, I was reminded of Ruskin's dictum, "There is no wealth but life."

A disturbing fad among American youngsters, especially girls, is self-injury—sometimes called "cutting" since it usually takes that form. There have been several movies and books about self-injury (have these movies fueled the fad?).

I was surprised to find an example of self-injury in *Hard Times*. In the following passage, Mr. Gradgrind's daughter, Louisa, has just received a kiss from Mr. Bounderby, whom she abhors:

> He went his way, but she stood on the same spot, rubbing the cheek he had kissed, with her handkerchief, until it was burning red. She was still doing this, five minutes afterwards. "What are you about, Loo?" her brother sulkily remonstrated. "You'll rub a hole in your face." "You may cut the piece out with your penknife if you like, Tom. I wouldn't cry!"

Louisa's self-injury is irrational, and shows that her father's rational system of education has failed, that man isn't rational. Tom, Louisa's brother, is as negative and irrational as Louisa:

> "I am sick of my life, Loo. I hate it altogether, and I hate everybody except you...." "I wish I could collect all the Facts we hear so much about," said Tom, spitefully setting his teeth, "and all the Figures, and all the people who found them out: and I wish I could put a thousand barrels of gunpowder under them, and blow them all up together!"

Tom even engages in some self-injury; he is described as "chafing his face on his coat-sleeve, as if to mortify his flesh, and have it in unison with his spirit."

In my old Norton edition of *Hard Times*, there's an essay called "The Brother-Sister Relationship in *Hard Times*," by Daniel P. Deneau. Deneau also finds perversion in Louisa and Tom, but not the same kind that I noticed. Deneau calls the relationship between Louisa and Tom "abnormal," and discusses a scene (Book 2, Ch. 8) that has "sexual overtones": "Dickens's reference to 'a loose robe' and Louisa's more pointed reference to her state of undress—'barefoot, unclothed'—are pretty insistent details." Deneau quotes Louisa's father: "I think there are qualities in Louisa, which—which have been harshly neglected, and—and a little perverted." Perhaps Deneau's incest argument and my self-injury argument strengthen each other, since they find perversion in the same two characters. Incest and self-injury are used by Dickens to build a case that the Gradgrind educational system is unhealthy, perverted.

Another example of perversion in *Hard Times* is Bounderby's behavior toward Louisa, when Louisa is still a child, and hasn't yet been married to Bounderby. Bounderby's behavior should probably be called sexual abuse, or sexual harassment, and it leaves Louisa with a horror of Bounderby.

These three cases of perversion in *Hard Times* strike me as psychologically accurate, or at least plausible. *Hard Times* depicts working-class characters (Stephen Blackpool and Rachael) in a way that's notoriously sentimental and unrealistic, but its depiction of various kinds of perversion seems true-to-life. Dickens has a firm grasp of the negative, irrational side of human nature.

ii. Irony and Sophistication

One of the characters in *Hard Times* is a suave aristocrat named James Harthouse. Harthouse has no enthusiasms or convictions. Harthouse says,

> I have not so much as the slightest predilection left. I assure you I attach not the least importance to any opinions. The result of the varieties of boredom I have undergone, is a conviction (unless conviction is too industrious a word for the lazy sentiment I entertain on the subject), that any set of ideas will do just as much good as any other set, and just as much harm as any other set.

Dickens speaks of "[Harthouse's] conviction that indifference was the genuine high-breeding (the only conviction he had)."

Readers of this e-zine will recall that, just as Dickens criticizes Harthouse for his lack of strong convictions, so I criticized the *New Yorker* magazine for a lack of strong convictions.[1] A lack of strong convictions is sophisticated and fashionable, and protects one from something that a person in society fears most: ridicule. Two years ago, I criticized Alain de Botton for his sophisticated tone:

> Alain de Botton's writings have the sophisticated tone that today's journalists strive for. But good literature, in my view, has a different tone—an unsophisticated, naive tone.... Good literature often has... a tone of conviction, passion, anger.[2]

Like Dickens, Proust noted that people in high society lack strong convictions. Proust said that Swann avoided

> saying in all seriousness what he thought about things.... Whenever he spoke of serious matters, whenever he used an expression which seemed to imply a definite opinion upon some important subject, he

---

1 ljhammond.com/phlit/2009-04b.htm#2

2 ljhammond.com/phlit/2006-10.htm#2

would take care to isolate, to sterilize it by using a special intonation, mechanical and ironic.[1]

iii. Shaw

My Norton edition of *Hard Times* contains an essay by George Bernard Shaw. Shaw argues that the first half of the 19th century was self-satisfied, and considered itself a very advanced civilization, while the second half of the 19th century considered itself to be on the wrong track, a deeply flawed civilization. Shaw says that *Hard Times*, which was written in 1854, represents a watershed in Dickens' work: before *Hard Times*, Dickens was "light-hearted and only occasionally indignant," while in *Hard Times* and his later works, one finds a "passionate revolt against the whole industrial order of the modern world." Shaw complains that critics generally prefer Dickens' early work, and overlook his later "masterpieces."

Another characteristic of Dickens' later work is that it has an elaborate plot, whereas his early work is sometimes a series of disconnected episodes. Here the "watershed work" is probably *Bleak House*; *Bleak House* is probably the first carefully-plotted Dickens novel.

Shaw points out that one of the themes of *Hard Times* is unhappy marriage. Dickens suggests that an unhappy marriage should be dissolved. Dickens had first-hand experience of unhappy marriage.

Surprisingly, Dickens was a fan neither of labor unions nor of democracy. According to Shaw, Dickens "adopts the idealized Toryism of Carlyle and Ruskin, in which the aristocracy are the masters and superiors of the people, and also the servants of the people and of God."

iv. Leavis

F. R. Leavis, perhaps influenced by Shaw, said "Dickens has no glimpse of the part to be played by Trade Unionism in bettering the conditions he deplores."[2] Leavis goes further, and says Dickens "has no notion of the part played by religion in the life of nineteenth century industrial England." Nonetheless, Leavis is a big fan of Dickens in general, and of *Hard Times* in particular. Leavis praises Dickens for his mastery of symbol and language. Leavis' essay on *Hard Times* is perhaps the best and most influential study of the novel.

According to Leavis, Dickens believes that we can't follow reason alone, we must connect to fairy-tale, art, feeling, the unconscious; we must be whole, not just rational. Morality must come from the heart, not the reason, and life must be lived from emotion, not intellect. As Leavis says, "Sissy [in *Hard Times*] stands for vitality as well as goodness—they are seen, in fact, as one." Sissy represents "the life that is lived freely and richly from the deep

---

1 *Swann's Way*, "Combray"

2 Leavis' essay on *Hard Times* can be found in the Norton Critical Edition of *Hard Times*, in Leavis' *Dickens: The Novelist*, and in Leavis' *Great Tradition.*

instinctive and emotional springs." The failure of calculating characters like Scrooge and Gradgrind is a failure of both morality and vitality.

Animals are connected to the "deep instinctive and emotional springs," and in *Hard Times*, the dog Merrylegs has an instinctive wisdom that resembles the highest flights of the human spirit. Merrylegs has a wisdom that is non-rational, and that defies rational explanation. Dickens tells us to admire the wisdom of the dog and the horse, rather than the calculations of the economist.

Just as Dickens criticizes Louisa's upbringing (in *Hard Times*), so he criticizes Judy's upbringing (in *Bleak House*): "Judy never owned a doll, never heard of Cinderella, never played at any game." Judy's brother is also deprived of play and fantasy, but he's helped by his friendship with Mr. Guppy, whom his elders dismiss as a "fool." Likewise, in *Dombey and Son*, Paul is helped by his friendship with "old Glubb."

So there's a recurring theme in the work of Dickens: life is desiccated by reason, calculation, and economics, and saved by feeling, fairy-tale, and play, and by people like Sleary (in *Hard Times*), Guppy (in *Bleak House*), and Glubb (in *Dombey and Son*).

Is this a timeless theme? Or is it a response to Dickens' historical situation? As we see in *Hard Times*, Dickens is critical of contemporary economics, and contemporary business. There was a trend, in Dickens' day, to prefer positivism over poetry, reason over faith. Dickens is reacting to this trend; he champions fairy-tale against science, feeling against reason. So the recurring theme in Dickens' work is a response to his historical situation. On the other hand, the claims of feeling and the unconscious are eternal, so there is a timeless quality to The Dickens Theme.

Leavis says that the best Dickens biography is John Forster's. Forster has "an intimate personal knowledge of his friend," and he "gives us the sense... of being in the same room as Dickens, and even, more important, of being really inward with Dickens' personality and character." The Forster biography is 900 pages long. In recent years, Dickens biographies have been published by Peter Ackroyd and Fred Kaplan.

v. General Remarks

Dickens' style is wordy and ornate. His style draws attention to itself, rather than shining a light on what he's describing. If a great style is (as Orwell put it) as clear as a window-pane, Dickens's style is like clouded glass, through which we see the world darkly. He never uses one word if he can use two or three. The speech of his characters is utterly unlike real speech. (Shaw says of Sissy Jupe's conversation, "This is the language of a Lord Chief Justice, not of the dunce of an elementary school.") When he isn't constructing long and ornate periods, he's writing dialect and jargon, so his language isn't easy for the modern reader. I recommend reading Dickens in an annotated version, such as the Norton Critical Edition. I like the old Nortons—the ones put together before the humanities were politicized.

Dickens deals with social issues like labor unions, and many of these issues are no longer relevant. He doesn't deal with the eternal facts of human life—birth, death, etc.—as Tolstoy does, and he doesn't deal with the eternal question of personal growth, as Lawrence does. Dickens' reputation is mixed: while many critics praise him, others (including Henry James and Virginia Woolf) are scornful of him. Though I enjoy Dickens, I can understand why E. M. Forster said that the great ages of English literature were the Elizabethan age and the Romantic age, not the Victorian age. Perhaps Dickens was the greatest writer of his time and place, but it wasn't a great time and place for writers.

One of the most obvious flaws in Dickens is that he covers romantic relationships with a thick layer of sugary, teary-eyed sentimentality. He also has a sentimental piety, an emotional Christianity. At times, sentimental romance combines with sentimental religion, and the reader feels like he's swimming through honey. This thick sentiment is one of the weaknesses of Victorian culture.

In *Hard Times*, the relationship between Harthouse and Louisa is devoid of physical passion, and Louisa's retreat to her father's house is utterly unrealistic, Victorian. One appreciates D. H. Lawrence more when one sees how Dickens handles man-woman relationships.

H. Stefan Zweig on Dickens

I wanted to read a short biography of Dickens, and found a book by Stefan Zweig called *Three Masters: Balzac, Dickens, Dostoyevsky*. I discovered, though, that the section on Dickens isn't a biography, and isn't literary criticism. It looks at Dickens in relation to his time and place. It gives the reader generalizations, not anecdotes. Zweig is an excellent writer—profound, poetic, readable. His eloquence shines through even in translation. What must he be like in the original German?!

Though Zweig was Jewish, he didn't identify with Jewry. He was an advocate of European unity, and a champion of European culture. In 1942, at the age of 61, Stefan was living in Brazil, and committed "double suicide" with his wife. "I think it better," he wrote, "to conclude in good time and in erect bearing a life in which intellectual labor meant the purest joy and personal freedom the highest good on Earth." "[Stefan Zweig's] autobiography *The World of Yesterday* is a paean to the European culture he considered lost."[1]

Though primarily known for his fiction, Stefan Zweig wrote numerous biographies—Nietzsche, Freud, Romain Rolland, Marie Antoinette, Magellan, etc. He said that his biography of the humanist Erasmus was a concealed autobiography. Perhaps we should see Zweig as the Erasmus of his time: a citizen of the world, a champion of the humanities and of Western literature. Zweig had a special interest in Balzac. When Zweig died, he left behind an unfinished biography of Balzac, which has been called his *magnum opus*.

Zweig begins his Dickens essay with a delightful little chapter called "A Writer Loved More Than All Others," in which he talks about Dickens' enormous popularity, and about how people in England eagerly awaited the

---

[1] Wikipedia article, "Stefan Zweig"

next monthly installment of his work, walking miles to the post-office (not patient enough to wait for the postman to reach their house), and reading as they walked home. Then he talks about the popularity of Dickens' public readings:

> In the [U.S.,] despite the wintry cold, people would camp in front of the box-office, catching what rest they could on the mattresses they had lugged along with them, satisfying their hunger with food brought to them by the waiters from a near-by restaurant. No hall proved large enough to accommodate the crowds, so that in the end a church in Brooklyn was converted into a huge reading room for this most popular of authors. Standing aloft in the pulpit, Dickens read the stories of Oliver Twist and of Little Nell.

Not content to describe Dickens' popularity, Zweig attempts, in the next chapter, to explain it. He says that most geniuses are in opposition to their times (as Kierkegaard put it, "Genius like a thunderstorm comes up against the wind"), but Dickens was in harmony with his times.

> Dickens [was] perfectly satisfied within the four walls of the English tradition. He felt at ease in this atmosphere, and never travelled beyond the frontiers of English art, morality, and aesthetics.

Zweig contrasts Dickens with other English writers—Byron, Shelley, Wilde—who tried to break free from England, and become citizens of the world (we might add D. H. Lawrence to this list).

In the third chapter, Zweig discusses Victorian society, and how Dickens' place in history destined him to be a certain kind of writer. Living at such a time, Dickens could not be Shakespeare. Shakespeare was the expression of a different era; Shakespeare could only have emerged when he did.

> [Dickens] was born out of due time, born into the Victorian era. Shakespeare, too, was the most superb literary and imaginative expression of his epoch; but his England, Elizabethan England, was a country full of youthful energy, eager for adventure, fresh in mind and spirit, ardent and vibrant, just beginning to stretch forth its vigorous hands to grasp at the *imperium mundi*.... Shakespeare was the incarnation of a heroic England; Dickens was the symbol of the middle classes.... [Dickens] was the citizen of a prudish, comfortable, well-ordered State, a State lacking verve and passionate enthusiasms.

The Victorian public preferred the sentimental to the tragic:

> In the books they read, just as in their everyday life, they wish for tempered passions; they have no desire for ecstasy, wanting merely to experience normal emotions that will run a demure course.

Dickens and his contemporaries were content, self-satisfied.

Zweig says that Dickens was the poet of the common man. "The wealthy, and people of aristocratic birth, all the spoiled darlings at life's table, were obnoxious to him." Dickens glorified the simple man's simple pleasures, and he appealed to middle-class readers because he

> was able to enhance their love for that which they already loved above all else in the world—their homes, with the cozy room, the fire crackling on the hearth, the logs spluttering and hissing, the tea-table, and the kettle singing on the hob—home, which shut them safely away from ravening storms and the mad, bad world without.

Zweig makes some penetrating criticisms of Dickens as a creator of characters:

> He cannot, as a matter of fact, be regarded as a great psychologist.... As soon as we enter the torrid zone of the passions, the drama melts like wax and becomes mere sentimentality; or it gets petrified into hatred, and shows conspicuous flaws. The most successful of his types are the perfectly straightforward ones; he is not happy in his depiction of those far more interesting natures which stand on the borderland of good and evil, which have elements of the divine intermingling with the satanic. That is why there is a certain measure of justification for the frequent criticism that in Dickens's books, as on the Day of Judgment, all men and women must be classed as "good" or "bad," and herded unhesitatingly with the sheep or the goats.

Zweig argues that Dickens is excessively moral and sentimental, and falls short of the heroic and tragic:

> Even today, the English find it hard to tolerate real drama, unless in the end it leaves them with the pleasant feeling that all is for the best in the best of all possible worlds. This typically English hypertrophy of the moral sense is responsible for the fact that Dickens's grandest and noblest inspirations fall flat, that he is never able to give us a tragedy in the sublimest sense of the word.... Dickens claps a censorship on to the emotions, instead of allowing them free vent.... When he died, the Bishop of Winchester declared with pride that Dickens's works could unhesitatingly be placed in the hands of any child. But this is what detracts from his achievement, this is what cuts the glory from his magnificent gifts—the fact that his books do not describe life as it really is, but only as a bishop would like to have it presented to children!

Zweig says that, in the Victorian period, adult Englishmen censored their feelings, but children were natural. Dickens had difficulty depicting adults as they really are, but he could depict children well; this is his specialty, "here he is incomparable." Zweig notes that he was also fond of depicting child-like adults—feeble-minded people who never grow up.

Zweig emphasizes Dickens' sunny humor:

> He travels through life aimlessly and complacently, with a mischievous twinkle in his eye, burlesquing the world as he goes, giving the people he encounters those diverting masks and queer lovable personalities we meet at every turn in his books, and thereby brightening the existence of millions here below.... Of Dickens we can say, and of him alone among literary geniuses of the nineteenth century, that he increased the joyousness of the world.

I hope these selections from Zweig's 50-page Dickens essay have thrown some light on Dickens, and also persuaded you that Zweig is both an elegant stylist and a deep thinker, who can give us a better appreciation of Dickens, though he doesn't discuss individual works in detail, and doesn't discuss the life of Dickens in detail.

I. Dickens' Influence On Dostoevsky

I knew that Tolstoy was a big fan of Dickens, and I recently discovered that Dostoyevsky was, too. In his *Diary of a Writer*, Dostoyevsky wrote

> We understand Dickens in Russia, I am convinced, almost as well as the English, and maybe even all the subtleties; maybe even we love him no less than his own countrymen; and yet how typical, distinctive, and national Dickens is.[1]

Dostoyevsky called Dickens "a 'great Christian,' admiring especially Dickens' humbler characters.... As Dickens determined to be their voice in Great Britain, so Dostoevsky determined to be their voice in Russia."

Dickens influenced not only Dostoyevsky's work, but also his life. When Dostoyevsky and his wife were living in Dresden, they read Dickens in translation; Dostoyevsky's wife said, "Dickens' sense of humor was part of our life." Dickens helped them to make light of their poverty; Dostoyevsky referred to himself as "Mr. Micawber," and to his wife as "Mrs. Micawber."

Dostoyevsky shared Dickens' skeptical attitude toward reason, and his belief in the wisdom of the heart. The protagonist of *Crime and Punishment*, Raskolnikov, is transformed much as Scrooge is. Early in the novel, Raskolnikov ponders the question that some rational thinkers were pondering: Who shall live, and who shall die? He decides that the old pawnbroker is one who should die, and murders her. Later in the novel, Raskolnikov's hard rationalism is softened.

Dostoyevsky's *Idiot* was influenced by Dickens' *Mutual Friend*. Dostoyevsky's saintly Prince Myshkin is reminiscent of Dickens' John Harmon. As Myshkin feels alienated from Russian aristocratic society, so Harmon

> feels deeply alienated from the main values of middle-class Victorian society.... Both have spent their youth abroad (in Brussels, and in Switzerland), and, after coming back to their native land, have inherited vast fortunes.... Defining the complex of common features in the characters of John Harmon and Prince Myshkin, one could not but mention their deep insight into human nature, their ability to understand refined and subtle spiritual processes, and, most obviously, their generosity.

44. *Cranford*

---

[1] "Dickens's Influence upon Dostoevsky, 1860-1870," by Irina Gredina and Philip V. Allingham, victorianweb.org/authors/dickens/gredina.html

"I remember the glow of his tender delight in that simple tale." This is how Jessie Chambers describes D. H. Lawrence's reaction to Elizabeth Gaskell's *Cranford.* When I read this in 2010, I had never heard of *Cranford. Cranford* isn't part of The Canon, it's on the edge of The Canon; one might say it's not part of the "core canon," it's part of the "extended canon."

Early in Gaskell's career, she received a letter from Dickens, who wanted her to write for his new magazine, *Household Words*. Gaskell had recently published her first novel, *Mary Barton*, and it had been an "enormous success." *Mary Barton* dealt with the poor whom Gaskell had known in Manchester, where her husband was a minister.

Dickens said that the purpose of his new magazine was "the raising up of those that are down, and the general improvement of our social condition." With her literary talent and urban experience, Gaskell seemed to be the perfect writer for *Household Words*. *Cranford* and many of Gaskell's other writings were initially published in *Household Words*. Hoping to reach a wide audience, Dickens set the price of his magazine at just two pence. *Household Words* was published every week for nine years.

Gaskell's writings were popular in her day; her ghost stories, such as "The Old Nurse's Story," were especially popular; she was acquainted with prominent writers like Charlotte Brontë, Dickens, and Ruskin. Three of her novels—*Cranford*, *North and South*, and *Wives and Daughters*—have been turned into TV dramas by the BBC.

Cranford is short, readable, humorous, touching. It depicts small-town life in England around 1840—the world that Gaskell knew first-hand. Of all her books, Gaskell seemed most fond of *Cranford.* She wrote to Ruskin in 1865, "It is the only one of my own books that I can read again."[1] What I most enjoyed about *Cranford* was Patricia Wolfe's essay on the novel.[2] She

---

1 The Oxford World's Classics edition of *Cranford* has three appendices. The first is a non-fiction essay by Gaskell called "The Last Generation in England." If you read *Cranford*, I would skip this essay, which repeats some of the stories told in the novel.

Clearly *Cranford* is based, at least partly, on true stories, as great fiction often is. In an earlier issue, I quoted Mark Twain: "If you found on fact in your personal experience, it is an acorn, a root, and every created adornment that grows out of it, and spreads its foliage and blossoms to the sun will seem reality, not invention."

The second appendix is a short story by Gaskell called "The Cage At Cranford." It features the familiar *Cranford* characters. If you liked the novel, you'll like the story.

The third appendix is a collection of materials called "*Cranford* in Context." I recommend it, it has interesting quotes from Dickens, Ruskin, Wilkie Collins, etc.

2 "Structure and Movement in Cranford," *Nineteenth-Century Fiction*, Vol. 23, No. 2 (Sep., 1968), pp. 161-176, jstor.org/stable/2932367

seemed to understand the novel far better than I did, I must be the world's worst novel-reader.

In the last issue, I discussed the moral aspect of literature—how literature can inspire us, change us, form us.[1] Wolfe's essay deals with the moral aspect of *Cranford.*

[Spoiler Warning: If you're thinking of reading *Cranford*, you may want to skip the rest of this section.]

Cranford begins with a female Declaration of Independence:

> Cranford is in possession of the Amazons; all the holders of houses, above a certain rent, are women.... The ladies of Cranford are quite sufficient. "A man," as one of them observed to me once, "is so in the way in the house!"

This attitude reaches an extreme when the women of Cranford become terrified of male robbers. They don't want to go to bed at night without peeking under the bed, to see if an invader is lurking there. After this fear of men reaches an extreme, the pendulum swings back, and the women become more receptive to male influence. By the end of the novel, several of the women have married, and the main character, Matilda ("Matty") Jenkyns, is living happily with her brother, Peter.

When Patricia Wolfe discusses the "robbery panic," she speaks of "the irrational fear of masculinity which characterizes the psychological condition of Miss Matty and the other Cranford ladies." Gaskell was married, and had numerous children. Is *Cranford* warning against a female Declaration of Independence? Does *Cranford* describe the positive aspects of male influence? If so, does it clash with the taste of our time? Is it politically-incorrect?[2]

Two of Gaskell's novels—*Mary Barton* and *North and South*—are in the series called Norton Critical Editions. As for *Cranford*, I recommend the version in Oxford World's Classics, which is available as an e-book as well as a paperback. The e-book is only $1.99. Oxford World's Classics seems to offer the best value for e-books.

1 See ljhammond.com/phlit/2019-04.htm#5

2 Perhaps Wolfe's essay is politically-incorrect; written in 1968, it may clash with the taste of today. The Oxford World's Classics edition of *Cranford* has a long list of essays on the novel, but Wolfe's essay is nowhere to be found.

"At the beginning of the story," Wolfe writes, "Cranford is pictured as a fortress of feminism defended by the indomitable Deborah." The second half of *Cranford* "relates Matty Jenkyns's struggle and triumph over the village's policy of feminine isolationism which her sister had initiated."

Some contemporary critics agree with Wolfe, at least partially. Dinah Birch, for example, says "The recognition of [Captain Brown's] merit is the first

Early in the novel, the reader is introduced to Deborah Jenkyns, Matty's older sister. Deborah has a rigid concept of social propriety. She admires the formal prose of Samuel Johnson, and scorns the lighter style of Dickens. Deborah has adopted the attitudes of her late father, a minister who was fond of Johnson's writings. Wolfe says that Deborah has an "immoderate attachment to the father-figure.... Even after his death her whole course of life is dominated by his personality.... Deborah existed simply as a shadow of the man she had most respected in her early life."

If Deborah has a "father complex," Matty has a mother complex.

> Mrs. Gaskell leaves no doubt in the reader's mind [Wolfe writes] as to which sister is the stronger. Shy Miss Matty has earned the role of Cranford's heroine. Significantly, in these critical chapters she is constantly associated with her mother. She only cries, for instance, when she thinks "how my mother would grieve if she could know" ....The point is unmistakable. Mrs. Gaskell has identified Deborah with the father-figure and Matilda with the image of motherhood. Deborah and her father shaped Cranford's social code; Matty and her mother, its moral and ethical standards.

Matty has a "distaste for the single life," and admits that "she is not a spinster by desire." She dreams about having a baby. And she's not alone: "Mrs. Brown demonstrated the same desire for feminine fulfillment when she struggled to leave India in order to save her one surviving child from an early death."

Deborah and her father prevent Matty from marrying Thomas Holbrook; they don't think Holbrook's social status is high enough. Holbrook is described as a man of genuine culture, with little regard for social convention. "He despised every refinement which had not its root deep down in humanity."[1]

---

stage in the lengthy process through which the ladies' stubborn wish to exclude men from the town is gently corrected." (Introduction to Oxford World's Classics edition) But Birch doesn't accept Wolfe's argument that the "robbery panic" is based on a fear of men. Birch argues that this panic is based on a fear of the foreign—the Muslim, the Turk, etc.

[1] When Holbrook shows the narrator around his farm, "he surprised me occasionally by repeating apt and beautiful quotations from the poets, ranging easily from Shakespeare and George Herbert to those of our own day. He did this as naturally as if he were thinking aloud, and their true and beautiful words were the best expression he could find for what he was thinking or feeling.... Altogether, I never met with a man, before or since, who had spent so long a life in a secluded and not impressive country, with ever-increasing delight in the daily and yearly change of season and beauty."

Then they tour the inside of Holbrook's house. "The rest of the pretty sitting-room—looking into the orchard, and all covered over with dancing tree-shadows—was filled with books. They lay on the ground, they covered the

Though he often quotes English poetry, Holbrook doesn't know Johnson's poetry well. In this respect, as in other respects, Holbrook contrasts with Deborah. Matty is inclined to blame Deborah for preventing her marriage to Holbrook. But Matty feels guilty for blaming Deborah, so she starts singing Deborah's praises, "she kept telling me how good and how clever Deborah was in her youth."

Matty's virtues are most apparent when a local bank goes bust, the bank-notes lose their value, and Matty loses her savings. She hears the news while shopping for clothes. When a farmer tries to buy something for his wife, the shopkeeper won't accept the farmer's bank-note. Matty offers to give the farmer gold coins in exchange for his worthless bank-note. Matty's kindness seems to inspire others to be kind, and it seems to rebound back to her. Matty's neighbors donate to a fund to help her.

In the last issue, I discussed how emotions like kindness or depression can spread through a group:

> Nicholas Christakis, a Yale professor, has argued that a network of people is a "super-organism." Within a network, emotions spread, emotions are contagious. Christakis wrote a book called *Connected: The Surprising Power of Our Social Networks*.

Cranford ends with the words, "We all love Miss Matty, and I somehow think we are all of us better when she is near us." Kindness is contagious. Fear is also contagious, as the "robbery panic" shows. Does a novel about a small town inevitably deal with emotional contagion?

Christakis was initially interested in The Widow Effect—how people often die after their spouse dies. Gaskell seems to be interested in this phenomenon, too. After Peter disappears in India, his mother dies of sorrow. After Gaskell's own brother disappeared in India, her father died.

Gaskell can discuss universal truths in lively language, as when she describes Matty and the narrator looking over old letters:

> I never knew what sad work the reading of old letters was before that evening, though I could hardly tell why. The letters were as happy as letters could be.... There was in them a vivid and intense sense of the present time, which seemed so strong and full, as if it could never pass away, and as if the warm, living hearts that so expressed themselves could never die, and be as nothing to the sunny earth.

Gaskell is a great writer with a deep interest in morality. In earlier issues, we've discussed numerous imaginative writers who are interested in morality. One might ask, are there any great imaginative writers who don't have a deep interest in morality?

45. Hardy's *Far from the Madding Crowd*

---

walls, they strewed the table.... They were of all kinds—poetry, and wild weird tales prevailing. He evidently chose his books in accordance with his own tastes, not because such and such were classical, or established favorites.

I just finished a Victorian novel, Thomas Hardy's *Far from the Madding Crowd*. In my salad days, I ignored Victorian fiction, I thought it was second-rate. Perhaps it is second-rate compared to Elizabethan drama, or Russian fiction, or Greek tragedy, but it may be more enjoyable to read than those first-raters. I hadn't read Hardy in many years, and I was impressed: the plot is enjoyable, there are beautiful scenes of rural life, and the ideas are interesting. Some say that Hardy uses cheap tricks, melodramatic devices, to stir up his plot, but I haven't read enough of this kind of fiction to become cynical about it. I've spent much of my time reading plotless writers like Proust and Joyce, so for me, an action-packed plot is a refreshing change.

As is my wont, I chose the Norton Critical Edition, which was made in 1986, and contains useful footnotes, good essays, and a bibliography that points you to more Hardy material. Many leading critics have written about Hardy, so there's a plethora of criticism to choose from.

The title (*Far from the Madding Crowd*) comes from a famous English poem, Thomas Gray's "Elegy Written in a Country Churchyard":

Far from the madding crowd's ignoble strife,
Their sober wishes never learned to stray;
Along the cool sequestered vale of life
They kept the noiseless tenor of their way.

Most of Hardy's novels are set in the countryside of southwest England—a region known as Wessex (sometimes called Dorsetshire; the county name is Dorset, the largest town is Dorchester). One might compare Hardy with Faulkner, who also wrote a series of novels about the rural area where he grew up. Hardy describes country life—shearing sheep, making hay, caring for bees, etc. These descriptions of country life are interwoven with his characters and his plot, so they're never tedious. Hardy tells us that, in the churchyard

> at six o'clock, the young men of the village gathered, as was their custom, for a game of Prisoners' Base. The spot had been consecrated to this ancient diversion from time immemorial, the old stocks conveniently forming a base facing the boundary of the churchyard, in front of which the ground was trodden hard and bare as a pavement by the players. She could see the brown and black heads of the young lads darting about right and left, their white shirt-sleeves gleaming in the sun; whilst occasionally a shout and a peal of hearty laughter varied the stillness of the evening air.

While Hardy praises country life, he doesn't thunder against industrialization as Lawrence does; Hardy ignores the city. One might say that Hardy is Lawrence without an edge.

In earlier issues, I discussed *frevel*—a teasing, childish kind of daring that stems from a lack of respect, and that often has dire consequences. (*Frevel* is a German word, related to the English "frivolous.") *Madding Crowd* includes a perfect example of *frevel*: Liddy and Bathsheba send Boldwood a teasing valentine, with a spurious suggestion of love and marriage.

This valentine has dire consequences. One might say that the plot of *Madding Crowd* hinges on this case of *frevel*. One wonders where Hardy acquired his understanding of *frevel*. Was it his own idea? Did he have experience of it? Did he find it in some philosophical writer, or in some fictional work?

D. H. Lawrence was a fan of Hardy, and wrote a book on his work; Hardy's candid treatment of sex in *Jude the Obscure* may have increased Lawrence's admiration for him.[1]

Hardy attempts humor, often at the expense of his rustics, but I don't find him funny. He often displays his erudition with references to history, literature, astronomy, etc.; these references are somewhat interesting, but also somewhat forced. Critics often find fault with Hardy's style, which is occasionally quirky and obscure.

[Spoiler Warning: If you're thinking of reading *Madding Crowd*, you may want to skip the rest of this essay.]

Hardy is by no means blind to the mysterious and occult; Hardy once said he would give ten years of his life to see a ghost, and Wikipedia speaks of his "fascination with the supernatural." Hardy notes that Bathsheba can feel when Gabriel is looking at her: "Rays of male vision seem to have a tickling effect upon virgin faces in rural districts; she brushed hers with her hand, as if Gabriel had been irritating its pink surface by actual touch." When Troy is reported to have drowned, his wife says that she feels he's alive: "From the first, I have had a strange unaccountable feeling that he could not have perished." And indeed, he hadn't perished. (In an earlier issue, I discussed a Sherlock Holmes story in which a woman feels that her "dead" husband is still alive.[2])

There's a clear class structure in Hardy's work. Employers are called "master" and "mistress," and a laborer is called "my man."

One essay in the Norton Edition is by Howard Babb. Babb argues that the theme of *Madding Crowd* is the goodness of nature, and the goodness of lives close to nature. He points out that positive characters in the novel have names taken from nature—Oak and Robin, for example—while negative characters have names that suggest civilization and business—Troy and Pennyways, for example. Babb points out that Hardy associates positive characters with beautiful scenes, negative characters with dismal scenes. Hardy's hero (Gabriel Oak) is introduced in connection with "the sublimity of Norcombe Hill," while Hardy's villain (Frank Troy) is introduced in a snow-

---

[1] In his *Study of Thomas Hardy*, Lawrence says that the theme of Hardy's work is, "The spirit of Love must always succumb before the blind, stupid, but overwhelming power of the Law." Those who take a chance on romance come to a bad end; one should follow the beaten path of convention, Hardy seems to say. Lawrence's view of *Madding Crowd* is that Bathsheba truly loves Troy ("the flower of imaginative fine love"), but this love is destroyed, so she settles for Gabriel.

[2] See ljhammond.com/phlit/2007-09.htm#5

covered landscape notable for its dreariness, somberness, and deathlike quality. Oak is in touch with nature, and reads nature's signs of a coming storm, while Troy is at odds with nature, and his attempt to plant flowers on his girlfriend's grave is ruined by a heavy rain. As for Bathsheba, when she's feeling low after breaking with her husband, she's "spiritually regenerated by a night in a thicket." So Hardy doesn't just offer us descriptions of nature, he uses nature to illustrate character and theme; one might even say that nature *is* a character in Hardy's novel.

Another essay in the Norton Edition is by Roy Morrell. Morrell points out that the relationship between Gabriel and Bathsheba is healthy because it develops "in the interstices of a mass of hard prosaic reality." On the other hand, the relationship between Boldwood and Bathsheba is unhealthy because it's based on airy romanticism; the relationship between Bathsheba and Troy is also romantic and unhealthy. "Hardy is disparaging romance, the dream and the dreamer. He is suggesting, instead, that one should live... in accordance with reality."

Another essay in the Norton Edition is by Alan Friedman. Friedman argues that, at the start of *Madding Crowd*, Bathsheba is described as high-spirited, headstrong, un-tamed, because the theme of the novel is the taming of Bathsheba. Bathsheba's world expands in the course of the novel—she becomes a landowner, a wife, etc. This expansion reaches a bursting point when her marriage with Troy collapses, and when Boldwood shoots Troy at the Christmas party. Bathsheba's life has become impossible, she wonders how she can continue living. Friedman's analysis of the novel is penetrating; he connects it not only to literature in general but also to life:

> In fiction, those moments—or those many pages—which render a central character's realization that life has become morally impossible are often accompanied (is it only in fiction?) by the onset of illness and fever: the very intensity of the moral explosion brings on a physical deterioration. And not infrequently, those fully expanded and intensified moments in the structure are also accompanied by the suggestion of mental derangement [one thinks of Hamlet]. Perhaps we are justified in regarding these processes as literary "rituals" or conventions—drawn of course from cultural conventions and psychological observation—which not only render but also mark the fullness of the formal expansion of experience.

Our headstrong ways get us into trouble, we get stuck, life becomes impossible. Through suffering we attain wisdom, we learn humility. Bathsheba's expansion, Friedman argues, is followed by the containment of that expansion. Bathsheba's health revives, her spirits revive. By the end of the novel, she's ready for a modest, un-romantic match with Gabriel—a match that she spurned at the start of the novel. She's older and wiser; "she never laughed readily now." She has become serious, she's no longer a *freveler*.

As I read *Madding Crowd*, I wondered if Boldwood had some of Hardy's own traits. Boldwood is a shadow figure, reminding me of Hamlet and Ahab. When Gabriel Oak is shearing sheep,

> Oak's belief that [Bathsheba] was going to stand pleasantly by [was] painfully interrupted by Farmer Boldwood's appearance in the extremest corner of the barn. Nobody seemed to have perceived his entry, but there he certainly was. Boldwood always carried with him a social atmosphere of his own, which everybody felt who came near him; and the talk, which Bathsheba's presence had somewhat suppressed, was now totally suspended.

In my book of aphorisms, I discussed Hamlet's shadowy tendencies, and said that Shakespeare himself probably shared them. Boldwood is the antithesis of Troy, and surely Hardy himself was also the antithesis of Troy.

Surely Troy has his faults, and surely he does much harm to Fanny Robin, but he's one of the most striking characters in *Madding Crowd*, he's one of Hardy's finest creations, and he has some positive traits. He has a remarkable capacity for action, as is clear from his swordsmanship, his circus act, etc.; Hardy speaks of "the lightning action in which he was such an adept." Troy has no concern with the past or the future, but there's a certain Zennish wisdom in that attitude, as Hardy realizes: "it may be argued with great plausibility that reminiscence is less an endowment than a disease, and that expectation [is] a constant fluctuation between pleasure and pain."

Madding Crowd contains a striking criticism of specialized knowledge. Bathsheba tells Gabriel,

> When I want a broad-minded opinion for general enlightenment, distinct from special advice, I never go to a man who deals in the subject professionally. So I like the parson's opinion on law, the lawyer's on doctoring, the doctor's on business, and my business-man's—that is, yours—on morals.

46. W. Somerset Maugham

A. General Remarks

I received an e-mail from a neighbor:

> I got addicted to Maugham's short stories when I lived in Taiwan. I don't usually like short stories, but I was desperate for something to read in English and all I could find were some yellowed Penguin paperbacks on the bottom shelf in a little shop run by an Indian. I bought the first volume and was instantly addicted. Gradually I read all of Maugham's short stories as well as his famous novel, *The Razor's Edge*. I also was riveted to *The Narrow Corner*. If you have a way to get movies, get *The Painted Veil* (2006), based on [Maugham's] novel. It haunted me for days. It's about a woman who goes to the Orient with her doctor-husband in the 1920s. An excellent movie. My favorite short story is "The Book-Bag."

After reading this, I figured, "If his short stories are that good, and if 'The Book-Bag' is his best story, then I can't miss with 'The Book-Bag.'" So I read "The Book-Bag," and soon I was addicted, too. Maugham's stories are so enjoyable to read that it's difficult to read only one. He's a master of story-telling, a master of plot. Like all great storytellers, he draws you in, he persuades you that his characters are real people, he makes you "suspend your disbelief." He's always intelligent, sometimes humorous, and occasionally profound. His writing is clear, direct, readable. Orwell said, "The modern writer who has influenced me most is Somerset Maugham, whom I admire immensely for his power of telling a story straightforwardly and without frills."[1]

There are several parallels between Maugham and Orwell. In Maugham's *Summing Up*, he looked back on the sufferings of his youth:

> I was small; I had endurance but little physical strength; I stammered; I was shy; I had poor health. I had no facility for games.

Orwell echoed this passage in his essay, "Such, Such Were the Joys": "I had no money, I was weak, I was ugly. I was unpopular, I had a chronic cough, I was cowardly, I smelt."[2]

Both Maugham and Orwell skipped college, partly because they didn't win a scholarship, partly because their parents couldn't afford to send them. Both of them are known for lucid prose. "Good prose," wrote Maugham, "should be like the clothes of a well-dressed man, appropriate but unobtrusive."[3]

But while there are similarities between Maugham and Orwell, there are also differences. Orwell was about thirty years younger than Maugham. Orwell is the quintessential 20th-century writer, renowned for his depiction of totalitarianism. Maugham, on the other hand, came of age in the 19th century, in the confident years before World War I. Maugham writes about colonialism, not totalitarianism. In Maugham's world, one Englishman can rule an island in the South Pacific, and enjoy doing it.[4]

I mentioned above that Maugham stammered. He isn't the only prominent writer who stammered, there seems to be a link between writing and

---

1 *Somerset Maugham: A Life*, by Jeffrey Meyers, Ch. 22, #3, pp. 343, 344

2 Maugham's *Summing Up* was published in 1938, about a year before Orwell began writing "Such, Such Were the Joys." The parallels between Maugham and Orwell are discussed in *Somerset Maugham: A Life*, by Jeffrey Meyers, Ch. 22, #3, p. 344

3 Meyers, p. 345

4 As Joseph Warren Beach put it, Maugham's "cool blood was warmed by an afterglow of Victorianism and he never seriously questioned the basic premises of that nineteenth-century culture of which he was a distinguished exponent. With all his irony, his cynicism, his uncanny faculty for reducing human motives to their lowest common denominator, he has long stood for a humanism which cherished the surface values of civilization even when it could not quite recall the grounds on which they were based." (*W. Somerset Maugham: The Critical Heritage*, edited by Anthony Curtis and John Whitehead, Ch. 121, pp. 352, 353) Beach is a fine critic, a Minnesota professor who wrote studies of Henry James, George Meredith, etc.

stammering. Perhaps the stammerer takes to writing because speaking is difficult for him.

> For the stammerer who wishes to express himself without the risks inherent in speech, there is an obvious alternative: writing. On the page, even the most unruly words can be brought into line, so it may be no coincidence that many of the finest writers have suffered from a stammer: Lewis Carroll, Arnold Bennett, Somerset Maugham, Aldous Huxley, Elizabeth Bowen, Philip Larkin, Henry James, Charles Kingsley, Leigh Hunt, Margaret Drabble, and many more.[1]

Maugham was born in 1874, so he was an exact contemporary of Churchill (he was also a friend of Churchill). Maugham also died in the same year as Churchill (1965). Maugham was a popular writer during most of his long life. When he was just 23, Maugham published his first novel, *Liza of Lambeth*, which sold well, prompting Maugham to abandon his medical career and devote himself to writing.

Maugham's most popular novel, *The Razor's Edge* (1944), sold more than 5,000,000 copies—a tribute to Doubleday's marketing skill as well as Maugham's literary skill. Maugham sold more books, and made more money, than any writer of his time. His most highly-regarded novel is *Of Human Bondage*, which is his most personal, most autobiographical work; one might say that while his other works were manufactured, *Human Bondage* burst out of him, it obsessed him, it demanded to be written. As Maugham put it,

> I was but just firmly established as a popular playwright when I began to be obsessed by the teeming memories of my past life.... It all came back to me so pressingly, in my sleep, on my walks, when I was rehearsing plays, when I was at a party, it became such a burden to me that I made up my mind I could only regain my peace by writing it all down in the form of a novel. I knew it would be a long one, and I wanted to be undisturbed, so I refused the contracts managers were anxious to give me and temporarily retired from the stage.[2]

The phrase "human bondage" refers to obsessive love, and is borrowed from Spinoza.

On the whole, Maugham's childhood wasn't happy. He was very close to his mother, and she died when he was 8 (for the rest of his life, Maugham kept a photo of her at his bedside).[3] His father died when he was 10. He was

---

[1] telegraph.co.uk

[2] From Maugham's *The Summing Up*

[3] One psychologist argued that a factor in the origin of genius is "Jocasta mothering"—that is, a mother who is in love with her son, as Jocasta was with Oedipus. He cited Maugham as an example of a genius who experienced Jocasta mothering. Perhaps Proust and Hitler also experienced this sort of mothering. See Matthew Besdine, "The Jocasta Complex, Mothering

sent to the home of an uncle, who was "cold and emotionally cruel."[1] His uncle sent him to boarding school, where he was unhappy.

Perhaps these experiences contributed to the tone of Maugham's writing, which has been described as "astringent cynicism."[2] Perhaps we should ascribe Maugham's cynicism and coldness, not simply to an unhappy childhood, but rather to the contrast between his mother's deep love and the world's cruelty. An Eskimo who's raised in the Arctic doesn't suffer from the cold as much as someone who's raised in the Tropics, then suddenly transplanted to the Arctic. Maugham was surrounded by deep love, then suddenly transplanted to indifference.

Maugham found happiness in Heidelberg, where he went at age 16, and remained for 18 months. In Heidelberg, Maugham attended lectures on Schopenhauer, and was converted to Schopenhauer's pessimistic worldview. He also had a homosexual experience in Heidelberg; Maugham remained homosexual for the rest of his life, though he also had liaisons with women, an unhappy marriage, and one child.[3] He spent much of his adult life at his mansion on Cap Ferrat, in the French Riviera; perhaps he felt that France was more tolerant of his lifestyle than England. Many literary people visited Maugham at his mansion, which was called the Villa Mauresque.

B. "The Outstation"

After I finished "The Book-Bag," I read one of Maugham's most highly-regarded stories, "The Outstation." Like many of Maugham's stories, "The Outstation" takes place in The East, in the British colony on the Malay Peninsula. Maugham knew such places from firsthand experience; he travelled widely, perhaps even more widely than Graham Greene. "The Outstation" is a story about animosity, about hatred between two men. This is one of the ancient themes of world literature, and Maugham handles it superbly.

The protagonist of "The Outstation" is 54-year-old George Warburton, who

---

and Genius," *Psychoanalytic Review* (this is a 2-part article, both parts are in volume 55, both were published in 1968; part one is pages 259-277, part two is pages 574-600).

[1] See Wikipedia's article "W. Somerset Maugham"

[2] See Encyclopedia Britannica's article "W. Somerset Maugham." The critic Raymond Mortimer spoke of Maugham's "distrust of life, presumably the sour fruit of a most miserable childhood." (*Somerset Maugham: A Life*, by Jeffrey Meyers, Ch. 21, #1, p. 327) The writer C. P. Snow said that Maugham's friendliness "was a very astringent sort of friendliness, no nonsense about it and no sentimentality about it, but just hard, rather like visiting one's family lawyer." (Meyers, Ch. 11, #3, p. 175)

[3] Maugham excoriated his ex-wife in a late memoir, *Looking Back*, which Graham Greene called "the sick Maugham's senile and scandalous work." (*Somerset Maugham: A Life*, by Jeffrey Meyers, Ch. 21, #2, p. 331)

> was a figure in the society of London in the early nineties, and society then had not lost its exclusiveness nor its brilliance. The Boer War which shook it was unthought of; the Great War which destroyed it was prophesied only by the pessimists.

Thus, Maugham notes the decline of aristocratic society; this is a central theme in the work of Proust, who was just three years older than Maugham.

There's a hint of synchronicity in "The Outstation": the dramatic climax of the quarrel is foreshadowed by the natural world:

> Mr. Warburton went down to the river and sat in his arbor. But peace was denied him. The river flowed ominously silent. It was like a great serpent gliding with sluggish movement towards the sea. And the trees of the jungle over the water were heavy with a breath-less menace. No bird sang. No breeze ruffled the leaves of the cassias. All around him it seemed as though something waited.[1]

C. "Mackintosh"

"Mackintosh" also deals with animosity, and it resembles "The Outstation." Walker rules a Pacific island, and he's loathed by his bookish lieutenant, Mackintosh. Mackintosh arranges Walker's murder semi-consciously:

> He felt as though something possessed him so that he acted under the compulsion of a foreign will. Himself did not make the movements of his body, but a power that was strange to him.

One thinks of Ibsen's *Wild Duck*, in which Gregers gives a pistol to Hedvig, a teenage girl, and thus semi-consciously arranges Hedvig's suicide.[2]

Perhaps Walker rules a bit too long. He seems to represent the aging king, the "fisher king" whose power is slipping away:

> "They were saying in Apia it was about time Walker retired. He ain't so young as he was. Things have changed since he first come to the islands and he ain't changed with them." "He'll go too far," said the old chiefess. "The natives aren't satisfied."

D. "Lord Mountdrago"

Another Maugham story, "Lord Mountdrago," deals with what might be called "occult animosity"—in other words, animosity that expresses itself in occult ways. Two men appear to be dreaming the same dreams—communicating through their dreams, battling through their dreams. "Lord Mountdrago" resembles a Poe story.

---

[1] V. S. Naipaul was fascinated by Maugham, and Naipaul's novel *A Bend in the River* takes its title from the opening paragraph of "The Outstation."

[2] For more on *Wild Duck*, see ljhammond.com/phlit/2002-08a.htm. In *Hedda Gabler*, Hedda gives a pistol to Eilert; this pistol also leads to suicide.

"Lord Mountdrago" deals with one of Maugham's recurring themes: behind the veil of decorum and respectability lurk the savage and the criminal. Many of Maugham's stories deal with the rending of this veil.

> He knew how often in men who to all appearance were healthy and normal, who were seemingly devoid of imagination, and who fulfilled the duties of common life with credit to themselves and with benefit to their fellows, when you gained their confidence, when you tore away the mask they wore to the world, you found not only hideous abnormality, but kinks so strange, mental extravagances so fantastic, that in that respect you could only call them lunatic.[1]

Occasionally, though, the rending of the veil reveals goodness, not savagery. At the end of "Mackintosh," for example, Walker seems to be a good man, perhaps a better man than Mackintosh. And at the end of "Mr. Know-All," Max Kelada appears in a good light, though much of the story deals with his vices.

Why did I choose to read "Lord Mountdrago," which isn't one of Maugham's better-known stories? I read it because I'm interested in D. H. Lawrence, and I heard that "Lord Mountdrago" takes a jab at Lawrence. Here's the passage that seems aimed at Lawrence:

> His father's a miner, and he worked in a mine himself when he was a boy; he's been a schoolmaster in the board schools and a journalist. He's that half-baked, conceited intellectual, with inadequate knowledge, ill-considered ideas and impracticable plans, that compulsory education has brought forth from the working-classes.

The quarrel in "Lord Mountdrago" begins with ridicule:

> In the House of Commons the most devastating weapon is ridicule: I mocked him; I bantered him; I was in good form that day and the House rocked with laughter. Their laughter excited me and I excelled myself. The Opposition sat glum and silent, but even some of them couldn't help laughing once or twice; it's not intolerable, you know, to see a colleague, perhaps a rival, made a fool of. And if ever a man was made a fool of I made a fool of Griffiths.

I'm reminded of Dostoyevsky's aphorism, "Ridicule is the world's strongest weapon."[2] And because it's a strong weapon, ridicule often leads to enduring animosity, such as we find in "Lord Mountdrago."

---

1 At the end of *Razor's Edge*, Isabel is revealed to be a killer, behind a facade of good manners and good looks.

2 *The Possessed*, supplementary chapter, "At Tihon's." Maugham seems to be keenly aware of the power of ridicule. In "Mackintosh," Mackintosh's hatred of Walker is prompted by Walker's jests: "Walker little knew that there was nothing Mackintosh could stand less than chaff. He would wake in the night, the breathless night of the rainy season, and brood sullenly over the gibe that Walker had uttered carelessly days before. It rankled. His heart

I experienced something similar to what happens in "Lord Mountdrago": I dreamed of quarreling with my cousin, and when I saw my cousin the next morning, he was somewhat distant, as if he had experienced the "dream quarrel," too. Perhaps we should speak of "co-dreaming," or perhaps we should say that telepathic communication takes place not only on the conscious level, but also on the unconscious level, the dream level.

Like many of Maugham's stories, "Lord Mountdrago" draws on Maugham's own experience—more specifically, it draws on Maugham's experience with a psycho-therapist, whom he saw for his stutter. Maugham's stories are often built on something he experienced or observed—a person he met, a story he heard on his travels. Imaginative literature is often not imaginary. In an earlier issue, I wrote,

> Most of the characters in *Huck Finn* are based on people Twain knew: Pap, Huck, Tom, Jim, the duke and the dauphin, Boggs and Col. Sherburn. Twain's fiction has a ring of truth because it's based on fact; as Twain put it, "If you attempt to create a wholly imagined incident, adventure or situation, you will go astray and the artificiality will be detectable, but if you found on fact in your personal experience, it is an acorn, a root, and every created adornment that grows out of it, and spreads its foliage and blossoms to the sun will seem reality, not invention."[1]

E. "Gigolo and Gigolette"

Maugham's story "Gigolo and Gigolette" is based on something he witnessed: in 1931, Maugham saw a woman dive from a high platform into a shallow pool of water, to entertain customers at a casino. Maugham's story suggests that the will can shape the outcome, and that the diver can anticipate success or disaster. The diver's husband tries to encourage her: "You know and I know, there's no risk, not if you keep your nerve." "But I've lost my nerve, Syd. I shall kill myself."

F. "The Letter"

One of Maugham's best-known stories is "The Letter." Like many of Maugham's stories and novels, "The Letter" was made into a movie—actually, it was made into a movie four times. "The Letter" was also made into a play and an opera. Again we find the theme of savagery lurking behind the veil of aristocratic grace. Again we have a plot that's based on an actual event.

---

swelled with rage, and he pictured to himself ways in which he might get even with the bully." Likewise, the natives can't endure ridicule: "There is nothing the Kanaka can endure less than ridicule." I've even heard people say that dogs don't like to be laughed at.

[1] See ljhammond.com/phlit/2007-12.htm#9

Maugham's grandfather, father, and three older brothers were lawyers; Maugham himself might have been trained for the law if it weren't for his stutter. "The Letter" draws on Maugham's familiarity with legal matters.

G. "The Unconquered"

"The Unconquered" is one of Maugham's best stories. It deals with war and love, and like many of Maugham's stories, it has a dramatic ending. (Maugham had firsthand experience of war; at the start of World War I, he was in the ambulance corps, along with several other writers. Late in 1915, Maugham joined British intelligence, and worked as a spy in Switzerland. In 1917, he worked as a spy in Russia, trying to prevent a Bolshevik takeover. Maugham earned high marks for his espionage work.)

"The Unconquered" has the best description of falling-in-love that I've ever read:

> She wasn't his type. She wasn't very pretty. There was nothing to her. Why should he have all of a sudden this funny feeling for her? It wasn't a pleasant feeling either, it was a pain. But he knew what it was all right; it was love, and it made him feel happier than he had ever felt in his life. He wanted to take her in his arms, he wanted to pet her, he wanted to kiss those tear-stained eyes of hers. He didn't desire her, he thought, as a man desires a woman, he wanted to comfort her.

The man tells the woman, "It's not only that I love you, I admire you. I admire your distinction and your grace. There's something about you I don't understand. I respect you."[1]

Maugham was equally adept at describing the death of love—that is, the gradual withering-away of passion, respect, love. He describes the death of love in his story "Red":

> For many years now they had lived together bound by the ties of habit and convenience, and it was with a smile that he looked back on his old passion.... The tragedy of love is not death or separation.... It is dreadfully bitter to look at a woman whom you have loved with all your heart and soul, so that you felt you could not bear to let her out of

---

[1] Maugham's description of falling-in-love in *Human Bondage* is similar: "He did not know how he was to get through the hours that must pass before his eyes rested on her again. He thought drowsily of her thin face, with its delicate features, and the greenish pallor of her skin. He was not happy with her, but he was unhappy away from her. He wanted to sit by her side and look at her, he wanted to touch her, he wanted… the thought came to him and he did not finish it, suddenly he grew wide awake… he wanted to kiss the thin, pale mouth with its narrow lips. The truth came to him at last. He was in love with her. It was incredible.... He had thought of love as a rapture which seized one so that all the world seemed spring-like, he had looked forward to an ecstatic happiness; but this was not happiness; it was a hunger of the soul, it was a painful yearning, it was a bitter anguish, he had never known before." (Ch. 57)

> your sight, and realize that you would not mind if you never saw her again. The tragedy of love is indifference.[1]

"The Unconquered" was published in 1943, and deals with the German occupation of France. Maugham shrewdly describes how the war looked from a German perspective. A German soldier asks a Frenchwoman, "Why did you want to fight for the Poles? What were they to you?" "You're right. If we had let your Hitler take Poland he would have left us alone."[2]

Maugham also makes a shrewd remark about politics in his novel *Ashenden*. When the Polish agent Herbartus says that World War II will give his country freedom, Ashenden responds, "What will your country do with it when it gets it?"[3] Many wars were fought in the 20th century to expel foreign powers and gain independence, but did countries like Algeria and Vietnam flourish once they were independent? One is reminded of children who look forward eagerly to Christmas, only to be disappointed when it finally comes. Now Muslim extremists are fighting to create a caliphate and impose *sharia* law, but how grim, sterile, and disappointing this would be if it were ever realized!

Like other Maugham stories, "The Unconquered" has contrasting characters—in this case, a loving man and a hating woman. But this isn't a case of "simple animosity," such as we find in "The Outstation" or "Mackintosh" or "Lord Mountdrago." This is a case of wartime animosity; "The Unconquered" shows how war between nations creates animosity between individuals.

H. "Rain"

Perhaps Maugham's most celebrated story is "Rain," which deals with American missionaries in the Pacific. Again we find contrasting characters: moralizing missionaries contrast with easy-going natives, and the missionaries also contrast with a high-spirited prostitute. Again we find the theme of the proper, respectable character who harbors animal impulses.

One of the missionaries deplores how the natives dance:

> It's not only immoral in itself, but it distinctly leads to immorality. However, I'm thankful to God that we stamped it out, and I don't think I'm wrong in saying that no one has danced in our district for eight years.

---

[1] In an earlier issue, I discussed the death of love in the work of D. H. Lawrence (see ljhammond.com/phlit/2010-09c.htm). I also discussed a *NewYorkTimes* article on the death of love (see ljhammond.com/phlit/2012-12.htm#4).

[2] Some non-Germans took a similar view. Hoffer and Jung, for example, felt that the only way for the Allies to avoid world war was to let Hitler drive east (see ljhammond.com/phlit/2011-05b.htm#2).

[3] Ch. 13, "The Flip of a Coin"

The missionaries are equally horrified by native clothing—or rather, the lack of it—and one of them says, "the inhabitants of these islands will never be thoroughly Christianized till every boy of more than ten years is made to wear a pair of trousers." The chief goal of the missionaries is to convince the natives that they're sinners:

> When we went there they had no sense of sin at all. They broke the commandments one after the other and never knew they were doing wrong. And I think that was the most difficult part of my work, to instill into the natives the sense of sin.

But the missionaries are confident of eventual success: "We'll save them in spite of themselves."

One of Maugham's novels, *The Moon and Sixpence*, is based on Gauguin, who was a "reverse missionary"—that is, he went to the South Seas in the belief that primitive life was better than European life.[1]

Maugham's dim view of missionaries is part of something larger—his dim view of Christianity. In *Razor's Edge*, he writes,

> I couldn't but surmise that the devil, looking at the cruel wars that Christianity has occasioned, the persecutions, the tortures Christian has inflicted on Christian, the unkindness, the hypocrisy, the intolerance, must consider the balance sheet with complacency. And when he remembers that it has laid upon mankind the bitter burden of the sense of sin that has darkened the beauty of the starry night and cast a baleful shadow on the passing pleasures of a world to be enjoyed, he must chuckle.[2]

I. "The Bum"

"The Bum" is in a volume of stories called *Cosmopolitans*; the stories in this volume are shorter than most of Maugham's stories, and they aren't highly-regarded. "The Bum" is about a gifted young writer who fails to break through, fails to gain recognition, and becomes a beggar. Maugham's description of the young writer is excellent:

> He was not popular among us because he was arrogant and we were none of us old enough to take the arrogance of youth with tolerance.

---

[1] The conclusion of "Rain"—suicide prompted by feelings of guilt—resembles the conclusion of "Mackintosh."

Rebecca West argues that the end of "Rain" is shocking not because of orgy or suicide, but because "the missionary's wife, on hearing the news of his death, instantly knows what has happened. 'Her voice was hard and steady. Dr. Macphail could not understand the look in her eyes. Her pale face was very stern.' And from that one knows what a foul den of lust and suspicion of lust these people's hearts had been." (*W. Somerset Maugham: The Critical Heritage*, edited by Anthony Curtis and John Whitehead, Ch. 48, p. 154)

[2] Ch. 5, #4, p. 228

> He thought us poor fish and did not hesitate to tell us so. He would not show us his work, because our praise meant nothing to him and he despised our censure. His vanity was enormous. It irritated us; but some of us were uneasily aware that it might perhaps be justified. Was it possible that the intense consciousness of genius that he had, rested on no grounds? He had sacrificed everything to be a writer. He was so certain of himself that he infected some of his friends with his own assurance. I recalled his high spirits, his vitality, his confidence in the future and his disinterestedness.

J. *The Razor's Edge*

After reading several short stories by Maugham, I decided to read his novel *The Razor's Edge*. I figured, "If it was so popular, surely I'll enjoy it." But I found it somewhat disappointing, and I never quite understood why it was so popular. The protagonist, Larry Darrell, loses his faith in God and the world after witnessing the horrors of World War I. Larry travels the world in search of the meaning of life. He's particularly impressed with the wisdom of India. (The phrase "razor's edge" comes from the Upanishads: "The sharp edge of a razor is difficult to pass over; thus the wise say the path to Salvation is hard.")

But Larry's spiritual quest is too remote from Maugham's own experience. Maugham was intent on crafting novels, not discovering Truth. *Razor's Edge* is crafted, not lived. It's entertaining and readable, like all of Maugham's work, but it isn't Maugham at his best, and I can understand why the critics panned it. Tolstoy was so intent on finding ultimate truth that he turned his back on fiction. Maugham, on the other hand, turned his back on ultimate truth, and focused on writing fiction.

During World War II, Maugham spent several years in the U.S. He was employed by Hollywood studios to work on screenplays. In California, he met three younger Englishmen who were devoted to Eastern philosophy—Christopher Isherwood, Aldous Huxley, and Gerald Heard. The character of Larry in *Razor's Edge* is based on these three Englishmen (especially Isherwood) and their spiritual quest. Other characters in *Razor's Edge* are also based on real people: Elliott Templeton is based on Henry Channon, Gray Maturin is based on Maugham's American publisher, Nelson Doubleday.[1]

Eventually Larry turns his back on India, and its philosophy, and returns to the U.S. to be an auto mechanic and writer. Larry has decided that Indian philosophy is too nihilistic, too hostile to life:

> The Aryans when they first came down into India saw that the world we know is but an appearance of the world we know not; but they welcomed it as gracious and beautiful; it was only centuries later... when the debilitating climate had sapped their vitality... that they saw only evil in life and craved for liberation from its return.... It was not for me

---

[1] I found an interesting *New York Times* article on the Doubleday publishing empire at nytimes.com/1996/10/06/nyregion/once-doubleday-was-a-king-now-house-gets-a-new-look.html

> to leave the world and retire to a cloister, but to live in the world and love the objects of the world, not indeed for themselves, but for the Infinite that is in them.... I wanted to live again and again. I was willing to accept every sort of life, no matter what its pain and sorrow.[1]

Thus, Larry reaches a conclusion that reminds us of Nietzsche: an affirmation of life, and an affirmation of the "eternal recurrence" of life. But Maugham doesn't mention Nietzsche in *Razor's Edge*. Perhaps Maugham reached his Nietzschean conclusion independently of Nietzsche.

As in "The Unconquered" and "Rain," we find contrasting characters in *Razor's Edge*. The bohemian Larry contrasts sharply with the conventional, bourgeois Isabel. Larry's bohemian bent foreshadows the counter-culture movement of the 1960s. As one critic put it, "Maugham had encouraged his readers, especially affluent young post-World War II Americans, to examine and even question their own postwar values."[2]

Despite its flaws, *Razor's Edge* is a brave attempt, and a partly-successful attempt, to depict the enlightened person, the saint. Thus, it can be compared to Dostoyevsky's *The Idiot*, which attempts to portray a Christ figure in Prince Myshkin. Larry, Maugham's saint, is child-like, and gets along well with children:

> He was sweet with Odette [Suzanne Rouvier's daughter] and she adored him. I had to prevent her from making a nuisance of herself, but he never seemed to mind how much she pestered him. It used to make me laugh, they were like two children together.[3]

Larry wanted to marry Sophie Macdonald, a drug addict and nymphomaniac. He says that Sophie had "spiritual beauty.... a lovely soul, fervid, aspiring and generous. Her ideals were greathearted. There was even at the end a tragic nobility in the way she sought destruction."[4] Sophie started down the road to ruin after experiencing death at close range, just as Larry begins his spiritual quest after witnessing death.[5]

Larry has no use for academia, and doesn't pursue a degree. Instead, he studies the classics on his own, and goes into raptures over Homer, Spinoza, etc. "I want to learn as passionately as—Gray, for instance, wants to make pots of money."[6] Perhaps the book he reads most assiduously is William

---

[1] Ch. 6, #8, pp. 303, 304

[2] *A William Somerset Maugham Encyclopedia*, by Samuel J. Rogal, "*The Razor's Edge*," p. 232

[3] Ch. 4, #9

[4] Ch. 7, #2, pp. 323, 324

[5] As Joseph Warren Beach writes, Sophie is "a spirit akin to Larry's, whose vision of Evil is too much for her, and drives her the way of sin and death where Larry goes the way of life and sanctity."

[6] Ch. 2, #4, p. 74

James' *Principles of Psychology*, which Maugham praises for its historical importance, and for being "exceedingly readable."[1]

K. Maugham's Critics

Maugham has no truck with the experimental or avant-garde. He's more popular with the general public than with highbrow critics; one might describe him as a middlebrow writer.[2] Rebecca West faulted Maugham for lacking a philosophical vision, a positive worldview. Reviewing Maugham's story-collection *The Trembling of a Leaf,* West said that Maugham's

> cheap and tiresome attitude towards life nearly mars these technically admirable stories. They are charged with a cynicism which one feels Mr. Maugham has stuffed into them to conceal his lack of any real philosophy.[3]

Maugham is long on cynicism, short on enthusiasm.

The Irish writer Kate O'Brien criticized *Razor's Edge* for its charming surface, for "that gloss, that convenient, amusing *chic*, that curious ChampsElysées *décor* which this author finds irresistible and which he does so well; indeed, excessively, sterilizingly well."[4]

One of Maugham's toughest critics is Diana Trilling, who speaks of "the failure of [Maugham's] whole literary career."[5] Trilling complains that *Razor's Edge* lacks deep emotion, and she quotes Maugham's own remark: "A chill went down my spine as it strangely does when I am confronted with deep and genuine emotion. I find it terrible and rather awe-inspiring." Trilling says that Maugham was drawn to mysticism since it promised to still emotions: "Mysticism [is] bound to be inviting to the person who is afraid of the deep emotions."

The critic Cyril Connolly takes a more positive view of *Razor's Edge*. He speaks of, "the sheer delight that I and all my friends have received from this novel," and he says that it "perfectly recaptures the graces that have vanished." Perhaps we can describe Maugham as the last of the 19th-century

---

1 Ch. 1, #7, p. 32. *The Razor's Edge* has been made into a movie at least twice. I thought the 1984 movie was quite good, though Bill Murray was rougher, less gentle than Maugham's Larry.

2 In the Norton Critical Editions, Maugham is nowhere to be found.

3 *W. Somerset Maugham: The Critical Heritage*, edited by Anthony Curtis and John Whitehead, Ch. 48, p. 153. In *Human Bondage*, Maugham ponders the meaning of life, and develops a positive worldview (see ljhammond.com/phlit/2017-02b.htm#2).

4 *W. Somerset Maugham: The Critical Heritage*, edited by Anthony Curtis and John Whitehead, Ch. 123, p. 357. As the American critic Joseph Warren Beach put it, "In Maugham there are few intentions that lie much deeper than the surface.... The people say just what they mean, no more and no less.... There is little to distinguish one person's speech from another."

5 *W. Somerset Maugham: The Critical Heritage*, Ch. 122, p. 355

novelists. Connolly notes that *Razor's Edge* isn't Maugham's first foray into mysticism: "In all [Maugham's] previous work there has always been a strong inclination to mysticism."[1] Connolly calls *Razor's Edge*, "A considerable addition to the literature of non-attachment, [it] ranks with Huxley's *Grey Eminence* and Heard's *Man the Master*." On the other hand, Connolly scoffs at the Hindu theories and hypnotic tricks in Maugham's novel.

In an earlier issue, I mentioned Caroline Gordon, an American novelist and critic, and I said that Gordon was a mentor to Flannery O'Connor.[2] Gordon was married to the writer Allen Tate, and they maintained a literary salon in Clarksville, Tennessee (Gordon had grown up nearby, in southern Kentucky).

> Their guests included some of the best-known writers of their time, including F. Scott Fitzgerald, Ernest Hemingway, William Faulkner, Flannery O'Connor, T. S. Eliot, Robert Penn Warren, and Ford Madox Ford.[3]

Gordon was a harsh critic of Maugham, comparing him unfavorably to Chekhov.[4] In Chekhov's work, Gordon says, "Each detail not only vibrates with a life of its own but 'acts' upon the neighboring detail." Gordon quotes Chekhov's maxim, "If a gun hangs on the wall in one of the first scenes of a story it must be discharged before the end of the story." Chekhov's "greatest disciple," Gordon says, is Joyce; Joyce's story "The Dead" is a Chekhovian masterpiece.

Gordon thinks that Maugham doesn't work hard enough; she disapproves of Maugham's idea that a writer should "do only as well as it lies in him easily to do." Gordon insists that a writer should not "stop short of the final, exhausting, almost superhuman efforts which result in the production of masterpieces." I think Maugham is right. Many first-rate writers wrote "easily" and rapidly: Nietzsche wrote some of his best books in a week, Kafka wrote some of his best stories in a night (van Gogh could complete a painting in a day). But perhaps the important thing isn't ease or effort, but whether a writer is committed to his subject, loves his subject, etc.

L. *Of Human Bondage*

Of Human Bondage is often called Maugham's best novel, but it isn't as engrossing as his short stories. The main theme is the protagonist's obsessive love for a woman. One might compare *Human Bondage* to Proust's *Swann's Way*, which also deals with obsessive love. No literary work depicts

---

1 Ibid, Ch. 124, p. 358

2 See ljhammond.com/phlit/2014-11b.htm#7

3 See Wikipedia's article "Caroline Gordon"

4 "Notes on Chekhov and Maugham," by Caroline Gordon, *The Sewanee Review*, Vol. 57, No. 3 (Summer, 1949), pp. 401-410. In this essay, Gordon discusses Maugham's story "Rain" and Chekhov's story "On the Road." She explains the symbolism of "On the Road," but one wonders how many readers appreciate this symbolism.

obsession ("bondage") in stronger colors than Maugham's *Of Human Bondage*.

Maugham's intelligence is apparent in his philosophical remarks, as when he discusses fate and freedom:

> "The illusion of free will is so strong in my mind that I can't get away from it, but I believe it is only an illusion. But it is an illusion which is one of the strongest motives of my actions. Before I do anything I feel that I have choice, and that influences what I do; but afterwards, when the thing is done, I believe that it was inevitable from all eternity." "What do you deduce from that?" asked Hayward. "Why, merely the futility of regret. It's no good crying over spilt milk, because all the forces of the universe were bent on spilling it."

Maugham seemed to view *Human Bondage* as his *magnum opus*, so it's more philosophical, and less entertaining, than his short stories.

When you read a novel from a different era, you learn about the details of life in that era. For example, Maugham describes a hospital as a place for poor people; apparently the affluent didn't go to hospitals in Maugham's day, they were treated at home. Employees, in Maugham's day, were often given housing and food by their employer (this was true in China until recently). Sometimes the concerns of Maugham's characters are the same as our concerns, as when he describes someone who's afraid that if he uses pain-killers, he'll become addicted to them.

M. Concluding Remarks

Like Graham Greene, Maugham wrote travel books as well as fictional works. Maugham's *Don Fernando* is about Spain and its Golden Age; Maugham's *Land of the Blessed Virgin* is about Andalusia. Maugham wrote about China in *On a Chinese Screen*, and Southeast Asia in *The Gentleman in the Parlour*. In the twilight of his career, Maugham wrote two historical novels: *Then and Now* is about Machiavelli, and uses a plot from a Machiavelli comedy; *Catalina* is about 17th-century Spain.

Maugham's autobiographical works *The Summing Up* (1938) and *A Writer's Notebook* (1949) are well-regarded. Maugham was a private person, not given to confiding and confessing, so these autobiographical works deal more with his literary career than with his life. Stephen Vincent Benét said of *The Summing Up*, "The whole book gives a picture of the progress and development of a craftsman that is truly remarkable in its intellectual frankness."[1] Ted Morgan's 1980 biography of Maugham is well-regarded.[2]

47. George Orwell

---

1 *W. Somerset Maugham: The Critical Heritage*, Ch. 110, p. 321

2 Much Maugham material can be found at mymaughamcollection.blogspot.com, and Maugham texts can be found at unz.org

A. Marrakech

The local Great Books group recently read an Orwell essay, "Marrakech." It's a short essay describing the poverty of the people in Marrakech—Arabs, Jews, blacks. It was written in 1939, when colonial empires were in disrepute, when people had forgotten how bad things were before the European powers came, and hadn't yet learned that things would get a lot worse when the European powers left. It describes sights and experiences, it's a kind of journalism; it doesn't offer deep ideas or flights of imagination.

I was never an Orwell fan, and I don't mention him in my *Realms of Gold*; I don't regard him as a great thinker or a great artist. His most famous works, *Animal Farm* and *Nineteen Eighty-Four*, are neither pure fiction nor pure philosophy, they're fables, designed to make political points. One might compare them to *Gulliver's Travels*, of which Orwell was a big fan.

But if Orwell has weaknesses, he has strengths, too. He's a good stylist and a penetrating observer, and his work is leavened with wit. I don't regret reading "Marrakech," and I'd probably enjoy his other writings.

I knew that Orwell had written about poor people in books like *Down and Out in Paris and London*, so I assumed that he was poor himself. I was surprised to learn that his family was quite well-to-do, and that poverty was a role that he played in order to learn about the poor, and write about them. He was inspired by Jack London, who had studied the London poor by pretending to be one of them.

Since Orwell was a mediocre student at Eton, he despaired of winning a scholarship to college, and joined the civil service. His first posting was to Burma, and this experience was the basis of his first novel, *Burmese Days*.

Orwell was born in 1903 in India, where his father was a civil servant (Orwell's mother brought him to England when he was one year old). Orwell's grandmother lived in Burma, hence he chose to go to Burma rather than India. His real name was Eric Arthur Blair—"George Orwell" was a pen name.

After about four years in Burma, he returned to England, hoping to make his way as a writer. He lived among the poor, and got himself arrested, hoping to learn about prison life (Jack London had been imprisoned, and had written about prison life). Later, Orwell worked as a teacher, while continuing to write essays and novels.

In 1936, he travelled to northern England, and observed the life of working people; this experience was the basis for a non-fiction work, *The Road to Wigan Pier*. Like many of his writings, *Wigan Pier* was published by a firm that specialized in socialist literature. Orwell was critical of both capitalism and totalitarianism; he subscribed to "democratic socialism."

Late in 1936, Orwell set out for Spain, to fight the Fascists, and to write about the situation there. He spent about six months in Spain; he was in combat, was wounded, and witnessed the internecine conflicts of leftist groups. This experience was the basis for his book *Homage to Catalonia*. When Orwell had health problems, he and his wife went to Morocco, where it was hoped the climate would be good for him (this trip was the basis for the essay that I read, "Marrakech").

During World War II, Orwell made radio broadcasts for the British government, and wrote numerous book reviews and essays. He also wrote a short fable, *Animal Farm*, that satirized Stalin's regime; it includes the famous line, "All animals are equal, but some animals are more equal than others." *Animal Farm* was published in 1945, and made Orwell internationally famous. After the war, he began writing *Nineteen Eighty-Four*, which was published in 1949.

Orwell criticized English intellectuals, especially those on the Left, for denigrating England. He also criticized intellectuals who denigrated the U.S.:

> To be anti-American nowadays is to shout with the mob.... I do not believe the mass of the people in this country are anti-American.... But politico-literary intellectuals are not usually frightened of mass opinion. What they are frightened of is the prevailing opinion within their own group. At any given moment there is always an orthodoxy, a parrot-cry which must be repeated, and in the more active section of the Left the orthodoxy of the moment is anti-Americanism.[1]

Orwell died of tuberculosis in 1950, at the age of 46.

B. Jeffrey Meyers on Orwell

One of the best literary magazines in the U.S. is Roger Kimball's *New Criterion*, which started about thirty years ago. *The New Criterion* published an excellent essay on Orwell by Jeffrey Meyers, who wrote a biography of Orwell, as well as biographies of many other modern writers. Meyers writes frequently for *The New Criterion.*

Orwell has many fans. Indeed, one might say that he has nothing but fans. Is anyone critical of Orwell? Meyers has collected numerous tributes to Orwell, such as this by Kingsley Amis: "No modern writer has his air of passionately believing what he has to say and of being passionately determined to say it as forcefully and simply as possible." Edmund Wilson praised Orwell's "readiness to think for himself, courage to speak his mind, tendency to deal with concrete realities rather than theoretical positions, and prose style that is both downright and disciplined." Veronica Wedgwood, an English historian, noted that Orwell combined passion with restraint: "the strength of his feelings and his determination that they should not intrude make his style spare and economical, while his acute observation and sensibility make its very bleakness the more powerful."

Maugham was born in 1874, about thirty years before Orwell, so he was old enough to be (in Orwell's eyes) established and respected, but not so old as to seem antiquated. Meyers wrote a biography of Maugham.

Meyers notes that both Maugham and Orwell were impressed with Milton's language:

---

1 Quoted in Norman Podhoretz, *The Bloody Crossroads*, "If Orwell Were Alive Today"

> Despite their preference for simplicity, both were also deeply moved when young by the rich sounds and exotic associations of John Milton's high style. Maugham noted "the exultation, the sense of freedom which came to me when first I read in my youth the first few books of *Paradise Lost*." Orwell also recalled that "when I was about sixteen I suddenly discovered the joy of mere words.... The lines from *Paradise Lost*... sent shivers down my backbone."

I had a similar experience with Milton.

When Orwell became an editor, he had difficulty rejecting manuscripts. Later he wrote, "It is questionable whether anyone who has had long experience as a free-lance journalist ought to become an editor. It is too like taking a convict out of his cell and making him governor of the prison." Orwell was a master of metaphor.

Like Orwell himself, the protagonists of Orwell's novels are often struggling writers, constantly short of money. Only during his four years as a Burma policeman did Orwell receive a reliable paycheck. "In August 1941, when he took a job at the BBC and earned a salary of £640 a year, for the first time since 1925 he made more money than he had as a policeman in Burma."

Orwell was a big fan of Swift, often re-read *Gulliver's Travels*, and admired Swift's essays on the art of writing. "Swift emphasized clarity," Meyers writes, "particularly disliked the 'use of obscure terms,' and urged the young clergyman to address his congregation 'in a manner to be understood by the meanest among them.'"

In his essay "Why I Write," Orwell discussed his political views.

> He called the Spanish Civil War, in which he fought on the Loyalist side and was shot through the throat, the great turning point in his life. After that, every line of his serious work—and in his view no work could be serious without a political purpose—was written "against totalitarianism and for democratic Socialism."

Orwell's goal was to

> make people "see the Soviet régime for what it really was" and destroy the Soviet myth in order to revive the real Socialist movement. Inspired by seeing a little boy whip a huge farm horse, Orwell imagined a revolution of oppressed beasts.

The result was his popular fable, *Animal Farm*, which satirized the Soviet system.

Since there are few defenders of the Soviet system around today, is Orwell's work still relevant? Orwell's political purposes make his work seem dated; the political debates of his day are of little interest nowadays. Great literature deals with eternal questions; Orwell often deals with topical questions.

Orwell became famous in 1945, with the publication of *Animal Farm*. He retreated to the island of Jura (on the west coast of Scotland) in order to find quiet, and complete his last novel, *Nineteen Eighty-Four*. His health was failing (he had tuberculosis). After completing *Nineteen Eighty-Four*, Orwell went to a sanatorium for treatment. Meyers says that Orwell's description of the protagonist of *Nineteen Eighty-Four* fits Orwell himself:

> "The truly frightening thing was the emaciation of his body. The barrel of the ribs was as narrow as that of a skeleton.... The curvature of the spine was astonishing. The thin shoulders were hunched forward so as to make a cavity of the chest, the scraggy neck seemed to be bending double under the weight of the skull." When Orwell was in the sanatorium, the doctors had to take extreme measures to prevent him from writing. The medical staff, insisting on complete physical and mental rest, confiscated his typewriter. When he kept on writing with a ball-point pen, they put his right arm in plaster.

48. J. B. Priestley

Meyers' essay on Orwell drew my attention to an English novelist named J. B. Priestley, whom Orwell speaks of with respect. Priestley's family seems to have been upper-class, or upper-middle-class; his father was a headmaster. Priestley fought in World War I, and later attended Cambridge. "Priestley's first major success came with a novel, *The Good Companions* (1929), which earned him the James Tait Black Memorial Prize for fiction and made him a national figure." Later he became a prominent playwright. Perhaps his best-known play is *An Inspector Calls* (1945), in which Priestley expressed his socialist views. Priestley also expressed his socialist views in *English Journey*, which is said to have inspired Orwell's *Road to Wigan Pier*. In 1958, Priestley joined a campaign for nuclear disarmament.

Priestley was interested in the paranormal, and studied the writings of J. W. Dunne, who argued that the future already exists, and can be perceived in dreams. Several of Priestley's plays drew on Dunne's ideas; critics speak of Priestley's "Time Plays." When he was interviewed on British TV in 1963, he asked viewers to send him their paranormal experiences. These submissions became part of Priestley's book *Man and Time*.[1]

During World War II, Priestley was a popular radio broadcaster; only Churchill drew larger audiences. (E. M. Forster was also a radio broadcaster.)

Priestley wrote an autobiographical work, *Margin Released*. He died in 1984, at the age of 89. J. B. Priestley (John Boynton Priestley) should not be confused with Joseph Priestley, an 18th-century intellectual who is sometimes credited with discovering oxygen.

49. Proust

---

[1] One is reminded of Koestler's 1974 appeal to newspaper readers to submit striking coincidences.

A. Proust and Ruskin

When Ruskin died in 1900, Proust wrote an obituary, and several articles about Ruskin. Though not known for his terse style, Proust began his obituary "*Ruskin est mort.*" Proust's attitude toward Ruskin was reverential and filial. He translated two of Ruskin's books (*The Bible of Amiens* and *Sesame and Lilies*), laboring over every word, embellishing his translations with footnotes that quoted relevant passages from other Ruskin books. "During the four years that I have worked on *The Bible of Amiens*," Proust wrote, "I have learned it entirely by heart."[1]

To a reviewer who had reviewed his translation, Proust wrote,

> You know what admiration I have for Ruskin. And since I believe that each of us has charge of the souls that he particularly loves, charge of making them known and loved, of avoiding for them the slights of misunderstandings, and the night... of oblivion, you know with what hands—scrupulous—but pious also and as gently as I could—I have touched that soul.

Did a reader ever have a more reverential attitude toward a writer than Proust had toward Ruskin? Perhaps a writer's reverence for past writers is a good indication of his own merit as a writer, and nothing does Proust more credit than his reverence for Ruskin. Ruskin was one of the great writers of that period, and he's still of deep interest to our time; Proust chose his master well.

Proust took several "Ruskinian pilgrimages" to places that Ruskin had written about. For example, he went to Rouen to find a tiny carving of which Ruskin was fond:

> "I went to Rouen as if obeying a dying wish, and as if Ruskin, upon dying, had in some way entrusted to his readers the poor creature to which he had given life again by speaking of it, and which, unknowingly, had just lost forever the person who had done for it as much as its first sculptor." [Proust] tells the story of his search for the carving, recounting his difficulty in identifying the tiny figure among the crowd of sculptures on the cathedral portal, followed by his delight as his companion recognizes it.[2]

Ruskin was a second father to Proust. Proust's reverence for Ruskin was a stage in his development. He had to outgrow this reverence before he could find himself, attain maturity, and become creative, just as Nietzsche had to outgrow his reverence for Schopenhauer and Wagner. The mature Proust was less reverential toward Ruskin than the young Proust.

What an assortment of talents Proust had! He could write about Ruskin with profound piety, he could write about philosophical ideas with seriousness and penetration, and he could write about social gatherings with wit and

---

[1] *The Cambridge Companion to Proust*, "Ruskin and the cathedral of lost souls", by Diane R. Leonard, p. 49
[2] Ibid, p. 47

vivacity. Since Proust had a deep interest in philosophy, it's surprising that he had little interest in the most famous philosopher of his day, Nietzsche. Proust doesn't write about the questions that engaged Nietzsche and Dostoyevsky—the death of God and the death of morality. Proust matured just before Nietzsche became famous, so the teachers who influenced Proust weren't familiar with Nietzsche, and didn't introduce Proust to Nietzsche. Proust seems to have been interested chiefly in Kantian idealism and in Schopenhauer.

Proust made the following remark on Schopenhauer:

> The capacity for profitable reading [is] far greater with the thinkers than with the great imaginative writers. Schopenhauer, for instance, offers us the image of a mind whose vitality bears lightly the most enormous reading.[1]

B. Proust and Perversity

November 13, 2006

One of the strangest scenes in the "Combray" section of *Swann's Way* is the scene between Mlle. Vinteuil and her female friend, a scene that blends the homo-erotic and the sadistic. The two women desecrate the memory of Mlle. Vinteuil's late father, calling him an "ugly old monkey," and spitting on a photo of him. Proust uses various arguments to justify the behavior of Mlle. Vinteuil. Does this strange scene re-enact a scene that Proust himself performed? Is this passage a confession and an apologia?

Proust's biographer, George Painter, says that "cerebral sadism was a constant element in Proust's own ambivalent love-hatred for his mother, both in her lifetime and long after her death."[2] Proust's love-hatred for his mother resembles that of Mlle. Vinteuil for her father. Displacement from mother to father is the sort of displacement that we often find in Proust.

Proust excuses Mlle. Vinteuil's behavior on various grounds. He speaks of "the instinctive generosity of her nature," and its "genuine goodness." Proust's desire to justify Mlle. Vinteuil's conduct would be difficult to account for if his own conduct didn't resemble hers. Proust's insight into Mlle. Vinteuil's motives would be difficult to account for if these motives weren't his own. And his choice of subject matter would be difficult to account for if he weren't driven to confess and explain his own conduct.

Because Proust's work is connected so closely to his life, Proust is a challenge to those who maintain that literature is objective, that literature isn't connected to the author's own life. Proust's work is based on his fondest childhood memories, just as Ruskin's autobiography, *Praeterita*, is based on childhood memories. But Proust's work is also based on his strangest impulses, and on his most painful experiences (such as his mother's death). Writing about his perversities and sufferings met a psychological need, helped Proust to overcome these experiences, served a cathartic function.

---

[1] "On Reading"

[2] Vol. II, ch. 3

Proust enjoyed writing about the experiences that meant the most to him—his fondest memories, and also his most perverse actions and his most agonizing sufferings.

January 19, 2007
When Proust was a young man, and was still living with his mother, he wrote her the following letter:

> As I'm unable to speak to you, I'm writing to tell you that I simply can't understand your behavior. You know, or must guess, that I've spent every night since I came back in weeping, and not without good cause; and all day long you say things to me like: 'I couldn't sleep last night because the servants didn't go to bed till eleven o'clock.' I only wish it was nothing worse than that that keeps *me* from sleeping! ....Thanks to you I was in such a state of nerves that when poor Fénelon came... I went for him with my fists... and without knowing what I was doing I took the new hat he'd just bought, stamped on it, tore it to pieces and ripped out the lining. As you might think I'm exaggerating I enclose a piece of the lining so that you can see it's true.[1]

Proust must have realized that such behavior was bizarre and not at all admirable. Small wonder that Proust was eager to separate a writer's everyday self from his "greater self," his literary self. The separation between the "everyday person" and the "creative person" is one of the themes of Proust's work; Proust depicts great artists like Vinteuil and Elstir as ordinary people, un-impressive people, and other characters are surprised to discover their hidden greatness.

Indeed, Proust goes further, and says that great artists are not only ordinary, they're worse than ordinary. In the following passage from *Within A Budding Grove*, Proust describes the artist as "vicious" and "wicked," and he distinguishes between the artist's "personal life" and his "true life":

> Perhaps it is only in really vicious lives that the moral problem can arise in all its disquieting strength. And of this problem, the artist finds a solution in the terms not of his personal life but of what is for him the true life, a general, literary solution.... Great artists, while being thoroughly wicked, make use of their vices in order to arrive at a conception of the moral law which is binding upon us all.[2]

Elsewhere Proust describes the modern artist as "hopelessly enslaved to sin," and as regarding his own behavior as "scandalous."[3] Perhaps the tension between Proust's personal life and his "true life" fueled his creativity; it's difficult to imagine Proust without his vices and sins. In an earlier issue, we discussed Luther's advice "sin boldly."[4] This was Proust's maxim, too.

---

[1] Quoted in *A Reader's Guide to Marcel Proust*, by Milton Hindus

[2] Quoted in *A Reader's Guide to Marcel Proust*, ch. 1, p. 6

[3] Ibid, p. 7

[4] See bookmark or ljhammond.com/phlit/2005-09b.htm#2

As Proust was more creative on account of his vices, so too a character in *Swann's Way*, Odette, is more charming on account of her vices. As M. Verdurin says of Odette, "Does it matter so very much whether she is virtuous or not? You can't tell; she might be a great deal less charming if she were." We recall that Proust himself possessed a good deal of social charm; like Odette, Proust may have been more charming on account of his vices.

I'm now reading one of the most celebrated sections of Proust's work—the Saint-Euverte party near the end of "Swann in Love." Proust's party scenes are filled with scathing remarks about people; Proust's descriptions of people are satirical, if not sadistic. I'd like to quote one such satirical description, which includes Proust's favorite kind of metaphor—the culture metaphor, in which something mundane is compared to something from the world of high culture. Describing Mme. de Gallardon, Proust says that she was very proud of her kinship with the Guermantes family:

> When she found herself seated next to someone whom she did not know... she suffered acutely from the feeling that her own consciousness of her Guermantes connection could not be made externally manifest in visible characters, like those which, in the mosaics in Byzantine churches... inscribe in a vertical column by the side of some Sacred Personage the words which he is supposed to be uttering.

C. Proust Notes

I've been looking at *A Reader's Guide to Marcel Proust*, by Milton Hindus. Hindus notes several differences between the real Marcel and the fictionalized Marcel:

> Marcel in the novel is not homosexual but heterosexual, and this is only one of a number of respects in which he differs from his creator. He appears to be, for instance, completely non-Jewish; the closest he comes to the Jews in the novel is that some of his friends and acquaintances are Jewish. No hint is given that the narrator's mother is Jewish, as Proust's was. And, as a final change, the narrator, so far as we can tell, is an only child; Proust's younger brother Robert nowhere appears in the story of *Remembrance.*[1]

Proust studied philosophical idealism—that is, the doctrine that the world is our idea of the world, we can't know the real world, we can't know the "thing-in-itself." Proust's idealism leads him to describe the world that his characters perceive, not the "real world." This leads Proust to criticize the school of literature known as realistic (or naturalistic or social). Proust prefers the symbolists to the realists.

Proust is less concerned with the real Venice than with the Venice of the narrator's imagination. Hindus speaks of

> Marcel's recollection of the fascination which railway timetables had for him as a boy when he dreamed of seeing for the first time Balbec,

---

[1] Ch. 1, p. 6

> Venice, Florence. [As Cicero said, *Omne ignotum pro magnifico* (Everything unknown is regarded as magnificent).] What magic resided in "mere" names for the young Marcel, names that became so much more gorgeous than reality to him that they "aggravated the disenchantment that was in store for me when I set out upon my travels." ....Reality, in fact, is a drab thing to Marcel without the embellishment of the imagination.

Marcel's imagination is fired by books, so one might say that books are to blame for cutting him off from reality, and for making reality seem drab. Marcel enjoys literature, but suffers from reality. Perhaps Marcel's imagination is fired by youth, as well as by books, perhaps youth always romanticizes.

Hindus discusses Proust's interior drama, psychological drama. While some say that Proust's work isn't dramatic, "It should be a truer criticism of Proust to say that his psychological drama... verges perilously upon melodrama than that he is not dramatic enough."[1] I had the same feeling as I read *Swann's Way*, I felt that Proust was sometimes melodramatic, as when he says that the sight of a steeple in Paris reminded him of the Combray steeple, aroused childhood memories, and caused him to stand gazing for an hour or more.

The madeleine dipped in tea revives the past, brings back the Narrator's childhood. This experience fascinates Proust, revealing a parallel universe where time doesn't exist, as Freud said that time doesn't exist in the unconscious.

> The joy he feels arises not from the mere repetition in the present of an insignificant experience from the past but from the essence that is common to them both, so that what one experiences is neither in the past nor in the present but is outside time altogether, perhaps in a universe where time has no meaning, a paradise where everything is bathed in the radiance of eternity.[2]

One might say the theme of unconscious memory is related to the theme of immortality. The resurrection of a long-lost memory is like the resurrection scenes in Shakespeare's last plays—it transcends this world, it transcends the world of death and time. Is this also true of the Narrator's aesthetic experiences, his experiences of beautiful art and music—do these experiences also transcend the world of death and time?

Though the madeleine-dipped-in-tea is the most famous example of unconscious memory in Proust's work, there are several other such examples in the "Combray" chapter. Hindus points out that Proust didn't discover unconscious memory; Hindus mentions other writers who explored that subject—Ruskin, Chateaubriand, Wilkie Collins, etc.

---

[1] Ch. 2, p. 23

[2] see the essay on Proust by F. Hemmings, in the Scriber Writers Series

Hindus compares Proust with Wagner. Just as Wagner has a certain melody (leitmotif) for each character, so Proust has certain phrases for each character; these phrases are a leitmotif, and recur again and again.

> Wagner was much on Proust's mind while he was writing *Remembrance* and he spoke of his own composition's leitmotifs.... *Remembrance* is a behemoth of a composition, which is the literary counterpart of Wagner's *Ring*—that is to say, an artistic undertaking the vast extent of which in itself is enough to constitute it one of the wonders of the world.

Unlike most novelists, Proust views love as separate from physical desire. The Narrator's love for Gilberte is "violent and painful... although the two hardly exchange a kiss." The narrator is fascinated by girls working in the fields, but it's their souls, not their bodies, that fascinate him. As for Swann, his passion for Odette can't be explained in terms of physical beauty.

Hindus calls jealousy "the great theme of Proust's entire work.... Jealousy is, to Proust, 'the shadow of love'.... There is no love, in his pages, which does not have its counterpart in jealousy." This applies not only to Swann's love for Odette, and the narrator's love for Albertine, but also to the narrator's love for his mother.

In Proust, love is a jealous desire for complete possession of another's soul: "suddenly we experience the anxious need for her very being," Proust wrote, "an absurd need which the laws of the universe prevent us ever from satisfying and from which we can wean ourselves only with difficulty—the irrational, agonizing need to possess her." The lover wants the beloved to be devoted to him, the lover can't stand the thought of losing the beloved. And it's this fear of loss, not a physical passion, that inspires the Narrator's jealous love for his Mother: "The dread of loss, of being deprived of the comfort and reassurance of a kiss of reconciliation, can perfectly well precede the awakening of sexual instinct."[1] And it's this dread of loss that prompts the lover to make the beloved a prisoner, a captive.

When Proust was 32, his father died, and when he was 34, his mother died. "It is arguable that this double bereavement, once the shock was over, released some hidden spring in the writer's inmost self."[2] The deaths of his parents enabled Proust to mature as a man and as a writer. After these deaths, Proust set to work, knowing that time was short. Proust anticipated that he would die young, and spoke of "the premature evening of my life, a life that seemed destined to be as brief as a winter's day."

50. Ruskin

---

1 ibid

2 ibid

I recently came across a Ruskin quote: "Taste [is] the only morality. Tell me what you like, and I'll tell you what you are."[1] This quote is strikingly similar to a passage in Nietzsche:

> How can man know himself? Let the youthful soul look back on life with the question: what have you truly loved up to now, what has elevated your soul, what has mastered it and at the same time delighted it?[2]

There's a deep kinship between Ruskin and Nietzsche; Ruskin and Nietzsche lived at about the same time, had similar personalities/lifestyles, and similar philosophic genius.

Ruskin goes on to say, "Good taste is essentially a moral quality." Education is the forming of character—in other words, the forming of taste, the shaping of likes and dislikes.

> The entire object of true education [Ruskin writes] is to make people not merely *do* the right things, but *enjoy* the right things—not merely industrious, but to love industry—not merely learned, but to love knowledge—not merely pure, but to love purity—not merely just, but to hunger and thirst after justice.... What we *like* determines what we *are*, and is the sign of what we are; and to teach taste is inevitably to form character.

Art, in Ruskin's view, should not only give pleasure to the receiver, it should also show the pleasure of the artist; only what is created with love can be beautiful. Thus, Ruskin's aesthetic theory is closely related to his moral theory and his educational theory.

Ruskin seems completely unaware of Asian culture, but his ideas about art are similar to Chinese ideas. The Chinese viewed art as a manifestation of the artist; Chinese critics "did not confine their attention to the art object itself, but focused it also on the painter as a man, and on the painting as a revelation of the man."[3] The Chinese respected art that was plain, bland, unspiced, un-skillful.[4] Tranquil art, the reflection of a tranquil mind.

---

[1] This quote is from Ruskin's essay "Traffic." I read this essay years ago, made a note of this quote, but forgot it. I recently came across it on the *WeeklyStandard* website.

[2] "Schopenhauer as Educator," #1

[3] James Cahill, *Chinese Painting*, Preface. "Poetry and music, and later calligraphy, had long been treated in Confucian writings as vehicles for embodying one's personal thought and feeling, for conveying to others something of one's very nature.... The quality of a painting, said the literati writers, reflects the personal quality of the artist."

[4] "An outward 'plainness,' both in subject and style, they regarded as a virtue, and their aim was to produce within this plainness something moving, subtly exciting, personal—'flavor within blandness,' as Wu Chen puts it. No painter achieves this better than Huang Kung-wang. Cool and reserved, his

The Chinese would say that only a good man can write good prose, or paint a good painting. Ruskin would add, "And only a good man can appreciate good prose and good paintings."

A writer who deals with literature, film, etc. is educating, is forming taste, is shaping character. Literature and film (and other arts) should be seen as part of philosophy. Ruskin writes about art, and should be seen as a philosopher.

If Ruskin could see our society's art, what would he say? Is anything more characteristic of our society than a corruption of taste?

51. Whistler vs. Ruskin

I read an article called "A Sense of Justice: Whistler, Ruskin, James, Impressionism."[1] The author discusses Whistler's libel suit against Ruskin, and he argues that this suit was closely watched by Henry James, and influenced the novel that James wrote after the suit: *A Portrait of a Lady*. I found the essay unconvincing, but it raises some interesting issues.

The essay views Ruskin as a precursor of impressionism, and speaks of "Ruskin's proto-impressionist emphasis on the use of pure, vibrant color to capture nature in its most animated state." But Ruskin's impressionism wasn't completely subjective and individualistic. Ruskin believed that a critic could create a "cultural conversation," a "moral community."

Whistler argued that painting should have no connection to anything outside painting—pure art, art for art's sake. James thought Whistler had gone too far, complaining about Whistler's "exaggerated emphasis on subjective perception."[2] James insisted that "a picture should have some relation to life as well as to painting." The Chinese would agree.

But James criticized Ruskin for assuming tyrannical power over the art world:

> Art is the one corner of human life [James writes] in which we may take our ease.... One may read a great many pages of Mr. Ruskin without getting a hint of this delightful truth.... And as for Mr. Ruskin's world's being a place—his world of art—where we may take life easily, woe to the luckless mortal who enters it with any such disposition. Instead of a garden of delight, he finds a sort of assize court in perpetual session. Instead of a place in which human responsibilities are lightened and suspended, he finds a region governed by a kind of Draconic legislation.

---

paintings represent for the Chinese the perfect expression of an ideal scholarly temperament." (Cahill, Ch. 10)

[1] By Adam Parkes, *Victorian Studies*, Volume 42, Number 4, Summer 1999/2000, pp. 593-629

[2] I'm quoting the author (Adam Parkes), not James.

So James thought Whistler too subjective, Ruskin too tyrannical. James wrestled with "these paradoxes of freedom and legislation," hoping to find a happy medium between these extremes.

In James' *Portrait of a Lady*, the protagonist, Isabel Archer, is brought up in a free-spirited environment. As a result, Isabel's spirit is too free: "Isabel's education has weakened her character by overstimulating her imagination (the seat of private aesthetic experience) at the expense of good judgment." As Isabel matures, she develops

> a mode of vision that is wedded to sound judgment: one cannot live, James implies, by first impressions alone. And what this teaches her is that freedom means nothing, can be nothing, without a profound sense of constraint.

Isabel stays with her husband, though she probably doesn't love him or respect him. While Isabel is a model of conjugal fidelity, some may say that she's too faithful: "Not only does Isabel remain committed to Osmond, but in doing so she seems to renounce life, even to commit a kind of suicide." Thus, the aesthetic paradox of freedom vs. law becomes the ethical paradox of freedom vs. law.

I was struck by the contrast with Conrad's famous character, Kurtz, whose great weakness is his lack of restraint. Kurtz achieves freedom—no mean feat—but fails to achieve a balance between freedom and law. Isabel achieves this balance—or at least comes close to it.

52. *Dracula*

Dracula displays a wide knowledge of folklore and the occult; Bram Stoker studied folklore for many years before writing the novel. The setting is Transylvania, in the Carpathian mountains of western Romania; this area is known for its abundance of folk beliefs. Stoker probably thought he was writing another Gothic novel, but today *Dracula* is regarded as the first horror novel.

Stoker has a firm sense of place, of geography. First you follow the English clerk (Jonathan Harker) from England to Munich, and from Munich east through Vienna and Budapest to Transylvania (in Romania). Later Stoker describes Whitby, a town on the northeast coast of England. Then he describes the voyage from Varna (on the Black Sea) to Whitby. Do the horror writers of today have such a firm sense of geography? I recommend reading *Dracula* with a map at hand.

Stoker mentions Whitby Abbey, which was sacked by Danish Vikings in 867, rebuilt, then damaged again during the Reformation. Perhaps this east coast of England was particularly susceptible to Danish incursions and Danish influence, while the west coast of England (Wales, etc.) preserved its Celtic heritage, and is sometimes called The Celtic Fringe. At any rate, we meet an old man in Whitby who speaks a local dialect, and he uses a Danish word (the only Danish word I know): "kirkgarth." This word, Stoker's character says, has "something to do with the church." It means churchyard, and it can also be spelled Kierkegaard.

Dracula is an example of an evil character who has a touch of greatness. Professor van Helsing says,

> He must, indeed, have been that Voivode Dracula who won his name against the Turk.... If it be so, then was he no common man, for in that time, and for centuries after, he was spoken of as the cleverest and the most cunning, as well as the bravest of the sons of the "land beyond the forest." That mighty brain and that iron resolution went with him to his grave, and are even now arrayed against us. The Draculas were... a great and noble race.... There have been from the loins of this very one great men and good women.... This evil thing is rooted deep in all good.

[Spoiler Warning: If you think you might read *Dracula*, you should skip the rest of this paragraph.] The Norton Critical Edition of *Dracula* is mediocre. Its numerous footnotes distract rather than enlighten. There is, however, an interesting footnote at the end of the novel, an alternative ending that Stoker later abandoned. In this version, Dracula's castle collapses at the moment Dracula himself dies; there's a "volcano burst... a terrible convulsion of the earth." Here we have a synchronistic link between nature and man, between the castle and Dracula.

Dracula is about vampires, a subject that Stoker has clearly studied. It's not a subject that I find pleasant or interesting, but it raises a larger subject: the occult in general, how we approach it, how we deal with things that reason says are impossible. Stoker's hero, Professor Van Helsing, believes that vampires are about, but he doesn't express this belief to his friends, who probably don't believe in vampires.

As the evidence mounts, and his friends question him more and more, the Professor begins to speak. He tries to persuade his friend to have an open mind toward the occult in general, toward things that seem impossible:

> You are a clever man, friend John. You reason well, and your wit is bold, but you are too prejudiced. You do not let your eyes see nor your ears hear.... Do you not think that there are things which you cannot understand, and yet which are, that some people see things that others cannot? ....Ah, it is the fault of our science that it wants to explain all, and if it explain not, then it says there is nothing to explain.... Let me tell you, my friend, that there are things done today in electrical science which would have been deemed unholy by the very man who discovered electricity, who would themselves not so long before been burned as wizards. There are always mysteries in life.

Stoker was a student of physiognomy, a science that tried to grasp human nature by studying the shape of the face. The Swiss writer Lavater had pioneered this science around 1780, and it enjoyed considerable popularity in Stoker's youth. But it wasn't the same science that Lavater had developed, it had changed during the course of the 19th century as a result of an interest in race.

> The world of *Dracula* was very much a world of "ethnological physiognomies" in which racial identities were assumed to be plainly readable from appearances and, more than this, these readings could be used as data from which to extrapolate judgments as to a nation's social and moral wellbeing.[1]

Stoker was a fan of Whitman, wrote him letters in his youth, and visited him when he went to the U.S. In an early letter to Whitman, he spoke of his interest in physiognomy, and he described his own appearance. In *Dracula*, Stoker is careful to describe the facial features of his characters.

> Not only are Count Dracula's malevolent powers recognizable from his "fixed and rather cruel-looking" mouth or his "peculiarly arched nostrils," but when we meet Dr. Van Helsing, the man who will orchestrate the vampire's downfall, moral fitness can be immediately discerned from his "large, resolute, mobile mouth" and his "good-sized nose... with quick, sensitive nostrils, that seem to broaden as the big, bushy eyebrows come down and the mouth tightens."[2]

I finally found a top-notch *Dracula* essay: "*Dracula*: The Gnostic Quest and Victorian Wasteland," by Mark Hennelly. Hennelly's essay illuminates the novel, it raises one's opinion of the novel, and it makes one glad that one read the novel.

According to Hennelly, both Victorian England and Dracula's Transylvania are spiritually impoverished, both need the other in order to be rejuvenated. In an earlier issue, I quoted a philosopher from India, who described Western thought as a 'life-giving leaven.' I asked, "Isn't this how Westerners regard Eastern thought? Perhaps the beneficial influence operates in both directions."[3] This mutual benefit is, according to Hennelly, what we find in *Dracula*: England needs Transylvania, and Transylvania needs England.

In folklore, when a king ages, his kingdom declines into a wasteland. There's nothing left for the king to do except go fishing, hence the motif of the Fisher King. Hennelly views Dracula as an aged Fisher King—energetic in his younger days, but now in decline. He must be replaced by someone young and vigorous. At the end of the novel, the new king is born, "the Harker child through whose veins run not only the Victorian blood of his parents but also the vitality of the Count whose blood Mina has drunk." The Harker child is "appropriately born on the anniversary of Dracula's death."

Hennelly argues that other Victorian novelists also describe a "Gnostic quest," a quest for knowledge and spiritual growth. Hennelly quotes another critic:

> [Victorian novelists] stand as transitional figures between the confidence in objective fact that characterizes the age of reason and the unabashed solipsism

---

1 "Bram Stoker and the Crisis of the Liberal Subject," by David Glover, *New Literary History*, 1992, 23: 983-1002

2 ibid

3 See below or ljhammond.com/phlit/2008-01b.htm#2

that came into fiction in the present century through the stream of consciousness technique.

Hennelly points out that Stoker uses neither an omniscient narrator, nor a stream of consciousness, but rather a collection of diaries: "The disappearance of an omniscient narrator in *Dracula* reflects the atrophy of God and traditional faith so symptomatic of the Victorian wasteland." Hennelly's essay not only teaches one about *Dracula*, it also teaches one about the society that produced *Dracula*.

Hennelly devotes a paragraph to each of the novel's major characters:

Renfield	"Renfield's wish to 'not deceive myself' allows him to distinguish between 'dream' and 'grim reality' and makes this 'sanest lunatic' an epistemological model for the other Victorians. As Van Helsing admits, 'I may gain more knowledge out of the folly of this madman than I shall from the teaching of the most wise.'"
Quincey Morris	"Quincey Morris, the Texan and prior suitor of Lucy, is not quite as simple-minded as he seems; or at least his simple-mindedness finally becomes an analogue of open-mindedness. Like Van Helsing and Dracula, he represents a foreign quality which the Victorians need to absorb."
Arthur Holmwood	"Arthur Holmwood, or *Lord* Godalming, emblemizes class, wealth, and aristocratic values, all instances of decay in the Victorian wasteland.... His bride-to-be is appropriately seduced by Dracula, the demiurge of the natural world; and Arthur's sterile lack of open-minded belief renders him unable 'to believe things we know to be untrue.'"
Dr. Seward	"Dr. Seward represents Science but is also the detached alter-ego of the sceptical Victorian reader since his diary consumes so much of the narrative and since what he calls 'the dogged argumentativeness of my nature' provokes him repeatedly to question belief in the unknown: 'Surely there must be *some* rational explanation of all these mysterious things.'"
Harker	Harker "begins the novel on an 'unknown night-journey.'" Harker is the "actively questing knight errant.... Throughout the novel, this Galahad-figure's fate tacitly hinges upon Dracula's, the Fisher King. When he finally returns to the Perilous Castle and with the phallic Kikri knife helps to slay Dracula, Harker no longer 'felt impotent' but reclaims the sexual prerogatives which Dracula had usurped and produces a new male heir on the very anniversary of the Count's ritualistic beheading and symbolic castration, or 'sterilization.'"
Lucy	Lucy is Guinevere, "scapegoat of an unnatural and wasted courtly-love code.... As Lucy's transformation indicates, the stereotyped Victorian woman, elevated on a pedestal or embowered in an ivory tower like the Lady of Shalott, denies belief in the

	life-giving forces of carnal nature and produces the wasteland nightmare."
Mina	"If the blood of Dracula lethally drowns hitherto one-sided Lucy, it therapeutically baptizes, and provides rebirth for, diminutive *Mina.*" Early in the novel, Mina is an "emblem of angelic Victorian morality." Later, however, "her open-minded epistemology balances the close-minded gnoses of the vampire hunters: 'her tender faith against all our fears and doubting.'" Mina drinks Dracula's blood, which "provides an antidote by a kind of homeopathic magic to wasteland sterility.... Her repeated slogan becomes a liberating epigram for the theme of the entire novel: 'There must be no concealment... Alas! We have had too much already.'"
Van Helsing	"Van Helsing and Dracula himself are both quite similar and represent vital, foreign imports which the insular Victorian creed must smuggle in for restoration of domestic tranquility. Like the Count, Van Helsing transfuses blood, has had his blood 'sucked' by Seward, is an isolated, enigmatic personality, and is also the same kind of 'master amongst men' that Dracula is.... [Van Helsing's] personal life too has become a wasteland: 'My life is a barren and lonely one, and so full of work that I have not had much time for friendships'.... Still armed with his Catholic faith, so foreign to low-church Protestantism, and his 'open mind,' he is the primary savior of the wasteland. His gospel finally becomes the redeeming deed of the novel: 'I may err—I am but man; but I believe in all I do.'"
Dracula	"One of Dracula's opening speeches to Victorian Harker heralds his role as redeeming Gnostic: 'There is reason in all things as they are, and did you see with my eyes and know with my knowledge, you would perhaps better understand.'" Renfield even calls Dracula "God," reminding us of Jung's conception of God as both good and evil.

The novel teaches a Jungian message: "There are darknesses in life, and there are lights." Victorian society stressed the lights, and *Dracula* restores the balance by stressing the darknesses, just as Jung stressed God's darkness.

53. Mary Shelley's *Frankenstein*

April 10, 2004

A. The Culture Theme

Our book group recently read Mary Shelley's *Frankenstein*. Nobody disliked it, but nobody was enthusiastic about it either. It seemed rather gloomy: several characters say, "no one in the history of the world has ever been as miserable and unhappy as I am." One character, Victor Frankenstein, has discovered the secret of making a living being, or reviving a dead person. But good people are continually dying, and none of the deceased are revived. One has little sense of distinct characters: one is told that a character is full of virtues and talents, but one never feels that he is a distinct person, a 3-dimensional character.

When you finish the novel, you say to yourself, "I can understand why it's a well-known novel, a respected novel, but I can also understand why it isn't considered a top-notch novel, equal to the novels of Dostoyevsky and Tolstoy." *Frankenstein*'s reputation is an accurate indicator of its merit (as often happens); it has a high reputation (and deserves it), but it doesn't have a *very* high reputation (and doesn't deserve it).

As I read *Frankenstein*, I was impressed by the teenage author's excellent prose. I was also impressed by her broad education, and by her love of culture—especially literary classics. Even the monster, though raised in isolation, manages to obtain a good general education. The monster eavesdrops as a tutor (Felix) instructs a student (Safie): "The book from which Felix instructed Safie was Volney's *Ruins of Empires*.... Through this work I obtained a cursory knowledge of history." Later the monster begins to read the classics himself. He finds a satchel in the woods containing Plutarch's *Lives*, *Paradise Lost*, and Goethe's *Sorrows of Young Werther*. "The possession of these treasures gave me extreme delight; I now continually studied and exercised my mind upon these histories." Doubtless Mary Shelley herself received a similar education from her father, the philosopher and novelist William Godwin.

If the monster has a good general education, his maker, Victor Frankenstein, has an even better education. Victor's friend, Walton, says "on every point of general literature [Victor] displays unbounded knowledge, and a quick and piercing apprehension." Victor's friend, Henry Clerval, is also well-educated; while Henry is living in London, he

> desired the intercourse of the men of genius and talent who flourished at this time.... His mind expanded in the company of men of talent, and he found in his own nature greater capacities and resources than he could have imagined himself to have possessed while he associated with his inferiors.

Thus, social life overlaps with the life of the mind; doubtless this was also true in the Godwin-Shelley circle.

So *Frankenstein* presents two channels of culture: books and social life. It also presents a third channel of culture: travel. The reader is continually hearing about European locations that are notable for their history or their scenery. For example, the author speaks thus of Oxford:

> As we entered this city, our minds were filled with the remembrance of the events that had been transacted there more than a century and a half before [during the English Civil War].... The colleges are ancient and picturesque; the streets are almost magnificent; and the lovely Isis, which flows beside it through meadows of exquisite verdure, is spread

> forth into a placid expanse of waters, which reflects its majestic assemblage of towers, and spires, and domes, embosomed among aged trees.

Mary Shelley's education made her receptive to travel, and also to nature. Though she admires the mountains of Switzerland, she prefers the scenery along the Rhine:

> The mountains of Switzerland are more majestic and strange; but there is a charm in the banks of this divine river, that I never before saw equaled. Look at that castle which overhangs yon precipice; and that also on the island, almost concealed amongst the foliage of those lovely trees.

When our book group discussed *Frankenstein*, I talked about the prominent role of culture in the novel, and I said that contemporary writers don't discuss culture in this way. Our society has lost this conception of culture, this conception of general education, this conception of the classics. Our society doesn't have a leisure class, a class for which culture is a serious occupation.

B. Godwin on Solitude vs. Society

We chose the Norton Critical Edition of *Frankenstein*. Usually I enjoy the critical essays in this series, but this time I didn't. Perhaps *Frankenstein* is too popular with contemporary critics, with critics who view literature from a political or feminist perspective. Though I didn't enjoy the critical essays, I did benefit from the bibliography, which lists various studies of *Frankenstein*. I found two interesting essays in this bibliography: a 1965 essay called "Philosophical and Literary Sources of *Frankenstein*," and a psychoanalytic study of *Frankenstein*. The 1965 essay called my attention to a 1959 essay.

I greatly enjoyed these three essays—more than I enjoyed *Frankenstein* itself. Readers of Phlit have heard me say this before, have heard me say that I enjoyed the critical essays more than the book itself. I could almost say, "I don't read critical essays in order to understand novels, I read novels in order to understand critical essays."

The first essay I read was "Philosophical and Literary Sources of *Frankenstein*" (1965).[1] This essay points out that one of the purposes of *Frankenstein* (according to Mary's husband, Percy Bysshe Shelley) is "the exhibition of the amiableness of domestic affection, and the excellence of universal virtue." There are indeed many passages that describe "domestic affection"; for example, Victor's description of his childhood:

> No human being could have passed a happier childhood than myself. My parents were possessed by the very spirit of kindness and indulgence. We felt that they were not the tyrants to rule our lot according to their caprice, but the agents and creators of all the many delights

---

[1] "Philosophical and Literary Sources of Frankenstein," by Burton R. Pollin, *Comparative Literature*, vol. xvii, #2, spring 1965

> which we enjoyed. When I mingled with other families, I distinctly discerned how peculiarly fortunate my lot was, and gratitude assisted the development of filial love.

Mary's father, William Godwin, also wrote novels that stressed "the importance of companionship and the social affections,"[1] and Godwin's novels were a major influence on his daughter's work. The theme of *Frankenstein* is that those who follow a solitary path in the hope of reaching a lofty goal will come to grief; *Frankenstein* contrasts the happiness of family life and friendship with the misery of solitude. This theme plays an important role in Godwin's philosophy. Thus, *Frankenstein* can be described as a philosophical idea in fictional form. We'll follow this train of thought further when we discuss the second essay I read, the 1959 essay. First, however, a couple points raised in the 1965 essay deserve mention.

C. Locke's Sensationalism and *Frankenstein*

As she was writing *Frankenstein*, Mary was studying John Locke's *Essay Concerning Human Understanding*. Locke argued that there are no innate ideas, all ideas come from sensation (and from our reflections on our sensations). Locke's argument influenced the French materialists and the French Encyclopaedists, such as Condillac; these French thinkers, in turn, influenced Godwin. Locke's theory is known as sensationalism, and it found its way into *Frankenstein*. "Mary Shelley presents the process whereby consciousness dawns, objects are differentiated and are given intellectual significance, and language develops."[2]

Here is how the monster describes the first moments of his life: "A strange multiplicity of sensations seized me, and I saw, felt, heard, and smelt, at the same time; and it was, indeed, a long time before I learned to distinguish between the operations of my various senses." The monster's final words are also imbued with Locke's sensationalism:

> I shall no longer see the sun or stars, or feel the winds play on my cheeks. Light, feeling, and sense will pass away; and in this condition must I find my happiness. Some years ago, when the images which this world affords first opened upon me, when I felt the cheering warmth of summer, and heard the rustling of the leaves and the warbling of the birds, and these were all to me, I should have wept to die; now it is my only consolation.

Thinkers who subscribed to the theory of sensationalism, like Godwin, took a keen interest in education. Since they believed that the mind is a blank slate, a *tabula rasa*, they thought that man had an infinite capacity to be molded, educated. And if all young people were sent to free schools, then the world's problems could be solved, and the Golden Age would come again. For radicals like Godwin, public education and democracy were the great hopes for the future.

---

[1] ibid

[2] ibid

Another influence on Mary, besides the sensationalism of Locke and his followers, was the primitivism of Rousseau. Mary began *Frankenstein* when she was in Switzerland with the Shelley-Byron circle. One of their pastimes was visiting places that figure in Rousseau's novels. Mary's interest in education corresponds to Rousseau's interest in education, which is apparent in his novel, *Emile*. One of the characters in *Emile* is named Sophie; this may be the source of Mary's character, Safie.

Before I turn to the 1959 essay, permit me to mention one more point raised by the 1965 essay. I knew that Mary had some interest in alchemy, and had mentioned it in *Frankenstein*. What I failed to realize is that *Frankenstein* deals with a central issue of alchemy: the elixir of life. A school of alchemy that seemed to be particularly important in England was Rosicrucianism, and Mary's father had written novels that dealt with Rosicrucian ideas. When *Frankenstein* was published, it was condemned by conservative journals as a Rosicrucian heresy.

D. *Frankenstein* on Solitude vs. Society

Now let's turn to the 1959 essay, "Moral and Myth in Mrs. Shelley's *Frankenstein*."[1] This essay points out that Captain Walton is ambitious and knowledge-hungry, just like Victor Frankenstein; Walton "has been inspired since early youth to satiate an ardent curiosity about the unknown regions of the earth." Like Victor, Walton is lonely and therefore unhappy. He feels his solitude to be "a most severe evil"; he longs for "intimate sympathy with a fellow mind.... A man could boast of little happiness, who did not enjoy this blessing." When he meets Victor, Walton finally tastes the pleasures of friendship. Victor, however, warns Walton that his pursuit of knowledge will ruin his life, as it has ruined Victor's:

> You seek for knowledge and wisdom, as I once did; and I ardently hope that the gratification of your wishes may not be a serpent to sting you, as mine has been. I do not know that the relation of my disasters will be useful to you; yet, when I reflect that you are pursuing the same course, exposing yourself to the same dangers which have rendered me what I am, I imagine that you may deduce an apt moral from my tale.

Doubtless Mary Shelley intended this "apt moral" for her readers as well as for Walton.

Victor tells Walton how his unremitting study of alchemy and science "secluded me from the intercourse of my fellow-creatures, and rendered me unsocial." Finally, after prolonged effort, Victor succeeds in making a human being—or rather, a monster that resembles a human being. What an achievement! The monster destroys, one by one, all of Victor's friends and family members. Though Victor curses the monster, he admits that his own curiosity, his own quest for knowledge, is responsible for the deaths of his friends and relatives. He feels as if he has "committed some great crime." The author of this essay, Milton Goldberg, quotes Jung:

---

1 Milton Allan Goldberg, *Keats-Shelley Journal*, VIII (Winter, 1959), 27-38

> every step towards greater consciousness is a kind of Promethean guilt: through knowledge, the gods are as it were robbed of their fire, that is, something that was the property of the unconscious powers is torn out of its natural context and subordinated to the whims of the conscious mind.

We recall that the title of the novel is *Frankenstein; or, the modern Prometheus*. Is every intellectual a Frankenstein, a Prometheus? Is every quest for knowledge accompanied by a feeling of guilt? Mary Shelley's novel is a warning to intellectuals: don't pursue knowledge at the expense of fellow-feeling.

Walton and Frankenstein are both preoccupied with knowledge, and neglect fellow-feeling, love, sympathy. They start out with benevolent intentions, but they end with "misguided pride, a selfish pursuit aimed at self-glory." Their sin is different (according to Goldberg) from the sins depicted by the Greeks, and the sins depicted by Milton. They don't sin against God, they sin against society. This sin is characteristic of Mary Shelley's time, and it's described by other writers of her time, such as Mary's husband, Percy Shelley.

Percy Shelley argued that love is the sole law of the moral world. If one can't love people, one loves nature. If one doesn't love anything,

> man becomes the living sepulcher of himself, and what yet survives is the mere husk of what once he was.... Those who love not their fellow-beings, live unfruitful lives, and prepare for their old age a miserable grave.

Godwin believed that "virtue is essentially social." Goldberg traces this view to Adam Smith and the Scottish Common-Sense School, then back to Shaftesbury and Hutcheson, then back to the 17th century. This view was opposed by (among others) La Rochefoucauld, Hobbes, and Mandeville "for whom man was basically selfish and non-social."[1]

More than twenty years ago, when I first subscribed to Freud's theory of life- and death-instincts, I looked for thinkers who had expounded a similar view, and Shaftesbury was one of the thinkers I found. Freud and Shaftesbury felt that man has a life-instinct, that man is naturally social, that man's instincts prompt him to help others, to help society, to help his species. This argument can be strengthened by looking at other species (ants, bees, etc.) where social behavior is obvious. Freud argued that all organisms, including man, have a life-instinct. Freud complemented the theory of a life-instinct with the theory of a death-instinct; the death-instinct prompts man to be hostile, violent, and unsocial. Godwin and Shaftesbury were probably

---

[1] Goldberg points out that Thomas Paine shared Godwin's view. Perhaps this view was widespread among radicals like Godwin and Paine, while conservatives like Hobbes, who were wary of democracy, believed that man is naturally unsocial, and must be restrained by authority, force. In short, the radicals took an optimistic view of human nature, while the conservatives took a pessimistic view.

more optimistic than Freud, and placed more emphasis on man's social nature.

Frankenstein is a story within a story within a story; it is the monster's story within Frankenstein's story within Walton's story—three concentric circles. All three stories have the same theme: solitude is poisonous, companionship is essential.

> The sympathies of Walton and Frankenstein have been rendered torpid by their monomaniacal pursuit of knowledge which removes them increasingly from a compassionate society; similarly, the creature discovers that his sympathies are perpetually blunted by the misery of loneliness and isolation, estranged as he must be from human kind.

The Walton-Frankenstein theme is "knowledge without society is worthless." The monster theme is "virtuous inclinations, if they have no outlet in society, wither, and are replaced by criminal inclinations." Whatever deficiencies *Frankenstein* may have as a novel, it must be considered a most interesting example of philosophy fictionalized.

E. Godwin's Opponents: Kierkegaard, Nietzsche, etc.

What was Godwin (and others) arguing against? What worldview was supplanted by this Godwin-Shelley worldview? We mentioned before that La Rochefoucauld, Hobbes, and Mandeville (among others) had argued that man is essentially selfish and unsocial. But this isn't the only worldview that Godwin was arguing against. He was also arguing against the old Christian view that a man's most important relationship is his relationship with God, and that your eternal salvation depends on your relationship with God. Godwin was no mystic. Godwin was arguing against the introverted worldview, against the view that what matters most is the state of your own soul.

The Godwin-Shelley worldview (the view that fellow-feeling is essential, and virtue is social), though popular in the modern West, has not been universally accepted. Indeed, one could say that there has been a backlash against it. Schopenhauer—who was born in 1788, nine years before Mary Shelley—believed that a great thinker is solitary, and only a mediocre person is popular. Schopenhauer doubted whether true friendship really exists: "True friendship belongs to that class of things—the sea-serpent, for instance—with regard to which no one knows whether they are fabulous or really exist somewhere or other."[1]

Kierkegaard, who was born in 1813, seemed to feel the rising tide of "Godwinian fellow-feeling," and he vehemently rejected the Godwinian position. Like other Christians, Kierkegaard felt that the God relationship should be paramount, the inner life should be paramount. Kierkegaard deplored the present age as a time

---

[1] *Counsels and Maxims*, §3

> when people's attention is no longer turned inwards, when they are no longer satisfied with their own inner religious lives, but turn to others and to things outside themselves.[1]

Kierkegaard perceived that modern man was "other-directed" (to use Riesman's term).

Kierkegaard tried to remind his contemporaries of the old ideal:

> The man who can really stand alone in the world only taking counsel from his conscience; that man is a hero....[2] The yardstick for a human being is: how long and to what degree he can bear to be alone, devoid of understanding with others.[3]

Kierkegaard not only preached this ideal, he lived it, too.

Nietzsche, who was born in 1844, wasn't familiar with Kierkegaard's writings, but he was in complete agreement with Kierkegaard's conclusions, and he rejected the Godwin-Shelley position even more vehemently than Kierkegaard did. "Flee into your solitude!"[4] Zarathustra tells his disciples. Nietzsche says that one who communes with the great writers of the past

> has no need of company, except now and then so as afterwards to embrace his solitude the more tenderly; as a substitute for the living he has the dead, and even for friends he has a substitute: namely the best who have ever lived.[5]

In *Frankenstein*, Captain Walton eventually abandons his lofty goals, and turns his ship homeward. But Nietzsche advises against this course: "By my love and hope I entreat you: do not reject the hero in your soul! keep holy your highest hope![6].... Rather despair than submit."[7]

Nietzsche was reacting against the other-directed trend that became increasingly strong as the 19th century proceeded. On the other hand, Godwin & Company may have been reacting against a tendency that existed in the late 1700s, namely, a tendency to pursue a solitary path toward ambitious goals. The arguments of Godwin & Company have little meaning for our time, since in our time, people rarely pursue a solitary path toward ambitious goals. As Nietzsche said, philosophy is the bad conscience of its time, it says what people don't want to hear, it goes "against the grain," it's an antidote to the excesses of its time. Since our time isn't disposed toward the solitary-

---

1 *The Present Age*

2 *The Journals of Soren Kierkegaard*, edited by A. Dru, long version, Oxford University Press, 1938, §1155

3 *The Diary of Soren Kierkegaard* (edited by Peter Rohde, Philosophical Library, 1960) V, 3 (1854)

4 *Thus Spoke Zarathustra*, "Of the Flies of the Market-place"

5 *Daybreak* [also known as *Dawn*], §566, translated by R. J. Hollingdale, Cambridge Univ. Press, 1982

6 *Thus Spoke Zarathustra*, "Of the Tree on the Mountainside"

7 *Thus Spoke Zarathustra*, "Of the Higher Man"

heroic, we don't need to be warned (as *Frankenstein* warns its readers) about the dangers of the solitary-heroic.

F. A Freudian View of *Frankenstein*

Before concluding these remarks on *Frankenstein*, I'd like to discuss the third essay I read, a psychoanalytic study of *Frankenstein*.[1] The author, Harry Keyishian, describes Victor Frankenstein as "an intellectually ambitious, moody, willful young man (rather like Mary's husband Percy, many scholars have observed)." Victor has lofty goals, he "dreams of performing unprecedented feats," he creates an ideal self.

Keyishian views Victor through the lens of a Freudian study by Karen Horney. According to Horney, the self-idealizing individual "endows himself with unlimited powers and with exalted faculties; he becomes a hero, a genius, a supreme lover, a saint, a god."[2] His search for glory "can be like a demoniacal obsession, almost like a monster swallowing up the individual who has created it." The parallel with Victor could scarcely be closer.

Horney continues:

> If a man's thinking and feeling are primarily focused upon the infinite and the vision of possibilities, he loses his sense for the concrete, for the here and now. He loses his capacity for living in the moment.

Doubtless every ambitious intellectual has been down this road. Such people have a special need for Zen, since Zen connects one to the concrete, to the here and now. Victor says that his ambitions and labors made him "insensible to the charms of nature." Here again, it seems that Victor needs a dose of Zen, since Zen sharpens one's appreciation of nature.

After Victor succeeds in making a living being, he is horrified by the result, "a miserable monster." Here again, says Keyishian, there is a close parallel with Horney's self-idealizing individual:

> The glorified self becomes not only a *phantom* to be pursued: it also becomes a measuring rod with which to measure his actual being. And this actual being is such an embarrassing sight when viewed from the perspective of godlike perfection that he cannot but despise it.

While he dreams of high ideals, he keeps bumping into lowly reality: "Because reality keeps interfering with the flight to glory," writes Keyishian, "the individual grows to hate it, and to hate himself."[3]

---

[1] "Vindictiveness and the Search for Glory in Mary Shelley's *Frankenstein*," by Harry Keyishian, *The American Journal of Psychoanalysis*, vol. 49, #3, 1989

[2] ibid. Quotations from Karen Horney are from her book *Neurosis and Human Growth* (1950).

[3] As Kierkegaard put it, "we human beings have our heads full of great imaginings, and then comes existence and offers us the commonplace." (*Concluding Unscientific Postscript*, II, 4, 2, A, 3)

Horney speaks of the "pride system," and says that "pride and self-hate are actually one entity." The ideal person and the actual person are in conflict. "Self-hate, Horney says, 'makes visible a rift in the personality that started with the creation of an idealized self.'" Keyishian says that Victor's hatred for the monster is a dramatization of self-hatred, a dramatization of the self-idealizing individual's hatred for his actual self.

So much for Victor's situation. Now Keyishian turns to the monster, and credits Mary Shelley with skillfully describing the origin of the monster's vindictiveness. Mary's description agrees with Horney's. Horney says that the arrogant-vindictive individual was mistreated early in life, gives up "all hope of being loved," and longs for "vindication, revenge, and triumph." The monster, says Keyishian, "was deprived of the experience of total acceptance and uncritical love which is one of the saving legacies of normal infantile development." The monster has been rejected by mankind, and is consumed with envy, which Horney calls "the emotion... that most contributes to the callousness which vindictive individuals demonstrate toward others." Keyishian compares the monster to Richard III, who (according to Freud's interpretation) feels that he has been wronged (he is deformed), and therefore he has the right to mistreat others.

According to Keyishian, each of Mary Shelley's characters dramatizes an aspect of Karen Horney's theory: Victor shows the consequences of self-idealization and the search for glory, the monster shows how vindictiveness arises from a "pathogenic childhood environment," and Walton shows how one can finally turn away from the quest for glory, accept reality, and accept one's limitations. When Walton meets Victor, he acquires a friend, a wise counselor, one might even say a therapist.

One must be impressed by Mary Shelley's achievement—impressed by her understanding of human nature, and by her ability to express this understanding in fictional form.

54. Byron

In an earlier issue, I discussed an essay on Hawthorne by Paul Elmer More.[1] I recently read More's essay on Byron, and was much impressed by More's elegant style and deep ideas.[2] More's essay deals with one of the central questions in aesthetics: the difference between Classic and Romantic. Byron was a champion of the Classic, a critic of the Romantic.

> Byron condemned the romantic spirit, and waged continuous if often indiscreet warfare for Milton and Dryden and Pope. His indifference to Shakespeare proves the sincerity of his opinion, however it may expose the narrowness of his judgment.

Writing in 1898, More notes that Byron is out of fashion:

---

1 See bookmark or ljhammond.com/phlit/2016-06.htm#3

2 theatlantic.com

> So much has been written of late years about Wordsworth and Shelley, while their quondam rival has been treated with much contumelious silence, that the disdainers of Byron had begun to feel that the ground was entirely their own.

Byron is still out of fashion today—perhaps even more so than in More's day.

One of the chief characteristics of Romanticism is its worship of nature. More notes that the worship of nature arose when religious faith declined: "By the closing years of the eighteenth century the long illusion of man's personal value in the universe had been rudely shattered; his anchor of faith had been rent away." More argues that the Romantic poet's worship of nature causes him to lose sight of man:

> In this flattering absorption into nature the poet was too apt to forget that, after all, the highest and noblest theme must forever be the struggle of the human soul; he was too ready to substitute vague reverie for honest thought, and to lose his higher sympathy with man in the eager pursuit of minute phenomena.... Wordsworth has made a stir over the small celandine, and Tennyson has discovered that ash-buds are black in March; the present generation must, for originality, examine the fields with a botanist's lens, while the poor reader, who retains any use of his mind, is too often reminded of the poet Gray's shrewd witticism, that he learnt botany to save himself the trouble of thinking.[1]

The Classic writer focuses on man; as More says, "The preponderance of human interest is an essential feature of the classical spirit... this human interest is everywhere present in Byron's work." Byron has "intense human passions and personality." Byron focuses on "simple, fundamental passions.... I hardly know where in English literature, outside of Shakespeare, one is to find the great passions of men set forth so directly and powerfully as in Byron." More's remarks remind me of Tolstoy; Tolstoy exemplifies the Classic approach.

More says that Romantics like Wordsworth and Shelley possess a "subtle grace," their style is "wayward and effeminate," they view poetry as "a vehicle for the emotions and imaginations of the heart alone." On the other hand, Classic poetry has a "predominance of intellect and breadth of expression." More says that the best poets, like Homer and Shakespeare, have both Classic and Romantic qualities, they combine "subtle grace" with vigorous breadth.

Though Byron admired the Classic style, he couldn't achieve it himself, his work is mixed with Romantic qualities. In his day, Christian ideals were crumbling, and it wasn't clear how they could be replaced; as More says, Byron "revolted from the past, and still felt himself homeless and unattached

---

[1] More quotes Pope: "The proper study of mankind is man." He also quotes St. Augustine: "And abroad to gaze at the lofty mountains, and the great waves of the sea, and the wide flowing of rivers, and the circle of ocean, and the revolutions of the stars, and pass themselves, the crowning wonder, by."

in the shadowy ideals of the future." So it wasn't an auspicious time for Classic serenity and restraint. Byron exemplifies the world-weariness (*Weltschmerz*) of his time.

> Classical art [More writes] should result in self-restraint and perfection of form, but to this Byron never attained except spasmodically, almost by accident it would seem. So far is he classical that he almost universally displays predominance of intellect, breadth of treatment, and human interest; but side by side with this principle of limitation runs the other spirit of revolt, producing at times that extraordinary incongruity of effect which has so baffled his later audience.

More finds the "spirit of revolt" in Byron's private life, as well as his writings: "Many times [Byron] refers to the ruin of his own life, and always he puts his finger on the real source of the evil, his lack of self-restraint and his revolt from conventions."[1] One of Byron's girlfriends called him, "Mad, bad, and dangerous to know." Byron's art reflects his life. In both his art and his life, Classic serenity, restraint, and moderation eluded him.

Perhaps Byron's early success contributed to his lack of self-restraint. Byron became famous at 24, with the publication of *Childe Harold's Pilgrimage*. As Byron put it, "I awoke one morning and found myself famous."

By age 28, however, Byron was embroiled in scandal and mired in debt. After Byron had numerous affairs, his wife left him and took their daughter, Ada Lovelace. Byron was accused of incest with his half-sister, Augusta, and he was rumored to be the father of one of Augusta's children. Byron was probably bisexual, and his affairs with men probably contributed to the cloud of scandal that surrounded him.

His personal life in tatters, Byron left England at 28, and never returned. He spent much of his remaining eight years in Italy, often in the company of the poet Shelley. Byron died at 36, while helping Greece in its war for independence from the Ottoman Empire.

Though Byron died young, it seems that his life was complete. Goethe wrote,

> Although Byron has died so young, literature has not suffered an essential loss.... Byron could, in a certain sense, go no further. He had reached the summit of his creative power.[2]

As Byron put it in his "Epistle to Augusta,"

I have outlived myself by many a day...

---

[1] As Byron wrote in "Epistle to Augusta,"

I have been cunning in mine overthrow,
The careful pilot of my proper woe.
Mine were my faults, and mine be their reward.

More praises Byron's "Epistle to Augusta," calling it "perhaps the noblest of all his shorter poems."

[2] *Conversations With Eckermann*, 5/18/1824

I had the share
Of life which might have filled a century,
Before its fourth in time had passed me by.

In our time, it's easy to forget what an impression Byron made on his contemporaries. Goethe advised his friend Eckermann to learn English in order to read Byron. Goethe said, "a character of such eminence had never existed before, and probably would never come again."[1]

55. Conrad

A. A Sketch of His Life

Joseph Conrad was born in 1857 in Berdychiv, which is now in Ukraine. He was born into the Polish nobility, the landowning class, but this class had been declining since the Russians took over in the late 1700s (Poland had been divided in the late 1700s between Russia, Austria, and Prussia). Conrad's father wasn't a member of the landed gentry, he was a member of the "working intelligentsia."[2]

Conrad's father introduced Conrad to Polish Romantic poets like Adam Mickiewicz. Conrad's father and grandfather had aided the Polish independence movement, which aimed to throw off the Russian yoke. Conrad's grandfather had fought in Napoleon's army, during Napoleon's invasion of Russia. Conrad's father was imprisoned by the Russians in the Warsaw Citadel. Conrad later wrote, "In the courtyard of this Citadel—characteristically for our nation—my childhood memories begin."

Conrad and his parents (Conrad was an only child) were later exiled for eight months to a city north of Moscow, a city "known for its bad climate."[3] Conrad's mother died when he was 8, his father when he was 11; both died of tuberculosis. One might say that Conrad imbibed anti-Russian feelings with his mother's milk. For the young Conrad, politics was a matter of life and death.

---

[1] *Conversations With Eckermann*, 10/19/1823

[2] Wikipedia > Joseph Conrad. The quotes in this section (section A) and in the following five sections (sections B through F) are from Wikipedia or from Conrad's essay "Autocracy and War," unless otherwise indicated.

One might compare Poland to Korea. As Poland was squeezed between Russia, Austria, and Prussia, and struggled to maintain its independence, so Korea was squeezed between Russia, China, and Japan.

[3] The city was Vologda. A monument to Conrad was erected there in 2013, and taken down in 2016. Perhaps it was erected when Russians were ready to admit their past mistakes, ready to admit their harsh foreign policy, ready to honor a writer who was virulently anti-Russian. Then it was taken down when Russians became more nationalistic, and didn't want to admit past mistakes.

The region where Conrad was born was at a crossroads—an intersection of various peoples and nations. Poles like Conrad's father would say that the region was rightfully Polish, and had been part of the Polish-Lithuanian Commonwealth for 300 years. But many of the people who lived in Berdychiv, where Conrad was born, were Jewish, and many of the people in the countryside were Ukrainian. While Poles tried to expel Russians, Ukrainians might try to expel Poles; Ukrainians might say that the region was Ukrainian before it was Polish.

Beginning in his childhood, Conrad had various physical and mental ailments. His physical ailments were regarded as psycho-somatic—an offshoot of his mental state. As a boy, Conrad enjoyed sea stories, like those written by Frederick Marryat. At 13, Conrad "announced his intention to become a sailor." The young Conrad seemed more at home in the world of his imagination than in the real world. "A playmate of his adolescence recalled that Conrad spun fantastic yarns, always set at sea, presented so realistically that listeners thought the action was happening before their eyes."

After his parents died, Conrad was cared for by his maternal uncle. When Conrad was 15, his uncle sent him to a boarding school in what is now western Ukraine. The owner's daughter later recalled,

> He stayed with us ten months... Intellectually he was extremely advanced but [he] disliked school routine, which he found tiring and dull; he used to say [he] planned to become a great writer.... He disliked all restrictions. At home, at school, or in the living room he would sprawl unceremoniously. [He suffered] from severe headaches and nervous attacks.[1]

At 16, Conrad was sent to Marseilles to join the French merchant marine. At 20, his career stalled after he had a problem with his papers (immigration papers); he fell into debt and attempted suicide "by shooting himself in the chest with a revolver."[2] At 21, he joined the British merchant marine, and remained there until he was 36, working his way up to captain. He interrupted his tenure in the British merchant marine to work briefly for a Belgian ship on the Congo River, an adventure that inspired his novella, *Heart of Darkness*.

At 36, Conrad left the merchant marine because his health was poor, and because he wanted to make his way as a writer. At 38, he published his first novel, *Almayer's Folly*, which was set in Borneo. At 39, he married an Englishwoman, Jessie George. "Jessie was an unsophisticated, working-

---

[1] Genius often has psychological problems, problems that are apparent in childhood. When I discussed Gide, I said "Like Jung, Gide had a childhood neurosis that kept him out of school for long periods." (See my *Realms of Gold* ==> "Literature" ==> "Gide"

[2] Conrad seems to have had gambling losses, too. The Conrad scholar Zdzislaw Najder speaks of Conrad's "youthful casino debacle in Monte Carlo, which ended with an attempted suicide."(*Conrad in Perspective*, Ch. 10)

class girl, sixteen years younger than Conrad. To his friends, she was an inexplicable choice of wife."[1] When I wrote about the psychology of genius, I noted that Goethe and Heine married lower-class women.[2] Conrad and Jessie had two children.

After meeting Conrad and Jessie, Ottoline Morrell wrote, "His manner was perfect, almost too elaborate; so nervous and sympathetic that every fiber of him seemed electric." Morrell described Jessie as "a good and reposeful mattress for this hypersensitive, nerve-wracked man, who did not ask from his wife high intelligence, only an assuagement of life's vibrations." Bertrand Russell described Conrad thus:

> He spoke English with a very strong foreign accent, and nothing in his demeanor in any way suggested the sea. He was an aristocratic Polish gentleman to his fingertips.... At our very first meeting, we talked with continually increasing intimacy. We seemed to sink through layer after layer of what was superficial, till gradually both reached the central fire.... We looked into each other's eyes, half appalled and half intoxicated to find ourselves together in such a region.

Conrad and Russell remained friends until Conrad's death.

At 47, Conrad published *Nostromo*, often called his best novel (F. Scott Fitzgerald said that *Nostromo* was "the great novel of the past fifty years").

According to Wikipedia, Conrad had "a genius for companionship," and he was on friendly terms with many of the writers of his day, including Henry James, André Gide, and Ford Madox Ford. As a teenager in Marseilles, "Conrad had an intensive social life, often stretching his budget." At 31, when he was on the island of Mauritius, Conrad's "excellent French and perfect manners opened all local salons to him."

Though Conrad's early works brought him a reputation in the literary world, popular success eluded him, and he was often short of money. At 56, he finally achieved popular success with the novel *Chance*, "which is often considered one of his weaker novels."

At 66, Conrad died of a heart attack. His grave in Canterbury is inscribed with a quotation from Spenser, a quotation that he had used as an epigraph for his last novel:

Sleep after toil, port after stormy seas,
Ease after war, death after life, doth greatly please.

B. On Russia

Conrad had a deep grasp of politics. For him, the great powers of Europe were like chess-pieces, and he could anticipate, not just the next move, but the move after that. When World War I broke out, Conrad predicted that Poland would gain its independence if the Central Powers (Germany and

---

1 After Conrad died, Jessie wrote several books about him. Conrad's son Borys also wrote a book about him.

2 See ljhammond.com/phlit/2020-10b.htm

Austria) defeated Russia, and then the Allied Powers (France and Britain) defeated the Central Powers.[1]

But no sooner did Poland gain its independence than it had to fight to protect its borders from Ukrainians and from the new Soviet regime in Russia. The borders that were awarded at the conference table would need to be vindicated on the battlefield. In 1920, Conrad's hometown of Berdychiv became part of the reborn Polish state, but it was soon torn away by Ukraine, which became part of the Soviet Union.

In 1905, Conrad wrote an essay on world affairs called "Autocracy and War." The essay begins by discussing an ongoing war, the Russo-Japanese War. The war wasn't going well for Russia, and inside Russia there were uprisings against the Czar's regime, just as, ten years later, World War I didn't go well for Russia, and there were more uprisings against the Czar's regime. Conrad's essay was published in July, 1905, just two months before Russia and Japan signed a peace treaty in Portsmouth, New Hampshire. The war had begun in early 1904; it lasted 18 months, and ended with a Japanese victory.[2]

Conrad at 47

---

[1] Conrad wasn't the only novelist with a deep grasp of politics. In earlier issues, I noted how Graham Greene anticipated how events would unfold in Vietnam (ljhammond.com/phlit/2016-07.htm#6), and E. M. Forster anticipated how events would unfold in India (ljhammond.com/phlit/2008-01b.htm#7).

[2] In earlier issues, I discussed two other essays written shortly before World War I—one by Lewis Namier (ljhammond.com/phlit/2017-10.htm#7), and another by Guglielmo Ferrero (ljhammond.com/phlit/2020-10.htm#2).

around the time he wrote "Autocracy and War"

Conrad describes the Russo-Japanese War as a kind of rehearsal for World War I. He speaks of, "the struggles in Manchuria engaging half a million of men on fronts of sixty miles, struggles lasting for weeks, flaming up fiercely and dying away from sheer exhaustion." Conrad says that, when we read about these faraway battles in the newspaper, they don't trouble us much. But Conrad foresees, with the prophetic gift of genius, that soon there will be battles closer to home:

> We shall have a wealth of appallingly unpleasant sensations brought home to us with painful intimacy, while the apostles of war's sanctity will crawl away swiftly into the holes where they belong, somewhere in the yellow basements of newspaper offices.... War is with us now; and, whether this one ends soon or late, war will be with us again. And it is the way of true wisdom for men and states to take account of things as they are.

Conrad notes that modern war destroys the soul as well as the body:

> In both armies, many men are driven beyond the bounds of sanity by the stress of moral and physical misery. Great numbers of soldiers and regimental officers go mad.

(In an earlier issue, I discussed the English poet Wilfred Owen, one of those whose mind was unhinged by World War I.[1])

In 1905, the war was far away, but Conrad could sense that the atmosphere in Europe was darkening. He describes an early-Victorian "sentimentalist" who looked at the crowds on Fleet Street, and "wept for joy at seeing so much life." But no one would weep for joy at such a sight today, Conrad says. "I should think that now, after eighty years, the emotion would be of a sterner sort."

In the novels of Dickens, tears flow frequently, but Conrad is known for restrained emotion: "He scorned sentimentality; his manner of portraying emotion in his books was full of restraint, skepticism and irony."[2] So Conrad differs from Dickens, who was born about forty years before Conrad. Conrad's restrained emotion reminds one of Hemingway, who was born about forty years after Conrad; Hemingway was a big fan of Conrad, as I noted in an earlier issue.[3]

One might say that our response to a crowd on Fleet Street is an individual matter, not a reflection of the atmosphere of the age. But Conrad points out that the individual is molded by his time, and reflects his time: "The psychology of individuals, even in the most extreme instances, reflects the general effect of the fears and hopes of the time." As the psychologist Erik Erikson put it, "We cannot separate personal growth and communal

---

[1] See ljhammond.com/phlit/2018-11.htm#4

[2] Who was the early-Victorian "sentimentalist"? Was it Dickens? Despite their differences, Conrad seems to have been a fan of Dickens.

[3] See ljhammond.com/phlit/2008-05c.htm#5

change, nor can we separate [the] identity crisis in individual life and contemporary crises in historical development."[1]

We saw above how Conrad's hatred of Russia had been building up for generations. In the essay "Autocracy and War," the dam breaks, the hatred pours forth. I never heard anyone criticize any nation as harshly as Conrad criticizes Russia.

He says that the Czar's regime was born in "an unspeakable baseness of subjection to the Khans of the Tartar Horde." The Czar's regime "has never been sanctioned by popular tradition, by ideas of loyalty, of devotion.... Its only sanction has been the fear of the lash." The Czars are

> mere owners of slaves.... In whatever upheaval Autocratic Russia is to find her end, it can never be a revolution fruitful of moral consequences to mankind. It cannot be anything else but a rising of slaves.... It is safe to say that tyranny, assuming a thousand protean shapes, will remain clinging to [Russia's] struggles for a long time.[2]

In light of the history of Russia in the 20th century, Conrad's criticisms seem justified. The tyranny of the Soviet regime makes Czarist tyranny seem mild and benevolent. Is it surprising that Russia's current government has tyrannical features—murdering journalists on the street, poisoning opposition leaders, etc.?

Conrad describes Russia as

> a bottomless abyss that has swallowed up every hope of mercy, every aspiration towards personal dignity, towards freedom, towards knowledge; every ennobling desire of the heart, every redeeming whisper of conscience....
>
> This despotism has neither a European nor an Oriental parentage.... It is a visitation, like a curse from heaven falling in the darkness of ages upon the human plains of forest and steppe, lying dumbly on the confines of two continents: a true desert harboring no spirit either of the East or of the West. This pitiful fate of a country, held by an evil spell....

---

1 *Youth: Identity and Crisis*, Prologue, #3. If philosophy can change the atmosphere, change the "fears and hopes," then this change will seep into all individuals. A more hopeful philosophy, a more optimistic answer to the ultimate questions, will affect all individuals.

2 One wonders if Conrad's essay was read by George Kennan, who criticized the Czar's regime in books like *Siberia and the Exile System* (1891). Wikipedia calls Kennan "an ardent critic of the Russian autocracy." When the Bolsheviks seized power in 1917, Kennan realized that they would be no better than the Czar's regime, and Kennan wanted Woodrow Wilson to take strong measures against the Bolsheviks. Kennan's younger relative, also named George Kennan, was one of the leading Russia experts of his time.

> From the very first ghastly dawn of her existence as a state, she had to breathe the atmosphere of despotism, she found nothing but the arbitrary will of an obscure Autocrat at the beginning and end of her organization.

Conrad is contemptuous of Russia's performance on the battlefield:

> As a military power, it has never achieved by itself a single great thing.... Even the half-armed were always too much for the might of Russia.... It was victorious only as against the practically disarmed.... In its attacks upon its specially selected victim, this giant always struck as if with a withered right hand.

As for Russia defeating Napoleon, Conrad concedes that Russia was "able to repel an ill-considered invasion, but only by having recourse to the extreme methods of desperation." Forty years after Conrad wrote this, Russia repelled another "ill-considered invasion." Russian patriots will long remember Russia's victories over Napoleon and Hitler.

C. On Dostoyevsky

Did Conrad extend his criticism to Russian writers like Dostoyevsky and Tolstoy? Conrad says that "the poison of slavery drugged the national temperament into the apathy of a hopeless fatalism. It seems to have gone into the blood, tainting every mental activity in its source by a half-mystical, insensate, fascinating assertion of purity and holiness." This half-mystical assertion of holiness is what one finds in Dostoyevsky and Tolstoy.

Conrad took a dim view of Dostoyevsky: "The detested Dostoyevsky," one Conrad scholar writes, "was for Conrad practically identified with Russianness." "He is too Russian for me," Conrad wrote of Dostoyevsky, "it sounds to me like some fierce mouthings from prehistoric ages." Dostoyevsky's political views may have contributed to Conrad's animosity; "of Poles and their national aspirations [Dostoyevsky] was openly contemptuous."[1]

And there was a philosophical difference between Dostoyevsky and Conrad. "For Dostoyevsky, God was necessary for the existence of a moral order." On the other hand, Conrad was an agnostic who found Christianity "distasteful." Conrad "believed that moral norms are man-made, shaped and passed on by tradition.... His ethical dramas were played out in the categories of duty, fidelity and honor." While Dostoyevsky and Tolstoy remain within the "gravitational field" of Christianity, Conrad subscribes to a non-Christian morality; this may be one reason why Conrad was idolized by later writers like Hemingway and Fitzgerald.[2]

---

[1] The quotes in this paragraph, and the next three paragraphs (ending with "the cool, controlled Flaubert"), are from Najder's *Conrad in Perspective*, Ch. 10, "Conrad, Russia and Dostoyevsky."

[2] Perhaps we should compare Conrad to Kipling, who was born in 1865, eight years after Conrad. Like Conrad, Kipling advocated a morality of duty and stoicism, the sort of morality that you might find in an army, or on a

And finally, there was an aesthetic difference between Dostoyevsky and Conrad. Dostoyevsky was "verbose, disorderly in construction of his stories, wallowing in exhibitionist introspection." Conrad, on the other hand, "declares his repugnance at the 'open display of sentiment' and preaches restraint."

Conrad was more respectful toward Tolstoy, but it was a moderate respect. Conrad criticized Tolstoy's "anti-sensualism," and he criticized the "monstrous stupidity" of Tolstoy's *Kreutzer Sonata.* Conrad's favorite Russian writer was the mellow Ivan Turgenev. In general, Conrad preferred French writers to Russian writers, and his favorite French writer was Flaubert—the cool, controlled Flaubert.

When I discussed the fiction of Mark Twain, I said that his characters and incidents were usually based on real characters and real incidents.[1] Conrad also drew on real characters and real incidents; he often named characters after people he knew. He would have agreed with Twain's remark,

> If you attempt to create a wholly imagined incident, adventure or situation, you will go astray and the artificiality will be detectable, but if you found on fact in your personal experience, it is an acorn, a root, and every created adornment that grows out of it... will seem reality, not invention.

D. On Germany

Conrad says that Europeans don't realize "the worth and force of the inner life," and don't realize that "even in the greatest darkness there is nothing that we need fear." So they want to assert themselves by physical activity. "'Let us act lest we perish' is the cry."

European nations long to "grow in territory, in strength, in wealth, in influence—in anything but wisdom and self-knowledge." And so they turn to war to satisfy their longing for action and growth. "Never before has war received so much homage at the lips of men, never has it reigned with less undisputed sway in their minds." The apostles of war preach "the gospel of the mystic sanctity of its sacrifices."

Conrad looks back nostalgically on the old monarchies; he speaks of, "the regard paid to certain forms of conventional decency." But now Europe has no such regard for decency, no principle capable of restraining ambition, greed, and national aspirations. Conrad says prophetically, Beware Germany:

> It is a powerful and voracious organism, full of unscrupulous self-confidence, whose appetite for aggrandizement will only be limited by the power of helping itself to the severed members of its friends and neighbors. The era of wars, so eloquently denounced by the old republicans as the peculiar blood-guilt of dynastic ambitions, is by no means over yet.

---

ship. Like Conrad, Kipling is known for writing about foreign climes, not life in England.

1 ljhammond.com/phlit/2007-12.htm#9

Conrad says that the Franco-Prussian War of 1870 was characterized by "a special intensity of hate." Bismarck wanted "to see men, women and children—emphatically the children, too—of the abominable French nation massacred off the face of the earth."

E. Pessimism

Nietzsche called himself an immoralist, and he felt that civilization advanced, not by grand moral ideals, but by the conquests of the powerful. Nietzsche admired conquerors like Caesar and Napoleon. Conrad, on the other hand, put his faith in moral ideals, and felt that Napoleon had done great harm. Conrad speaks of, "the solidarity of Europeanism which must be the next step towards the advent of Concord and Justice; an advent that has been and remains the only possible goal of our progress." But Conrad saw little chance of this goal being reached.

Conrad is pessimistic, perhaps because he lived in a dark time, perhaps because of personal factors—his tendency toward depression, the early deaths of his parents, the plight of his homeland, etc. He sometimes embraces "a sort of blanket incredulity... the negation of all faith, devotion, and action."[1] He compared the universe to a machine:

> The most withering thought is that the infamous thing has made itself; made itself without thought, without conscience, without foresight, without eyes, without heart. It is a tragic accident... you can't even smash it.... It knits us in and it knits us out. It has knitted time, space, pain, death, corruption, despair and all the illusions—and nothing matters.

This passage shows how, when people lost their faith in God, it was difficult to take an upbeat view of the world. This passage also shows how a mechanical view of the world can lead to pessimism, hence an organic view of the world is man's best hope.

In a letter to a friend, Conrad wrote, "In this world—as I have known it—we are made to suffer without the shadow of a reason, of a cause or of guilt.... There is no morality, no knowledge and no hope." Conrad takes a bleak view of the end of the world: "A moment, a twinkling of an eye and nothing remains—but a clod of mud, of cold mud, of dead mud cast into black space, rolling around an extinguished sun. Nothing. Neither thought, nor sound, nor soul. Nothing." (In an earlier issue, I took a more upbeat view of the end of the world.[2]) Conrad's pessimism is evident in his fiction: "In keeping with his skepticism and melancholy, Conrad almost invariably gives lethal fates to the characters in his principal novels and stories."

In the passage I quoted earlier, Conrad spoke of, "the solidarity of Europeanism." Both Conrad and Nietzsche wanted to see Europe become more

---

1 Will a future novelist, who isn't burdened by this pessimistic worldview, achieve more than Conrad?

2 ljhammond.com/phlit/2016-06.htm

united.[1] Conrad felt that, after the Napoleonic Wars, Europe seemed to be coming together; he speaks of, "The idea of a Europe united in the solidarity of her dynasties, which for a moment seemed to dawn on the horizon of the Vienna Congress."

But this hope has been dashed by the rise of an aggressive, ruthless Prussia. Quoting a "distinguished statesman of the old tradition," Conrad writes, "'*Il n'y a plus d'Europe!*' There is, indeed, no Europe.... There is only an armed and trading continent, the home of slowly maturing economical contests for life and death." Conrad concludes his essay thus: "So far as a future of liberty, concord and justice is concerned, '*Le Prussianisme—voilà l'ennemi!*'"[2]

F. Further Reading

If you want to learn more about Conrad, Zdzislaw Najder wrote *Joseph Conrad: A Life* (revised edition 2007), Frederick Karl wrote *Joseph Conrad: The Three Lives*, and Albert Guerard wrote a critical study of Conrad called *Conrad the Novelist*. Robert Hampson has edited several Conrad volumes, and his biography (*Joseph Conrad*) has been called "the best short guide to Conrad's life." Conrad wrote two autobiographical works, *The Mirror of the Sea*, and *A Personal Record* (also known as *Some Reminiscences*).

There are several Conrad associations, and they each have a website; the American association is at josephconrad.org, the British at josephconradsociety.org.

---

1 One of Conrad's friends, the Pole Jozef Retinger, was the co-founder of the European Movement, a precursor of the European Union. Retinger wrote a book called *Conrad and His Contemporaries*.

2 Conrad speaks of, "the envious acquisitive temperament of the last comer amongst the great Powers of the Continent [i.e., Germany], whose feet are not exactly in the ocean—not yet, whose head is very high up." This implies German hubris ("whose head is very high up"). Does hubris lead to destruction? Doesn't the Bible say, "Pride goeth before a fall"? Conrad doesn't predict Germany's defeat, but it probably wouldn't surprise him.

While Nietzsche and Dostoyevsky foresaw genocide, Conrad probably didn't. And Conrad didn't foresee that Japan might be as aggressive as Germany; he praises Japan for defeating Russia, for performing "an important mission in the world's struggle against all forms of evil." Conrad didn't realize that Japan itself was a form of evil. And Conrad felt that nothing could be worse than the Czar's regime, he didn't suspect that Stalin and Hitler would be far worse.

Now that Germany has been defeated, and Europe has grown weary of war, the idea of European unity has again come to the fore. But there's still no principle capable of restraining ambition and national aspirations, there are still rogue nations (Russia, China, Iran, etc.) that seem intent on disturbing the peace, as Germany and Japan once did.

G. *The Nigger of the "Narcissus"*

December 20, 2003
A couple months ago, our book group read a short novel by Joseph Conrad, *The Nigger of the "Narcissus"*. I was struck by the similarity between Conrad and Nietzsche. Both were aristocrats who were inclined to despise the lower class. Conrad's lower-class character, Donkin, is portrayed in an entirely negative way. Conrad insinuates that Donkin was an illegitimate child, calling him "the independent offspring of the ignoble freedom of the slums."[1] Conrad says that the forecastle

> was his refuge; the place where he could be lazy; where he could wallow, and lie and eat—and curse the food he ate; where he could display his talents for shirking work, for cheating, for cadging; where he could find surely someone to wheedle and someone to bully.

Conrad says that every Donkin the world over is "the pet of philanthropists." Nietzsche shared Conrad's dim view of compassion and philanthropy. It would be difficult to find a character anywhere in literature for whom the author has more loathing than Conrad has for Donkin.

The ship that Conrad describes is a little aristocracy, in which the few govern the many. The captain and his two mates are portrayed in a positive way. Some of the old salts among the crew are portrayed as quiet heroes, obedient sailors, while others (like Donkin) are engaged in what Nietzsche would call a "slave revolt" against the rulers of the ship. Since Conrad himself was, at various times, a captain, and a captain's mate, it isn't surprising that his sympathies are with the rulers, not the rebels.

We read *The Nigger of the "Narcissus"* in the Norton Critical Edition. One of the essays in this edition is a personal reminiscence by Edward Garnett, Conrad's literary agent.

> I first met Conrad [Garnett writes] in November 1894.... My memory is of seeing a dark-haired man, short but extremely graceful in his nervous gestures, with brilliant eyes, now narrowed and penetrating, now soft and warm, with a manner alert yet caressing.... I had never seen before a man so masculinely keen yet so femininely sensitive.

Genius is often hermaphroditic—masculine and feminine.

H. The Secret Sharer

"The Secret Sharer" is about a sea captain who shelters a wanted man, and helps him escape. (A common figure in Conrad's work is the stranger, the outcast, the quasi-criminal.) According to the Jungian view, the wanted man is the captain's shadow, the captain's dark side. And indeed, Conrad often refers to the wanted man as the captain's "shadow", or "double," or "reflection."

At the beginning of the story, the captain admits to being young and inexperienced: "I was somewhat of a stranger to myself." By the end of the

[1] ch. 1, p. 6 (of the Norton Critical Edition)

story, however, the captain has become wiser, perhaps because he has encountered his own shadow. According to a Jungian essay,

> Not infrequently consciousness of the shadow side of our own personality is forced upon us when life presents us with some new demand for which we do not feel ourselves entirely adequate. If the new task needs a bigger man than we are, obviously other parts of the psyche beyond the conscious ego will have to be called on to fill out the need. This was the case with the hero of Conrad's story, "The Secret Sharer." There a young man who had so far only acted as first officer was called upon to take over command of a strange ship whose crew were quite unknown and who were rather suspicious of him as a newcomer.[1]

A man who committed a crime on a different ship takes refuge on the young captain's ship. Since the wanted man is a reflection or shadow of the captain, he resembles the captain in innumerable ways. Both he and the captain are, like Conrad himself, from the upper class of society. This created some tension on the wanted man's original ship, the Sephora. Conrad himself was a gentleman who doubtless felt somewhat out-of-place on many ships.

Before he fled the Sephora, the wanted man had killed a seaman, perhaps accidentally. But he had also saved the ship in a time of danger. Conrad describes his action thus: "The same strung-up force which had given twenty-four men a chance, at least, for their lives, had, in a sort of recoil, crushed an unworthy mutinous existence." The phrase "unworthy mutinous existence" reminds me of the contempt that Conrad pours on Donkin in *The Nigger of the Narcissus*. Surely Conrad was no stranger to contempt and hatred, and perhaps no stranger to homicidal impulses.

When the captain speaks of his inner struggles, one suspects that Conrad experienced similar struggles. The captain says, "I think I had come creeping quietly as near insanity as any man who has not actually gone over the border." Such inner struggles provided Conrad with the material for great introspective literature.

Because the captain is divided within, he lacks wholeness and harmony, and thus he lacks spontaneity. This affects his performance as captain:

> There are to a seaman certain words, gestures, that should in given conditions come as naturally, as instinctively as the winking of a menaced eye. A certain order should spring on to his lips without thinking; a certain sign should get itself made, so to speak, without reflection. But all unconscious alertness had abandoned me. I had to make an effort of will to recall myself back (from the cabin) to the conditions of the moment. I felt that I was appearing an irresolute commander to those people who were watching me more or less critically.

---

[1] "The Shadow," by Esther M. Harding, *Spring: A Journal of Archetype and Culture*, 1945. Though this essay doesn't discuss "The Secret Sharer" in detail, it's a good general treatment of The Shadow, and could serve as an introduction to this important Jungian concept.

I. *Heart of Darkness*

Our book group recently discussed Conrad's famous novella, *Heart of Darkness*. It's a profound work, and highly respected, but not as clear, readable, and popular as Conrad's other famous novella, *The Secret Sharer*. I enjoyed *Heart of Darkness*, but I enjoyed the essays on it even more. There are many fine essays on it—essays that bring out the Jungian significance, the mythical significance, etc.[1]

One of the most interesting essays on *Heart of Darkness* is an unpublished essay that I found on the Internet; it's a Jungian interpretation by Colleen Burke. As I read this essay, I was surprised at how many parallels there were between Conrad's novella and Jung's theories, and I was also surprised that I didn't notice these parallels when I read the novella.

Heart of Darkness is narrated by a sea-captain, Marlow, who travels upriver into the interior of Africa, where he meets Kurtz. Kurtz was once gifted

---

[1] I recommend the following essays:

- "The Journey Within," by Albert J. Guerard, in the volume *Conrad the Novelist*; a classic essay by the dean of Conrad critics; good general study; takes a psychological approach, but doesn't adhere to a particular school of psychology
- "Myth and Archetype in Heart of Darkness," by James Mellard; views Conrad's story from the perspective of mythology—more specifically, Joseph Campbell's theory of mythology; also makes use of the critical theories of Northrop Frye; *Tennessee Studies in Literature*, 13 (1968): pp. 1-15
- "Marlow's Quest," by Jerome Thale; views Marlow's journey as a Grail quest, a quest for the self and for freedom; *University of Toronto Quarterly*, XXIV (July, 1955), pp. 351-358
- "The Narrator As Hero," by Jerome Thale; compares Conrad's story to *The Great Gatsby*; argues that the heroes of the two stories are the narrators, Marlow and Nick Carraway; Marlow and Nick achieve self-knowledge and personal growth by observing other characters, Kurtz and Gatsby; Kurtz and Gatsby are initially impressive, then they're perceived in a negative way, but finally they're vindicated, and the narrators come back to their original positive view of Kurtz and Gatsby; *Twentieth-Century Literature*, III (July, 1957), pp. 69-73
- "The Journey to Hell: Satan, The Shadow, and The Self," by Charlotte K. Spivack; focuses on Dante's journey to hell; views Dante from a Jungian perspective; includes brief discussions of other "journeys to hell", such as *Heart of Darkness*, Hesse's *Steppenwulf*, Golding's *Lord of the Flies*, and two works by Dostoyevsky; *Centennial Review*, 9:4 (1965): pp. 420-437
- "Conrad's Heart of Darkness: An Aspect of the Shadow," by Dorsha Hayes; a Jungian study; argues that Kurtz is not only a personal shadow but a collective shadow, the shadow of European civilization; *Spring: A Journal of Archetype and Culture* (Spring, 1956, pp. 43-47)

and high-minded, but he has become savage and tyrannical. "Marlow encounters his double," Burke writes, "in the powerful image of ivory-obsessed Kurtz, the dark shadow of European imperialism."[1] In imaginative literature, one personality is often split into two characters; one character is the shadow of the other, or the "double" of the other. Kurtz is Marlow's shadow or double. Kurtz indulges the savage desires that civilized man represses. At the end of the novella, however, when Kurtz is on his deathbed, he has a moment of enlightenment, or at least reflection, and he says, "The Horror! The Horror!"

Conrad refers to Kurtz as a "shadow," sometimes even capitalizing the S; Conrad uses the word "shadow" just as Jung uses it. Burke writes thus:

> When the pilgrims first carry Kurtz on a stretcher out of his cabin, Marlow describes Kurtz, observing, "This shadow looked satiated and calm." When Marlow later discovers Kurtz missing from his steamer cabin and determines to find and capture him on shore, he comments, "I was anxious to deal with this shadow by myself alone." Overtaking the escaping Kurtz crawling in the bush, Marlow comments, "This clearly was not a case for fisticuffs, even apart from the very natural aversion I had to beat that Shadow—this wandering and tormented thing."

Confronting one's shadow is an important part of personal growth. Jung described the shadow as "the negative side of the personality, the sum of all those unpleasant qualities we like to hide."[2] If one doesn't acknowledge one's shadow, one projects it on the outside world; "where the shadow is not recognized it is projected."[3] "The effect of projection," Jung wrote, "is to isolate the subject from his environment.... Projections change the world into the replica of one's own unknown face." Jung speaks of a "feeling of sterility" that is "explained by projection as the malevolence of the environment."[4]

Jung used the term "individuation" to refer to personal growth, becoming oneself, finding one's center. Confronting one's shadow is part of the journey of individuation. "*Heart of Darkness*," Burke writes, "holds three journeys of individuation: those of Marlow, of Kurtz—and of Conrad himself." Conrad's own experience on the Congo River resembles Marlow's in many ways, and Conrad's river journey was a turning-point in his life; "before the Congo," Conrad said, "I was just a mere animal." While he was in Africa, Conrad became seriously ill, and was close to death—an experience that probably contributed to his personal growth.

Not only does Conrad use the word "shadow" in a Jungian sense, he also uses the word "soul" in a Jungian sense. Jung uses the word "anima" to refer to a man's female soul (just as he uses the word "animus" to refer to a woman's male mind). Of course, Jung was aware that "anima" is the Latin

---

1 "Joseph Conrad's *Heart of Darkness*: A Metaphor of Jungian Psychology"

2 Quoted in the Burke essay

3 Quoted in the Hayes essay

4 Quoted in the Hayes essay

word for soul, and that the gender of anima is feminine. While Kurtz represents the shadow, two characters represent the anima: Kurtz's African mistress, and his European mistress. The word "soul" is used of the African mistress (just as the word "shadow" is used of Kurtz). Here is Conrad's description of the African mistress:

> She was savage and superb, wild-eyed and magnificent; there was something ominous and stately in her deliberate progress. And in the hush that had fallen suddenly upon the whole sorrowful land, the immense wilderness, the colossal body of the fecund and mysterious life seemed to look at her, pensive, as though it had been looking at the image of its own tenebrous and passionate soul.

Again, I'm amazed at how Conrad and Jung are following the same path—using the same language, the same images—independently of each other. Kurtz's European mistress (also known as his Intended) uses the same gestures as his African mistress, and when Marlow meets this European mistress, he's struck by her resemblance to the African mistress. Just as meeting one's shadow can be considered part of the process of individuation, so too meeting one's anima (if one is a man) can be considered part of the process of individuation.

On the surface, it may seem that Kurtz is "the bad guy" in *Heart of Darkness*. But Kurtz has redeeming features, and he's compared favorably to the other Europeans who work in the ivory trade. After Marlow talks to one of these traders, he says, "It seemed to me I had never breathed an atmosphere so vile, and I turned mentally to Kurtz for relief—positively for relief." Marlow tells the trader, "I think Mr. Kurtz is a remarkable man."

Kurtz follows his nature, he acts freely and decisively. The vile traders, on the other hand, follow rules, principles, methods, judgment; they act from their mind, not their soul. One trader says to Marlow,

> "There is no disguising the fact, Mr. Kurtz has done more harm than good to the Company. He did not see the time was not ripe for vigorous action. Cautiously, cautiously—that's my principle. We must be cautious yet.... Look how precarious the position is—and why? Because the method is unsound." "Do you," said I, looking at the shore, "call it 'unsound method?'" "Without doubt," he exclaimed hotly. "Don't you?" "...No method at all," I murmured after a while. "Exactly," he exulted. "I anticipated this. Shows a complete want of judgment. It is my duty to point it out in the proper quarter".... It seemed to me I had never breathed an atmosphere so vile.

Marlow has a certain respect for the natives, who represent "truth," who have a "terrible frankness." This truth and frankness are a challenge to the Europeans. Conrad says, "He must at least be as much of a man as these on the shore. He must meet that truth with his own true stuff—with his own inborn strength. Principles won't do." The traders follow rules, methods, principles, but Conrad scorns principles. Conrad respects those who follow their nature—like Kurtz and the natives.

It should be noted that Conrad isn't alone in scorning principle. Jung, too, tried to act out of his whole nature, out of his center, rather than following principles. His disciples could never predict how he would respond to a situation, because he didn't follow general principles, he followed his feelings, intuitions, hunches. Zen, too, has no use for principles.[1]

Luther said "sin boldly [*pecca fortiter*]." And this is Kurtz's strength, this is why Kurtz stands above the ivory traders, with their small virtues and small vices: Kurtz sinned boldly. "Sooner murder an infant in its cradle," wrote Blake, "than nurse unacted desires." Kurtz didn't nurse unacted desires, he acted his desires. Kierkegaard wrote,

> Let others complain that the age is wicked; my complaint is that it is paltry; for it lacks passion.... The thoughts of their hearts are too paltry to be sinful.... [One thinks of Conrad's ivory traders.] My soul always turns back to the Old Testament and to Shakespeare. I feel that those who speak there are at least human beings: they hate, they love, they murder their enemies, and curse their descendants throughout all generations, they sin.[2]

Kierkegaard would have understood Marlow's admiration for Kurtz. Kurtz sinned, he sinned boldly.

One Conrad commentator, Jerome Thale, says that "in the depths of Africa Kurtz is not hampered by outside restraint.... Away from the grooves that society provides for keeping us safely in a state of subsisting, we can discover that we are free to be, to do anything, good or evil." Thale speaks of Kurtz's "radical freedom" and Kurtz's "acceptance of his freedom."

> Kurtz commits himself totally to evil, the manager keeps up appearances. Kurtz throws himself into action, though evil; the manager, ruled by caution, murmurs, and does evil by omission.... [Kurtz's] choice is for evil, but it is a human choice—and it is to this humanity that Marlow turns with positive relief, even though it is a nightmare.

If Kurtz lacked restraint, others have too much restraint—they never do what they want. Joseph Campbell's favorite maxim was "follow your bliss." He loved to tell of the man he overheard in a restaurant: the man reproached his son for something, his wife said, "let him do what he wants," and the man said, "I never did a thing I wanted to do in my whole life." Perhaps there are slaves of virtue, as well as slaves of vice.

Zen speaks much of freedom, but is silent about virtue and vice. Zen is restraint, meditation is restraint—sitting still with back straight. But through this self-imposed restraint, Zen sharpens the feeling of freedom. Zen is a union of freedom and restraint. In *Heart of Darkness*, restraint is symbolized by the cannibals who endure hunger stoically while traveling up-river; restraint is also symbolized by the seaman who writes a manual on marine

---

[1] For more on this subject, see the section "Beyond Ethics" in the Ethics chapter of my *Conversations With Great Thinkers*.

[2] *Either/Or*, Part I, "Diapsalmata"

matters, a manual that shows "simple-hearted devotion to the right way of doing things."[1]

One of the most interesting essays on *Heart of Darkness* is "Myth and Archetype in *Heart of Darkness*," by James Mellard. It compares Conrad's novella to myths, using Joseph Campbell's theory of myth. Just as Burke's essay could serve as an introduction to Jungian psychology, so Mellard's essay could serve as an introduction to Campbell's theory of myth.

Mellard was influenced not only by Campbell, but also by the famous Canadian critic, Northrop Frye. Frye argued that literature is based on archetypes. Frye's best-known work is *The Anatomy of Criticism*. Frye attained such prominence that he appeared on a postage stamp—a rare distinction for a literary critic.

Mellard says that *Heart of Darkness*

> contains at least twelve of the twenty-four possibilities Campbell lists on his graph for the "adventure of the hero." Including, of course, the basic threefold plan of separation, initiation, and return, *Heart of Darkness* shows these elements: the call to adventure, the threshold crossing with the aid of helpers, the night-sea journey or wonder journey, underworld tests and helpers, father atonement, the elixir theft, flight, and threshold struggle, resurrection, and return with the possibility of granting the elixir.

Mellard says that the elixir in Conrad's story is the "bundle of papers" that Kurtz gave to Marlow, and that Marlow brings with him when he returns to the "upper world." Mellard describes Marlow as a "savior or redeemer" who replaces Kurtz. Kurtz was once a redeemer himself, but he has aged and weakened and become a "tyrant ogre." So Marlow and Kurtz are both redeemers—Marlow is ascending, Kurtz descending. The youthful redeemer replaces the aged tyrant. This is a common motif in mythology: "inertia, dissolution, age, death, are followed by vitality... renewed youth and life." As Campbell put it, "a regular alternation of fair and foul is characteristic of the spectacle of time." The golden age alternates with the wasteland. (A similar alternation can be found in my theory of history.)

Although Marlow replaces Kurtz, *Heart of Darkness* doesn't end on a positive note, and doesn't emphasize "renewed youth and life." On the contrary, *Heart of Darkness* ends on a negative note, and emphasizes "the downward movement of the cycle." Thus, Conrad probably belongs among the many modern writers who are gloomy and pessimistic.

---

[1] "Marlow's Quest," by Jerome Thale, *University of Toronto Quarterly*, XXIV (July, 1955), pp. 351-358

56. Arthur Conan Doyle

I knew that Arthur Conan Doyle had a keen interest in the occult, so when I read some of his Sherlock Holmes stories, I was surprised to find that he emphasized Holmes' reasoning powers, rather than any psychic (or occult) powers. I gradually realized, though, that Doyle emphasizes intuition as much as reasoning. He often describes his hero reclining on a couch, his head wreathed in smoke—the picture of relaxation. Holmes unravels mysteries by relaxing; relaxation allows the unconscious to speak, allows the intuition to speak. I'm reminded of *Zen in the Art of Archery*, in which the archer relaxes with a cup of tea before drawing his bow.[1]

Certain passages in Doyle's stories explicitly refer to occult matters. For example, a story called "The Man With The Twisted Lip" describes a missing husband; when Holmes tells the distraught wife that her husband may have been murdered, she replies,

> I know that all is well with him. There is so keen a sympathy between us that I should know if evil came upon him. On the very day that I saw him last he cut himself in the bedroom, and yet I in the dining-room rushed upstairs instantly with the utmost certainty that something had happened. Do you think that I would respond to such a trifle, and yet be ignorant of his death?

The woman trusts her intuition, her telepathic power, and this trust proves to be well-founded—her husband is indeed alive.

The Sherlock Holmes stories are, in my view, well-written, intelligent, and thoughtful, but they fall short of first-rate literature. Arthur Conan Doyle also wrote several novels featuring a character named Professor Challenger. The most popular of the Challenger novels is *The Lost World*, which inspired a host of LostWorld novels. Another Challenger novel, *The Land of Mist*, deals with the occult. Doyle also wrote historical novels, such as *The White Company*, which is set during the Hundred Years War. According to Wikipedia, *The White Company*

> is relatively unknown today, though it was very popular up through the Second World War. In fact, Doyle himself regarded this and his other historical novels more highly than the Sherlock Holmes adventures for which he is mainly remembered.

---

[1] Maria Konnikova has written a book called *Mastermind: How to Think Like Sherlock Holmes*. She notes that Holmes' approach involves relaxing, "'throwing his brain out of action,' as Dr. Watson puts it." "More often than not, when a new case is presented, Holmes does nothing more than sit back in his leather chair, close his eyes and put together his long-fingered hands in an attitude that begs silence. He may be the most inactive active detective out there." Konnikova notes that Holmes' approach is related to meditation, to mindfulness; meditation also 'throws the brain out of action.'

57. Mysteries

A. *Murder on the Orient Express*

I read Agatha Christie's *Murder on the Orient Express*. It's easy to see why such books are popular; *Orient Express* is concise, clear, readable. It grabs your attention on the first page, and holds your attention to the last page; you want to learn the solution to the puzzle, you want to know who did it. There are no wasted words, no flowery language, no digressions; as they say in politics, Christie "stays on message." Every page is a pleasure, an effortless pleasure. The author uses an astonishing amount of cleverness, reasoning; one might compare the author to a chess player. Christie gives us very little Christie, she reveals very little about herself; her writing is objective, not subjective.

Since Christie's work is so concise, it's suitable for reading aloud, and since it's so clear, it's suitable for young readers, and for foreigners who are trying to learn English. It could persuade youngsters that reading is pleasurable.

Christie's writing has dignity, courtesy, taste. She doesn't use the vulgar device, popular in Hollywood, of ridiculing the nobility. Her detective, Poirot, puts faith in Count Andrenyi's "word of honor," and this faith proves justified.

While the strengths of such novels are obvious, so are the weaknesses. The characters aren't three-dimensional and life-like, the story is utterly unrealistic. There are no deep feelings or thoughts; the reader is neither moved nor enlightened, merely entertained. The author doesn't create a world; she merely creates a puzzle. Edmund Wilson criticized this genre in his essay "Who Cares Who Killed Roger Ackroyd?" while Jacques Barzun defended it in *The Delights of Detection*.

Christie's detective-hero, Hercule Poirot, is Belgian, and he seems to use intuitions and feelings more than an Englishman would. As Poirot says to Mary Debenham, "An English inquiry.... would be cut and dried—it would all be kept to the facts—a well-ordered business."

Orient Express was published in 1934, and is based on the Lindbergh kidnapping, which occurred in 1932. When Christie wrote *Orient Express*, she was married to an archeologist who was working in the Middle East. When she visited him in 1931, she travelled via the Orient Express, and her train was forced to stop because of bad weather; this incident influenced her novel, in which the train is stopped by heavy snow. Christie's time in the Middle East influenced her 1936 novel, *Murder in Mesopotamia*.

The 1974 film version of *Orient Express* is one of the most popular film adaptations of Christie's works.

Christie began her career with *The Mysterious Affair at Styles* (1920). Her early work was influenced by the Sherlock Holmes stories, as those stories were influenced by Poe's "Murders in the Rue Morgue."

B. Chesterton

I read a detective story called "The Bottomless Well," by G. K. Chesterton. It was published in 1922 in a volume of stories called *The Man Who Knew Too Much*. But I didn't find it in that volume, I found it in a volume called *The Delights of Detection*, an anthology of detective stories edited by Jacques Barzun.

I enjoyed "The Bottomless Well." It starts slowly, but then becomes engrossing. You learn something about the British Empire in the early 1900's. I view Agatha Christie's detective fiction as purely a game, but Chesterton seems to use fiction as a vehicle for his ideas on politics, religion, etc. Chesterton's prose isn't as simple and straightforward as Christie's, so Chesterton may not be suitable for reading aloud or for young readers. Chesterton was slightly older than Christie, and his prose is more ornate, more 19th-century, than Christie's.

The story takes a dim view of the British Empire. Chesterton was a "Little Englander," that is, he thought that England should "stay home," and avoid foreign entanglements. There's a strong anti-Semitic element in the story: Chesterton blames the Jews for pushing England to defend their own far-flung business interests. One of his characters says,

> It's bad enough that a gang of infernal Jews should plant us here, where there's no earthly English interest to serve, and all hell beating up against us, simply because Nosey Zimmern has lent money to half the Cabinet. It's bad enough that an old pawnbroker from Baghdad should make us fight his battles....

Earlier the same character said that "the Zimmernes" wanted to extend British authority "as far as the canal... though everybody knows adding provinces doesn't always pay much nowadays." The tacit assumption is that "the Zimmernes" have invested in "the canal," and want England to defend it.

This anti-Semitic element was probably so well-known in Chesterton, and in that whole generation, that Barzun scarcely noticed it when choosing stories for his anthology. In an earlier issue, we discussed anti-Semitism in D. H. Lawrence. Wikipedia notes an anti-Semitic element in Hemingway's *The Sun Also Rises*.

Chesterton also expresses his religious views (he was a steadfast Christian). He suggests that God has influenced the action of the story, in accordance with justice. Speaking of a revolving bookcase, he says

> [Boyle] barely touched the thing, and it went round as easily as the world goes round. Yes, very much as the world goes round, for the hand that turned it was not his. God, who turns the wheel of all the stars, touched that wheel and brought it full circle, that His dreadful justice might return.

The story suggests that Chesterton was not blind to the occult dimension. At the first hint of trouble, one of the characters suspects foul play; the character is described as "a person of a curious and almost transcendental sensibility to atmospheres, and he already felt the presence of something more than an accident."[1]

C. Dorothy Sayers

After the Chesterton story, I read another story from the Barzun anthology, "The Professor's Manuscript" by Dorothy Sayers. It has a scholarly setting, like several Sayers works. Unlike Agatha Christie, who was home-schooled, Sayers was university-educated. Sayers' father was a rector, and that was also an influence on her work. One of her best-known novels, *The Nine Tailors*, describes an old church in detail.

Like Christie, Sayers is considered a representative of "the golden age of detective fiction." Many Sayers novels feature a detective named Lord Peter Wimsey. In addition to fiction, Sayers wrote plays, poetry, essays, etc.; she was especially proud of her Dante translation (she also translated *The Song of Roland*). She was a friend of C. S. Lewis, and like Lewis, she wrote books about Christianity. Sayers also wrote a series of plays about the life of Jesus; the series is called *The Man Born to be King*. Lewis said that he read the series every Easter. Like Christie, Sayers has been accused of anti-Semitism.

D. Raymond Chandler

I recently read Raymond Chandler's *The Big Sleep*. The plot is somewhat confusing, and the novel has a sordid atmosphere, but on the whole, I enjoyed it. There were times when I felt, like one of Chandler's characters, that "The smart thing for me to do was to take another drink and forget the whole mess," but the ending is good, and there are many good critical essays on the novel. As you've heard me say before, the essays were more interesting than the novel itself—you should read the novel in order to understand the essays.

Chandler can't be dismissed lightly. Writers like Somerset Maugham and Evelyn Waugh had a high opinion of Chandler, and even called him the best American novelist of his time. Chandler's protagonist, the detective Philip Marlowe, deals with various moral questions; *The Big Sleep* has been praised by business schools as offering a model of professional ethics. Chandler still has fans today, and I've received e-mails telling me that I should try him. Many academics are interested in Chandler.

Chandler was a successor of Dashiell Hammett, for whom he had high praise, and Chandler inspired younger mystery writers like Robert B. Parker. (While Chandler's work is often set in Los Angeles, Parker's is often set in

---

[1] Elsewhere in *The Man Who Knew Too Much*, we find this comment about atmosphere: "Do you know, I was half expecting something like that.... It was quite irrational, but it was hanging about in the atmosphere, like thunder in the air."

Boston.) Chandler and Hammett are the chief representatives of the hard-boiled school of detective fiction.[1]

The hard-boiled school is a sharp departure from the English school of Agatha Christie, Dorothy Sayers, etc. The English school depicts a peaceful, orderly world, often a country house, and a lone criminal who disrupts this Eden. The clever detective unravels the mystery with no risk to himself, exposes the criminal, and restores peace.

A Chandler novel, on the other hand, is usually set in a messy urban environment, an environment that has "a smell of fear"; evil spreads its tentacles far and wide, and can never be entirely eradicated. The detective confronts evil at the risk of life and limb. Chandler was a harsh critic of the English school, and wrote an essay called "The Simple Art of Murder," describing the differences between the English school and the hard-boiled school.[2]

Chandler regarded Hammett as part of a broader movement, a movement in modern fiction as a whole, a movement toward gritty realism and colloquial language, a movement exemplified by Hemingway, Dreiser, etc. The English school was satisfied to create an entertaining puzzle, Chandler had vaster ambitions. Dorothy Sayers had said, "The detective story does not, and by hypothesis never can, attain the loftiest level of literary achievement." Chandler responded, "[Hammett] demonstrated that the detective story can be important writing. *The Maltese Falcon* may or may not be a work of genius, but an art which is capable of it is not 'by hypothesis' incapable of anything. Once a detective story can be as good as this, only the pedants will deny that it could be even better." Of course, Chandler aspired to make it "even better."

Just as Chandler was scornful of the English school of mystery, so too he was scornful of literary writers with literary ambitions. His own work was somewhere between the popular and the serious; he aspired to the popularity of Christie, and he also aspired to the realism of Dreiser. After observing how popular mysteries are, Chandler wrote

> This is very annoying to people of what is called discernment. They do not like it that penetrating and important works of fiction of a few years back stand on their special shelf in the library marked "Best-Sellers of Yesteryear," and nobody goes near them but an occasional shortsighted customer who bends down, peers briefly and hurries away; while old ladies jostle each other at the mystery shelf to grab off some item of the same vintage with a title like *The Triple Petunia Murder Case*, or *Inspector Pinchbottle to the Rescue*. They do not like it that "really important books" get dusty on the reprint counter, while *Death Wears*

---

1 Chandler and Hammett met, and seemed to like each other, but didn't stay in touch.

2 The typical crime novel ends with the capture of the criminal, but in *The Big Sleep*, Eddie Mars is alive and well at the end. Hollywood couldn't accept this, so in the film version of *The Big Sleep*, Mars gets his just reward.

Yellow Garters is put out in editions of fifty or one hundred thousand copies.

Chandler had a lively sense of humor. After watching him mimic Hollywood personalities, his friends agreed that, if he weren't a professional writer, he could have been a professional entertainer.

Chandler was born in the U.S., but his family moved to London when he was 12, and he attended private school in England. Though he didn't go to college, he studied French in France, and German in Germany. When he was 24, he returned to the U.S., moved to Los Angeles, and married a woman 18 years older than himself. After taking a correspondence course in bookkeeping, he began working for an oil company, eventually becoming a high-paid executive. Soon, however, he was fired for "alcoholism, absenteeism, promiscuity with female employees and threatened suicides."[1]

He became intrigued by pulp fiction, studied it closely, and began writing short stories for a penny a word. In 1939, at age 51, Chandler published his first novel, *The Big Sleep*. He published six more novels before his death in 1959. His novels were commercially successful, and his screenwriting work in Hollywood was even more lucrative. "By 1945 Chandler was earning enough that he paid $50,000 in income tax."[2]

When his wife died in 1954, Chandler's drinking got out of control, he attempted suicide, and was placed in the psychiatric ward of a hospital. After his release, he went to England, where he was greeted as a literary star. Chandler met Ian Fleming, author of the James Bond novels, and encouraged him before his books became popular. (Fleming's books became bestsellers after President Kennedy expressed a liking for them, just as Tom Clancy became well-known after Reagan praised his *Hunt for Red October*.)

If one considers Hammett's novels and Chandler's novels as one body of work, an interesting pattern emerges. Hammett's first two novels feature a detective who works for a firm, but his third novel features a detective who owns his own firm, and has no employees except one secretary. Chandler's first novel, *The Big Sleep*, takes this trend one step further; it features a detective who has no employees at all.

This trend toward independence mirrors a trend in the lives of the authors. Hammett worked for the Pinkerton Detective Agency, then later became a self-employed writer. Likewise, Chandler worked for an oil company, then later became a self-employed writer. In *The Big Sleep*, Marlowe is hired by an oil tycoon, General Sternwood, whose life has become complicated as a result of his two daughters. But Marlowe himself is independent, and has no romantic entanglements. So Hammett and Chandler are presenting a picture of the American male as free and independent in his professional life and his personal life. Is this freedom part of the allure of the hard-boiled school of detective fiction?

---

1 See Wikipedia's article, "Raymond Chandler"

2 detnovel.com/Chandler.html

As Chandler grew older, independence seemed to become less attractive to him. After his wife's death, he tried to find a relationship that would alleviate his loneliness—like Poe after his wife died.

> Chandler's last five years—after Cissy's death—bear an uncanny resemblance to those of the inventor of the detective genre after the death of Virginia Poe. Trying desperately to reestablish the secure domesticity he had lost, Poe engaged in a series of quixotic courtings of, proposals to, and refusals by various women friends, interspersed with alcoholic episodes—a pattern repeated by Chandler.[1]

This shift from loner to suitor is mirrored in Chandler's fiction. In his last completed novel, *Playback*, Marlowe becomes romantically involved. "Time and loneliness have finally worn him down, turning the hard-boiled Marlowe, so it seems, into the hero of a Harlequin romance."[2]

The Goncourt brothers said that Poe, with his stories about the detective Dupin, shifted the focus of fiction from the heart to the head, from romance to ratiocination. The hard-boiled school shifted the focus from reasoning to working,

> from personal relationships to professional ones, from love, not to deductions, but to work. For what the hard-boiled fiction of Hammett and Chandler did was not just to transform the amateur sleuth of the analytic genre into a salaried or self-employed private eye but also to annex to the imagining of professional detective work questions about the place of work in the American psyche, in gender relations, in notions of personal success or failure, of freedom or its lack.[3]

Poe focuses on plot, as does Agatha Christie and other representatives of the English school. Hammett and Chandler focus more on character, and explore moral questions such as what the detective is willing to do for a client, when he will accept payment, etc.

---

1 "Being boss: Raymond Chandler's *The Big Sleep*," by John T. Irwin, *The Southern Review*, Baton Rouge: Spring 2001. Vol. 37, Iss. 2; pg. 211. "Anyone who has lived past a certain age in this country," Irwin writes, "knows that philosophies of self-sufficiency are one thing at high noon in bright sunshine when you are twenty-five or thirty but a far different thing at three A.M. when one is about to be jettisoned into the penultimate void of retirement."

2 "Being boss: Raymond Chandler's *The Big Sleep*". As Chandler grew older, his fiction became more cynical. "The increasing cynicism, weariness, and disillusion, not to say bitterness, that critics have noted in Marlowe as the novels progress seem more characteristic of a man's transition from his early fifties to mid-sixties than from his early thirties to early forties." In other words, the increasing cynicism seems to reflect Chandler's own aging process rather than Marlowe's.

3 "Being boss: Raymond Chandler's *The Big Sleep*"

Chandler said that the English school emphasizes plot, and how the story is resolved at the end, but the hard-boiled school is interested in scenes, and believed that you could have a good crime novel even if the end were missing. Perhaps the most memorable scene in *The Big Sleep* is the gambling scene in which Vivian Regan is winning at the roulette table.

But even this scene can't match the gambling scene in Pushkin's "Queen of Spades." Pushkin explores the power of fate, the power of occult forces, unconscious forces, but Chandler stays closer to the surface, and doesn't explore the depths. Chandler may do a fine job of exploring the ethical choices faced by his protagonist, but he doesn't explore the murky world below consciousness, below ethics.

At the end of *The Big Sleep*, Vivian offers Marlowe $15,000, as a kind of bribe or blackmail. Marlowe refuses the money. Marlowe often puts principle over profit. Since he's a single man who lives frugally, he doesn't have to make lots of money. Both his apartment and his office are spartan. Marlowe has much in common with his employer, Sternwood: "Both proud, both insubordinate, one financially independent because he has all the money he'll ever need, the other because he's willing to adjust his lifestyle to his income."[1] Chandler insisted that the protagonist of a crime novel should be a modern hero, a modern knight:

> Down these mean streets a man must go who is not himself mean, who is neither tarnished nor afraid. The detective in this kind of story must be such a man. He is the hero, he is everything. He must be a complete man and a common man and yet an unusual man. He must be, to use a rather weathered phrase, a man of honor, by instinct, by inevitability, without thought of it, and certainly without saying it.

Like a medieval knight, Marlowe is loyal to his liege lord (i.e., his employer, Sternwood), and he chastely refuses the sexual favors offered by Sternwood's daughters. Marlowe has firm principles, but he doesn't have a high place in society. In *The Long Goodbye*, a mobster mocks Marlowe: "No dough, no family, no prospects, no nothing."

A writer's first book often expresses what he cares about most.[2] His later books often ring changes on the theme of his first book. In an earlier issue, I said that "Proust saw in Hardy's *Jude the Obscure*, *The Well-Beloved*, and *A Pair of Blue Eyes* the same nucleus. He recognized the same basic content in all the work of any one artist."[3] It has been argued that Chandler's *Long Goodbye* repeats the basic structure of *The Big Sleep*:

> In reworking the materials of *The Big Sleep* in *The Long Goodbye*, Chandler repeats virtually every major element in the earlier story, some changed slightly, some substantially. In place of the millionaire

---

1 Ibid

2 As Josephine Tey says in *The Daughter of Time*, "Most people's first books are their best anyway; it's the one they wanted most to write."

3 See "Shakespeare's Themes," ljhammond.com/phlit/2003-07.htm#4

General Sternwood and his two spoiled daughters, there is now the millionaire Harlan Potter and his two spoiled daughters, Linda Potter Loring and Sylvia Potter Lennox.[1]

In an earlier issue, I discussed Conrad's influence on Hemingway—more specifically, the influence of Conrad's novella "Youth" on Hemingway's *The Old Man and the Sea*.[2] Conrad probably influenced Chandler, too. One critic, Peter Rabinowitz, says that Chandler may have named his detective Marlowe after Conrad's protagonist (Marlow). Rabinowitz says that *The Big Sleep* and *Heart of Darkness* have the same "general drift":

> Both tell of idealists whose adventures seem destined to bring them in contact with some kind of truth, but who in fact find only a hollowness and a horror. Significantly, both these lovers of truth learn that the only way to deal with the horror they have exposed is to bury it once again with a lie, a lie that leaves the hero perhaps wiser, but also more bitter; and a lie that leaves the evil fundamentally untouched.

Rabinowitz says that *The Big Sleep* ends on a pessimistic note, like Conrad's "Youth." Chandler's hero asks,

> What did it matter where you lay once you were dead? In a dirty sump or in a marble tower on top of a high hill? You were dead, you were sleeping the big sleep, you were not bothered by things like that. Oil and water were the same as wind and air to you. You just slept the big sleep, not caring about the nastiness of how you died or where you fell.

Conrad's "Youth" also ends on a dismal note:

> You simply can do nothing, neither great nor little, not a thing in the world.... Youth, strength, genius, thoughts, achievements, simple hearts—all dies.... No matter.

We saw such pessimism earlier, when we discussed the American novelist Nathanael West.[3] It seems to be common among the writers of this period.

Some readers find anti-Semitism in Chandler's description of the owner of a store that sells jewelry on credit: "a tall handsome white-haired Jew in lean dark clothes, with about nine carats of diamond on his right hand." Anti-Semitism is often encountered in the literature of the early 1900s. In an earlier issue, I discussed anti-Semitism in the work of D. H. Lawrence. The main villain in *The Big Sleep* is Eddie Mars, whom Marlowe describes as "a pornographer, a blackmailer, a hot car broker, a killer by remote control, and a suborner of crooked cops." Is it not significant that Mars is described as having a "hooked nose"? Isn't Chandler insinuating that Mars is Jewish?

- best critical essay on *The Big Sleep*: "Being boss: Raymond Chandler's *The Big Sleep*," by John T. Irwin, *The Southern Review*

---

1 "Being boss: Raymond Chandler's *The Big Sleep*"

2 See bookmark or ljhammond.com/phlit/2008-05c.htm#5

3 See bookmark or ljhammond.com/phlit/2012-11.htm#2

- excellent essay on *The Big Sleep*: "Rats Behind the Wainscoting: Politics, Convention, and Chandler's *The Big Sleep*," by Peter J. Rabinowitz, *Texas Studies in Literature and Language*, Vol. 22, No. 2, summer 1980, pp. 224-245
- good essay on *The Big Sleep*: "'I'm in the Business Too': Gothic Chivalry, Private Eyes, and Proxy Sex and Violence in Chandler's *The Big Sleep*," by Charles J. Rzepka, *MFS Modern Fiction Studies*, Volume 46, Number 3, Fall 2000, pp. 695-724
- good discussion of business ethics in *The Big Sleep*: "'The Client Comes First, Unless He's Crooked': Legal And Professional Ethics In Raymond Chandler's *The Big Sleep*," by Joseph Allegretti, *Creighton Law Review*, vol. 44, p. 581
- *Raymond Chandler's Philip Marlowe: The Hard-Boiled Detective Transformed*, by John Paul Athanasourelis, notes that Marlowe rarely uses force; he talks, negotiates, compromises. Marlowe doesn't represent old-fashioned individualism, the author argues, but rather Dewey's new individualism, which emphasizes our "social interdependencies."[1] Marlowe engages in "'shuttle diplomacy' among clients, criminals, and police."

E. Van Dine

I discovered an American mystery writer, S. S. Van Dine (real name: Willard Huntington Wright). In his early years, Van Dine had literary ambitions, writing serious fiction and a study of Nietzsche. In the 1920s, he made an exhaustive study of detective fiction, and wrote a detective novel called *The Benson Murder Case*. He followed this with eleven more novels, all featuring the detective Philo Vance. Vance shared his creator's intellectual and artistic interests. Van Dine's novels were initially popular, but the later ones weren't well received by the public or by critics. His career is foreshadowed in one of his characters, Stanford West, who begins by writing serious literary works, then later becomes a popular author of light literature. Van Dine once wrote an article called, "I used to be a Highbrow and Look at Me Now."

58. P. G. Wodehouse

Like the mystery genre, the comic works of Wodehouse are a game, a diversion, with no purpose beyond entertainment. But Wodehouse has more literary talent, more genius, than the mystery writers. His style has more grace and wit, his metaphors more poetry. There are many mystery writers, but only one Wodehouse. Will his popularity endure in an un-literary age?

Wodehouse is best known for his Jeeves series, a series of stories and novels about a valet named Jeeves and his boss, Bertie Wooster. The Jeeves series started in 1915 (with one short story), and continued with *The Inimitable Jeeves* (1923), *Carry On, Jeeves* (1925), etc., and finally concluded

---

[1] In earlier issues, we've often discussed the modern tendency to see interdependencies rather than independence, "inter-being" rather than being; this tendency is apparent in literary criticism, physics, etc. See, for example, ljhammond.com/phlit/2003-07.htm or ljhammond.com/phlit/2007-09.htm#7

with *Aunts Aren't Gentlemen*, which was published in 1974, when Wodehouse was 93.

Wodehouse also wrote a series of works about "Blandings Castle" and its dim-witted proprietor, Lord Emsworth. One of Lord Emsworth's chief goals is growing prize pumpkins, raising prize pigs, etc. One morning, he's concerned because his pig, Empress of Blandings, has stopped eating, and the vet confesses himself baffled.

> The effect of the veterinary surgeon's announcement on Lord Emsworth was overwhelming. As a rule, the wear and tear of our complex modern life left this vague and amiable peer unscathed. So long as he had sunshine, regular meals, and complete freedom from the society of his younger son Frederick, he was placidly happy. But there were chinks in his armor, and one of these had been pierced this morning. Dazed by the news he had received, he stood at the window of the great library of Blandings Castle, looking out with unseeing eyes.

Wodehouse has considerable culture. For example, he alludes to Scottish history when he describes Angus McAllister, Lord Emsworth's Scotch gardener; when McAllister is angry with Emsworth, Wodehouse says he has "the look of a man who has not forgotten Bannockburn, a man conscious of belonging to the country of William Wallace and Robert the Bruce." Wodehouse's cultural references are natural, unforced, tongue-in-cheek.

59. A Fox-Hunting Man

I wanted to do some light reading, so I chose Siegfried Sassoon's *Memoirs of A Fox-Hunting Man*. Published in 1928, it deals with the author's rustic pre-war life, and then his WorldWarOne experiences. It has little humor or suspense or thought. It has become a minor classic because of its tone and atmosphere. The tone is intimate, self-deprecating, nostalgic, and the prose is first-rate. It was well-received by the reading public, and won both the James Tait Black Prize and the Hawthornden Prize. Sassoon followed *Fox-Hunting Man* with two more volumes of fictionalized autobiography, *Memoirs of An Infantry Officer* and *Sherston's Progress*.

This photo was taken in 1915, when Sassoon was 28

Fox-Hunting Man is an un-bookish book: it rarely mentions anything intellectual, focusing instead on horses, fox-hunting, and cricket. It depicts small-town life and upper-class sports. One of the few books that Sassoon mentions is Edmund Gosse's acclaimed memoir *Father and Son*. Gosse's memoir probably influenced Sassoon; Gosse's memoir is said to have "gentle wit," and this is also true of *Fox-Hunting Man*. Sassoon knew Gosse personally—Gosse was close friends with Sassoon's maternal uncle, the sculptor Hamo Thornycroft. When Sassoon started writing *Fox-Hunting Man*,

> he sent some manuscript pages to Gosse, who replied: "I think you will be anxious for a word from me, and so I write provisionally to say that I am delighted with it so far. There is no question at all that you must go on steadily. It will be an extraordinarily original book."

Sassoon was also influenced by Proust, and the nostalgic tone of his work is somewhat Proustian. I suspected the influence of Proust after reading the following passage, which deals with a wartime experience:

> We had some tea.... If I could taste that tea out of the dixies now I should write it all very much as it was. Living spontaneity would be revived by that tea, the taste of which cannot be recovered by any effort of memory.

Proust is famous for emphasizing unconscious memory, the memory preserved by tastes and smells.

Memoirs of A Fox-Hunting Man reminds us how important hunting was, especially in the life of the upper classes. Sassoon and his cohorts don't hunt once a month, or once a week; they hunt four or five times a week. In Central Europe, hunting was as popular as it was in England; the Archduke Franz Ferdinand kept records of his hunts, and counted 275,000 animals killed. The Romans were also very fond of hunting. A group hunt can be considered eminently "natural," it has deep roots in human nature and human history. Our species engaged in group hunts for a million years or more. Of course, there's something cruel about hunting in general, and fox-hunting in particular; Sassoon mentions this but doesn't lose sleep over it.

Sassoon at age 20, during his brief stint as a Cambridge student. He was a rather shy, diffident youth.

When the war starts and death is near, Sassoon appreciates life more: "Never before had I known how much I had to lose. Never before had I looked at the living world with any degree of intensity." He says that the war taught him "one useful lesson—that on the whole it was very nice to be alive at all."

When Sassoon is sent to the front lines, he gains a reputation for wild courage, then becomes known as an anti-war protester. He writes "A Soldier's Declaration," in which he explains why he's refusing to fight:

> I am making this statement as an act of wilful defiance of military authority, because I believe that the war is being deliberately prolonged by those who have the power to end it. I am a soldier, convinced that I am acting on behalf of soldiers. I believe that this war, upon which I entered as a war of defence and liberation, has now become a war of aggression and conquest. I believe that the purposes for which I and my fellow-soldiers entered upon this war should have been so clearly stated as to have made it impossible to change them, and that, had this been done, the objects which actuated us would now be attainable by negotiation. I have seen and endured the sufferings of the troops, and I can no longer be a party to prolong these sufferings for ends which I believe to be evil and unjust....

Sassoon's Declaration was read aloud in the House of Commons. Later, however, Sassoon feels guilty that others are fighting while he's resting, so he returns to the Front, and is shot in the head by friendly fire (the wound wasn't fatal, Sassoon survived the war and lived to be 80).

It was believed, Sassoon says, that young men should have courage. But what if their courage has no purpose? What if they're dying for no reason? What if their courage is exploited? When Sassoon first joined the Army, he believed that

> the War was inevitable and justifiable. Courage remained a virtue. And that exploitation of courage, if I may be allowed to say a thing so obvious, was the essential tragedy of the War, which, as everyone now agrees, was a crime against humanity.

Sassoon is known for his war poems, which depict the war with brutal realism. The following lines are from a poem called "Counter-Attack":

The place was rotten with dead; green clumsy legs
High-booted, sprawled and grovelled along the saps
And trunks, face downward, in the sucking mud,
Wallowed like trodden sand-bags loosely filled;
And naked sodden buttocks, mats of hair,
Bulged, clotted heads slept in the plastering slime.
And then the rain began—the jolly old rain!

In an earlier issue, I discussed a CivilWar memoir that describes how the marching soldiers sometimes broke into song.[1] Sassoon apparently witnessed something similar, and wrote a poem called "Everyone Sang":

Everyone suddenly burst out singing;
And I was filled with such delight
As prisoned birds must find in freedom,
Winging wildly across the white
Orchards and dark-green fields; on—on—and out of sight.

Everyone's voice was suddenly lifted;
And beauty came like the setting sun:
My heart was shaken with tears; and horror
Drifted away....

In *Fox-Hunting Man*, Sassoon describes the underground life of the WorldWarOne soldier:

> Pushing past the gas-blanket, I blundered down the stairs to the company headquarters' dug-out. There were twenty steps to that earthy smelling den, with its thick wooden props down the middle and its precarious yellow candlelight casting wobbling shadows. Barton was sitting on a box at the rough table, with a tin mug and a half-empty whisky bottle. His shoulders were hunched and the collar of his trench-coat was turned up to his ears. Dick was in deep shadow, lying on a bunk (made of wire-netting with empty sandbags on it). It was a morose

---

[1] *Company Aytch* by Sam Watkins. See ljhammond.com/phlit/2014-09b.htm.

> cramped little scene, loathsome to live in as it is hateful to remember. The air was dank and musty; lumps of chalk fell from the "ceiling" at intervals. There was a bad smell of burnt grease.

During the war, Sassoon became friends with the poets Robert Graves and Wilfrid Owen. Owen's war experience seems even grimmer than Sassoon's:

> Outfitted in hip-length rubber waders, on 8 January [Owen] had waded through two and a half miles of trenches with "a mean depth of two feet of water." By 9 January [1917] he was housed in a hut where only seventy yards away a howitzer fired every minute day and night. On 12 January [they] marched three miles over a shelled road and three more along a flooded trench, where those who got stuck in the heavy mud had to leave their waders, as well as some clothing and equipment, and move ahead on bleeding and freezing feet. They were under machine-gun fire, shelled by heavy explosives throughout the cold march, and were almost unconscious from fatigue when the poison-gas attack occurred....[1]

The war doesn't start until near the end of *Fox-Hunting Man*; most of the book deals with horses, horse races, and fox-hunting. The protagonist and narrator, who is called George Sherston, frequently buys new horses. One of these purchases involves an experience of *déjà vu*:

> The horse stood there as quiet as if he were having his picture painted. "I wish to goodness someone would give me fifty pounds for him," exclaimed Lewison petulantly, and I had that queer sensation when an episode seems to have happened before. The whole scene was strangely lit up for me; I could have sworn that I knew what he was going to say before a single word was out of his mouth. And when, without a second's hesitation, I replied, "I'll give you fifty pounds for him," I was merely overhearing a remark which I had already made.

Psychologists like Freud have offered various explanations for the feeling of *déjà vu*. I would explain this feeling by saying that we often anticipate the future, and when something that we anticipated comes to pass, it feels that we already experienced it, we've been here before.

Sassoon has some family money, and this enables him to spend his time on sport and literature. His father's family was one of the wealthiest Jewish families in the world. The Sassoons were based in Iraq and India, and controlled the opium trade with China; they were known as the Rothschilds of the East. Sassoon's father was disinherited because he married a non-Jewish woman, so as a young man, Sassoon had to be somewhat careful with his expenditures—he was wealthy, but only moderately so.

In my book of aphorisms, I argue that boys who are raised primarily by their mother are more apt to become homosexual, and I cite Proust as an

---

[1] poetryfoundation.org/poets/wilfred-owen

example.[1] Sassoon is another example; his father left the family when Sassoon was five, and died soon after. (Sassoon's fictional alter-ego, George Sherston, is raised by "Aunt Evelyn.") Sassoon had numerous homosexual affairs, in addition to a wife and child. According to the critic Paul Fussell, one of Sassoon's goals as a writer was "registering subtly and in the process justifying his homosexuality." Sassoon seemed to long for a world where "creatures of my temperament" could lead a "free and unsecretive existence."

Fox-Hunting Man contains no explicit comments on homosexuality, but Sassoon records his fondness for fellow-soldiers, especially Dick Tiltwood:

> I saw my new companion for the first time. He had unpacked and arranged his belongings, and was sitting on his camp-bed polishing a perfectly new pipe. He looked up at me. Twilight was falling and there was only one small window, but even in the half-light his face surprised me by its candour and freshness. He had the obvious good looks which go with fair hair and firm features, but it was the radiant integrity of his expression which astonished me.... His was the bright countenance of truth; ignorant and undoubting; incapable of concealment but strong in reticence and modesty. In fact, he was as good as gold, and everyone knew it as soon as they knew him. Such was Dick Tiltwood.

Perhaps the hero of Sassoon's 3-volume work is the psychiatrist who treated him, Dr. Rivers. Thirty years after this treatment, Sassoon wrote, "I should like to meet Rivers in 'the next world.' It is difficult to believe that such a man as he could be extinguished."[2]

60. War or Peace? (Part I)

In the last issue, I mentioned Siegfried Sassoon's anti-war protest. Sassoon decided that World War I was a "crime against humanity," a crime perpetrated by the politicians, by the generals, and perhaps by the people at home. There was a stalemate on the Western Front, and millions were dying for no apparent reason. Was each side motivated by hatred of the other side? Or was each side motivated by pride—was each side too proud to call for negotiations and make concessions?

In the following poem, Wilfred Owen suggests that the killing could have stopped if one of the armies had been willing to swallow its pride:

So Abram rose, and clave the wood, and went,
And took the fire with him, and a knife.
And as they sojourned both of them together,
Isaac the first-born spake and said, My Father,

---

1 See *Conversations With Great Thinkers* ==> "Genius" ==> "Genius and Homosexuality"

2 The movie *Regeneration* (1997) deals with Sassoon and Rivers, as well as Wilfred Owen. *Regeneration* should be included on any list of good movies about World War I. Consider also a one-hour BBC documentary called *War Poet Wilfred Owen—A Remembrance Tale.*

Behold the preparations, fire and iron,
But where the lamb for this burnt-offering?
Then Abram bound the youth with belts and straps,
and builded parapets and trenches there,
And stretchèd forth the knife to slay his son.
When lo! an angel called him out of heaven,
Saying, Lay not thy hand upon the lad,
Neither do anything to him. Behold,
A ram, caught in a thicket by its horns;
Offer the Ram of Pride instead of him.

But the old man would not so, but slew his son,
And half the seed of Europe, one by one.

Wilfred Owen

Swallowing one's pride can be very difficult, especially for one who has a lot of pride. Near the end of the Civil War, it was clear that the South was beaten, but Lee was extremely reluctant to surrender. "There is nothing left for me to do," Lee said, "but go and see General Grant, and I would rather die a thousand deaths."

If a war drags on for years, each side has invested vast amounts of blood and treasure in the effort. Each side feels that they must win to justify this huge investment; if they stop fighting, their investment will be lost, wasted. One of the most famous WorldWarOne poems says that the living should continue the fight, lest the dead should have died in vain:

In Flanders fields the poppies grow
Between the crosses, row on row,

That mark our place; and in the sky
The larks, still bravely singing, fly
Scarce heard amid the guns below.

We are the Dead. Short days ago
We lived, felt dawn, saw sunset glow,
Loved and were loved, and now we lie
In Flanders fields.

Take up our quarrel with the foe:
To you from failing hands we throw
The torch; be yours to hold it high.
If ye break faith with us who die
We shall not sleep, though poppies grow
In Flanders fields.

This poem was written early in the war, before anti-war feeling became widespread. Notice how the author (John McCrae, a Canadian doctor) refers to the war as "our quarrel." In the last issue, I compared the wars of nations to the quarrels of individuals. There are numerous parallels between wars and quarrels—the role of pride, the role of hatred, the role of prior-investment.

Shakespeare had numerous quarrels, some of which resulted in sword-fights. In *Hamlet*, Shakespeare says that we should fight for a straw if our honor is involved:

Rightly to be great
Is not to stir without great argument,
But greatly to find quarrel in a straw
When honor's at the stake.

Fifty years ago, the U.S. was divided between those who wanted "peace now" (in Vietnam), and those who wanted "peace with honor."

In an earlier issue, I discussed Donald Kagan's views on the causes of wars: "Kagan says that war is often caused, not by the desire for money or land, but by the desire for honor, prestige, respect."[1] Respect is a factor not only in causing wars, but also in continuing wars that have already started. One cause of the 9/11 attacks, and other examples of "jihad," is a Muslim desire to strike at a Western world that dis-respects them, a Muslim desire to make the West tremble at Muslim power, as in the days of Saladin.

What conclusion should we draw? Should we conclude that courage, pride, and honor are virtues? Or should we conclude that they cause war and suffering? Perhaps we should conclude that no virtues are absolute; we must respect the situation, the moment, our own feelings.

61. War or Peace? (Part II)

---

[1] See ljhammond.com/phlit/2015-03.htm#2

On September 1, 1939, Hitler invaded Poland. He probably thought that the Allies would stand aside, rather than declaring war on Germany. He probably thought that the Allies wanted to avoid another world war—the memory of the first world war was still fresh in people's minds. And at that moment, Hitler was especially formidable since he had the Soviet Union on his side.

Should the Allies have stood aside, rather than declaring war? When should we resist evil, and when should we make concessions to evil? Should a decision of war-or-peace be based on a calculus of power? Or should we resist evil even when we're faced with overwhelming power? Should we prefer peace to war, even though choosing peace often means allowing evil to triumph?

Let's assume that Hitler's principles were

- peace isn't valuable
- land is valuable (*Lebensraum* is valuable)

If the Allies declare war on Germany, are they accepting Hitler's principles? When we choose to resist evil, are we accepting our enemy's principles, and betraying our own principles?

Let's pretend someone steals your ring. Should you say to yourself, "I'll just let him have it, he evidently thinks that such things are important. I have different principles, higher principles. If I resist him, I'm descending to his level. As Jesus said, Resist not evil."

Or should you say to yourself, "What he did is evil/unjust. I should resist injustice, I should show him that 'crime doesn't pay.' Every decent person should love justice, and resist injustice."

Decisions of war and peace—between individuals and between nations—are so difficult and complex that no general rule can govern them, we can only wrestle with them on a case-by-case basis. And whatever decision we make, our critics will be able to find fault. Since these decisions are so difficult, societies are often bitterly divided over war vs. peace.

62. Owen and Sassoon

During World War I, Wilfred Owen met Siegfried Sassoon, and greatly admired him, perhaps because Sassoon had been decorated for bravery, perhaps because Sassoon was famous for protesting against the war, perhaps because Sassoon was a published author and accomplished poet. To Owen, Sassoon was "Keats and Christ and Elijah."

Sassoon encouraged Owen to write poetry about the war, made marginal notes on Owen's poems, and helped to publish Owen's poems after his death (Owen died in combat at age 25). Owen wrote to Sassoon, "You have fixed my life—however short."[1] Both Sassoon and Owen wrote poetry that described the war in lucid language; they had no use for the obscurities of T. S. Eliot, and Eliot had no use for their poetry. As Owen said, "I am not concerned with Poetry. My subject is War, and the pity of War. The Poetry is in the pity."

When Owen met Sassoon, Owen was 24, Sassoon 31. Sassoon had been a diffident youth, but became more confident and assertive during the war,

---

[1] These words suggest that Owen may have anticipated his early death. When he was going to France for the last time, he recited a Tagore poem to his mother:

When I go from hence
let this be my parting word,
that what I have seen is unsurpassable....

In this playhouse of infinite forms
I have had my play
and here have I caught sight of him that is formless....

and if the end comes here, let it come
— let this be my parting word.

In his last tour of duty, Owen displayed the sort of wild courage that Sassoon displayed, and Owen was awarded the Military Cross, as Sassoon was. Does this wild courage indicate a suicidal tendency?

perhaps because he was in charge of younger men.[1] His men liked him; one of them said, "It was only once in a blue moon that we had an officer like Mr. Sassoon."

63. E. M. Forster

A. *A Room With A View*

I enjoyed Forster's *Room With A View*. It's short, readable, full of life, and often philosophical. In 1985, it was made into a popular film by Merchant & Ivory.

As I read *Room With A View*, I sometimes felt that I was reading a JaneAusten novel—the guy and girl seem destined to come together, but all sorts of obstacles are thrown in their way. The plot consists of overcoming these obstacles, untangling these knots. We know that Forster was influenced by Austen. When he was asked what he had learned from her, he replied, "I learned the possibilities of domestic humor. I was more ambitious than she was, of course; I tried to hitch it on to other things."[2] *A Room With A View* has humor, but it also deals with personal growth, the ideal person, the beautiful soul. It's remarkable that Forster achieved so much at such a young age; much of the novel was written in 1902, when he was just 23.

The first half of the novel takes place in Florence. Chapter 1 is set in a hotel ("pension") that's full of English tourists. We meet Mr. Emerson, who seems to represent the archetypal Wise Old Man. He isn't well-dressed or well-mannered, but he has a beautiful soul. There's "something childish" in his eyes, and when Charlotte refuses his offer to trade rooms, he thumps the table with his fists "like a naughty child."

One character says that Mr. Emerson is "not tactful; yet, have you ever noticed that there are people who do things which are most indelicate, and yet at the same time—beautiful?" Charlotte doesn't understand this, she equates beauty with delicacy, propriety, manners. When she finally accepts the rooms with views, her young cousin, Lucy, wonders "whether the acceptance might not have been less delicate and more beautiful."

In Chapter 2, Lucy (the protagonist) meets Mr. Emerson in a church. He scorns religious formalities and churches, but says "I do believe in those who make their fellow-creatures happy." Mr. Emerson says he raised his son, George, "free from all the superstition and ignorance that lead men to hate one another in the name of God."

Mr. Emerson's saintliness puts him at odds with society. George tells Lucy that most people are kind "because we think it improves our characters.

---

[1] In an earlier issue, I described how Harry Truman, like Siegfried Sassoon, grew during wartime: "In World War I, [Truman] gained valuable experience and self-confidence, serving as a captain. He earned the respect of his men by his courage under fire and his leadership ability. When the U.S. entered World War I, Truman was already 33—older than most of the soldiers—so he naturally assumed a leadership role."

[2] 1952 interview. See *Howards End*, Norton Critical Edition, p. 293

But he is kind to people because he loves them; and they find him out, and are offended, or frightened."

George has imbibed some of his father's ways; when Lucy speaks of "a kind action done tactfully," George is disgusted at the notion of tact, and throws up his head "in disdain". What the tour guide says about St. Francis seems applicable to Mr. Emerson: "full of innate sympathy... quickness to perceive good in others... vision of the brotherhood of man..." Like Dostoyevsky in *The Idiot*, Forster is attempting to depict the beautiful soul, the saint, the Christ figure. Surely this is one of the chief themes of world literature.[1] *A Room With A View* is a novel of 'domestic humor' that's 'hitched onto other things.'

In Forster's society, young women are taught to be wary of men, but Mr. Emerson urges Lucy to get closer to George:

> Let yourself go. Pull out from the depths those thoughts that you do not understand, and spread them out in the sunlight and know the meaning of them. By understanding George you may learn to understand yourself. It will be good for both of you.

Life seems hard and meaningless, Mr. Emerson tells Lucy; "the things of the universe... won't fit." The universe has no plan: "We come from the winds... we shall return to them." George is depressed by this aspect of life, Mr. Emerson says, but we shouldn't let it depress us. "Let us rather love one another, and work and rejoice. I don't believe in this world sorrow." We should make the best of the situation, we should call the glass half-full instead of half-empty.

In the early chapters of the novel, Lucy seems stuck in the world of tact and propriety, and she regards Mr. Emerson as "a very foolish old man." But Lucy has the potential for growth, as we see in her piano-playing. Mr. Beebe says, "If Miss Honeychurch ever takes to live as she plays, it will be very exciting both for us and for her." Lucy plays passionately, and this alarms her mother, who "doesn't like one to get excited over anything."

Her mother seems oblivious of all beauty except "beautiful manners"; she finds beautiful manners in Cecil, Lucy's bookish suitor. Cecil only kisses Lucy after asking permission, while George kisses her without any preamble.

Lucy chafes under Charlotte's control. Lucy wants to be free, to spread her wings. She doesn't want to stay in the background, and help men "by means of tact and a spotless name." Forster sympathizes with the independent woman of his day:

> She too is enamored of heavy winds, and vast panoramas, and green expanses of the sea. She has marked the kingdom of this world, how full it is of wealth, and beauty, and war—a radiant crust, built around the central fires, spinning towards the receding heavens.

Mr. Emerson looks forward to a day when the sexes are equal, when men and women are "comrades."

---

[1] Kipling attempted to depict the saint in his novel *Kim*, as we saw in an earlier issue (ljhammond.com/phlit/2012-04.htm#10).

Lucy's discontent starts the plot moving. "This afternoon she was peculiarly restive. She would really like to do something of which her well-wishers disapproved." Lucy wants to do something "unladylike."

Forster admires instinct more than intelligence, and he admires Italians for being closer to their instincts than the English. Forster tells us that the Italian cab-driver "had played skillfully, using the whole of his instinct, while the others had used scraps of their intelligence." The English "gain knowledge slowly, and perhaps too late."

Forster rejects the English, Protestant, Victorian world, as Lucy rejects the advice of her older cousin, Charlotte. Charlotte had presented to Lucy

> the complete picture of a cheerless, loveless world in which the young rush to destruction until they learn better—a shamefaced world of precautions and barriers which may avert evil, but which do not seem to bring good, if we may judge from those who have used them most.

For Forster, Italy seems to represent instinct, wholeness, personal growth. Lucy returns from Italy "with new eyes.... Italy was offering her the most priceless of all possessions—her own soul."

Like his contemporary D. H. Lawrence, Forster respects instinct and the body. Mr. Emerson says, "The Garden of Eden... which you place in the past, is really yet to come. We shall enter it when we no longer despise our bodies."

Mr. Emerson's scorn for social propriety is matched by his love of natural beauty, and doubtless Forster shares both. When Lucy's brother says, "I must... have the pleasure of calling on you later on, my mother says," Mr. Emerson responds, "CALL, my lad? Who taught us that drawing-room twaddle? Call on your grandmother! Listen to the wind among the pines! Yours is a glorious country."

Forster touches on one of the deepest philosophical questions: coincidence, synchronicity, fate. Mr. Beebe says, "When I was a young man, I always meant to write a History of Coincidence." But George doesn't believe in coincidence: "Everything is Fate. We are flung together by Fate, drawn apart by Fate." What appears to be coincidence, George thinks, is actually Fate.

Near the end of the novel, Mr. Emerson tells Lucy that when George was twelve, he had a serious case of typhoid. When he recovered, his mother (Mr. Emerson's wife) became sick and died. It sometimes seems that one person dies in another's stead, as if Death must take somebody, but doesn't care who. When Jung was gravely ill, he had a vision of his doctor dying; soon Jung recovered, and his doctor died in his stead.[1]

[Spoiler Warning: Don't read the rest of this section if you're planning to read *Room With A View*.] After Lucy breaks her engagement to Cecil, Mr. Emerson talks with Lucy, and steers her toward George.

> [Mr. Emerson] had robbed the body of its taint, the world's taunts of their sting; he had shown her the holiness of direct desire. She "never exactly understood," she would say in after years, "how he managed to

[1] *Memories, Dreams, Reflections*, Ch. 10

> strengthen her. It was as if he had made her see the whole of everything at once."

Isn't this the philosopher's goal—to present "the whole of everything at once"? Mr. Emerson is indeed the Wise Old Man.

B. Brander on *A Room With A View*

I'm a fan of the critic Laurence Brander, whom I discussed in connection with Forster's *Passage to India*. When Brander discusses *A Room With A View*, he compares Mr. Emerson to Gino, a character in Forster's first novel, *Where Angels Fear to Tread*. Both Mr. Emerson and Gino are "completely out of tune with the others, a real person among Edwardian marionettes." Mr. Emerson puts "truth and passion before the suburban niceties."[1]

Brander points out that it is Mr. Emerson who offers Lucy and Charlotte the rooms with views. "The offer becomes a symbol. The old man who made it will help the girl to see things she might never have seen in her stuffy Edwardian suburban life."

Brander describes Cecil Vyse as "a Meredithian character who will mold the woman to his design." George Meredith was from an older generation; perhaps in Meredith's day, men often molded women. Among younger novelists like Hardy, Kipling, and Lawrence, one finds a different theme: men who are dominated, crushed by their wives.[2] Forster doesn't seem to deal with the theme of men dominated by women, he seems more interested in the theme of women dominated by men, women striving for freedom.

C. Forster and Lawrence

One critic (David Ellis) argued that both Forster and D. H. Lawrence aimed at "the presentation of a unified whole."[3] Forster and Lawrence didn't celebrate "the fragmentary nature of modern experience," as the Futurists did. After Lawrence visited the studio of painter Duncan Grant, he said, "Tell [Grant] not to make silly experiments in the futuristic line.... It is the Absolute we are all after, a statement of the whole scheme." Lawrence and Forster wanted an artistic wholeness that stayed close to life; they had no use for a modernism that "simplified the problem of 'wholeness' by disconnecting art from life (so that unity in art became a formal matter only)."

Forster met Lawrence in 1915. At first, they got along well, and Forster visited Lawrence and his wife Frieda at their house in the country. In a letter, Forster wrote, "The Lawrences I like—especially him." Forster described "walking in 'the glorious country' listening to Lawrence's account of his background (his 'drunken father, sister who married a tailor, etc.')." Forster was then 36, Lawrence 29. Both were already established writers.

---

1 *E. M. Forster: A Critical Study*

2 See ljhammond.com/phlit/2012-04.htm#6

3 "Lawrence and Forster in 1915," by David Ellis, *The Cambridge Quarterly*, Vol. 27, No. 1 (1998), pp. 1-14, jstor.org/stable/42967889

Later Lawrence quizzed Forster about his bachelor lifestyle. Forster wasn't open about his homosexuality, and Lawrence wondered, "Why can't he act? Why can't he take a woman and fight clear to his own basic, primal being?" Lawrence wasn't known for tact, he was known for complete openness. Forster became annoyed; the friendship was heading for the rocks.

A few days later, Forster wrote the Lawrences and said that he liked Frieda, and he liked the D. H. Lawrence who "sees birds" etc., "but I do not like the deaf impercipient fanatic who has nosed over his own little sexual round until he believes that there is no other path for others to take." The friendship that had blossomed quickly died just as quickly, and it never revived. But it should be noted that after Lawrence's early death, Forster was a champion of his work.

Forster dealt with homosexuality in his novel *Maurice*, but he didn't publish *Maurice* during his lifetime. Forster regarded *Maurice* as a groundbreaking work; he said he had

> created something absolutely new, even to the Greeks. Whitman nearly anticipated me but he didn't really know what he was after, or only half knew—shirked, even to himself, the statement.

Critics are cool toward *Maurice*; few critics regard it as one of Forster's best works. Forster himself eventually cooled toward *Maurice*, and wondered if it was worth publishing. The film version of *Maurice*, made by Merchant & Ivory, also has few admirers.

David Ellis argues that several people, including Forster, suspected that Lawrence himself had homosexual inclinations. In Forster's view, Lawrence didn't understand his own sexuality, yet he presumed to lecture others about their sexuality. Lawrence himself said, "nearly every man that approaches greatness tends to homosexuality, whether he admits it or not; so that he loves the *body* of a man better than the body of a woman." Ellis notes that both Lawrence and Forster were brought up by "a loved but dominating mother."

At their 1915 meeting, Lawrence and Forster agreed that capitalism was bad, and socialism was better; the time had come for revolution, or at least bold reforms. Lawrence advocated "a program of mass nationalization which will ensure that every man 'shall have his wages whether he is sick or well or old.'" Until the economic problem is solved, literature is pointless:

> I am ashamed [Lawrence said] to write any real writing of passionate love to my fellow men. Only satire is decent now.... Forster knows, as every thinking man now knows, that all his thinking and his passion for humanity amounts to no more than trying to soothe with poetry a man raging with pain that can be cured. Cure the pain, don't give the poetry.

Though Lawrence and Forster agreed about politics, their disagreement about personal matters ruined their rapport. Lawrence summarized their conversation thus:

> We have talked so hard—about a revolution—at least I have talked...
> and now I wonder, are my words gone like seed spilt on a hard floor....
> I must tell you I am very sad, as if it hurt me very much.

Lawrence said, "I get a feeling of acute misery from [Forster]... the acute, exquisite pain of cramps." David Ellis spoke of "the paralysis or blockage which Lawrence felt he had detected in his visitor." This blockage may be connected to Forster's sexuality. This blockage also has a literary aspect: Forster wrote only one novel in his last fifty years.

Perhaps one reason why Forster stopped writing is that his "domestic humor," his satire of suburbia, was out of place in an age of World War. The critic P. N. Furbank suggests another reason why Forster stopped writing. Furbank says that Forster belongs among those whom Freud called "wrecked by success." Ellis speaks of the "enormous success" of Forster's *Howards End* (1910), and the "spectacular success" of Forster's *Aspects of the Novel* (1927). Ellis wrote,

> Like the Greeks [Forster] seemed to feel that any good luck was always likely to be followed by its opposite. Furbank records how, after the spectacular success of *Aspects of the Novel*, [Forster] told the other Lawrence (T. E.), "a sort of nervousness—glancing at my stomach for the beginnings of cancer—seems to gather in me." It would no doubt be possible to trace this... common form of superstition to Freudian concepts of guilt.

If you want to learn more about Forster, consider Furbank's biography, which Ellis speaks highly of.

D. Deconstruction

Perhaps the best way to approach Deconstruction is by looking at its antecedents, its foundations.

Scientific truths (for example, that the earth is round, not flat) aren't really understood unless they're challenged and questioned. As Mill put it, "Both teachers and learners go to sleep at their post, as soon as there is no enemy in the field."[1] To understand a widely-accepted scientific truth, we need to look at the arguments for it and against it, we need to bring ourselves back to a time when it was fighting for acceptance. If we simply tell a young student, "the earth is round, though it appears to be flat," he won't understand it as well as someone who has to look at the evidence, make up his own mind, and defend his view against people who maintain a contrary view.

What is true in the intellectual sphere is also true in the religious sphere. A religion that is widely accepted receives passive assent, while a religion that is fighting for acceptance receives enthusiastic adherence. If people are born Christian, and raised in a predominantly Christian society, they passively accept Christianity. Kierkegaard asked, "how does one become a Christian in a country where almost everyone is born Christian?" How can

---

[1] *On Liberty*, ch. 2

we bring ourselves back to the time when Christianity was fighting for acceptance? How can we regain the passionate faith of early Christians, who suffered and died for their belief?

Kierkegaard tried to awaken people from their pseudo-Christian slumber, and make them realize what it meant to be a Christian. He wanted people to think for themselves, choose for themselves, not just receive the official religion of their nation. Kierkegaard argued that if we simply give people The Truth, they won't understand it; if we simply tell people, "the earth is round," they won't understand it. They must reach it by themselves, fight for it.

In *Either/Or*, Kierkegaard presented two worldviews—the aesthetic worldview of a young art-lover, and the ethical worldview of a mature family man. Then he said to the reader, "You choose. You choose either the aesthetic or the ethical. Don't expect someone to tell you who you are, to tell you that you're a Christian. Don't expect someone to tell you what is The Truth. Find it for yourself. Choose."

Kierkegaard opposed Hegel's approach because Hegel attempted to set forth The Truth. Kierkegaard felt that Hegel's approach would put the individual to sleep; Kierkegaard wanted to awaken the individual, present him with choices, insist that he fight his way to truth.

Kierkegaard admired Socrates because Socrates didn't claim to possess Truth; Socrates said, "the only thing I know is that I know nothing." Socrates questioned established views, and tried to rouse people to think for themselves; Socrates referred to himself as a midwife, because he tried to draw out of people what was within them, instead of handing them Truth on a platter, and saying "swallow." Socrates spoke not with authority but with irony. Socrates and Kierkegaard used an indirect approach, while Hegel used a direct approach. The Socratic method has long been respected as an educational technique because it stirs students to think for themselves, to earn truth instead of just passively receiving it. Kierkegaard created various pseudonyms to present various viewpoints, and force the reader to choose among them; he didn't want to build up his own authority as a author, he didn't want the reader to receive Truth from him. Existentialism, which Kierkegaard pioneered, says we must choose for ourselves, we can't rely on Truth—objective, absolute, universal Truth—to tell us what to do.

Kierkegaard's indirect approach has influenced Deconstruction, which believes that an author doesn't directly state The Truth. Deconstruction concerns itself with what an author doesn't directly state; Deconstruction reads between the lines, it interprets an author's silences. This enables critics to keep themselves busy, but it can lead to some wild and groundless interpretations. A commentator on Kierkegaard, for example, after pointing out that Kierkegaard never mentioned his mother in his writings, declares that "Kierkegaard's mother, who was not well educated, is represented in his writings by the mother-tongue (Danish)."[1] This without even a "probably" or a "perhaps"!

Most writers communicate directly, not indirectly; Kierkegaard is one of the few to employ an indirect approach. But Deconstruction assumes that all writers communicate indirectly, that all writers use Kierkegaard's approach. Furthermore, Deconstruction applies Kierkegaard's insights to a field they weren't intended for; Kierkegaard's goal was spiritual awakening, not literary interpretation. Surely Kierkegaard would disapprove of the use that is being made of his work.

Deconstruction is popular with academics, but of no interest to laymen. Deconstruction leads to over-reading and over-interpreting. Among modern critics, "simple" has become a pejorative term, and the most strained interpretation is considered the deepest. Modern critics have forgotten that simplicity has long been considered a sign of truth, an aesthetic virtue, a moral virtue—even a virtue for literary critics. One of the greatest critics praised Tolstoy for the "rock-like" simplicity of his literary criticism.[2] Modern critics have forgotten that simplicity is a characteristic of good prose; their prose is an obscure, technical jargon.

Surely the Deconstruction trend will fade away, just as earlier trends in literary criticism faded away. The next generation of critics will take a different tack; as Proust said, "the critics of each generation confine themselves to maintaining the direct opposite of the truths admitted by their predecessors."[3]

E. Deconstruction and E. M. Forster

Now let's see how one of today's deconstructors deals with a classic of modern fiction, Forster's *Howards End*. Forster's genius shows itself in deep thought, as well as in sparkling wit and superb prose. Like many modern intellectuals, Forster realizes that Christianity has had its day:

> I cannot believe that Christianity will ever cope with the present world-wide mess.... It was a spiritual force once, but the indwelling spirit will

---

1 McDonald, William, "Søren Kierkegaard", The Stanford Encyclopedia of Philosophy (Winter 2001 Edition)

2 see G. Wilson Knight's *Wheel of Fire*, "Tolstoy's Attack on Shakespeare", §2. Deconstruction might be compared with the Straussian approach, developed by Leo Strauss. Strauss believed that philosophers don't say what they mean, that philosophers conceal their views from fear of persecution, and from fear that their views will have a harmful effect on society. Straussians argue, for example, that many philosophers, from Machiavelli on, were atheists, but concealed their atheism. Strauss looked for hidden meanings and secret codes; he even hired someone who had been a code-breaker for the U.S. Army to study Machiavelli! Like Deconstruction, the Straussian approach is very popular in academia, but of no interest to laymen.

3 *The Guermantes Way*, Part II, ch. 1

> have to be restated if it is to calm the waters again, and probably restated in a non-Christian form.[1]

Forster was a great admirer of Whitman, and read Whitman just before writing *Howards End*, which is suffused with the Zen spirit of Whitman. Here's an example of the Zen spirit in *Howards End*:

> The present flowed by them like a stream. The tree rustled. It had made music before they were born, and would continue after their deaths, but its song was of the moment. The moment had passed. The tree rustled again. Their senses were sharpened, and they seemed to apprehend life. Life passed. The tree rustled again. "Sleep now," said Margaret. The peace of the country was entering into her. It has no commerce with memory, and little with hope.... It is the peace of the present, which passes understanding. Its murmur came "now," and "now" once more as they trod the gravel, and "now," as the moonlight fell upon their father's sword.[2]

Notice the Zennish emphasis on the present moment, and notice the Zennish awareness of the world around us.

When Forster says, "the indwelling spirit [of Christianity] will have to be restated," it suggests that there is a kernel of truth in Christianity, a mystical core that deserves respect, a mystical core that is similar to (perhaps even identical with) the mystical core in Islam, Buddhism, and other religions. An example of the mystical spirit in Christianity is this passage from the New Testament:

> Take no thought for your life, what ye shall eat, or what ye shall drink.... Which of you by taking thought can add one cubit unto his stature?.... Consider the lilies of the field, how they grow; they toil not, neither do they spin.[3]

In *Howards End*, Forster often expresses a similar thought, often says that we shouldn't spend the Present preparing for the Future. When one character says, "It's as well to be prepared," another character responds, "'No—it's as well not to be prepared'.... She could not explain in so many words, but she felt that those who prepare for all the emergencies of life beforehand may equip themselves at the expense of joy."[4]

---

[1] *Two Cheers For Democracy*, "What I Believe"

[2] ch. 40

[3] Matthew, 6:25

[4] ch. 7. Forster expresses the same idea in Chapter 12: "Our national morality.... assumes that preparation against danger is in itself a good, and that men, like nations, are the better for staggering through life fully armed.... Margaret hoped that for the future she would be less cautious, not more cautious, than she had been in the past." Thoreau also speaks of the folly of spending your life preparing for the future, the folly of over-preparation: "Men say that a stitch in time saves nine, and so they take a thousand stitches

Forster points out that the thought of death focuses us on the present moment, the thought of death leads us to Zen. If we lived forever, it might make sense to accumulate for the future, to accumulate money, but since we can die tomorrow, we should experience today, we should appreciate the present moment. When Leonard Bast, plagued by poverty, says "The real thing's money and all the rest is a dream," Helen responds, "You've forgotten Death.... If we lived forever what you say would be true. But we have to die, we have to leave life presently.... I love Death—not morbidly, but because He explains. He shows me the emptiness of Money.... Death destroys a man: the idea of Death saves him."[1]

But today's deconstructors don't find any Zen in Forster, or any philosophical ideas except those that they discover "between the lines." They believe that Forster hides behind the narrator of *Howards End*, that Forster is being ironic, duplicitous, evasive, that Forster is "playing games with the reader," that Forster doesn't mean what he says, or say what he means, that the countless thoughts and feelings expressed by the narrator aren't those of Forster himself (though the narrator's thoughts frequently agree with the thoughts that Forster expresses in his essays, letters, etc.). "He winks at us as if to acknowledge that the beliefs he offers are only that—beliefs that can be played with and used to create a posture." In short, today's deconstructors regard this delightful novel as a complicated game of hide-and-seek—so complicated that generations of readers missed Forster's irony, and failed to join in the game.[2]

Even when Forster expresses his love for his native land, the modern critic finds ambiguity and irony. Forster writes thus of the Isle of Wight:

> Seen from the west, the Wight is beautiful beyond all laws of beauty. It is as if a fragment of England floated forward to greet the foreigner—chalk of our chalk, turf of our turf, epitome of what will follow. And behind the fragment lie Southampton, hostess to the nations, and Portsmouth, a latent fire, and all around it, with double and treble collision of tides, swirls the sea. How many villages appear in this view! How many castles! How many churches, vanished or triumphant![3]

Though it may seem that here, surely, Forster is speaking from the heart, the modern critic speaks of "the irony of the extravagant prose," which calls for

---

today to save nine tomorrow."(*Walden*, ch. 2). A writer on Zen, Alan Watts, wrote a book on the folly of over-preparation (*The Wisdom of Insecurity*). Watts points out that "[Christ's] life was from the beginning a complete acceptance and embracing of insecurity. 'The foxes have holes, and the birds of the air have nests, but the Son of Man hath not where to lay his head.'"(ch. 1)

[1] ch. 27

[2] See Paul Armstrong, "The Narrator in the Closet: The Ambiguous Narrative Voice in *Howards End*", *Modern Fiction Studies* 47.2 (Summer 2001): 306-28

[3] ch. 19

"critical scrutiny." The modern critic fails to see that writers usually mean just what they say; the modern critic is "too clever by half."

While Forster's humor entertains the reader, and his profundity impresses the reader, perhaps Forster's chief virtue as a writer is his taste. He treats the reader well, he treats the reader as a friend. Every sentence is clear, every page is a pleasure. Wit and wisdom is everywhere. Even Miss Avery, a minor character, expresses the deepest wisdom when she says that the world is better than nothing.[1] A pessimist can point out many flaws in the world—death, suffering, injustice, etc.—but only the most extreme pessimist could take issue with Miss Avery's view that the world is better than nothing. Forster makes the same argument in one of his essays: "Though I am not an optimist, I cannot agree with Sophocles that it were better never to have been born."[2] Though life has many flaws, it is better than non-existence.

Miss Avery's deep wisdom is completely missed by the modern critic, who is convinced that *Howards End* doesn't contain philosophical ideas because it is a novel, and novels don't contain philosophical ideas. But Forster himself said that he had large ambitions; when he was asked what he had learned from Jane Austen, he replied, "I learned the possibilities of domestic humor. I was more ambitious than she was, of course; I tried to hitch it on to other things."[3]

Some critics complained that Forster's ambitions were too large. Virginia Woolf, for example, wished that Forster would "write comedy only," and Woolf said that when Forster "forgets that he should solve the problem of the universe, he is the most diverting of novelists." Roger Fry made a similar criticism: "I wish [Forster] weren't a mystic, or that he would keep his mysticism out of his books."[4]

Woolf and Fry understood that Forster is presenting profound ideas, not just playing with profound ideas. Forster grasped the spiritual crisis of his time, and saw a solution to it. Naturally, he didn't want to hide his light under a bushel. Woolf and Fry would have preferred that Forster merely entertain the reader, but Forster wanted to be a philosophical novelist, as well as a humorous novelist.

If Forster's chief virtue is taste, one may wonder, where does taste come from? Forster's taste probably stems from his sunny disposition, from his deep understanding of literature, and from his deep love of literature. He was suffused with literature, it ran through his veins. He knew that literature could take over one's life, hence he struggled against it. In *Howards End*, he often says that culture isn't an end, that great writers are only sign-posts, and we shouldn't "mistake the sign-post for the destination."[5] One of the novel's

---

1 ch. 33

2 *Two Cheers For Democracy*, "What I Believe"

3 1952 interview. See *Howards End*, Norton Critical Edition, edited by P. Armstrong

4 ibid

5 ch. 14

chief characters, Margaret, grows in wisdom as the novel proceeds, and at the end of the novel, she has little interest in new books, or in other forms of culture:

> As for theaters and discussion societies, they attracted her less and less. She began to "miss" new movements, and to spend her spare time re-reading or thinking, rather to the concern of her Chelsea friends.... She had outgrown stimulants, and was passing from words to things. It was doubtless a pity not to keep up with Wedekind or John, but some closing of the gates is inevitable after thirty, if the mind itself is to become a creative power.[1]

Of Nietzsche, too, it may be said that he was suffused with literature, it ran through his veins, and of Nietzsche, too, it may be said that he struggled against it. Nietzsche agreed with Forster that the mind can't be a "creative power" if one is continually reading and learning:

> Scholars who at bottom do little nowadays but thumb books... ultimately lose entirely their capacity to think for themselves.... They *respond* to a stimulus (a thought they have read).... They themselves no longer think.... Early in the morning, when day breaks, when all is fresh, in the dawn of one's strength—to *read a book* at such a time is simply depraved![2]

Great minds think alike, and whatever genre they choose becomes a vehicle for their thoughts. Forster presents ideas in his novels that resemble the ideas Nietzsche presents in his philosophical works.

Forster's view of love is similar to Schopenhauer's. In a journal entry, Forster wrote, "We like the like and love the unlike."[3] Friendship is based on similarity of character, while love is often based on difference ("opposites attract"). *Howards End* deals with 'loving the unlike', it deals with love between a Schlegel (Margaret) and a Wilcox (Henry), it deals with love between two opposite types.

Schopenhauer also believed that opposites attract; Schopenhauer argued that a masculine man would love a feminine woman, and a feminine man would love a masculine woman. Jungians argue that people usually marry their opposites; for example, an extrovert-rational person will marry an introvert-feeling person. According to Jungians, marriage means seeking wholeness by joining with someone who complements you, someone who supplies your deficiencies. On the subject of love, as on other subjects, Forster shows himself to be a deep thinker, someone whose thoughts should be taken seriously, not dismissed as ironic.

Margaret speaks of "personal relations, that we think supreme."[4] Margaret is here expressing Forster's own view; in one of his essays, Forster

---

1 ch. 31. Wedekind was a German dramatist, John a British painter.

2 *Ecce Homo*, "Why I Am So Clever," #8

3 See *Howards End*, Norton Critical Edition, p. 269

4 ch. 4

wrote, "My books emphasize the importance of personal relationships and the private life, for I believe in them."[1] This suggests that Forster's novels are vehicles for Forster's own views, that Forster meant what he said, that he wasn't hiding his meaning, that he wasn't being ironic.

The epigraph of *Howards End* is "Only connect..." and connecting is one of its chief themes. The following passage deals with Margaret's attempt to guide Henry toward spiritual growth:

> She need trouble him with no gift of her own. She would only point out the salvation that was latent in his own soul, and in the soul of every man. Only connect! That was the whole of her sermon. Only connect the prose and the passion, and both will be exalted, and human love will be seen at its height. Live in fragments no longer. Only connect, and the beast and the monk, robbed of the isolation that is life to either, will die.[2]

Here, surely, Forster is giving us the best advice that he has to give. The theme of connecting complements the mystical theme. Eastern mysticism doesn't emphasize connecting since the opposites (conscious/unconscious, reason/feeling, etc.) aren't as far apart in the Eastern psyche as in the Western; there is no need to connect what was never disconnected. In the West, however, the opposites are far apart, and there is an urgent need to connect in order to reach wholeness.

Forster sees this, and speaks frequently of the need to connect. But today's deconstructors insist that Forster is being "deeply ironic"[3] when he speaks of connecting. And if generations of readers thought that he meant what he said, and took his advice to heart, aren't the deconstructors forced to conclude that Forster has deceived generations of readers, has led them astray?

Margaret's attempt to foster Henry's spiritual growth is a brave attempt for "it was hard-going in the roads of Mr. Wilcox's soul. From boyhood he had neglected them. 'I am not a fellow who bothers about my own inside....'"[4] Henry is a "persona character"; he has a well-developed persona, plays his social role competently, and achieves success in the business world, but his inner life is undeveloped. One might compare him with Tolstoy's "persona character", Alexey Karenina (Anna's husband).

Henry's wife, Ruth Wilcox, is the opposite of Henry, and while Henry is depicted in a negative light, Ruth is idealized. One might compare Ruth to Prince Myshkin, the protagonist of Dostoyevsky's novel, *The Idiot*. Myshkin is Dostoyevsky's attempt to depict an ideal person, Myshkin is Christ-like. But Forster's ideal person isn't Christ-like because Forster's ideals don't come from Christianity; Forster's ideal person is connected to nature

---

1 See "The Challenge of Our Time"

2 ch. 22

3 Paul Armstrong

4 ch. 22

and to herself, devoted to things rather than words, Zennish. Ruth and Myshkin both have undeveloped personas, they're somewhat naive, and somewhat awkward in social situations (the same is true of Mr. Emerson in Forster's *Room With A View*).

Forster himself aspired to live the quiet life that Ruth lived. "Let me not be distracted by the world," Forster wrote in his journal in 1910; "never forget nature and to look at her freshly. Don't advance *one step more* into literary society than I have."[1] But for today's critics, Ruth isn't Forster's ideal, she is merely the narrator's ideal. Today's critics, influenced by the deconstruction fad, rob *Howards End* of its ideals and its wisdom, and leave nothing behind but irony and humor.

F. Queer Theory and E. M. Forster

Another modern literary theory that has been applied to *Howards End* is Queer Theory. This theory sees Forster as a "queer artist" who is trying "to pass for normal even while secretly rebelling against the normative."[2] Thus, instead of trying to communicate thoughts and feelings, Forster is playing another game of hide-and-seek, "a game so subtle and slippery that it can pass without notice."[3]

Queer Theory, Feminist Theory, Race Theory—all these theories view writers in terms of their group, rather than their individuality; these theories politicize the humanities. A great writer is highly individual, transcends his group, attains universality, and speaks to people in distant times and places. Shakespeare, for example, transcends his nation and class, and speaks to people in distant times and places.

Instead of speaking of a "queer writer," a "female writer," etc., we should speak of a writer who happens to be queer, a writer who happens to be female, etc. The mystical theme in *Howards End* is similar to the mystical theme in the work of Thoreau, who wasn't queer. Likewise, the connecting theme in *Howards End* is similar to the connecting theme in Jung, who wasn't queer. Forster's sexual orientation has little impact on the major themes of *Howards End.*

Today's colleges strive for racial diversity, gender diversity, etc. But diversity isn't about race and gender, it's about individuality. The Concord intellectuals—Emerson, Thoreau, Hawthorne and Alcott—were a diverse group, though not diverse in terms of race or gender. The diversity of the Concord intellectuals is real diversity, the diversity of individual thought and personality.

---

1 see *Howards End*, Norton Critical Edition, p. 274

2 Paul Armstrong

3 Ibid. Paul's remarks remind me of Edward Shils' comment on intellectual fashions: "The most frequent fatality of all intellectual activities in our contemporary societies is the gratifying ease of reiterating what is currently fashionable.... To run with the intellectual mob is a common pitfall into which many intellectuals fall."

G. Skepticism

The modern critic believes that Forster is hiding behind the narrator, playing games with the reader, and being ironic, not striving to discover truth, and communicate truth as clearly as he can. Likewise, the modern critic believes that Kierkegaard hides behind pseudonyms, he doesn't strive to discover and communicate truth. And the modern critic thinks that Nietzsche doesn't believe in truth; he describes Nietzsche as a "German philosopher who argued that truth is not absolute but varies with perspective."[1]

The modern critic is a skeptic, and doesn't believe in truth, hence he sees Forster, Kierkegaard and Nietzsche as skeptics. The modern critic overlooks the fact that Nietzsche explicitly rejected skepticism, and that Nietzsche's "perspectivism" is one more theory, one more attempt to discover and communicate truth. Nietzsche realized the popularity of skepticism: "Skepticism is the most spiritual expression of… nervous debility and sickliness…. Our present-day Europe [is] skeptical in all its heights and depths."[2]

Truth entails responsibilities, and affects one's life. Skepticism is alluring because it doesn't entail responsibilities, it lets one live as one wishes. Furthermore, truth is threatening because someone else may lay claim to truth, and may act on it. Hitler, Marx, bin Laden—all lay claim to truth, and all act on it. Nietzsche wrote,

> When a philosopher nowadays makes known that he is not a skeptic… he is henceforth said to be dangerous. With his repudiation of skepticism, it seems to them as if they heard some evil-threatening sound in the distance, as if a new kind of explosive were being tried somewhere… perhaps a newly discovered Russian nihilism, a pessimism… that not only denies, means denial, but—dreadful thought!—*practices* denial.[3]

Since truth brings responsibilities and threats, today's intellectuals eagerly embrace skepticism, they turn to what Nietzsche called "the mild, pleasing, lulling poppy of skepticism."[4] Today's intellectuals are fond of saying, "there is no truth," or "all truth is relative," or "all truth depends on one's perspective." Skepticism corrodes the life of the mind. We should believe in truth, and strive to discover it and communicate it, though it may be elusive, though it may bring with it threats and responsibilities.

---

1 see *Howards End*, Norton Critical Edition, p. 329

2 *Beyond Good and Evil*, §208. Hegel said, "It marks the diseased state of the age when we see it adopt the despairing creed that our knowledge is only subjective." (*Encyclopedia of the Philosophical Sciences*, Logic, Introduction, #22)

3 ibid

4 Ibid. "There are two ways to slide easily through life; to believe everything or to doubt everything. Both ways save us from thinking."
--Alfred Korzybski

H. Does Culture Matter?

Forster came of age before World War I, and lived through both World Wars. Forster came of age in a world that respected culture, and lived to see a world that had little use for culture, and little respect for tradition. Forster decried this change, and championed culture and tradition. "That clamor for art and literature," Forster wrote, "which Ruskin and Morris thought they detected has died down.... There is a hostility to cultural stuff today which is disquieting." Forster realized that, in the modern world,

> there will be work for all and play for all. But the work and the play will be split; the work will be mechanical and the play frivolous. If you drop tradition and culture you lose your chance of connecting work and play and creating a life which is all of a piece.

Forster argues that culture isn't a pastime for epicures: "The higher pleasures.... resemble religion, and it is impossible to enjoy them without trying to hand them on." Forster tried to "hand them on" through his criticism, his essays, and his lectures. The best way to champion culture, Forster argues, is to enjoy it, and let others see that you enjoy it:

> Let one's light so shine that men's curiosity is aroused, and they ask why Sophocles, Velasquez, Henry James should cause such disproportionate pleasure. Bring out the enjoyment. If 'the Classics' are advertised as something dolorous and astringent, no one will sample them. But if the cultured person [is] obviously having a good time, those who come across him will be tempted to share it and to find out how.[1]

Forster is one of the 20th century's great humanists; he reminds one of Bernard Berenson and André Gide. Forster was a champion neither of popular culture nor of scholarly culture, but rather of culture that is connected to life, that aims at The Good Life, that is as serious as religion and as playful as a child's game, that links our generation to previous generations in a great conversation.

I. Edmundson

While many modern scholars insist that authors like Forster are subtle, slippery, and ironic, one modern scholar, Mark Edmundson, became famous by taking a different tack, by arguing that literature advises us how to live, and changes our life. Edmundson argued that studying literature doesn't mean learning to interpret, rather it means having one's life and personality challenged. According to Edmundson, an author advises us how to live either directly or indirectly, either by precept or by example, either by his works or by his life. Students should "measure themselves against what they've read."[2] The study of literature should be life-changing, inspiring.

Edmundson complains that today's students are too self-satisfied to be inspired:

---

1 *Two Cheers For Democracy*, "Does Culture Matter?"

2 "On the uses of a liberal education," *Harper's Magazine*, Sept. 1, 1997

> some measure of self-dislike, or self-discontent... seems to me to be a prerequisite for getting an education that matters. The pervading view is the cool consumer perspective, where passion and strong admiration are forbidden.

Edmundson's work struck a chord, since it was clear that the study of literature had become over-specialized, divorced from life, interesting to no one except academics. Indeed, many publishers had decided not to publish literary criticism because it didn't interest the public.

Edmundson takes a dim view of today's students and today's universities, but he thinks that literature will survive as long as the isolated individual finds a great book, and is inspired, transformed.

J. *A Passage to India*

The Indian writer Nirad Chaudhuri wrote an essay on E. M. Forster's novel, *A Passage to India*. Chaudhuri found fault with Forster's depiction of India.[1] (Chaudhuri later wrote a book called *Passage to England*, a book that Forster reviewed.) I recommend Chaudhuri's essay. What's more interesting than listening to a great writer discuss another great writer?

Chaudhuri blames Forster for arousing British opposition to Britain's empire:

> Mr Forster's novel became a powerful weapon in the hands of the anti-imperialists, and was made to contribute its share to the disappearance of British rule in India.... The British people taken in the mass were never deeply involved in this empire, emotionally or intellectually. To them it was rather a marginal fact of British history than what it really was—a major phenomenon in the history of world civilization. Mr Forster's book not only strengthened the indifference, it also created a positive aversion to the empire by its unattractive picture of India and Anglo-Indian life and its depiction of Indo-British relations as being of a kind that were bound to outrage the English sense of decency and fair play. Thus, the novel helped the growth of that mood which enabled the British people to leave India with an almost Pilate-like gesture of washing their hands of a disagreeable affair.

Forster made a point of ignoring politics: "his is an appeal in a political case to the court of humane feelings." But, Chaudhuri cautions, "the most obvious moral judgment on a political situation is not necessarily a right judgment, and for humane feelings to go for a straight tilt at politics is even more quixotic than tilting at windmills." Perhaps "humane feelings" would suggest that the British can't rule India, but political wisdom might suggest that a British withdrawal would trigger catastrophe; the policy dictated by "humane feelings" might be an unwise policy.

---

[1] *A Routledge Literary Sourcebook on E. M. Forster's* A Passage to India, edited by Peter Childs; Extract from Nirad Chaudhuri, "Passage To and From India"

Chaudhuri says that, in India, the Muslims hated the British more than the Hindus did, because the Muslims had been deprived of an empire by the British. On the other hand, the Muslims knew that the Hindu nationalists could bear most of the weight of expelling the British, so they could afford to be friendly to the British. "This game, played with boldness and hard-headed realism, succeeded beyond expectation and created an independent state for the Muslims of India." (Chaudhuri himself was from a Hindu family.)

But while Muslim leaders were successfully playing "a colossal Machiavellian game of politics," the majority of Muslims were either filled with a "barren and rancorous hatred" or pining for British patronage. Forster's Indians are among those pining for British patronage:

> Aziz and his friends belong to the servile section and are all inverted toadies. With such material, a searching history of the Muslim destiny in India could have been written, but not a novel on Indo-British relations, for which it was essential to have a Hindu protagonist.

Chaudhuri notes that the British and Indians both speak Indo-European languages, because they both are Indo-European peoples. He notes that some Indian thinkers celebrated this kinship, but the British were more attracted by the simplicity of Muslim monotheism than by any British-Hindu kinship:

> There was between European civilization and the Hindu in its stricter form a common Indo-European element, which was discovered and described by British Orientalists in the first century or so of British rule, but which came to be forgotten and ignored by Englishmen in later times. Modern Hindu thinkers did not, however, lose sight of the affinity. Swami Vivekananda, speaking at the end of the last century, said that two branches of the same people placed in different surroundings in Greece and India had worked out the problems of life, each in its own particular way, but that through the agency of the British people the ancient Greek was meeting the ancient Hindu on Indian soil, and thus "slowly and silently the leaven has come, the broadening out, the life-giving revivalist movement that we see all around us." The British in India never gave this fruitful idea any encouragement. They were taken in by the deceptive simplicity of the Muslim and repelled by the apparent bizarrerie of Hinduism and its rococo excrescences. I wonder if it was the Hebraic element in the British ethos which was responsible for this.

Notice how Swami Vivekananda regards Western thought as a "life-giving leaven." Isn't this how Westerners regard Eastern thought? Perhaps the beneficial influence operates in both directions.

Chaudhuri concludes his essay thus:

> My most serious criticisms [of *Passage to India*] are the following. It shows a great imperial system at its worst, not as diabolically evil but as drab and asinine; the rulers and the ruled alike are depicted at their smallest, the snobbery and pettiness of the one matching the imbecility

> and rancor of the other.... When I consider all this I feel Mr Forster's literary ability, which has given the book its political importance, as a grievance.

Chaudhuri was a man of vast learning, and his writings are filled with literary allusions; he mentions Don Quixote tilting at windmills, Pilate washing his hands, Swami Vivekananda, British Orientalists, a Machiavellian game, etc. But despite this plethora of allusions, Chaudhuri's tone is lively, not pedantic. Chaudhuri must be regarded as one of the best English stylists of the 20th century.

A critic named Laurence Brander discusses various characters in *A Passage to India.*[1] Brander says that Godbole represents universal love (the Hindu theme), while Aziz represents friendship (the Muslim theme). Brander summarizes Forster's characters thus:

> The two ladies are middle class Edwardians, untouched by the suburbanism of Sawston, representing the grace of age in Mrs Moore and intellectual emancipation in Adela Quested. They resemble Ruth Wilcox and the Schlegel girls [in *Howards End*]. Sawston and suburbanism is found in the little English community, friendship is found among the Muslims and Universal Love is found in the one Hindu of any consequence in the book, the old Brahmin teacher, Professor Godbole.... The theme of friendship, the Muslim theme, was introduced in the mosque. The theme of universal love is introduced at the very end of the next chapter. There is no apparent reason for recording that Mrs Moore noticed a wasp asleep on the peg: "Going to hang up her cloak she found the tip of the peg was occupied by a small wasp... 'Pretty dear,' said Mrs Moore to the wasp." Two years later in time and away across the great Indian plain we shall see Professor Godbole in his annual religious festival realizing universal love and the images that come to his mind are the wasp and Mrs Moore and universal love embraces them both.

Just as universal love seems higher than friendship, so Forster regards Hinduism as higher than Islam. Forster takes a dim view of simple, rational, Muslim monotheism. Brander quotes Forster:

> "'There is no God but God' doesn't carry us far through the complexities of matter and spirit; it is only a game with words, really, a religious pun, not a religious truth." Mrs Moore had dismissed "poor little talkative Christianity". Now Islam is rejected. Hinduism is left.

But while Forster is impressed with Hinduism as philosophy, he isn't impressed with it as everyday ethics. Forster thinks India is divided between the mystical and the mundane:

> There "is scarcely anything in that tormented land," Forster wrote in 1922, "which fills up the gulf between the illimitable and the inane,

---

1 *E. M. Forster: A Critical Study*, by Laurence Brander, "A Passage to India"

and society suffers in consequence. What isn't piety is apt to be indecency; what isn't metaphysics is intrigue."

Perhaps what India lacks is an ethical system to fill up the gap between the mystical and the mundane. Perhaps India needs absolute morality, black-and-white morality. This may be a social need, but not a philosophical need. Society may benefit from black-and-white morality, but philosophy is more profound if it sees morality as grey and relative, not absolute.

Brander mentions Adela's car accident, and the ghost she sees. Brander says that Forster's novel deals with "things outside normal experience." Like most people who are interested in the mystical, Forster was interested in the occult, and there are occult phenomena in *Howards End* as well as *Passage to India*.

Forster had a good grasp of world affairs. Writing in the early 1920s, he understood Hindu-Muslim hostility, the rising power of Japan, and the likelihood that, if Britain became involved in another major war, India would seize the opportunity to break away from the British Empire.[1] He says that atheism is growing in England, but people "don't like the name. The truth is that the West doesn't bother much over belief and disbelief in these days."[2]

The decline of religious belief, says Forster, has brought with it a decline of morality. At this point in the conversation, an Indian says, "Excuse the question, but if this is the case, how is England justified in holding India?" Forster understands the decline of religion and morality, and he understands that Britain can't rule an empire if it doesn't believe in itself, if its own *Weltanschauung* is eroding; nihilism can't be imperial.

Perhaps Forster's toughest critic was Virginia Woolf. I wouldn't be surprised if her criticism was a factor in prompting Forster to abandon novel-writing. Woolf described *Howards End* as a "failure." She says, "Elaboration, skill, wisdom, penetration, beauty—they are all there, but they lack fusion; they lack cohesion; the book as a whole lacks force."[3]

There is some truth to Woolf's criticism. Perhaps Forster himself wasn't a forceful person. But what he does, he does very well, and he achieves things of great importance. I find Forster's works very enjoyable, and isn't enjoyment worth something? Shouldn't enjoyment be an argument in the field of aesthetics? I also find a deep wisdom in both Forster's novels and his essays. Isn't wisdom worth something—even in a work of art? Woolf is focusing on Forster's weaknesses instead of his strengths. Woolf was a contemporary of Forster's, and judged him too harshly. Perhaps with the benefit of time, we can reach a truer and more favorable estimate of Forster's work.

---

[1] When Aziz tells Fielding that the English should "clear out," Fielding asks, "Who do you want instead of the English? The Japanese?" Aziz says, "Until England is in difficulties we keep silent, but in the next European war—aha, aha! Then is our time."(ch. 37)

[2] *A Passage to India*, ch. 9

[3] See the Norton Critical Edition of *Howards End*, edited by P. Armstrong

K. Forster on Modern Writers

I read a lecture that Forster delivered in Glasgow in 1944, "English Prose Between 1918 and 1939." The lecture is in Forster's volume of essays/lectures, *Two Cheers For Democracy*, which was published in 1951. (In 1936, Forster published a volume of essays called *Abinger Harvest*.)

a. War and Industrialization

In his Glasgow lecture, Forster says that the literature written between 1918 and 1939 is influenced by war, world war, total war. Earlier writers could feel "tranquil" during wartime (as an example, he mentions Jane Austen writing during the Napoleonic wars). But modern war destroys tranquility. The literature of this period displays "unrest or disillusionment or anxiety," it's the product of "a civilization which feels itself insecure." The writers of this period realize "what a mess the world is in."

But the writers of this period aren't influenced only by war.

> There is a huge economic movement which has been taking the whole world, Great Britain included, from agriculture towards industrialism.... Normal life today is a life in factories and offices... farming has become scientific... insurance has taken the place of charity.

Forster leaves us no doubt as to his attitude toward industrialization: "Personally I hate it. So I imagine do most writers." Forster seems to regard the Industrial Age as permanent, he seems to have no inkling that, a few years after he delivered this lecture, the Industrial Age would begin to give way to the Information Age.

b. Modern Psychology

While he hates industrialization, Forster welcomes another contemporary trend: psychology. "Man is beginning to understand himself better and to explore his own contradictions." Forster says that earlier writers, like Shakespeare, were aware of the unconscious, but their awareness didn't rise to the level of conscious knowledge. "Conscious knowledge of it only comes at the beginning of the century, with Samuel Butler's *The Way of All Flesh*." Of course, Forster gives credit to Freud for spreading knowledge of the unconscious.

Modern psychology, Forster says, has been a boon for modern writers. "What a rich harvest they have reaped!" Proust explored the unconscious, Forster says, as did Joyce, D. H. Lawrence, and Virginia Woolf.

Historians, too, have benefited from modern psychology; Forster mentions Aldous Huxley's *Grey Eminence*, and Livingston Lowes' *The Road to Xanadu*. Forster praises Toynbee's *Study of History*, calling it "the great work of a Christian historian [which] regards history as a record of what men think and feel as well as of what they assert and achieve."

Forster's favorite book from the period between the wars is Lytton Strachey's biography of Queen Victoria. Forster says that Strachey's book exemplifies the modern psychological approach. Forster says that Strachey's *Victoria* is

> an achievement of genius, and it has revolutionized the art of biography. [Strachey] did what no biographer had done before: he managed to get inside his subject. [He] makes his people move; they are alive, like characters in a novel.

Forster also says that Einstein has had an impact on modern writers, even if they don't understand his theories. The idea of relativity is 'in the air,' so novelists see human character as relative, not as absolutely good or absolutely evil. Proust, Forster says, is especially adept at depicting characters who are a blend of good and evil. I suspect that Forster errs in giving Einstein credit for this tendency; even before Einstein, novelists like Stevenson were creating characters who were a mix of good and evil. Perhaps Einstein himself was part of a larger trend.

c. Lawrence of Arabia

Forster praises *The Seven Pillars of Wisdom*, by T. E. Lawrence; he speaks of the book's "greatness," and praises its "brilliant descriptions of scenery." *Seven Pillars* is an account of Lawrence's adventures in Arabia. Lawrence helped the Arabs to overthrow their Ottoman rulers; he's often called "Lawrence of Arabia." Forster quotes a passage from *Seven Pillars*; in this passage, Lawrence seems to anticipate contemporary Arab terrorism, or something like it:

> Their mind was strange and dark, full of depressions and exaltations, lacking in rule, but with more of ardor and more fertile in belief than any other in the world.... They were as unstable as water, and like water would perhaps finally prevail.... In fullness of time the sea shall be raised once more.

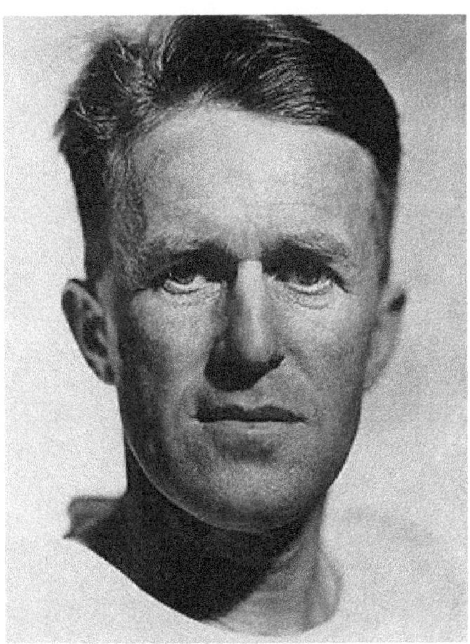

T. E. Lawrence

In a passage that Forster doesn't quote, Lawrence writes,

> At the first meeting with them, was found a universal clearness or hardness of belief, almost mathematical in its limitation, and repellent in its unsympathetic form.... They were a people of primary colors, or rather of black and white.... They were a dogmatic people, despising doubt, our modern crown of thorns. They did not understand our metaphysical difficulties, our introspective questionings. They knew only truth and untruth, belief and unbelief, without our hesitating retinue of finer shades.... Their thoughts were at ease only in extremes.... They never compromised.

If anyone could have foreseen today's terrorism in 1920, it was Lawrence, with his intellectual gifts and his first-hand knowledge of the Arabs.

d. Rose Macaulay

Forster mentions a writer I had never heard of: Rose Macaulay. She's best known for "her award-winning novel *The Towers of Trebizond*, about a small Anglo-Catholic group crossing Turkey by camel." For 25 years, she carried on a secret affair with a married man. She wrote,

> Adultery is a meanness and a stealing, a taking away from someone what should be theirs, a great selfishness, and surrounded and guarded by lies lest it should be found out. And out of meanness and selfishness and lying flow love and joy and peace beyond anything that can be imagined.

In addition to numerous novels, Rose Macaulay wrote a biography of Milton, studies of Forster and Evelyn Waugh, travel books about Portugal, etc. She was apparently a descendant of the famous historian and man-of-letters Thomas Babington Macaulay.

e. Two Tendencies in Modern Literature

Forster says that there are two tendencies in modern prose, a popular tendency and an esoteric tendency. He says that the popular tendency "absorbs what is passing," like the newspaper, while the esoteric tendency "rejects it, and tries to create through art something more valuable than monotony and bloodshed." The word "esoteric" sometimes means "occult." I once believed that Forster was using "esoteric" as a synonym for "occult," but now I'm unsure. He may mean occult, but he may also mean subjective, or he may mean arcane/hidden/obscure, or he may mean all these things. Forster says that "the best work of the period has [an] esoteric tendency." Writers with this tendency, Forster says, are Joyce, Woolf, Lytton Strachey, T. E. Lawrence, etc. These writers aren't known for dealing with the occult.

Forster briefly mentions Christopher Isherwood, saying that his novel *Mr. Norris Changes Trains* is a "popular" (as opposed to "esoteric") work, and an example of "democratic good manners." Wikipedia says that Forster and Isherwood were close friends, and Forster was a mentor to Isherwood. Isherwood was also friends with W. H. Auden, Aldous Huxley, Truman Capote, Stephen Spender, etc. Huxley introduced Isherwood to Eastern religion, and Isherwood wrote several books on the subject, including *Essentials of Vedanta*, and *Ramakrishna and His Disciples*. In his latter years, Isherwood lived mostly in the U.S. Isherwood was gay, and his 1964 novel *A Single Man* depicts "a day in the life of George, a middle-aged, gay Englishman who is a professor at a Los Angeles university."[1]

In conclusion, Forster says that some fine literature was created between the wars. And indeed, I'm astonished at how many good books emerged from Britain in these decades.

---

[1] Forster mentions Hemingway among the "popular" writers; he says that Hemingway "introduces a new technique of conversation." Forster dismisses Graham Greene and Evelyn Waugh, saying that world war and industrialization made these two writers feel lost and disgusted. Forster mentions Elizabeth Bowen and Dorothy Richardson among the writers who explored the unconscious.

www.ingramcontent.com/pod-product-compliance
Lightning Source LLC
Chambersburg PA
CBHW031230090426
42742CB00007B/143

* 9 7 8 0 9 8 3 8 2 7 0 4 7 *